Prentice Hall

LITERATURE

Timeless Voices, Timeless Themes

English Learner's Companion Teacher's Edition

BRONZE LEVEL

Upper Saddle River, New Jersey
Glenview, Illinois
Needham, Massachusetts

ISBN 0-13-063102-7

2 3 4 5 6 7 8 9 10 06 05 04 03 02

Acknowledgments

Grateful acknowledgment is made to the following for permission to reprint copyrighted material:

Miriam Altschuler Literary Agency
"Treasure of Lemon Brown" by Walter Dean Myers from *Boy's Life Magazine*, March 1983. Copyright © 1983, by Walter Dean Myers.

AMG
"A Christmas Carol: Scrooge and Marley" by Israel Horovitz, an adaptation of Charles Dickens's *A Christmas Carol.* Copyright © 1994 by Fountain Pen, Inc. All rights reserved.

Arte Publico Press
"Maestro" by Pat Mora is reprinted with permission from the publisher of *Borders* (Houston: Arte Publico Press-University of Houston, 1986).

Susan Bergholz Literary Services, New York
"Four Skinny Trees" from *The House on Mango Street.* Copyright © 1984 by Sandra Cisneros. Published by Vintage Books, a division of Random House, Inc., and in hardcover by Alfred A. Knopf in 1994. All rights reserved.

Curtis Brown Ltd.
"Ribbons" by Laurence Yep, copyright © 1992 by Laurence Yep from *American Girl*, Jan/Feb 1992.

Brandt & Hochman Literary Agents, Inc.
"The Third Wish" from *Not What You Expected: A Collection of Short Stories* by Joan Aiken. Copyright © 1974 by Joan Aiken.

Delacorte Press, a division of Random House, Inc.
"The Luckiest Time of All" from *The Lucky Stone* by Lucille Clifton. Copyright © 1979 by Lucille Clifton. All rights reserved.

Don Congdon Associates, Inc.
"All Summer In A Day" by Ray Bradbury, published in *The Magazine of Fantasy and Science Fiction*, March 1, 1954. Copyright © 1954, renewed 1982 by Ray Bradbury.

Farrar, Straus & Giroux, Inc.
"The Cat Who Thought She Was a Dog and the Dog Who Thought He Was a Cat" from *Naftali the Storyteller and His Horse, Sus* by Issac Bashevis Singer. Copyright © 1973, 1976 by Isaac Bashevis Singer.

M.W. Farrell, executrix for the Estate of Juliet Piggot Wood
"Popocatepetl and Ixtlaccihuatl" from *Mexican Folk Tales* by Juliet Piggott. Copyright © 1973 by Juliet Piggott.

Golden Books Family Entertainment
"The Bride of Pluto" (retitled "Demeter and Persephone") from *Golden Treasury of Myths and Legends* by Anne Terry White. Copyright © 1959 Western Publishing Company, Inc. All rights reserved.

G.P Putnam's Sons, a division of Penguin Putnam, Inc.
"Two Kinds" by Amy Tan from *The Joy Luck Club.* Copyright © 1989 by Amy Tan. "Our Finest Hour" from *The Osgood Files* by Charles Osgood. Copyrigh © 1986, 1987, 1988, 1989, 1990, 1991 by Charles Osgood.

Harcourt, Inc.
Excerpt from *In Search of Our Mother's Gardens: Womanist Prose*, copyright © 1983 by Alice Walker. "Seventh Grade" from *Baseball in April and Other Stories*, copyright © 1990 by Gary Soto.

HarperCollins Publishers, Inc.
"How the Snake Got Poison" from *Mules and Men* by Zora Neale Hurston. Copyright © 1935 by Zora Neale Hurston. Copyright renewed 1963 by John C. Hurston and Joel Hurston. From *An American Childhood* by Annie Dillard. Copyright © 1987 by Annie Dillard.

John Hawkins & Associates Inc.
"My Furthest-Back Person—The African" by Alex Haley, published July 16, 1972, by *The New York Times Magazine.* Copyright © 1972 by Alex Haley.

Bill Hilgers, Esq., for the Estate of Barbara Jordan
"All Together Now" by Barbara Jordan, originally published in *Sesame Street Parents*, July/August 1994.

(Acknowledgments continue on page viii)

Contents

Unit 5: Just For Fun

Unit 6: Short Story

Unit 7: Nonfiction

Unit 8: Drama

Unit 9: Poetry

Unit 10: Legends, Folk Tales, and Myths

Part 2: Selection Summaries in Six Languages With Alternative Reading Strategies . . . 327

Unit 1: Independence and Identity

Unit 2: Common Threads

Unit 3: What Matters

Unit 4: Meeting Challenges

Unit 5: Just For Fun

Unit 6: Short Story

Unit 7: Nonfiction

Unit 8: Drama

Unit 9: Poetry

Unit 10: Legends, Folk Tales, and Myths

(Acknowledgments continued from page ii)

Helmut Hirnschall
"I Am a Native of North America" by Chief Dan George, from *My Heart Soars*. Copyright © 1974 by Clarke Irwin.

International Paper Company
"How to Enjoy Poetry" by James Dickey from *The Power of the Printed Word Program.*

Alfred A. Knopf Children's Books, a division of Random House, Inc.
"People Could Fly" from *The People Could Fly: American Black Folktales* by Virginia Hamilton, copyright © 1985 by Virginia Hamilton.

Charles Neider
Excerpt from "The Californian's Tale" by Mark Twain, from *The Complete Short Stories of Mark Twain.* Copyright © 1957 by Charles Neider.

Hugh Noyes, on behalf of the Trustees of Alfred Noyes
"The Highwayman" from *Collected Poems* by Alfred Noyes (J.B. Lippincott).

Random House, Inc.
"Melting Pot" from *Living Out Loud* by Anna Quindlen, copyright © 1987 by Anna Quindlen.

William Saroyan Foundation for the Trustees of Leland Stanford Junior University
"The Hummingbird That Lived Through Winter" by William Saroyan, from *Dear Baby*. Copyright © 1935, 1936, 1939, 1941, 1942, 1943, 1944 by William Saroyan.

St. Martin's Press, Inc., and Harold Ober Associates, Inc.
"Cat on the Go" from *All Things Wise and Wonderful* by James Herriot. Copyright © 1976, 1977 by James Herriot.

Scribner, a division of Simon & Schuster Inc.
"A Day's Wait" from *Winner Take Nothing* by Ernest Hemingway. Copyright © 1933 Charles Scribner's Sons. Copyright renewed © 1961 by Mary Hemingway.

Simon & Schuster Books for Young Readers, an imprint of Simon & Schuster Children's Publishing Division
"Papa's Parrot" by Cynthia Rylant from *Every Living Thing* by Cynthia Rylant. Copyright © 1985 Cynthia Rylant.

Piri Thomas
"Amigo Brothers" by Piri Thomas from *El Barrio.* Copyright © 1978 by Piri Thomas.

Rosemary A. Thurber and The Barbara Hogensen Agency
"The Night The Bed Fell" by James Thurber. Copyright © 1933, 1961, James Thurber, from *My Life and Hard Times*, published by Harper & Row.

Viking Penguin, a division of Penguin Putnam
"Was Tarzan a Three-Bandage Man?" from *Childhood* by Bill Cosby. Copyright © 1991 by William H. Cosby. Reprinted by permission of Viking Penguin, a division of Penguin Putnam Inc.

Note: Every effort has been made to locate the copyright owner of material reprinted in this book. Omissions brought to our attention will be corrected in subsequent editions.

To the Teacher

As you face the challenge of heterogeneous classes, you will find a wide variety of abilities and strengths among your students. This book is aimed at English learners who have difficulty with their grade-level textbook. You can use it to keep your classes reading the same selections, but getting the instruction and reading support at the appropriate level. This book provides extended support for those students who need more guidance with reading strategies, literary analysis, and critical thinking skills.

Factors that Affect Reading Success

There are four key factors that influence students' ability to achieve reading success. These factors, alone and in combination, determine how well a student will learn, grow, and succeed as a reader. To understand the students in your classroom, consider these factors:

(a) **Kinds of Learners** Consider each student's background, previous learning experiences, and special needs. In addition to students who read fluently at grade level, you may find a mix of the following learning characteristics in your classroom:

- *Students who speak a language other than English at home* Unlike their fully fluent counterparts, these students often speak English only at school. This situation leaves them limited hours in which to learn the grammar, vocabulary, idioms, and other intricacies of English.
- *Students who have recently moved to this country* These students may be highly capable students without the specific language skills to function academically in English.
- *Students with learning disabilities* These students may have cognitive, behavioral, social, or physical challenges that make reading more difficult.

(b) **Kinds of Skills and Instruction** Students' reading ability is influenced by the skills they bring to the task. Students must master the skills of decoding, activating and building prior knowledge, and making connections among experiences and new information. Other factors include a student's knowledge of the English language and vocabulary, and a student's ability to apply reading comprehension strategies.

Active reading, including the practice of summarizing, questioning, setting a purpose, and self-monitoring, is key to successful reading. For those students who have not yet developed such skills, your classroom instruction is critical. You should model such skills and encourage students to practice them. Through practice, students should be able to internalize the strategies of active reading.

(c) **Kinds of Texts** Just as students and their backgrounds and skills vary, so do the texts presented in a language arts curriculum. The grade-level language arts classroom curriculum traditionally addresses fiction, nonfiction, poetry, and drama. Each of these forms presents unique challenges to students. Each writer and selection also presents challenges in the difficulty of the concepts addressed or in the coherence of the writing. For example, you may find that students are more comfortable with narratives than with expository writing. Focused reading strategies that you model and reinforce can help students tackle texts that are more dense or difficult for them to master.

(d) **Classroom Environment** The classroom environment affects everything and everyone within it. Research suggests that students learn best in a friendly, respectful setting categorized by these criteria:

- Students feel a sense of safety and order.
- They feel comfortable taking risks.
- They understand the purpose and value of the tasks presented.
- Students have high expectations and goals for learning.
- They feel accepted by their teachers and peers.

Students performing below grade level may be especially self-conscious. Therefore, these criteria are key to helping students take full advantage of the opportunities the classroom affords. Set your classroom as a caring yet on-purpose environment that helps students achieve.

Researchers encourage teachers to be truthful with students about the work it will take to build and master abilities in the language arts. Tell your students that improving reading, writing, speaking, and listening takes a great deal of practice. You need to be prepared to provide direct instruction, guided practice, specific feedback, coaching, and more. Then, encourage your students to understand their responsibilities as active, self-directed learners as well.

The English Learner

English language learners are those students whose first language is not English. For these students, the challenge of an average language arts classroom looms large.

There are very few generalities to draw about this group of students, beyond their need to develop English fluency. Some are high functioning in their home language with a strong understanding of the routines and expectations of schools. Others are severely underschooled and therefore, they need to learn school routines, the vocabulary for studying English, and English itself. Some are not literate in their home language.

For English learners, initial reading and writing will be slower because the students struggle with fluency. Consequently, the following conditions result:

- These learners may revert to poor reading strategies to accommodate difficulty with language. For example, they may not read in sentences and instead tackle each word individually.
- Students may have a cultural disadvantage because they have less relevant prior knowledge or background information. Even if students can decode the selection, they may have difficulty in constructing meaning from the text or simply relating to its topic.
- These students are less familiar with academic language—the language of directions, content analysis, and school routines.

English learners may benefit from a separate reading support classroom to help them master reading English. In a heterogeneous classroom, however, English learners will benefit from the specific steps you take to support them.

- Present extensive and dynamic pre-teaching instruction to help students meet the literacy challenge.
- Explain critical concepts and key vocabulary in advance. Particularly, focus on classroom activities that build conceptual and linguistic foundation.
- Show students text organizations.
- Model appropriate comprehension strategies.
- Provide a clear purpose for reading.

Overview of Components for Universal Access

The *Prentice Hall Literature: Timeless Voices, Timeless Themes* program includes an array of products to provide universal access. Fully integrated, these materials help teachers identify student needs or deficiencies and teach to the varying levels in a classroom, while providing the quality that literature teachers expect.

As your main resource, the *Annotated Teacher's Edition* provides a lesson plan for every selection or selection grouping. In addition to teaching notes and suggestions, it also includes cross-references to ancillary material. Customize for Universal Access notes help teachers direct lessons to the following groups of students: special needs students, less proficient readers, English learners, gifted and talented students, and advanced readers. In addition to teaching notes and suggestions, it also includes cross-references to ancillary material such as the *Reader's Companion*, the *Adapted Reader's Companion*, and the *English Learner's Companion*.

The ***Teaching Guidebook for Universal Access*** gives you proven strategies for providing universal access to all students. In addition to its general teaching strategies and classroom management techniques, this component explains how the parts of the Prentice Hall program work together to ensure reading success for all student populations.

The ***Reading Diagnostic and Improvement Plan***—part of the Reading Achievement System— provides comprehensive diagnostic tests that assess students' mastery of reading skills. The book also includes charts that help you map out an improvement plan based on students' performance on the diagnostics.

You can use the ***Basic Reading Skill: Comprehensive Lessons for Improvement Plan***—also part of the Reading Achievement System— to give instruction and practice that bring students up to grade level, enabling them to master the skills in which they are deficient. For each skill covered, you'll find the following materials:

- lesson plan with direct instruction
- teaching transparency
- blackline master for student application and practice

The ***Reader's Companion*** and ***Reader's Companion Teacher's Edition*** are consumable components of the Reading Achievement System. The books contain the full text of approximately half of the selections from the student book. Questions prompt students to interact with the text by circling, underlining, or marking key details. Write-on lines in the margins also allow for students to answer questions. You can use this book in place of the student book to help students read interactively. In addition, a summary and a reading-skill worksheet support every selection grouping in the student book.

The ***Adapted Reader's Companion*** and ***Adapted Reader's Companion Teacher's Edition*** are another set of consumable components of the Reading Achievement System. These books use the same format and contain the same selections as the *Reader's Companion.* However, the selections are abridged and appear in a larger font size. The questions are targeted toward special education students. You can use this book as a supplement to or in place of the student book for certain selections to enable special education students to experience the same literature and master the same skills as on-level students. These components also contain a summary and a reading-skill worksheet to support every selection grouping in the student book.

The ***English Learner's Companion*** and ***English Learner's Companion Teacher's Edition*** are a third set of consumable components of the Reading Achievement System. These books use the same format and contain the same selections as the *Reader's Companion.* Again, the selections are abridged and appear in a larger font size. The questions are targeted toward English learners. You can use this book as a supplement to or in place of the student book for certain selections to enable English learners to experience the same literature and master the same skills as students who are native English speakers. These components also contain summaries in English, Spanish, Chinese, Vietnamese, Cambodian, and Hmong, along with a reading-skill worksheet to support every selection grouping in the student book.

Listening to Literature Audiotapes and CDs These components feature professional recordings of every selection in the student book. To support student reading, you can play the selections, in part or in full, before students read them.

Spanish/English Summaries Audio CD Audio summaries in both English and Spanish are provided for every selection. You can play these selection summaries for struggling readers, special education students, and English learners before they read the actual texts.

Basic Language Skills: Reteaching Masters With the reteaching masters, you can provide basic-level instruction and practice on grammar and language skills.

Interest Grabber Videos These videos are an optional enrichment resource designed to provide background for a selection or otherwise motivate students to read the selection. There is a video segment for every selection or selection grouping in the student book.

About the *English Learner's Companion*

The *English Learner's Companion* is designed to support your students whose first language is not English. Its two parts offer different levels of support.

Part 1: Selection Adaptations with Excerpts of Authentic Text

Part 1 will guide English learners as they interact with half the selections from *Prentice Hall Literature: Timeless Voices, Timeless Themes.* This range of selections includes the more challenging selections, the most frequently taught selections, and many examples of narrative and expository writing. Part 1 provides pre-reading instruction, larger print summaries of literature selections with passages from the selection, and post-reading questions and activities.

The ***Preview*** page will help your students get the general idea of the selection and therefore be better equipped to understand it. Both written and visual summaries preview the selections before students read the adapted versions.

The ***Prepare to Read*** page is based on its parallel in *Prentice Hall Literature: Timeless Voices, Timeless Themes.* It introduces the same literary element and reading strategy addressed in the textbook, and provides a graphic organizer to make the information more accessible.

The ***selection*** pages present the text in a larger font size. Interspersed among blocks of authentic text, the companion also provides summaries of episodes or paragraphs to make the selections more accessible to your students.

The ***side notes*** make active reading strategies explicit, asking students to look closely at the text to analyze it in a variety of ways. Notes with a *Mark the Text* icon prompt students to underline, circle, or otherwise note key words, phrases, or details in the selection. Notes with write-on lines offer students an opportunity to respond in the margin to questions or ideas. These notes offer focused support in a variety of areas:

> **Literary Analysis** notes provide point-of-use instruction to reinforce the literary element introduced on the Preview page. By pointing out details or events in the text in which the literary element applies, these notes give students the opportunity to revisit and reinforce their understanding of literature.
>
> **Reading Strategy** notes help students practice the skill introduced on the Preview page. These notes guide students to understand when, how, and why a strategy is helpful.
>
> **Stop to Reflect** notes ask students to reflect on the selection or on a skill they are using. By encouraging students to solidify their own thinking, these notes help to develop active reading skills.

Reading Check notes help students to confirm their comprehension of a selection. These notes help to make explicit a critical strategy of active reading.

Read Fluently notes provide students with concrete, limited practice reading passages aloud with fluency.

Vocabulary and Pronunciation notes address specific points of language development for English learners. For example, notes might explain English word parts, teach the multiple meanings of words, point out and show the pronunciation of new words, or ask students to make comparisons with English words and those in their home language.

English Language Development notes deal with concepts including spelling, grammar, mechanics, and usage. They call out for students the finer points of text written in English.

Culture Notes explain aspects of American culture that students new to the country might not understand. These notes, explaining traditions such as holiday celebrations and leisuretime activities, are especially helpful to students who may be able to read the selection fluently but not understand its context as well.

Background notes provide further explanation of a concept or detail to support student understanding.

The ***Review and Assess*** questions following the selection ensure students' comprehension of the selection. Written in simple language, they assess students' understanding of the literary element and the reading strategy. In addition they offer a scaffolded guide to support students in an extension activity based on either a writing or listening and speaking activity in the *Student Edition* of the grade-level textbook.

Part 2: Selection Summaries in Six Languages with Alternative Reading Strategies

Part 2 contains summaries of all selections in *Prentice Hall Literature: Timeless Voices, Timeless Themes.* Summaries are provided in English, Spanish, Vietnamese, Cantonese, Hmong, and Cambodian. These summaries can help students prepare for reading the selections in English. Alternatively, the summaries may serve as a review tool.

This section also includes alternative reading strategies to guide students as they read selections. The strategies may be useful for reviewing selection events and ideas or to reinforce specific reading strategies for students.

How to Use the *English Learner's Companion*

When you are planning lessons for heterogeneous classes, this companion reader offers you an opportunity to keep all the students in your class reading the same selection and studying the same vocabulary, literary element, and reading strategy but getting the support they need to succeed. Here are some planning suggestions for using the book in tandem with the grade-level volume of *Prentice Hall Literature: Timeless Voices, Timeless Themes.*

Use the *Annotated Teacher's Edition* and the *Student Edition* of the grade-level textbook as the central text in your classroom. The *Annotated Teacher's Edition* includes *Customize for Universal Access* notes throughout each selection. In addition, it identifies when use of the *English Learner's Companion* is appropriate.

TEACHING SELECTIONS INCLUDED IN PART ONE

PRE-TEACH with the Full Class

Consider presenting the* Interest Grabber *video segment. This optional technology product can provide background and build motivation.

Preview the selection. To help students see the organization of a selection, or to help them get a general idea of the text, lead a quick text pre-reading or "text tour" using the textbook. Focus student attention on the selection title, the art accompanying the text, and any unusual text characteristics. To build connections for students, ask them to identify links between the selection and other works you have presented in class, or to find connections to themes, activities, or other related concepts.

Build background. Use the Background information provided in the *Student Edition.* Whether explaining a historical time period, a scientific concept, or details about an idea that may be unfamiliar to students, this instruction presents useful information to help all students place the literature in context.

Focus vocabulary development. The student edition includes a list of vocabulary words included in the selection or selection grouping. Instead of attempting to cover all of the vocabulary words you anticipate your students will not know, identify the vocabulary that is most critical to talking and learning about the central concepts. However, for the words you do choose to teach, work to provide more than synonyms and definitions. Using the vocabulary notes in the *Annotated Teacher's Edition,* introduce the essential words in more meaningful contexts: for example, through simple sentences drawing on familiar issues, people, scenarios, and vocabulary. Guide students in internalizing the meanings of key terms through these familiar contexts and ask them to write the definitions in their own words. Look at these examples of guided vocabulary instruction:

Point out the word *serene* and explain that it means "calm or peaceful." Then, provide the following scenarios and ask students to determine whether the situations are *serene* or not: an empty beach at sunset *(yes);* a playground at recess (no). You might also ask students to provide their own examples of *serene* situations.

Point out the word *intervals* and explain that it means "the period of time between two events or point of time." Ask students to identify the interval between Monday and Wednesday *(two days)* and the interval between one Monday and the next Monday *(one week).*

You might also take the opportunity to teach the prefix *inter-*, meaning "between." Then, discuss with students the following group of words:

interview (a meeting between two or more people);
interstate (between two or more states);
international (between nations);
intervene (to come between two sides in a dispute).

Introduce skills. Introduce the *Literary Analysis* and *Reading Strategy*, using the instruction in the *Student Edition* and the teaching support in the *Annotated Teacher's Edition.*

Separate the class. As average level students begin reading the selection in the *Student Edition*, have English learners put their textbooks aside. Direct these students to the *English Learner's Companion* for further pre-teaching.

PRE-TEACH for English Learners Using the *English Learner's Companion*

Reinforce the general idea. Use the selection and visual summaries presented on the first page of every selection in the *English Learner's Companion.* These summaries will give students a framework to follow for understanding the selection. Use these tools to build familiarity, but do not use them as a replacement for reading.

Present audio summaries. The *Spanish/English Summaries Audio CD* can reinforce the main idea of a selection.

Reinforce skills instruction. Next, use the Prepare to Read page to reinforce the *Literary Analysis* and *Reading Strategy* concepts. Written in simpler language and in basic sentence structures, the instruction will help students better grasp these ideas.

Provide decoding practice. Because many English learners lack strategies for decoding bigger words, give them guided practice with the vocabulary words for the selection. Using the list, model a strategy for decoding polysyllabic words. First, show students how to break the word into parts and the put the parts back together to make a word.

> For the word *mimic*, ask students to draw a loop under each word part as they pronounce it.
>
> *mim ic*　　　*fright en ing*

Using this strategy, you can encourage students to look for familiar word parts and then break the rest of the word down into its consonant and vowel sounds. By building this routine regularly into your pre-teaching instruction, you reinforce a key reading skill for your students.

Prepare for lesson structure. To build students' ability to complete classroom activities, examine your lesson to see what types of language functions students will need to participate. Look at these examples:

> If students are being asked to make predictions about upcoming paragraph content in an essay, review the power of transition words that act as signals to meaning. Rather than teaching all transitions, limit your instruction to the ones in the passages. Identify the key transition words and point out their meaning. In addition, teach students some basic sentence patterns and verbs to express opinions. Model for students statement patterns such as:
>
> *I predict that . . .*
>
> *Based on this transition word, I conclude that . . .*

TEACH Using the English Learner's Companion

As average achieving students in your class read the selection in the textbook, allow English learners to read the adapted version in the *English Learner's Companion.* Whenever possible, give these students individualized attention by pairing them with aides, parent volunteers, or student peers.

Set purposes and limits. To keep students focused and motivated, and to prevent them from becoming overwhelmed as they read a selection, clearly establish a reading purpose for students before assigning a manageable amount of text. Once you identify a focus question or a purpose, revisit the question occasionally as students read. You can do this with a brief whole-group dialogue or by encouraging students in pairs to remember the question. In addition, your effective modeling will also provide the scaffolding for students to begin internalizing these strategies for effective reading.

Model your thinking. Describe and model strategies for navigating different kinds of text. Use the questions raised in the side notes as a starting point. Then, explain how you arrive at an answer. Alternatively, ask a student to explain his or her responses to classmates.

Reinforce new vocabulary. Present key words when they occur within the context of the reading selection. Review the definition as it appears on the page. Then, make the words as concrete as possible by linking each to an object, photo, or idea.

Build interactivity. The side notes in the *English Learner's Companion* are an excellent way to encourage student interactivity with the selections. To build students' ability to use these notes, model several examples with each selection. These are not busy work; they are activities that build fluency and provide the scaffolding necessary for student success.

Whenever possible, get students physically involved with the page, using *Mark the Text* icons as an invitation to use highlighters or colored pencils to circle, underline, or number key information. In addition, some students may find that using a small piece of cardboard or heavy construction paper helps to focus and guide their reading from one paragraph or page to the next.

Vary modes of instruction. To maintain student attention and interest, monitor and alternate the mode of instruction or activity. For example, alternate between teacher-facilitated and student-dominated reading activities. Assign brief amounts of text at a time, and alternate between oral, paired, and silent reading.

Monitor students' comprehension. As students use the side notes in the margins of the *English Learner's Companion,* build in opportunities to ensure that students are on purpose and understanding. Consider structured brief conversations for students to share, compare, or explain their thinking. Then, use these conversations to praise the correct use of strategies or to redirect students who need further support. In addition, this is an excellent chance for you to demonstrate your note-taking process and provide models of effective study notes for students to emulate.

Reinforce the reading experience. When students read the selection for the first time, they may be working on the decoding level. If time allows, students should read the selection twice to achieve a greater fluency and comfort level.

REVIEW AND ASSESS Using the *English Learner's Companion*

Reinforce writing and reading skills. Assign students the extension activity in the *English Learner's Companion.* Based on an activity presented the grade-level text, the version in the *English Learner's Companion* provides guided, step-by-step support for students. By giving students the opportunities to show their reading comprehension and writing skills, you maintain reasonable expectations for their developing academic competence in English.

Model expectations. Make sure that students understand your assessment criteria in advance. Provide models of student work whenever possible for them to emulate, along with a non-model that fails to meet the specified assessment criteria. Do not provide exemplars that are clearly outside of their developmental range. Save student work that can later serve as a model for students with different levels of academic preparation.

Lead students to closure. To achieve closure, ask students to end the class session by writing three to five outcome statements about their experience in the day's lesson, expressing both new understandings and needs for clarification.

Encourage self-monitoring and self-assessment. Remember to provide safe opportunities for students to alert you to any learning challenges they are experiencing. Consider having students submit anonymous written questions (formulated either independently or with a partner) about confusing lesson content and process. Later, you can follow up on these points of confusion at the end of class or in the subsequent class session.

EXTEND Using the *Student Edition*

Present the unabridged selection. Build in opportunities for students to read the full selection in the grade-level textbook. This will allow them to apply familiar concepts and vocabulary and stretch their literacy muscles.

Play an audio reading of the unabridged selection. Use the *Listening to Literature Audiotapes* or *CDs*. Students may benefit from reading along while listening to a professional recording of the selection. Encourage students to use their fingertips to follow the words as they are read.

Invite reader response. When students have finished reviewing the selection—whether in the companion or in the grade-level textbook—include all students in your class in post-reading analysis. To guide an initial discussion, use the Respond question in the *Thinking About the Selection* in the textbook. You will find that questions such as the following examples will provide strong springboards for classroom interaction:

> **Respond:** What advice would you have given the mother and daughter? Why?
>
> **Respond:** What questions would you like to ask the writer about his experience?
>
> **Respond:** Do you find the boy's actions courageous, touching, or silly? Explain your answer.

Encourage students to explain their answers to these questions by supporting their ideas with evidence from the text or their own lives. In addition, invite students to respond to classmates' ideas. These questions will lead students from simply getting the gist of a selection to establishing a personal connection to the lesson content.

Direct student analysis with scaffolded questions. When you are ready to move students into the Review and Assess questions, let your average achieving students use the instruction and questions in the grade-level textbook. At the same time, encourage English learners to use the questions in the *English Learner's Companion.*

- Questions in the companion, written in more simple language and providing more explicit support, will be more accessible to these students. Students will be applying concepts and practicing strategies at their own level.
- Some English learners may be prepared to answer questions in the grade-level text. The two-part questions in the *Thinking About the Selection* section are written to build and support student analysis. First, students use lower-level thinking skills to identify information or to recall important details in a selection. For the second part, students use a higher-level thinking skill based on the answer to the first part.

Look at these examples of scaffolded questions from the grade-level textbook:

(a) Recall: Why does the boy tell his father to leave the sickroom?
(b) Infer: What does this reveal about the boy?

(a) Recall: Why does the boy think he will die?
(b) Infer: What is the meaning of the title?

Revisit and reinforce strategies. Recycle pre- and post-reading tasks regularly, so students can become more familiar with the task process and improve their performance. If they are constantly facing curricular novelty, English learners never have the opportunity to refine their skills and demonstrate improved competence. For example, if you ask them to identify a personality trait of an essential character in a story and then support this observation with relevant details in an expository paragraph, it would make sense to have them write an identical paragraph in the near future about another character.

Show students how to transfer skills. Consider ways in which students can transfer knowledge and skills gleaned from one assignment/lesson to a subsequent lesson. For example, discuss with students the ways in which they can apply new vocabulary and language strategies outside of the classroom. In addition, demonstrate the applicability of new reading and writing strategies to real-world literacy tasks. Include periodic writing tasks for an authentic audience other than the teacher: another class, fellow classmates, local businesses, family, etc.

Offer praise and encourage growth. Praise students' efforts to experiment with new language in class, both in writing and in speaking.

USING PART TWO

For selections that are not presented as adaptations in Part One, use the summaries and activities in Part Two to support your English learners.

PRE-TEACH

In addition to the pre-teaching strategies listed on page xvi, consider these strategies to accommodate English learners.

Provide students a "running start." Use the selection summaries provided in the *English Learner's Companion.* These summaries, provided in six languages, will give students a framework for understanding the selection to follow.

Build interest. To take full advantage of the summaries, ask students to write one or two questions that the summaries raise in their minds. Share these questions in a discussion before reading the full text.

TEACH

As your students read the full selection in the textbook, provide English learners with support and individualized attention by pairing them with aides, parent volunteers, or student peers. In addition to the suggestions on page xviii, consider these additional strategies.

Model your thinking for side-column questions. To help these students practice the *Literary Analysis* skill and the *Reading Strategy,* use the questions raised in the side notes as a starting point. If students have difficulty answering the questions, review the concept for students and model your thinking process. Look at these examples of modeling explicit thinking:

Reading Strategy: Making Inferences

Remind students that, in a work of fiction, a writer expects readers to make connections with what they already know or have read in an earlier passage. Show students how to make inferences based on the side-column question and the appropriate text. Look at this passage from a selection as an example:

> "Mary, you oughta write David and tell him somebody done opened his letter and stole that ten dollars he sent," she said.
>
> "No mama. David's got enough on his mind. Besides, there's enough garden foods so we won't go hungry."

Then, use language like this to model your thinking process:

I'm not sure who the characters are talking about. There hasn't been any David mentioned in the story. What's this about an envelope? First, I ask myself what information there is in the passage. Mama sounds like she cares about this person; it's probably a friend or a family member. David sends money to the family, so he must be in another place. I'll ask myself what I know from what I've already read. Do I know anything about characters who live far away? Earlier, Mama said the father worked in Louisiana so that he could support the family. Could David be the father? I think so! He probably sends his wages back to Mississippi. That's the part about the envelope! Somebody opened up one of the letters and took the money.

Reading Strategy: Interpreting Poetic Language

In poetry, writers may describe an event in very different language from what they might use in writing an essay. Students can increase their understanding of poetry by learning to interpret poetic language. To help them, use the side notes and any marked texts to model your thinking process. Look at this example based on the following poetic lines:

> You crash over the trees,
> you crack the live branch—
> the branch is white,
> the green crushed,

Then, use language like this to model your thinking process:

I am not sure exactly what is being desc'ribed in the last two lines. What do the colors mean? Why is the branch white? What is the author referring to by "green crushed"? I'll start by figuring out what I do know. This poem is about a storm. From the second line, I can figure out that lightning or wind has struck the tree and cracked a branch. Green is the color of leaves. When a storm cracks a branch, it may fall to the ground. The leaves are crushed by the fall; this must be "the green crushed." But branches aren't white; they're brown or gray. However, if they're cracked open, the wood inside is white. The storm has cracked the branch and exposed its white insides.

***Use the* Reading Check *questions in the* Student Edition.** Consider pairing students, working with small groups, or setting brief instructional time for *Reading Check* questions that appear with every selection. These recall-level questions can be answered based on information in the text. Ask students to point to their answers in the selection before returning to reading.

REVIEW AND ASSESS

In addition to the suggestions on page xix, consider these additional strategies:

Build tests using the computer test bank. The computer test bank allows you to sort questions by difficulty level. Use this feature to generate tests appropriate to English learners.

Part 1

Selection Adaptations With Excerpts of Authentic Text

Part 1 will guide and support you as you interact with selections from *Prentice Hall Literature: Timeless Voices, Timeless Themes.* Part 1 provides summaries of literature selections with passages from the selection.

- Begin with the Preview page in the *English Learner's Companion.* Use the written and visual summaries to preview the selections before you read.
- Then study the Prepare to Read page. This page introduces skills that you will apply as you read selections in the *English Learner's Companion.*
- Now read the selection in the *English Learner's Companion.*
- Respond to all the questions along the sides as you read. They will guide you in understanding the selection and in applying the skills. Write in the *English Learner's Companion*—really! Circle things that interest you. Underline things that puzzle you. Number ideas or events to help you keep track of them. Look for the **Mark the Text** logo for help with active reading.
- Use the Review and Assess questions at the end of each selection to review what you have read and to check your understanding.
- Finally, do the Writing or the Speaking and Listening activity to extend your understanding and practice your skills.

Interacting With the Text

As you read, use the information and notes to guide you in interacting with the selection. The examples on these pages show you how to use the notes as a companion when you read. They will guide you in applying reading and literary skills and in thinking about the selection. When you read other texts, you can practice the thinking skills and strategies found here.

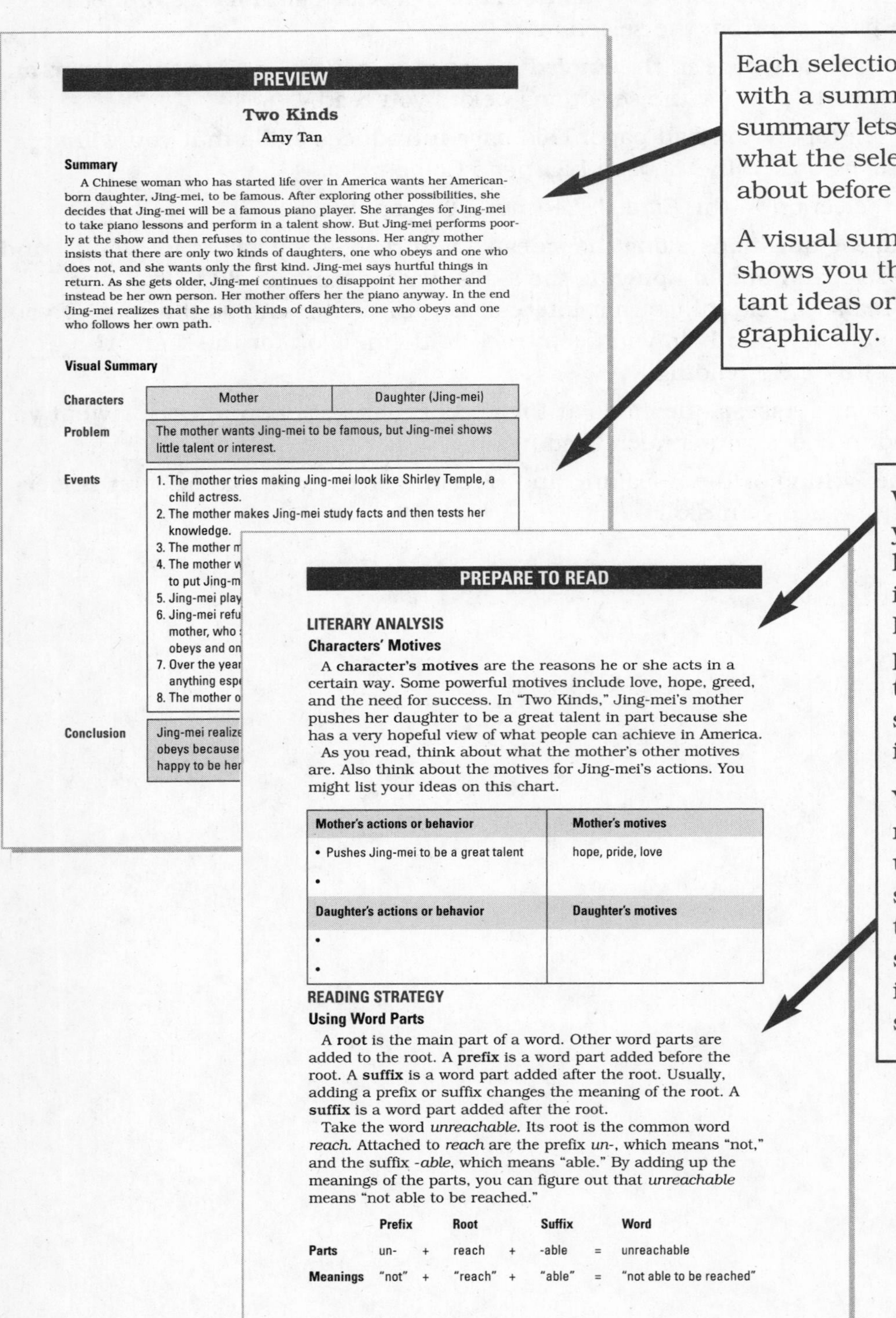

Each selection begins with a summary. The summary lets you know what the selection is about before you read.

A visual summary shows you the important ideas or details graphically.

With each selection, you will study a literary element. It is introduced on the Prepare to Read page. Later, notes in the margins of the selection help you identify this element.

You are also given a reading strategy to use as you read the selection. Notes in the margins of the selection guide you in applying this strategy as you read.

Text set in a narrow margin provides a summary of selection events or details.

Text set in a wider margin provides the author's actual words.

Two Kinds

Amy Tan

The mother in this story was born in China. She fled during the communist revolution of 1949. She lost everything in the revolution: her parents, her first husband, her two baby daughters, her family home. But in America she married again and had a new daughter, Jing-mei. It is Jing-mei who tells the story:

◆ ◆ ◆

My mother believed you could be anything you wanted to be in America. You could open a restaurant. You could work for the government. . . . You could become rich. You could become instantly famous.

◆ ◆ ◆

Jing-mei's mother decides that her daughter can be a prodigy, or supertalented child. First, she plans to make Jing-mei a movie star and has Jing-mei's hair cut just like the popular child actress Shirley Temple's. Then, the mother gets a better idea: She makes Jing-mei study books and magazines and tests her on the facts. When Jing-mei's performance is disappointing, her mother gives up on that idea too.

◆ ◆ ◆

Two or three months had gone by without any mention of my being a prodigy again. And then one day my mother was watching *The Ed Sullivan Show* on TV. . . .

◆ ◆ ◆

On the show, a young Chinese girl is playing the piano. When she is done, she

Vocabulary Development

prodigy (PRAH di gee) *n.* a child of unusually high talent

◆ **Reading Check**

Mark the Text

What does Jing-mei's mother believe anyone can be in America? Circle three answers.

◆ **Reading Strategy**

Mark the Text

Super- is a prefix meaning "over; above; beyond normal." Circle the three **word parts** in the word *supertalented.* Then, complete this sentence: A *supertalented* child is a child who ____________________

Use write-on lines to answer the questions. You may also want to use the lines for your own notes or for questions you have.

When you see this symbol, follow the directions to underline, circle or mark the text as indicated.

REVIEW AND ASSESS

1. How does Jing-mei disappoint her mother in the story? Answer by circling the word or phrase in parentheses that best completes each sentence:

   The mother wants Jing-mei to be (famous, beautiful, contented, sent away).

   But Jing-mei can only be (brilliant, pleading, a child, herself).

2. What does the mother say are the two kinds of daughters?

   Kind 1: ________________ Kind 2: ________________

3. In the end, what does Jing-mei realize about the kind of daughter she is? ________________________

4. **Reading Strategy:** For each word on the right, add up the meanings of the word parts to figure out the meaning of the word. Write the meaning on the line below the word.

	Prefix		Root	Word
	un-	+	like	= unlike
Meanings	"not"	+	"similar to"	= __________
	Root		**Suffix**	**Word**
	child	+	-ish	= childish
Meanings	"young person"	+	"like"	= __________

5. **Literary Analysis:** Fill out this chart by putting at least one **motive** in the second column of each item.

Mother's actions or behavior	Mother's motives
• pushes Jing-mei to be famous	__________
• arranges for a talent show	__________
• offers to give Jing-mei the piano	__________

Questions after every selection help you think about the selection. You can use the write-on lines or charts to answer the questions.

The Cat Who Thought She Was a Dog and the Dog Who Thought He Was a Cat

Isaac Bashevis Singer

Summary

Jan Skiba lives in a small hut with his wife, his daughters, a dog, and a cat. They are poor, but they don't really notice. Even the dog and cat get along, for they do not realize that they are different from each other. Then one day the Skibas buy a mirror. For the first time, they see what they look like. They notice flaws in their appearance and begin to long for changes in their lives. The dog and cat realize that they are different and begin to fight. Finally, Jan decides that the mirror is no good. He returns it, and the family returns to normal.

Visual Summary

What are things like at first? →

Skiba family
- very poor
- live in a small hut

Burek the dog
- thinks he is a cat
- plays with Kot

Kot the cat
- thinks she is a dog
- plays with Burek

What happens after the family buys a mirror? →

Jan Skiba
- dislikes his thick lips and buck teeth

Marianna Skiba
- thinks missing tooth makes her ugly

Skiba daughters
- dislike something about their looks

Burek the dog
- gets angry at his reflection
- fights with Kot

Kot the cat
- becomes confused
- fights with Burek

What happens after Jan gets rid of the mirror?

Burek the dog
- again thinks he is a cat
- plays with Kot

Kot the cat
- again thinks she is a dog
- plays with Burek

Skiba daughters
- make good marriages

Skiba family
- returns to normal

PREPARE TO READ

LITERARY ANALYSIS

The Moral of a Story

A **moral** is a message about how people behave or how they should behave. The events in many stories point to a moral.

Example 1: Suppose you read a story about someone who works hard and does well in life. The moral of that story might be: "Hard work is often rewarded."

Example 2: Suppose you read a story about a lion who is kind to a mouse. The moral of that story might be: "Be kind to those who are weaker than you."

Singer's story has more than one moral. To figure out the morals, answer these questions:

1. What does the story show about the importance of owning things?
2. What does the story show about the importance of a person's looks?
3. What does the story show are the most important things in life?

READING STRATEGY

Clarifying Word Meanings

When you read, you will often come across words you aren't sure about. How can you figure out their meaning? One way is to look at nearby words and sentences, which often help make the meaning clear. For example, Singer's story uses the word word *mimic*, which you may not know. But the next sentence gives you an example of how Burek the dog and Kot the cat *mimic* each other. From it, you can tell that to mimic must mean "to imitate" or "to act like someone else."

Filling out a chart like this might help you with other unfamiliar words in the story.

Unfamiliar Word	Burek and Kot . . . tried to mimic each other.
Nearby Words	When Burek barked, Kot tried to bark along, and when Kot meowed, Burek tried to meow too.
Meaning of Word	to imitate; to act like someone else

The Cat Who Thought She Was a Dog and the Dog Who Thought He Was a Cat

Isaac Bashevis Singer

◆ Reading Strategy

Circle the words that help you understand the meaning of *peasant*.

Jan Skiba was a peasant, or poor farmer. He lived in a tiny hut far from town with his wife Marianna and their three daughters. The Skibas were so poor that they didn't own very much. In fact, they didn't even own a mirror. But they did have a dog named Burek and a cat named Kot. The animals had been born within a few days of each other. Even though the family was poor, Jan Skiba never let the dog and the cat go hungry.

◆ ◆ ◆

◆ Vocabulary and Pronunciation

In English, dogs *bark* and cats *meow*. Both words come from the sounds these animals make. What words does your native language use for the sounds dogs and cats make? Write them here:

dogs: ______________________

cats: ______________________

Since the dog had never seen another dog and the cat had never seen another cat and they saw only each other, the dog thought he was a cat and the cat thought she was a dog. True, they were far from being alike by nature. The dog, like most dogs, barked and went after rabbits. The cat, like most cats, meowed and lurked after mice. But . . . Burek and Kot lived on good terms, often ate from the same dish, and tried to mimic each other.

◆ ◆ ◆

◆ Reading Strategy

Circle the words in the bracketed passage that help you understand the meaning of *peddler*. Then, write the meaning here.

peddler: ______________________

____

____

In those days, peddlers traveled from door to door, buying and selling things. Because the Skibas were poor, peddlers never stopped at their house—the Skibas had nothing to buy or sell. Then one day a peddler did stop. He had jewelry, kerchiefs and other trinkets to sell.

◆ ◆ ◆

Vocabulary Development

lurked (lerkd) *v.* waited quietly

But what enthralled the women of the house most was a mirror set in a wooden frame.

♦ ♦ ♦

The peddler agreed to let them give him a small amount of money each month until the mirror was paid for. After he left, the Skibas kept looking in the mirror. They saw problems they had never noticed before.

♦ ♦ ♦

Marianna was pretty but she had a tooth missing in front and she felt that this made her ugly. One daughter discovered that her nose was too snub and too broad; a second that her chin was too narrow and too long; a third that her face was sprinkled with freckles. Jan Skiba too caught a glimpse of himself in the mirror and grew displeased by his thick lips and teeth, which protruded. . . .

♦ ♦ ♦

The women ignored their chores and kept looking in the mirror. The first daughter kept pinching her nose to try to make it narrower. The second kept pushing her chin to try to make it shorter. The third wondered if she could go to the city and buy something to remove her freckles. Her mother thought of visiting a city dentist and getting a new tooth. But all this would cost more than they could afford.

♦ ♦ ♦

Vocabulary Development

enthralled (in THRAWLD) *v.* fascinated; excited; charmed
snub (SNUB) *adj.* short and turned up
protruded (proh TROO did) *v.* stuck out

♦ Vocabulary and Pronunciation

English speakers pronounce *mirror* differently in different areas. Some say each syllable. Others say the word so that it almost sounds like the one-syllable word *mere*. How do most people say *mirror* where you now live? Circle the answer:
1 syllable 2 syllables

♦ Vocabulary and Pronunciation

Many English words start with *dis-*. This prefix means "not" or "the opposite of." Explain the meanings of these words.

displeased: ________________

disbelief: ________________

disappear: ________________

♦ Culture Note

Ideas about beauty change from place to place and time to time. Today, many people consider freckles cute. In the past, that was not always the case. What are some ideas about beauty in your native land? Have they changed over time? Write your answers here.

____

____

____

____

◆ **Vocabulary and Pronunciation**

Read this bracketed sentence aloud. Are there any words that look or sound a lot like words with the same meaning in your native language? If so, circle them.

◆ **Literary Analysis**

What does Jan Skiba now think is important in life? Complete this **moral** based on what Jan thinks.

______________________ is/are

more important than __________

__________________________.

◆ **Literary Analysis**

What does the priest think is important in life? Complete this **moral** based on what the priest says.

____

______________________ is/are

more important than __________

____

__________________________.

For the first time the Skiba family deeply felt its poverty and envied the rich.

◆ ◆ ◆

The dog and cat also became unhappy. They now saw themselves in the mirror and realized they were different. They began biting and clawing each other until they had to be separated.

◆ ◆ ◆

When Jan Skiba saw the disruption the mirror had created in his household, he decided a mirror wasn't what his family needed.

◆ ◆ ◆

Jan thought they should look at things like the sun and the moon. He returned the mirror to the peddler in exchange for kerchiefs and slippers. Without the mirror in the house, things went back to being the way they had been. The cat and the dog stopped fighting because, once again, the cat thought she was a dog and the dog thought he was a cat. The daughters quit worrying about what was wrong with their looks.

◆ ◆ ◆

When the village priest heard what happened, he pointed out that a glass mirror shows only the outside of a person. The real image of a person comes from his or her being willing to help family and, if possible, others. This real image shows what is on the inside—the person's soul.

Vocabulary Development

envied (EN veed) *v.* was jealous of

disruption (dis RUP shun) *n.* a confused situation; a situation that does not go smoothly

REVIEW AND ASSESS

1. Write three words that describe the Skibas' life when the story opens.

   1. ____________ 2. ____________ 3. ____________

2. Complete this chart that lists the problems each character has after looking in the mirror.

Jan Skiba	lips too thick, teeth stick out
Marianna Skiba	
first daughter	
second daughter	
third daughter	
Burek	realizes he is not a cat
Kot	

3. Why does Jan give back the mirror?

   ____

   ____

4. **Reading Strategy:** A *trinket* is a small, pretty item that is not worth very much money. In paragraph 3 (page 6) of the story, which words help you understand the meaning of *trinket*?

   trinket: ____________________________________

   ____

5. **Reading Strategy:** Use the words near *glimpse* in paragraph 3 (page 7) to help you figure out the meaning of *glimpse*.

   glimpse: ____________________________________

   ____

(Continued)

6. **Literary Analysis:** Put a check in front of each sentence that you think is a **moral** of this story.

____ What makes people unhappy is not doing without things but wanting more than they have.

____ Beautiful people have an easy life.

____ Never buy something you cannot afford.

____ It is better to look at the world and not be so interested in looking at yourself.

____ You show your true self by your actions, not your appearance.

Writing

A **fable** is a simple story that teaches a moral. Usually it has animal characters who act like human beings. Write down your ideas for a fable about Burek the dog and Kot the cat. Explain how they will act and what will happen to them. Start by stating what the moral of the fable will be.

Moral:

____

____

____

Ideas:

____

____

____

____

____

PREVIEW

Two Kinds

Amy Tan

Summary

A Chinese woman who has started life over in America wants her American-born daughter, Jing-mei, to be famous. After exploring other possibilities, she decides that Jing-mei will be a famous piano player. She arranges for Jing-mei to take piano lessons and perform in a talent show. But Jing-mei performs poorly at the show and then refuses to continue the lessons. Her angry mother insists that there are only two kinds of daughters, ones who obey and ones who do not, and she wants only the first kind. Jing-mei says hurtful things in return. As she gets older, Jing-mei continues to disappoint her mother and, instead, be her own person. Her mother offers her the piano anyway. In the end Jing-mei realizes that she is both kinds of daughters, one who obeys and one who follows her own path.

Visual Summary

Characters	Mother	Daughter (Jing-mei)
Problem	The mother wants Jing-mei to be famous, but Jing-mei shows little talent or interest.	
Events	1. The mother tries making Jing-mei look like Shirley Temple, a child actress. 2. The mother makes Jing-mei study facts and then tests her knowledge. 3. The mother makes Jing-mei take piano lessons with Mr. Chong. 4. The mother wants to show off her daughter and gets Mr. Chong to put Jing-mei in a talent show. 5. Jing-mei plays badly in the talent show. 6. Jing-mei refuses to continue piano lessons and fights with her mother, who says that there are two kinds of daughter, ones who obey and ones who do not. 7. Over the years, Jing-mei is true to herself but does not do anything especially well. 8. The mother offers her the piano for her thirtieth birthday.	
Conclusion	Jing-mei realizes that she is both kinds of daughter, one who obeys because she needs the approval of others and one who is happy to be herself.	

PREPARE TO READ

LITERARY ANALYSIS

Characters' Motives

A **character's motives** are the reasons he or she acts in a certain way. Some powerful motives include love, hope, greed, and the need for success. In "Two Kinds," Jing-mei's mother pushes her daughter to be a great talent in part because she has a very hopeful view of what people can achieve in America.

As you read, think about what the mother's other motives are. Also think about the motives for Jing-mei's actions. You might list your ideas on this chart.

Mother's actions or behavior	Mother's motives
• Pushes Jing-mei to be a great talent •	hope, pride, love
Daughter's actions or behavior	**Daughter's motives**
• •	

READING STRATEGY

Using Word Parts

A **root** is the main part of a word. Other word parts are added to the root. A **prefix** is a word part added before the root. A **suffix** is a word part added after the root. Usually, adding a prefix or suffix changes the meaning of the root.

Take the word *unreachable*. Its root is the common word *reach*. Attached to *reach* are the prefix *un-*, which means "not," and the suffix *-able*, which means "able." By adding up the meanings of the parts, you can figure out that *unreachable* means "not able to be reached."

	Prefix		Root		Suffix		Word
Parts	un-	+	reach	+	-able	=	unreachable
Meanings	"not"	+	"reach"	+	"able"	=	"not able to be reached"

Two Kinds

Amy Tan

The mother in this story was born in China. She fled during the communist revolution of 1949. She lost everything in the revolution: her parents, her first husband, her two baby daughters, her family home. But in America she married again and had a new daughter, Jing-mei. It is Jing-mei who tells the story:

◆ ◆ ◆

My mother believed you could be anything you wanted to be in America. You could open a restaurant. You could work for the government. . . . You could become rich. You could become instantly famous.

◆ ◆ ◆

Jing-mei's mother decides that her daughter can be a prodigy, or supertalented child. First, she plans to make Jing-mei a movie star and has Jing-mei's hair cut just like the popular child actress Shirley Temple's. Then, the mother gets a better idea: She makes Jing-mei study books and magazines and tests her on the facts. When Jing-mei's performance is disappointing, her mother gives up on that idea too.

◆ ◆ ◆

Two or three months had gone by without any mention of my being a prodigy again. And then one day my mother was watching *The Ed Sullivan Show* on TV. . . .

◆ ◆ ◆

On the show, a young Chinese girl is playing the piano. When she is done, she

Vocabulary Development

prodigy (PRAH di gee) *n.* a child of unusually high talent

◆ Culture Note

Mark the Text

Many people come to America to escape war or confusion in their native lands. Most see America as a land of great opportunity. What were some of the reasons your family came to America? Write your answer on these lines.

____

____

____

____

◆ Reading Strategy

Mark the Text

Super- is a prefix meaning "over; above; beyond normal." Circle the three **word parts** in the word *supertalented*. Then, complete this sentence: A *supertalented* child is a child who ____________________

____

____

______________________________.

◆ Vocabulary and Pronunciation

Many words about music came to English from Italian. The *piano* was originally called a *pianoforte*, from the Italian words for "soft" and "loud." How do you say piano in your native language? Write it here:

______________________________.

◆ Vocabulary and Pronunciation

The word *whine*, which means "to complain," is usually pronounced like *wine*. Some English speakers add a tiny breath after the w to made it sound a bit different. Circle at least two more words in the bracketed paragraphs that start with the same sound.

Mark the Text

◆ English Language Development

Jing-mei's mother does not yet speak perfect English. Her verbs often have the wrong endings, and she sometimes leaves out words. For example, "Who ask you be genius?" should really be "Who asked you to be a genius?" Fix the underlined sentences by squeezing in missing words and verb endings.

Mark the Text

◆ Vocabulary and Pronunciation

Bass has two pronunciations, each with a different meaning. Pronounced with a short *a*, to rhyme with *class*, it is a type of fish. Pronounced with a long *a*, the same as *base*, it has the meaning in the story. Say the word in the story, and then write the meaning here.

____

____

____

makes a sweeping curtsy in her fluffy white dress. The mother decides that Jing-mei will take piano lessons too. She speaks with Mr. Chong, a retired piano teacher who lives in the same apartment building. She agrees to clean his apartment if he will give lessons to Jing-mei.

◆ ◆ ◆

When my mother told me this, I felt as though I had been sent to hell. I whined and then kicked my foot a little when I couldn't stand it anymore.

"Why don't you like me the way I am? I'm not a genius! I can't play the piano. And even if I could, I wouldn't go on TV if you paid me a million dollars!" I cried.

My mother slapped me. "Who ask you be genius?" she shouted. "Only ask you be your best. For your sake. You think I want you be genius? Hnnh! . . ."

◆ ◆ ◆

Jing-mei secretly nicknames the piano teacher Old Chong and begins taking lessons from him. She does not do very well, for there is a serious problem.

◆ ◆ ◆

I soon found out why Old Chong had retired from teaching piano. He was deaf. . . .

Our lessons went like this. He would open the book and point to different things, explaining their purpose: "Key! Treble! Bass! No sharps or flats. So this is C major! Listen now and play after me!"

Vocabulary Development

curtsy (KERT see) *n.* a polite action in which a female bends her knees and lowers her body
treble (TRE bul) *n.* the higher sounds in music
bass (BAYS) *n.* the lower sounds in music

And then he would play the C scale a few times, a simple chord, and then, as if inspired by an old, unreachable itch, he gradually added more notes and running trills and a pounding bass until the music was really something quite grand.

I would play after him, the simple scale, the simple chord, and then I just played some nonsense that sounded like a cat running up and down on top of garbage cans. Old Chong smiled and applauded and then said, "Very good! But now you must learn to keep time!"

◆ ◆ ◆

Jing-mei never mentions Old Chong's problem to anyone. She continues to take lessons from him. One day she hears her mother talking to Lindo Jong, a close family friend that Jing-mei calls her aunt. Lindo brags about her daughter Waverly, a chess champion.

◆ ◆ ◆

"She bring home too many trophy. . . . You lucky you don't have this problem," said Auntie Lindo with a sigh to my mother.

And my mother squared her shoulders and bragged: "Our problem worser than yours. If we ask Jing-mei wash dish, she hear nothing but music. It's like you can't stop this natural talent."

◆ ◆ ◆

A few weeks later, Jing-mei's mother gets Old Chong to plan a talent show in which Jing-mei and others will perform. Jing-mei is supposed to learn by heart a

Vocabulary Development

inspired (in SPĪ rd) *v.* influenced; aroused; caused to create

trills (TRILZ) *n.* musical sounds that go rapidly back and forth between the same notes

champion (CHAMP ee un) *n.* someone who has won many games or contests

◆ **Reading Strategy**

Mark the Text

Unreachable means "not able to be reached." Circle the prefix and suffix in the word. Below, explain what those **word parts** mean.

un-: ________________

-able: ________________

◆ **Vocabulary and Pronunciation**

Mark the Text

The word *chord* refers to a blend of musical sounds. In the word, the *ch* is pronounced like a */k/*. In the bracketed sentence, circle three other words with a */k/* sound spelled in a different way.

◆ **Vocabulary and Pronunciation**

Mark the Text

A *trophy* is a gold cup or a similar prize given to the winner of a game or contest. Circle the letter or letters in *trophy* that have the sound of */f/*.

◆ **English Language Development**

Mark the Text

Many English adjectives have a comparative form to compare two things. Most short adjectives use *-er* for this form:

He is *nice* but she is *nicer*.

The adjectives *good* and *bad* have irregular comparative forms:

He is *good* but she is *better*.

This is *bad* but that is *worse*.

Circle and fix the incorrect comparative form in the mother's remarks.

piece called "Pleading Child" from a work called *Scenes from Childhood*. But she has trouble practicing.

◆ ◆ ◆

The part I liked to practice best was the fancy curtsy: right foot out, touch the rose on the carpet with a pointed foot, sweep to the side, left leg bends, look up and smile.

◆ ◆ ◆

Jing-mei's parents invite all their friends and relatives to the show, including Auntie Lindo and Waverly the chess champion. After some other children dance, sing, recite poems, and play tunes, it is Jing-mei's turn.

◆ ◆ ◆

And I started to play. It was so beautiful. I was so caught up in how lovely I looked that at first I didn't worry how I would sound. So it was a surprise to me when I hit the first wrong note and I realized something didn't sound quite right. And then I hit another and another followed that. A chill started at the top of my head and began to trickle down. . . .

◆ ◆ ◆

After the awful performance, the whole room is quiet except for Old Chong, who cheers loudly. Jing-mei leaves the stage and returns to her seat in shame. When the show is over, people in the audience talk together before leaving.

◆ ◆ ◆

Waverly looked at me and shrugged her shoulders. "You aren't a genius like me," she said. . . . And if I hadn't felt so bad, I would have pulled her braids and punched her stomach.

◆ ◆ ◆

As Jing-mei and her parents return home, Jing-mei's mother says nothing. She

Vocabulary Development

pleading (PLEED ing) *adj.* asking; begging

◆ Culture Note

A *curtsy* is a traditional way for a woman to show respect. What special actions or movements show respect in your native land? Do they differ between men and women? Write your answers on the lines below.

____

____

____

◆ Culture Note

Auntie is an affectionate form of *aunt,* the English word for a mother's or father's sister. But in China, it is the custom also to use the Chinese word for *aunt* for family friends like Lindo. Write the term for a mother's or father's sister in your native land:

____

Is it ever used for other women too ? ____________

◆ Vocabulary and Pronunciation

Mark the Text

In the word *chord* from earlier in the story, the *ch* is pronounced like */k/.* Now circle the word in the bracketed sentence with a *ch* also pronounced like */k/.*

seems to be in a state of shock. Yet two days later, she expects Jing-mei to begin practicing the piano again. But Jing-mei has had enough.

◆ ◆ ◆

"I'm not going to play anymore. . . . Why should I? I'm not a genius."

◆ ◆ ◆

Her mother insists that Jing-mei play, but Jing-mei refuses.

◆ ◆ ◆

"No!" I said, and I now felt stronger, as if my true self had finally emerged. So this was what had been inside me all along.

"No! I won't!" I screamed.

◆ ◆ ◆

As her mother drags her to the piano, Jing-mei begins to cry.

◆ ◆ ◆

"You want me to be someone that I'm not!" I sobbed. "I'll never be the kind of daughter you want me to be!"

"Only two kinds of daughters," she shouted in Chinese. "Those who are obedient and those who follow their own mind. Only one kind of daughter can live in this house. Obedient daughter!"

"Then I wish I wasn't your daughter. I wish you weren't my mother," I shouted. As I said these things I got scared. It felt like worms and toads and slimy things crawling out of my chest, but it also felt good, as if this awful side of me had surfaced at last.

"Too late change this," said my mother shrilly.

I could sense her anger rising to its breaking point. I wanted to see it spill over. And that's

Vocabulary Development

emerged (ee MERGD) *v.* came out
obedient (oh BEE dee ent) *adj.* doing what others say; obeying
surfaced (SER fisd) *v.* came to the top; showed itself

◆ **English Language Development**

Mark the Text

In the bracketed paragraph, circle the adjective that uses the comparative form.

◆ **English Language Development**

Mark the Text

In these two bracketed paragraphs, circle all the quotation marks that show when Jing-mei and her mother are speaking. How does the author show a change of speaker?

____

____

____

____

◆ **Literary Analysis**

Mark the Text

Circle the sentence that helps explain Jing-mei's **motive** for making these very hurtful remarks to her mother. Also circle the feeling or emotion that is part of the motive for both her and her mother's behavior here.

when I remembered the babies she had lost in China, the ones we never talked about. "Then I wish I'd never been born!" I shouted. "I wish I were dead! Like them."

◆ ◆ ◆

Stunned by these words, the mother leaves the room. She stops trying to get her daughter to play the piano. As the years pass, Jing-mei also disappoints her mother in other ways: She does not get straight A's or become class president. She does not get accepted to Stanford University. She even drops out of college.

◆ ◆ ◆

For unlike my mother, I did not believe I could be anything I wanted to be. I could only be me.

◆ ◆ ◆

For years, the two never mention what happened with the piano lessons. Then, on Jing-mei's thirtieth birthday, her mother offers her the piano. Jing-mei sees this as a sign of forgiveness. After her mother dies, she takes the piano. In the piano bench she finds the music from *Scenes from Childhood*, with the piece she played at the talent show, "Pleading Child."

◆ ◆ ◆

I played a few bars, surprised at how easily the notes came back to me.

And for the first time, or so it seemed, I noticed the piece on the right-hand side. It was called "Perfectly Contented." I tried to play this one as well. . . . "Pleading Child" was shorter but slower; "Perfectly Contented" was longer, but faster. And after I played them both, I realized they were two halves of the same song.

◆ Reading Check

Number four things that Jing-mei does that disappoint her mother.

◆ Reading Strategy

The suffix *-ness* means "act; state; condition." Put a line between the root and suffix in the word *forgiveness*. Then, explain the meaning of the word.

forgiveness: ____________________

____

____

◆ Vocabulary and Pronunciation

The word *bars* has many meanings, some of which appear below. Circle the letter of the meaning here.

(a) long pieces of metal, wood, etc.

(b) stripes or bands

(c) sections of notes in a piece of music

(d) blocks; prevents

Now circle two other words in the sentence that make the meaning clear.

Vocabulary Development

contented (cuhn TENT ed) *adj.* happy with the way things are; satisfied

REVIEW AND ASSESS

1. How does Jing-mei disappoint her mother in the story? Answer by circling the word or phrase in parentheses that best completes each sentence:

   The mother wants Jing-mei to be (famous, beautiful, contented, sent away).

   But Jing-mei can only be (brilliant, pleading, a child, herself).

2. What does the mother say are the two kinds of daughters?

   Kind 1: ______________________ Kind 2: ______________________

3. In the end, what does Jing-mei realize about the kind of daughter she is? ____

   ____

4. **Reading Strategy:** For each word on the right, add up the meanings of the word parts to figure out the meaning of the word. Write the meaning on the line below the word.

	Prefix		Root	Word
	un-	+	like	= unlike
Meanings	"not"	+	"similar to"	= ______________________
	Root		**Suffix**	**Word**
	child	+	-ish	= childish
Meanings	"young person"	+	"like"	= ______________________

5. **Literary Analysis:** Fill out this chart by putting at least one **motive** in the second column of each item.

Mother's actions or behavior	Mother's motives
• pushes Jing-mei to be famous	______________________
• arranges for a talent show	______________________
• offers to give Jing-mei the piano	______________________

(Continued)

Daughter's actions or behavior	Daughter's motives
• agrees to take piano lessons	
• refuses to take any more piano lessons	
• says hurtful words to her mother	

Writing

Imagine that the same story was told by Jing-mei's mother instead of Jing-mei. What thoughts and feelings would the mother describe? Write at least two thoughts or feelings for each item on this list.

- the mother's thoughts or feelings about America

- the mother's thoughts or feelings about her daughter being famous

- the mother's thoughts or feelings about the talent show

- the mother's thoughts or feelings when she and Jing-mei have their big fight after the show

- the mother's thoughts or feelings years later

My Furthest-Back Person (The Inspiration for *Roots*)

Alex Haley

Summary

Alex Haley tells how he traced his family's roots to Africa. Checking government records from just after the Civil War, he was excited to find that relatives he'd heard about had actually lived. He then began checking his grandmother's story of the family's "furthest-back person" in America. Some of the strange words she had used turned out to be from an African language. Also *Kin-tay*, the name she called the "furthest-back person," turned out to be the old West African family name *Kinte*. Traveling to Africa, Haley found his distant Kinte relatives and heard the family history from a traditional oral historian. Piecing together all his research, he confirmed his grandmother's story: His "furthest-back person" in America was Kunta Kinte, a 16-year-old African kidnapped near the Gambia River in 1767, shipped to Annapolis, Maryland, and sold into slavery.

Visual Summary

Starting Point: Grandmother's stories of relatives include the family's "furthest-back person" in America, a man named Kin-tay, who was kidnapped in Africa, brought to 'Naplis, and sold into slavery.

Research in America	Research in Africa	Research in England
1. Census records confirm 1800s relatives 2. Cousin Georgia repeats story of furthest-back relative Kin-tay 3. Professor identifies strange African words; one is Gambia River 4. Dr. Curtin identifies Kin-tay as old African family name Kinte 9. Records in Maryland show arrival and sale of 98 slaves Sept./Oct. 1767	5. Gambians confirm terms are Gambia River and Kinte 6. Traditional storyteller tells of Kinte family history and disappearance of 16-year-old Kunta in time of "king's soldiers"	7. Records show soldiers sent mid-1767 to protect Britain's James Fort on Gambia River 8. Shipping records show British ship with 140 slaves left Gambia for Annapolis on July 5, 1767

Conclusion: Research confirms that Haley's family's "furthest-back person" in America was Kunta Kinte, a kidnapped Gambian brought to Annapolis, Maryland, in 1767, and sold into slavery.

PREPARE TO READ

LITERARY ANALYSIS

Personal Essay

An **essay** is a short piece of nonfiction writing on a particular topic. In a **personal essay**, the topic is usually an experience in the writer's life. The writer shares thoughts about what happened and shows why it was important. The style of the writing is conversational, as if the writer were talking to you.

As you read Haley's essay, answer these questions.

1. What personal experience is Haley's essay about?
2. What are his thoughts and feelings about the experience?
3. Why is the experience so important to him?

READING STRATEGY

Breaking Down Long Sentences

Sometimes it is hard to follow a long sentence. It helps if you **break down long sentences** and think about how the different parts are related.

Step 1. Put lines between groups of words that you think work together. There is no one right way to divide a sentence—just divide it into groups of words that seem best to you.

Step 2. Think about what the different groups of words are saying. Then, underline the key group or groups that tell you what happened. This sample sentence from the essay is divided into five groups with key words underlined:

> After about a dozen microfilmed rolls, | <u>I was beginning to tire</u>, | when in utter astonishment | <u>I looked upon the names of Grandma's parents</u>: | Tom Murray, Irene Murray . . .

Step 3. Decide what the other groups of words in the sentence tell you. To show their relationship to the other groups of words, you might create a chart like the one below.

Sentence Part	What the Part Tells
After about a dozen microfilmed rolls	tells when first thing happened
I was beginning to tire	first thing that happened (key group)

My Furthest-Back Person

(The Inspiration for *ROOTS*)

Alex Haley

As a boy, Alex Haley often sat on his grandmother's front porch, listening to her stories of family history going back to the days of slavery. The "furthest-back person" she spoke about was an African who was kidnapped from his homeland, shipped to Annapolis, Maryland, and sold as a slave. Years later, in 1965, Haley walked past the National Archives in Washington, D.C. His grandmother's stories came to mind, and he decided to go inside. In the main reading room, where people do research, he spoke with the man at the desk.

◆ ◆ ◆

I wouldn't have dreamed of admitting to him some curiosity hanging on from boyhood about my slave forebears. I kind of bumbled that I was interested in census records of Alamance County, North Carolina, just after the Civil War.

◆ ◆ ◆

The records were stored on rolls of microfilm that Haley viewed on a special machine.

◆ ◆ ◆

After about a dozen microfilmed rolls, I was beginning to tire, when in utter astonishment I looked upon the names of Grandma's parents: Tom Murray, Irene Murray . . . older

Vocabulary Development

archives (AR kīvz) *n.* a place where records are stored
forebears (FOHR bayrz) *n.* relatives who came before; ancestors
census (SEN sus) **records** *n.* official lists of people living in a particular area

◆ **English Language Development**

Instead of saying "person who is furthest back," the grandmother takes a shortcut. She uses the compound adjective *furthest-back* to describe the noun *person.* A compound adjective contains two or more words, usually joined with hyphens (-). It comes before the noun it describes. Shorten each of these phrases by writing a compound adjective on each line.

an African who is 16 years old:

a ________________ African

a fort that is held by the British:

a ________________ fort

◆ **Culture Note**

The American Civil War was fought from 1861 to 1865. The official United States census, which counts the people in the country, is taken every ten years in a year that ends in *0.* In which year's census do you think Haley found his grandmother's parents listed? Write it here:

____

◆ **Reading Strategy**

Mark the Text

To help you understand this sentence, use lines to break it into parts. Then, answer this question: Who were Tom and Irene Murray? Circle the letter of the answer.

(a) Haley's parents

(b) Haley's grandparents

(c) Haley's grandmother's parents

(d) the grandmother's sister and brother

◆ English Language Development

An **apostrophe (')**, pronounced "uhPOSStruhfee", shows where a letter or letters are left out when words are shortened. The shortened word is called a contraction. The word *wasn't*, for example, is a contraction of *was not*, with the apostrophe showing where the *o* was left out. Circle two more contractions in these sentences. In each, squeeze in the missing letter or letters that the apostrophe stands for.

◆ English Language Development

To show that Cousin Georgia dropped some sounds when she spoke, Haley drops the letters that make those sounds. He uses apostrophes in place of the missing letters. Squeeze in the letters that the apostrophes stand for in *an', an', choppin'*, and *'im*.

sisters of Grandma's as well—every one of them a name that I'd heard countless times on her front porch.

It wasn't that I hadn't believed Grandma. You just *didn't* not believe my Grandma. It was simply so uncanny actually seeing those names in print and in official U.S. government records.

◆ ◆ ◆

Having seen proof of some of his grandmother's stories, Haley grew more curious about the family's "furthest-back person." Since his grandmother was no longer alive, he went to visit his elderly Cousin Georgia in Kansas City, Kansas.[1]

◆ ◆ ◆

Wrinkled, bent, not well herself, she was so overjoyed, repeating to me the old stories and sounds. . . . "Yeah, boy, that African say his name was '*Kin-tay*'; he say the banjo was '*ko*,' an' the river '*Kamby Bolong*,' an' he was off choppin' some wood to make his drum when they grabbed 'im!"

◆ ◆ ◆

Haley now realized that the strange words in the story must be from an African language. But he had no idea which one. So he met with Dr. Jan Vansina, a professor in Wisconsin who had studied African languages. Vansina recognized that some of the words were from a West African language called Mandinka.

◆ ◆ ◆

Among Mandinka stringed instruments, Dr. Vansina said, one of the oldest was the "kora."

Vocabulary Development

uncanny (un CAN ee) *adj.* strange; weird

1. **Kansas City, Kansas:** A smaller city near Kansas City, Missouri.

"*Bolong*," he said, was clearly Mandinka for "river." Preceded by "Kamby," it very likely meant "Gambia River."

◆ ◆ ◆

Vansina phoned another expert on Africa, Dr. Philip Curtin. Curtin said that "*Kin-tay*" was how you pronounced "*Kinte*," the name of a clan going back to the old African kingdom of Mali, near where the Gambia River flows.

◆ ◆ ◆

I knew I must get to the Gambia River.

◆ ◆ ◆

Haley traveled to the African nation of Gambia and told his family's story to many people in the capital. They felt that the key to finding more information was in the name "Kinte."

◆ ◆ ◆

Then they told me something I would never ever have fantasized—that in places in the back country lived very old men, commonly called *griots*, who could tell centuries of the histories of certain very old family clans. As for *Kintes*, they pointed out to me on a map some family villages, Kinte-Kundah, and Kinte-Kundah Janneh-Ya, for instance.

◆ ◆ ◆

Not long afterward, Haley traveled with others into the back country to meet a griot named Kebba Kanga Fofana. As the group headed up the Gambia River, they passed the ruins of an old British fort called James Fort. There, for two centuries, Africans had been loaded onto ships and brought to the Americas as slaves.

Vocabulary Development

clan (CLAN) *n.* a group of people with a common ancestor
fantasized (FAN tuh sizd) *v.* dreamed; imagined

◆ Vocabulary and Pronunciation

Mark the Text

Try saying the words *Kamby* and *Gambia* so that they sound alike. Can you see why the professor thinks the river is the Gambia? Circle your answer:

yes no

◆ Stop to Reflect

Where do you think Haley will go next? Circle the letter of your answer.

(a) Washington, D.C.

(b) Kansas City, KS

(c) Wisconsin

(d) Africa

Explain your answer.

____

____

____

◆ Reading Strategy

Mark the Text

Use lines to break this bracketed sentence into parts. Then circle two parts that give information about what *griots* are. To show you understand the sentence, explain what a *griot* is on these lines.

griot:

____

____

____

____

____

____

____

◆ Vocabulary and Pronunciation

The word *bank* can mean a place where you save money or the side of a river. Which is the meaning here?

Mark the Text

Circle two other words in the same sentence that help make the meaning clear.

◆ Culture Note

The *griot* uses "rains" for *years* because there is one part of each year when it usually rains a lot in the area. So 30 rainy seasons would be the same as 30 years. In other words, Omoro got married when he was 30 years old. How old was Kunta Kinte when he disappeared?

◆ Literary Analysis

Circle three words in this bracketed paragraph that help reveal the sorrow about slavery that Haley expresses in this **personal essay**. What other emotion comes through strongly in this paragraph? Circle the best answer:

Mark the Text

anger fear joy jealousy

◆ ◆ ◆

Then we continued upriver to the left-bank village of Albreda, and there put ashore to continue on foot to Juffure,[2] village of the griot.

◆ ◆ ◆

The griot recited the history of the Kinte clan, which he knew by heart. Every few sentences he would pause for his words to be translated into English. He told of the clan's beginnings in Old Mali. He spoke of one clan member, Kairaba Kunta Kinte, who came to Gambia and settled right there in Juffure. Kairaba's youngest son, Omoro, had about 30 "rains," or years, when he married a woman named Binta Kebba. Omoro and Binta had four sons.

◆ ◆ ◆

"About the time the king's soldiers came, the eldest of these four sons, Kunta, when he had about 16 rains, went away from his village, to chop wood to make a drum . . . and he was never seen again. . . ."

◆ ◆ ◆

When Haley heard this, he grew very excited. The details matched the story his grandmother had always told! Learning how the stories matched, the griot and other villagers welcomed Haley as a long-lost relative. Haley was deeply moved.

◆ ◆ ◆

Let me tell you something: I am a man. But I remember the sob surging up from my feet, flinging up my hands and bawling as I had not done since I was a baby. . . . If you really knew the odyssey of us millions of black Americans, if you

Vocabulary Development

bawling (BAWL ing) *v.* crying loudly
odyssey (AH duh see) *n.* a very long journey

2. **Juffure** (joo foo ray)

really knew how we came in the seeds of our forefathers, captured, driven, beaten, inspected, bought, branded, chained in foul ships, if you really knew, you needed weeping . . .

◆ ◆ ◆

Haley decided to write the story of his family, which he felt was like the story of so many African Americans. But he needed more details. What ship had brought Kinte to America? Since the griot had spoken of he arrival of "king's soldiers," Haley went to Britain to continue his research. In British government records he found what he was looking for.

◆ ◆ ◆

Feverish searching at last identified . . . "Colonel O'Hare's Forces," dispatched in mid-1767 to protect the then British-held James Fort whose ruins I'd visited.

◆ ◆ ◆

So if Kinte was caught soon after British soldiers came to Gambia, the ship bringing him to America must have sailed around then. Haley began checking British shipping records for 1767.

◆ ◆ ◆

And then early one afternoon I found that a *Lord Ligonier* under a Captain Thomas Davies had sailed on the Sabbath of July 5, 1767. Her cargo: 3,265 elephants' teeth, . . . 800 pounds of cotton, 32 ounces of Gambian gold and 140 slaves; her destination: "Annapolis."

Vocabulary Development

forefathers (FOHR fa therz) *n.* ancestors
foul (FOWL) *adj.* filthy and disgusting
feverish (FEE ver ish) *adj.* very excited; frantic
dispatched (dis PATCHD) *v.* sent
destination (des tuh NA shun) *n.* the place being traveled to

◆ Vocabulary and Pronunciation

Colonel is a rank in the army. Because the word was once *coronel*, it is still pronounced as if it had an *r* in it. It is also slurred into just two syllables. Practice saying the word out loud. It sounds like *kernel*, the word for a grain of corn.

◆ English Language Development

Mark the Text

A singular noun means one of the noun. A plural noun means more than one. Most nouns add *s* or *es* to form the plural:

Singular	Plural
one *slave*	two *slaves*
one *porch*	two *porches*

Some nouns form the plural in an irregular way. *Feet*, for example, is the irregular plural of *foot*. Circle the word in the bracketed passage that is an irregular plural. Write the singular form here:

____

◆ ◆ ◆

Back in America, Haley visited the Annapolis Historical Society. He found records of the arrival of the *Lord Ligonier* on Sept. 29, 1767. Only 98 slaves had survived the trip, but one of them must have been 16-year-old Kunta Kinte. Haley also found, on microfilm, a copy of the *Maryland Gazette* for Oct. 1, 1767. On page 2, the newspaper announced a sale:

◆ ◆ ◆

"from the River GAMBIA, in AFRICA . . . a cargo of choice, healthy SLAVES . . ."

◆ English Language Development

In modern American English, the word *River* usually comes after the actual name of the river: *Gambia River*. However, in past times, the word *River* was often used before the name: the *River Gambia*. How are rivers named in your native language? Write an example here:

____

◆ Literary Analysis

Based on the other details in this **personal essay**, circle three words in the newspaper ad that you think would make Haley especially angry.

Mark THE Text

Vocabulary Development

cargo (CAR goh) *n.* the load carried by a ship

REVIEW AND ASSESS

1. Who was Kunta Kinte in relation to Alex Haley and his family?

____

____

____

2. What apparently happened to Kinte in 1767, when he was about 16?

____

____

____

3. List five items of information Haley found in his research. Also write the person or organization that supplied the information and the place where he found it. An example is done for you.

Information	Person or Organization	Place
census records of grandmother's parents and sisters	National Archives	Washington, DC
____________	____________	____________
____________	____________	____________
____________	____________	____________
____________	____________	____________
____________	____________	____________

4. **Reading Strategy:** Draw lines to break this sentence from the essay into smaller parts. Then, show that you understand the sentence by answering the following questions.

Then we continued upriver to the left-bank village of Albreda, and there put ashore to continue on foot to Juffure, village of the *griot*.

(Continued)

Where did the travelers leave their boat?

____

Who or what was Juffure?

____

5. **Literary Analysis:** Why are the experiences in Haley's **personal essay** so important to him? Give two reasons.

1. ____

____

2. ____

____

Writing

Haley's book *Roots* is based on his and his family's experiences in this essay. Like all authors, he had to persuade a publisher to publish *Roots*. What do you think he said? Write your ideas on a separate paper. Your ideas should include answers to the questions below. Many of the questions can have more than one answer, so you decide what *you* would have said if you were Haley.

- What is the main topic of the book? ____________________
- When and where will the book begin? ____________________

____

- Who is the first main person the book will be about? __________

____

- What will the book show about slavery? ____________________

____

- Why will the book be important to African Americans? __________

____

____

PREVIEW

A Day's Wait

Ernest Hemingway

Summary

When Schatz has the flu, his father calls the doctor. The doctor says that Schatz's temperature is 102 degrees. Later that day, Schatz asks about his temperature. He is very quiet and worried, and his father cannot understand why. Finally, Schatz asks when he is going to die. His father says he is not that ill and will not die. Schatz says that boys at school in France told him a person could not live with a temperature of 44 degrees. His father then realizes that Schatz has been waiting to die all day, ever since he heard the doctor. The father explains that in France they use a different kind of thermometer. On that thermometer a normal temperature is 37 degrees. On the thermometer the doctor used, normal is 98 degrees. Schatz is very relieved by the explanation.

Visual Summary

A Day's Wait: The story takes place in one day			
Early Morning to 11 AM			
Schatz comes down with flu. →	Father calls doctor. →	Doctor says temperature is 102 degrees. →	Father tries to read to Schatz.
11 AM to Late Afternoon			
Schatz sends father away. →	Father goes hunting. →	Father returns to house. →	Father learns Schatz wouldn't see anyone all day.
Late Afternoon to Early Evening			
When Schatz asks about dying, father says Schatz won't die. →	Schatz says in France such high temperature meant certain death. →	Father explains that Schatz confused two types of thermometers. →	Father realizes Schatz has spent all day in bed expecting to die.

LITERARY ANALYSIS

Internal Conflict

Most stories center on a **conflict**, or struggle between two forces. Sometimes the struggle is an **internal conflict**, taking place in the character's mind.

For example, in "A Day's Wait," Schatz struggles between his desire to be brave and his fear and worry about his illness. We see Schatz's tension in his own words and behavior.

> "I don't worry," he said, "but I can't keep from thinking."
>
> "Don't think," I said. "Just take it easy."
>
> "I'm taking it easy," he said and looked straight ahead. He was evidently holding tight on to himself about something.

As you read "A Day's Wait," pay careful attention to Schatz's words and actions. Look for signs that he is going through an internal conflict.

READING STRATEGY

Identifying Word Roots

A **root** is the main part of a word. Other parts are added to word roots. Some of the roots in English words come from other languages, especially Latin and Greek. You can often get an idea of a word's meaning if you know the meaning of its Latin or Greek root.

Study this chart of Latin and Greek roots, their meanings, and examples of words in which they appear. Look for these roots in "A Day's Wait."

Root	Meaning	Word with Root	Word's Meaning
-vid- *or* -vis-	see	evidently	in a way that is easily seen; clearly
-medic-	doctor	medicine	something a doctor recommends to fight an illness
-therm-	heat	thermometer	an instrument that measures heat

A Day's Wait

Ernest Hemingway

In "A Day's Wait," a father tells the story of an amazing day in the life of his nine-year-old son. As the story opens, the son comes into the bedroom, where his parents are sleeping. The boy does not look or act like he feels well. He is pale and shivering. He looked as though it ached to move.

◆ ◆ ◆

"What's the matter, Schatz?"[1]

"I've got a headache."

"You better go back to bed."

"No, I'm all right."

◆ ◆ ◆

The father tells his son to go back to bed. But when he comes downstairs, the boy is dressed and sitting by the fire. His son looks sick and miserable. When he feels his son's forehead, it's obvious the boy has a fever. The doctor comes to check on the boy and takes his temperature. When the father asks what it is, the doctor states that it is one hundred and two. Downstairs, the doctor identifies the boy's illness as influenza, or flu. He leaves three kinds of medicine for the boy to take at different times throughout the day. The father returns to the boy's room after writing down the doctor's instructions. The boy lay still. The father noticed that his son's face was pale with dark circles under his

◆ Vocabulary and Pronunciation

The word *ached*, which means "hurt," rhymes with *baked*. Circle another word a few lines below in which the *ch* is also pronounced like a /k/.

◆ Vocabulary and Pronunciation

Forehead is a compound word in which two smaller words are combined: *fore*, which means "front," and *head*. The *forehead* is the front of the head—that is, the part above the eyebrows and below the hairline. Circle another compound word in the bracketed passage, and draw a line to show the two words that make it up. Then, write its meaning here:

____

____

____

◆ Vocabulary and Pronunciation

The illness *influenza* is usually called *flu* for short. Below are some other English words that are often shortened. Write the short forms on the lines after the words.

advertisement: ______________

bicycle: ______________

Vocabulary Development

fever (FEE ver) *n.* a condition in which a person's body temperature is higher than normal

1. **Schatz** (SHAHTZ): A loving nickname that comes from the German word for "treasure" or "dear."

◆ English Language Development

The verb *lay* means "to put or place (something down)." Its past tense is *laid*. The verb *lie* means "to be resting." Its past tense is *lay*. Which *lay* is used here? Circle the correct answer.

- present tense, "to put or place"
- past tense of *lie*, "to be resting"

◆ Culture Note

We never learn why the father uses the German nickname *Schatz*—perhaps he once lived in Germany. Are there nicknames in your native land that parents use to show love or affection? If so, write one on this line:

____

◆ Vocabulary and Pronunciation

Latin roots like *-medic-* also appear in Spanish, French, Italian, and other languages that come from Latin. On the chart below, list examples of words from your native language that contain the Latin roots listed. If your language does not use the roots, leave the chart blank.

Root	Meaning	Word
-medic-	doctor	______
-scrib-/-scrip-	write	______
-vid-/-vis-	see	______

eyes. Despite the fact that the boy seems detached and listless, the father offers to read to him from a book about pirates. While he was reading, the boy lay still, but did not seem to be listening.

◆ ◆ ◆

"How do you feel, Schatz?" I asked him.
"Just the same, so far," he said.

◆ ◆ ◆

The father sits at the foot of the bed, looking at the book himself. He is waiting until it is time to give the boy more of the prescribed medicine. The boy's father notices that his son has a strange look on his face. He suggests to his son that he sleep until it's time for the capsules that are his next dose of medicine. The boy, however, wants to stay awake.

◆ ◆ ◆

After a while he said to me, "You don't have to stay in here with me, Papa, if it bothers you."

"It doesn't bother me."

"No. I mean you don't have to stay if it's going to bother you."

◆ ◆ ◆

The father thinks his son is feeling light-headed from being sick and taking medicine. After he gives his son the prescribed medicine late in the morning he leaves for a while.

When he leaves the house, the father goes hunting for quail, a type of bird that is usually hunted with the help of a dog. The dog that the father takes with him is a young

Vocabulary Development

detached (dee TACHD) *adj.* not connected to
prescribed (pree SCRĪBD) *adj.* ordered in writing
capsules (CAP soolz) *n.* medicine enclosed in small containers that a person can swallow like pills

Irish setter. The two slide along the frozen creek. Then the dog drives some quail from the bushes. Since it is so icy, it isn't easy to shoot at the flying birds. But the father still manages to kill two. He and the dog then return to the house.

While the father is gone, the boy doesn't let anyone come near him. He warns everyone not to come in the room because they must not get what he has. The father ignores what the boy says and goes in. He finds him in exactly the position he left him in.

♦ ♦ ♦

I took his temperature.

"What is it?"

"Something like a hundred," I said. It was one hundred and two and four tenths.

"It was a hundred and two," he said.

"Who said so?"

"The doctor."

♦ ♦ ♦

The father assures his son that his temperature is all right and nothing to worry about. He also suggests that the boy just take it easy and gives him another dose of medicine. The boy evidently isn't taking it easy because he asks whether taking the medicine will do any good. The father reassures his son and sits down and starts reading aloud from the pirate book again. And again, the boy doesn't pay attention. So the father stops.

♦ ♦ ♦

"About what time do you think I'm going to die?" he asked.

Vocabulary Development

evidently (ev uh DENT lee) *adv.* clearly

◆ Literary Analysis

Mark the Text

Circle two details in the bracketed paragraph that show Schatz is going through an **internal conflict**. Then, complete this sentence to show what you think the conflict is about: Schatz's inner struggle seems to be between

____

____

and

____

______________________.

◆ Vocabulary and Pronunciation

Use nearby words to help you understand the meaning of the expression "take it easy." Circle the letter of the meaning.

(a) relax (c) raise it slowly

(b) worry (d) remove it quickly

"What?"

"About how long will it be before I die?"

"You aren't going to die. What's the matter with you?"

♦ ♦ ♦

As the father talks with his son, he realizes that the boy has been waiting all day to die—ever since he overheard the doctor say that his temperature was one hundred and two. The boys at his school in France, told him that a person can't survive a fever of forty-four degrees. The boy believes that he is dying because his temperature is a hundred and two. When the father discovers the cause of his son's worry, he explains the difference between thermometers and their temperature readings. Thirty-seven degrees is a normal temperature on the kind of thermometer that the boys at school were talking about.

♦ ♦ ♦

"Are you sure?"

"Absolutely," I said. "It's like miles and kilometers.[2] You know, like how many kilometers we make when we do seventy miles in the car?"

"Oh," he said.

But his gaze at the foot of the bed relaxed slowly. The hold over himself relaxed too, finally, and the next day it was very slack and he cried very easily at little things that were of no importance.

◆ Reading Strategy

Circle the two words in the bracketed passage that contain the Greek **root** *-meter-*, which means "measure." Since the Greek root *-therm-* means "heat," what do you think a *thermometer* measures?

Mark the Text

____

◆ Culture Note

In your native land, which is used to measure distance, kilometers or miles?

____

If you answered *kilometers*, explain why you like or don't like that system.

____

____

Vocabulary Development

degrees (duh GREEZ) *n.* the units of measure that show heat or body temperature

slack (SLAK) *adj.* loose

[2]**kilometers** (KIL oh MEET erz): Units for measuring distance used instead of miles in many other nations, including France. A kilometer is 1000 meters or about 5/8 of a mile.

REVIEW AND ASSESS

1. In the story, what does Schatz confuse? Circle the letter of the correct answer.

   (a) kilometers in France and miles in America

   (b) kilometers in France and degrees in America

   (c) thermometers in France and America

   (d) school in France and America

2. Why does his mistake cause Schatz to think he will die? Write your answer on the lines.

   ____

   ____

3. Write two words that describe the father in this story.

   1. ____________________ 2. ____________________

4. **Literary Analysis:** Explain Schatz's internal conflict by choosing four words from the Word Box to complete the sentence. Then, in the columns, list examples from the story to illustrate the words you chose.

Word Box: brave mean noisy scared spoiled unselfish worried

Schatz is (A) ________________ and (B) ________________, BUT he tries to be (C) ________________ and (D) ________________ .

Examples of (A) and (B)	Examples of (C) and (D)

(Continued)

5. **Reading Strategy:** Use the meaning of each **word root** to help you explain the meaning of the word in which it appears. Write the meanings of the word on the lines provided.

Root	Meaning of Root	Word	Meaning of Word
-vid-	see	evidently	
-scrib-	write	prescribed	
-tach-	stick; connect	detached	

Listening and Speaking

Work in a group of four students. Take turns explaining the mistake Schatz made and listening to the explanations of your classmates. After you listen to an explanation, give feedback on how it might be improved. Use these questions as a guide.

	Yes	No
1. Was the explanation clear and easy to understand?	_____	_____
If not, what changes might improve it?		

____

____

	Yes	No
2. Was the information right?	_____	_____
If not, which details need to be corrected?		

____

____

	Yes	No
3. Was the speaker's voice clear?	_____	_____
Was he or she interesting to listen to?	_____	_____
If not, what could be improved?		

____

____

PREVIEW

Was Tarzan a Three-Bandage Man?

Bill Cosby

Summary

When Bill Cosby was young, he and his friends tried to act cool by imitating their sports heroes. Bill's mother pokes fun at him for walking funny to copy famous ball players. She scolds him for putting bandages on his face to imitate champion boxers. Cosby now realizes it might have been better to imitate the boxers who gave injuries rather than those who received them.

Visual Summary

Cosby and Friends' Actions	Cosby's Mother's Reaction	Adult Cosby's Reaction
• Copy walk of Jackie Robinson, fastest man in baseball • Copy walk of football player Buddy Helm • Imitate boxers like Sugar Ray Robinson by wearing a bandage above an eye	• Pokes fun by questioning Robinson's shoes and whether walk slows speed • Pokes fun at how son twists his legs to copy these men's walks • Suggests son is being stupid and needs better role models; makes him remove his bandage	• Pokes fun by saying walk was painful • Pokes fun by suggesting the behavior made little sense

PREPARE TO READ

LITERARY ANALYSIS

Anecdote

An **anecdote** is a short account of an interesting incident in a person's life. Usually it is something that happened to the author. In "Was Tarzan a Three-Bandage Man?" the author tells an anecdote from his own childhood.

One reason Bill Cosby tells his anecdote is to entertain. His childhood actions are very funny, and so are his mother's comments about them:

> "Why you walkin' like that?" said my mother one day.
> "This is Jackie Robinson's walk," I proudly replied.
> "There's somethin' wrong with his shoes?"
> "He's the fastest man in baseball."
> "He'd be faster if he didn't walk like that. . . ."

As you read the anecdote, think about Cosby's purposes in telling it. Focus on these questions:

- What is funny or entertaining about the anecdote?
- Why do you think the events are important to the author?
- What general points do you think he is trying to make about life or human behavior?

READING STRATEGY

Using Context Clues

The **context** is the situation or surroundings in which a word appears. Often a word's context will give you clues to its meaning. For example, read this passage from the selection.

> In fact, they were such heroes to me and my friends that we even imitated their walks. When Jackie Robinson, a pigeon-toed walker, became famous, we walked pigeon-toed. . . .

The term *imitated* may be unfamiliar, but the context gives clues to its meaning. The first sentence says that Cosby and his friends *imitated* the heroes' walks. The next sentence says that Jackie Robinson was a pigeon-toed walker and that they too "walked pigeon-toed." From this context, you can tell that *imitated* must mean "copied."

Was Tarzan[1] a Three-Bandage Man?

Bill Cosby

Bill Cosby recalls events when he was young, in the late 1940's. Then, athletes were sports stars even before they started to incorporate themselves by selling products. One of the biggest sports heroes of the time was Jackie Robinson, the first African American to play in major-league baseball. Bill and his friends were so impressed with Robinson and other sports heroes that they copied the way the athletes walked.

♦ ♦ ♦

When Jackie Robinson, a pigeon-toed[2] walker, became famous, we walked pigeon-toed, ...

"Why you walkin' like that?" said my mother one day.

"This is Jackie *Robinson's* walk," I proudly replied.

♦ ♦ ♦

Bill's mother is both amused and annoyed by her son's behavior. When he explains that Robinson is the fastest man in baseball, she remarks that he'd be faster if he walked normally. Bill finds that walking pigeon-toed is a painful form of locomotion.

When football season starts, Bill tries to walk like Buddy Helm, a football player. His mother asks more questions. This time she asks why he's walking bowlegged.[3]

Vocabulary Development

athletes (ATH leetz) *n.* someone who is good at sports

incorporate (in CORP uh rayt) *v.* to form a business

1. **Tarzan** (tar ZAN): a popular movie hero who swung from vines in the jungle.
2. **pigeon-toed** (PIJ un tohd) *adj.* having the toes or feet turned in toward each other.
3. **bowlegged** (BOH leg id) *adj.* having legs that are curved outward.

◆ Reading Strategy

What do you think *locomotion* means? Circle the letter of the answer.

(a) moving from one place to another

(b) a subway train

(c) a baseball game

(d) feeding food to birds in the park

Now circle the **context clues** that helped you figure out the meaning.

◆ English Language Development

The comparative form of an adjective compares two things. The superlative compares more than two. Most short adjectives add *-er* for the comparative and *-est* for the superlative.

Comparative: He's *smarter* than I am.

Superlative: She's the *smartest* of all.

Circle and label the comparative and superlative forms in the bracketed paragraph. Then, complete this sentence: The comparative form is comparing

____

and

____________________.

◆ Reading Strategy

What do you think *emulate* means?

emulate: ____________________

Now circle the **context clues** that helped you figure out the meaning.

Cosby continues his anecdote by explaining that prizefighters, or boxers, like Sugar Ray Robinson were bigger heroes than baseball and football stars. The way to emulate a fighter was to wear a Band-Aid. Since boxers often had cuts around their eyes, the Band-Aid needed to be worn on the face. Bill and his friends hoped that people would understand that they were worshipping boxers and not trying to cover up their acne.

Of course, Bill's mother asks what the bandage over his eye is for. His muttered reply of "nuthin" doesn't impress her.

◆ ◆ ◆

"Now that's a new kinda stupid answer. That bandage gotta be coverin' somethin'—besides your entire brain."

◆ ◆ ◆

◆ Vocabulary and Pronunciation

To capture the sound of spoken English, the author uses odd spellings and apostrophes for dropped sounds. For instance, he uses *kinda* instead of *kind of* and *coverin'* instead of *covering.* Fix the odd spellings in the bracketed section by making small changes and squeezing in missing letters.

Bill explains that the Band-Aid is just for show and that he wants to look like Sugar Ray Robinson. His mother thinks Bill means Robinson, the baseball player. Bill explains that it's a different Robinson. Then his mother asks if he's going to imitate the Swiss Family Robinson next. They were children's book characters who had to live all alone on an island after their ship was lost at sea. Bill wants to know if the Swiss Family Robinson is a family that lives in the projects.[4] Bill's mother suggests that if he read more books instead of walking funny or wearing bandages that he'd know who they are.

◆ Culture Note

What are the most popular sports in your native land? Write your answer here:

____

____

4. **projects** (prah jektz): inexpensive apartment houses in poor neighborhoods.

Bill's mother thinks he should copy a person like Booker T. Washington[5] instead of an athlete. Bill doesn't know who this particular Washington is so he asks, "Who does he play for?" His mother doesn't answer him, but tells him that he can't wear the bandage.

♦ ♦ ♦

". . . You take off that bandage right now or I'll have your father move you up to stitches."

♦ ♦ ♦

The next morning, Bill tells his friends Fat Albert, Junior, and Eddie that his mother won't let him wear a bandage.

♦ ♦ ♦

"What's wrong with that woman?" said Fat Albert. "She won't let you do *nuthin'*."

♦ ♦ ♦

One of Bill's other friends tells him that it's okay that he can't wear the bandage—the tough guys wear two bandages—one is not enough anyway. The boys discuss what being a two-bandage man might be about. Eddie decides he "wouldn't want to mess with no two-bandage man."

Bill Cosby goes on to recall that the toughest guys wore the largest bandages. He finds it all very funny and ridiculous now.

♦ ♦ ♦

Our hero worshipping was backwards: we should have been emulating the men who had caused the *need* for bandages.

◆ Reading Check

What does "Who does he play for" mean?

(a) What team does he play for?

(b) Why is he famous?

(c) Who are his friends?

◆ Reading Check

What is the mother threatening to have the father do?

(a) remove the bandage

(b) hit Bill if he doesn't start behaving

(c) tell jokes that keep Bill in stitches

◆ English Language Development

Mark the Text

A double negative is the incorrect use of two negative words when you really mean just one. For example, if you say, "I can't talk no louder," you really mean "I can talk no louder" or "I can't talk *any* louder." Circle the two negative words that Eddie uses. Then, correct the sentence.

◆ Literary Analysis

Mark the Text

Circle the main point about young people's behavior that Cosby makes near the end of his **anecdote**.

5. **Booker T. Washington** (1856-1915): A famous African American educator who stressed the importance of education.

REVIEW AND ASSESS

1. Why do Bill and his friends imitate the sports stars?

____

____

2. Label each statement about the mother *T* if it seems true or *F* if it seems false.

_____ The mother thinks Bill's behavior is silly.

_____ The mother is a friend of Jackie Robinson's mother.

_____ The mother thinks Bill's feet will fall off.

_____ The mother has a good sense of humor.

_____ The mother knows the names of all the popular sports heroes.

3. Explain what is funny about Eddie's fear of "two-bandage men."

____

____

4. What do you think the anecdote's title means?

____

____

5. **Reading Strategy:** Circle the **context clues** that help you figure out the meaning of *acne*. Then, circle the letter of the meaning.

People with *acne* walked around that way too, but we hoped it was clear that we were worshipping good fists and not bad skin.

Acne means (a) a skin condition (b) a type of boxing (c) on tiptoes (d) height

6. **Literary Analysis:** List examples that show each of Cosby's three purposes in telling this **anecdote**.

- **Purpose: to tell a funny, interesting story** (list three examples)

1. ______________________________

2. ______________________________

3. ______________________________

- **Purpose: to describe something important to him** (list one example)

____

____

- **Purpose: to make a point about life or people's behavior** (list two examples)

1. ______________________________

2. ______________________________

Writing

Should young people make heroes of sports stars? On a separate sheet, write a paragraph expressing your opinion about this question. First, follow these four steps:

1. List your ideas in a two-column chart like this one.

Why it might be good to make heroes of sports stars	Why it might not be good
______________	______________
______________	______________

2. Study your chart and decide where you stand.
3. Open your paragraph with a statement of your opinion. For example, you might say, "I believe (*or* I do not believe) that young people should make heroes of sports stars."
4. Explain your opinion by giving reasons, examples, and other details. List them here.

____

____

from In Search of Our Mothers' Gardens

Alice Walker

Summary

Alice Walker praises her mother and other African American women like her. Walker sees her mother as an artist whose talents helped make Walker the writer she is today. Her mother revealed her artistic talent in the stories she told and in the flower gardens she grew. Being poor and working hard all her life did not stop her from taking time to grow these lovely gardens. Walker admires how black women of her mother's generation managed to "hold on" despite the difficulty of their lives. From these women, Walker has inherited a respect for strength as well as a love of beauty.

Visual Summary

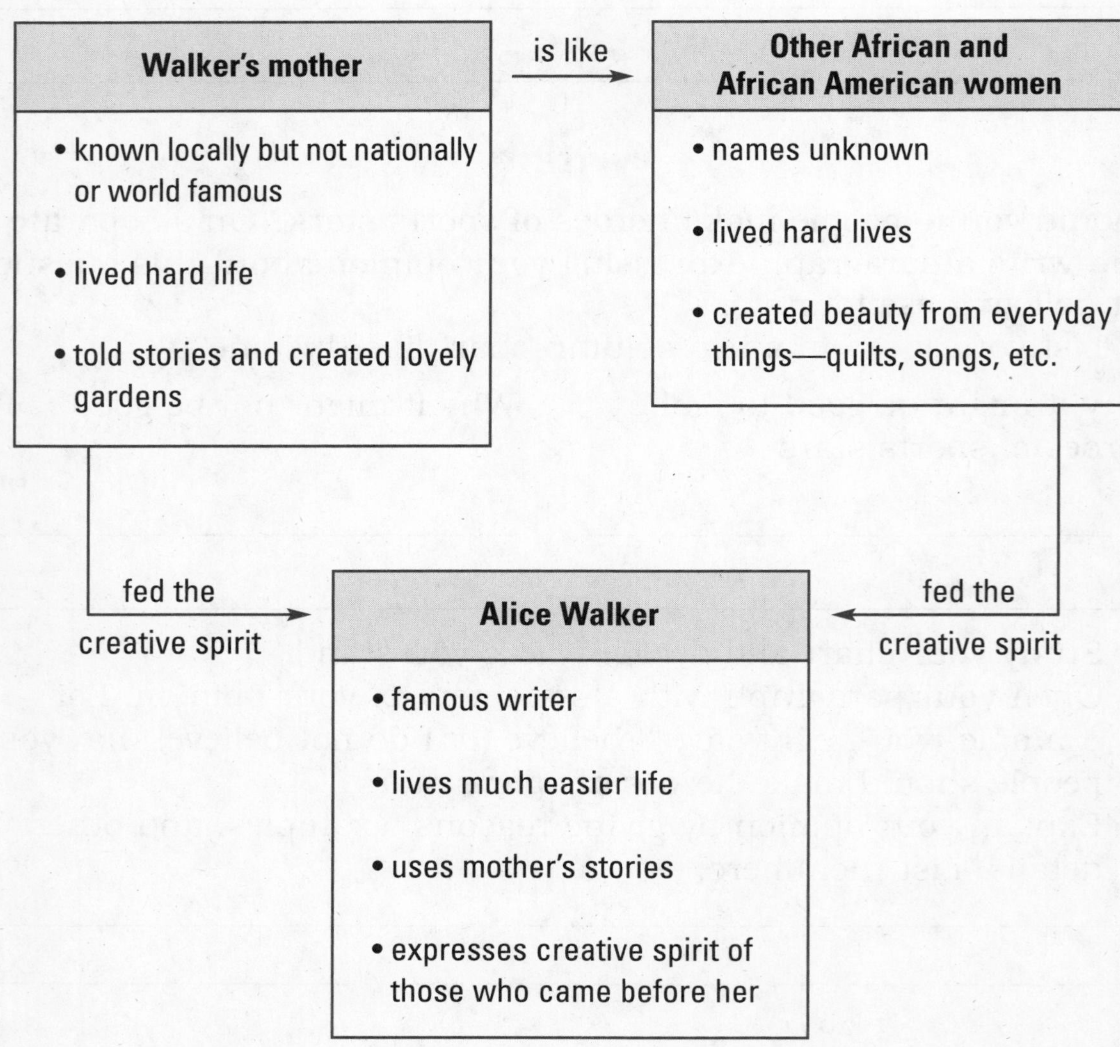

PREPARE TO READ

LITERARY ANALYSIS

Tribute

A **tribute** is a piece of writing that expresses thanks or admiration to a special person. It includes details about that person's life. It also explains why the person is important to the writer.

"In Search of Our Mothers' Gardens" is Alice Walker's tribute to her mother. In it, Walker considers what she as a writer owes to her mother. She provides many specific details about her mother's life to show why she admires her mother:

> She planted ambitious gardens—and still does—with over fifty different varieties of plants. . . . Whatever she planted grew as if by magic, and her fame as a grower of flowers spread over three counties.

As you read Walker's tribute, focus on these questions:

- What does Walker admire about her mother?
- In what ways does the mother contribute to Walker's own creative life as a writer?

READING STRATEGY

Recognizing Word Roots

A **root** is the main part of a word. Other parts are added to root words. Many English words have roots that come from Latin and Greek. Learning some of these common roots will help you understand whole groups of words.

For example, consider the Latin root *-herit-*, which means "heir." (An *heir* is someone who has property or something else passed down to him or her. For example, a daughter may be the *heir* to her father's money or her mother's temper.) Once you know the root, you have an idea of the meanings of the whole group of words that contain it.

English Words with the Latin Root *-herit-* ("heir")	
inherit:	to have property or something else passed down to you
inheritance:	the property or other things that are passed down to you
heritage:	the cultural or family traditions passed down to you
disinherit:	to take away someone's right to have property passed down

from In Search of Our Mothers' Gardens

Alice Walker

Now a famous writer, Alice Walker came from a poor farm family in Georgia. Her mother was weighed down with household chores and back-breaking farm work all her life. She canned vegetables and fruits. She sewed all of the clothes the family wore, even her brother's overalls. She also sewed the towels, sheets, and quilts they used.

◆ ◆ ◆

During the "working" day, she labored beside—not behind—my father in the fields. Her day began before sunup, and did not end until late at night.

◆ ◆ ◆

It would seem that Walker's mother had no time to be creative. And yet, it is to her mother that Walker looks when she wants to understand her own creative spirit.

◆ ◆ ◆

But when, you will ask, did my overworked mother have time to know or care about feeding the creative spirit?

The answer is so simple that many of us have spent years discovering it.

◆ ◆ ◆

To answer that question, Walker feels that we must look high—and low. Among the places Walker herself looks is one of the famous Smithsonian Institution museums in Washington, D.C., where she finds a beautiful quilt made a hundred years ago by an

Vocabulary Development

labored (LAY berd) *v.* worked

◆ Vocabulary and Pronunciation

Overalls are work pants with a connected top that covers the front of a shirt. They are called *overalls* because they go *over all.*

In the bracketed paragraph, find and circle another word made up of two words put together. Put a line between the two words. Then, use the parts to figure out the meaning of the whole word. Write the meaning here:

Mark THE Text

____

____

____

◆ Reading Strategy

The **root** *-spir-* in *spirit* means "breath." Since breath is associated with life, what do you think *spirit* means? Circle the letter.

(a) life force; soul

(b) a drawing of the human body

(c) loss of hope

(d) a bad cough

◆ Reading Check

What does Walker mean by looking *high* and *low* for creative spirit?

(a) look on mountains and in valleys

(b) look in the attic and in the basement

(c) look among trained artists and those who create art from everyday things

(d) look at both the happy times and the sad times

anonymous black woman in Alabama. The quilt is unusual. It is so valuable that it's beyond price. To Walker, the woman who made the quilt is one of her grandmothers, an artist who left her mark in one of the few ways possible for her at the time.

♦ ♦ ♦

And so our mothers and grandmothers have, more often than not anonymously, handed on the creative spark, the seed of the flower they themselves never hoped to see; or like a sealed letter they could not plainly read.

♦ ♦ ♦

Walker knows that her mother won't have her name on any work of art or piece of writing either. Yet so many of the stories that Walker writes are her mother's stories.

♦ ♦ ♦

Only recently did I fully realize this: that through years of listening to my mother's stories of her life, I have absorbed not only the stories themselves but something of the manner in which she spoke.

♦ ♦ ♦

Walker explains that her mother's creative spark also expressed itself in another way. Besides telling stories, she also created beautiful flower gardens. No matter how poor or plain a house the family was forced to live in, Walker's mother always decorated it with flowers.

♦ ♦ ♦

She planted ambitious gardens—and still does. . . . Before she left home for the fields, she watered her flowers, chopped up the grass,

Vocabulary Development

anonymous (a NAHN i muhs) *adj.* with no known name; unknown

ambitious (am BISH us) *adj.* involving a lot of work or effort

◆ Culture Note

The museums of the Smithsonian Institution are among the many famous buildings in the American capital, Washington, D.C. What is the capital city of your native land?

____

◆ English Language Development

Mark the Text

In English, *-ly* often turns adjectives into adverbs that tell *how.* In the previous paragraph, the adjective *anonymous* described the Alabama woman whose name is unknown. Here, the *-ly* ending turns the adjective into an adverb telling us how the mothers and grandmothers have often handed down the creative spark. They have done it *without having their names known.* Circle another *-ly* adverb in the bracketed paragraph. Write what it means here:

____

____

◆ **Vocabulary and Pronunciation**

The word *beds* is not used here in its most common meaning, "furniture on which people sleep." Instead, it has a special meaning related to gardening—"a piece of ground where plants are grown." Circle another gardening term in the next sentence that has a more common, everyday meaning. Write the more common meaning on these lines:

____

____

Mark the Text

◆ **Reading Strategy**

Latin roots like *-magni-* also appear in Spanish, French, Italian, and other languages that come from Latin. On the chart below, list examples of words from your native language that contain the Latin roots listed. If your language does not use the roots, leave the chart blank.

Root	Meaning	Word
-magni-	large	__________
-liter-	letter	__________
-spir-	breath	__________

and laid out new beds. When she returned from the fields she might divide clumps of bulbs,[1] dig a cold pit,[2] uproot and replant roses, or prune branches from her taller bushes or trees—until night came and it was too dark to see.

Whatever she planted grew as if by magic, and her fame as a grower of flowers spread over three counties.

◆ ◆ ◆

Walker revisits her memories of people coming from all over to see her mother's garden. They are drawn to the flowers and trees that bloom profusely. They admire her mother's ability to turn any soil into a magnificent garden—her art. Many ask for cuttings from the flowers so they can take a piece of the beauty home with them.

Her mother's creativity in the garden drew on color and design. Strangers still come by the house in Georgia and ask to stand or walk in Walker's mother's garden.

Walker observes that when her mother is at work in her garden, her face brightens and she seems fully alive. The work she does in the garden is for her soul—she creates her own conception of beauty. Even though her

Vocabulary Development

profusely (pro FYOOS lee) *adv.* in great number; freely; plentifully
prune (PROON) *v.* to cut off branches of a plant
creativity (KREE ay TIV i tee) *n.* imagination; artistic talent
conception (kon SEP shun) *n.* idea

1. **bulb:** a short thick underground stem covered by thick fleshy leaves that stores the food for a shoot to grow. Tulips and daffodils grow from bulbs.
2. **cold pit:** a hole in which small plants are placed at the beginning of spring.

mother has been hindered and had her work intruded upon by daily responsibilities, she has created her art every day of her life.

♦ ♦ ♦

This ability to hold on, even in very simple ways, is work black women have done for a very long time.

♦ ♦ ♦

Walker's mother values life and all it has to offer—the bad as well as the good. She has passed her attitude down to her children. Walker is moved by her mother's example and writes a poem to her. Walker does not feel that her poem is enough, but she thinks it is something of a tribute—to honor the woman who brought beauty and creativity into her life, and who literally covered holes in the wall with sunflowers.

Walker thinks of other proud women in Africa more than two hundred years ago. She wonders if they struggled to express themselves. Maybe they sang or painted bright colors on their hut walls. Perhaps the mother of Phillis Wheatley, the first African American poet in America, was a poet too. Walker realizes her own desire to write comes from the efforts of her mother and of black women who came before her. These nameless women, living in hard times, still managed to create something beautiful out of the simple things around them.

♦ ♦ ♦

Guided by my heritage of a love of beauty and a respect for strength—in search of my mother's garden, I found my own.

Vocabulary Development

hindered (HIN derd) *adj.* held back
literally (LIT er uh lee) *adv.* actually

◆ Reading Strategy

The **root** *-trud-* means "push." What do you think "intruded upon" means?

(a) helped (c) being an artist
(b) interrupted (d) praised

How does the root point to the meaning?

____

____

◆ Vocabulary and Pronunciation

Mark the Text

In English, a single *l*—as in *holes*—sounds the same as a double *l*—as in *walls*. Say "holes" and "walls" aloud. Then, find and circle another single *l* and double *l* in this paragraph, and again say the words aloud.

◆ Vocabulary and Pronunciation

The word *guided* rhymes with *sided:* the *u* is not pronounced. Usually, *u* after *g* and before *a, e, i,* or *y* is not pronounced. Say these words correctly:

guess	guard	guitar
guest	guilt	disguise
guy	vague	guarantee

After *ng*, *u* is often pronounced. It sounds like /*w*/. Say these words:

language distinguish bilingual

The *u* is also pronounced in some English words from other languages, like the Italian pasta *linguine*, the tropical fruit *guava*, or the island of *Guam*.

REVIEW AND ASSESS

1. To whom does Walker feel she and other African American women owe their creative spirit?

____

2. Check the statements that apply to Alice Walker's mother.

   ____ She spent most of her life in poor neighborhoods in large cities.

   ____ She and her husband worked hard on their farm.

   ____ No matter how plain their house, she always planted a garden.

   ____ People from counties all around came to hear her wonderful stories.

   ____ She made a lovely quilt that hangs in the Smithsonian Institution in Washington, D.C.

3. What main point is made about the story of the quilt in Washington? Circle the letter of your answer.

   (a) Poor people have little time to be creative.

   (b) Poor people can still be creative with everyday things.

   (c) Fame is a terrible thing; it is better for no one to know your name.

   (d) Making quilts is a difficult and tiring household chore.

4. What does the mother's garden seem to represent to Walker? Circle the letter of your answer.

   (a) a work of art where her mother expresses her personal ideas of beauty

   (b) her cultural heritage as an African American

   (c) a place where creative spirit is nurtured or cared for

   (d) all of the above

5. **Literary Analysis:** Based on this **tribute**, list at least four qualities or talents that Walker admires in her mother.

1. ______________________________

2. ______________________________

3. ______________________________

4. ______________________________

6. **Reading Strategy:** Complete the chart below by writing another word with each root and explaining its meaning.

Root	Meaning	Word	Meaning	Word	Meaning
-liter-	letter	literally	To the letter; actually		
-nym-	name	anonymous	With no known name		
-magni-	large	magnitude	large and impressive		

Listening and Speaking

Alice Walker feels that a person can be creative in everyday activities like gardening. Give a **how-to** speech to classmates. In your speech, explain how to do an everyday activity or chore. Try to pick one that you think can be creative.

- Choose an activity or chore that you know.
- Identify the activity or chore at the beginning of your speech. You might say something like, "I am explaining how to __________."
- When you give your speech, explain the activity in steps your classmates can follow. Use words like *first, second, third, next, then,* or *last* to make the order clear.
- On another piece of paper, list the steps in the activity. Then, put a number next to each to show the order in which the steps must be done.

Seventh Grade

Gary Soto

Summary

On his first day of seventh grade, Victor signs up for French because Teresa is taking the class. He hopes Teresa will be his girlfriend this year. In the hallway, he runs into his friend Michael, who is also trying to attract girls. Teresa is in Victor's homeroom but not in his other classes except for French. In their first French class, Victor embarrasses himself by pretending to speak the language. The French teacher is not fooled, but Teresa is. Impressed, she asks Victor to help her with French during the year. Victor happily heads for the library to take out some French textbooks.

Visual Summary

Setting

Place: a school in Fresno, California
Time: the first day of seventh grade

Problem

Victor doesn't know how Teresa feels about him.

Goal

Victor wants Teresa to be his girlfriend this year.

Events

- Victor knows Spanish but signs up for French because Teresa is taking the class.
- In homeroom, Victor makes sure Teresa notices him but is awkward when she says "Hi."
- When his English teacher asks for a noun that names a person, Victor says "Teresa."
- In French class, Victor pretends to know French, though the teacher soon realizes he doesn't.
- Victor is embarrassed and runs off quickly when the bell rings but then must return for a book.

Climax

Teresa is impressed that Victor knows French and asks if he can sometimes help her study.
The teacher hears them talking but does not give away Victor's secret.

Conclusion

Victor agrees to help Teresa with French and heads for the library to take out some French books.

PREPARE TO READ

LITERARY ANALYSIS

Tone

The **tone** of a work is the attitude the writer expresses. For example, the tone could be serious or humorous. It could be happy or angry or sad. In "Seventh Grade," Gary Soto uses a sympathetic tone to describe Victor and his problems. Soto's tone is also amused at times, as he gently pokes fun at Victor.

> His brown face blushed. Why hadn't he said, "Hi, Teresa," or "How was your summer?" or something nice?
>
> As Teresa walked down the hall, Victor walked the other way, looking back, admiring how gracefully she walked, one foot in front of the other.

As you read, look for details that convey Soto's amused but sympathetic tone. List them on a chart like this one.

Sympathetic Tone	Amused Tone
Victor blushes and wonders why he didn't say "something nice"	Victor admires how gracefully Teresa walks, "one foot in front of the other"

READING STRATEGY

Identifying Idioms

An **idiom** is an expression that means something different from the words that make it up. For example, this sentence from "Seventh Grade" uses the idiom *bump into*:

> He wanted to leave when she did so he could bump into her and say something clever.

To *bump* is to knock against someone or something. *Bump into* is an idiom that means "meet in a casual or unplanned way."

As you read "Seventh Grade," list other idioms from the story on a chart like this one.

Idiom	What Separate Words Mean	What Idiom Means
bump into	knock against; knock into	meet casually or unexpectedly

Seventh Grade

Gary Soto

It was the first day of seventh grade for Victor Rodriguez. When he signed up for classes, Victor had a choice about which language to study. Taking Spanish would probably have been easy, since he was of Mexican background. But he signed up for French instead. Victor thought he might like to visit France someday to see the sights and people. He also knew that a girl named Teresa was taking French. He hoped they'd be in the same class.

♦ ♦ ♦

Teresa is going to be my girl this year, he promised himself as he left the gym full of students in their new fall clothes. She was cute.

♦ ♦ ♦

Victor ran into his friend Michael Torres, who looked very strange.

♦ ♦ ♦

"How come you're making a face?" asked Victor.

"I ain't making a face. . . . This *is* my face."

♦ ♦ ♦

Michael explained that he had changed his expression over the summer, after he saw a copy of the men's magazine *GQ*. All of the male models were with beautiful women and had the same look on their faces—in all of the pictures they would scowl. Michael figured that the scowl must somehow be attractive so he decided to copy it.

♦ ♦ ♦

◆ Culture Note

Do you agree that it would be easier to study your native language than one you don't know? Circle *yes* or *no*. Then, explain your answer.

yes no

___

___

___

___

◆ English Language Development

English speakers often express the future by using the phrases *am going to, is going to,* or *are going to* followed by a verb.

Future tense: She will be my girl.

Future with *go*:

She is going to be my girl.

Rewrite these sentences to express the future with *go* followed by an infinitive.

They will study French:

___

___

___

___

He will visit France someday:

___

___

___

___

Vocabulary Development

scowl (SKOWL) *v.* to lower the eyebrows and corners of the mouth in an angry or annoyed look

"What classes are you taking?" Michael said, scowling.

"French. How 'bout you?"

"Spanish. I ain't so good at it, even if I'm Mexican."

"I'm not either, but I'm better at it than math, that's for sure."

♦ ♦ ♦

As Victor headed to his homeroom, he wondered about Michael's idea. Could making a face make him seem handsome? He tried it and felt silly, until he noticed a girl looking at him. Maybe scowling worked.

♦ ♦ ♦

In homeroom, . . . Victor sat calmly, thinking of Teresa, who sat two rows away, reading a paperback novel. This would be his lucky year. She was in his homeroom, and would probably be in his English and math classes. And, of course, French.

♦ ♦ ♦

When the bell rang, most of the students raced to their first class. But Teresa stayed to talk to the homeroom teacher. Victor lingered too. If he left at the same time Teresa did he could talk to her. He wanted to say something clever to her. So he waited and watched Teresa on the sly.

♦ ♦ ♦

As she turned to leave, he stood up and hurried to the door, where he managed to catch her eye. She smiled and said, "Hi, Victor."

He smiled back and said, "Yeah, that's me." His brown face blushed. Why hadn't he said, "Hi, Teresa," or "How was your summer?"

♦ ♦ ♦

Vocabulary Development

lingered (LING erd) *v.* was slow to leave; continued to stay

◆ English Language Development

Mark the Text

When conversations leave out tag lines like "Victor asked" or "Michael said," you can still figure out who is speaking by following the punctuation and paragraphing and knowing who spoke first. For example, in this bracketed conversation, you know Michael spoke before Victor. Label the rest of the remarks with the name of each speaker.

◆ Vocabulary and Pronunciation

Mark the Text

The letter *l* is often silent when it comes before an *m*. Circle the silent *l* in *calmly*, and say the word aloud.

◆ Reading Strategy

Mark the Text

Sly means "sneaky." What do you think the **idiom** "on the sly" means?

on the sly: ______

Circle another idiom in the next paragraph. Explain its meaning here:

______

______

◆ **Literary Analysis**

Reread Victor's conversation with Teresa at the bottom of p. 57. Think about Victor's reaction as she walks away. Do the details make you like or dislike Victor? Explain your answer on these lines.

____

____

____

____

◆ **Vocabulary and Pronunciation**

The word *crush* here means "a strong but temporary liking, usually of a romantic kind." However, the word is more often used as a verb with another meaning. Write that meaning.

crush:

____

____

____

____

◆ **Vocabulary and Pronunciation**

Sign here means "indication or trace." The g is silent, as it is in several English words that have *g* before *n* in the same syllable. Pronounce the word *sign*, which rhymes with *line*. Then, try saying these words:

reign (rhymes with *main*)

campaign (rhymes with *main*)

align (rhymes with a *mine*)

gnat (rhymes with *fat*)

Victor watched Teresa as she headed toward her next class. He thought she looked graceful as she walked. As it turned out, Teresa was not in Victor's English class. The English teacher began reviewing parts of speech. Victor was called on for an example of a noun that names a person.

◆ ◆ ◆

"Teresa," Victor said automatically.

Some of the girls giggled. They knew he had a crush on Teresa. He felt himself blushing again.

◆ ◆ ◆

After English, Victor had math and then social studies. Teresa was in neither class. At lunchtime, he went to the cafeteria and sat with Michael. Michael practiced his scowl and was excited when some girls noticed him.

Victor wasn't interested in Michael's scowl because he was thinking about Teresa. He didn't see her in the cafeteria. It was possible that she had brought her lunch from home and was eating outside. He decided to go out to the bag lunch area and check it out. Victor opened his math book and pretended to read from it. With his eyes lowered, he looked to the left and didn't see her. Then he looked for her to the right.

◆ ◆ ◆

Still no sign of her. He stretched out lazily in an attempt to disguise his snooping.

Then he saw her. . . . Victor moved to a table near her and daydreamed about taking her to a movie.

◆ ◆ ◆

Vocabulary Development

automatically (aw toh MA tic lee) *adv.* without pausing or thinking

Victor and Teresa went to French class separately. There, the teacher, Mr. Bueller, said hello in French and asked if anyone knew the language. Wanting to impress Teresa, Victor raised his hand, The teacher asked him a question in French. Victor didn't really know French, so he didn't understand the question. What made it worse was that he couldn't answer in French.

♦ ♦ ♦

. . . He tried to bluff his way out by making noises that sounded French.

"La me vave me con le grandma," he said uncertainly.

♦ ♦ ♦

Mr. Bueller asked Victor to speak up.

♦ ♦ ♦

Great rosebushes of red bloomed on Victor's cheeks. . . . He felt awful. Teresa sat a few desks away, no doubt thinking he was a fool.

♦ ♦ ♦

Victor mumbled something else that he thought might sound like French.

♦ ♦ ♦

"Frenchie oh wewe gee in September."

♦ ♦ ♦

But Mr. Bueller realized Victor didn't know French, and turned back to the rest of the class. Mr. Bueller continued with the lesson, but Victor could no longer concentrate. Victor was completely embarrassed and miserable.

When the bell rang, Victor raced from the room, but realized he had forgotten his math book. He had to go back. Mr. Bueller was still there, erasing the board. Teresa was there too. Victor was terrified she would learn the truth.

♦ ♦ ♦

♦ Culture Note

Though Victor knows very little about French, he seems to know *oui*, the word for "yes," which is pronounced "wee."

Mark the Text

Circle his made-up word in the bracketed text that sounds like "yes yes" in French. Then, write the word for *yes* in your own native language:

____

♦ English Language Development

Embarrassed, which means "ashamed," is a tricky word to spell. But lots of people use memory devices to remember tricky English spellings. For example, to remember that *embarrassed* has two *r*'s, think of Victor's two *r*ed cheeks. Try creating a memory device to help you with another tricky word from the story, such as *sign*. Write your memory device here:

____

◆ Stop to Reflect

In exchange for Victor's help in French, what subject could Teresa help Victor with? Write it here: ____________________

What do you predict will happen when Victor helps Teresa with French?

____

____

____

____

◆ Culture Note

Bonjour means "hello" or "good day" in French. Write a word with a similar meaning in your own language.

____

◆ Vocabulary and Pronunciation

Many English words with silent letters come from French. An example is the word *bouquets*, which means "bunches of cut flowers." *Bouquets* rhymes with trays. Circle the silent consonant in the word.

Mark the Text

"I didn't know you knew French," she said. "That was good."

◆ ◆ ◆

Victor tried to send a message to Mr. Bueller with his eyes. Victor silently begged his teacher not to let Teresa know that he didn't know French. Mr. Bueller seemed to get Victor's message. Better yet, he seemed to understand the situation. He said nothing. Victor's situation brought back Mr. Bueller's own embarrassing moments from his own past. As Mr. Bueller thought about a time when he had tried to impress a new girlfriend, Teresa asked Victor if he would help her with her French.

◆ ◆ ◆

"Sure, anytime," Victor said.

"I won't be bothering you, will I?"

"Oh, no. I like being bothered."

◆ ◆ ◆

The two left together and stopped outside Teresa's next class. She smiled and said "Bonjour," the term for "good day" that Mr. Bueller had taught them.

◆ ◆ ◆

"Yeah, right, *bonjour*," Victor said. . . . The rosebushes of shame on his face became bouquets of love. Teresa is a great girl, he thought. And Mr. Bueller is a good guy.

◆ ◆ ◆

Victor's happiness caused him to sprint to his next two classes. After he left school that day, he raced to the public library. He was in a hurry to check out some French textbooks so he could help Teresa with her French.

◆ ◆ ◆

He was going to like seventh grade.

Vocabulary Development

sprint (SPRINT) *n.* a race or run at full speed

REVIEW AND ASSESS

1. Write a reason for each of these story events.

Event	Reason
Victor signs up for French.	____________________
Victor is slow to leave homeroom.	____________________
Victor goes outside during lunch.	____________________
Victor pretends to know French.	____________________
Victor gets French books at the library.	____________________

2. List at least three times in the story when Victor feels embarrassed or ashamed.

   1. ____

   2. ____

   3. ____

3. What impression does the story give of seventh grade? Answer by completing this sentence.

   Seventh grade is a time of ____________________________

   ____

   ____

4. **Literary Analysis:** List six details from the story that illustrate Soto's amused but understanding tone.

Amused	Understanding
____________________	____________________
____________________	____________________
____________________	____________________

(Continued)

5. **Reading Strategy:** On the lines below, define these **idioms** from the story.

making a face:

catch her eye:

Writing

Victor is just starting seventh grade. On a separate paper, write a paragraph about seventh grade that might be helpful to someone like Victor. Explain what seventh grade is like by comparing and contrasting it to sixth grade.

- List several similarities and differences between sixth and seventh grade. They can be about schoolwork, social life, or any other similarity or difference that you think is important.

6th grade	7th grade

- Make a general statement about how seventh grade is like or unlike sixth grade. For example: Seventh grade is like sixth grade, only more fun. Or: Seventh grade is much harder than sixth grade. Or: In seventh grade, you are on your own more than in sixth grade.
- Use your general statement to open your paragraph. Then, support that statement with some of the similarities and differences you listed.

PREVIEW

Melting Pot

Anna Quindlen

Summary

The author describes her New York City neighborhood as a mixture of different ethnic and social groups. She sees the idea of the American melting pot existing where she lives, but only on a person-to-person level. In groups, the people often don't get along, but as individuals they usually do.

Visual Summary

Question: Does America's Melting Pot Exist?

Yes	No
• Author's children are friends with family from Ecuador next door.	• Author's mother as a girl is insulted for being Italian American.
• Neighbors of all backgrounds are friendly because their children play together.	• Author's immigrant grandfather was told "No Irish Need Apply."
• Person-to-person, people get along pretty well.	• Old-timers resent the young professionals, whose moving in causes prices to rise.
• Italian-American old-timers accept author, a young professional, because of her Italian roots.	• The young professionals resent being blamed for high prices.
• People join together on issues that affect them all.	• Old immigrants are suspicious of new immigrants.
• Both "them" and "us" attitudes exist.	• New immigrants think old ones are "bigots."
	• Looked at in broad strokes, the neighborhood is a pressure cooker of groups who don't always mix well.

Conclusion: Melting pot exists person to person but not group to group

PREPARE TO READ

LITERARY ANALYSIS

Tone

Tone is the attitude a writer expresses in a work. For instance, the writer's tone might be serious or lighthearted, angry or joyful, happy or sad. In "Melting Pot," Anna Quindlen uses an informal tone to explore her subject. To understand how she creates that tone, read this passage:

> It took awhile. Eight years ago we were the new people on the block. . . . We thought we could feel people staring at us from behind the sheer curtains on their windows. We were right.

Now, think about how the passage would be different if it were part of a formal paper about America's melting pot. Such a paper would not be likely to use informal language, personal details, and humor.

As you read Quindlen's essay, look for more details that convey her informal tone. You might list them on a chart like this one.

Informal Language	Personal Details	Humor
It took awhile; on the block	personal experiences eight years ago; how she and her family felt	"We were right"—the neighbors are nosey

READING STRATEGY

Identifying Idioms

An **idiom** is an expression that means something different from the words that make it up. An example is the expression *melting pot*, which Quindlen uses as the title of her essay. A real *melting pot* means just what each of the words mean, a pot in which things are melted. But the idiom *melting pot* refers to a place where people from many different backgrounds come together in a unified way. With people from all over the world coming to its shores and becoming American citizens, the United States itself is often called a *melting pot*.

Idiom	What Separate Words Mean	What Idiom Means
melting pot	a container in which things are heated until they melt	a country or an area where people of many backgrounds join or blend together

Melting Pot

Anna Quindlen

In Anna Quindlen's New York City neighborhood, there are people who came to America from all over the world. Right now, her children are next door having dinner with a family from the Spanish-speaking nation of Ecuador.

♦ ♦ ♦

The father speaks some English, the nother less than that. The two daughters are luent in both their native and their adopted anguages but the youngest child, a son, a close friend of my two boys, speaks almost 10 Spanish.

♦ ♦ ♦

The boy's parents want him to speak English instead of Spanish because he is an American, living in an American city. Quindlen isn't surprised at how the parents feel because her mother was raised as an American—speaking English—among Italians in her family.

Yet Quindlen wonders if America really is a melting pot where people of different backgrounds join together. Her mother was called nasty names when she was a girl—simply for being Italian American. When Quindlen's Irish grandfather first came to America and looked for work, signs said "No Irish Need Apply." Quindlen still sees dislike and suspicion among different groups in

◆ **Literary Analysis**

Mark the Text: Circle at least one detail that contributes to the essay's informal tone. Explain your choice.

______

______

______

◆ **Culture Note**

In your experience, is it a good idea for a family who came from another country to raise an American child to know only English? List one good point and one bad point of this practice.

Good Point:

______

______

Bad Point:

______

______

Vocabulary Development

fluent (FLOO ent) *adj.* able to write or speak easily and smoothly

◆ English Language Development

Verb forms that end in *-ed* and are used as adjectives are called **participles**:

the *tired* professionals

Moneyed is unusual because there is really no verb "to money." Nevertheless, the noun *money* has here been turned into a participle used as an adjective to describe *professionals*. Write the meaning of moneyed on the lines.

moneyed:

____

____

◆ Vocabulary and Pronunciation

The letters *gh* are often silent, as they are in *eight*. Say the word *eight* aloud—it sounds just like *ate*. Then, circle another word in the next paragraph that contains a silent *gh*. Say those words aloud too.

Mark the Text

◆ Stop to Reflect

Why do you think old-timers find the author different from the other young professionals moving into the neighborhood?

____

____

her neighborhood. For instance, the old-timers are suspicious of the new moneyed professionals. They think they are taking over. At the same time the professionals think that everyone in the neighborhood blames them for rising rents. In fact, they are the ones that are moving in and having to pay the high rents.

◆ ◆ ◆

The old immigrants are suspicious of the new ones. The new ones think the old ones are bigots.

◆ ◆ ◆

Yet on a person-to-person level, members of all these groups usually get along. Quindlen herself is friendly with neighbors of many backgrounds simply because her children play with theirs. She recalls that their friendliness didn't happen overnight. When she and her family moved in they thought people were watching them. The old-timers of the neighborhood were, indeed, watching them.

◆ ◆ ◆

Eight years ago we were the new people on the block. . . .

◆ ◆ ◆

Quindlen recalls her first New York apartment in an old Italian American neighborhood where young professionals were moving in. Though she too was a young professional, the old-timers accepted her because of her Italian background.

◆ ◆ ◆

Vocabulary Development

professionals (pro FESH uh nuhlz) *n.* people whose jobs require advanced education and training

bigots (BIG ots) *n.* very narrow-minded, prejudiced people

I remember sitting . . . with a group of half a dozen elderly men, . . . watching a glazier[1] install a great spread of tiny glass panes to make one wall of a restaurant.

♦ ♦ ♦

The men were convinced that the window panes soon would be broken and the restaurant wouldn't last. Despite their predictions, the restaurant became busy and successful. Two years later, all but three of the men had moved or died. The remaining men still sat and watched the restaurant. But now they dolefully watched people waiting in line to eat there. Quindlen even ate at the restaurant. However, the old men didn't have hard feelings toward Quindlen because she ate there. They said she wasn't one of "them."

♦ ♦ ♦

It's an argument familiar to members of almost any embattled race or class: I like you, therefore you aren't like the rest of your kind, whom I hate.

♦ ♦ ♦

The neighborhood where Quindlen now lives has also changed. Not only young professionals but also many new immigrant groups have arrived. She doesn't think change comes easy to people in America. However, she notes that change is constant. Some people deal with it better than others. The antiques store used to be the butcher shop—the butcher now sits sadly outside the pizzeria[2] because his shop is gone. Quindlen

Vocabulary Development

dolefully (DOHL ful lee) *adv.* sadly; glumly
embattled (em BAT ld) *adj.* in conflict; forced to fight

1. **glazier** (GLA zher) *n.* a person who cuts and installs glass.
2. **pizzeria** (PEETS uh REE uh) *n.* pizza shop.

♦ Vocabulary and Pronunciation

Mark the Text

A **homophone** is a word that sounds just like another word. The word *panes* is a homophone of *pains.* Write the meaning of each of these words on the lines below.

panes:

____

pains:

____

In the bracketed paragraph, find and circle homophones of these two words: *won* and *grate.*

◆ Reading Check

Squid is a type of sea creature with long arms, like an octopus. Bait here is a small piece of seafood that is used to catch a fish. Label the three views of squid—as calamari, as sushi, and as bait—with the letter of the group who views the squid that way:
(a) Italian American old-timers;
(b) a Japanese American;
(c) groups who would never eat squid and would only use it to catch other fish.

Mark the Text

◆ Reading Strategy

Think about how the underlined idioms are used in the selection. Then, circle the correct meaning of the idiom from the two choices given.

1. drawn in broad strokes: swimming very hard *or* described in a general way
2. pressure cooker: a very tense place *or* a place where groups blend
3. oil and water: two things that go together *or* two things that don't mix easily

◆ Literary Analysis

Is the writer happy with her neighborhood? Below, write the sentence that tells you.

____

____

sees the changes reflected in the types of stores and the items they sell.

◆ ◆ ◆

About a third of the people in the neighborhood think of squid as calamari,[3] about a third think of it as sushi,[4] and about a third think of it as bait.

◆ ◆ ◆

Quindlen thinks the neighborhood has reached a nice mix. People get along, even if there are still some tensions.

◆ ◆ ◆

Drawn in broad strokes, we live in a pressure cooker: oil and water, us and them.

◆ ◆ ◆

The groups of people are still different. And their differences can cause problems. At times, however, people from all the different groups gather together to complain about things they have in common. If they can agree, they can get along.

◆ ◆ ◆

We melt together, then draw apart. I am the granddaughter of immigrants, a young professional—either an interloper or a longtime resident. . . . I am one of them, and one of us.

Vocabulary Development

interloper (IN ter LOP er) *n.* someone who intrudes on another's rights or territory

3. **calamari** (KAL uh MAR ee) *n.* squid cooked as food, especially in Italian dishes.
4. **sushi** (SOO she) *n.* Japanese rice cakes cooked with vegetables and seafood, including squid.

REVIEW AND ASSESS

1. On the lines, explain what people mean when they call America a melting pot.

____

____

____

____

2. According to Quindlen, when is her neighborhood most like a melting pot? Put a check in front of the correct answer.

____ It is most like a melting pot when people deal with each other person-to-person.

____ It is most like a melting pot when people deal with each other group-to-group.

3. On the lines below, list the main groups in conflict in the neighborhood. Choose from these groups: old-timers, old immigrants, new immigrants, young professionals.

____________________ vs. ____________________

____________________ vs. ____________________

4. Explain how Anna Quindlen belongs to at least three of the four groups listed in item 3.

____

____

____

____

____

(Continued)

5. **Reading Strategy:** Read this sentence from the selection. Then, explain the meaning of the underlined **idiom**.

The old-timers are angry because they think the new moneyed professionals are taking over their town.

taking over: ______________________________

6. **Literary Analysis:** List two examples of each of these four kinds of details that convey Quindlen's informal **tone**.

personal experiences:

1. ______________________ 2. ______________________

personal feelings:

1. ______________________ 2. ______________________

informal language:

1. ______________________ 2. ______________________

humor:

1. ______________________ 2. ______________________

Listening and Speaking

Imagine that a neighborhood group is trying to solve a problem between two residents. With other students, role-play the meeting of such a group.

- Think of a situation or problem that has two sides—for example, a disagreement over building something, where one person wants to build it and one person doesn't.
- Two students, both pretending to be local residents, should present each side of the issue.
- The rest of your group should act as the neighborhood group's board members. The board should ask the residents questions to learn more information. The board should then discuss the situation among themselves and try to come up with a solution to the problem.

PREVIEW

The Hummingbird That Lived Through Winter

William Saroyan

Summary

Old Dikran, an Armenian immigrant to California, is nearly blind. One cold winter day, he finds a hummingbird. Though the bird is near death, he nurses it back to health and lets it go. The narrator is not sure if the bird survives the rest of winter. However, the next summer, the narrator sees many hummingbirds. Old Dikran says that each of them is the hummingbird they saved.

Visual Summary

DIKRAN

Description	Actions
• narrator's neighbor in Fresno, CA • immigrant from Armenia • past 80 years old • wife nearly as old • big, rough peasant's hands • nearly blind	• grows lovely garden • rescues dying hummingbird in winter • with narrator's help, saves hummingbird's life • has narrator let hummingbird go • tells narrator hummingbird survived winter • tells narrator they saved all the hummingbirds

PREPARE TO READ

LITERARY ANALYSIS

Symbol

A **symbol** is something that conveys an idea or meaning beyond what it actually is. For example, a dove actually is a bird. However, it often conveys the idea of peace. When it does, it is a symbol.

A symbol does not always stand for just one thing. Sometimes a symbol can stand for several ideas at once. Sometimes the same symbol means different things to different readers.

To understand what a symbol means, you need to look at the details about it. In Saroyan's story, the hummingbird is a symbol. It has been near death, but later it takes on a new life:

> It spun about in the little kitchen, going to the window, coming back to the heat, suspending, circling as if it were summertime and it had never felt better in its whole life.

As you read, list all the details about the hummingbird. Then, decide on its meaning as a symbol.

READING STRATEGY

Using Word Parts

One way to figure out the meaning of an unfamiliar word is to look for a part you recognize. The familiar part can give you a clue to the meaning of the whole word. For example, consider the word *guardian* in the story.

> Plants, bushes, trees—all strong, in sweet black moist earth whose guardian was old Dikran.

As you read the story, underline unfamiliar words and circle the parts that help you figure out their meanings. Keep track of the words and their meanings on a chart like this one.

Unfamiliar Word	Familiar Part	Meaning of Part	Probable Meaning of Word
guardian	guard	to watch over; to take care of	someone who watches over; a caretaker

The Hummingbird That Lived Through Winter

William Saroyan

Old Dikran (DEEK ran) was once a peasant, or poor farmer, in the southeastern European nation of Armenia. After fleeing hardship in his homeland, he settled with his wife in a California neighborhood where many other Armenian Americans live. The boy who tells the story lives just across the street and is also of Armenian background. He recalls a winter day when his neighbor old Dikran made an unusual discovery.

♦ ♦ ♦

There was a hummingbird once which in the wintertime did not leave our neighborhood in Fresno, California.

♦ ♦ ♦

As the narrator, the boy begins to tell the story. Dikran and his wife are about eighty years old. Old Dikran can hardly see. The couple keep an neat house—inside and outside. Dikran has a wild and wonderful garden with all kinds of plants, bushes and trees. He looks after his garden with care. Everything that flies in the sky comes to this place. It is a special spot in the poor neighborhood in which they live. Dikran loves the creatures that came to his garden.

One of these creatures from the sky is a hummingbird that has managed to survive into winter. This is unusual, because hummingbirds are creatures of summer who do not take to winter's cold.

♦ ♦ ♦

One freezing Sunday, in the <u>dead of winter</u>, as I came home from Sunday School, I saw old Dikran standing in the middle of the street.

♦ ♦ ♦

◆ Culture Note

Many immigrants choose to live in areas where others from their homeland have settled. List one reason this is a good idea and one reason it is not.

Good Point:

____

____

____

Bad Point:

____

____

____

◆ Vocabulary and Pronunciation

Mark the Text

The *neigh* in *neighborhood* rhymes with *pay*; the *gh* is silent. Say *neighborhood* aloud. Then, find another word in the next paragraph where *eigh* has the same sound as it does in *neighborhood.* Circle that word, and also say it aloud.

◆ Vocabulary and Pronunciation

What do you think "dead of winter" means here? Circle the letter of your guess. Then, explain why you think that is the meaning.

(a) a mild winter

(b) the coldest part of winter

(c) the end of winter, when it warms up

(d) people or animals who die in winter

◆ Reading Check

Does the explanation in the bracketed paragraph clearly explain what a hummingbird is? Write *yes* or *no*. If you say *yes*, list the information you found helpful. If you say *no*, write what you think is missing.

____

____

◆ English Language Development

To form the **present participle** (*-ing* form) of the verb *die*, you change the *ie* to *y* before adding the *-ing*:

die + -ing = dying

What is the present participle of the verb *lie*? Write it here:

____

◆ Literary Analysis

Mark the Text

Circle three details describing a hummingbird in summer and box three contrasting words that describe the bird now. Based on these contrasts, what might the hummingbird be a **symbol** of? Circle the letter of your answer.

(a) the joys of both summer and winter

(b) luck or good fortune

(c) the wonder and beauty of nature

(d) the fragile or delicate nature of life

Dikran holds out his hand to the boy. Speaking in Armenian, he asks the boy what is in his hand. The boy looks and tells Dikran that it's a hummingbird. Dikran is not familiar with the English word and too blind to see the bird itself. The boy describes a hummingbird to old Dikran. He tells him it is the little summer bird with wings that beat fast. He says it "stands in the air" before it "shoots away." He also tells Dikran that the bird is dying.

Because Dikran's wife is still at church, he asks the boy to help him care for the bird. He has the boy look at the bird again and report its condition.

◆ ◆ ◆

It was a sad thing to behold. This wonderful little creature of summertime in the big rough hand of the old peasant. Here it was the cold of winter, absolutely helpless and pathetic, not suspended in a shaft of summer light.

◆ ◆ ◆

Again, the boy tells the old man that the bird is dying. Old Dikran gently blows warm breath on the bird he cannot see. He speaks to the bird in Armenian, reassuring the bird that it is not long until summer.

He heads for his kitchen, where he has the boy warm some honey on the stove and put the honey in his hand. Soon the hummingbird begins to recover. The dying bird is showing new signs of life.

◆ ◆ ◆

Vocabulary Development

behold (bee HOLD) *v.* to see

pathetic (pa THET ic) *n.* causing pity, sorrow, or sympathy; very sad

suspended (sus PEND ed) *adj.* hanging in the air

shaft (SHAFT) *n.* a column of light; a beam

The warmth of the room, the vapor of the warm honey—and, well, the will and love of the old man.

◆ ◆ ◆

As the hummingbird begins to eat the honey, Old Dikran declares that it will live. He urges the boy to stay and watch what happens. The boy is amazed by the change in the bird.

◆ ◆ ◆

It spun about in the little kitchen, going to the window, coming back to the heat.

◆ ◆ ◆

The bird circles and flies as though it is outside on a summer's day. It also seems far from dying now. The old man sits in his plain chair, paying careful attention to what is happening, even though he cannot see. The boy describes the bird's behavior.

◆ ◆ ◆

When the bird was restless and wanted to go, the old man said, "Open the window and let it go."

◆ ◆ ◆

The boy is unsure. He asks whether the bird will live if it goes outside. Old Dikran announces that the bird is alive now. He points out to the boy that it wants to go outside. Then he commands the boy to open the window for it to fly out.

When the boy opens the window, the bird seems to test the cold air a bit and then flies off. The boy closes the window and talks a little more with Dikran before going home. Dikran continues to claim that the hummingbird lived through winter. The boy isn't so sure.

Vocabulary Development

vapor (VAY pur) *n.* mist or steam floating in the air

◆ Literary Analysis

Mark the Text

Circle at least one detail in this passage that suggests the hummingbird may be a **symbol** of hope.

◆ Reading Strategy

Mark the Text

The word part *-less* often means "without." Draw a line to break the word *restless* into two parts. Then, use the **word parts** to help you figure out the meaning of the full word. Write it here.

restless:

______

______

______

◆ **Think Ahead**

Do you think the hummingbird will live? Make a prediction and then explain it.

____

____

____

◆ **English Language Development**

In English, *-ly* often turns adjectives into adverbs that tell *how*. For example, the adjective swift means "quick." Adding *-ly* turns it into an adverb meaning "in a quick manner; quickly." Circle another *-ly* adverb in the final paragraph. Write the adjective from which it comes and the spelling change that took place when the *-ly* was added:

Mark THE Text

____

____

____

Now, write the meaning of the word:

____

____

____

When summer comes, the boy sees hummingbirds about but can't tell them apart. Finally he again asks Dikran if the bird lived. Dikran tells the boy to look around. He then asks the boy if he sees the bird.

◆ ◆ ◆

"I see humming*birds*," I said.

"Each of them is our bird," the old man said. "Each of them, each of them," he said swiftly and gently.

REVIEW AND ASSESS

1. On the lines, list three things that Dikran or the boy do for the ailing hummingbird.
   - ____________________
   - ____________________
   - ____________________

2. Why do you think Dikran wants the bird freed even though the winter cold might kill it?

   ____

   ____

3. Put a check in front of each statement that you think applies to Dikran.

   ____ He can barely see.

   ____ He is very wealthy.

   ____ He loves and respects nature.

   ____ He respects the freedom of living things.

   ____ He has a dark, negative view of the future.

4. **Literary Analysis:** Check the ideas on the left that you think the hummingbird might be a **symbol** of. Then, on the right, explain why the bird might be a symbol of each idea you checked.

Checklist of Possible Symbols	Explanation
___ hope or renewal ___ the fragile or delicate nature of life ___ youth and old age ___ the beauty and wonder of nature ___ human selfishness and greed	

(Continued)

5. **Reading Strategy:** Use the **word parts** to help you explain the meaning of these words from the story.

hummingbird: ______________________________

helpless: ______________________________

heartbreaking: ______________________________

Writing

A **database** is a catalog of information for use on a computer. Prepare a database of at least ten works about birds or other animals.

- Include the same information for each work, and put it in the same place. Follow this model.

Model Database Record	
Title of Work:	
Type of Work: Encyclopedia ☐ Book ☐ Magazine ☐ Other ☐	Quality: Excellent ☐ Good ☐ Poor ☐
Summary:	

- For *Type of Work*, indicate whether the work is a movie, book, story, poem, or true story. Try to list at least two examples of each of these types.

- For *Quality*, indicate whether you think the work is excellent, good, fair, or poor.

- For *Summary*, tell what the work is about in a sentence or two.

PREVIEW

The Third Wish

Joan Aiken

Summary

One evening, while driving through a forest, Mr. Peters discovers a swan tangled in a bush. He frees the swan, who turns into a little man, the King of the Forest. The King agrees to grant Mr. Peters three wishes and gives him three leaves to wish on. He warns that people who use wishes often end up worse off than before. Mr. Peters wants very little, and he is aware of the trouble wishes often bring. But he is lonely, so he decides to wish for a beautiful wife. His wish is granted with the arrival of Leita, a former swan, whom he then marries. But Leita misses her swan's life and her swan sister Rhea. And in time Mr. Peters realizes that Leita will never be happy as a human being. So he uses his second wish to turn her back into a swan. He and the two swans remain close. Those who know his situation are surprised that he never uses his third wish to ask for another wife. But he says that two wishes are enough for him, and that he prefers to stay true to Leita. One morning he is found dead with a smile on his face and a leaf and white feather in his hands.

Visual Summary

1	2	3	4	5
It is a spring evening. Mr. Peters is driving through the forest.	Mr. Peters hears a noise. He rescues a swan tangled in bushes. The swan turns into the King of the Forest. He gives Mr. Peters three magical leaves that will grant three wishes. Mr. Peters wishes for a wife. The next day he gets a wife who was once a swan. She loves him but desperately misses her old life and swan sister.	Mr. Peters uses his second wish to turn his wife back into a swan.	The wife joins her swan sister. The two stay close with Mr. Peters. He says two wishes are enough and won't wish for another wife.	Mr. Peters is found dead in bed with a smile on his face and the third leaf and a white feather in his hands.

PREPARE TO READ

LITERARY ANALYSIS

Modern Fairy Tale

Fairy tales are stories that often include one or more of these:

- imaginary creatures, such as fairies, elves, giants, and ogres (monsters)
- animals with unusual abilities, such as being able to talk
- wishes that come true and other magic
- mysterious and fantastic events

Most fairy tales take place a long time ago and were written long ago as well. But in more recent times, some writers have created **modern fairy tales**. They combine the elements of fairy tales with aspects of modern life. In "The Third Wish," for example, Mr. Peters meets a magical creature in the forest. He meets that creature while driving through the forest in a car.

As you read, list the elements of this modern fairy tale on a chart like the one below. On the left, list elements like those in a regular fairy tale. On the right, list the details about modern life from "The Third Wish."

Fairy-Tale Elements	Modern Elements
Mr. Peters encounters the magical King of the Forest.	Mr. Peters drives a car through the forest.

READING STRATEGY

Clarifying Word Meanings

Often when you are reading, you will come across words with confusing or unclear meanings. To **clarify word meanings**, or make their meanings clear to you, look for clues in nearby words and sentences. Take this example from "The Third Wish":

> The only thing that troubled him was that he was a little lonely, and had no <u>companion</u> for his old age.

The word *companion* may be unfamiliar, but the surrounding words and phrases give clues to its meaning. They indicate that a *companion* will stop the man from being lonely. So *companion* probably means "someone to be with" or "someone who keeps you company."

The Third Wish

Joan Aiken

One evening in early spring, Mr. Peters was driving through the forest. As he came to a stretch of empty road, he heard an odd cry.

◆ ◆ ◆

He left his car and climbed the mossy bank beside the road. . . . As he neared the bushes he saw something white among them which was trying to extricate itself; coming closer he found that it was a swan that had become entangled in the thorns growing on the bank of the canal.

◆ ◆ ◆

When he tried to help, the swan hissed and pecked at him. Still, Mr. Peters managed to untangle it.

◆ ◆ ◆

. . . And in a moment, instead of the great white bird, there was a little man all in green with a golden crown and long beard, standing by the water.

◆ ◆ ◆

The little green man did not seem grateful to be rescued. Instead, he spoke in a threatening way.

◆ ◆ ◆

"You think that because you have rescued—by pure good fortune—the King of the Forest from a difficulty, you should have some fabulous reward."

"I expect three wishes, no more and no less," answered Mr. Peters. . . .

"Three wishes he wants, the clever man! Well, I have yet to hear of the human being who made any good use of his three wishes—they mostly

Vocabulary Development

fortune (FOR chuhn) *n.* luck

◆ Reading Strategy

Mark the Text

Circle the letter of the correct meaning of *extricate*.

(a) untangle (b) scratch

(c) grow thickly (d) entertain

Now, circle the nearby word or words that helped you figure out the meaning of extricate.

◆ Culture Note

Many European fairy tales feature little people all in green—sometimes called *elves* (singular, *elf*). In Ireland, these creatures are known as *leprechauns* (with the *ch* pronounced like a *k*). What are some imaginary creatures from older stories in your native land? Name and describe one:

____

____

____

◆ Literary Analysis

Think about Mr. Peters's behavior in this **modern fairy tale**. Why does he expect three wishes? Do characters in regular fairy tales usually know what to expect? Write your answers on the lines.

____

____

____

end up worse off than they started. Take your three wishes then"—he flung three dead leaves in the air—"don't blame me if you spend the last wish undoing the work of the other two."

◆ ◆ ◆

Mr. Peters caught the leaves and put them in his briefcase. He spent some time thinking about what his wishes should be. He knew the stories of wishes being granted only to bring trouble to those who made them. He wanted to avoid that. Besides, he didn't need many things.

◆ ◆ ◆

The only thing that troubled him was that he was a little lonely, and had no companion for his old age. He decided to use his first wish and to keep the other two in case of an emergency. . . .

◆ ◆ ◆

Holding one of the leaves, Mr. Peters looked at the forest all around him and made his wish:

◆ ◆ ◆

"I wish I had a wife as beautiful as the forest."

A tremendous quacking and splashing broke out on the surface of the water. He thought that it was the swan laughing at him.

◆ ◆ ◆

Mr. Peters ignored the noise, returned to his car, and went to sleep in it. When he awoke, it was morning.

◆ ◆ ◆

Coming along the track towards him was the most beautiful woman he had ever seen, with eyes as blue-green as the canal, hair as dusky as the bushes, and skin as white as the feathers of swans.

"Are you the wife that I wished for?" asked Mr. Peters.

"Yes, I am," she replied. "My name is Leita."

◆ ◆ ◆

◆ English Language Development

Some nouns that end in *f* change the *f* to *v* and add *es* for their plural form.

Singular	**Plural**
one leaf	three leaves

On the lines, write the plurals of these words.

elf: ________ half: ________

◆ Reading Check

Circle and number the two reasons that Mr. Peters decides to wish for a wife.

◆ Vocabulary and Pronunciation

In English, the letter combination *gh* is sometimes silent, sometimes sounds like *f*, and sometimes sounds like *g*. Circle each *gh* combination in this sentence, and label it *silent*, *f*, or *g* to show what it sounds like.

◆ Literary Analysis

What **fairy-tale** event happens to Mr. Peters?

____

____

____

____

Leita and Mr. Peters drove to a nearby church to get married. He then took her to his home in a lovely valley. She was especially glad to see a river nearby.

◆ ◆ ◆

"Do swans come up there?" she asked.

"Yes. I have often seen swans there on the river," he told her, and she smiled.

◆ ◆ ◆

Leita was a good and loving wife. But as time passed, Mr. Peters saw that she was not really happy. She wandered around outside and sometimes disappeared with no explanation. One evening he saw her down by the river, hugging a swan and crying. Tears rolled from the swan's eyes too.

◆ ◆ ◆

"Leita, what is it?" he asked, very troubled.

"This is my sister," she answered. "I can't bear being separated from her."

Now he understood that Leita was really a swan from the forest, and this made him very sad because when a human being marries a bird it always leads to sorrow.

◆ ◆ ◆

He offered to use his second wish to give Leita's sister human form. Then the two sisters could be companions.

◆ ◆ ◆

"No, no," she cried. "I couldn't ask that of her."

"Is it so very hard to be a human being?" asked Mr. Peters sadly.

"Very, very hard," she answered.

"Don't you love me at all, Leita?"

"Yes, I do. I do love you," she said, and there were tears in her eyes again. "But I miss the old life in the forest. . . ."

◆ ◆ ◆

Mr. Peters then offered to turn Leita back into a swan again. But she refused.

◆ ◆ ◆

◆ Stop to Reflect

Why do you think Leita likes living near the river and asks this question? ______________________

____

____

____

◆ Literary Analysis

A character in an old fairy tale would probably not have this thought. Why would a character in a **modern fairy tale** know this?

(a) He knows more about science.

(b) He knows more about nature.

(c) He knows more about marriage.

(d) He knows more about what happens in fairy tales.

◆ Vocabulary and Pronunciation

Mark the Text

Many words have different meanings, but *tears* also has different pronunciations to go with those meanings. When it means "rips," it rhymes with *cares*. When it means "water droplets from the eyes," it rhymes with *fears*. Which pronunciation does it have here? Circle your answer:

rhymes with cares

rhymes with fears

◆ **Vocabulary and Pronunciation**

Clothes has the same *o* sound as the first syllable of *clothing*. In its plural noun form, it also means clothing. It appears without the *s* only as a verb, to *clothe*, which means "to give clothing to." Which meaning is used here? Answer on the line.

____

◆ **Read Fluently**

Read this speech aloud. Who do you think Rhea is?

Write your answer on the lines below.

____

____

____

____

◆ **English Language Development**

Circle all the question marks in the King's speech. Then, to practice getting the right tone for a question, say the King's speech aloud.

"No, I could not be as unkind to you as that. I am partly a swan, but I am also partly a human being now. I will stay with you."

Poor Mr. Peters . . . did his best to make her life happier, taking her for drives in the car, finding beautiful music for her to listen to on the radio, buying <u>clothes</u> for her and even suggesting a trip around the world. But she said no to that; she would prefer to stay in their own house near the river.

◆ ◆ ◆

Mr. Peters built his wife a special seat down by the river so that she could spend more time with her sister. But Leita still continued to grow thin and pale. One night her husband found her weeping in her sleep and calling out:

◆ ◆ ◆

"Rhea! Rhea! I can't understand what you say! Oh, wait for me, take me with you!"

Then he knew that it was hopeless and she would never be happy as a human. He stooped down and kissed her goodbye, then took another leaf from his notecase, blew it out of the window, and used up his second wish.

◆ ◆ ◆

Mr. Peters used his second wish to turn Leita back into a swan. He brought her down to the river. After resting her head lightly on his hand, she flew away. Mr. Peters heard a nasty laugh behind him and turned to find the old King there.

◆ ◆ ◆

"Well, my friend! You don't seem to have managed so wonderfully with your first two wishes, do you? What will you do with the last? Turn yourself into a swan? Or turn Leita back into a girl?"

"I shall do neither," said Mr. Peters calmly. "Human beings and swans are better in their own shapes."

◆ ◆ ◆

After that, Mr. Peters was often seen spending time with two swans. One swan wore a gold chain just like a chain he had given Leita. Some people were a little afraid of him. Others were amazed at how happy he seemed. Sometimes people who knew his story would ask why he didn't use his last wish for another wife.

◆ ◆ ◆

"Not likely," he would answer serenely. "Two wishes were enough for me. . . . I've learned that even if your wishes are granted they don't always better you. I'll stay faithful to Leita."

◆ ◆ ◆

One autumn night, people heard the sad song of two swans at Mr. Peters' home.

◆ ◆ ◆

In the morning Mr. Peters was found peacefully dead in his bed with a smile of great happiness on his face. In his hands, which lay clasped on his breast, were a withered leaf and a white feather.

◆ Vocabulary and Pronunciation

Mark the Text

The *w* in *answer* is silent; the word sounds like ann-sir. Find and circle another silent *w* in this paragraph.

◆ Literary Analysis

Mark the Text

Did Mr. Peters ever use his third wish? Write *yes* or *no*: ________

Now, circle the detail in the last paragraph that tells you the answer to this question.

Vocabulary Development

serenely (suh REEN lee) *adv.* peacefully
withered (WITH erd) *adj.* dried up; wrinkled

REVIEW AND ASSESS

1. What does Mr. Peters do to get the three wishes? Write your answer on the line.

____

2. What seems to be the attitude of the King of the Forest? Circle the best answer.

   (a) He seems grateful to be rescued.

   (b) He seems fed up with granting wishes and makes fun of human beings.

   (c) He feels deep sympathy and pity when Mr. Peters loses his wife.

   (d) He is devoted to nature and all its creatures.

3. Why do you think Mr. Peters was smiling when he died? Answer on the lines below.

____

____

4. Which of these points do you think the story makes? Check more than one.

   ____ We are never comfortable when we try to be what we are not.

   ____ Love will always be enough to keep a marriage together.

   ____ Love sometimes means letting go so that the person you love can do what makes him or her happy.

   ____ It is selfish and wrong to wish for things.

   ____ What we wish for does not always turn out the way we expected.

   ____ There are many different kinds of love.

5. **Literary Analysis:** List at least three details in each column to show that the story displays the elements of a **modern fairy tale**.

Fairy-Tale Elements	Details of Modern Life
______________________	______________________
______________________	______________________
______________________	______________________
______________________	______________________

6. **Reading Strategy: Clarify word meanings** by using nearby words to figure out the meaning of each underlined word. Then circle the letter of the correct meaning from the choices given.

- *He left his car and climbed the mossy bank beside the road.*

  bank:
  (a) a place where money is kept (c) a roadway
  (b) to save money in such a place (d) the side of a road or waterway

- *Coming along the track towards him was the most beautiful woman he had ever seen, with eyes as blue-green as the canal, hair as dusky as the bushes, and skin as white as the feathers of swans.*

  dusky:
  (a) plain (b) blue-green (c) dark (d) light

Writing

Choose "Cinderella," "Jack and the Beanstalk," "Little Red Riding Hood," or any other fairy tale you know. Then, in a paragraph or two, retell it as a modern fairy tale.

- Keep the basic plot, but make the events and settings more modern. For example, instead of a ball, Cinderella might go to a line dance or a night club.
- Keep the main characters, but make their backgrounds and experiences more modern. For example, Little Red Riding Hood might be a fourth-grade student.
- Keep the fairy-tale elements, though you can change details about them. For example, Jack would still grow a beanstalk from magic beans, but he might order them over the Internet.

The Charge of the Light Brigade

Alfred, Lord Tennyson

Summary

Six hundred lightly armed British troops on horseback attack an enemy position. Since the enemy are heavily armed with cannon, the British soldiers know that something was wrong with their orders. Still, they follow their orders bravely, as good soldiers do. Many are killed, but their courage will be honored always.

Visual Summary

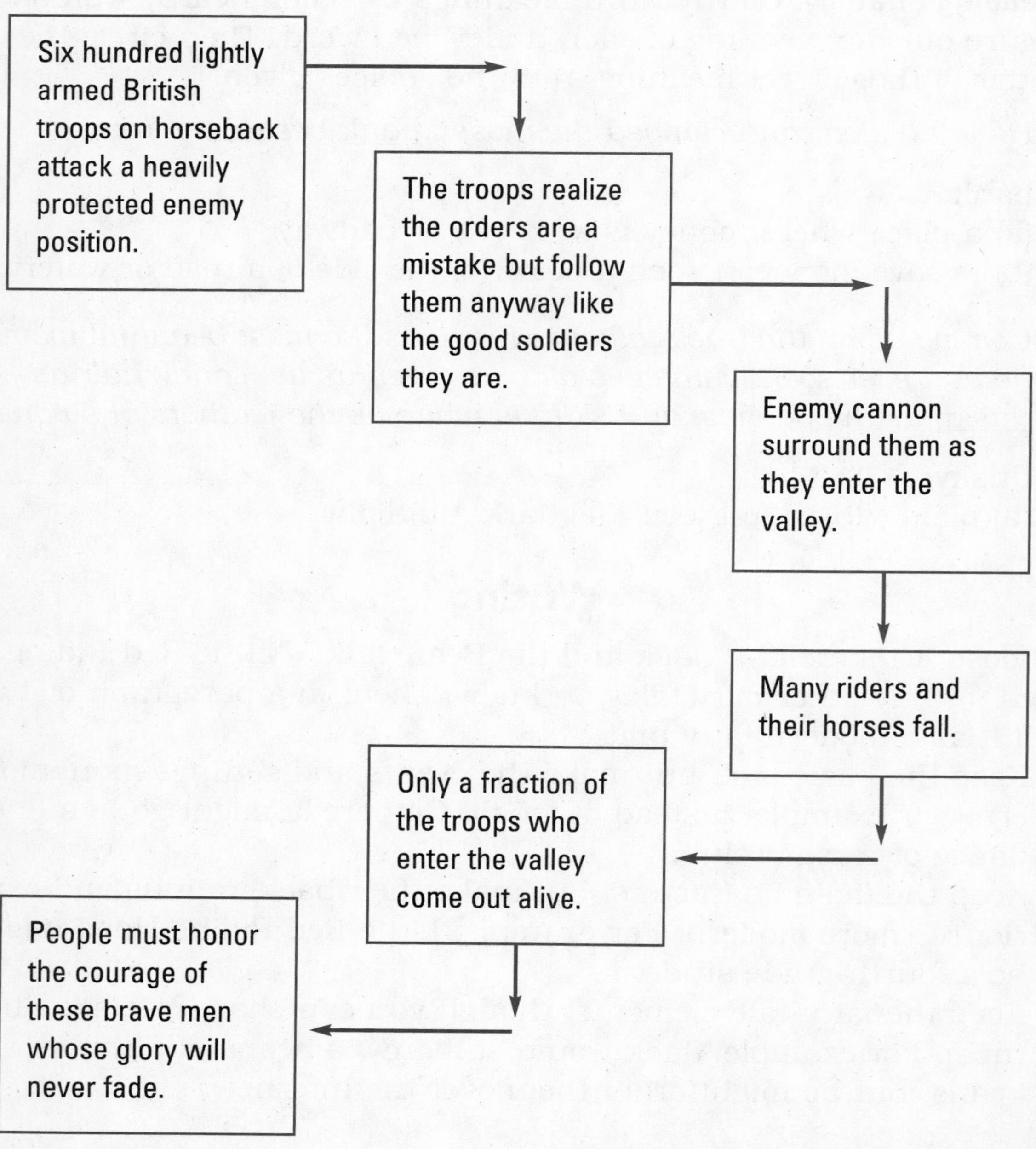

PREPARE TO READ

LITERARY ANALYSIS

Repetition

Repetition is the repeated use of the words or sounds. Poets use repetition to add to the music of their poems. Repetition also stresses ideas and helps create a mood or atmosphere. Read aloud these famous lines about the soldiers in "The Charge of the Light Brigade":

Theirs not to make reply,
Theirs not to reason why,
Theirs but to do and die.

The repetition in this example helps create the musical rhythm in the poem. It also stresses the idea that the soldiers had no say in the decision to attack.

As you read, look for other examples of repetition. List them on a chart like this one.

Example of Repetition	What It Does
theirs not to/theirs not to/ theirs but to	adds to musical rhythm; stresses the idea that the soldiers have no say in the decision to attack

READING STRATEGY

Using Word Parts

You can use **word parts** to help you understand the meanings of related words. For example, take these lines from "The Charge of the Light Brigade":

Half a league, half a league,
Half a league onward,

You may not know what *onward* means, but you probably recognize its parts. The word part *-ward-* appears in common words like *forward*, *toward*, and *backward*. *-ward-* clearly has something to do with movement. One meaning of *on* is "ahead" (as in "move *on* to the next topic"). So you can figure out that *onward* probably means "move ahead; go forward."

As you read, look for other words whose parts are familiar. Figure out what they mean from their parts.

The Charge of the Light Brigade

Alfred, Lord Tennyson

British poet Alfred, Lord Tennyson, writes here about the Battle of Balaklava in the Crimean War. Britain and Russia fought that war in the 1850s. In this battle, 600 lightly armed British troops attacked an area held by heavily armed Russian troops.

◆ ◆ ◆

Half a league,[1] half a league,
Half a league onward,
All in the valley of Death
  Rode the six hundred.
"Forward, the Light Brigade![2]
Charge for the guns!" he said:
Into the valley of Death
  Rode the six hundred.

"Forward, the Light Brigade!"
Was there a man dismayed?
Not though the soldier knew
  Someone had blundered:
Theirs not to make reply,
Theirs not to reason why,
Theirs but to do and die,
Into the valley of Death
  Rode the six hundred.

1. **league** (LEEG) *n.* three miles.
2. **light brigade** (LĪT bri GAYD) *n.* lightly armed troops on horseback.

Vocabulary Development

dismayed (dis MAYD) *adj.* upset; afraid; without confidence
blundered (BLUN derd) *v.* made a foolish mistake

◆ Literary Analysis

Circle examples of **repetition** in these lines. What sound is Tennyson most likely trying to imitate with his repeated rhythms? Circle the letter of your answer.

(a) the sound of horses' hooves

(b) the sound of beautiful music

(c) the sound of the sea

(d) the sound of army helicopters

◆ English Language Development

Circle the words spoken aloud. What punctuation shows they are being spoken? Write your answer here:

____

____

Who is speaking them? Circle the letter.

(a) the commanding officer

(b) the enemy's commanding officer

(c) the king of England

(d) each soldier, speaking together

◆ Stop to Reflect

Why don't the soldiers question the orders?

(a) They aren't smart enough.

(b) They agree with the orders.

(c) They hate the enemy and want to attack as soon as possible.

(d) Good soldiers do not question orders.

Cannon to right of them,
Cannon to left of them,
Cannon in front of them
  Volleyed and thundered. . . .
Stormed at with shot and shell,
While horse and hero fell,
They that had fought so well
Came through the jaws of Death,
Back from the mouth of Hell,
All that was left of them,
  Left of six hundred.

When can their glory fade?
O the wild charge they made!
  All the world wondered.
Honor the charge they made!
Honor the Light Brigade.
  Noble six hundred!

◆ ◆ ◆

Six hundred British troops rode into battle that day. Three quarters of them were killed. The charge was a terrible mistake. But the men who fought so bravely are forever remembered because of this famous poem.

◆ Reading Check

Did any of the six hundred soldiers survive? Circle the answer.

yes *no*

How do you know? Circle the words in the text that tell you.

◆ Vocabulary and Pronunciation

Charge can be a noun meaning "an attack" or a verb meaning "to attack." Which way is it used here? Label it *n* for noun or *v* for verb. Then, use *n* or *v* to show whether charge is a noun or a verb in its three other appearances in the poem (including the title).

Vocabulary Development

volleyed (VAHL eed) *v.* fired together

REVIEW AND ASSESS

1. Put a check in front of each statement that accurately describes the soldiers' situation.

   ____ They are riding into battle on horses.

   ____ They are lightly armed, while the enemy is heavily armed.

   ____ They greatly outnumber the enemy.

   ____ They have no idea what they are facing.

   ____ They are attacking because someone made a mistake and ordered them to.

2. With what attitude do the soldiers make their charge? Circle the letter of the best answer.

   (a) They go forward bravely without question.

   (b) They are full of questions for those who ordered the attack.

   (c) They fear the enemy and hold back as long as possible.

   (d) They feel a violent hatred for the enemy and cannot wait to fight.

3. What happens to the soldiers making the attack? Write your answer on the lines.

   ____

   ____

   ____

4. How does the speaker of the poem seem to feel about the soldiers? Circle the letter of the correct answer.

   (a) He is worried that they will be forgotten.

   (b) He is proud of their bravery.

   (c) He is hopeful that they all will survive.

   (d) He is angry and bitter that so many died.

5. **Literary Analysis:** Read these lines from the poem. Then complete the statements about the **repetition** in them.

Cannon to right of them,
Cannon to left of them,
Cannon in front of them
Volleyed and thundered.

• The repetition in the lines includes the words	_______________
• The repetition stresses the idea that the soldiers are	_______________
• The repetition helps capture the sound of the	_______________

6. **Reading Strategy:** Use the main **word part** in *stormed* to figure out what it means to be "*stormed* at with shot and shell." Write the meaning on the line below.

stormed: ____

Writing

Choose a battle you have learned about in school. Write a paragraph telling what happened.

- Do research using your social studies book or another source to get information.
- Indicate the war in which the battle took place.

____

- Include the time and place of the battle.

____

- Make clear the sides that were fighting.

____

- Give some idea of the number of troops that fought and the number that died.

____

- Indicate who won the battle or, if no one won, make that clear.

____

- Write your completed paragraph on another piece of paper.

PREVIEW

The Californian's Tale

Mark Twain

Summary

A man hunting for gold in California comes to the attractive, well-kept cabin of a miner named Henry. Henry invites the man in. He credits the loveliness of his home to his young wife who is away until Saturday night. He urges the visitor to stay until she returns. Henry's friends come over on Saturday and give Henry a drug that puts him to sleep. They explain that Henry's wife has been dead for 19 years. Every year, at the time of her death, they go through the act of pretending she's returning. They do this so that Henry doesn't go wild with anger and grief.

Visual Summary

Wednesday	Thursday	Friday	Saturday
• Narrator (storyteller) is hunting for gold. • He meets Henry outside a miner's cabin much nicer than others. • Henry explains that the pretty, comfortable home is the work of his wife, who is visiting relatives. • He insists that the narrator stay until Saturday, when his wife will return.	• Tom, a miner from three miles away, comes to visit that evening. • Henry reads him part of his wife's letter. • Tom promises to return to celebrate her homecoming on Saturday.	• Joe, another miner from nearby, comes to visit. • Henry reads him part of his wife's letter. • Joe too promises to return for the homecoming.	• The narrator checks his watch several times, eager for the wife's arrival. • Charley, Joe and Tom arrive. • Joe serves a drink to toast the wife before she arrives. • Henry is drugged by the drink and falls asleep. • Joe explains that Henry's wife has been dead for 19 years but that they pretend she is alive to keep Henry from going wild with grief.

PREPARE TO READ

LITERARY ANALYSIS

Local Color

Local color is the use of details specific to a region. Those details may include

- descriptions of places and things found in the region
- information about activities and customs in the region
- portraits of people typical of the region, including their way of speaking

"The Californian's Tale" takes place in the mining region of California in the years after the Gold Rush of 1849. In this passage, Mark Twain captures the emptiness of the landscape now that most of the Gold Rush miners have left.

> *It was a lonesome land! Not a sound in all those peaceful expanses of grass and woods but the drowsy hum of insects; no glimpse of man or beast; nothing to keep up your spirits and make you glad to be alive.*

As you read the story, look for other details that capture the local color of the California mining area.

READING STRATEGY

Summarizing

Summarizing means stating just the main points and important details of something you have read. You will often understand stories better if you pause after each paragraph or conversation to summarize what you have just read. For example, here is a paragraph from "The Californian's Tale":

> *A fiddle, a banjo, and a clarinet—these were the instruments. The trio took their places side by side, and began to play some rattling dance-music, and beat time with their big boots.*

You might summarize this paragraph with a single sentence:

> Three musicians played lively dance music.

As you read "The Californian's Tale," stop to summarize paragraphs and conversations. You can do the summaries in your head or write them down on a separate sheet of paper.

The Californian's Tale

Mark Twain

The narrator, or storyteller, recalls the time when he was hunting for gold in California some years after the Gold Rush of 1849.

◆ ◆ ◆

◆ Vocabulary and Pronunciation

Like many fields, prospecting, or hunting for gold, has its own **jargon**, or special vocabulary. Often jargon words have another, more common meaning. For example, a *pick* is an ax used for chopping up rocks when looking for gold. But one of its more common meanings is "to choose." Circle two more words in the paragraph that are part of the field of prospecting. Write them on these lines, along with a more common meaning.

____

____

____

____

Thirty-five years ago I was out prospecting on the Stanislaus,[1] tramping all day long with pick and pan and horn,[2] and washing a hatful of dirt here and there, always expecting to make a rich strike, and never doing it.

◆ ◆ ◆

Since the Gold Rush is over, the narrator finds many of the mining towns empty.

◆ ◆ ◆

◆ Reading Strategy

Circle the sentence in this paragraph that **summarizes** its main point.

It was a lonesome land! Not a sound in all those peaceful expanses of grass and woods but the drowsy hum of insects; no glimpse of man or beast; nothing to keep up your spirits and make you glad to be alive.

◆ ◆ ◆

Every so often the narrator comes across a cabin where a miner from the Gold Rush days still lives. At night the narrator stays in these cabins, which are very bare and simple. Then, one afternoon he meets a man named Henry standing outside a cabin of a different sort.

◆ ◆ ◆

Vocabulary Development

prospecting (PRAH spek ting) *n.* searching for gold
strike (STRĪK) *n.* discovery of gold
expanses (ek SPAN sez) *n.* fairly large stretches of land

1. **Stanislaus** (STAN uh slawz) a river in California.
2. **pick and pan and horn** equipment used in hunting for gold.

It had the look of being lived in and petted and cared for and looked after; and so had its front yard. . . . I was invited in, of course, and required to make myself at home—it was the custom of the country.

♦ ♦ ♦

The narrator is delighted to be in such a place—a real home with wallpaper and pretty chairs and and all the little bits of decoration he associates with a woman's touch. The man notices the narrator's delight.

♦ ♦ ♦

"All her work," he said, caressingly[3]; "she did it all herself—every bit," and he took the room in with a glance which was full of affectionate worship.

♦ ♦ ♦

The narrator wants to wash his hands so the man takes him into the bedroom. The narrator describes another beautifully decorated room with:

♦ ♦ ♦

. . . white counterpane, white pillows, carpeted floor, papered walls, pictures, dressing-table, with mirror and pin-cushion and dainty toilet things; and in the corner a washstand.

♦ ♦ ♦

As Henry continues to praise his wife, the narrator looks around the pretty room. He sees a picture on the far wall and studies it more closely.

♦ ♦ ♦

Vocabulary Development

counterpane (KOWNT uhr payn) *n.* bedspread; bed cover

3. **caressingly** (kuh RES ing lee) *adv.* lovingly.

◆ **Literary Analysis**

Mark the Text

Local color includes the customs of an area. What custom is discussed here? Write your answer on the lines:

____

____

____

____

Now, circle the part of the paragraph that pointed to your answer.

◆ **Vocabulary and Pronunciation**

Compound words have more than one part. They may have hyphens (-), like *dressing-table*. They may be written as one word, like *washstand*. A *dressing-table* is a table for dressing. What is a washstand?

washstand:

____

____

____

◆ English Language Development

The **past tense** shows action in the past. **Regular verbs** in English form their past tense by adding *ed*:

contain + ed = contained

Irregular verbs form their past tense in different ways. For example, *had* is the past tense of *have*. Circle one more regular verb in the same sentence as *contained* and label it *reg*. Then circle two more irregular verbs in the next sentence and label them *irreg*.

◆ English Language Development

A **contraction** is a shortened word that uses an **apostrophe (')**, pronounced uh-POS-truh-fee, to show where letters were left out. The word *o'clock*, for example, is a contraction of *of the clock,* with the apostrophe showing where the *f* and *the* were left out. Circle another contraction in this sentence. Write it on the line below, and explain what words were shortened.

Mark THE Text

____

◆ Read Fluently

Read the bracketed sentence aloud in the tone you think Henry might have used. Why do you think he is so eager for the narrator to stay until his wife gets home? Write your answer here:

____

____

____

It contained the sweetest girlish face, and the most beautiful, as it seemed to me, that I had ever seen. The man drank the admiration from my face, and was fully satisfied.

"Nineteen her last birthday," . . . ; "and that was the day we were married. When you see her—ah, just wait till you see her!"

◆ ◆ ◆

The narrator asks where the wife is. Henry explains that she went to see her family forty or fifty miles away. She has been gone for two weeks already.

◆ ◆ ◆

"She'll be back Saturday, in the evening—about nine o'clock, likely."

I felt a sharp sense of disappointment.

"I'm sorry, because I'll be gone by then," I said, regretfully.

"Gone? No—why should you go?

◆ ◆ ◆

Henry goes on to tell the narrator it would disappoint her not to meet him. He describes how much his wife likes to visit with people. He talks about the books she reads and what she knows. He suggests that the narrator would be just the kind of visitor his wife would like. Then he urges the narrator to stay until she returns.

The narrator feels a strange longing to meet Henry's wife. But he decides that he really ought to leave. But Henry brings his wife's picture over to his guest.

◆ ◆ ◆

"There, now, tell her to her face you could have stayed to see her, and you wouldn't."

◆ ◆ ◆

The narrator finds it impossible to say no, and agrees to stay until Saturday. He spends a pleasant, comfortable evening talking with Henry of many things, especially

Henry's wife. Then, on Thursday evening, a big miner named Tom, who lives three miles away, comes to visit Henry.

♦ ♦ ♦

"I only just dropped over to ask about the lit-
le madam, and when is she coming home. Any
ıews from her?"

"Oh, yes, a letter. Would you like to hear it,
Tom?"

♦ ♦ ♦

As he listens to parts of the letter, Tom's eyes get moist. Henry teases him, and Tom tries to explain his tears.

♦ ♦ ♦

"I am getting old, you know, and any little
lisappointment makes me want to cry. I
hought she'd be here herself, and now you've
got only a letter."

"Well, now, what put that in your head? I
hought everybody knew she wasn't coming till
Saturday."

♦ ♦ ♦

Tom is just one of several lonely miners still in the area from the Gold Rush. When he thinks about it, he says he did know she was due on Saturday. He has to leave, but says he'll be back for her arrival.

♦ ♦ ♦

Late Friday afternoon another gray veteran
ramped over from his cabin a mile or so away,
and said the boys wanted to have a little gaiety
and a good time Saturday night, if Henry
hought she wouldn't be too tired after her long
ourney to be kept up.

♦ ♦ ♦

Vocabulary Development

veteran (VET er uhn) *n.* someone with long experience in a particular job or activity

gaiety (GAY uh tee) *n.* joy; fun

◆ Stop to Reflect

Do you think Tom is really giving the true reason for his tears? Write *yes* or *no*, and explain your answer.

____

____

____

____

◆ Vocabulary and Pronunciation

Mark the Text

The word *journey*, which means a long trip, ends in the sound of *ee*. In *journey*, that sound is spelled *ey*—as it is at the end of *key*, *money*, and several other words. Even more common spellings for *ee* are *e*, *ea*, *ee*, and just *y*. Find and circle two more examples in this paragraph that show different spellings for *ee*.

Henry says that, of course, she won't be tired. She'll want to see everyone of the boys.

The veteran, Joe, also asks to hear the letter and reacts as Tom did. He explains how much everyone misses Henry's wife. The narrator is just as eager to see her. Saturday afternoon, the narrator finds himself anxiously waiting for her. He's checking his watch a lot, and Henry notices.

◆ ◆ ◆

"You don't think she ought to be here so soon, do you?"

◆ ◆ ◆

Embarrassed, the narrator explains that he is simply in the habit of checking his watch whenever he expects anything. But Henry gets more and more nervous. The two men walk up the road and look for her four times.

◆ ◆ ◆

"I'm getting worried. I'm getting right down worried.

◆ ◆ ◆

Henry continues to worry out loud about his wife. He admits that she is not due home until later. But he still worries out loud. Then he asks the narrator whether he thinks something has happened.

The narrator tells Henry he is being foolish. Then, a miner named Charley shows up and does his best to get Henry to stop worrying. Soon Joe and Tom arrive. They all help decorate the house with flowers. Joe, Tom, and Charley take out musical instruments, a fiddle, a banjo, and a clarinet. They say they need to tune up before Henry's wife and the other guests arrive.

◆ ◆ ◆

◆ Literary Analysis

"Right down" used in this way is part of Henry's regional speech, or **dialect**. Twain includes dialect to add **local color** to his tale. Use the context or surroundings to figure out the meaning of "right down" as it is used here.

right down: ______________________

____

____

____

◆ Vocabulary and Pronunciation

Mark THE Text

Trio (p. 101), which is from Italian, means "a group of three musicians." It contains the Latin word part *tri-*, which means "three." Circle the names of the instruments in the trio.

The trio took their places side by side, and began to play some rattling dance-music, and beat time with their big boots.

♦ ♦ ♦

Joe brings out several glasses for a final toast before Henry's wife arrives. When the narrator is about to take one of the last two glasses, Joe orders him to take the other. Joe then serves Henry the first. Soon Henry grows pale and has to lie down on the sofa. Then he lifts his head.

♦ ♦ ♦

"Did I hear horses' feet? Have they come?"

One of the veterans answered, close to his ear: "It was Jimmy Parrish come to say the party got delayed but they're right up the road. . . . Her horse is lame, but she'll be here in half an hour."

♦ ♦ ♦

Henry falls fast asleep, and the three miners carry him to bed. As they prepare to leave, the narrator stops them.

♦ ♦ ♦

"Please don't go, gentlemen. She won't know me; I am a stranger."

They glanced at each other. Then Joe said:

"She? Poor thing, she's been dead nineteen years!"

"Dead?"

♦ ♦ ♦

Joe explains that Henry's wife went to see her folks half a year after she married. On the Saturday when she was returning, she was captured by Indians five miles away. She has never been heard of since.

♦ ♦ ♦

"And he lost his mind in consequence?"

♦ ♦ ♦

◆ Literary Analysis

Mark the Text

Circle five details in the bracketed paragraph that add to the **local color** of the story.

◆ English Language Development

Mark the Text

The **singular** form of a noun means one of the noun; the **plural** means more than one. Most nouns form their plural by adding *s* or *es*:

Singular			Plural
veteran +	*s*	=	veterans
glass	+ *es*	=	glasses

Feet is the irregular plural of the noun *foot*. Find and circle another irregular plural in the next ten lines of the story. Then, on the line below, write the singular form of the noun.

____

◆ Reading Strategy

Circle the letter of the best **summary** of this story.

(a) Henry lost his mind when he lost his wife, and he gets worse on the anniversary of that loss. His friends play along to try to help him get through it.

(b) Henry goes insane for a few days on the anniversary of his wife's death but then returns to normal afterward.

(c) Henry has friends who will come to his aid whenever he is in need. He is a lucky man in spite of his troubles.

(d) Henry's friends bring flowers into the house and get ready for a dance.

◆ Stop to Reflect

Why do you think Henry's friends help him in this way?

(a) They care about him.

(b) They cared about his wife.

(c) They are kindhearted and help neighbors out when they can.

(d) all of the above

Joe tells the narrator that Henry hasn't been sane since it happened. Around the time of year that it happened, Henry gets worse. To make him feel better, his friends come by three days before his wife is supposed to come home. They ask after her as if she'll really be coming home. Then on that Saturday they decorate the house and have a dance. They've been doing it for nineteen years. Joe explains that twenty-seven people came by the first year. Now there are only the three of them left.

◆ ◆ ◆

"We drug him to sleep, or he would go wild; then he's all right for another year—thinks she's with him till the last three or four days come round; then he begins to look for her, and gets out his poor old letter, and we come and ask him to read it to us. Lord, she was a darling!"

REVIEW AND ASSESS

1. What makes Henry's house so special for the narrator? Circle the letter of the answer.

   (a) It is the only one with anyone inside.

   (b) It full of fancy foreign furnishings that cost a small fortune.

   (c) There is room for him to sleep there.

   (d) It is pretty and shows a woman's touch.

2. Write *T* in front of the true statements and *F* in front of the false ones.

   ____ Henry talks about his nineteen-year-old wife.

   ____ Henry lost his wife nineteen years ago.

   ____ Henry's wife was an orphan with no family of her own.

   ____ Henry's wife was well liked in the neighborhood.

   ____ Henry's wife was an educated woman who liked to read.

   ____ Henry's wife knew little about housekeeping.

3. Why do the miners pretend that Henry's wife is coming home? Write your answer on the lines.

   ____

   ____

4. What does the story show about life on the California frontier? Circle the letter of your answer.

   (a) It could be lonely but those who were there were often friendly.

   (b) It drove most people mad with grief and sorrow.

   (c) It was an easy life because so many found gold.

   (d) It was a hard life because no one ever offered a helping hand.

(Continued)

5. **Literary Analysis:** What details add **local color** to the story? List at least one of each of these kinds of details.

Local character:	
Local way of speaking:	
Local place:	
Local activity:	

6. **Reading Strategy:** On the lines below, write a one-sentence **summary** of this paragraph from the story.

Thirty-five years ago I was out prospecting on the Stanislaus, tramping all day long with pick and pan and horn, and washing a hatful of dirt here and there, always expecting to make a rich strike, and never doing it.

____

____

____

Writing or Listening and Speaking

In groups of five, act out the ending of "The Californian's Tale." Think of it as a short scene you might see in a play or on TV.

- Each person in your group, male or female, should take a different role—Henry, the narrator, Joe, Tom, and Charley.
- Follow any directions Twain gives about how words should be spoken or what body language you should use.
- Use the conversation that is there, and add more if necessary.

Four Skinny Trees

Sandra Cisneros

Summary

The speaker admires four skinny trees that grow outside the window of her city apartment. They possess a secret strength and keep surviving in spite of their surroundings. The trees inspire the speaker to keep going too.

Visual Summary

How Trees Are Similar to Speaker	How Speaker Is Similar to Trees
• Are only ones who understand speaker • Have skinny necks and pointy elbows • Do not belong in surroundings	• Is only one who understands the four trees • Has skinny neck and pointy elbows • Does not belong in her surroundings

Speaker will try to be like the four trees in other ways.

What Trees May Teach Speaker
• Have secret strength in hidden roots • Grab the earth with hairy toes • Bite sky with violent teeth • Stay angry and survive • How to survive • Grow despite concrete • Never forget to reach

LITERARY ANALYSIS

Levels of Meaning

Many works of literature contain different **levels of meaning.** On one level is the **literal meaning**—what the words are actually saying. Often there is also a deeper meaning of more importance. For example, on the literal level, "Four Skinny Trees" is about four trees that grow outside a young woman's window.

> Four skinny trees with skinny necks and pointy elbows like mine. Four who do not belong here but are here. Four raggedy excuses planted by the city. . . . They send ferocious roots beneath the ground.

The speaker compares the trees with herself. She speaks of the trees' struggle to survive in a place where they do not belong. Clearly she is talking about more than just four trees. On a deeper level, she is talking about the difficulties of growing up in a tough city neighborhood and about how all young people, wherever they live, struggle to make a place for themselves.

READING STRATEGY

Interpreting Figurative Language

Figurative language means something different than its literal, word-for-word meaning. For example, when the speaker says the four trees grew in spite of "concrete," she is not just talking about the concrete that blocked the soil and so made it hard for the trees to grow. She is talking about the many problems and obstacles that the four trees—and young people—faced in her neighborhood.

In order to understand the deeper level of "Four Skinny Trees," you need to understand its figurative language. As you read, you might fill out a chart like this one.

Author's Language	Literal Meaning	Meaning on a Deeper Level
"concrete"	hard building or paving material made from cement mixed with sand or small rocks and water	problems and obstacles

Four Skinny Trees

Sandra Cisneros

The speaker lives in a poor city neighborhood. It is not a place where gardens grow. Yet outside her window are four trees.

◆ ◆ ◆

They are the only ones who understand me. I am the only one who understands them. Four skinny trees with skinny necks and pointy elbows like mine. Four who do not belong here but are here. Four raggedy excuses planted by the city. From our room we can hear them, but Nenny[1] just sleeps and doesn't appreciate these things.

◆ ◆ ◆

The speaker admires the trees for being strong enough to keep, or survive, in unfriendly surroundings.

◆ ◆ ◆

Their strength is secret. They send ferocious roots beneath the ground. They grow up and they grow down and grab the earth between their hairy toes and bite the sky with violent teeth and never quit their anger. This is how they keep.

Let one forget his reason for being, they'd all droop like tulips in a glass, each with their arms around the other. Keep, keep, keep, trees say when I sleep. They teach.

◆ ◆ ◆

◆ Reading Check

What are the trees like? Circle the letter of your answer.

(a) thin and scrawny

(b) large and lush

(c) young and beautiful

(d) old and diseased

Now, circle two words in the paragraph that are clues to the answer.

◆ Vocabulary and Pronunciation

Keep is usually a verb that takes a direct object—in other words, you do not just keep, you keep *something*. The speaker here uses it poetically as a verb, with no object. What does she mean by *keep*? Circle the letter of the best answer.

(a) stay; endure; refuse to give up

(b) own; possess

(c) run a home, store, or business

(d) blow in the wind

Vocabulary Development

raggedy (RAG i dee) *adj.* ragged or tattered

ferocious (fuh ROH shuhs) *adj.* with the strength of a wild animal; fierce.

1. **Nenny** (NEN ee) the relative with whom the speaker shares a room.

◆ **Reading Strategy**

Interpret the figurative language here. What do you think the speaker means by a "tiny thing against so many bricks"? Circle the letter of your answer.

(a) a superhuman being bursting through walls

(b) an atom

(c) alone in a difficult world

(d) an insect thrown against a wall

When the speaker feels weak or hopeless, the trees inspire her.

◆ ◆ ◆

When I am too sad and too skinny to keep keeping, when I am a tiny thing against so many bricks, then it is I look at trees. When there is nothing left to look at on this street. Four who grew despite concrete. Four who reach and do not forget to reach. Four whose only reason is to be and be.

Vocabulary Development

despite (di SPĪT) *prep.* in spite of

REVIEW AND ASSESS

1. How are the speaker and the trees physically alike? Write your answer on the lines.

____

____

____

2. In what sort of neighborhood do the trees and speaker grow up?

____

3. Put a check in front of at least three values or attitudes that the trees teach the speaker.

____ strength ____ sorrow ____ greed

____ stubbornness ____ hope ____ pride

4. **Literary Analysis:** The sentences on the left illustrate the literal **level of meaning** in "Four Skinny Trees." Next to each, write a deeper meaning that you think the author communicates about a young person growing up or struggling to survive.

Literal Meaning	Deeper Meaning
The four trees do not belong here but are here.	
They send ferocious roots beneath the ground.	
They reach for the sky.	

5. **Reading Strategy: Interpret figurative meanings** by showing what each phrase from "Four Skinny Trees" literally means. Circle the letter of your answer

- "hairy toes" (p. 107) really means (a) roots (b) stems (c) tree toads (d) tulip bulbs

How do you know? ____

____

- "violent teeth" (p. 107) really refers to (a) the trees' beauty (b) the trees' branches (c) woodpeckers (d) insects called termites eating the tree from the inside

How do you know? ____

____

Listening and Speaking

What do you think the street with the four trees is like? What do you think it *sounds* like? Working in a small group, create a tape of background noises that would sound like that street.

- Discuss and list the sounds you hope to record. Consider those you will have to find, like the sounds of cars or of wind blowing in trees. Also consider those you can create yourself, like the sounds of car horns or of banging garbage cans. Write your ideas here.

____

____

____

____

____

____

____

- Record as many of the sounds as you can.
- Take notes as you record each sound so that you know what the sound is.
- Present the final tape to classmates, and be prepared to explain what the sounds are.

PREVIEW

The Night the Bed Fell

James Thurber

Summary

James Thurber recalls the chain of events that led to confusion one night when he was a boy. His father went to sleep in the attic to do some thinking. His mother was afraid the wobbly attic bed would collapse. During the night, young James accidentally tipped over his cot. The noises caused his mother to scream. This woke his brother Herman, who yelled at the mother to calm herself. This woke Briggs, a visiting cousin, who spilled on himself because he thought he had stopped breathing. By this time James's other brother, Roy, and the dog Rex were also awake, with Rex barking and attacking Briggs. All the noise woke the father, who came down from the attic and asked what was going on.

Visual Summary

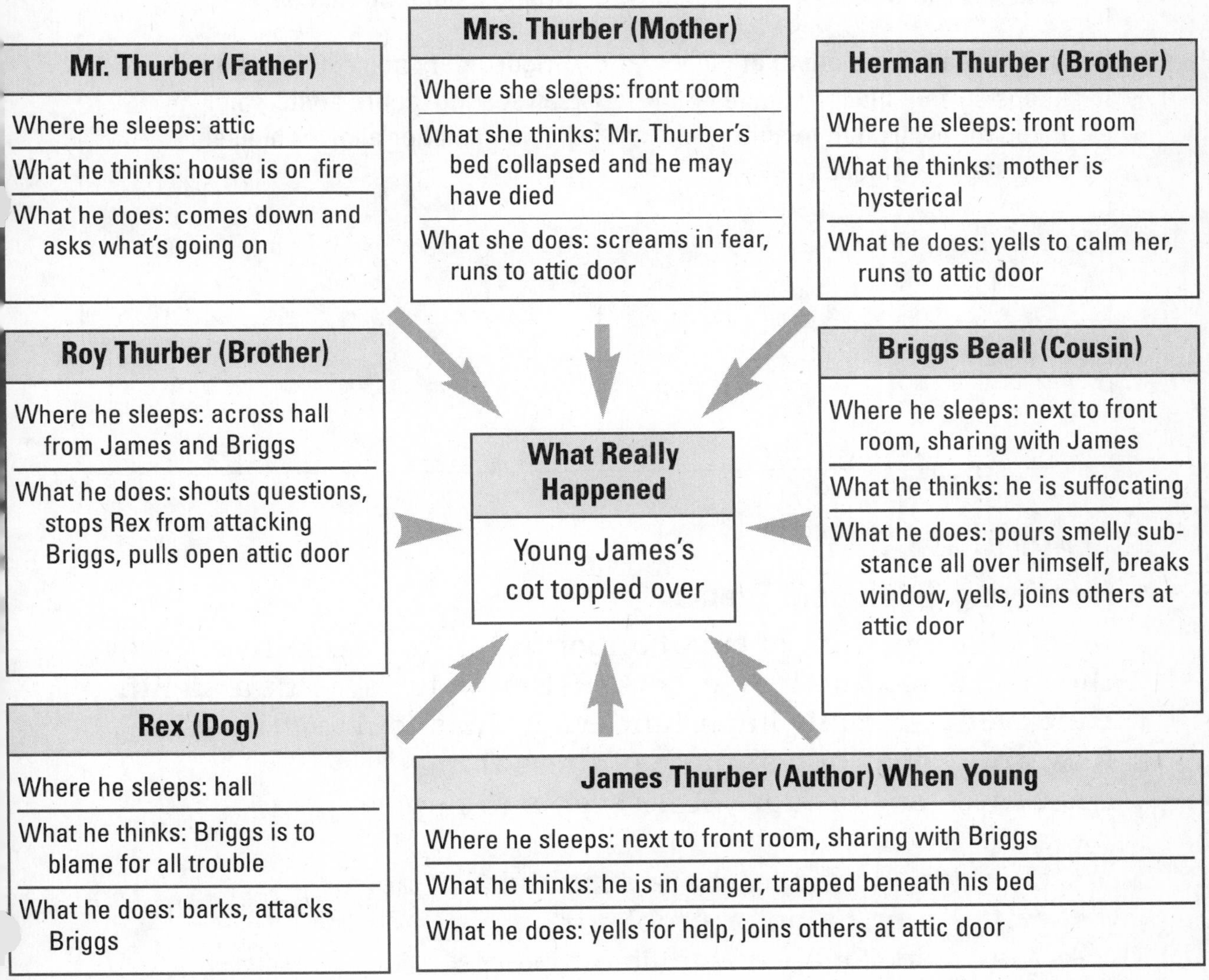

Mr. Thurber (Father)
- Where he sleeps: attic
- What he thinks: house is on fire
- What he does: comes down and asks what's going on

Mrs. Thurber (Mother)
- Where she sleeps: front room
- What she thinks: Mr. Thurber's bed collapsed and he may have died
- What she does: screams in fear, runs to attic door

Herman Thurber (Brother)
- Where he sleeps: front room
- What he thinks: mother is hysterical
- What he does: yells to calm her, runs to attic door

Roy Thurber (Brother)
- Where he sleeps: across hall from James and Briggs
- What he does: shouts questions, stops Rex from attacking Briggs, pulls open attic door

What Really Happened

Young James's cot toppled over

Briggs Beall (Cousin)
- Where he sleeps: next to front room, sharing with James
- What he thinks: he is suffocating
- What he does: pours smelly substance all over himself, breaks window, yells, joins others at attic door

Rex (Dog)
- Where he sleeps: hall
- What he thinks: Briggs is to blame for all trouble
- What he does: barks, attacks Briggs

James Thurber (Author) When Young
- Where he sleeps: next to front room, sharing with Briggs
- What he thinks: he is in danger, trapped beneath his bed
- What he does: yells for help, joins others at attic door

LITERARY ANALYSIS

Humorous Essay

A **humorous essay** is a short piece of nonfiction writing meant to be funny. In "The Night the Bed Fell," the humor comes from the characters' odd ideas and behavior and their mistakes and confusion on the night Thurber describes. Thurber also exaggerates, or stretches the truth, to add to the humor.

One character with odd ideas is Cousin Briggs. See the chart for a description of his behavior.

As you read, use this chart to keep track of the family's odd ideas, mistakes, and confusion.

Odd Ideas and Behavior	Mistakes and Confusion
• Briggs fears suffocating at night, keeps strong-smelling liquid camphor by his bed to sniff if he starts to choke	Briggs hears noise, thinks he is suffocating, pours awful-smelling liquid camphor all over himself
•	•
•	•

READING STRATEGY

Identifying Significant Events

Not all events are of equal importance. In a humorous essay, the author may include events just to be funny. But a **significant event**—a really important event—has to move the story forward. It does one or more of these things:

- causes one or more other events to happen
- adds a new complication
- changes the way a character thinks or acts
- settles a question or problem

As you read, look for significant events.

The Night the Bed Fell

James Thurber

James Thurber grew up about a hundred years ago in Columbus, Ohio. His noisy home included his mother, his father, brothers Herman and Roy, a dog named Rex, and other relatives.

◆ ◆ ◆

It happened . . . that my father had decided to sleep in the attic one night, . . . My mother opposed the notion strongly because, she said, the old wooden bed up there was unsafe: it was wobbly and the heavy headboard would crash down on father's head in case the bed fell, and kill him.

◆ ◆ ◆

In spite of the mother's worries, the father heads up to the attic bed.

◆ ◆ ◆

Grandfather, who usually slept in the attic bed, . . . had disappeared some days before. On these occasions he was usually gone eight days and returned growling and out of temper.

◆ ◆ ◆

A cousin of Thurber's is visiting and sharing his room. Briggs Beall is the nervous type. He thinks he needs to wake up every hour. Otherwise he might suffocate to death. To keep from choking, Briggs likes to set an alarm to ring throughout the night. James won't allow that. So Briggs instead puts liquid camphor on the table beside his bed. He figures he can sniff this strong-smelling

Vocabulary Development

opposed (ah POZD) *v.* was against
notion (NOH shun) *n.* idea

◆ **Vocabulary and Pronunciation**

A **prefix** is a word part added to the start of words. *Un-* is one of many prefixes that make words mean their opposite. *Un-* + *safe* = *unsafe*, which means "the opposite of *safe*" or "dangerous." Combine each of the following words with *un-* to make an opposite.

un + happy = ______________

un + friendly = ______________

un + known = ______________

◆ **Vocabulary and Pronunciation**

When you run *out* of something, you no longer have it. "Out of temper" really means "out of good temper"—the grandfather has run out of his good mood and is now in a bad one. Explain what these expressions mean.

out of your mind:

____

out of practice:

____

◆ **Literary Analysis**

Mark the Text

Thurber sometimes exaggerates, or stretches the truth, in this **humorous essay**. Circle the parts of Briggs's odd behavior that you think may be exaggerated.

◆ Reading Strategy

Would you say that the bracketed passage describes a **significant event**? Write *yes* or *no*, and explain your answer.

____

____

____

____

◆ Vocabulary and Pronunciation

In *shoe*, the letters *oe* have the sound of /*oo*/—*shoe* rhymes with *goo*. This is unusual; *oe* usually sounds like long /*o*/—*toe* rhymes with *go*. Circle a word in this paragraph where *oe* has the more common long /*o*/ sound.

Mark the Text

◆ Reading Check

Show that you understand the layout by filling out who slept where on the floor plan below.

Top Floor Attic: ______________ ______________

Next Room:	In Hall:	Across Hall:
________ ________ ________	________ ________ ________ ________	________ ________ ________

Floor Below Attic: Front Room: ______________

substance to revive himself if his breathing stops.

◆ ◆ ◆

Briggs was not the only member of his family who had his crotchets[1].

◆ ◆ ◆

Aunt Sarah Shoaf is afraid of burglars so she stacks cash and valuables outside her bedroom every night. She leaves a note telling the burglars it is all she has, asking them not to harm her. Another aunt, Gracie Shoaf, is sure burglars have been getting into her house every night for forty years. She has never found anything missing, but she says that's because she scares them off by throwing shoes. She prepares for the burglars each night by piling shoes close to her bed.

◆ ◆ ◆

Five minutes after she had turned off the light, she would sit up in bed and say "Hark!"[2] . . . Presently she would arise, tiptoe to the door, open it slightly, and heave a <u>shoe</u> down the hall.

◆ ◆ ◆

After describing various family members, Thurber returns to his tale of the night the bed fell. Everyone in the house was in bed by midnight.

◆ ◆ ◆

In the front room upstairs (just under father's attic bedroom) were my mother and my brother Herman, who sometimes sang in his sleep, . . . Briggs Beall and myself were in a

---

1. **crotchets** (KRAHCH ets) *n.* peculiar ideas
2. **Hark!** Listen!—an old-fashioned word even when Thurber was young.

room adjoining this one. My brother Roy was in a room across the hall from ours. Our bull terrier, Rex, slept in the hall.

♦ ♦ ♦

Thurber sleeps on a metal cot that tips over easily. At two in the morning. Thurber rolls out of bed, and the cot rolls over on top of him.

♦ ♦ ♦

Always a deep sleeper, . . . I was at first unconscious of what had happened.

♦ ♦ ♦

Thurber still does not wake up completely. But the noise wakes his mother up. She thinks the bed has fallen on father. She starts yelling which wakes Herman, who yells "You're all right!" to try to calm her. Briggs wakes up and concludes that he is suffocating.

♦ ♦ ♦

With a low moan, he grasped the glass of camphor at the head of his bed and instead of sniffing it poured it over himself. The room reeked of camphor. "Ugf, ahfg," choked Briggs, like a drowning man.

♦ ♦ ♦

He rushes to the window and knocks out the glass to get some air. This fully awakens James, who now realizes he is under his bed.

♦ ♦ ♦

"Get me out of this!" I bawled. . . . "Gugh," gasped Briggs.

♦ ♦ ♦

Vocabulary Development

reeked (REEKT) *v.* smelled really bad

◆ Reading Strategy

What do you think will happen when the mother hears James's bed tip over?

____

____

____

____

Do you think this is a **significant event?**

yes no

◆ English Language Development

Mark the Text

The *ph* in *camphor* has the sound of /*f*/. This sound is more often spelled with an *f* or *ff*. Circle two words in the paragraph that have the sound of /*f*/.

◆ Literary Analysis

Mark the Text

These funny, made-up words try to show the sounds Briggs makes. Circle another made-up word in the next two paragraphs.

While Thurber and Briggs are struggling, mother and Herman reach the attic door. They are frantic—and still yelling—because they think father's body is under the wreckage of the bed. The attic door is jammed. As they try to open the door, they make more noise. Roy is also awake and noisily trying to find out what is happening. Rex is barking. The noise finally wakes the father in the attic. He thinks the house is on fire and yells "I'm coming." But the mother thinks he is trapped under his bed.

♦ ♦ ♦

"He's dying!" she shouted.

"I'm all right!" Briggs yelled. . . . He still believed that it was his own closeness to death that was worrying mother. . . . The dog, who never did like Briggs, jumped for him—assuming he was the culprit.

♦ ♦ ♦

Roy rescues Briggs and manages to open the attic door. A sleepy father comes down and everyone finds out that he is safe and sound. He is, however, irritable about being waked. The mother starts to cry when she realizes he is okay. The dog responds by howling. Father demands to know what is going on.

♦ ♦ ♦

The situation was finally put together like a gigantic jigsaw puzzle. Father caught a cold from prowling around in his bare feet but there were no other bad results. "I'm glad," said mother, who always looked on the bright side of things, "that your grandfather wasn't here."

Vocabulary Development

irritable (IR i tuh buhl) *adj.* cranky

◆ Vocabulary and Pronunciation

In *wreckage,* which means "something wrecked or destroyed," the *w* is silent. Say the word out loud. Then, on the line below, write two more words that start with a silent *w* followed by an *r.*

1. ____________________

2. ____________________

◆ Literary Analysis

Much of the humor in this **humorous essay** comes from characters' mistakes about what has happened. Circle three mistakes.

◆ English Language Development

An **adjective** is a word that describes a noun or a pronoun. In this paragraph, circle the noun that the adjectives *sleepy, irritable, safe,* and *sound* all describe.

◆ Stop to Reflect

Do you think this essay is funny? Why, or why not?

____

____

____

____

REVIEW AND ASSESS

1. Which description best fits most of Thurber's relatives? Circle the letter of your answer.

   (a) They have odd ideas.
   (c) They are mean to each other.
   (b) They never worry.
   (d) They are a quiet bunch.

2. Why does Cousin Briggs set an alarm clock to ring all night and keep liquid camphor by his bed? Write your answer on the lines.

   ____

   ____

3. **Literary Analysis:** A lot of the humor in this **humorous essay** comes from the mistakes each character makes. What funny mistakes do these characters make? Fill in the chart.

Mother:	
Cousin Briggs:	
Rex the Dog:	

4. **Literary Analysis:** List three details that you think Thurber exaggerates to make his **humorous essay** funnier.

   - ____
   - ____
   - ____

5. **Reading Strategy:** Put a check in front of the **significant events**. Then, circle the event that you think causes all the confusion.

   ____ The father goes up to the attic to sleep.

   ____ Cousin Briggs sets an alarm clock to ring all night.

   ____ Aunt Sarah piles her valuables by her door and leaves a note for the burglars.

____ Aunt Grace throws shoes at imaginary burglars.

____ Young James Thurber's cot collapses.

____ The mother fears the attic bed fell and hurt or killed the father.

____ Brother Herman yells to try to calm mother.

____ Cousin Briggs pours camphor all over himself.

____ Rex attacks Briggs.

____ The father thinks the house is on fire and comes downstairs.

Listening and Speaking

With other classmates, act out the confusing scene near the end. Each of you take on a different role—the mother, James, and so on.

- Use actual words from characters' conversations in the essay. Mark the words you will use.
- Add more conversation to the scene. Write three additions here.

____

____

____

____

- Use hand and body movements to show characters' feelings.
- Use sound effects—Rex the dog's barking, for example. Write one more sound effect to use.

____

____

All Summer in a Day

Ray Bradbury

Summary

On the planet Venus, seven years of rain is about to stop for a short while. The other students in Margot's class have forgotten what the sun is like. They look forward to seeing it. They tease Margot, who came from Earth and remembers what the sun is like. Margot is an outsider who does not join in most of their games. As a cruel joke, they lock her in a closet before going out to play in the only hour of sunshine they will see in seven years. When the rain starts up again, the children sadly return indoors. They realize they made Margot miss the sunshine. Knowing how cruel they have been, they slowly go to the closet to let her out.

Visual Summary

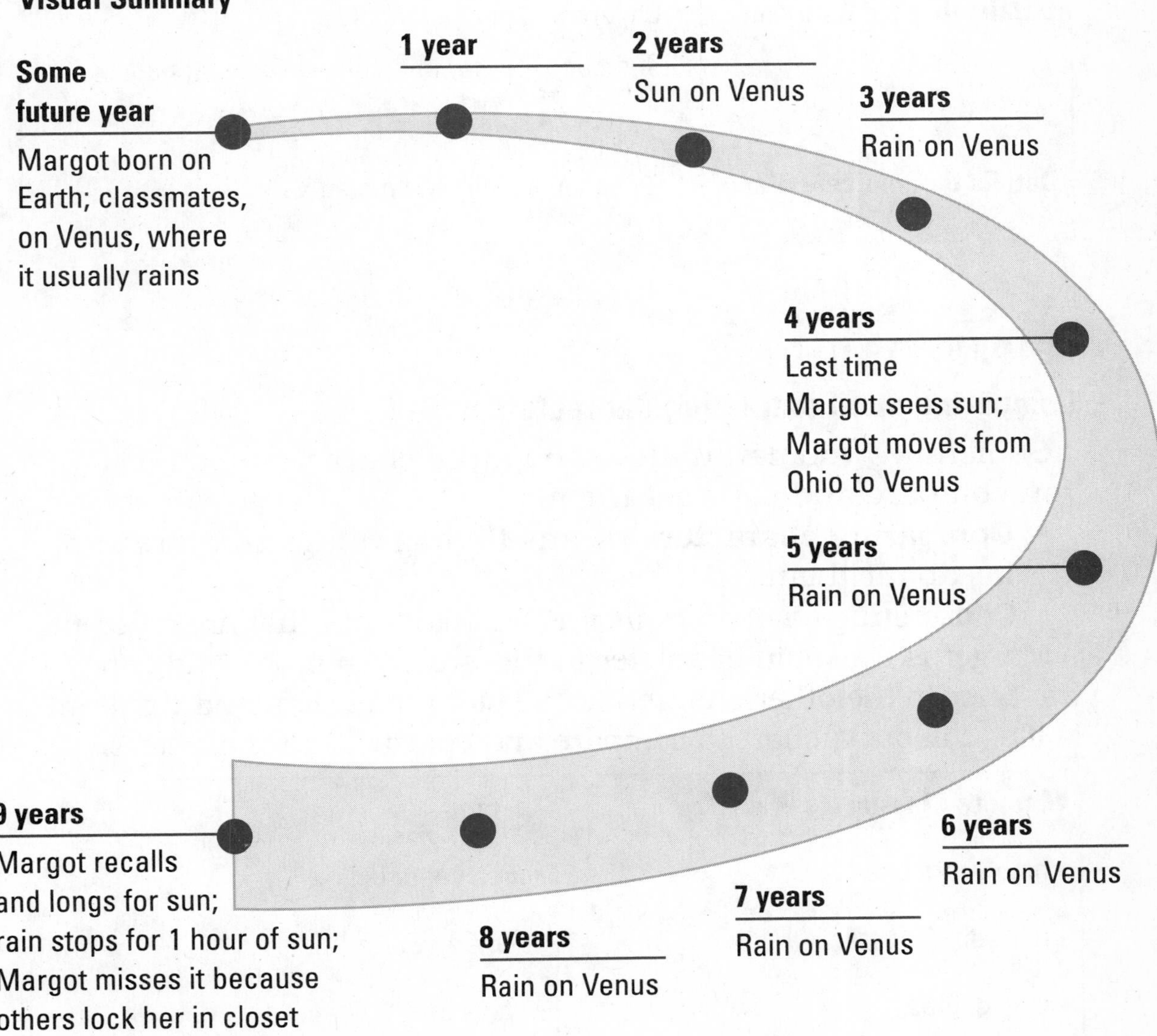

LITERARY ANALYSIS

Setting

The **setting** is the time and place of a story. "All Summer in a Day" is a science-fiction story. It takes place on the planet Venus in the future. The author provides many details to help us imagine what life there would be like. We learn, for example, that Venus is so rainy that children who were born there cannot remember ever seeing the sun.

As you read the story, use this chart to list details that help you understand the setting.

SETTING: Venus in the Future	
Details that indicate time	• Children all nine years old • Sun came out for one hour seven years ago •
Details that indicate place	• Rains almost all the time on Venus • •

READING STRATEGY

Comparing and Contrasting Characters

Sometimes you can understand story characters better if you compare and contrast them.

- **Comparing characters** means finding things that are similar about them.
- **Contrasting characters** means finding things that are different.

Margot is the main character in this story. Compare and contrast her to the other children in the story to understand what she is like. Fill out a chart to compare and contrast the characters.

Margot's Classmates	**Margot**
• nine years old	• nine years old
• born on Venus	• born on Earth
• play games	• stays apart

All Summer in a Day

Ray Bradbury

On the planet Venus some time in the future, Margot's[1] classmates are standing at the window.

♦ ♦ ♦

"Ready?"
"Ready."
"Now?"
"Soon."
"Do the scientists really know? Will it happen today, will it?"
"Look, look; see for yourself!"
The children pressed to each other like so many roses, so many weeds, intermixed, peering out for a look at the hidden sun.

♦ ♦ ♦

For seven years, Venus has known nothing but rain. Sometimes there were light showers; sometimes there were heavy storms; but always there was rain.

♦ ♦ ♦

A thousand forests had been crushed under the rain and grown up a thousand times to be crushed again. And this was the way life was forever on the planet Venus.

♦ ♦ ♦

Margot's classmates are used to it. They are the children of the rocket men and women who came to Venus from Earth to set up a space colony there. Margot isn't really part of the group of children.

◆ English Language Development

Mark the Text

The many questions show how excited the children are about what is going to happen. Circle the punctuation that shows they are asking questions. What other punctuation mark here shows excitement? Put a box around it.

◆ Literary Analysis

Mark the Text

Circle the words in the bracketed paragraphs that describe the **setting** of the story.

◆ Reading Check

Why do these children live on venus?

____

____

____

Vocabulary Development

peering (PEER ing) *n.* looking out at

1. **Margot** (MAR goh)

The children are nine years old. The only time the sun was out was when they were two. The sunshine only lasted an hour. They can't remember what it was like.

In class, they have been reading about the sun—how it looks and feels.

♦ ♦ ♦

And they had written small stories or essays or poems about it.

♦ ♦ ♦

The others cannot remember what the sun is like. But Margot can. She writes her poem from her memories. Then she quietly reads it aloud.

♦ ♦ ♦

I think the sun is a flower,
That blooms for just one hour. . . .

"Aw, you didn't write that!" protested one of the boys.

"I did," said Margot. "I did."

"William!" said the teacher.

♦ ♦ ♦

Today, as everyone waits for the sun, William shoves Margot. The others move away from her. She is a thin, lost-looking girl who often daydreams about the past. She behaves like an outsider, and her classmates treat her like one. She doesn't play games with the rest of the children in the echoing tunnels of their underground city. When the class sings, she only joins in when the songs are about the sun. She sings the songs and looks at the drenched windows.

◆ Vocabulary and Pronunciation

Flower rhymes with *hour*, even though they are spelled differently. Say both words aloud. Then, on the lines, write four more words that rhyme with them.

____

____

____

____

◆ Reading Strategy

How is Margot different from William? On the lines below, put a check before the qualities each child has.

Margot	**William**
___ quiet	___ quiet
___ shy	___ shy
___ bold	___ bold
___ mean	___ mean

◆ English Language Development

Verb forms that end in *ed* and *ing* can be used as adjectives. Here, *echoing* is used as an adjective to describe *tunnels*. Find and circle another verb form used as an adjective in this paragraph. Draw an arrow to the word it describes.

Mark the Text

Vocabulary Development

protested (proh TEST ed) *v.* complained
drenched (DRENCHT) *adj.* completely wet

For the rest of the class, Margot's biggest crime is having lived on Venus for only five years. Before that, she lived on Earth. She and her family lived in Ohio until she was four years old. Because of this, she remembers the sun. The rest of the children have lived all of their lives on Venus. Because they were only two when they saw the sun, they don't remember it. Out of the entire class, Margot is the only one who remembers the sun.

♦ ♦ ♦

"It's like a penny," she said once, eyes closed.

"No, it's not!" the children cried.

"It's like a fire," she said, "in the stove."

"You're lying, you don't remember!" cried the children.

♦ ♦ ♦

But Margot remembers. And because she does, she hates the rain. A month before, she refused to go into the school shower because she couldn't bear for any more water to touch her head. Since then, her classmates have realized that she is different from them. Margot's parents are thinking of moving back to Earth. She hopes very much that they do.

♦ ♦ ♦

And so, the children hated her for all these reasons. . . . They hated her pale snow face, her waiting silence, her thinness, and her possible future.

"Get away!" The boy gave her another push. "What're you waiting for?"

♦ ♦ ♦

◆ Reading Strategy

Mark the Text

Put circles around the **contrasts** between Margot and her classmates. Why do the others think Margot's past experience is a "crime"? Write your ideas here.

◆ English Language Development

The word *lying* combines *lie* + *ing*. When the *ing* is added, the *ie* turns into a *y*. Think of another word in which *ie* turns to *y* when *ing* is added. (Hint: It means the opposite of *live*.) Write both forms of the word on the line below.

◆ Reading Strategy

Mark the Text

What is Margot's possible future? Circle the detail in the bracketed paragraph that tells you. Why do you think this future makes the children hate her? Write your answer on these lines.

◆ Reading Check

When did Margot come to Venus?

Where did she come from?

◆ **Reading Strategy**

Circle three details that show Margot is scared and sad. What are the other children like in this paragraph? Write your answer here.

____

____

____

____

Mark the Text

Thinking about the sun, Margot looks at William for the first time. He tells her that the sun really isn't going to come out, that it is all a joke. The other students back him up. They begin shoving Margot roughly.

◆ ◆ ◆

They surged about her, caught her up and bore her, protesting, and then pleading, and then crying, back into a tunnel, a room, a closet, where they slammed and locked the door.

◆ ◆ ◆

The children can tell that Margot is pounding on the inside of the closet door. They also can hear her muffled yells to let her out. They don't care. The are smiling as they head back through the tunnel. Just then their teacher arrives.

◆ ◆ ◆

"Ready, children?"

◆ ◆ ◆

Glancing at her watch, the teacher asks if everyone is there; the children say yes. She doesn't notice that Margot is missing. The group crowds into the doorway. Then the rain stops.

◆ ◆ ◆

The silence was so immense and unbelievable that you felt your ears had been stuffed or you had lost your hearing altogether.

◆ ◆ ◆

The door opens. The children can smell the world outside. It is waiting for them. Then they see the sun.

◆ ◆ ◆

◆ **English Language Development**

You can often figure out the meaning of a word by studying its parts. *Unbelievable* contains the prefix *un-*, which means "not," and the suffix *-able*, which means "able." What does *unbelievable* mean?

unbelievable: ______________

____

____

____

Mark the Text

Vocabulary Development

surged (SURJD) *v.* moved in a swelling motion, like a wave

bore (BOHR) *v.* carried

muffled (MUF uhld) *adj.* quieted; stifled

immense (IM mens) *adj.* huge; very large

It was the color of flaming bronze and it was very large. And the sky around it was a blazing blue tile color. And the jungle burned with sunlight as the children, released from their spell, rushed out, yelling, into the springtime.

♦ ♦ ♦

The teacher cautions them that they will only have two hours in the sun. The children play and run and jump. In the sunlight, they are joyful. They play games such as hide-and-seek and tag. They only know the warmth of sun lamps so the sun's warmth amazes them.

♦ ♦ ♦

Like animals escaped from their caves, they ran and ran in shouting circles. They ran for an hour and did not stop running.

And then—

♦ ♦ ♦

One of the girls wails, and all the children stop. They see a raindrop lying in the open palm of her hand. Looking at it, she starts to cry. The children glance quietly at the sky. They hear thunder and watch the lightning get closer and closer. The sky darkens. The children stand at the door until the rain is coming down hard again.

♦ ♦ ♦

[They] heard the gigantic sound of the rain falling in tons and avalanches,[2] everywhere and forever.

"Will it be seven more years?"

"Yes. Seven."

Then one of them gave a little cry.

"Margot!"

"What?"

"She's still in the closet where we locked her."

♦ ♦ ♦

◆ Culture Note

Hide-and-seek and tag are popular American children's games. Both involve running around and finding or tapping others. What similar games do children play in your native land? Write one on this line: ____________________

◆ Vocabulary and Pronunciation

In the word *palm*, the *l* is silent. Say the word aloud. Then, circle all the silent letters in the words listed below:

calm climb island overwhelm

◆ Vocabulary and Pronunciation

Mark the Text

The letter *g* may have a "hard" sound, as in *good*, or a "soft" sound, as in *age*. When soft, it sounds like a *j*. Say the word *gigantic* out loud. Then, label the two *g*'s hard or soft.

◆ Read Fluently

Read the bracketed dialogue out loud with a partner. Each line is a different speaker.

---

2. **avalanches** (AV a LANCH iz) *n.* large amounts.

◆ Stop to Reflect

How do you think Margot will feel about what happened? Write your answer on these lines.

____

____

____

____

The children now feel terrible about what they did to Margot. They can barely look each other in the eye. They slowly walk back to the room. The sounds and sights of the rainstorm are with them as they go to the closet door. They stand there.

◆ ◆ ◆

Behind the closet door was only silence.

They unlocked the door, even more slowly, and let Margot out.

REVIEW AND ASSESS

1. What is odd about the weather on Venus?

____

____

2. In the paragraph below, circle the choice in parentheses that best completes each sentence.

Margot's classmates are jealous of her because (she is from Earth and remembers the sun, she is an outsider and stands apart). Because they are jealous, they (try to be nice to her, are mean to her). In the end they (regret, are happy about) their treatment of Margot.

3. What does the title of the story mean? Circle the letter of your answer.
   (a) Margot remembers good times in Ohio.
   (b) The sunny season lasts only a short time.
   (c) Children like to play in summer.
   (d) Margot will not see the sun today.

4. Put a check in front of each thing the story shows about the way people behave.

	Children are kinder than adults.
	Children can be mean to one another.
	Only children can really enjoy nature.
	Outsiders are often treated badly.
	People are mean when it rains.
	If you are mean, you may regret it later.

5. **Literary Analysis:** List three details in the story that help you picture the **setting**.

____

____

(Continued)

6. **Reading Strategy:** On the chart below, **compare and contrast** Margot with the rest of her classmates. List at least three similarities and three differences.

	Margot and Her Classmates
Similarities	1. ______________________
	2. ______________________
	3. ______________________
Differences	1. ______________________
	2. ______________________
	3. ______________________

Writing

In the story, Ray Bradbury describes the planet Venus as he imagines it to be. Write a paragraph in which you describe a setting. It can be a place and time you know or that you just imagine.

- Choose a time and place as your setting. Write what they are here.
  Time: ______________________ Place: ______________
- Think of details about the way the setting looks, sounds, feels, and maybe even smells. Write them down here.

____

____

____

____

____

- On a separate sheet of paper, write your paragraph using some or all of the details you listed.

PREVIEW

The Highwayman

Alfred Noyes

Summary

A dashing highwayman, or thief of the road, rides to an inn to see his love, the innkeeper's beautiful daughter Bess. He promises to return by the next night. The stable worker Tim, in love with Bess himself, overhears the couple. The next day soldiers hunting for the highwayman arrive at the inn. They gag and tie up Bess, tying a gun to her body, and tell her to keep watch. She hears her love riding closer. With no other way to warn him, she pulls the trigger of the gun, killing herself. The highwayman hears the shot and flees. The next day, when he learns what happened, he returns and is shot and killed. The ghosts of the highwayman and Bess are said to haunt the inn.

Visual Summary

1

The story takes place on a winter night in England of the 1700s.

2

The highwayman rides to the inn to visit Bess, the innkeeper's daughter.

He promises to return by the next night at the latest.

Tim, a stable worker in love with Bess, overhears.

The next day soldiers hunt down the highwayman. They tie and gag Bess with a gun tied to her body.

Bess hears her love approaching.

3

As the highwayman nears, Bess warns him of danger by pulling the trigger and killing herself.

4

The highwayman flees when he hears the shot.

The next day he learns what happened to Bess and returns, only to be shot and killed.

5

The ghosts of the highwayman and Bess haunt the inn.

LITERARY ANALYSIS

Suspense

Suspense is the tension or nervousness that you feel when you do not know what is going to happen. Writers use suspense to make things interesting. It keeps readers reading.

In "The Highwayman," suspense increases as the highwayman rides closer and closer to the inn. We know a trap has been set for him, but we don't know what will happen to him. Each new detail adds to the suspense.

Tlot-tlot; tlot-tlot! *Had they heard it? The horse hoofs ringing clear;*

Tlot-tlot, tlot-tlot, *in the distance? Were they deaf that they did not hear?*

Down the ribbon of moonlight, over the brow of the hill,
The highwayman came riding—
Riding—riding—

As you read "The Highwayman," look for other details that create suspense.

READING STRATEGY

Identifying Causes and Effects

You will understand events better if you can identify both causes and effects.

- **Causes:** events that bring about other events
- **Effects:** events that result from other events

Sometimes the effect of one event can be the cause of another. As you read "The Highwayman," show the causes and effects on a diagram like this one.

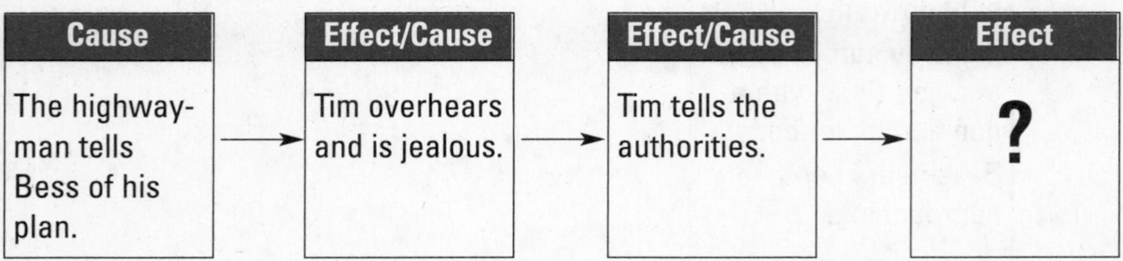

The Highwayman

Alfred Noyes

This poem takes place in England in the 1700s. People then still traveled on horseback or in horse-drawn coaches. The highways, or roads, had many inns where travelers stopped at night. Sometimes travelers were held up by robbers called highwaymen, like the one in this poem.

◆ ◆ ◆

The wind was a torrent of darkness among the
  gusty trees,
The moon was a ghostly galleon[1] tossed upon
  cloudy seas,
The road was a ribbon of moonlight over the
  purple moor,[2]
And the highwayman came riding—
  Riding—riding—
The highwayman came riding, up to the old
  inn door.

He'd a French cocked-hat on his forehead, a
  bunch of lace at his chin,
A coat of the claret[3] velvet, and breeches of
  brown doeskin.[4]
They fitted with never a wrinkle. His boots
  were up to the thigh.
And he rode with a jeweled twinkle,
  His pistol butts a-twinkle,
His rapier hilt[5] a-twinkle, under the jeweled
  sky.

◆ Vocabulary and Pronunciation

Moonlight is a compound word. It is made up of the words *moon* and *light*. What do you think it means?

Mark the Text

____

____

◆ Stop to Reflect

What do the details tell you about the highwayman? Circle the letter of your answer.

Mark the Text

(a) He is handsome and well dressed.

(b) He is dull and ordinary.

(c) He is not capable of love.

(d) He is evil and wicked.

Now, circle five details that pointed to your answer.

Vocabulary Development

torrent (TOHR uhnt) *n.* flood
gusty (GUS tee) *adj.* windy

1. **galleon** (GAL yon) *n.* a Spanish sailing ship.
2. **moor** (MOOR) *n.* open, rolling land.
3. **claret** (KLAR et) *adj.* wine-colored.
4. **breeches** (BREECH es) **of brown doeskin** knee-length pants of brown deerskin.
5. **rapier** (RAY pee er) **hilt** large sword handle.

◆ **English Language Development**

English speakers often turn phrases describing nouns into compound adjectives before the nouns. For example, "daughter *with black eyes*" becomes "*black-eyed* daughter." On the lines, write a compound adjective for each phrase.

coat of claret velvet:

____

lips that are red as blood:

____

◆ **Literary Analysis**

Tim loves Bess. How do you think Tim feels about the highwayman?

____

____

What do you think he will do?

____

____

◆ **Reading Strategy**

What earlier event do you think **caused** the soldiers to come looking for the highwayman?

Write your answer on these lines.

____

____

____

____

Over the cobbles he clattered and clashed in
the dark inn yard,
And he tapped with his whip on the shutters,
but all was locked and barred;
He whistled a tune to the window, and who
should be waiting there
But the landlord's[6] black-eyed daughter,
Bess, the landlord's daughter,
Plaiting a dark red love knot[7] into her long
black hair.

◆ ◆ ◆

Tim takes care of horses in the inn's stable. An ugly man, he loves beautiful Bess. Now he hears the highwayman and Bess making plans.

◆ ◆ ◆

"One kiss, my bonnie[8] sweetheart, I'm after a
prize tonight,
But I shall be back with the yellow gold before
the morning light;
Yet, if they press me sharply, and harry[9] me
through the day,
Then look for me by moonlight,
Watch for me by moonlight,
I'll come to thee by moonlight, though hell
should bar the way."

◆ ◆ ◆

The highwayman cannot reach Bess's lips, but he kisses her hair before riding off.

◆ ◆ ◆

He did not come in the dawning; he did not
come at noon;
And out of the tawny sunset, before the rise o'
the moon,

Vocabulary Development

shutters (SHUT erz) *n.* wooden window covers
tawny (TAW nee) *adj.* golden brown in color

---

6. **landlord's** (LAND lordz) *n.* owner of the inn's; innkeeper's.
7. **Plaiting** (PLAYT ing) **a dark red love knot** braiding a dark red ribbon.
8. **bonny** (BON ee) *adj.* beautiful.
9. **press . . . and harry** (HAR ee) close in on and attack.

When the road was a gypsy's ribbon, looping
  the purple moor,
A redcoat troop came marching—
  Marching—marching—
King George's men came marching, up to the
  old inn door.

◆ ◆ ◆

The soldiers in red coats, or redcoat troop, serve England's King George. They are hunting for the highwayman. They gag Bess and tie her to her bed by the window. They tie a gun called a musket to her, with the barrel below her heart. "Now keep good watch!" they laugh. Looking out the window, she can see the road her love promised to come down that night.

◆ ◆ ◆

She twisted her hands behind her; but all the
  knots held good!
She writhed her hands till her fingers were wet
  with sweat or blood!
They stretched and strained in the darkness,
  and the hours crawled by like years,
Till, now, on the stroke of midnight,
  Cold, on the stroke of midnight,
The tip of one finger touched it! The trigger at
  least was hers!

◆ ◆ ◆

Tied up and gagged, Bess desperately wants to warn her love of the danger that awaits him. Soon she hears a sound.

◆ ◆ ◆

Tlot-tlot; tlot-tlot! Had they heard it? The horse
  hoofs ringing clear;
Tlot-tlot, tlot-tlot, in the distance? Were they
  deaf that they did not hear?
Down the ribbon of moonlight, over the brow of
  the hill,

Vocabulary Development

writhed (RĪTHD) *v.* twisted

◆ Culture Note

Moor, which means "open rolling land with swamps," is mainly a British word. You hear it in the U.S. mostly in stories and poems about Britain. Write a word in your own native language for a swampy area:

____

◆ Literary Analysis

Circle the words that add to the suspense of the story.

Mark the Text

◆ Vocabulary and Pronunciation

When a word starts with *kn*, the *k* is silent. Say the word *knots* aloud. Then say each word below that begins with *kn*, and write another word on the line that sounds like it. An example is done for you.

knot: ____not____

knight: ________

know: ________

knew: ________

◆ Read Fluently

Read this stanza aloud. Make it as exciting as possible. What rhythm will you try to sound like in the third and fourth lines? Circle the letter of your answer.

(a) the rhythm of rain

(b) the rhythm of a train

(c) the rhythm of horses' hoofs

(d) the rhythm of Bess's breathing

The highwayman came riding—
  Riding—riding—
The redcoats looked to their priming![10] She
  stood up, straight and still!

Tlot-tlot, in the frosty silence! *Tlot-tlot,* in the
  echoing night!
Nearer he came and nearer! Her face was like a
  light!
Her eyes grew wide for a moment; she drew
  one last deep breath,
Then her finger moved in the moonlight,
  Her musket shattered the moonlight,
Shattered her breast in the moonlight and
  warned him—with her death.

◆ ◆ ◆

The highwayman hears the warning shot and rides away. The next morning he learns what happened—how Bess died to save him.

◆ ◆ ◆

Back, he spurred like a madman, shrieking a
  curse to the sky,
With white road smoking behind him, and his
  rapier brandished high!
Blood-red were his spurs in the golden noon,
  wine red was his velvet coat,
When they shot him down on the highway,
  Down like a dog on the highway,
And he lay in his blood on the highway, with a
  bunch of lace at his throat.

And still of a winter's night, they say, when the
  wind is in the trees,
When the moon is a ghostly galleon tossed upon
  cloudy seas,

◆ Literary Analysis

Circle the words or phrases that add to the **suspense** here. What do you wonder about at this point in the poem? Write your answer on these lines.

◆ Literary Analysis

Why do you think the highwayman goes back? Write your answer on these lines.

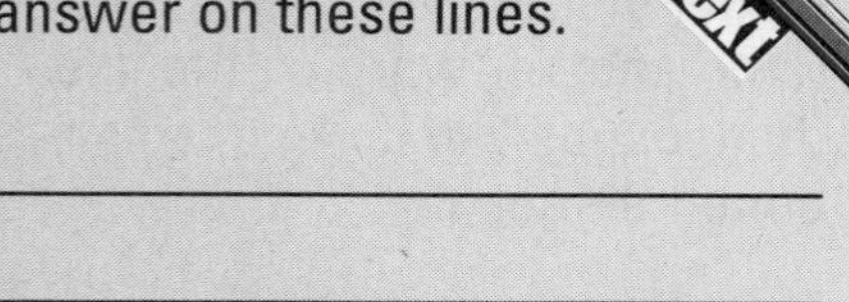

Now, circle any words here that point to your answer.

◆ Reading Check

What did Bess do?

Vocabulary Development

brandished (BRAN dishd) *v.* waved in a threatening way

10. **priming** (PRIM ing) *n.* explosive used to set the charge on a gun.

When the road is a ribbon of moonlight over the purple moor,
A highwayman comes riding—
Riding — riding —
A highwayman comes riding, up to the old inn door.

Over the cobbles he clatters and clangs in the dark innyard;
And he taps with his whip on the shutters, but all is locked and barred;
He whistles a tune to the window, and who should be waiting there
But the landlord's black-eyed daughter,
Bess, the landlord's daughter,
Plaiting a dark red love knot into her long black hair.

◆ Reading Check

What are the highwayman and Bess in this part of the poem? Circle the letter of your answer.

(a) travelers (c) ghosts

(b) old people (d) enemies

REVIEW AND ASSESS

1. Why do you think the highwayman whistles to Bess, instead of going through the inn? Write your answer on the lines below.

____

____

2. Circle the words that tell what the highwayman, Bess, and Tim are like.

Highwayman: dashing cowardly romantic honest loyal mean

Bess: beautiful romantic giggling brave loyal jealous

Tim: handsome jealous happy brave loving

3. What is the effect of the poem's rhythm? Circle the letter of the answer.

(a) It captures the sound of the highwayman riding his horse.

(b) It adds to the excitement of the story.

(c) It makes the poem more musical.

(d) all of the above

4. **Literary Analysis:** List three details that help build **suspense**.

____

____

____

5. **Reading Strategy:** What do you think **causes** the soldiers to show up at the inn? Write your answer on the lines.

____

____

6. **Reading Strategy:** What **causes** Bess to pull the trigger? What are two **effects** of her pulling it? Write your answers on the lines.

Cause:

____

____

Two Effects:

1. ____

2. ____

Writing

Prepare a wanted poster that the soldiers might have written to help catch the highwayman.

- Review the poem for words describing the highwayman's appearance and activities. Write the words here.

____

____

____

- Use your imagination to add other details to put on the poster. For instance, you might list crimes the highwayman committed. You might mention a reward for his capture. Write these details here.

____

____

____

- Use some or all of the words you list in your final poster. Write the final words of your poster here.

____

____

____

____

Amigo Brothers

Piri Thomas

Summary

The "Amigo Brothers" are close friends of seventeen. They grew up in the same building in a poor neighborhood of New York City. They are very different in appearance, but they share a common passion: boxing. For years they have trained together, but now they must fight each other in the very important division finals. They train separately and worry about hurting each other. Yet, in the end, they throw their toughest punches. They realize that their friendship will endure no matter who wins. When the time comes to announce the winner of the match, the two friends have already embraced and left the ring.

Visual Summary

Setting	Place: poor neighborhood of New York City Time: July and August
Main Characters	Antonio Cruz and Felix Vargas, two 17-year-old boys
Background	Grew up in the same building. Are as close as brothers.
Goal	To be champion lightweight boxers
Problem	Must fight each other in important boxing match
	• Don't want to hurt each other • Must do their best • Only one winner possible
	• Find it awkward to discuss upcoming fight • Agree to stop training together in last week • Fight with all they have, pulling no punches • Even have trouble stopping at final bell
	• Leave ring together before winner is announced • Realize friendship is more important than winning

PREPARE TO READ

LITERARY ANALYSIS

Third-Person Point of View

Point of view is the angle from which story events are told. In the **third-person point of view**, the storyteller sees the events from outside the story and is not a character in the story. The storyteller uses pronouns like *he* or *she* (not *I*) for all the characters. There are two types of third-person point of view:

- **third-person omniscient** (ahm NISH unt) The storyteller knows and tells the thoughts and feelings of all the characters. *Omniscient* means "all knowing."
- **third-person limited:** The storyteller tells the thoughts and feelings of only one character.

As you read "Amigo Brothers," pay attention to the thoughts and feelings of the characters. Decide if the story uses third-person omniscient or third-person limited point of view.

READING STRATEGY

Drawing Inferences

An **inference** is a logical guess you make based on the information provided. For instance, in "Amigo Brothers," the author provides this information about Antonio and Felix:

> Each youngster had a dream of someday becoming lightweight champion of the world. Every chance they had the boys worked out, sometimes at the Boys Club on 10th Street and Avenue A and sometimes at the . . . gym on 14th Street. Early morning sunrises would find them running along the East River Drive. . . .

From this information, you can **infer**, or conclude, that each boy worked hard to achieve his goal of becoming a boxing champion.

As you read, use the information in the story to make more inferences about Antonio and Felix.

Amigo[1] Brothers

Piri Thomas

Antonio Cruz and Felix Vargas were both 17. They grew up in the same building in a poor part of New York City. They were just close friends, or amigos, but thought of themselves as brothers. Yet they looked very different: Antonio was tall and fair; Felix was short and dark.

◆ ◆ ◆

Each youngster had a dream of someday becoming lightweight[2] champion of the world. Every chance they had the boys worked out, sometimes at the Boys Club on 10th Street and Avenue A and sometimes at the . . . gym on 14th Street. Early morning sunrises would find them running along the East River Drive. . . .

◆ ◆ ◆

The two boys read about boxing and went to lots of matches. They boxed often and won many medals. They were both good but had different styles: Antonio moved better, but Felix's punches were stronger and more damaging.

◆ ◆ ◆

Now . . . they had been informed that they were to meet each other in the division finals that were scheduled for the seventh of August, two weeks away—the winner to represent the Boys Club in the Golden Gloves Championship Tournament.

The two boys continued to run together along the East River Drive. But even when joking with each other, they both sensed a rising wall between them.

◆ ◆ ◆

◆ Vocabulary and Pronunciation

A *gym* is a place for exercise and sports. The word rhymes with *him.* Circle the man's name below that sounds just like *gym.*

Joe Jim Jay James

◆ Reading Check

What event will be held in two weeks? Circle the information, and label it *What?* On what date will it be held? Circle the information, and label it *When?*

Mark THE Text

◆ Reading Strategy

Based on the information presented, what do you think has caused this wall between the two friends? Write your **inference** on these lines.

____

____

____

____

1. **amigo** (ah MEE goh) *adj.* Spanish for "friend."
2. **lightweight** (LĪT WAYT) referring to boxers weighing under 135 pounds.

Early one morning, a week before the big match, the two were running together as usual.

◆ ◆ ◆

After a mile or so, Felix puffed and said, "Let's stop a while, bro. I think we both got something to say to each other."

Antonio nodded. It was not natural to be acting as though nothing unusual was happening. . . . "It's about our fight, right?"

"Yeah, right." Felix's eyes squinted at the rising orange sun.

"I've been thinking about it too. . . . In fact, since we found out it was going to be me and you, I've been awake at night. . . ."

"Same here. It ain't natural not to think about the fight. I mean, we both . . . want to win. But only one of us can win. . . ."

Antonio nodded quietly. "Yeah. We both know that in the ring the better man wins. Friend or no friend, brother or no. . . ."

◆ ◆ ◆

Even though they didn't want to hurt each other, Felix knew they could not "pull their punches," or hold back when they fought.

◆ ◆ ◆

"When we get into the ring, it's gotta be like we never met. We gotta be like two . . . strangers that want the same thing and only one can have it. You understand, don'tcha?"

◆ ◆ ◆

The two agreed not to meet again before the fight. Felix went to stay with an aunt in another part of the city and trained at

◆ Vocabulary and Pronunciation

Bro is a slang term short for *brother*. What short term do you think some people use for *sister*? Write your answer on the line.

____

◆ Literary Analysis

Mark the Text

Who is thinking this thought? Circle the earlier words that tell you, and underline the character's name.

◆ Reading Check

Mark the Text

Is it possible for the upcoming fight to end in a tie? Circle *yes* or *no*:

yes no

Now, circle the words here that told you the answer.

◆ Vocabulary and Pronunciation

Mark the Text

The author uses *gotta* and *don'tcha* to show how Felix speaks. Write their proper English spellings.

gotta ____________________

don'tcha ____________________

◆ Literary Analysis

Circle any character's thoughts that appear in these paragraphs. Label them *Felix* or *Antonio*. Based on these details, is the narrator omniscient or limited?

____

◆ Vocabulary and Pronunciation

The words *affect* and *effect* are often confused. *Effect* is usually a noun meaning "result." *Affect* is a verb meaning "to change in some way." Circle the correct form of the word in each of these sentences.

- Would the fight (affect, effect) the friendship of the boys?
- Would it have no (affect, effect)?

◆ Vocabulary and Pronunciation

What does *trunks* mean in this sentence? Circle the letter of your answer below. Then, circle the nearby words that helped you figure out the meaning.

Mark the Text

(a) large suitcases

(b) shorts worn for sports or swimming

(c) thick woody parts of trees

(d) long noselike body parts on elephants

the gym there. He also went to see a movie about a boxer.

◆ ◆ ◆

When Felix finally left the theatre, he had figured out how to psyche himself[3] for tomorrow's fight. It was Felix the Champion vs.[4] Antonio the Challenger.

◆ ◆ ◆

Meanwhile, on the roof of their apartment house, Antonio was also thinking of the fight.

◆ ◆ ◆

How would the fight tomorrow affect his relationship with Felix? After all, fighting was like any other profession. Friendship had nothing to do with it. . . . Felix, his *amigo* brother, was not going to be Felix at all in the ring. Just an opponent with another face. Antonio went to sleep hearing the opening bell for the first round.

◆ ◆ ◆

The division finals drew such a large crowd that they were held outdoors in Tompkins Square Park.

◆ ◆ ◆

Antonio wore white trunks, black socks, and black shoes. Felix wore sky blue trunks, red socks, and white boxing shoes. Each had dressing gowns to match their fighting trunks with their names neatly stitched on the back.

◆ ◆ ◆

After about six other matches, it was time for Felix and Antonio to face each other.

◆ ◆ ◆

As the two climbed into the ring, the crowd exploded with a roar. . . . Antonio tried to be cool, but even as the roar was in its first birth,

---

3. **psyche** (SIK) **himself** slang for "put himself in the right frame of mind."
4. **vs.** short for versus (VER suhs) meaning "against; competing with."

he turned slowly to meet Felix's eyes looking directly into his. Felix nodded his head and Antonio responded. And both as one, just as quickly, turned away to face his own corner.

◆ ◆ ◆

An announcer spoke in English and Spanish.

◆ ◆ ◆

"Ladies and Gentlemen. *Señores y Señoras.*"[5] . . . In this corner, weighing 134 pounds, Felix Vargas. And in this corner, weighing 133 pounds, Antonio Cruz. The winner will represent the Boys Club in the tournament of champions, the Golden Gloves. . . . May the best man win."

◆ ◆ ◆

The crowd cheered while the referee told the two boxers the rules for keeping it a fair fight. The two touched gloves and went to their corners. Then the bell rang and the fight began.

◆ ◆ ◆

BONG! BONG! ROUND ONE. Felix and Antonio turned and faced each other squarely in a fighting pose. Felix wasted no time. He came out with a straight left. He missed a right cross as Antonio slipped the punch and countered with one-two-three lefts that snapped Felix's head back. . . . If Felix had any small doubt about their friendship affecting their fight, it was being neatly dispelled.

Antonio danced, a joy to behold. His left hand was like a piston[6] pumping jabs one

Vocabulary Development

countered (KOWN terd) *v.* came back with

dispelled (di SPELD) *v.* driven away; made to disappear

5. **Señores** (sen YO res) **y Señoras** (se NYO ras) Spanish for "Ladies and Gentlemen."

6. **piston** (PIS tuhn) *n.* engine part that moves quickly back and forth.

◆ Culture Note

Many nations use kilograms, or kilos, instead of *pounds* as the basic unit of weight. A kilogram is about 2.2 pounds. Which would Felix be in your native land? Circle the answer.

134 pounds about 61 kilos

◆ Vocabulary and Pronunciation

Mark the Text

Antonyms are words with opposite or nearly opposite meanings. Circle the word in the same sentence that is an antonym for *left*.

◆ Reading Strategy

Mark the Text

How are the two boxers different? Circle the letter of the best answer below. Also circle details in the paragraph that helped you make your **inference**.

(a) Antonio is more experienced.

(b) Felix is more graceful.

(c) Antonio can stand more punches than Felix can.

(d) Felix is shorter.

right after another with seeming ease. Felix . . . never stopped boring in. He knew that at long range he was at a disadvantage. Antonio had too much reach on him. Only by coming in close could Felix hope to achieve the dreamed-of knockout.

◆ ◆ ◆

Finally the bell signaled the end of round one. Both fighters returned to their corners. All too soon, the bell rang again. The two resumed fighting with all their strength. Then Antonio hit Felix right on the chin.

◆ ◆ ◆

Felix's legs momentarily buckled. He fought off a series of rights and lefts and came back with a strong right that taught Antonio respect. . . .

Rights to the body. Lefts to the head. Neither fighter was giving an inch. Suddenly a short right caught Antonio squarely on the chin. His long legs turned to jelly. . . . Fighting off the growing haze, Antonio struggled to his feet, got up, ducked, and threw a smashing right that dropped Felix flat on his back.

Felix got up as fast as he could. . . . In a fog, he heard the roaring of the crowd, who seemed to have gone insane. His head cleared to hear the bell sound at the end of the round. He was very glad.

◆ ◆ ◆

The bell again rang for round three, the last round. Antonio came in fighting hard and drove Felix to the ropes. Then Felix went on the attack.

◆ ◆ ◆

◆ English Language Development

Most English verbs form the past tense by adding *ed*. **Irregular verbs** form it in other ways; for example, *fought* is the past tense of *fight*. Circle two more irregular forms in this sentence.

Mark THE Text

◆ Vocabulary and Pronunciation

Say *crowd* aloud. Find and underline two more words in the next sentence that have the same sound as the *ow* in *crowd*. Circle the letters that have the /*ow*/ sound.

Mark THE Text

Vocabulary Development

boring (BOHR ing) *n.* forcing your way in
buckled (BUK ld) *v.* bent and gave way

Both pounded away. Neither gave an inch and neither fell to the canvas.[7] Felix's left eye was tightly closed. . . . Blood poured from Antonio's nose. They fought toe-to-toe.

The sounds of their blows were loud in contrast to the silence of a crowd gone completely mute. The referee was stunned by their savagery.

Bong! Bong! Bong! The bell sounded over and over again. Felix and Antonio were past hearing. Their blows continued to pound on each other like hailstones.

◆ ◆ ◆

Finally, the referee broke up the fight by pouring cold water on the boys. Because neither had knocked the other to the canvas, officials would have to decide the winner. But the boxers suddenly rushed toward each other.

◆ ◆ ◆

A cry of alarm surged through Tompkins Square Park. Was this a fight to the death instead of a boxing match?

The fear soon gave way to wave upon wave of cheering as the two amigos embraced.

No matter what the decision, they knew they would always be champions to each other.

◆ ◆ ◆

The announcer began to declare the winner.

◆ ◆ ◆

"Ladies and Gentlemen. *Señores y Señoras.* The winner and representative to the Golden Gloves Tournament of Champions is . . ."

Vocabulary Development

mute (MYOOT) *adj.* silent
savagery (SAV ij ree) *n.* wildness; violence

7. **canvas** (CAN vuhs) *n.* the floor of the boxing ring.

◆ Reading Check

Who is winning the fight?

______

______

◆ Cultural Note

Bong is the sound a bell makes in English. What sound does a bell make in your native language?

______

◆ Reading Strategy

Mark the Text

What do the boys realize here? Circle the letter of the best answer. Also circle the words that helped you make your **inferences**.

(a) They fought their best.

(b) They are still friends.

(c) Their friendship matters more than winning.

(d) all of the above

◆ Reading Check

Who does the announcer say is the winner?

____

____

Why?

____

____

____

The announcer turned to point to the winner and found himself alone. Arm in arm the champions had already left the ring.

REVIEW AND ASSESS

1. Circle the letter of the statement that best describes Antonio and Felix.

   (a) They are brothers.

   (b) They are close friends and neighbors who feel like brothers.

   (c) They were friends until one moved out of the neighborhood.

   (d) They were once friends but are now jealous of each other.

2. On the lines, explain how boxing brings the two boys together but also drives them apart.

   How it brings them together: ______________________________

   ____

   ____

   ____

   How it drives them apart: ______________________________

   ____

   ____

   ____

3. In front of each detail, write *A* if the detail describes Antonio. Write *F* if it describes Felix.

   ____ tall ____ boxes better when he comes in close

   ____ short ____ boxes more gracefully

   ____ dark ____ has better moves as a boxer

   ____ fair ____ keeps boring down on his opponent

4. Complete this sentence to show what the two boys learn in the story.

   ________________ is more important than ________________.

5. **Literary Analysis:** Prove that this story uses third-person omniscient point of view by listing different characters' thoughts and impressions.

Felix (list 2 thoughts):
1. ______________________________
2. ______________________________
Referee (list 1 thought): ______________________________
Crowd (list 1 thought): ______________________________

6. **Reading Strategy:** Put a check in front of each **inference** you can draw from the information provided in the story.

____ Antonio and Felix are Irish American.

____ Antonio and Felix work very hard to fulfill their dreams about boxing.

____ The two boys often face each other in important boxing matches.

____ The Golden Gloves is an important tournament in the world of boxing.

____ Felix is the clear winner of the boxing match.

Listening and Speaking

Imagine that you are raising money for neighborhood sports. Give a **persuasive talk** to convince a group of community business people to donate money. Before you give your talk, be sure you have your facts and details straight.

- List three neighborhood sports that the business people might support. For each sport, list the equipment and other things that need to be paid for.

____

- List at least three reasons for supporting neighborhood sports.

____

- Organize your information into your talk. Then, practice delivering it. When you are ready, present your talk to a small group or to your class.

PREVIEW

Our Finest Hour

Charles Osgood

Summary

TV reporter Charles Osgood describes a series of mistakes on the night he was the substitute anchor on the *CBS Evening News*. First the lead story he introduced did not appear on the monitor—a different story ran instead. Then the next report didn't appear either. Then there was no commercial when there was supposed to be. Later a peculiar news story that no one had checked in advance showed up on the monitor and had to be cut in the middle. Then the executive producer's angry scream in the studio was picked up by a microphone and broadcast on the air. To top it all off, journalists from China were visiting the studio that night to observe the news.

Visual Summary

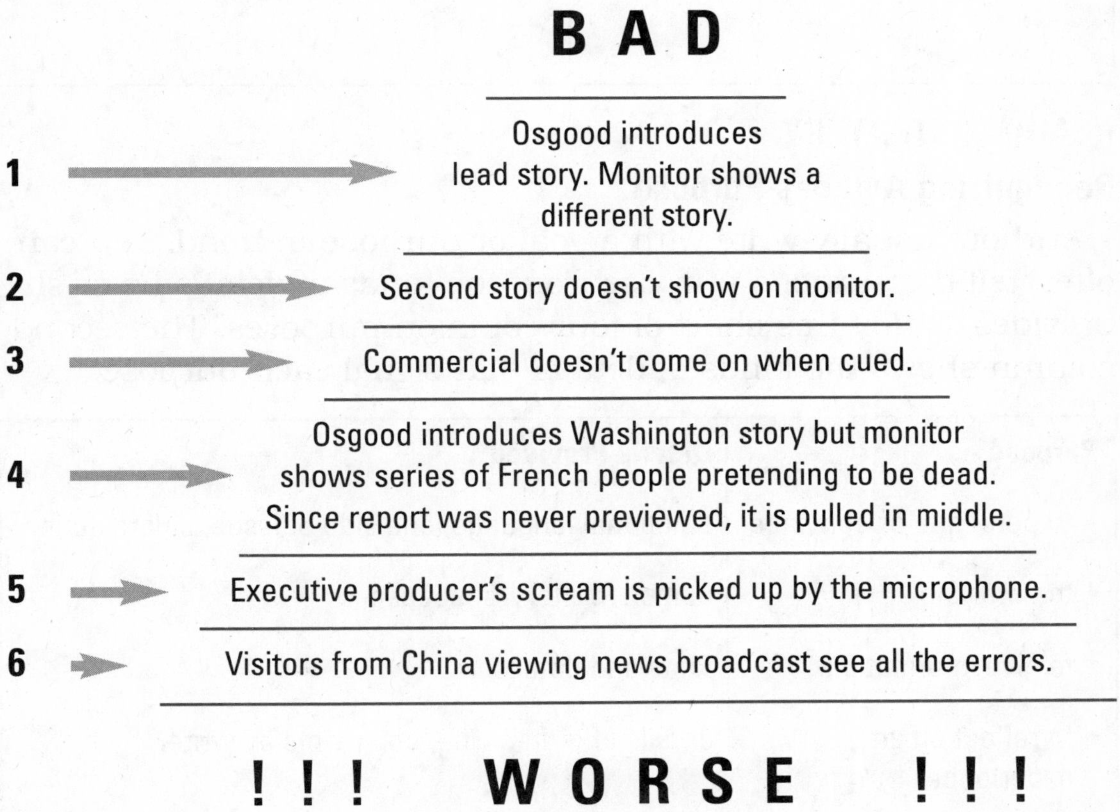

B A D

1 → Osgood introduces lead story. Monitor shows a different story.

2 → Second story doesn't show on monitor.

3 → Commercial doesn't come on when cued.

4 → Osgood introduces Washington story but monitor shows series of French people pretending to be dead. Since report was never previewed, it is pulled in middle.

5 → Executive producer's scream is picked up by the microphone.

6 → Visitors from China viewing news broadcast see all the errors.

! ! ! W O R S E ! ! !

PREPARE TO READ

LITERARY ANALYSIS

Humor

Humor is writing or speech that tries to make people laugh. Describing real-life bloopers, or mistakes, is often a good way to create humor. One person's embarrassing moments often seem funny to others. In fact, over time, even the embarrassed person often finds the experience funny.

In "Our Finest Hour," the news show that Charles Osgood anchors becomes a series of bloopers. As you read, list the mistakes that take place on a chart like this one.

Supposed to Happen	Actually Happened
Osgood announces first story and first story appears on monitor.	Osgood announces first story and second story appears on monitor.

READING STRATEGY

Recognizing Author's Purpose

Authors usually write with a goal or **purpose** in mind. You can often tell the author's purpose from the kinds of details he or she provides. Study this chart of four common purposes. The second column shows the kinds of details that signal each purpose.

Purpose	Details Provided
• to persuade or convince	emotional language, one side of issue, call to action
• to entertain	humor, mystery, suspense
• to give information	facts and details
• to reflect on an experience	details of writer's life, comments by writer

As you read "Our Finest Hour," look for the kinds of details in the selection. Use them to help you determine the author's purpose.

Our Finest Hour

Charles Osgood

In this essay, Charles Osgood recalls events that took place soon after he began working for CBS News. In those days, he worked mainly as a TV reporter and radio announcer.

◆ ◆ ◆

Only occasionally do most reporters or correspondents get to "anchor" a news broadcast. Anchoring, you understand, means sitting there in the studio and telling some stories into the camera and introducing the reports and pieces that other reporters do.

It looks easy enough. It is easy enough, most of the time. . . .

◆ ◆ ◆

But the first time Osgood did it, it turned out not to be so easy.

◆ ◆ ◆

It was a Saturday night and I was filling in for Roger Mudd[1] on the *CBS Evening News.* Roger was on vacation. The regular executive producer[2] of the broadcast, Paul Greenberg, was on vacation, too.

◆ ◆ ◆

Also on vacation were the cameraman, editor, and director who usually worked on the show. The show was live, as the TV news usually is.

◆ ◆ ◆

◆ Reading Check

Mark the Text

What is "anchoring"? Circle the words that tell you. Based on your answer, what is an "anchor" on a TV news show? Circle the letter of the best definition below.

(a) the main announcer

(b) the sports reporter

(c) a camera used to film the show

(d) something that hooks a TV news helicopter to the roof

◆ Culture Note

People in the United States plan vacations to take a rest from work. Vacations are usually one or two weeks. Many families travel during their vacations. They may visit family or they may see tourist attractions.

Vocabulary Development

correspondents (car reh SPAHN duhntz) *n.* person hired by a news organization to report news from a distant place

broadcast (BRAWD kast) *n.* an airing of a TV show

[1]**Roger Mudd:** CBS news reporter who usually anchored the news on weekends.

[2]**executive producer:** main person in charge of a TV show.

I said "Good evening" and introduced the first report and turned to the monitor to watch it. What I saw was myself looking at the monitor. Many seconds passed. Finally there was something on the screen. A reporter was beginning a story. It was not the story I had introduced.

◆ ◆ ◆

Osgood realized the reporter was doing what should have been the second story. So he found his notes for that story. When the report was done, Osgood explained it. He then reintroduced the first story, which he figured would now come second. Only it didn't. Finally, the director signaled him to move on to the third story.

◆ ◆ ◆

So I introduced the next report. It didn't come up either, so I said we'd continue in just a moment. Obvious cue for a commercial, I thought, but it took a while. . . .

◆ ◆ ◆

Finally the commercial came on. Everyone rushed to fix the problems. They didn't. After the commercial, Osgood introduced a political story from Washington, DC. But what came up on the monitor were pictures of people in a small town in France. The people were pretending to be dead to show the dangers of smoking. People in the news studio were frantic. They were trying to fix the problems with the broadcast.

◆ ◆ ◆

It was a nice story well told, but since nobody in authority at CBS News, New York, had seen it or knew what was coming next, they decided to dump out of it and come back to me. I, of course, was sitting there looking at

Vocabulary Development

monitor (MON i ter) *n.* TV screen
cue (KYEW) *n.* signal

◆ Vocabulary and Pronunciation

The prefix *re-* means "again" or "over." Is this the first or second time that Osgood introduced the first story? Circle your answer below.

first time second time

◆ Literary Analysis

On the lines below, explain what is funny about the incident in the bracketed passage.

____

____

____

____

◆ English Language Development

The **perfect tenses** use forms of the helping verb *have* along with the main verb. They are used to show relationships between different points in time. Look at three underlined verbs in this sentence. Then number them *1*, *2*, and *3* to show the order of the action.

Mark the Text

the piece with bewilderment written all over my face, when suddenly, in the midst of all these French people pretending to be dead, I saw myself, bewilderment and all.

◆ ◆ ◆

Finally, Osgood introduced the last story, which was supposed to be about rafting. Nothing happened on the monitor, however.

◆ ◆ ◆

"What is going on?" screamed the fill-in executive producer. I could hear him perfectly clearly, and so could half of America. The microphone on my tie-clip was open. Standing in the control room watching this with what I'm sure must have been great interest, was a delegation of visiting journalists from the People's Republic of China. They must have had a really great impression of American electronic journalism.

◆ ◆ ◆

On Monday, the head of CBS News came to see Osgood. "What *was* going on?" he asked.

◆ Literary Analysis

Mark the Text

Circle the words that tell what two things Osgood saw the monitor. Which one is funny?

____

____

Why? _______________

____

____

◆ Vocabulary and Pronunciation

Mark the Text

What is the meaning of *fill-in* in this sentence? Circle the letter of your answer below.

(a) a test item where you write in the blank

(b) substitute; temporary

(c) to put something in an empty place or space

◆ Vocabulary and Pronunciation

The suffix *-ism* means "the belief or practice of." If a *journalist* is a reporter, what is *journalism*?

journalism:

____

____

____

____

Vocabulary Development

bewilderment (bee WIL duhr muhnt) *n.* puzzlement; confusion
delegation (DEL e GAY shun) *n.* group sent by others
journalists (JUR nal istz) *n.* reporters
impression (im PRESH un) *n.* idea or image that stays in the mind

REVIEW AND ASSESS

1. What is probably the reason so many things go wrong on the night of Osgood's broadcast? Circle the letter of the best answer.
   (a) Osgood has little experience as a news anchor and does a bad job.
   (b) New equipment at CBS is not working properly.
   (c) The news people are very nervous about the foreign visitors.
   (d) Many people who usually work on the news are on vacation.

2. How would you describe Osgood's behavior during the broadcast? Circle *two* words.

   calm   panicked   angry   professional   joking

3. At the end of the essay, do you think the head of CBS News was mad at Osgood? Write *yes* or *no* on these lines, and then tell why.

   ____

   ____

   ____

4. **Literary Analysis:** What bloopers, or mistakes, help create the **humor**? On the chart below, explain what was supposed to happen and what actually happened in at least three of the bloopers.

Supposed to Happen	Actually Happened

5. **Reading Strategy:** List three details that show that the author's purpose is mainly to entertain.

- ____
____
- ____
____
- ____
____

Writing

A **summary** of a work gives just its main ideas or events. Write a one-paragraph summary of "Our Finest Hour." Follow these steps.

- Complete this sentence and use it to open your summary.

In "Our Finest Hour," ____________________ tells of the series of humorous ____________________ that occurred on the night he ____
____
____

- List at least five main events to include in your summary.

____
____
____
____
____

- Now, create your one-paragraph summary on a separate sheet of paper. Use the opening sentence and main events you listed above.

Cat on the Go

James Herriot

Summary

Animal doctor James Herriot and his assistant Tristan save the life of a badly injured stray cat brought to their office. Herriot's wife Helen then cares for the cat in their home and names it Oscar. The cat is unusually friendly. After he recovers, he disappears one evening and shows up at a church meeting. Another night, he sits in on a darts championship. After the third such incident, the Herriots realize that Oscar enjoys large gatherings of people. One day the cat's previous owners, who live some distance away, show up after a long search to claim him. The Herriots sadly give him up. Then they decide to visit him. Oscar is out when they arrive but greets them warmly when he returns—from sitting in on a local yoga class.

Visual Summary

Oscar the Stray	Oscar the Herriot Pet	Oscar Back with His Owners
• Found by Marjorie Simpson, postman's teenaged daughter • Is badly injured and near death • Brought to animal doctor James Herriot and his assistant Tristan • Saved by unusual surgery • Nursed to health by Helen Herriot, who calls him Oscar	• Becomes one of the family • Visited often by Tristan • Vanishes one night and is brought back from a church meeting • Disappears again and is brought back from a darts championship • Goes off again, this time to a Women's Institute meeting • Continues to appear at neighborhood gatherings	• Was pet of a Gibbons family, who finally locate and claim him • Leaves the Herriots, who miss him a lot • Is not home at first when the Herriots pay a visit • Recognizes them and seems happy to see them • Had been sitting in on a local yoga class when they arrived

LITERARY ANALYSIS

Character Traits

The qualities displayed by a human or animal character are called **character traits**. They are the details that tell you what a character is like. They show a character's personality.

Sometimes authors tell you these traits directly. Sometimes you have to figure them out from a character's words or behavior. For example, in "Cat on the Go," Oscar the cat often sits in on people's meetings and other group activities. We can tell from his behavior that he is a friendly cat.

As you read "Cat on the Go," keep track of character traits by completing this diagram.

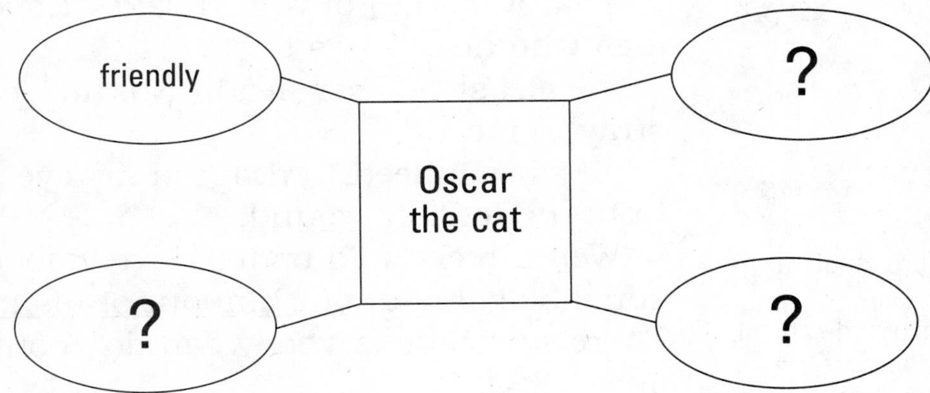

READING STRATEGY

Interpreting Idioms

An **idiom** is an expression with a meaning different from what the words actually say. For example, "on the go" is an idiom. If you think of the words separately, they don't make much sense. The expression, however, has a meaning different from its separate words. It means "to be active" or "to be out and busy."

As you read, list the idioms in "Cat on the Go" on a chart like the one below. Use the words nearby to help you figure out the meanings of unfamiliar idioms.

Idiom	Meaning
on the go	to be active; to be out and busy

◆ Culture Note

In England, many people speak local versions of English in which they drop *h*'s at the start of words and also drop other sounds. Circle three places where Herriot shows the girl's pronunciation by using apostrophes to replace missing letters. Then squeeze in the missing letters.

Mark THE Text

◆ Literary Analysis

When one character mentions a **character trait** of another, you need to decide if the first character is right. Circle two details in this section that prove the girl is kind.

Mark THE Text

◆ Vocabulary and Pronunciation

The word *wound* pronounced "WOOND" means "injury." However, the same word spelled the same way can also be the word *wound*, which rhymes with *found* and means "turned." Which pronunciation and meaning for *wound* is used here?

◆ Reading Strategy

Circle the letter of the meaning of "put him out of his misery."

(a) put him out of the house

(b) kill him to end his suffering

(c) make him happy

(d) make him well

On the lines below, explain how nearby words helped you figure out the meaning of this idiom.

____

____

Cat on the Go

James Herriot

James Herriot writes of his experiences as a veterinarian, or animal doctor, in the farm communities of northern England. Herriot and his assistant Tristan treat all kinds of animals, including household pets. One day the postman's daughter brings in a cat so badly injured that his guts are spilling from his body.

◆ ◆ ◆

"I saw this cat sittin' in the dark. . . . Then I saw 'e was badly hurt and I went home for a blanket and brought 'im round to you."

"That was kind of you," I said. "Have you any idea who he belongs to?"

The girl shook her head. "No, he looks like a stray to me."

"He does indeed." I dragged my eyes away from the terrible wound. . . .

"Well, I reckon I'd better leave 'im with you. You'll be going to put him out of his misery. There's nothing anybody can do about . . . about that?"

I shrugged and shook my head. The girl's eyes filled with tears, she stretched out a hand and touched the emaciated animal then turned and walked quickly to the door.

◆ ◆ ◆

The doctors are both very sad about having to end the poor cat's life. When Tristan gently strokes his cheek, the cat purrs.

◆ ◆ ◆

Vocabulary Development

emaciated (e MAY shee AYT ed) *adj.* extremely thin; starving

"My God, do you hear that?"

"Yes . . . amazing in that condition. He's a good-natured cat."

Tristan, head bowed, continued his stroking. . . . At last he looked up at me and gulped. "I don't fancy[1] this much, Jim. Can't we do something?" . . .

"But the bowels are damaged—they're like a sieve in parts."

"We could stitch them, couldn't we?"

I lifted the blanket and looked again. . . . "Come on, then," I said. "We'll have a go."

◆ ◆ ◆

Herriot and Tristan carefully clean and stitch the cat's insides, trying to put everything back in place. Herriot still believes the cat will die. But his wife Helen brings the cat home to try to nurse it back to health. For the next few days she carefully spoons milk, broth, and expensive baby foods down his throat. She names him Oscar. The cat does better than Herriot ever expected.

◆ ◆ ◆

It was as though Oscar's animal instinct told him he had to move as little as possible because he lay absolutely still day after day and looked up at us—and purred.

His purr became part of our lives and when he eventually left his bed . . . it was a moment of triumph. . . . From then on it was sheer joy to watch the furry scarecrow fill out and grow

Vocabulary Development

bowels (BOW uhlz) *n.* intestines; guts
sieve (SIV) *n.* a metal strainer with many holes
instinct (IN stinkt) *n.* inborn understanding
triumph (TRY umf) *n.* victory

1. **fancy** (FAN see) *v.* feel in the mood for; want; wish.

◆ Think Ahead

What do you think will happen to the cat? Write your prediction on the lines below.

◆ Reading Strategy

Use the words nearby to help you figure out the meaning of the British **idiom** "have a go." Circle the letter of the correct meaning below.

(a) try (c) leave
(b) cry (d) busy

◆ Stop to Reflect

Why is it important for the cat to remain still? Write your ideas on the lines below.

◆ Reading Check

Mark the Text

What change takes place in Oscar? Circle the letter of your answer below. Also circle the story details that point to your answer.

(a) He becomes fat and lazy.
(b) He fills out and becomes a nice-looking cat.
(c) After he gains weight, he looks like a furry scarecrow.
(d) He is no longer good-natured.

strong, and as he ate and ate and the flesh spread over his bones the true beauty of his coat showed. . . .

◆ ◆ ◆

Tristan visits, teasing Oscar playfully. Oscar also gets along well with the Herriots' dog. But one night, James comes home to find his wife very upset. Helen has hunted everywhere, and Oscar is missing! Then the doorbell rings.

◆ ◆ ◆

I could see Mrs. Heslington, the vicar's[2] wife, through the glass. I threw open the door. She was holding Oscar in her arms.

"I believe this is your cat, Mr. Herriot," she said.

"It is indeed, Mrs. Heslington. Where did you find him?"

She smiled. "Well it was rather odd. We were having a meeting of the Mothers' Union at the church house and we noticed the cat sitting there in the room . . . as though he were listening to what we were saying and enjoying it all. It was unusual. When the meeting ended I thought I'd better bring him along to you."

◆ ◆ ◆

Not long afterward, Oscar disappears again. The man who brings him back explains that he showed up at a local darts tournament, sat with the players, and seemed to enjoy himself. Three nights later, Oscar appears at the local Women's Institute. A woman from the meeting reports that he enjoyed the slides and was very interested in the cakes. After she leaves, James share his thoughts with his wife.

◆ ◆ ◆

◆ Literary Analysis

What personality traits do you see in the bracketed description of Oscar? Write your ideas on the lines below.

____

____

____

◆ English Language Development

Use an apostrophe and *s* to show possession with most singular nouns. Use just an apostrophe after a plural noun that ends in *s*.

Singular: vicar's wife (one vicar)

Plural: vicars' wives (many vicars)

Find and circle another possessive noun in the second bracketed paragraph. Label it *sing* if it is singular or *pl* if it is plural.

◆ Literary Analysis

Circle the **character traits** in the bracketed passage that show Oscar's personality.

2. **vicar** (VIK er) *n.* local priest in the Church of England, where priests can marry.

"I know about Oscar now," I said.

"Know what?"

"Why he goes on these nightly outings. He's not running away—he's visiting."

"Visiting?"

"Yes," I said. "Don't you see? He likes getting around, he loves people, especially in groups, and he's interested in what they do. He's a natural mixer."

Helen looked down at the attractive mound of fur curled on her lap. "Of course . . . that's it . . . he's a . . . cat-about-town!"

◆ ◆ ◆

One evening a farm worker named Sep Gibbons visits James Herriot's office with his two little boys. They live a few towns away and have been hunting for their lost cat for months. Sep describes a cat that looks like Oscar and always goes to gatherings. James thinks they must be looking for Oscar. Deeply upset, James takes them home and explains the situation to Helen.

◆ ◆ ◆

She stood very still for a moment and then smiled faintly. "Do sit down. Oscar's in the kitchen. I'll bring him through."

She went out and reappeared with the cat in her arms. She hadn't got through the door before the little boys gave tongue.

"Tiger!" they cried. "Oh, Tiger, Tiger!"

The man's face seemed lit from within. He walked quickly across the floor and ran his big work-roughened hand along the fur. . . .

As the two little boys rolled on the floor our Oscar rolled with them, pawing playfully, purring with delight. . . .

Helen said it for me. "Well, Mr. Gibbons." Her tone had an unnatural brightness. "You'd better take him."

◆ English Language Development

Mark the Text

When you add *ing* to a one-syllable word that ends in a single vowel + a single consonant, you double the consonant.

run + ing = running

Find and circle another word two paragraphs down that follows the same spelling rule.

◆ Vocabulary and Pronunciation

Say the word *tongue* aloud. Circle the letters that are silent. On the line here, write a word that rhymes with *tongue*:

____

◆ Literary Analysis

Helen is upset to lose Oscar, but she welcomes Sep into her home. List two **character traits** that you think Helen shows in this section.

1. ____________________

2. ____________________

◆ **Vocabulary and Pronunciation**

Circle two places in this sentence where Herriot tries to show Sep's pronunciation by using words with unusual spellings or apostrophes to replace missing letters. Squeeze in the correct words or letters.

Mark the Text

◆ **Vocabulary and Pronunciation**

The past tense of a verb is usually formed by adding *ed*. An **irregular verb** forms its past tense in other ways. For example, *strode* is the irregular past tense form of *stride*, "to take large, bold steps." Circle all the past-tense forms in the bracketed paragraph. Label them *R* for *regular* verb and *I* for *irregular*.

Mark the Text

The man hesitated, "Now then, are ye sure, Missis Herriot?"

"Yes . . . yes, I'm sure. He was your cat first."

◆ ◆ ◆

The Herriots miss Oscar a lot. One night after seeing a movie near the Gibbons's home, they drop by to visit. Sep and his wife make them welcome, but there is no sign of Oscar.

◆ ◆ ◆

"How—" I asked. . . . "How is—er—Tiger?"

"Oh, he's grand," the little woman replied briskly. She glanced up at the clock on the mantelpiece.[3] "He should be back any time now, then you'll be able to see 'im."

As she spoke, Sep raised a finger. "Ah think ah can hear 'im now."

He walked over and opened the door and our Oscar strode in with all his old grace and majesty. He took one look at Helen and leaped onto her lap. With a cry of delight she put down her cup and stroked the beautiful fur. . .

"He knows me," she murmured. "He knows me."

. . . I went over and tickled Oscar's chin, then I turned to Mrs. Gibbons. "By the way, it's after nine o'clock. Where has he been till now?" . . .

"Let's see, now," she said. "It's Thursday, isn't it? Ah yes, it's 'is night for the Yoga class."

Vocabulary Development

hesitated (HEZ i TAYT ed) *v.* waited or paused because of feeling uncertain

3. **mantelpiece** (MAN tuhl pees) *n.* the shelf over a fireplace.

REVIEW AND ASSESS

1. Why does Oscar survive? Circle the letter of the best answer.

   (a) He is not as seriously injured as he seems.

   (b) He is a very active cat and refuses to be still for a moment.

   (c) He is a good patient and gets lots of loving care.

   (d) all of the above

2. List two ways in which Oscar surprises James Herriot.

   - ______________________________
   - ______________________________

3. How do the Herriots feel about returning Oscar to the Gibbons family? Answer the question by completing this sentence.

   The Herriots are very ____________ about returning Oscar, but they also realize that ____________ ______________________________ ____________.

4. What does the story show about pets? Circle the letter of your answer.

   (a) Pets can cause danger to people.

   (b) Pets can be like members of the family.

   (c) Pets can make people do things they regret.

   (d) all of the above

   Explain how the story shows this idea. ______________________________ ______________________________

(Continued)

5. **Literary Analysis:** Put a check in front of the words or phrases that name or describe the **character traits** of each character below.

Oscar the Cat	James Herriot	Helen Herriot
____ friendly	____ skilled as a doctor	____ caring
____ bad tempered	____ good storyteller	____ selfish
____ affectionate	____ no sense of humor	____ shy

6. **Reading Strategy:** On the line, explain the meaning of the **idiom** in italics. Use the story context as a clue.

Oscar was always *on the go*: Oscar was always ________________.

Let's *have a go* p. 159: Let's ________________________________.

The two boys *gave tongue* p. 161: The two boys ______________.

Writing

Write a paragraph describing a character in the story. Show what the character is like by focusing on his or her character traits.

- Choose the character you want to describe. Write the character's name in the chart below.
- List the character's three main personality traits. For each, give an example from the story.

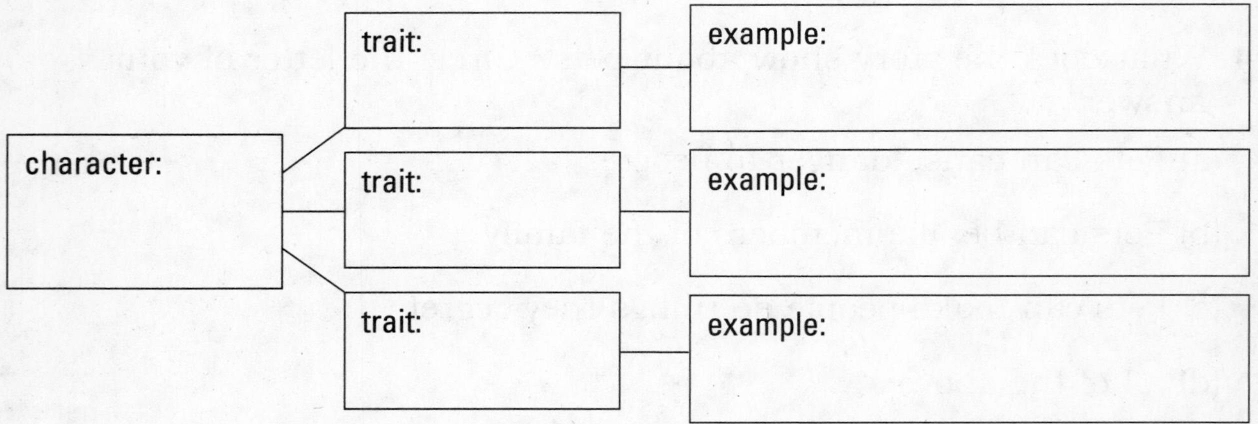

- Write your paragraph on a separate sheet of paper. Discuss the three traits. Support each trait with the examples you have listed.

The Luckiest Time of All

Lucille Clifton

Summary

Elzie tells her great-granddaughter Tee the story of how she and her friend Ovella ran off to see the Silas Greene show, a kind of traveling circus, when they were young. On the show grounds, a cute dancing dog amused the crowd. Seeing people toss coins at the dog, Elzie threw her "lucky stone." But the stone hit the dog on the nose, and he began chasing Elzie. She was then rescued by a boy named Amos Pickens. Meeting Amos changed her life, since he would later become her husband. So the stone proved very lucky indeed!

Visual Summary

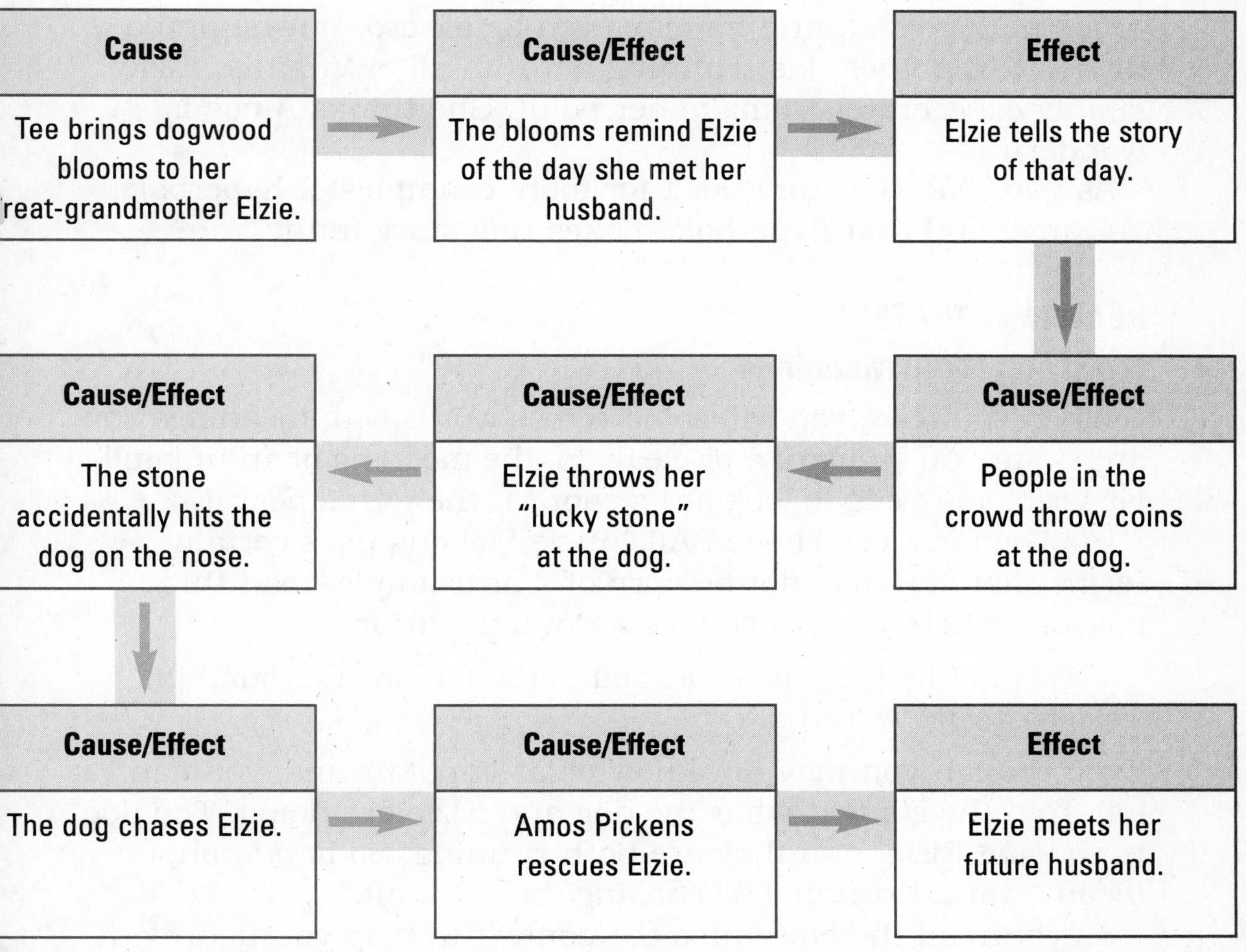

LITERARY ANALYSIS

Hyperbole

Hyperbole (hī PUHR boh lee) is exaggeration done for effect. People use hyperbole all the time to make a story funny or to make a point.

If you say "I'm hungry enough to eat a horse," that is hyperbole. You don't really mean that you would eat a whole horse. You are exaggerating to stress the idea that you are hungry.

In "The Luckiest Time of All," Elzie uses hyperbole to describe Amos Pickens on the day she met him. Look at this example:

> Right behind me was the dancin dog and right behind him was *the finest fast runnin hero in . . . Virginia*.

Amos may be fast, and he may even be a hero, but he probably isn't "the finest fast-running hero" in all of Virginia. Elzie simply exaggerates to make her point. She thinks Amos is wonderful.

As you read the story, look for more examples of hyperbole. You may find that hyperbole makes this story funny.

READING STRATEGY

Clarifying Word Meanings

When you read, you will come across words with meanings you aren't sure of. To **clarify**, or clear up, the meaning of an unfamiliar term, you need to look at its context, the words near it.

In "The Luckiest Time of All," Elzie Pickens uses certain terms that you may not be sure of. For example, read this passage where Elzie describes a dog's behavior.

> Well, . . . he *lit out* after me and I flew! Round and round the Silas Greene we run. . . .

Even though you may not know what *lit out* means, you can tell from the context what the dog and Elzie are doing. The dog is chasing Elzie, and they are both running. So *lit out* must mean "started running or chasing" or "took off."

As you read the story, use the context to help you figure out the meanings of other unfamiliar terms.

The Luckiest Time of All

Lucille Clifton

Elzie F. Pickens is rocking in a chair on her porch when her great-granddaughter Tee visits. Tee brings her blooms from a dogwood tree that remind Elzie of the day she met Amos Pickens, her husband and Tee's great-grandfather.

◆ ◆ ◆

"It was just this time, spring of the year, and me and my best friend Ovella Wilson, who is now gone, was goin to join the Silas Greene. Usta be a kinda show went all through the South, called it the Silas Greene show. Somethin like the circus. Me and Ovella wanted to join that thing and see the world. Nothin wrong at home or nothin, we just wanted to travel and see new things. . . ."

◆ ◆ ◆

So the two girls got all dressed up. They headed for the show. They decided to explore the grounds before signing up to join.

◆ ◆ ◆

"While we was viewin it all we come up on this dancin dog. Cutest one thing in the world next to you, Sweet Tee, dippin and movin and head bowin to that music. Had a little ruffly skirt on itself and up on two back legs twistin and movin to the music. Dancin dancin dancin till people started throwin pennies out of they pockets."

◆ ◆ ◆

Ovella and Elzie joined the others who were throwing money for the dog. Ovella tossed the dog a tiny pin she had won in Sunday school. Elzie threw her lucky stone. But the stone hit the dog in the nose!

◆ ◆ ◆

◆ Vocabulary and Pronunciation

Like many people, Elzie speaks in a **dialect**, a form of English different from standard English. Lucille Clifton uses unusual spellings to show the way Elzie speaks; for example, she drops the *g* in *ing* endings, writing *goin* instead of *going*. How would you write "Usta be a kinda show went all through the South" in standard English? Write it on the lines below.

Mark the Text

◆ Reading Strategy

What is the Silas Greene? Circle the words nearby context clues to help you **clarify the meaning**.

Mark the Text

◆ Culture Note

In parts of America, iced tea with sugar is called "sweet tea." Why do you think Elzie calls Tee, her great-granddaughter, "Sweet Tee"? Write your ideas on these lines.

◆ English Language Development

In standard English, it is the custom to put yourself last in a compound *(Ovella and me)*. On the lines below, write this portion of the underlined sentence in standard English. You will need to change the pronoun *me* to *I* to make the sentence correct.

____

____

____

____

◆ Vocabulary and Pronunciation

The word *loose*, which rhymes with goose, means "not tight." It is often confused with *lose*, which rhymes with *ooze* and means "to misplace." Circle the correct form in the sentences below.

Elzie did not want to (lose, loose) her lucky stone.

When the dog was (lose, loose), it chased Elzie.

"Well, . . . he lit out after me and I flew! Round and round the Silas Greene we run, <u>through every place me and Ovella had walked before</u>, but now that dancin dog was a runnin dog and all the people was laughin at the new show, which was us!

"I felt myself slowin down after a while and I thought I would turn around a little bit to see how much gain that cute little dog was makin on me. When I did I got such a surprise! Right behind me was the dancin dog and right behind him was the finest fast runnin hero in . . . Virginia."

◆ ◆ ◆

The hero was Amos Pickens, who would later be Elzie's husband. Amos twirled some twine around in his hand, like a cowboy in the Silas Greene show. He then looped the twine over the back leg of the dancin dog, bringing it down.

◆ ◆ ◆

"I stopped then and walked slow and shy to where he had picked up that poor dog to see if he was hurt, cradlin him and talking to him soft and sweet. That showed me how kind and gentle he was, and when we walked back to the dancin dog's place in the show he let the dog <u>loose</u> and helped me to find my stone. . . . We searched and searched and at last he spied it!"

◆ ◆ ◆

By this time, Ovella and Elzie had changed their minds about joining the Silas Greene show. Instead, they decided it was time to leave the show. They began walking home.

◆ ◆ ◆

"And a good little way, the one who was gonna be your Great-granddaddy was walkin on behind. Seein us safe. Yes," Mrs. Pickens' voice trailed off softly and Tee noticed she had a little smile on her face.

"Grandmama, that stone almost got you bit by a dog that time. It wasn't so lucky that time, was it?"

Tee's Great-grandmother shook her head and laughed out loud.

"That was the luckiest time of all, Tee Baby. It got me acquainted with Mr. Amos Pickens, and if that ain't luck, what could it be! Yes, it was luckier for me than for anybody, I think. Least mostly I think it."

◆ Read Fluently

Practice reading aloud Elzie's remarks here. What is funny about the last sentence? Write your ideas on the lines below.

REVIEW AND ASSESS

1. What words below describe Elzie and Ovella as girls? Circle at least two of the words.

   adventurous stingy fun-loving cruel shy

   On the lines below, write one circled word. Then, explain how you know the word describes the girls.

   ____

   ____

2. Circle all the words that seem to describe Elzie's opinion of Amos.

   heroic thoughtful mean protective bossy nice

3. In what way was Elzie's stone unlucky? In what way was it lucky? Answer these questions on the lines below.

   It was unlucky because ______________________________

   ____.

   It was lucky because ______________________________

   ____.

4. **Literary Analysis:** On the lines below, list two examples of **hyperbole** in the story.

   - ____

     ____

   - ____

     ____

5. **Literary Analysis:** Elzie tells the story of an adventure she had many years ago. How might the time that has passed help Elzie remember events and use hyperbole?

   ____

   ____

   ____

6. **Reading Strategy:** Use the words in the rest of each sentence to help you clarify the meaning of the word in italics. Then, circle the meaning from the choices given.

We searched and searched and at last he *spied* it!

spied: (a) lied (b) snooped (c) spotted (d) crawled

. . . where he had picked up that poor dog to see if he was hurt, *cradlin* him and talking to him soft and sweet.

cradlin: (a) throwing (b) holding gently (c) biting hard (d) whistling loudly

Listening and Speaking

With a partner, act out a short conversation that might have taken place between two characters in the story. It could be between Tee and Elzie, Elzie and Ovella, or Elzie and Amos.

- Name the characters you have chosen.

____________________ and ____________________

- List a few words to describe each character

FIRST CHARACTER	SECOND CHARACTER
____________________	____________________
____________________	____________________
____________________	____________________

- Reread all or part of the story for ideas about what the characters might say.

____

____

- In the space below, list some ideas about what these characters might say to each other.

____

____

- Act out the conversation using appropriate tones, movements, and body language.
- Practice until you feel comfortable with your work and then share it with a group of classmates.

PREVIEW

How the Snake Got Poison

Zora Neale Hurston

Summary

The snake went up to God and explained how dangerous it was crawling around on his belly in the dust. So God gave him poison to protect himself. But then he bit and killed so many small animals that they complained to God. So God sent for the snake and asked why he was biting everything instead of using the poison only to protect himself. The snake explained that he could not tell who was friend and who was foe and had to bite everything to protect himself. So God gave the snake a kind of bell to tie on his tail. That way, those who weren't out to harm the snake would avoid him when they heard the warning sound. And that is how the snake got his poison and his rattles.

Visual Summary

Problem		Solution
• Snake complains that, because he crawls on his belly in the dust, everyone stamps on and kills him.	→	• God gives him poison for protection.
• Snake still does not know who is friend and who is foe.	→	• Snake bites and kills everything with his poison.
• Small animals complain snake is killing them off.	→	• God gives snake bells, or rattles, to warn away those not trying to harm him. Snake will then bite only those who come near.

PREPARE TO READ

LITERARY ANALYSIS

Character's Perspective

A **character's perspective** is the way a character sees events in a story. A character's perspective will depend on the character's background. It may also depend on the character's experiences. For example, a character who is a student may have an entirely different point of view than a character who is a teacher—just as a student and teacher might in real life.

In "How the Snake Got Poison," the snake sees events very differently than the other small animals do.

Snake	sees getting poison as a means of protection
Other Animals	see the snake's getting poison as a deadly danger

As you read Hurston's tale, look for other ways in which the characters' perspectives differ.

READING STRATEGY

Evaluating an Author's Message

The **author's message** is a main idea that a writer wants you to understand through a piece of writing. For example, one idea that Hurston wants to show in "How the Snake Got Poison" is that animals have special traits or abilities that help them survive.

To **evaluate** an author's message, first figure out the idea the author is presenting. Then, decide whether it is true. Ask yourself these questions:

- What message is the author trying to convey?
- What details or examples does the author give to support the message? How good is the author's support?
- Does the message seem reasonable based on my own knowledge and experiences? Why, or why not?

How the Snake Got Poison

Zora Neale Hurston

Zora Neale Hurston retells an old African-American folktale that was first told orally. To show the sound of the spoken story, she uses a non-standard form of English with many unusual spellings. The folktale tries to explain how snakes came to have poison.

◆ ◆ ◆

◆ English Language Development

Suit is one of many words with both noun and verb meanings.

suit (noun): a set of clothes worn together

suit (noun): an action in a court of law

suit (verb): to go well with

Circle the meaning of *suit* as it is used in the first paragraph of the selection.

Well, when God made de snake he put him in de bushes to ornament de ground. But things didn't suit de snake so one day he got on de ladder and went up to see God.

"Good mawnin', God."

"How do you do, Snake?"

◆ Read Fluently

Read the snake's remarks out loud. What words does he use for *I* and *the*? Circle both words, and mark them *I* and *the*.

"Ah ain't so many,[1] God, you put me down here on my belly in de dust and everything trods upon me and kills off my generations. Ah ain't got no kind of protection at all."

God looked off towards immensity and thought about de subject for awhile, then he said, "Ah didn't mean for nothin' to be stompin' you snakes lak dat. You got to have some kind of a protection. Here, take dis poison and put in yo' mouf and when they tromps on you, protect yo'self."

◆ Culture Note

The story uses a **dialect**, in this story. Dialect is a non-standard form of English. It imitates spoken English. This particular dialect is African American. Circle five dialect words or spellings in the bracketed paragraph. Then, write their meanings or correct forms on the lines below.

Mark THE Text

____

____

____

____

◆ ◆ ◆

The snake took the poison and went away. But after a time a group of small animals such as mice and rats went up to speak with God.

◆ ◆ ◆

Vocabulary Development

ornament (OR na ment) *v.* decorate
generations (JEN er AY shuns) *n.* children, grandchildren, and so on
immensity (i MEN si tee) *n.* endless space

1. **ain't so many:** I am not doing so well.

"Good evenin', God."

"How you making it,[2] varmints?"

"God, please do something' 'bout dat snake. He' layin' in de bushes there wid poison in his mouf and he's strikin' everything dat shakes de bushes. He's killin' up our generations. Wese skeered to walk de earth."

◆ ◆ ◆

So God sent for the snake. He told the snake that He had given him poison for protection. He did not expect the snake to kill every single creature that came near him.

◆ ◆ ◆

De snake say, "Lawd, you know Ah'm down here in de dust. Ah ain't got no claws to fight wid, and Ah ain't got no feets to git me out de way. All Ah kind see is feets comin' to tromple me. Ah can't tell who my enemy is and who is my friend. You gimme dis protection in my mouf and Ah uses it."

◆ ◆ ◆

God thought about the situation for a time. Finally he spoke again:

◆ ◆ ◆

"Well, snake, I don't want yo' generations all stomped out and I don't want you killin' everything else dat moves. Here take dis bell and tie it to yo' tail. When you hear feets comin' you ring yo' bell and if it's yo' friend, he'll be keerful. If it's yo' enemy, it's you and him."

So dat's how de snake got his poison and dat's how come he got rattles.

---

2. **How you making it, varmints:** How are you getting by, creatures? How are things going, creatures?

◆ Literary Analysis

How does these **characters' perspective** differ from the snake's perspective? Answer by completing the sentence below.

The snake feels he needs

____

but the small animals feel they need ______________________

______________________________.

◆ Vocabulary and Pronunciation

Use the context to figure out the meaning of *Wese skeered.* Circle the letter of the correct meaning.

(a) We're sure.

(b) We're scared.

(c) We screamed.

(d) Wheeze, scarred.

◆ Reading Strategy

Based on God's remarks, what seems to be the **author's message** about the animal world?

(a) In nature, only the strongest and fittest animals survive.

(b) All types of animals are part of creation and should not be allowed to be hurt.

(c) Only animals useful to human beings are worth protecting.

(d) Animals are kind and generous.

On the lines below, explain why you agree or disagree with the message.

____

____

____

____

REVIEW AND ASSESS

1. According to the story, why does God give the snake poison? Write your answer on the lines below.

____

____

____

2. According to the story, how are the snake's rattles supposed to work? Circle the letter of the correct answer.

   (a) by attracting enemies

   (b) by frightening enemies

   (c) by warning friends

   (d) by attracting friends

3. The snake's problems could have been solved if God gave him legs or claws. Why do you think the story couldn't end that way? Answer on these lines.

____

____

____

____

____

4. **Literary Analysis:** Complete these sentences to show the different characters' perspectives.

   The small animals complain that the snake's poison is

____

____

   The snake explains that he has to _______________________

   because _______________________________________.

5. **Reading Strategy:** Put a check in front of the statements that you think show the **author's messages**.

____ A snake's rattles protect the snake from large animals.

____ A snake's rattles protect small animals from the snake.

____ All types of animals created by God deserve to remain on earth.

____ Animals have special traits or abilities to help them survive.

____ Only the strongest and fittest animals should survive.

Then, **evaluate** those messages. Circle the ones that you think are true.

Listening and Speaking

With a partner, find three unusual facts about an animal. Then include those facts in an oral story about the animal.

- Do research to find your three unusual facts. List them here.

1. ______________________________
2. ______________________________
3. ______________________________

- Working with your partner, decide what problem the animal in your story will face. Write the problem on these lines.

____

____

Next, outline a very short story that includes the three unusual facts. Write your plan on these lines.

____

____

- Practice your story aloud. You and your partner should each present a different part of the story. Work until you feel comfortable telling the story. Then present the story to classmates.

Rikki-tikki-tavi

Rudyard Kipling

Summary

In this story set in India, Rikki-tikki-tavi is a mongoose, a small furry animal that eats snakes. When a flood washes him from his underground home, he is adopted by the family of a young boy named Teddy. Exploring the garden, he meets Nag and Nagaina, two deadly cobras. Later he rescues Teddy by killing a smaller poisonous snake. That night he overhears the cobras' plot to enter the house and kill Teddy's family. Rikki attacks Nag in the bathroom, fighting until Teddy's father shoots the cobra. The next day Rikki finds Nagaina's eggs and begins crushing them. When she threatens to kill Teddy, Rikki draws her away by threatening to destroy her last egg. Rikki then chases her into her hole and kills her. Teddy's family and the garden animals hail Rikki as a hero.

Visual Summary

Who?	Rikki-tikki-tavi, a small furry animal called a mongoose
Where?	house and grounds of a British family in India
When?	late 1800s, when India was a British colony
What?	saves the lives of Teddy and the rest of the family
How?	fights with and kills several poisonous snakes
Why?	likes the family who adopted him; is natural enemy of snakes

LITERARY ANALYSIS

Plot

The **plot** is the arrangement of events in a story. It usually has the following parts or sections:

- The **exposition** is the background that sets up the situation.
- In the **rising action**, a problem gets worse.
- The **climax** is the high point of tension.
- In the **falling action**, events after the climax lead to the ending.
- The **resolution** is the final outcome, in which all loose ends are tied up.

This diagram shows how the five parts are organized into a plot. As you read, identify the five parts of this story's plot.

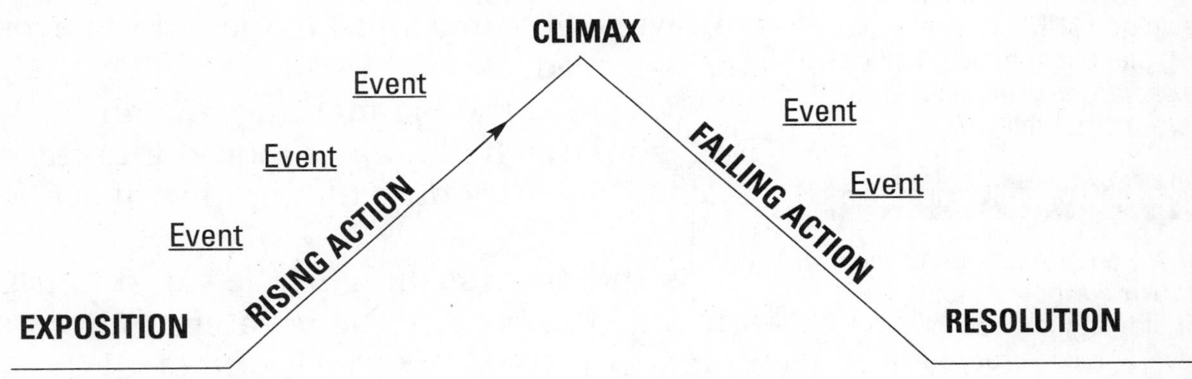

READING STRATEGY

Predicting

When you read a good story, you wonder what will happen next. Often you will **predict**, or make an educated guess, about what is coming next. The details you know can help you predict what you don't know.

As you read the story, try to predict what will happen. Use the details you know as clues. Look at this example.

Clues	Prediction
• Rikki is the natural enemy of snakes • Rikki likes Teddy and his family • Nag is sneaking into the house to kill the family	Rikki will try to stop Nag from killing the family

Rikki-tikki-tavi

Rudyard Kipling

◆ Reading Check

Circle the words that explain what a mongoose is. What other word is explained in this paragraph? Put a box around the word, and circle its meaning.

This story takes place when India was a British colony. Rikki-tikki-tavi is a mongoose, a small furry animal that kills snakes. One day, a flood washes him from his underground home. It carries him to the grounds of a large bungalow, or one-story house, where a British family lives.

◆ ◆ ◆

◆ English Language Development

The **progressive tense** uses a form of *be* + the *ing* form of the main verb—*was saying, are going*. It is used to show action that is going on when another action takes place. What action was taking place when the small boy *was saying* what he said? Circle the words that tell you.

When he revived, . . . a small boy was saying: "Here's a dead mongoose. Let's have a funeral." . . .

They took him into the house, and a big man picked him up between his finger and thumb, and said he was not dead but half choked; so they wrapped him in cotton wool, and warmed him, and he opened his eyes and sneezed.

"Now," said the big man (he was an Englishman who had just moved into the bungalow); "don't frighten him, and we'll see what he'll do."

◆ Vocabulary and Pronunciation

Curiosity, the noun form of the adjective *curious*, means "the state of being curious, or nosey." The u is dropped in forming the noun:

curious + *-ity* = curiosity

The adjective *generous* follows the same pattern. On the lines below, write the noun form of *generous* and explain the noun's meaning.

Noun Form: ________________

Meaning: ________________

It is the hardest thing in the world to frighten a mongoose, because he is eaten up from nose to tail with curiosity. The motto of all the mongoose family is "Run and find out"; and Rikki-tikki was a true mongoose. He looked at the cotton wool, decided that it was not good to eat, ran all around the table, sat up and put his fur in order, scratched himself, and jumped on the small boy's shoulder.

"Don't be frightened, Teddy," said his father. "That's his way of making friends."

◆ ◆ ◆

Vocabulary Development

revived (ree VĪVD) *v.* became conscious again

Rikki eats and dries himself on the verandah, or porch. Then he explores his new home. At night he sleeps in Teddy's room. Teddy's mother worries he might bite Teddy, but the father says he will protect Teddy from snakes. The next day Rikki explores the gardens. There he meets Darzee the bird and his wife, who are crying.

◆ ◆ ◆

"We are very miserable," said Darzee. "One of our babies fell out of the nest yesterday, and Nag[1] ate him."

"H'm!" said Rikki-tikki, "that is very sad—but I am a stranger here. Who is Nag?"

. . . From the thick grass at the foot of the bush there came a low hiss—a horrid cold sound that made Rikki-tikki jump back two clear feet. Then inch by inch out of the grass rose up the head and spread hood of Nag, the big black cobra, and he was five feet long from tongue to tail. . . . "Who is Nag?" said he. "I am Nag."

◆ ◆ ◆

Nag recognizes Rikki as a natural enemy. He talks with Rikki while his wife Nagaina[2] sneaks up from behind. But Darzee sees her and warns Rikki. After the snakes slink off, Teddy comes to pet Rikki. Then a new danger threatens: Karait,[3] a tiny but deadly brown snake.

◆ ◆ ◆

Karait struck out. Rikki jumped sideways and tried to run in, but the wicked little dusty gray head lashed within a fraction of his shoulder, and he had to jump over the body, and the head followed his heels close.

1. **Nag** (NAG)
2. **Nagaina** (na GAYn uh)
3. **Karait** (kuh RAYT)

◆ Culture Note

Verandah, also spelled *veranda*, is a word for a wide porch that came to English from Portuguese. Portugal has coastal colonies in India before the British took over.

◆ English Language Development

The word *stranger* has noun and adjective meanings.

adjective: more unfamiliar; odder
noun: an unfamiliar person

You can tell it is used as a noun here because it is modified by an article (*a, an,* or *the*)—the sentence is about *a* stranger. Circle the meaning of *cold* as it is used in the underlined sentence.

adjective: not friendly; unkind
noun: an illness where you often have chills and a running nose

◆ Literary Analysis

In this passage, the problem with snakes gets worse. Which part of the **plot** is this event? Circle the letter of your answer.

(a) exposition

(b) rising action

(c) climax

(d) falling action

◆ Reading Strategy

Rikki decides not to eat Karait. He is afraid such a big meal will slow him down. What future event does he think he needs to be fast for? Answer on these lines.

____

____

____

Teddy shouted to the house: "Oh, look here! Our mongoose is killing a snake"; and Rikki-tikki heard a scream from Teddy's mother. His father ran out with a stick, but by the time he came up, Karait had lunged out once too far, and Rikki-tikki had sprung, jumped on the snake's back, dropped his head far between his forelegs, bitten as high up the back as he could get hold, and rolled away. That bite paralyzed Karait, and Rikki-tikki was just going to eat him up from the tail, after the custom of his family at dinner, when he remembered that a full meal makes a slow mongoose. . . .

◆ ◆ ◆

Teddy's parents hug Rikki and praise him for saving Teddy. That night Rikki patrols the house. He hears Nag enter on the bathroom drainpipe and hears Nagaina whispering. She reminds Nag their eggs may hatch the next day. She tells him to kill the family and return to hunt Rikki with her. Nag curls up by the water jar to wait for the man. Rikki waits too—until Nag falls asleep.

◆ ◆ ◆

◆ Reading Check

Circle the words that tell you what Rikki hopes to do on the first bite. Do you think he will do it?

Mark the Text

____

Why or why not? Answer on these lines.

____

____

____

Rikki-tikki looked at his big back, wondering which would be the best place for a good hold. "If I don't break his back at the first jump," said Rikki, "he can still fight; and if he fights—O Rikki!" He looked at the thickness of the neck below the hood. . . . "It must be the head," he said at last; "the head above the hood; and when I am once there, I must not let go."

Vocabulary Development

lunged (LUNJD) *v.* jumped
fore (FOHR) *adj.* front
paralyzed (pa ruh LĪZD) *v.* prevented from moving

Then he jumped. The head was lying a little clear of the water jar, under the curve of it; and, as his teeth met, Rikki braced his back. . . . He was battered to and fro as a rat is shaken by a dog—to and fro on the floor, up and down, and round in great circles. . . . He was dizzy, aching, and felt shaken to pieces when something went off like a thunder-clap just behind him; a hot wind knocked him senseless, and red fire singed his fur. The big man had been wakened by the noise, and had fired both barrels of a shotgun into Nag just behind the hood.

Rikki-tikki held on with his eyes shut, . . . and the big man picked him up and said: "It's the mongoose again, Alice; the little chap[1] has saved our lives now."

Rikki feels stiff from the fight but better in the morning. Skipping breakfast, he goes to the garden. Everyone there knows Nag is dead, for his body was thrown on the garbage heap.

"Nag is dead—is dead—is dead!" sang Darzee. The valiant Rikki-tikki caught him by the head and held fast. The big man brought the bang-stick, and Nag fell in two pieces! He will never eat my babies again."

◆ ◆ ◆

Rikki learns that Nagaina's eggs are in the melon bed. He gets there just in time—the baby cobras are due to hatch the next day. He has smashed all but one egg when Darzee's wife screams that Nagaina is heading for the house. Rikki races to the family, who are at breakfast.

◆ ◆ ◆

Vocabulary Development

battered (BAT erd) *v.* knocked
singed (SINJD) *v.* burned the edges
valiant (VAL yuhnt) *adj.* acting with courage; brave

4. chap (chap) *n.* fellow.

◆ **Vocabulary and Pronunciation**

Mark the Text

The expression *to and fro* means "forward and back" or "toward and away." Circle four more words in the paragraph that show direction or position.

◆ **Vocabulary and Pronunciation**

Mark the Text

Circle the made-up term that Darzee uses for the man's shotgun. Why is the term appropriate? Explain on the lines below.

______

______

◆ **Reading Strategy**

What do you **predict** Rikki will do soon? Circle the letter of the answer. Then, on the lines, explain why you think he will do that.

(a) try to kill Nagaina

(b) try to kill Darzee

(c) become like a father to Nag's fatherless children

(d) hide in the house

______

______

______

______

◆ **Vocabulary and Pronunciation**

What does "within easy striking distance" mean here? Circle the letter of your answer.

(a) at a great distance

(b) able to reach out and bite easily

(c) refusing to work

(d) able to pitch a baseball

◆ **English Language Development**

In commands or requests, the subject *you* is usually omitted but understood:

(You) Turn round Nagaina; (you) turn and fight.

Circle four more commands in the bracketed paragraphs. For each, squeeze in the subject *you* to show that it is understood.

Mark the Text

They sat stone-still, and their faces were white. Nagaina was coiled up on the matting by Teddy's chair, within easy striking distance of Teddy's bare leg. . . .

Rikki-tikki came up and cried: "Turn round Nagaina; turn and fight!"

"All in good time," she said, without moving her eyes. . . . "Look at your friends, Rikki-tikki. . . . They dare not move, and if you come a step nearer I strike."

"Look at your eggs," said Rikki-tikki, "in the melon bed near the wall. Go and look, Nagaina."

The big snake turned half round, and saw the egg on the verandah. "Ah-h! Give it to me," she said.

Rikki-tikki put his paws one on each side of the egg, and his eyes were blood-red. "What price for a snake's egg? For a young cobra? For a young king cobra? For the last—the very last of the brood?[5] . . ."

Nagaina spun clear round, forgetting everything for the sake of the one egg; and Rikki-tikki saw Teddy's father shoot out a big hand, catch Teddy by the shoulder, and drag him across the little table with the teacups, safe and out of reach of Nagaina.

◆ ◆ ◆

Nagaina throws herself at Rikki over and over, backing him away. Then she grabs the egg and runs. Darzee's wife flaps her wings near her head but fails to slow her. Rikki chases Nagaina down the rat hole where she lives.

◆ ◆ ◆

Darzee said: "It is all over with Rikki-tikki! We must sing his death song. Valiant Rikki-tikki is dead! For Nagaina will surely kill him underground."

5. **brood** (brood) *n.* all the eggs laid or cared for at one time.

So he sang a very mournful song that he made up on the spur of the minute, and just as he got to the most touching part the grass quivered again, and Rikki-tikki, covered with dirt, dragged himself out of the hole leg by leg, licking his whiskers. Darzee stopped with a little shout. Rikki-tikki shook some of the dust out of his fur and sneezed. "It is all over," he said. "The widow will never come out again."

Rikki-tikki curled himself up in the grass and slept where he was, . . . for he had done a hard day's work.

◆ ◆ ◆

The Coppersmith, a bird who spreads the news, sings of Rikki's triumph. The frogs join the song. Meanwhile, Rikki returns to the house.

◆ ◆ ◆

That night he ate all that was given him till he could eat no more, and went to bed on Teddy's shoulder, where Teddy's mother saw him when she came to look late at night.

"He saved our lives and Teddy's life," she said. . . .

Rikki-tikki had a right to be proud of himself; but he did not grow too proud, and he kept that garden as a mongoose should keep it, with tooth and jump and spring and bite, till never a cobra dared show its head inside the walls.

Vocabulary Development

mournful (MOHRN ful) *adj.* showing grief over a death; very sad

quivered (KWI verd) *v.* shook

◆ Literary Analysis

What happens to Nagaina? Write your answer on these lines.

____

____

____

How does this event help fix the problem?

____

____

____

◆ English Language Development

Some nouns ending in *f* or *fe* change *f* to *v* in their plural forms.

Singular	**Plural**
life	lives
elf	elves

On the lines below, write the plural form of each noun.

Singular: knife

Plural: ______________________

Singular: leaf

Plural: ______________________

Singular: wolf

Plural: ______________________

Singular: belief

Plural: ______________________

REVIEW AND ASSESS

1. Circle all the words that you think describe Rikki-tikki-tavi.

   brave nosey snobby sloppy shy

2. Why do Rikki and cobras fight? Write two reasons on these lines.

   1. ____

   2. ____

3. Why does Rikki destroy the eggs? Circle the letter of the best answer.

   (a) He is hungry.

   (b) He wants revenge for Nag's attack the night before.

   (c) He is mean and wants to torture Nagaina.

   (d) He wants to clear the garden of deadly cobras.

4. **Literary Analysis:** The problem in this story is the danger of the snakes. List three events that make up the **rising action**. These events show how dangerous the snakes are.

   1. ____

   2. ____

5. **Literary Analysis:** What is the **climax** of the story (When the trouble or problem is greatest)?

   Climax:

6. **Reading Strategy:** List a clue that helped you **predict** each event.

Event: Rikki will fight Nag one day.

Clue: ______________________________

Event: Rikki will try to destroy the cobra eggs.

Clue: ______________________________

Event: Rikki will fight Nagaina one day.

Clue: ______________________________

Writing

Do research to learn more about an unfamiliar animal, like a cobra or a mongoose. Then write a paragraph about the animal you research.

- Use reliable Internet or library sources. List two sources here.

____

____

- List key facts you learn about the animal. Focus on these questions:

  What does it look like? ______________________________

  ____

  ____

  Where is it found? ______________________________

  ____

  ____

  How does it behave? ______________________________

  ____

  ____

- Use your facts in a paragraph that you write on another sheet.

PREVIEW

After Twenty Years

O. Henry

Summary

One night a police officer walks the nearly empty streets of a New York business area. In a dark store doorway is a man named Bob waiting to meet his friend Jimmy Wells. Bob explains that he hasn't seen Jimmy since leaving New York twenty years ago to make his fortune out west. The two promised to meet in twenty years at Big Joe Brady's restaurant, now this store. Bob is sure Jimmy will show up. After the officer leaves, another man arrives and greets Bob by name. Bob soon realizes this man is not Jimmy. In fact he is a plainclothes officer who arrests "Silky Bob" for crimes in Chicago. He hands Bob a note from Jimmy, who actually was the first officer. Jimmy came to meet his old friend but recognized Bob as a wanted man. He didn't have the heart to arrest Bob himself, so he sent a fellow officer.

Visual Summary

Twenty Years Ago

Parting friends Jimmy Wells and Bob agree to meet again at Big Joe Brady's New York restaurant in twenty years

What Happens to Jimmy Wells	What Happens to Bob
• remains in New York City	• leaves New York to seek his fortune out west
• unknown to Bob and reader, becomes a New York City police officer	• unknown to Jimmy and reader, becomes "Silky Bob," gangster wanted in Chicago
• unknown to Bob and reader, keeps appointment outside closed store that was once Big Joe's	• keeps appointment outside closed store that was once Big Joe's
• recognizes Bob as a wanted man	• fails to recognize Jimmy in uniform
• doesn't have the heart to arrest his old friend	• is sure loyal friend Jimmy will keep appointment
• sends another officer to arrest Bob	• recognizes second arrival is not Jimmy
• sends note with second officer, explaining situation to Bob (and reader)	• learns the truth (as reader does) when he is arrested and reads Jimmy's note

PREPARE TO READ

LITERARY ANALYSIS

Surprise Ending

The events in most stories usually build to a climax, or high point. Then, they wind down to the ending. In some stories, however, there is a **surprise ending** that is different from what most readers expect. A good surprise ending comes as a surprise but it still makes sense to the reader. In some cases, earlier details may hint at the surprise. In other cases, earlier details make more sense once the surprise is revealed.

O. Henry is famous for his surprise endings. As you read his story, ask yourself these questions:

- How do you think the story will end?
- Which details seem to hint at the ending?

Once you finish the story, ask yourself these questions:

- Does the surprise ending seem believable? Why or why not?
- What earlier details gave hints about the ending?

READING STRATEGY

Breaking Down Sentences

Sometimes it is hard to understand the meaning of long, complex sentences. If you **break down sentences** into smaller groups of words, you can often understand them better. Underline the heart of the sentence—the main subject and action. Then break the sentence into logical chunks. Think about how those chunks relate to the main part.

In the sentence below, the main part is underlined. *A tall man* is the subject—the person or thing the sentence is about; *hurried across* is the main action he performs. The rest of the sentence is divided into logical chunks that tell you more about the man and from where he hurried.

> *A tall man* | *in a long overcoat,* | *with collar turned up to his ears,* | *hurried across* | *from the opposite side of the street.*

After Twenty Years

◆ Vocabulary and Pronunciation

What does *beat* mean here? Use the context, or surroundings, to help you figure it out. Then circle the letter of the meaning below.

(a) to hit or strike repeatedly

(b) a steady pulse, such as the heart makes

(c) a regular path or round that a person makes

It is ten o'clock on a rainy, windy night. A police officer in New York City walks his beat with his usual style, even though almost no one is there to see him. The neighborhood is a business area, and most of the stores and office buildings are closed for the night.

◆ ◆ ◆

◆ Reading Strategy

Circle the main subject and verb in this sentence. Then use straight lines to **break the sentence down** into parts you can understand it better.

About midway of a certain block the policeman suddenly slowed his walk. In the doorway of a darkened hardware store a man leaned, with an unlighted cigar in his mouth. As the policeman walked up to him the man spoke up quickly.

"It's all right, officer," he said, reassuringly. "I'm just waiting for a friend. It's an appointment made twenty years ago. . . . About that long ago there used to be a restaurant where this store stands—'Big Joe' Brady's restaurant."

◆ English Language Development

Nicknames are often put in quotation marks to show they are not the real name:

"Ma" Rainey

Nat "King" Cole

In American style, single quotation marks are used for items that are part of longer items in quotation marks. Circle the single and double quotation marks here.

"Until five years ago," said the policeman. "It was torn down then."

The man in the doorway struck a match and lit his cigar. The light showed a pale, square-jawed face with keen eyes, and a little white scar near his right eyebrow. His scarfpin was a large diamond, oddly set.

"Twenty years ago tonight," said the man, "I dined here at 'Big Joe' Brady's with Jimmy Wells, my best chum, and the finest chap[1] in the world. He and I were raised here in New York, just like two brothers, together. I was

Vocabulary Development

reassuringly (ree uh SHOOR ing lee) *adv.* in a way that eases concern; confidently

keen (KEEN) *adj.* sharp

chum (CHUM) *n.* friend; pal

1. **chap** (chap) *n.* slang for fellow; guy.

eighteen and Jimmy was twenty. The next morning I was to start for the West to make my fortune. You couldn't have dragged Jimmy out of New York; he thought it was the only place on earth. Well, we agreed that night that we would meet here again exactly twenty years from that date and time, no matter what our condition might be or from what distance we might have to come. We figured that in twenty years each of us ought to have our destiny worked out and our fortunes made, whatever they were going to be."

◆ ◆ ◆

The man explains that it was exactly ten o'clock when he and Jimmy parted twenty years before and that they are supposed to meet at the same time now. The policeman seems interested in the story. He asks if the man and Jimmy have been in touch. The man says they lost touch years before.

◆ ◆ ◆

"Did pretty well out West, didn't you?" asked the policeman.

"You bet! I hope Jimmy has done half as well. He was a kind of plodder, though, good fellow as he was. I've had to compete with some of the sharpest wits going to get my pile. . . ."

◆ ◆ ◆

The policemen continues on his beat. The man in the doorway feels a little silly to have come a thousand miles to keep an appointment made twenty years ago. Still, he smokes his cigar and continues to wait.

◆ ◆ ◆

Vocabulary Development

destiny (DES tin ee) *n.* future; fate
plodder (plod er) *n.* someone who moves slowly and carefully; a slowpoke

◆ Vocabulary and Pronunciation

Mark the Text

Say each number. Then show that you understand the amount by writing the numeral next to each word. For example, if the sentence said *ten*, you would write *10*.

◆ Vocabulary and Pronunciation

What do you think the expression "You bet" means? Circle the letter of the likely meaning.

(a) absolutely; yes indeed

(b) no, never

(c) risky; danger; beware

(d) I don't believe it!

◆ Reading Check

Mark the Text

Circle the words that show that the man is proud of what he has achieved.

A tall man in a long overcoat, with collar turned up to his ears, hurried across from the opposite side of the street. He went directly to the waiting man.

"Is that you, Bob?" he asked, doubtfully.

"Is that you, Jimmy Wells?" cried the man in the door.

"Bless my heart!" exclaimed the new arrival, grasping both the other's hands with his own. "It's Bob, sure as fate. I was certain I'd find you here if you were still in existence."

◆ ◆ ◆

The two men continue with warm greetings. They walk up the street arm in arm. The man from the West outlines his successful career; the other listens with interest. Then the two move into the glare of brightly lit drugstore window.

◆ ◆ ◆

The man from the West stopped suddenly and released his arm.

"You're not Jimmy Wells," he snapped. "Twenty years is a long time, but not long enough to change a man's nose from a Roman to a pug."[2]

"It sometimes changes a good man into a bad one," said the tall man. "You've been under arrest for ten minutes, 'Silky' Bob."

◆ ◆ ◆

The tall man turns out to be a plainclothes police officer. He explains that the Chicago police contacted New York to say that "Silky" Bob was heading that way. The Chicago police want to question Bob and asked that he be taken into custody. When the officer sees that Bob is going quietly with him, he pauses.

◆ ◆ ◆

◆ Literary Analysis

Circle the detail that suggests that the man is hiding his appearance. What sort of **surprise ending** might this detail hint at? Write your guess on the lines.

Mark the Text

____

____

____

____

◆ Stop to Reflect

What do you think the criminal nickname "Silky" Bob might mean?

Mark the Text

(a) Bob is known as a stylish dresser who likes to wear silk shirts.

(b) Bob is a slick or smooth operator—smooth as silk.

(c) Both *a* and *b* seem likely.

(d) Neither *a* nor *b* seems likely.

2. **change a man's nose from a Roman to a pug:** A Roman nose has a high, bony bridge; a pug nose is short, thick, and turned up at the end.

"Now, before we go to the station, here's a note I was asked to hand to you. You may read it here at the window. It's from Patrolman Wells."

The man from the West unfolded the little piece of paper handed him. His hand was steady when he began to read, but it trembled a little by the time he had finished. The note was rather short.

Bob: I was at the appointed place on time. When you struck the match to light your cigar, I saw it was the face of the man wanted in Chicago. Somehow I couldn't do it myself, so I went around and a got a plain clothes man to do the job. Jimmy.

◆ Literary Analysis

Were you surprised by the ending?

____

Did you think it made sense? On the lines below, explain your answer.

____

____

____

____

____

REVIEW AND ASSESS

1. On the lines below, sum up the agreement that Bob and Jimmy made twenty years ago.

____

____

2. Which statement best describes the relationship between Bob and Jimmy? Circle the letter of the best answer.

(a) They were close in childhood and are just as close now.

(b) They were close in childhood but have taken different paths in life.

(c) They are much closer today than they were in childhood.

3. Why do you think Bob keeps the appointment, even though he is a criminal? Check at least two possible reasons.

____ He wants to keep a promise to an old friend.

____ He wants to show off his success.

____ He is a hunted man and wants to escape capture.

____ Deep down he feels guilty and wants to be arrested.

____ He is curious to see his old friend.

4. Why is Jimmy unable to arrest Bob himself? Explain on these lines.

____

____

5. **Literary Analysis:** On the lines below, explain what happens in the **surprise ending**.

____

____

6. List two earlier details that point to the surprise, even though you may not have known that earlier.

1. ______________________________

2. ______________________________

7. **Reading Strategy:** Draw lines to **break down this sentence** into logical parts. Circle the main subject and action. Then answer the two questions about the sentence.

In the doorway of a darkened hardware store a man leaned, with an unlighted cigar in his mouth.

Where did the man lean? ______________________________

What was in his mouth? ______________________________

Listening and Speaking

Imagine that you are a radio announcer reading a news bulletin about the arrest of "Silky" Bob. On the lines, list information to include in your bulletin. Include details from the story and details you make up.

- What does "Silky" Bob look like? ______________________________

____

____

- What was Bob wearing? ______________________________

____

- Where is Bob wanted by the police? ______________________________

____

- Where was Bob captured? ______________________________

____

- What crimes is Bob suspected of committing? ______________________________

____

Now use the details in a news bulletin that you announce. Speak clearly, and raise and lower your voice for effect.

PREVIEW

Papa's Parrot

Cynthia Rylant

Summary

A boy named Harry Tillian once enjoyed visiting his father's candy store. As he grows older, however, he goes there less often. Meanwhile his father gets a talking parrot that he keeps in the store. Because his father talks so much to the parrot, Harry is embarrassed and goes to the store even less often. Then one day, Harry's father falls ills and has to go to the hospital. Harry goes to the store to help out. He is amazed when the parrot keeps saying, "Where's Harry? Miss him." Harry realizes the bird is echoing his father's words. After a long cry, Harry goes to visit his father at the hospital.

Visual Summary

Before Harry Starts Junior High	After Harry Starts Junior High	After Harry's Father Gets Ill
• Harry visits his father's candy and nut shop often.	• Harry stops going to his father's shop.	• Harry goes to his father's shop to take care of things.
• Harry's friends often stop by.	• His father gets a parrot that he names Rocky.	• The parrot keeps saying "Where's Harry?" and "Miss him."
	• Harry is embarrassed to see his father talking with the parrot.	• Harry realizes the parrot is echoing his father's words.
	• Harry's father gets ill and must go to the hospital.	• Harry weeps.
		• Harry goes to visit his father in the hospital.

PREPARE TO READ

LITERARY ANALYSIS

Characterization

Characterization is the way in which a writer tells readers about characters. There are two basic methods.

- In **direct characterization**, the author *tells* you a character's personality or attitudes.
- In **indirect characterization**, the author *shows* you what the character is like. From the character's actions and speech, you figure out his or her personality and attitudes.

As you read "Papa's Parrot," pay attention to the characterization of Harry and his father. You might fill in a characterization chart like this one.

Direct Characterization	"Harry Tillian liked his papa."
Indirect Characterization	"For years, after school, Harry had always stopped in to see his father at work."
What it shows	Harry Tillian liked his father.

READING STRATEGY

Identifying with a Character

You can understand a story better if you identify with the characters. To **identify with a character**, put yourself in his or her place. Think how you might react to the same situations.

As you read "Papa's Parrot," identify with either Harry or his father. For each main event, create an organizer like the one below. Identify the event, write the character's reaction, and write what you would have done or said in the same situation.

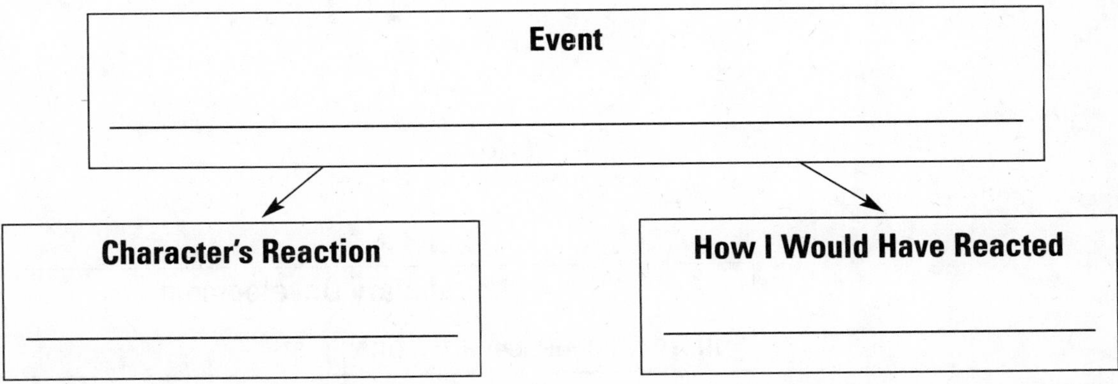

Papa's Parrot

Cynthia Rylant

◆ **Stop to Reflect**

Circle two words that make it seem like being fat and owning a candy and nut store are not the best things. Whose point of view is being expressed in this sentence? Circle the letter of your answer.

Mark THE Text

(a) the father's

(b) Harry's

(c) Harry's friends

(d) the author's

◆ **Vocabulary and Pronunciation**

The word *company* has several meanings. Circle the letter of the meaning used here.

(a) visitors; companionship

(b) a business firm

(c) unnamed business partners

(d) a unit of military troops

◆ **Culture Note**

The candy store described here is no longer as common in America as it used to be. Penny candy shops once sold candy by the piece. Children bought each piece for one cent. As the story shows, the children enjoyed selecting candy.

The main characters in this story are a boy named Harry Tillian and his father. There is also a bird named Rocky, a large parrot that can imitate the words spoken by human beings.

◆ ◆ ◆

Though his father was fat and merely owned a candy and nut shop, Harry Tillian liked his papa. . . . For years, after school, Harry had always stopped in to see his father at work. Many of Harry's friends stopped there too, to spend a few cents. . . . Mr. Tillian looked forward to seeing his son and his son's friends every day. He liked the company.

◆ ◆ ◆

When Harry and his friends start junior high school, they stop coming to the shop. They have other things to do like play video games and hang out at the burger place.

That same year, Harry's father bought a parrot at the pet store. Mr. Tillian named the parrot Rocky. He kept it at the candy store. Harry thought it was a strange thing for his father to do. But Mr. Tillian ignored his son's opinion. He found Rocky to be good company. When business was slow, he and the bird would sit and watch TV.

◆ ◆ ◆

Vocabulary Development

merely (MEER lee) *adj.* only; just

The more Mr. Tillian grew to like his parrot, and the more he talked to it instead of to people, the more embarrassed Harry became. Harry would stroll past the shop, on his way somewhere else, and he'd take a quick look inside to see what his dad was doing.

♦ ♦ ♦

Whenever Harry looks in the shop, he sees his father talking to the bird. Harry is embarrassed so he keeps walking.

Then, Mr. Tillian has a heart attack one day while he is opening the boxes of caramels. A customer comes into the shop and finds that Mr. Tillian has fallen. An ambulance is called, and Mr. Tillian goes to the hospital.

Harry visits his father in the hospital. Mr. Tillian asks him to take care of the store and to feed Rocky. So the next day after school, Harry goes to the store. He picks up the spilled caramels and puts them back in the box. Then he begins opening the other boxes of candy that his father never got to. Suddenly Rocky starts to talk.

♦ ♦ ♦

"Hello, Rocky!"

Harry stared at the parrot. . . . "Hello," Harry said.

"Hello, Rocky!" answered the parrot. . . .

"Is that all you can say, you dumb bird?" Harry mumbled. . . .

"Where's Harry?"

♦ ♦ ♦

Vocabulary Development

stroll (STROHL) *v.* walk slowly

◆ **Literary Analysis**

Mark the Text

Circle the words that show Harry's attitude toward his father. Also circle the actions that show his attitude. Label each circle *D* for **direct characterization** or *I* for **indirect characterization**.

◆ **Vocabulary and Pronunciation**

Caramels are sweet chewy candies. The word *caramel* has different pronunciations. In some areas, people say it in three syllables and pronounce the first syllable as it is pronounced in the name *Carrie*. In other areas, people say *caramel* in two syllables and pronounce the first syllable like the word *car*. Which way is said in your area? Circle the answer, and say the word.

2 syllables 3 syllables

◆ **Reading Check**

Mark the Text

Circle the words spoken out loud in this section. Then label each remark R if it is spoken by Rocky or H if it is spoken by Harry.

◆ Reading Fluently

In what tone of voice would you say Harry's underlined words? Circle the letter of the best answer.

(a) annoyed (c) silly

(b) joyous (d) excited

Now say the Harry's words aloud, trying to use the tone you circled.

◆ Stop to Reflect

Who does Harry realize has been saying "Where's Harry?" and "Miss him"? Write your answer on the line.

____

Harry looks at the bird as it keep repeating the same question. He wonders what it means.

◆ ◆ ◆

Harry swallowed and said, "I'm here. I'm here, you stupid bird."

"You stupid bird!" said the parrot.

◆ ◆ ◆

Harry thinks the bird has one thing right—it's stupid. But the parrot goes back to saying "Where's Harry?" and adds "Miss him."

Harry gets more upset as the bird keeps repeating "Where's Harry?" and "Miss him." He throws some peppermints at the bird. Then, he leans on a glass counter and begins to cry.

◆ ◆ ◆

"Papa." . . . Harry sighed and wiped his face on his sleeve.

◆ ◆ ◆

Harry has figured out that the bird is repeating what his father has been saying. As he thinks about how his father must have missed him, Harry finishes up his work in the shop.

◆ ◆ ◆

He checked the furnace so the bird wouldn't get cold. Then he left to go visit his papa.

Vocabulary Development

furnace (FUR nis) *n.* equipment like a boiler, used to heat a building

REVIEW AND ASSESS

1. Why does Harry almost never visit his father's candy and nut store any more? Put a check in front of all the reasons.

____ He has outgrown the store and no longer finds it as interesting.

____ He does not want to get fat like his father.

____ He and his friends now have more money and go to more places.

____ He does not like his father.

____ He is jealous of his father's parrot.

____ He is embarrassed that his father talks so much to a parrot.

2. Why does Harry's father buy a parrot to keep in his shop? Circle the letter of the best answer.

(a) He needs something to make noise at night and scare off robbers.

(b) He wants to insult some customers and uses the bird to do it.

(c) He wants to attract young children to his shop.

(d) He is lonely and misses his son's visits.

3. What does Harry learn from the bird's remarks? Write your answer on the lines below.

____

____

4. **Literary Analysis:** List one statement of **direct characterization** that tells us something about each of these characters.

Harry: ____

____

Mr. Tillian: ____

____

(Continued)

5. For each of Harry's qualities or attitudes below, write an example of **indirect characterization** that shows us the quality or attitude.

   He is embarrassed by his father: ______________________________

   ____

   He loves his father: ______________________________

   ____

6. **Reading Strategy:** Can you **identify** with the embarrassment Harry feels in parts of the story? Why or why not? Explain on these lines.

   ____

   ____

   ____

Writing

A summary is a short version of a story that tells only the main points and details. Write your own summary of "Papa's Parrot."

- Complete this story outline.

Story Outline
Setting: ______________________________
Characters: ______________________________
____
Events: ______________________________
____
____
Outcome: ______________________________
____

- Use the information in your outline in a summary that you write on a separate sheet of paper.

PREVIEW

Ribbons

Laurence Yep

Summary

Stacy's grandmother comes from Hong Kong to live with the family. It is difficult for the family and especially Stacy, who must give her grandmother her room. Grandmother knows some English, but she seems to favor Stacy's brother Ian, who has learned some Chinese. Then the grandmother gets upset with Stacy's ribboned ballet shoes and demands the ribbons be destroyed. Stacy is very upset until she learns that her grandmother, as a child in China, was forced to bind her feet with ribbons. This painful old practice supposedly made Chinese women more beautiful. But it has left the grandmother's feet all twisted and aching. She objected to the ribboned ballet shoes because she thought the custom was similar. But Stacy explains it is not and dances for her. The two finally bond.

Visual Summary

Grandmother	Grandfather
• feet bound in ribbons in China to be "beautiful" • removed ribbons created great pain • now comes to U.S. and stays in Stacy's room • reacts badly to Stacy's ballet-shoe ribbons • finally accepts Stacy's ballet dancing	• died in China
Stacy's Mother	**Stacy's Father**
• saved as baby by mother in China • tries to make mother comfortable in U.S. • takes Stacy's ballet-shoe ribbon at mother's request • has promised not to speak of mother's bad feet	• unpacks car for Grandmother • cannot afford Stacy's ballet and settling Grandmother • is not of Chinese background
Stacy	**Ian**
• gives up room and ballet lessons for Grandmother • thinks Grandmother likes Ian because he looks Chinese • doesn't understand Grandmother's reaction to her ballet-shoe ribbons • sees Grandmother's damaged feet and learns why Grandmother hated her shoe ribbons • shows the ballet she loves to Grandmother • bonds with Grandmother and realizes shared love	• younger than Stacy • bow of greeting pleases Grandmother • learns more Chinese to talk with Grandmother • looks more like Chinese mother than Stacy does

PREPARE TO READ

LITERARY ANALYSIS

Theme

The **theme** of a work is its central message. The story's details point to the theme, which is a general message about life or human behavior. For example, suppose a story is about a grandmother from China and granddaughter in America who come to understand each other. The theme might be "Love can span age and cultural differences." It might also be "The more time you spend with people, the more you will understand them."

Sometimes a theme is stated in a story. More often, it is not stated, and you must decide what theme the details suggest. Many stories have more than one theme.

As you read "Ribbons," think about its theme or themes. Consider what the details show about life or human behavior.

READING STRATEGY

Asking Questions

One way to understand a story and its themes is by **asking questions** as you read. For example, you might ask questions like these:

- Why is the author telling me this?
- Why does the character do, say, or think that?
- How does this event fit into what happened so far?

As you read "Ribbons," jot down questions and answers on a chart like this one.

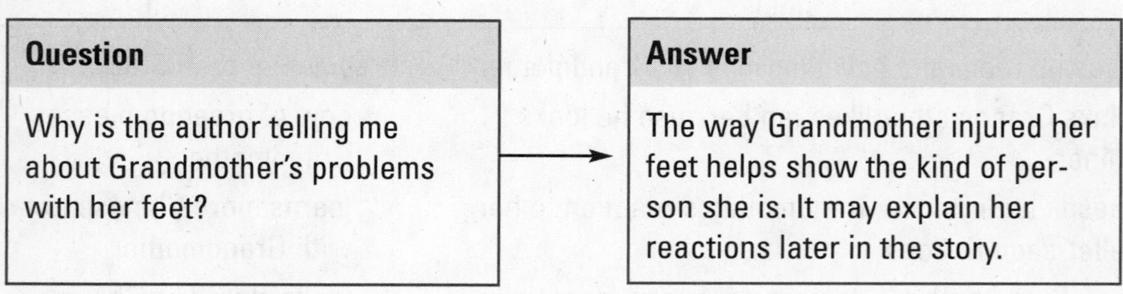

Question	Answer
Why is the author telling me about Grandmother's problems with her feet?	The way Grandmother injured her feet helps show the kind of person she is. It may explain her reactions later in the story.

Ribbons

Laurence Yep

Stacy and her younger brother Ian (EE uhn) are waiting for their Chinese grandmother. The grandmother fled communist China years ago, after she lost her husband. Strapping Stacy's mother—then a baby—to her back, she walked all the way to the British colony of Hong Kong. Now, many years later, she is coming to live with her daughter's family in San Francisco.

♦ ♦ ♦

A car stopped outside, and Ian rushed to the window. "She's here! She's here!" he shouted excitedly. "Paw-paw's here!" *Paw-paw* is Chinese for grandmother—for "mother's mother." . . .

Grandmother was a small woman in a padded silk jacket and black slacks. Her hair was pulled back into a bun behind her head. On her small feet she wore a pair of quilted cotton slippers shaped like boots, with furred tops that hid her ankles.

"What's wrong with her feet?" I whispered to Mom.

"They've always been that way. And don't mention it," she said. "She's sensitive about them."

♦ ♦ ♦

Stacy greets Grandmother with a big hug and kiss. But Grandmother seems to prefer Ian's Chinese-style bow. Walking with two canes, she goes up to the room where she'll be staying—Stacy's room. As Stacy's father goes back and forth unloading

Vocabulary Development

sensitive (SEN suh tiv) *adj.* easily hurt or annoyed; touchy

◆ **English Language Development**

Circle the punctuation that shows you Ian is excited.

◆ **Reading Check**

Circle the meaning of the Chinese word *paw-paw.* What does *paw* seem to mean? Write the meaning on the line below.

paw: ______________________

◆ **Reading Strategy**

Asking questions can help you understand the story. Circle the question that Stacy asks that you might ask too. Then, on the lines below, write one more question you have, based on the mother's words.

____

____

____

the car, Stacy stays outside to watch Grandmother's things.

♦ ♦ ♦

"Now that Grandmother's here, can I begin my ballet lessons again?" I asked.

Dad turned toward the house. "We'll see, hon."

Disappointment made me protest. "But you said I had to give up the lessons so we could bring her from Hong Kong," I said. "Well, she's here." . . .

"Try to understand, hon. We've got to set your grandmother up in her own apartment. That's going to take even more money. Don't you want your room back?"

♦ ♦ ♦

Stacy is very disappointed in the next few weeks. She has lost both her room and her ballet lessons. And Grandmother seems to prefer Ian. She had taught him to speak some Chinese. She even gives Ian an ice cream bar that Stacy bought for herself.

♦ ♦ ♦

When I complained to Mom about how Grandmother was spoiling him, she only sighed. "He's a boy, Stacy. Back in China, boys are everything."

♦ ♦ ♦

Stacy decides that the reason Grandmother likes Ian better is because he looks more Chinese. Ian looks a lot like their mother. Stacy looks more like their father, whose background is not Chinese. Stacy is upset to think that her own grandmother views her as an outsider.

♦ ♦ ♦

◆ Vocabulary and Pronunciation

Circle two silent letters in the word *ballet*.

◆ Reading Check

List the two things Stacy has given up because of her Grandmother's arrival.

1. ______________________

2. ______________________

◆ English Language Development

The **perfect tenses** are formed with a form of the helping verb *have* and the past participle of the main verb. Many past-participle forms end in *ed*. Some verbs do not follow this pattern. For example, *taught* is the irregular past participle of the verb teach: *had taught*. Circle the irregular past participle of each verb.

had bringed had brought

have buyed have bought

will have catched

will have caught

Vocabulary Development

protest (PROH test) *v.* complain

Even so, I kept telling myself: Grandmother is a hero. She saved my mother. She'll like me just as much as she likes Ian once she gets to know me. And, I thought in a flash, the best way to know a person is to know what she loves. For me, that was the ballet.

♦ ♦ ♦

Stacy takes out her ballet shoes to show Grandmother. When the satin ribbons on the shoes come off, Stacy decides to ask her grandmother for help. But instead of helping, Grandmother is horrified by the ribbons. She won't believe Stacy that they are for dancing shoes. The two argue until Stacy's mother runs into the room.

♦ ♦ ♦

"Stop yelling at your grandmother!" she said.

By this point I was in tears. "She's taken everything else. Now she wants my toe-shoe ribbons."

Grandmother panted as she learned on Mom. "How could you do that to your own daughter?"

"It's not like you think," Mom tried to explain. However, Grandmother was too upset to listen. . . . "Take them away. Burn then. Bury them."

Mom sighed. "Yes, Mother."

♦ ♦ ♦

Stacy can't understand. Her mother explains that to Grandmother, ribbons mean something awful, but she won't say what. Grandmother made her promise never to tell. The next day, Stacy is angry and won't talk to Grandmother. Later she goes into the bathroom and finds Grandmother sitting on edge of the bathtub, soaking her feet.

♦ ♦ ♦

"Don't you know how to knock?" she snapped, and dropped a towel over her feet.

◆ Literary Analysis

Mark the Text

Circle the words here that might state one of the story's **themes**.

◆ Reading Check

Circle three words for different family relationships.

◆ Vocabulary and Pronunciation

When *kn* starts a word, the *k* is usually silent. Say *knock* aloud. Then, read the following other *kn* words aloud.

knife	knee
knead	knee

◆ English Language Development

When a word with a short vowel sound ends in a single consonant, you double the consonant when you add a word part that starts with a vowel:

snap + ed = snapped

Mark the Text

If you did not double the consonant, the vowel sound would change to a long vowel (*snaped* would rhyme with *taped*).

Circle another word in the bracketed sentence that follows this rule.

◆ **Think Ahead**

What do you think Stacy is going to find out here in the bathroom? Write your ideas on the lines below.

____

____

____

◆ **Reading Strategy**

Circle one question you might ask here. Then, on the lines below, write one more question you might ask when you read these details.

Mark the Text

____

____

____

◆ **Literary Analysis**

To what **theme** might the mother's words point? Circle the letter of the best choice below.

(a) People try to spare their loved ones from pain.

(b) Uncomfortable shoes make people behave in odd ways.

(c) Grandparents want their grandchildren to be as much like them as possible.

(d) Pain in life cannot be avoided.

However, she wasn't quick enough, because I saw her bare feet for the first time. Her feet were like taffy that some had stretched out and twisted. Each foot bent downward in a way that feet were not meant to, and her toes stuck out at odd angles, more like lumps than toes. I didn't think she had all ten of them, either.

"What happened to your feet?" I whispered in shock.

◆ ◆ ◆

Grandmother won't answer Stacy's question. She orders her out of the bathroom. Later, Stacy's mother explains that Grandmother is too embarrassed to let anyone see her feet. The terrible damage was caused by the old Chinese custom of binding a girl's feet to give them a shape and small size considered beautiful.

◆ ◆ ◆

I shook my head. "There nothing lovely about those feet."

"I know. But they were usually bound up in silk ribbons." . . .

Finally the truth dawned on me. "And she mistook my toe-shoe ribbons for her old ones."

Mom . . . nodded solemnly. "And she didn't want you to go through the same pain she had."

◆ ◆ ◆

Later that night, Grandmother listens as Stacy reads Ian the story of the little mermaid. When Stacy comes to the part about the mermaid walking on land even though each step hurts, she looks up at Grandmother. At the end of the story, the mermaid turns to sea foam.

◆ ◆ ◆

Vocabulary Development

taffy (TAF ee) *n.* a type of candy that stretches
solemnly (SAHL um lee) *adv.* seriously

"I would rather have gone on swimming," he insisted.

"But maybe she wanted to see new places and people by going on the land," Grandmother said softly. "If she had kept her tail, the land people would have thought she was odd. They might even have made fun of her."

♦ ♦ ♦

Stacy realizes that Grandmother is talking about herself. Then Stacy tries to explain that her ribbons aren't like the silk ones Grandmother wore. To show they don't hurt, she puts her ballet shoes on and begins dancing.

♦ ♦ ♦

"See? I can move fine."

She took my hand and patted it clumsily. I think it was the first time she had showed me any sign of affection. "When I saw those ribbons, I didn't want you feeling pain like I do."

I covered her hands with mine. "I just wanted to show you what I love best—dancing."

"And I love my children," she said. I could hear the ache in her voice. "And my grandchildren. I don't want anything bad to happen to you."

Suddenly I felt as if there were an invisible ribbon binding us, tougher than silk and satin, stronger even than steel; and it joined her to Mom and Mom to me.

Vocabulary Development

invisible (in VIZ uh buhl) *adj.* unseen

♦ Literary Analysis

The story about the mermaid helps show a message. Put a check on the line in front of all the themes that you think the fairy tale helps express.

___ People will undergo hardship to experience more of life.

___ No one swims when they can walk.

___ People will do painful things to be more accepted.

___ Everyone likes to be different.

♦ Vocabulary and Pronunciation

Mark the Text

In *ache*, the letters *ch* are pronounced like a *k*: *ache* rhymes with *lake*. Circle a word in the next sentence where *ch* is pronounced differently. Then say both words aloud.

♦ Stop to Reflect

What is the invisible ribbon? Write your ideas on the lines below.

____

____

____

REVIEW AND ASSESS

1. Put a check in front of each true statement about Grandmother.

____ Grandmother is a brave woman who escaped communist China with her daughter.

____ Grandmother was too scared to go against the communists.

____ Grandmother hurt her feet escaping the communists.

____ Grandmother was a ballet dancer in China.

____ Grandmother values freedom and independence.

2. Why do you think Grandmother gives more attention to Ian than to Stacy? Circle the letter of the best answer.

(a) She dislikes Stacy because Stacy is a girl.

(b) She dislikes Stacy because Stacy doesn't look Chinese.

(c) She dislikes Stacy because of the ribbons on Stacy's ballet shoes.

(d) She can talk more with Ian, who has learned more Chinese.

3. What mistake does Grandmother make about the ribbons on Stacy's ballet shoes? Write your answer on the lines provided.

____

____

____

4. What is the "invisible ribbon" at the end of the story? Circle the letter of your answer.

(a) the memory of Grandmother's silk ribbons in China

(b) the satin ribbon on Stacy's ballet shoe

(c) Grandmother's Chinese heritage, which pulls her away from Stacy

(d) the loving family ties between Stacy, her mother, and Grandmother

5. **Literary Analysis:** Put a check in front of the statements that you think are **themes** in the selection.

____ Love and understanding can bring family members closer together.

____ Good health is very important.

____ People do unusual things to try to be different.

____ We don't want those we love to experience pain and suffering.

____ The best way to know a person is to know what he or she loves.

6. **Reading Strategy:** In the left column, list three **questions** you asked as you read the story. In the right column, write the answers.

Question	Answer
•	
•	
•	

Writing

Write a paragraph in which you state a theme of the story and show that it *is* one of the story's themes.

In the space below, list an important theme of the story.

____

List at least three details from the story that point to the theme.

- ____
____
- ____
____
- ____
____

Write your paragraph on a separate sheet of paper. State the theme, and then support it with the details you listed.

The Treasure of Lemon Brown

Walter Dean Myers

Summary

One night, Greg leaves home so he doesn't have to listen to his father's complaints about how badly Greg is doing in school. In an abandoned building near his home, Greg meets Lemon Brown, a homeless man who was once a noted blues musician. Brown proudly shows Greg old newspaper reviews of his performances—reviews that Brown's son was carrying when he died in the war. Greg returns home with a new respect for his own father.

Visual Summary

Greg's Attitude in the Beginning	Events That Change Greg's Attitude	Greg's Attitude in the End
• angry with father for lecturing him about schoolwork and not letting him play basketball • not interested in father's proud talk of passing test for postal service and years of hard work • tries to avoid father and ducks into empty building when rain starts	• meets Lemon Brown, who talks of his "treasure" • helps Brown frighten off troublemakers coming after Brown's treasure • looks at Brown's "treasure"—Brown's old harmonica and clippings about his successful blues career; Brown gave these to his son when his son went off to war. They were returned when his son died	• is happy to go home, even if only to his father's lecture • sees his father's hopes for him as a kind of treasure

PREPARE TO READ

LITERARY ANALYSIS

Theme

The **theme** of a story is its central message about life or human behavior. The story's details point to the theme. In some cases, the theme may be directly stated within the work. In other cases, it is suggested by the details. For example, suppose a character who used to be a blues musician places great value on his old harmonica. The theme might be one of these messages:

- Our past achievements are important
- The worth of something is not determined by money value alone.

Stories sometimes have more than one theme. As you read "The Treasure of Lemon Brown," identify the theme or themes. To do this, ask yourself what the details show about life or human behavior.

READING STRATEGY

Asking Questions

You can often understand a story and its themes better if you **ask questions** as you read. For example, you might ask questions like these:

- Why is the author telling me this?
- Why does the character do, say, or think that?
- How does this event fit into what happened so far?

As you read "The Treasure of Lemon Brown," write down your questions and answers on a chart like the one below.

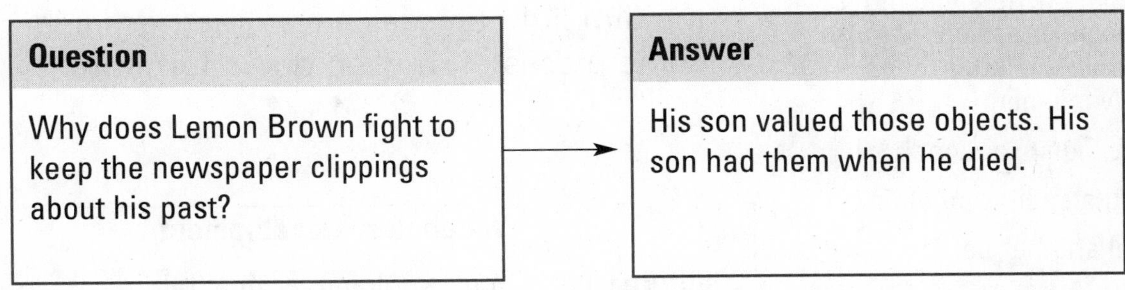

Question		Answer
Why does Lemon Brown fight to keep the newspaper clippings about his past?	→	His son valued those objects. His son had them when he died.

◆ Vocabulary and Pronunciation

Homophones are words with the same pronunciation but different spellings and meanings. Study these homophones.

principal: the head of a school

principle: a guiding value or belief

team: a group that works together

teem: to be filled to overflowing

Complete the sentences below with the right word.

1. Greg wants to join the Scorpions, a popular basketball __________ .
2. At Scorpion games, the stands __________ with fans.
3. The __________ tells Greg's father that Greg is failing math.
4. Greg's father has this ________: No basketball team until Greg's schoolwork improves.

◆ Reading Check

Circle a word in the bracketed paragraph that tells you Greg's mood.

◆ Vocabulary and Pronunciation

Use the context, or surroundings, to figure out the meaning of *hit* in the slang expression *hit those books.* Circle the letter of the most likely meaning.

(a) to slap, bump, or knock

(b) to read steadily and often

(c) to deal another card to

(d) to hide

The Treasure of Lemon Brown

Walter Dean Myers

Fourteen-year-old Greg Ridley has been invited to play basketball with a very good local team. But his father won't give him permission to join the team unless Greg does better in school. The principal just sent his father a letter warning that Greg is failing math.

◆ ◆ ◆

The dark sky, filled with angry, swirling clouds, reflected Greg Ridley's mood as he sat on the stoop[1] of his building. His father's voice came to him again. . . .

"I had to leave school when I was thirteen," his father had said. . . . "If I'd had half the chances that you have, I'd . . ."

Greg had sat in the small, pale green kitchen listening, knowing the lecture would end with his father saying he couldn't play ball with the Scorpions.

◆ ◆ ◆

Greg's father has told him he can't play basketball. He tells him to go to his room and "hit those books."

That was two nights ago. Now Greg cannot bring himself to go inside to hear more of the same. Instead he heads down the street and escapes the rain by entering an empty old apartment building there. In the dim light he sees a torn mattress and some pieces of broken-down furniture.

◆ ◆ ◆

Vocabulary Development

lecture (LEK chur) *n.* scolding; critical talk

1. **stoop** (STOOP) *n.* outdoor steps and small porch area in front of the door of a building.

He went to the couch. The side that wasn't broken was comfortable enough, though a little creaky. From the spot he could see the blinking neon sign over the bodega[2] on the corner. He sat awhile, watching the sign blink first green then red.

♦ ♦ ♦

Greg thought about the Scorpions. Then he started thinking about his father. He'd heard his father's story way too many times. But he knew his father had worked hard to pass the test for the post office. He was proud to be a postal worker.

♦ ♦ ♦

For a moment Greg thought he heard something that sounded like a scraping against the wall. He listened carefully, but it was gone. . . . Still, he thought, as soon as the rain let up he would leave. . . .

"Don't try nothin' 'cause I got a razor here sharp enough to cut a week into nine days!"

♦ ♦ ♦

Greg is scared until he realizes the voice belongs to an old man from the neighborhood. Greg has seen the man, dressed in rags, picking through trash cans.

♦ ♦ ♦

"Who are you?" Greg hardly recognized his own voice.

"I'm Lemon Brown," came the answer. "Who're you?"

"Greg Ridley."

"What you doing here?" The figure shuffled forward again, and Greg took a small step backward.

Vocabulary Development

shuffled (SHUF uld) *v.* walked slowly

2. **neon sign over the bodega:** Brightly lit outdoor sign over the Latino grocery store.

◆ Culture Note

A bodega usually sells all kinds of foods. Usually, it sells foods that are popular in the Latino community. Sometimes, those foods are hard to get in other stores.

◆ Vocabulary and Pronunciation

Mark the Text

Awhile is a term that provides clues about time. It helps you understand how long an event took. Circle four more time clues in the bracketed paragraph.

◆ Stop to Reflect

Why do you think Greg's father often tells Greg how hard he worked to pass the test? Write your ideas on the lines below.

◆ Reading Strategy

What **question** do you have about the figure? Write it here.

◆ English Language Development

Mark up Lemon Brown's words here to show how they would be said in standard English.

◆ Reading Strategy

On the lines below, write one **question** about Lemon Brown that you ask after reading the bracketed passage.

____

____

____

◆ Vocabulary and Pronunciation

Footstep is a **compound word** formed from two smaller words: *foot + step*. You can figure out its meaning by considering the meaning of the smaller words that make it up: A *footstep* is a step made by a foot, or the sound of such a step. Circle two more compound words in this sentence. Then, on the lines below, write the words and their meanings.

Mark THE Text

____

____

____

"It's raining," Greg said. . . .

"Ain't you got no home?"

"I got a home," Greg answered.

"You ain't one of them bad boys looking for my treasure, is you?" Lemon Brown cocked his head to one side and squinted one eye. "Because I told you I got me a razor."

"I'm not looking for your treasure," Greg answered, smiling. "*If* you have one."

"What you mean, *if* I have one," Lemon Brown said. "Every man got a treasure. You don't know that, you must be a fool!"

◆ ◆ ◆

The old man explains that he was once a blues singer nicknamed Sweet Lemon Brown because he sang so sweetly. He even had a boy just like Greg. While he and Greg continue talking, they hear noise. Three neighborhood troublemakers are breaking into the building. They are armed with pieces of pipe, and one of them carries a flashlight.

◆ ◆ ◆

"Hey! Rag man!" A voice called. "We know you in here. What you got up under them rags? You got any money? . . . We heard you talking about your treasure." The voice was slurred. "We just want to see it, that's all.". . .

There was a footstep on the stairs, and the beam from the flashlight danced crazily along the peeling wallpaper. . . .

Lemon Brown stood at the top of the stairs, both arms raised high above his head.

"There he is!" A voice cried from below.

"Throw down your money, old man, so I won't have to bash your head in!"

Vocabulary Development

cocked (KOKT) *v.* tilted

Lemon Brown didn't move. . . . He was an <u>eerie</u> sight, a bundle of rags standing at the top of the stairs, his shadow on the wall <u>looming</u> over him. Maybe, the thought came to Greg, the scene could be even eerier.

♦ ♦ ♦

So Greg begins howling while Lemon Brown throws himself directly at the trouble-makers. Between the two of them, they scare the three men off. Brown even winds up with their flashlight. Afterward, Greg asks about the treasure, and Brown offers to show it to Greg. He unties the rags on one leg and removes a piece of plastic that contains yellowed newspaper clippings and a bent harmonica. All the clippings are reviews from over fifty years ago. The reviews praise Sweet Lemon Brown, a blues singer and harmonica player.

Brown tells Greg how he used to travel around and perform his music to earn a living. He earned enough to take good care of his wife and son, Jesse. When Brown's wife died, Jesse went to live with his aunt. After he was grown, Jesse was a soldier in the war. By then, Brown's musical career wasn't what it had been. He didn't have anything to give to his son except his "treasure." Those things told his son who his father was and where he came from. Brown felt like his son would be able to do something since he knew his father had.

♦ ♦ ♦

Vocabulary Development

eerie (EER ee) *adj.* spooky; weird

looming (LOOM ing) adj. taking shape in a large or threatening way

◆ Vocabulary and Pronunciation

Mark the Text

The sound of long /*e*/ has many different spellings in English. Some common ones include

e, as in *me*
i, as in *spaghetti*
ea, as in *tea*   *ie*, as in *piece*
ee, as in *teen*   *y*, as in *funny*

Circle at least nine spellings of long /*e*/ in these two sentences.

◆ Read Fluently

Read the bracketed passage aloud as you think about how Lemon Brown might have told these things to Greg. What tone would he probably have used to say he took good care of his family? Circle the letter of your answer.

(a) sad   (c) proud
(b) angry   (d) snobby

◆ Literary Analysis

Mark the Text

Circle the sentence here that might state a **theme** of the story. What earlier behavior does this remark help explain? Circle the letter of the best answer.

(a) Greg's father not letting him join the basketball team

(b) Greg's anger at not being able to join the basketball team

(c) Greg's father telling how he studied hard to pass the postal test

(d) the troublemakers' attack on Lemon Brown

◆ **English Language Development**

What word or letters does the apostrophe stand for here? Squeeze in the missing word or letters.

◆ **Stop to Reflect**

What effect do you think the experiences that Lemon Brown shares may have on Greg's relationship with his own father?

Write your ideas on these lines.

____

____

____

____

____

◆ **English Language Development**

Many two-syllable adjectives add *er* for the comparative form and *est* for the superlative: *pretty, prettier, prettiest.* However, *foolish* is not one of them. Change *foolishest* to its standard form.

____

"Anyway, he went off to war, and I went off still playing and singing. 'Course by then I wasn't as much as I used to be, not without somebody to make it worth the while. You know what I mean?"

"Yeah," Greg nodded, not quite really knowing.

"I traveled around, and one time I come home, and there was this letter saying Jesse got killed in the war. Broke my heart, it truly did.

"They sent me back what he had with him over there, and what it was is this old mouth fiddle[3] and these clippings. Him carrying it around with him like that told me it meant something to him. That was my treasure, and when I give it to him he treated it just like that, a treasure. . . ."

"You really think that treasure of yours was worth fighting for?" Greg asked. "Against a pipe?"

"What else a man got 'cepting what he can pass on to his son, or his daughter, if she be his oldest?" Lemon Brown said, "For a big-headed boy you sure do ask the foolishest questions."

◆ ◆ ◆

Greg knows it is well past time to go home but does not like leaving Lemon Brown alone. Brown tells him not to worry—the troublemakers are too scared to come back that night, and he will be heading west in the morning. The rain has stopped as Greg makes his way home. Greg knows it's late and his father will have something to say about what time he is coming home. He thinks about whether he should tell his father about Lemon Brown. By the time he gets home, he has decided not to say anything

3. **mouth fiddle:** A slang term for a harmonica.

about Lemon Brown. The old man will be just fine with his memories and treasure.

♦ ♦ ♦

Greg pushed the button over the bell marked Ridley, thought of the lecture he knew his father would give him, and smiled.

◆ Stop to Reflect

Why do you think Greg smiles?

REVIEW AND ASSESS

1. Why doesn't Greg go home when it starts to rain? Circle the letter of the best answer.
   (a) He does not want his father to know that he is failing math.
   (b) He is angry that his father won't let him play basketball.
   (c) He is worried about Lemon Brown and wants to visit with him.
   (d) He is blocks from home, and the rain is very heavy.

2. Why do the troublemakers break in to Lemon Brown's house? Circle the letter of the correct answer.
   (a) They want to get out of the rain.
   (b) They are friends of Greg's and follow him there.
   (c) They have heard that Brown has a treasure and want to steal it.
   (d) They don't like Greg and want to frighten him.

3. Next to each description, list one or two details from the story to show how the description applies to Lemon Brown.

Description	Detail
poor	______________________
talented	______________________
loved family	______________________
proud	______________________
sad	______________________

4. What is the treasure of Lemon Brown? Describe it on these lines.

____

____

5. **Literary Analysis:** Put a check in front of the statements that you think are **themes** in the selection.

____ A real treasure is worth a lot of money.

____ A person's achievements are a treasure that can be passed down.

____ It is impossible to live up to a parent's achievements.

____ Basketball is less useful than math.

____ Just about everyone has a treasure of some kind.

6. **Reading Strategy:** In the left column, list three **questions** you asked as you read the story. In the right column, write the answers.

Question	Answer
•	
•	
•	

Listening and Speaking

With a group of other students, prepare an oral presentation about the blues. Include information you research. If possible, play music for classmates. For your research, use reliable Internet or library sources and information provided with CD recordings. Try to answer the following questions on a separate sheet of paper. Then include the information in your presentation.

- What is the blues?
- When did the blues develop?
- Who are some of the important early blues artists?
- How has the blues changed over the years?
- How does the blues continue to influence music today?

PREVIEW

I Am a Native of North America

Chief Dan George

Summary

The author of "I Am a Native of North America" remembers the culture in which he grew up. He reflects on the love that Native American people showed one another. He thinks about their great love of the earth and its precious gifts. he compares his culture with white society. He thinks that people in white society have to learn to appreciate one another. They have to learn to appreciate and respect nature. He thinks white society lacks love. In the end, he says, we all need love. He hopes that white society will take the gift of love from Native American culture.

Visual Summary

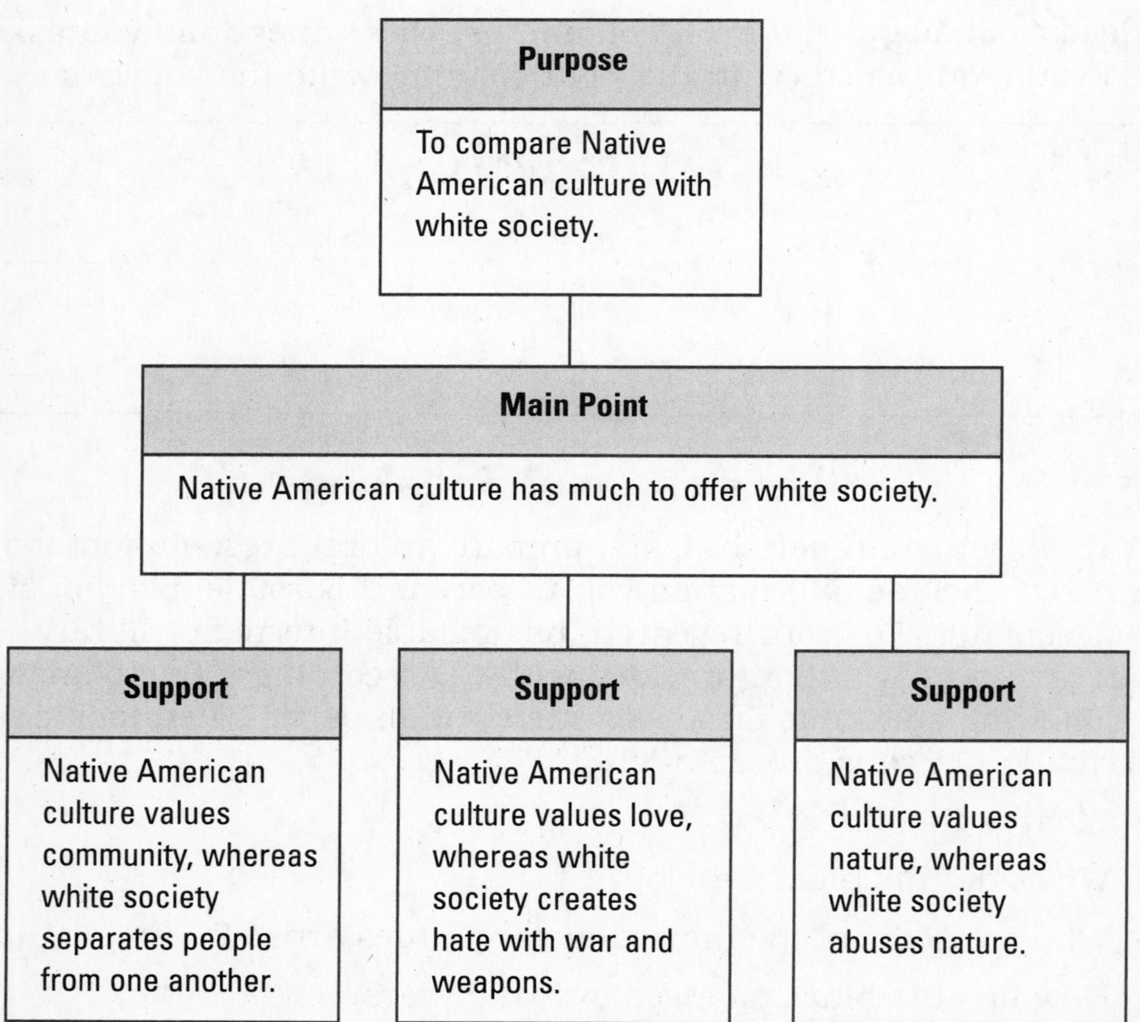

PREPARE TO READ

LITERARY ANALYSIS

Essay

An **essay** is a short piece of writing in which an author gives an opinion on a topic or experience. Chief Dan George's essay is a **reflective essay**. He presents his ideas about two different cultures. He explains how his own experiences shaped his point of view.

The chart below shows some of the author's ideas about each culture. As you read the essay, add other ideas to the chart.

Native American Culture	White Society
People learn to respect the rights of their neighbors through communal living.	People live near one another but do not know or care about their neighbors.
People love and respect nature.	People abuse nature.

READING STRATEGY

Evaluate Support

When authors make a statement, they should back it up with support or evidence. Readers should **evaluate the support** to decide whether they agree with the author. In "I am a Native of North American," the author makes many statements about the Native American culture and white society. For example, he tells us that white society abuses nature. He backs up this statement with the following support:

- They strip the land.
- They poison the water.
- They poison the air.

To evaluate this and other statements, ask yourself these questions: Is the supporting information logical? Is it true? Do I agree with what the author is saying?

◆ Culture Note

Compare Native American culture to white society. Name one way it is different

____

____

Name one way it is the same.

____

____

◆ Reading Check

What three things did people learn by living in communal houses?

1. ______________________

____

2. ______________________

____

3. ______________________

____

◆ Reading Strategy

Circle the information in this paragraph that supports the point that Native Americans respected nature.

I Am a Native of North America

Chief Dan George

In the course of my lifetime I have lived in two distinct[1] cultures. I was born into a culture that lived in communal houses. My grandfather's house was eighty feet long. . . . It stood down by the beach along the inlet.[2] All my grandfather's sons and their families lived in this large dwelling.

◆ ◆ ◆

The communal house had one fire in the middle. That open fire was used for all of their cooking. The areas where they slept had blankets hanging between them. The people of the tribe learned to live together well. They learned how to help each other and respect one another's rights. Children and adults shared the space. The children shared in the adult responsibilities. They weren't threatened by adults.

The author's culture also loved and respected nature. He says nature was considered a gift from the great spirit. The way to thank the great spirit was to treat nature well. As a child, the author fished with his father and saw him raise his arms to give thanks. Once the author went fishing just for fun. For this, his father scolded him. He told him that the fish were his brothers. They fed him when he was hungry and should be respected.

Vocabulary Development

communal (kah MYOO nuhl) *adj.* shared by all

1. **distinct** (di STINKT) *adj.* separate and different.
2. **inlet** (IN let) *n.* narrow strip of water jutting into a body of land from a river, a lake, or an ocean.

When the author grew older, he learned about a different culture, white culture. He says he did not understand how people could live near one another other but not know or care for one another. He could not understand all the hate among people. Wars and weapons did not make sense. He was saddened to see people abuse nature. They stripped the land and poisoned the water and air.

♦ ♦ ♦

My white brother does many things well for he is more clever than my people but I wonder if he knows how to love well.

♦ ♦ ♦

The author wonders whether the people of the white culture ever learned to love. He thinks that they may love the things they own. But this isn't love. Man must love the things that are beyond him. Chief Dan thinks that people must love all creation in order to love any of it.

♦ ♦ ♦

Man must love fully or he will become the lowest of the animals. It is the power of love that makes him the greatest of them all . . . for he alone of all animals is capable of love.

♦ ♦ ♦

The author explains the importance of love in everyone's life. He says that love is necessary for the spirit. Without love, people lose strength, self-esteem suffers, and courage fails. People that do not have love in their lives turn away from the world. When they turn inward, they eventually destroy themselves.

♦ ♦ ♦

◆ Reading Strategy

Mark the Text

What details **support** the idea that white society does not respect nature? Circle the details in the text.

◆ English Language Development

Mark the Text

Most English adjectives have different forms when they are used to make comparisons. The superlative form compares three or more things. Most short adjectives add *-est* for this form: Alex is the tallest player on the team. Find and circle two superlative adjectives in this paragraph.

◆ Literary Analysis

In the author's opinion, what happens without love?

____

____

____

◆ **Vocabulary and Pronunciation**

Possessions are things that people own. *Material* has several different meanings. To fully understand the meaning of the phrase, use context to figure out the meaning of the word *material*. Circle the correct meaning below.

(a) fabric

(b) necessary

(c) physical

(d) ideas or notes for a story

◆ **Reading Strategy**

How does the author **support** his statement that Native American culture will soon be forgotten? Underline the supporting information in the text.

◆ **Reading Check**

What is it that Native American culture must forgive?

____

____

____

You and I need the strength and joy that comes from knowing that we are loved.

◆ ◆ ◆

The author explains that Native American culture valued friendship and companionship. It did not value privacy because privacy divides people. He says that divided people do not trust one another. People from the author's culture did not collect <u>material possessions</u>. They believed that all things belonged to nature and should be shared. He says people should take only what they need.

The author wishes that white society would take some of these values from his Native American culture. Soon Native American culture will be forgotten. Many young people have forgotten the old ways. They have been made to feel ashamed of their Indian ways.

◆ ◆ ◆

The only thing that can truly help us is genuine love. You must truly love us, be patient with us and share with us. And we must love you—with a genuine love that forgives and forgets . . . a love that forgives the terrible sufferings your culture brought ours . . . with a love that forgets and lifts up its head and sees in your eyes an answering love of trust and acceptance.

This is brotherhood . . . anything less is not worthy of the name.

I have spoken.

REVIEW AND ASSESS

1. What two cultures does the essay compare?

____

____

2. How does Native American culture view nature?

____

____

3. Write a sentence that explains the author's idea of *brotherhood.*

____

____

4. **Literary Analysis:** In the chart below, give two ideas the author expresses about Native American culture and two ideas the author expresses about white society.

Native American Culture	White Society
1. ______________________	1. ______________________
______________________	______________________
______________________	______________________
2. ______________________	2. ______________________
______________________	______________________
______________________	______________________

5. **Reading Strategy:** Did the author provide convincing support for his main idea that Native American culture has something important to offer white society? Write a few sentences to explain your answer.

____

____

____

(Continued)

Writing

Summary of an Essay

Write a summary of the first page of the essay. Answer the questions below to help you. Write your final draft on a separate sheet of paper.

Main points:	How has the author lived over the course of his lifetime?	
Author's message in your own words	How does he describe the communal houses of his culture?	
Restate the main points in your own words.	What did people learn by living this way?	

Explain the author's message in your own words.

____

____

____

All Together Now

Barbara Jordan

Summary

In "All Together Now," Barbara Jordan appeals to Americans to be tolerant of other races. She encourages us to make friends with people of different background. She asks us to be open to the feelings and beliefs or other cultures. She asks parents to teach tolerance to their children. She believes that by working together—at home, at school, and at work—we can make the world a more loving and peaceful place.

Visual Summary

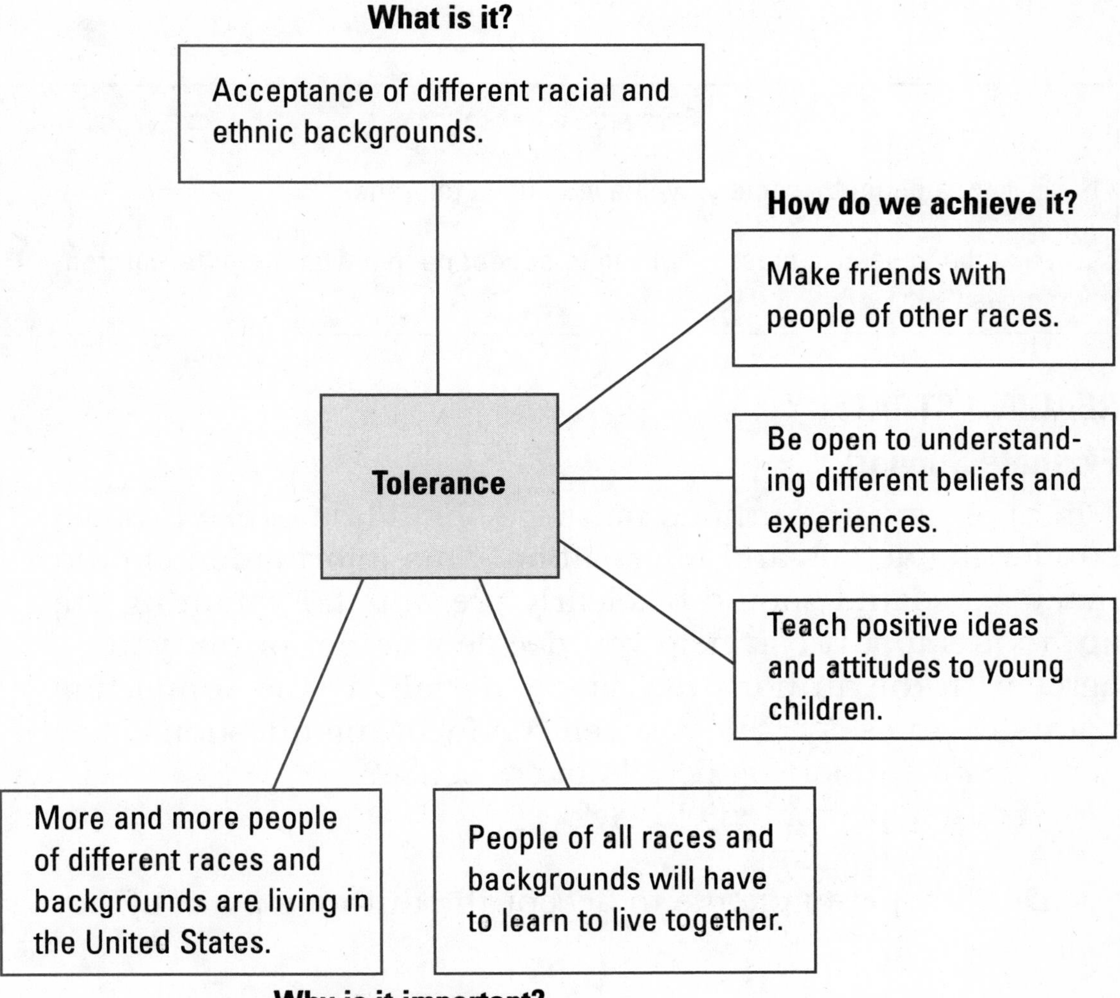

PREPARE TO READ

LITERARY ANALYSIS

Persuasive Essay

In an **essay**, a writer presents a topic from his or her point of view. Essays are written for different reasons, such as to entertain, to persuade, or to inform. "All Together Now" is written to inspire readers and **persuade** them that civil rights are very important. The writer wants readers to do something in response to her essay.

The chart below shows passages in which Barbara Jordan tries to persuade readers to accept her point of view. As you read the essay, notice other passages where Jordan uses persuasive language to make her point.

Persuasive Passages
If we want a peaceful society, we have to have tolerance.
We, as human beings, must be willing to accept people who are different from ourselves.

READING STRATEGY

Evaluate Support

In an essay, an author's message should be backed up with supporting details and information. This information should make sense and should be clearly presented. **Evaluating the author's support** can help you decide whether or not you agree with the author's message. To evaluate the supporting points in an essay, ask yourself the following questions:

- Do the supporting details make sense?
- Are they presented clearly?
- Are they logical?
- Do they persuade me to accept the author's point of view?

All Together Now

Barbara Jordan

The author begins by saying that the relationships between different races in America has improved. Laws have changed to be fairer to everyone. But the real race problem is not government. It is people. She says that individual people need to be more tolerant. And parents are very important in making a tolerant society.

Jordan explains that in the 1960s Dr. Martin Luther King, Jr. led marches and protests against segregation.[1] In 1964, President Lyndon B. Johnson helped pass the Civil Rights Act of 1964. The Voting Rights Act was passed in 1965 to make sure everyone could vote. The laws supported equal rights for all. But laws cannot create tolerance between groups of people. In order for that to happen, people's attitudes have to change.

She explains that Civil Rights issues are just as important today as they were in the past. More and more people of different races and backgrounds are living in America. If we want a peaceful society, we have to have tolerance.

◆ ◆ ◆

If we are concerned about community, if it is important to us that people not feel excluded, then we have to do something. Each of us can decide to have one friend of a different race or background in our mix of friends. If we do this, we'll be working together to push things forward.

Vocabulary Development

tolerant (TAHL er ent) *adj.* free from bigotry or prejudice
excluded (eks CLEWD id) *adv.* left out

. **segregation** (SEG ruh GAY shun) *n.* the practice of separating racial groups.

◆ Vocabulary and Pronunciation

The word *races* can have different meanings. Based on the way it is used, what is the meaning in this selection?

(a) contests to see who is the fastest

(b) strong, swift currents of water

(c) the major groups into which human beings are divided based on physical features

◆ Reading Check

Did civil rights laws bring peace among races? Circle one:

Yes No

Explain your answer.

____

____

____

____

____

◆ Literary Analysis

Mark the Text

What does the author want readers to do to help create tolerance? Underline the answer in the text.

◆ **English Language Development**

In English, a colon (:) can be used to introduce a sentence that summarizes or explains the sentence before it. Underline the passage in which a colon is used in this way.

◆ **Reading Strategy**

How does the author **support** the idea that young people can be a positive force for change? Underline two supporting statements in the text.

◆ **Literary Analysis**

In the final paragraph, circle a phrase that shows how Jordan hopes to inspire readers by her own example.

One thing is clear to me: We, as human beings, must be willing to accept people who are different from ourselves. I must be willing to accept people who don't look as I do and don't talk as I do. It is crucial that I am open to their feelings, their inner reality.

What can parents do? We can put our faith in young people as a positive force. I have yet to find a racist baby. Babies come into the world as blank as slates and, with their beautiful innocence, see others not as different but as enjoyable companions. Children learn ideas and attitudes from the adults who nurture them. I absolutely believe that children do not adopt prejudices unless they absorb them from their parents or teachers.

The best way to get this country faithful to the American dream of tolerance and equality is to start small. Parents can actively encourage their children to be in the company of people who are of other racial and ethnic backgrounds.

◆ ◆ ◆

The author concludes by saying that the rest of her life will be spent bringing people together. She loves other people because they are humans. And she hopes that her love will help others to love. Everyone can work toward racial peace—at home, school, and work.

Vocabulary Development

nurture (NUR chur) *v.* care for

prejudices (PREJ oo disis) *n.* unfair opinions based on someone's race

REVIEW AND ASSESS

1. Complete this sentence: The real problem in race relations is

____

2. Name two laws that support equal rights for all.

   1. ____

   2. ____

   Did these laws bring about racial tolerance? Why or why not?

   ____

   ____

3. What does the author mean when she says "Babies come into the world as blank as slates . . ."?

   ____

   ____

4. **Literary Analysis:** Why did Barbara Jordan write "All Together Now"?

   ____

   ____

   What does she want people to do?

   ____

   ____

5. **Reading Strategy:** Name two questions you used to evaluate Jordan's supporting information.

   1. ____

   ____

   2. ____

   ____

Was the support strong enough to convince you to do as she says? Why or why not?

Writing

Summary of an Essay

Follow the steps below to write a summary of the following paragraph from "All Together Now."

What can parents do? We can put our faith in young people as a positive force. I have yet to find a racist baby. Babies come into the world as blank as slates and, with their beautiful innocence, see others not as different but as enjoyable companions. Children learn ideas and attitudes from the adults who nurture them. I absolutely believe that children do not adopt prejudices unless they absorb them from their parents or teachers.

Write one sentence to explain each part of the paragraph.

Beginning	
Middle	
End	

Now combine your sentences to write one summary of the whole paragraph.

How to Enjoy Poetry

James Dickey

Summary

The author of this essay loves poetry. He wants to help others enjoy it, too. He talks about the connections that words have with our hearts. He explains how rhyme and rhythm leave lasting impressions. He suggests ways that readers can think about poetry. He even encourages them to try writing it. Reading poetry, he says, can change your life.

Visual Summary

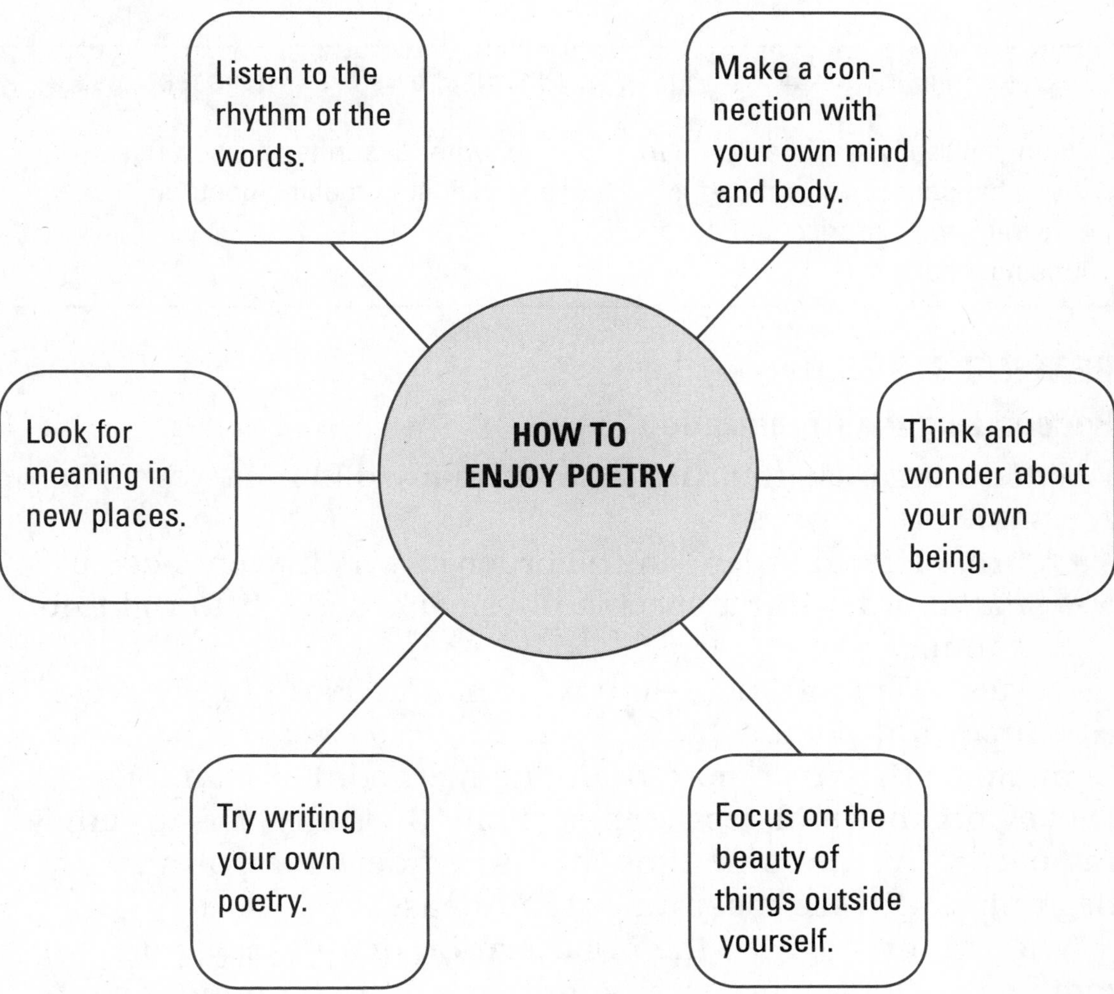

LITERARY ANALYSIS

Expository Essay

An essay is a short piece of writing about a topic. One type of essay is the expository essay. In an **expository essay**, the writer explains something or gives information about it. For example, "How to Enjoy Poetry" explains what readers can do to help themselves enjoy poetry.

The writer also includes his own feelings and opinions about his explanations. The chart below shows one example. As you read, look for other passages that show the author's opinion.

Passage from the essay	How it shows the writer's feelings
When you really feel it, a new part of you happens, or an old part is renewed, with surprise and delight at being what it is.	The writer describes his surprise and delight in reading poetry.

READING STRATEGY

Recognizing the Organization

Writers organize their material in many different ways. These are some of the ways:

- chronological order—in the order in which events occur
- spatial order—in a specific physical order, left to right, for example
- order of importance—in a way that leads up to the most important point

Sometimes they use more than one method. For example, Dickey organizes his essay in sections that offer tips for enjoying poetry. At the same time, he uses order of importance by beginning with his most important ideas.

When you **recognize the organization** of an essay, you can more easily follow its main points. As you read, notice the section headings. They will give you clues about the main point of each section.

How to Enjoy Poetry

James Dickey

What is poetry? And why has it been around so long? Many have suspected that it was invented as a school subject, because you have to take exams on it. But that is not what poetry is or why it is still around. That's not what it feels like, either. When you really feel it, a new part of you happens, or an old part is renewed, with surprise and delight at being what it is.

◆ ◆ ◆

Where Poetry Is Coming From

From the beginning, people have known that words and things, words and actions, words and feelings, go together, and that they can go together in thousands of different ways, according to who is using them. Some ways go shallow, and some go deep.

◆ ◆ ◆

Your Connection With Other Imaginations

The first thing to understand about poetry is that it comes to you from outside you, in books or in words, but that for it to live, something from within you must come to it and meet it and complete it. Your response with your own mind and body and memory and emotions gives the poem its ability to work its magic; if you give to it, it will give to you, and give plenty.

When you read, don't let the poet write down to you; read up to him. Reach for him from your gut out, and the heart and muscles will come into it, too.

◆ ◆ ◆

Vocabulary Development

gut (guht) *n.* innermost self

◆ Literary Analysis

Mark the Text

Underline the sentence that shows how the writer feels about poetry.

◆ English Language Development

Mark the Text

In English, authors sometimes repeat words in phrases to create a pattern in their writing. For example, in "Where Poetry is Coming From," the phrase *words and* is repeated three times. Underline two more phrases that are repeated in this paragraph.

◆ Vocabulary and Pronunciation

Shallow means "not serious in thought or feeling." When poetry explores something in a "shallow" way, it focuses on things that are easily noticed. These things are also usually less important. Explain what it means to explore something in a "deep" way.

____

____

____

____

Which Sun? Whose Stars?

People living thousands of years ago saw the same sun and stars that you see now. Poetry can describe the sun and stars in different ways and from different perspectives. So poetry can make the sun and stars personal for each of us.

The poet Aldous Huxley[1] wrote about Orion,[2] a constellation of stars in the winter sky. His poem shows the personal emotion he felt when seeing it.

◆ ◆ ◆

Up from among the emblems of the
  wind into its heart of power,
The Huntsman climbs, and all his
  living stars
Are bright, and all are mine.

◆ ◆ ◆

Where to Start

To begin enjoying poetry, you should start with yourself. You should think and wonder about your own being. Then, you might think about something outside of yourself. For example, you might focus on the beauty of a rock or a leaf. Or, you might focus on the sun, the source of all living things.

"Start with the sun," D. H. Lawrence[3] said, "and everything will slowly, slowly happen."

◆ ◆ ◆

The Poem's Way of Going

Part of the spell of poetry is in the rhythm of language, used by poets who understand how

◆ Reading Strategy

Underline the main point of the bracketed section "Which Sun? Whose Stars?"

◆ Literary Analysis

In the section "Where to Start," what does Dickey explain?

____

____

____

____

◆ Reading Check

What does the writer say you need to do to begin enjoying poetry?

____

____

____

____

Vocabulary Development

spell (spel) *n.* magic
rhythm (RI thum) *n.* sound and beat

1. **Aldous Huxley:** English poet, essayist, and novelist (1894–1963).
2. **Orion** (oh RI un)
3. **D. H. Lawrence:** English poet and novelist (1885–1930).

powerful a factor rhythm can be, how compelling and unforgettable. Almost anything put into rhythm and rhyme is more memorable than the same thing said in prose. Why this is, no one knows completely, though the answer is surely rooted . . . in the circulation of the blood that goes forth from the heart and comes back, and in the repetition of breathing.

◆ ◆ ◆

Some Things You'll Find Out

You might like to try writing poetry. Limericks are fun to write. And you can write about any topic. The rhymes in limericks make the poem complete and memorable.

◆ ◆ ◆

How It Goes With You

Reading poetry helps you to look at your own life differently. You will see that your own life is full of words, images, and rhythms. You will look for meaning and you will help others look for meaning. You will make connections between things that you never made before.

Vocabulary Development

compelling (kuhm PEL ling) *adj.* attractive; appealing
prose (prohz) *n.* Nonpoetic language
limericks (LIM er iks) *n.* type of funny poem that has five rhyming lines

◆ English Language Development

Mark the Text

Many English adjectives have a comparative form to compare two things. Most short adjectives use *-er* for this form. Longer adjectives use the words *less* or *more.* For example: Bet is *faster* than Bill, but Bill is *more careful.* In the bracketed section circle an adjective in the comparative form.

◆ Stop to Reflect

Do you think that writing poetry has the same effect as reading poetry? Circle one:

Yes No

Explain your answer.

____

____

____

____

◆ Reading Check

Mark the Text

According to the author, how does poetry help you in your own life?

____

____

____

____

REVIEW AND ASSESS

1. What does Dickey say is "the first thing to understand about poetry"? Circle the letter of the correct answer.

   a) poetry is fun to read

   b) poetry is difficult to understand

   c) poetry comes to you from outside you and something from within you must meet it

2. Reread "Your Connection With Other Imaginations." Explain what it means to "give" to poetry?

   ____

   ____

   ____

   ____

3. Why are rhythm and rhyme important to poetry?

   ____

   ____

   ____

4. **Literary Analysis:** Write two things that Dickey explains to readers in the opening paragraphs of the essay.

   1.____

   2.____

5. **Reading Strategy:** List three main points that Dickey makes in the essay. List them in the order in which Dickey states them.

   1.____

   ____

2. ____

____

3. ____

____

Writing

Write a paragraph explaining an activity that you enjoy. Your goal is to make the reader want to try the activity. To begin, complete the chart below. Then, use the information in the chart to write your paragraph on a separate sheet of paper.

Name three activities that you enjoy. Circle the one you want to write about.	Activity:	Activity:	Activity:
Jot down three reasons why you enjoy the activity that you circled.	Reason 1:	Reason 2:	Reason 3:
Turn each reason into a complete sentence.	1. ____________________		
	2. ____________________		
	3. ____________________		

from An American Childhood

Annie Dillard

Summary

In *An American Childhood*, the author describes an experience from her childhood. She tells us about a winter morning, shortly after Christmas, when she and some neighborhood friends were throwing snowballs at passing cars. The driver of one car surprised the children by stopping. He got out and chased them on foot for ten blocks before finally catching up with them. Dillard is impressed that the driver chases them over such a long distance. The experience strengthens her belief that people should throw themselves into an activity with all their energy if they want to win. She wishes the excitement of the chase could last forever.

Visual Summary

The Chase

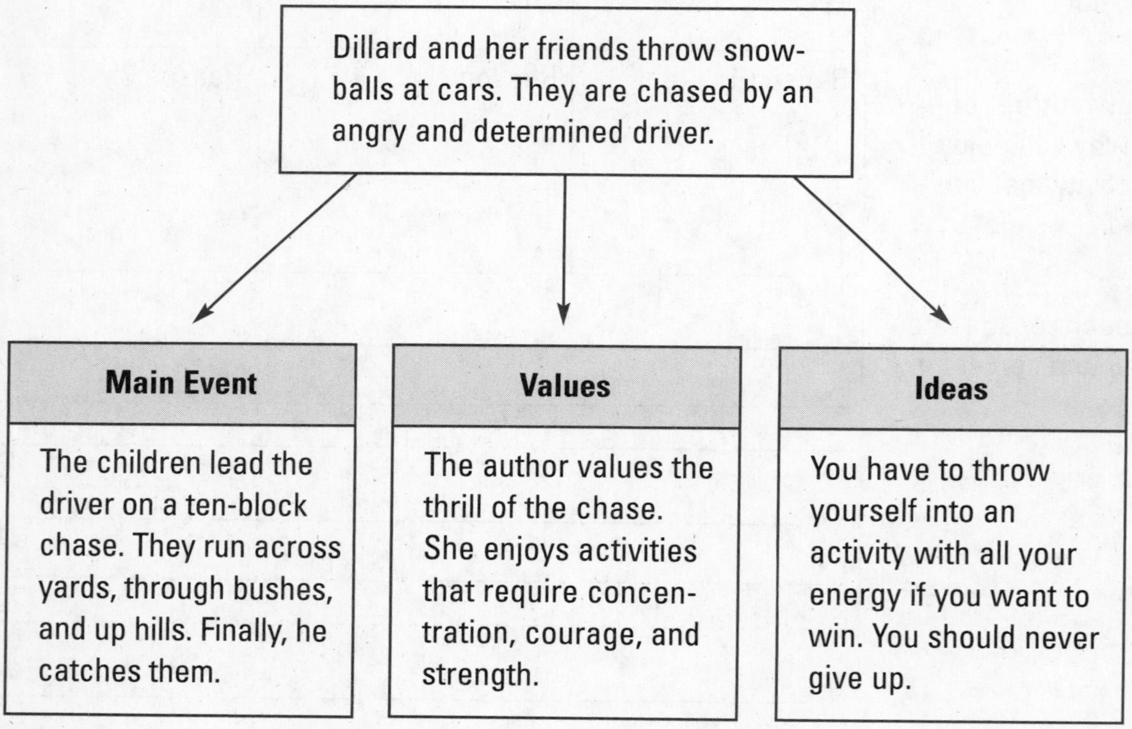

Dillard and her friends throw snowballs at cars. They are chased by an angry and determined driver.

Main Event	Values	Ideas
The children lead the driver on a ten-block chase. They run across yards, through bushes, and up hills. Finally, he catches them.	The author values the thrill of the chase. She enjoys activities that require concentration, courage, and strength.	You have to throw yourself into an activity with all your energy if you want to win. You should never give up.

PREPARE TO READ

LITERARY ANALYSIS

Autobiography

An **autobiography** is a person's life story written by that person. Autobiographies often show main events in the author's life. They also show the author's values, ideas, and struggles. For example, in *An American Childhood*, the author shows that she values a good challenge when she tells us how much she enjoys the chase. As you read, fill in the word web with other things that Dillard values.

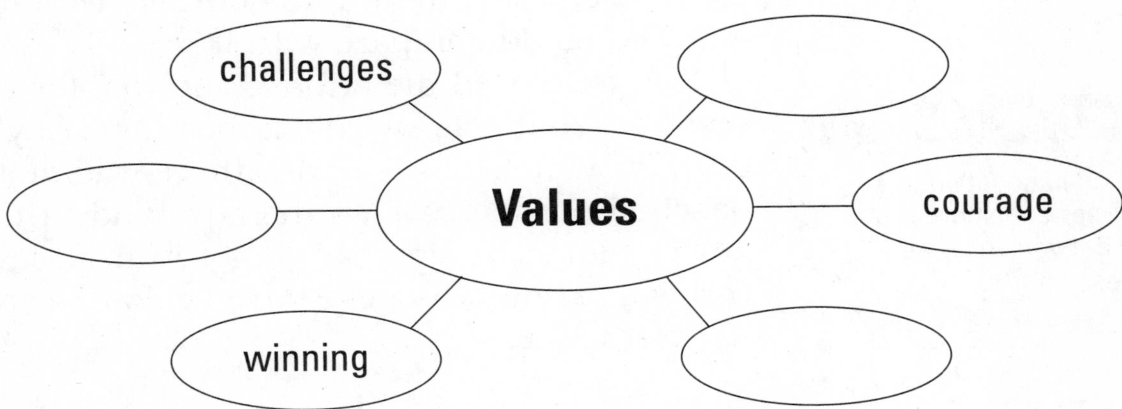

READING STRATEGY

Understanding the Author's Purpose

An **author's purpose** is his or her reason for writing. Authors who write autobiographies might write to entertain, teach a lesson, or explain themselves or their values. As the chart below shows, Annie Dillard has all three of these purposes for writing *An American Childhood*. As you read, look for passages that show each purpose.

Purpose	Example
To Entertain	Dillard amuses readers with an exciting and suspenseful account of the ten block chase.
To Teach	She shares a lesson about putting all of your energy into an activity in order to win.
To Explain	She explains something about herself by letting us know what qualities she values in herself and other people.

from An American Childhood

Annie Dillard

Some boys taught me to play football. This was fine sport. You thought up a new strategy for every play and whispered it to the others.

◆ ◆ ◆

Dillard also likes going out for a pass. Her favorite part of the game is tackling. She goes all out when she plays football.

◆ ◆ ◆

Your fate, and your team's score, depended on your concentration and courage. Nothing girls did could compare with it.

Boys welcomed me at baseball, too, for I had . . . what was weirdly known as a boy's arm. In winter, in the snow, there was neither baseball nor football, so the boys and I threw snowballs at passing cars. I got in trouble throwing snowballs, and have seldom been happier since.

◆ ◆ ◆

One winter morning when Dillard was seven, there was six inches of new snow. She and the boys waited for cars and pelted them with snowballs. Then, a black Buick came towards them. They spread out, aimed at the Buick, and threw.

◆ ◆ ◆

A soft snowball hit the driver's windshield right before the driver's face. It made a smashed star with a hump in the middle.

◆ ◆ ◆

Dillard and the others expected to hit the target—that's usually what happened when they threw snowballs. This time, it's different. The man stops the car and gets out. He leaves the car running, and he also leaves the door open.

◆ ◆ ◆

◆ English Language Development

Most verbs add *-ed* to form the past tense. For example: *whispered.* Verbs that do not follow this pattern are called irregular verbs. For example, the past tense of *teach* is *taught.* In the first paragraph, circle the past tense of the following irregular verb: *think.*

◆ Culture Note

Football and baseball are popular American sports. Explain what you know about one of these sports.

____

____

____

____

◆ Vocabulary and Pronunciation

Circle the words in the text that help you figure out the meaning of the word *pelted.* Write the meaning here:

____

____

____

____

He ran after us, and we ran away from him, up the snowy Reynolds sidewalk. At the corner, I looked back; incredibly, he was still after us. He was in city clothes: a suit and tie, street shoes. Any normal adult would have quit, having sprung us into flight and made his point. This man was gaining on us. He was a thin man, all action. All of a sudden, we were running for our lives.

♦ ♦ ♦

The group splits up. They are on their turf so they figure they can use what they know about the neighborhood to get away. Dillard sees Mikey Fahey heading around the corner of a house. She follows him. The man from the car picks the two of them to follow. He doesn't seem to have anywhere he has to be as he chases them.

The man chased Dillard and Mikey all over the neighborhood. They ran across yards, over driveways, up hills, through bushes, between houses, and across streets. Whenever Dillard looked back, the man was always there. She expected that he would eventually give up, but he didn't. Then she realized that the man knew the same thing she did: You have to throw yourself into an activity with all your energy if you want to win.

Dillard and Mikey kept running. Dillard felt cold and happy and scared all at the same time. After ten blocks, the man finally caught them by their jackets, and they all stopped.

♦ ♦ ♦

Vocabulary Development

turf (terf) *n.* an area considered to be under one's control

◆ Reading Strategy

Mark the Text

Circle the words in the bracketed paragraph that describe how the driver is dressed. What is Dillard's **purpose** in including this information?

◆ English Language Development

Mark the Text

Prepositions are words that show location or position. For example: *on* the table, *under* the table, *over* the table, *around* the table. Circle the prepositions in the underlined sentence.

◆ Stop to Reflect

Do you think the driver does the right thing by chasing the children? Circle your answer.

yes no

Why or why not?

◆ Literary Analysis

What does Dillard's view of the driver as a "hero" and her "excitement" tell you about her?

◆ Reading Strategy

Why does the author include details about the man's clothing after the chase?

◆ English Language Development

What does Dillard mean when she says the man "came down to earth"? Circle the letter of the correct answer. Explain your choice on the lines below.

(a) sat down on the ground

(b) calmed down and came back to reality

(c) returned from an outer space trip

We three stood there staggering, half blinded, coughing, in an obscure hilltop backyard: a man in his twenties, a boy, a girl. He had released our jackets, our pursuer, our captor, our hero: he knew we weren't going anywhere. We all played by the rules.

◆ ◆ ◆

There were tracks in the snow around them. Dillard and Mikey had been breaking new snow throughout their chase. They both unzipped their jackets. No one looked at anyone else. Dillard was cherishing her feeling of excitement at that point. The man's clothing and shoes showed signs of plowing through the snow—wet pants legs, cuffs full of snow, and his shoes and socks covered with snow. The three stand there with no one else around. They are the only players.

It's a long time before anyone can speak. Dillard, at first, can't even remember what has brought them here. Her lips, eyes, and lungs are feeling the effects of the chase.

◆ ◆ ◆

"You stupid kids," he began perfunctorily. We listened perfunctorily indeed, if we listened at all, for the chewing out was redundant, a mere formality, and beside the point. The point was that he chased us passionately without giving up, and so he had caught us. Now he came down to earth. I wanted the glory to last forever.

◆ ◆ ◆

Vocabulary Development

obscure (ahb SKYOOR) *adj.* difficult to see; isolated
cherishing (CHER ish ing) *v.* enjoying; valuing
perfunctorily (per FUNK tah rah lee) *adv.* without enthusiasm; routinely
redundant (ri DUN dent) *adj.* more than enough; not needed

But Dillard knew the glory couldn't last. Even if the man had chased them all over North America, the chase would have ended sometime. And he still would have called them stupid kids. She reflects that if the driver of the black Buick had cut off their heads, she would have died happy. That's because the chase in the snow required more of her than anything else ever has.

◆ Reading Check

What does Dillard feel was the most satisfying thing about her experience?

____

____

____

____

REVIEW AND ASSESS

1. Why does Dillard enjoy playing football?

____

____

2. Write two sentences to describe Dillard's personality.

   1.____

   ____

   2.____

   ____

3. **Literary Analysis:** How does the author feel about the man who catches them? Explain your answer.

____

____

____

____

4. **Reading Strategy;** Complete the chart by giving one passage that shows each purpose.

Passage that explains something about the author:	
Passage that entertains:	
Passage that teaches a lesson:	

Writing

Comparison-and-Contrast Paragraph

Follow the steps below to write a paragraph comparing and contrasting Annie Dillard with the man who chases her in *An American Childhood.*

1. Complete the Venn diagram to show the similarities and differences between Annie Dillard and the man.

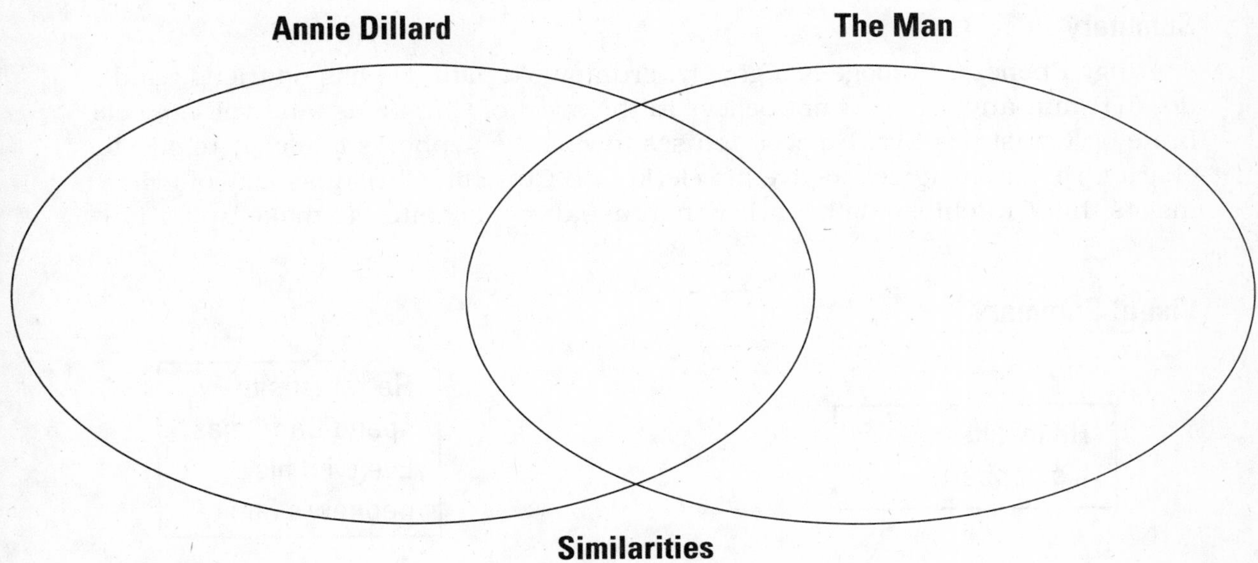

2. Use the information in the chart to write two sentences describing how they are similar.

3. Use the information in the chart to write two sentences describing how they are different.

4. Write your final draft on a separate sheet of paper.

PREVIEW

A Christmas Carol: Scrooge and Marley, Act 1, Scenes 1 and 2

Israel Horovitz

adapted from *A Christmas Carol* by Charles Dickens

Summary

Stingy Ebenezer Scrooge is a greedy, grumpy old man. He has no friends and doesn't want any. He does not believe in the spirit of Christmas, and will not celebrate on Christmas Eve. He even refuses to visit his nephew's family or to give to charity. He barely agrees to give his clerk, Bob Cratchit, Christmas Day off! He insists that Cratchit come in earlier than usual the day after, to make up for it.

Visual Summary

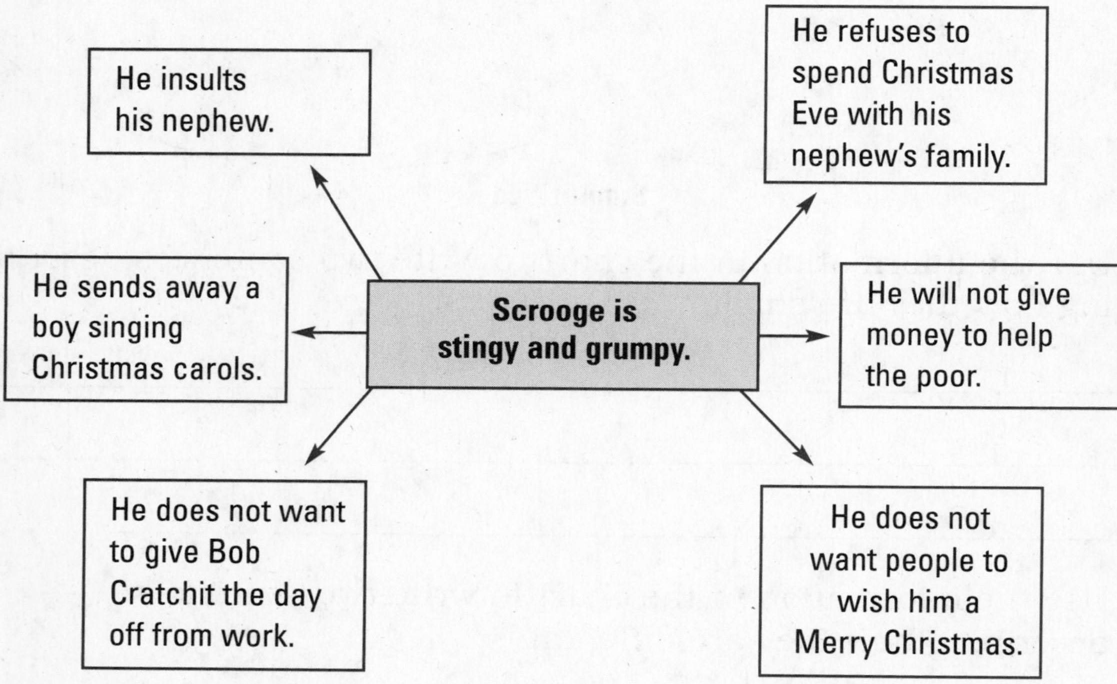

PREPARE TO READ

LITERARY ANALYSIS

Elements of Drama

In drama, characters reveal information about themselves through their actions and words. **Stage directions**, in square brackets, describe the setting. They also describe how the characters look, move, and speak. For example, the stage directions in the passage below show that Scrooge's nephew moves and speaks in a cheerful manner.

Example 1:

NEPHEW. [*Cheerfully; surprising SCROOGE*] A merry Christmas to you, Uncle! God save you!

READING STRATEGY

Picturing the Action

When you read drama, use descriptive details to create pictures in your mind. You will read those details in the stage directions and in the dialogue. Imagine the sights, sounds, and actions in each scene. When you **picture the action**, you increase your understanding of the play. You also make your reading experience more enjoyable and entertaining. To help yourself picture the action, draw a sketch of the stage in each scene. You can also jot down details that help you "see" each character. To do this, use this chart. Complete the chart as you read "A Christmas Carol."

Details About . . .	
MARLEY	
SCROOGE	
NEPHEW	cheerful, full of Christmas spirit, sneaks up on uncle
CRATCHIT	

A Christmas Carol: Scrooge and Marley, Act 1, Scenes 1 & 2

Israel Horovitz

adapted from *A Christmas Carol* by Charles Dickens

◆ **Reading Strategy**

To **picture the action** in this play, you will have to see Jacob Marley as a *specter*. A specter is a ghost. What do you think a specter looks like?

____

____

____

◆ **Vocabulary and Pronunciation**

Jocund (JAHK uhnd) means "cheerful." What word do you think is related to jocund. Circle the letter of the correct answer.

(a) Jack

(b) joke

(c) jog

(d) jock

THE PEOPLE OF THE PLAY

Jacob Marley, a specter
Ebenezer Scrooge, not yot dead, which is to say still alive
Bob Cratchit, Scrooge's clerk
Fred, Scrooge's nephew
Thin Do-Gooder
Portly Do-Gooder
Specters (Various), carrying money-boxes
The Ghost of Christmas Past
Four Jocund Travelers
A Band of Singers
A Band of Dancers
Little Boy Scrooge
Young Man Scrooge
Fan, Scrooge's little sister
The Schoolmaster
Schoolmates
Fezziwig, a fine and fair employer
Dick, young Scrooge's co-worker
Young Scrooge
A Fiddler
More Dancers
Scrooge's Lost Love
Scrooge's Lost Love's Daughter
Scrooge's Lost Love's Husband
The Ghost of Christmas Present
Some Bakers
Mrs. Cratchit, Bob Cratchit's wife
Belinda Cratchit, a daughter
Martha Cratchit, another daughter
Peter Cratchit, a son
Tiny Tim Cratchit, another son
Scrooge's Niece, Fred's wife
The Ghost of Christmas Future, a mute Phantom

Three Men of Business
Drunks, Scoundrels, Women of the Streets
A Charwoman
Mrs. Dilber
Joe, an old second-hand goods dealer
A Corpse, very like Scrooge
An Indebted Family
Adam, a young boy
A Poulterer
A Gentlewoman
Some More Men of Business

The action in these scenes takes place on Christmas Eve, 1843, in Ebenezer Scrooge's offices in London.

Scene 1

[Ghostly music in auditorium. A single spot light on JACOB MARLEY, D. C. He is ancient; awful, dead-eyed. He speaks straight out to auditorium.]

◆ ◆ ◆

MARLEY. [*Cackle-voiced*] My name is Jacob Marley and I am dead. [*He laughs.*] Oh, no, there's no doubt that I am dead. The register of my burial was signed by the clergyman, the clerk, the undertaker . . . and by my chief mourner . . . Ebenezer Scrooge . . . [*Pause; remembers*] I am dead as a doornail.

◆ ◆ ◆

Jacob Marley introduces Ebenezer Scrooge and says that Scrooge is a greedy old man. The audience sees Scrooge sitting in his office counting money. Scrooge cannot see Marley.

Marley tells the audience that he and Scrooge were business partners for many years. When Marley died, Scrooge was too stingy to remove Marley's name from the sign on their office. Scrooge has no friends. But he likes it that way.

◆ Vocabulary and Pronunciation

Poultry are animals raised for meat, such as chickens, turkeys, ducks, and geese. What do you think a *poulterer* does?

____

____

◆ Reading Check

On what night does the story take place?

____

◆ Vocabulary and Pronunciation

Stingy is pronounced (STIN jee). It is the opposite of generous. Circle the letter of the correct meaning.

(a) spending money freely

(b) spending money only when necessary

(c) giving money to orphans

◆ Reading Strategy

Circle all the details in Scene 1 that help you picture how Jacob Marley looks and sounds.

Marley tells the audience that it must watch to see what will happen to Scrooge. It is Christmas Eve and Scrooge is in his counting house. It's a bitterly cold night. Then Marley disappears.

Scene 2

This scene opens to the sound of Christmas music. Scrooge is sitting at his desk. His clerk, Bob Cratchit, is working in a cold and dark corner. He tries to warm himself. Scrooge's nephew enters, unseen.

◆ English Language Development

The expression *save your breath* means "don't bother talking." Underline the words in the paragraph that offer a clue to this meaning.

◆ ◆ ◆

SCROOGE. What are you doing, Cratchit? Acting cold, are you? Next, you'll be asking to replenish your coal from my coal-box, won't you? Well, save your breath, Cratchit! Unless you're prepared to find employ elsewhere!

◆ Reading Check

Why doesn't Scrooge think his nephew should be merry?

____

____

____

NEPHEW. [*Cheerfully; surprising SCROOGE*] A merry Christmas to you, Uncle! God save you!

SCROOGE. Bah! Humbug![1]

NEPHEW. Christmas a "humbug," Uncle? I'm sure you don't mean that.

SCROOGE. I do! Merry Christmas? What right do you have to be merry? What reason have you to be merry? You're poor enough!

◆ Vocabulary and Pronunciation

Writers sometimes offer clues to the meaning of unfamiliar words by using words with similar meanings nearby. Circle a word that has a similar meaning to *morose*.

NEPHEW. Come, then. What right have you to be dismal? What reason have you to be morose? You're rich enough.

Vocabulary Development

replenish (ri PLEN ish) *v.* to fill again
employ (em PLOY) *n.* work; a job
morose (muh ROHS) *adj.* gloomy; ill-tempered

1. **Humbug** (HUM BUG) *interj.* Nonsense!

SCROOGE. Bah! Humbug!

NEPHEW. Don't be cross, Uncle.

SCROOGE. What else can I be? Eh? When I live in a world of fools such as this? Merry Christmas? What's Christmastime to you but a time of paying bills without any money; a time for finding yourself a year older, but not an hour richer. If I could work my will, every idiot who goes about with "Merry Christmas" on his lips, should be boiled with his own pudding, and buried with a stake of holly through his heart. He should!

NEPHEW. Uncle!

SCROOGE. Nephew! You keep Christmas in your own way and let me keep it in mine.

NEPHEW. Keep it! But you don't keep it, Uncle.

SCROOGE. Let me leave it alone, then. Much good it has ever done you!

◆ ◆ ◆

Scrooge's nephew says that Christmas is the time when people open their hearts to each other. He invites Scrooge to eat with his family on Christmas. But Scrooge rudely refuses. He criticizes his nephew and Cratchit for having wives and children to support. After arguing, the nephew leaves.

Two kind men enter the office. They have come to ask Scrooge to give a donation for the poor and needy. Instead Scrooge tells the men that the prisons and workhouses are for the poor and needy. Both men are shocked at Scrooge's cold heart. Scrooge asks them to leave him alone and rudely returns to his desk. Bob Cratchit walks the men to the door and gives them a small amount of money as a donation.

◆ Literary Analysis

What phrase does Scrooge use several times that shows he is grumpy and rude?

____

◆ English Language Development

Mark the Text

Writers use exclamation marks to show strong emotion. Circle the exclamation marks in the bracketed passage. Then, read the dialogue aloud to show how Scrooge and his Nephew would speak it.

◆ Vocabulary and Pronunciation

Mark the Text

Circle the letter or letters in the word *nephew* that make the *f* sound. Then, in the paragraph that begins "Scrooge's nephew says," circle three other words that spell the *f* sound in a different way.

◆ English Language Development

On the lines below, write the meaning of the expression "the clock strikes six."

◆ Literary Analysis

Circle the stage directions that show how Cratchit responds when Scrooge says he should reduce his pay for missing work on Christmas Day.

◆ Reading Check

How many days off does Cratchit get each year?

◆ Reading Check

What does Cratchit want to say to Scrooge?

Why doesn't Scrooge want to hear it?

After the men leave, the clock strikes six and Cratchit prepares to go home.

◆ ◆ ◆

SCROOGE. Hmmm. Oh, you'll be wanting the whole day tomorrow, I suppose?

CRATCHIT. If quite convenient, sir.

SCROOGE. It's not convenient, and it's not fair. If I was to stop half-a-crown for it, you'd think yourself ill-used, I'll be bound?[2]

[*CRATCHIT smiles faintly.*]

CRATCHIT. I don't know, sir . . .

SCROOGE. And yet, you don't think me ill-used when I pay a day's wages for no work . . .

CRATCHIT. It's only but once a year . . .

SCROOGE. A poor excuse for picking a man's pocket every 25th of December! But I suppose you must have the whole day. Be here all the earlier the next morning!

CRATCHIT. Oh, I will, sir, I will. I promise you. And, sir . . .

SCROOGE. Don't say it, Cratchit.

CRATCHIT. But let me wish you a . . .

SCROOGE. Don't say it, Cratchit. I warn you . . .

◆ ◆ ◆

Cratchit leaves, saying "Merry Christmas" as he goes. A boy outside sings "Away in a Manger." Scrooge sends the boy away. Then he grumbles and turns off the lights.

---

2. **If I was to stop half-a-crown for it, you'd think yourself ill-used, I'll be bound?:** If I reduced your pay by half-a-crown for missing work, you'd think I had treated you poorly, wouldn't you?

[SCROOGE will walk alone to his rooms from his offices. As he makes a long slow cross of the stage, the scenery should change. Christmas music will be heard, various people will cross by SCROOGE, often smiling happily.

There will be occasional pleasant greetings tossed at him.

SCROOGE, in contrast to all, will grump and mumble. He will snap at passing boys, as might a horrid old hound . . . This statement of SCROOGE'S character, by contrast to all other characters, should seem comical to the audience. . . .]

◆ Reading Strategy

How does the scenery change when Scrooge leaves for his office?

____

____

____

◆ Literary Analysis

Use the stage directions to write a sentence comparing Scrooge to the other people in London.

____

____

____

REVIEW AND ASSESS

1. Who is Jacob Marley?

____

2. Where do Scenes 1 and 2 take place?

____

3. Why doesn't Scrooge want to give Bob Cratchit the whole day off on Christmas?

____

____

4. **Literary Analysis:** Give two examples of things Scrooge says and two examples of things he does that reveal his attitude towards Christmas.

Things Scrooge Says:

1. ____

____

2. ____

____

Things Scrooge Does:

1. ____

____

2. ____

____

5. **Reading Stategy:** In your own words, describe how you picture Scrooge as he walks from his offices to his rooms. How does he move? What are his facial expressions?
   - How he moves:

   ____

   ____

   ____

   - His facial expressions:

   ____

   ____

   ____

Listening and Speaking

In small groups, assign parts and then prepare and perform readings of scenes from *A Christmas Carol.*

- When you are assigned your role, read through your lines silently. Circle any words that you have trouble pronouncing. Ask your teacher to help you pronounce the words.
- Make sure that you understand the meaning of the lines you are to speak.
- Practice reading your lines aloud to yourself until you can read them smoothly. Then, read them and use the stage direcitons that are given for emotion and movement.
- Perform your scene for the rest of the class.

PREVIEW

A Christmas Carol: Scrooge and Marley, Act 1, Scenes 3, 4, and 5

Israel Horovitz

adapted from *A Christmas Carol* by Charles Dickens

Summary

At home on Christmas Eve, Scrooge is visited by the ghost of his dead business partner, Jacob Marley. The ghost warns Scrooge that he must be better to other people or he will end up a miserable, chain-dragging ghost like him. He tells Scrooge that three spirits will visit him during the next three nights. Then he disappears. Later, the Ghost of Christmas Past takes Scrooge back in time. Scrooge sees himself as a young schoolboy, an older schoolboy, and a young worker. Finally, he sees himself as a young man whose sweetheart leaves him because he thinks only about money. Scrooge becomes upset. He begins to regret the choices he has made in life. The ghost disappears, and Scrooge goes to sleep.

Visual Summary

Ideas	Evidence
Scrooge was not always a stingy, greedy, cold-hearted man.	As a young boy, he loved Christmas music even though he was lonely.
	As a 12-year-old, he loved his sister.
	As a young worker, he was happy with his friends and his boss.
	As a young man, he loved a young woman and planned to marry her.
Scrooge begins to regret the choices he has made in his life.	He wishes he had given something to the boy singing Christmas carols.
	He wishes he had treated Cratchit more kindly.
	He regrets that his greed caused the woman he loved to end their engagement.

PREPARE TO READ

LITERARY ANALYSIS

Elements of Drama

In drama, writers use action and dialogue to develop characters. They also use **stage directions** to describe each character's actions and appearance. Stage directions are not meant to be spoken. They give instructions about what is happening on the stage.

As you read Act I, Scenes 3–5 of *A Christmas Carol*, look for new information about Scrooge. Analyze his actions, his words, and the information in the stage directions. Use this information to complete the chart below.

New Information About Scrooge:
• Scrooge tries to ignore things he doesn't understand. • He is afraid of ghosts. • As a young boy, he was lonely

READING STRATEGY

Picturing the Action

Reading drama is like watching a movie in your head. As you read, **picture the action** so that it becomes real to you. Use the stage directions to help you see what is happening. For example, in the passage below, the Ghost of Christmas Past commands Scrooge to fly:

> **PAST.** [*Motioning to* SCROOGE *and taking his arm*] Rise! Fly with me! [*He leads* SCROOGE *to the window.*]
>
> **SCROOGE.** [*Panicked*] Fly, but I am a mortal and cannot fly!

The stage directions tell you that Scrooge panics. Bring this event to life by picturing *how* he panics. Does he stop walking? jerk his arm away? What are his facial expressions? Does his voice squeak when he talks?

A Christmas Carol: Scrooge and Marley, Act 1, Scenes 3–5

Israel Horovitz

adapted from *A Christmas Carol* by Charles Dickens

◆ Vocabulary and Pronunciation

The meaning of the prefix *dis-* is "to fail or stop." The word *appear* means "to come into sight or existence." Circle the prefix in the word *disappear*. Then, complete this sentence: When something disappears, it

____

◆ Reading Check

What does Scrooge see that startles him?

____

____

____

◆ Reading Strategy

Circle all the details that help you picture Marley's Ghost.

Mark the Text

Scene 3

Scrooge arrives home. As he unlocks his door, the door knocker changes into Marley's face. Scrooge is startled. Then, the face disappears. When Scrooge gets inside, he goes through the house looking to see if anyone is there. The pictures on the walls show Marley's face. Then, all the bells in the house begin to ring. Scrooge hears a loud chain dragging across his basement floor and up the stairs. He hears doors fly open. He refuses to believe these things are happening.

[MARLEY'S GHOST enters the room. He is horrible to look at: pigtail, vest, suit as usual, but he drags an enormous chain now, to which is fastened cash-boxes, keys, padlocks, ledgers, deeds, and heavy purses fashioned of steel. He is transparent. MARLEY stands opposite the stricken SCROOGE.]

◆ ◆ ◆

SCROOGE. Who are you?

MARLEY. Ask me who I *was*.

SCROOGE. Who *were* you then?

MARLEY. In life, I was your business partner: Jacob Marley.

SCROOGE. I see . . . can you sit down?

MARLEY. I can.

SCROOGE. Do it then.

MARLEY. I shall. [MARLEY *sits opposite* SCROOGE, *in the chair across the table, at the front of the fireplace.*] You don't believe in me.

SCROOGE. I don't.

◆ ◆ ◆

Marley screams a ghostly scream and removes his head from his shoulders. This convinces Scrooge that he is real. Marley says that he continues to walk the earth as a ghost because he did not care for other people during his life. He is forced to carry the chain because he cared too much for business and money.

Scrooge is frightened that a chain will appear around his body, but Marley cannot comfort him. However, he warns Scrooge that he has a chance to save himself. He tells him he will be haunted by Three Spirits. They are Scrooge's only hope. If he does not listen to the spirits, he will end up like Marley.

After Marley's Ghost leaves, Scrooge wonders if he imagined the whole thing.

Scene 4

Marley's Ghost appears to the audience. It tells them that they are going to witness a change in Scrooge.

A bell rings and Scrooge is awakened from his sleep. He sees a hand drawing back the curtains. A figure stands in front of Scrooge. It looks like both a child and an old man. It is the Spirit called PAST.

◆ ◆ ◆

SCROOGE. Who, and what are you?

PAST. I am the Ghost of Christmas Past.

SCROOGE. Long past?

PAST. Your past.

◆ Literary Analysis

Draw a sketch of the scene with Scrooge and Marley sitting in front of the fireplace.

◆ Culture Note

Marley and Scrooge spent much of their lives focusing on money. In the United States, money is measured in dollars and cents. How is money measured in your native land?

____

____

____

◆ Reading Check

How does Marley convince Scrooge that he is real?

____

____

____

◆ Stop to Reflect

How was Marley similar to Scrooge when he was alive?

____

____

____

◆ **Vocabulary and Pronunciation**

In the name *Scrooge*, the /oo/ sound is spelled *oo*. In the passage that begins "Not to sound ungrateful . . . ," circle two words in which the /oo/ sound is spelled differently.

Mark the Text

◆ **Literary Analysis**

Circle the word that describes how Scrooge feels after the Ghost of Christmas Past tells him to fly. Read his response aloud as he would say it.

Mark the Text

◆ **English Language Development**

Adjectives usually come before the nouns they describe. However, sometimes they follow a linking verb. For example: The air was *cold*. Circle all the adjectives in the stage directions for Scene 5. Which adjective follows a linking verb?

Mark the Text

SCROOGE. May I ask, please, sir, what business you have here with me?

PAST. Your welfare.

SCROOGE. Not to sound ungrateful, sir, and really, please do understand that I am plenty obliged for your concern, but, really, kind spirit, it would have done all the better for my welfare to have been left alone altogether, to have slept peacefully through this night.

PAST. Your reclamation, then. Take heed!

SCROOGE. My what?

PAST. [*Motioning to* SCROOGE *and taking his arm*] Rise! Fly with me! [*He leads* SCROOGE *to the window.*]

SCROOGE. [*Panicked*] Fly, but I am a mortal and cannot fly!

PAST. [*Pointing to his heart*] Bear but a touch of my hand here and you shall be upheld in more than this!

◆ ◆ ◆

[SCROOGE touches the spirit's heart and the lights dissolve into sparkly flickers. Lovely crystals of music are heard. The scene dissolves into another. Christmas music again.]

Scene 5

[SCROOGE and the GHOST OF CHRISTMAS PAST walk together across an open stage. In the background, we see a field that is open; covered by a soft, downy snow: a country road.]

Vocabulary Development

reclamation (REK luh MAY shun) *n.* reclaiming; rescuing or bringing something back

heed (HEED) *n.* attention or warning

mortal (MOR tul) *n.* a human being

SCROOGE. Good Heaven! I was bred in this place. I was a boy here!

◆ ◆ ◆

The Ghost of Christmas Past notices that Scrooge is crying. Four men pass by singing a Christmas carol. Scrooge remembers the beauty of the song. The Ghost is surprised that Scrooge has happy memories of Christmas.

Then they see a boy weeping in a schoolhouse. It is the young Scrooge, all alone. The real Scrooge sobs and says the little boy was very lonely. He thinks of the young caroler whom he shooed away from his office earlier that night. He says he wishes he had given him something. The Ghost smiles and takes Scrooge to another past Christmas.

This time, Scrooge is twelve. He is at the school where he lives with a harsh teacher. His six-year old sister Fan comes to take him home for Christmas. The real Scrooge says he loved his little sister very much. In real life, she is dead. But she had one child, Scrooge's nephew.

Next, the Ghost and Scrooge go to a warehouse where Scrooge worked as a young man. He sees his former boss and coworkers. They are dancing and playing music on Christmas Eve. The young Scrooge and his friends talk fondly of their boss. The real Scrooge regrets that he hasn't been kinder to his own employee, Bob Cratchit.

◆ ◆ ◆

[In a flash of light, EBENEZER is gone, and in his place stands an OLDER SCROOGE, this one a man in the prime of his life. Beside him stands a young woman in a mourning dress. She is crying. She speaks to the man, with hostility.]

◆ English Language Development

Mark the Text

The present participle form of a verb ends in *-ing* and describes an ongoing action. Circle five present participles in these four paragraphs.

◆ Reading Check

Who does Scrooge think about when he sees himself with his former boss and coworkers?

___

What does he wish?

___

___

◆ Reading Strategy

How do the stage directions that begin "In a flash of light . . . ," help you picture what is happening in the play?

___

___

___

◆ **Reading Check**

What is the golden idol that has taken the young woman's place in the young Scrooge's heart?

____

____

____

◆ **Reading Check**

Restate the underlined passage by completing the following sentences:

The world is hard on people who

____

____

______________________________.

It punishes people who

____

____

______________________________.

◆ **English Language Development**

Many English adjectives have a comparative form to compare two things. Most short adjectives use *-er* for this form. For example: She runs *faster* than he does. In the bracketed passage, circle two adjectives in the comparative form.

Mark the Text

WOMAN. It matters little . . . to you, very little. Another idol has displaced me.

MAN. What idol has displaced you?

WOMAN. A golden one.

MAN. This is an even-handed dealing of the world. There is nothing on which it is so hard as poverty; and there is nothing it professes to condemn with such severity as the pursuit of wealth!

WOMAN. You fear the world too much. Have I not seen your nobler aspirations fall off one by one, until the master-passion, Gain, engrosses you? Have I not?

SCROOGE. No!

MAN. What then? Even if I have grown so much wiser, what then? Have I changed towards you?

WOMAN. No . . .

MAN. Am I?

WOMAN. Our contract is an old one. It was made when we were both poor and content to be so. You *are* changed. When it was made, you were another man.

MAN. I was not another man: I was a boy.

WOMAN. Your own feeling tells you that you were not what you are. I am. That which promised happiness when we were one in heart is fraught with misery now that we are two . . .

SCROOGE. No!

Vocabulary Development

aspirations (AS puh RAY shuns) *n.* goals

WOMAN. How often and how keenly have I thought of this, I will not say. It is enough that I *have* thought of it, and can release you . . .

SCROOGE. [*Quietly*] Don't release me, madam . . .

MAN. Have I ever sought release?

WOMAN. In words. No. Never.

MAN. In what then?

WOMAN. In a changed nature; in an altered spirit. In everything that made my love of any worth or value in your sight. If this has never been between us, tell me, would you seek me out and try to win me now? Ah, no!

◆ ◆ ◆

The woman leaves the man, telling him to be happy in the life he has chosen. The real Scrooge cries out as she leaves. He begs the Spirit to take him away. In a flash of light, the Spirit is gone and Scrooge is back in his bedroom. Marley's Ghost appears again to tell the audience that Scrooge must sleep. He still has to meet Christmas Present and Christmas Future.

◆ Reading Check

What is the woman releasing the young Scrooge from?

____

____

____

◆ Vocabulary and Pronunciation

The *ch* sound as in *chair* can be spelled in many ways. In the woman's final passage, underline the words *changed* and *nature*. Circle the letters in each word that make the *ch* sound.

◆ Reading Check

Complete this timeline of the major events in Scenes 3–5

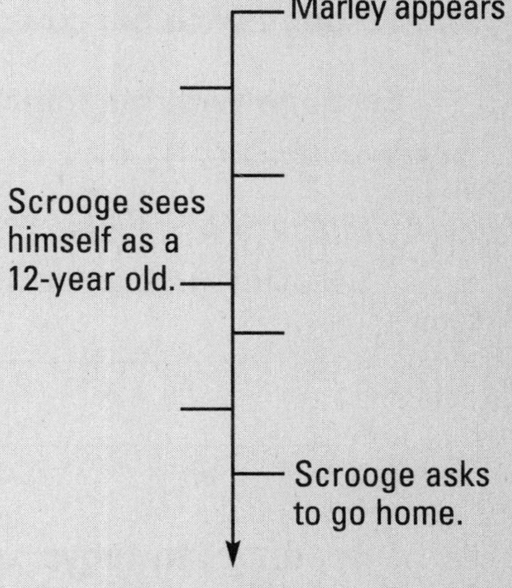

REVIEW AND ASSESS

1. Why must Marley's ghost carry a chain full of cash-boxes, keys, padlocks, ledgers, deeds, and heavy purses?

____

____

2. Who visits Scrooge after Marley leaves?

____

3. Complete the chart by describing how Scrooge responds to each of the past Christmases he visits.

Past Christmases	
Scrooge as a young boy: **Scrooge as a twelve-year-old boy:** **Scrooge with his coworkers:** **Scrooge with his fiancée:**	

4. **Literary Analysis:** List two new things you learned about Scrooge through his actions and dialogue.

   1. ____

   2. ____

5. **Reading Strategy:** In your own words, describe how Scrooge responds when the Ghost of Christmas Past tells him to fly.

____

____

Writing

Pretend that you are a drama critic for a newspaper. You have just seen a production of *A Christmas Carol*. Write a review of Act 1 of *A Christmas Carol*.

Answer the following questions to help you with your review.

- Write three things that you liked about the play.

___

___

___

- Write three things that you disliked about the play.

___

___

___

- Who is your favorite character? Explain why.

___

___

- Which character did you like the least? Explain why.

___

___

Now write a paragraph summarizing the answers to the questions. Conclude your paragraph by telling your readers whether you think they should see the play or not. Then, explain why you do or do not recommend the play.

___

___

___

The Cremation of Sam McGee

Robert Service

Summary

"The Cremation of Sam McGee" is the story of a Tennessee miner who hated the cold. Still, he joined the gold rush in northern Canada, where it is extremely cold. He knew he couldn't survive the cold, so he asked the narrator to cremate him when he died. When Sam dies from the cold, the narrator travels across the frozen landscape with Sam's corpse to find a place to cremate him. On a frozen lake, he finds an abandoned ship. He attempts to cremate Sam's body in the ship's furnace, but when the corpse is warmed by the fire, Sam comes back to life!

Visual Summary

Sequence of Events					
1. →	2. →	3. →	4. →	5. →	6.
Sam McGee and miners are working in northern Canada.	McGee asks narrator to cremate him when he dies.	McGee dies.	Narrator carries the body on the sleigh to find a place to cremate him.	Narrator attempts to cremate the body.	When narrator checks on the cremation, Sam McGee is alive in the fire.

PREPARE TO READ

LITERARY ANALYSIS

Types of Poetry

Poetry comes in different forms. "The Cremation of Sam McGee" is a **narrative poem**. Narrative poems tell stories. Like other poems, they also use rhythm, rhyme, and repetition.

- Narrative poems tell a story using characters, setting, and plot events.

Characters:	Sam McGee, the narrator who tells the story
Setting:	the Arctic
Plot events:	1. Sam McGee and the narrator search for gold in the Arctic. 2. Sam dies of the cold. 3. The narrator searches for a place to burn Sam's dead body. 4. He burns it in an old ship's furnace. 5. When he checks the furnace, he discovers that the heat has revived Sam.

- Narrative poems may use rhythm. In this line, notice the strong beat:

  Well he seemed so low that I couldn't say no

- Narrative poems may also use repetition. Repetition is the repeated use of words or lines.

READING STRATEGY

Interpreting Figures of Speech

A **figure of speech** is a creative way of expressing an idea. Usually a figure of speech makes a comparison between two things that are not alike. This chart shows common figures of speech.

Figure of speech	**Explanation**	**Example**
Simile (SIM uh lee)	A comparison using *like* or *as*	"the cold stabbed *like* a driven nail"
Hyperbole (hī PER buh lee)	exaggeration	"a smile you could see a mile"
Personification (per SAHN uh fi CAY shun)	giving something human qualities	"the stars . . . were dancing heel and toe"

The Cremation of Sam McGee

Robert Service

The narrator begins by saying that gold miners in the Arctic have many strange stories to tell. But the strangest thing the miners ever saw was the cremation of Sam McGee.

Sam McGee was from Tennessee, where the weather was warm. But he wanted to get rich, so he traveled to the North Pole to find gold. One Christmas Day, the miners walked through cold so bitter their eyelashes froze.

◆ ◆ ◆

Talk of your cold! through the parka's fold
it stabbed like a driven nail.
If our eyes we'd close, then the lashes froze
Til sometimes we couldn't see;
It wasn't much fun, but the only one
to whimper was Sam McGee.

◆ ◆ ◆

Sam McGee was miserable. That night he told the narrator he was going to die. But he had one final request.

◆ ◆ ◆

Well, he seemed so low that I couldn't say no;
Then he says with a sort of moan:
"It's the cursed cold, and it's got right hold
till I'm chilled clean through to the bone.
Yet 'tain't being dead—it's my awful dread
of the icy grave that pains;
So I want you to swear that, foul or fair,
you'll cremate my last remains."

Vocabulary Development

cremation (cree MAY shun) *n.* the burning of a dead body into ashes

whimper (HWIM per) *v.* make low, crying sounds; complain

◆ Culture Note

When gold was found in the North, many people rushed there to try to get rich. This was known as the "Gold Rush." Sam McGee and the narrator are in the North Pole during this Gold Rush.

◆ Reading Strategy

Underline the simile in the bracketed lines. Then tell what two things are being compared.

____

____

____

◆ Reading Check

Why was Sam McGee so miserable?

____

____

____

◆ Reading Strategy

Circle the **hyperbole** in this sentence.

◆ Reading Check

Look at the words around the phrase *last remains*. What do you think the phrase *last remains* means?

____

____

____

A pal's last need is a thing to heed,
so I swore I would not fail;
And we started on at the streak of dawn;
but God! he looked ghastly pale.
He crouched on the sleigh, and he raved all day
of his home in Tennessee;
And before nightfall a corpse was all
that was left of Sam McGee.

◆ ◆ ◆

The frightened narrator carried McGee's body on the sleigh. He had promised to cremate the body, and he was going to keep his promise. The next days were hard as he carried the body over the freezing land.

Finally the narrator came to the edge of a lake. He saw an old ship there. He took boards from the ship and lit a fire in the furnace. When it was hot, he pushed Sam McGee's body inside. Then he took a walk to get away from the sound of the burning body.

◆ ◆ ◆

I do not know how long in the snow
I wrestled with grisly fear;
But the stars came out and they danced about
ere again I ventured near;
I was sick with dread, but I bravely said:
"I'll just take a peep inside.
I guess he's cooked, and it's time I looked"; . . .
then the door I opened wide.

Vocabulary Development

ghastly (GAST lee) *adj.* ghostlike, frightful
grisly (GRIZ lee) *adj.* horrible

◆ Literary Analysis

In this part of the narrative poem, what happens to Sam McGee?

____

____

____

◆ Stop to Reflect

What do you think will happen in the rest of the poem?

____

____

____

____

____

◆ Literary Analysis

Mark the Text

Circle *snow*. Then, circle the word that rhymes with *snow*. Draw a box around *fear*. Then, draw a box around the word that rhymes with *fear*. Find and mark *out*, *dread*, *cooked*, and *wide*. For each, draw an arrow to the rhyming word.

◆ Literary Analysis

Check which of the following elements of a narrative poem are shown in the bracketed lines:

______ Character

______ Setting

______ Plot

Explain your answer.

____

____

____

____

____

And there sat Sam, looking cool and calm,
in the heart of the furnace roar:
And he wore a smile you could see a mile,
and he said, "Please close that door.
It's fine in here, but I greatly fear
you'll let in the cold and storm—
Since I left Plumtree, down in Tennessee,
it's the first time I've been warm."

◆ ◆ ◆

At the end of the poem, the narrator repeats the ideas from the beginning of the poem. He says the gold miners in the Arctic have many strange stories to tell. The narrator ends by saying that no story is stranger than the story of Sam McGee.

REVIEW AND ASSESS

1. Complete this sentence: Sam McGee thinks the weather in the Arctic is ______________________________.

2. Why doesn't Sam go home?

____

____

____

3. What does the narrator promise Sam McGee?

____

____

4. Why is the narrator determined to keep his promise?

____

____

5. What did the narrator find when he opened the door to the furnace?

____

____

____

6. **Literary Analysis:** Give examples from the poem of the following features of a narrative poem:

   - **a setting** (the time and place the events of a story occurs)

   ____

   - **characters** (the people in a story) ______________________________

   ____

   - **rhythm** (a strong beat) ______________________________

   ____

(Continued)

7. **Reading Strategy:** Look at the following examples of figures of speech. For each, explain what the comparison means.

Figure of speech	Example	What it means
simile	the cold stabbed like a driven nail	
hyperbole	he wore a smile you could see a mile	
personification	I wrestled with fear	

Writing

Write a paragraph to introduce "The Cremation of Sam McGee" to a friend. In your writing, point out two or three things you liked and that you think make the poem effective. You could mention the story, the rhythm, the rhyme, or the language.

- Use the chart below to list your ideas

What I like	Why it makes the poem effective

- Then write your final paragraph on another piece of paper

Annabel Lee

Edgar Allan Poe

Summary

The poem "Annabel Lee" tells of the deep love between the young man who tells the poem and Annabel Lee. Annabel Lee is a young woman who lives by the sea. When Annabel Lee dies from a chill, her lover grieves over her death. Still, he believes that their love is so deep that their souls are never truly separated.

Visual Summary

Setting	What Happens
• "kingdom by the sea" • "tomb by the sea"	• "The angels... / Went envying her and me" • "...the wind came out of a cloud, chilling / And killing my Annabel Lee" • "... the moon [brings] me dreams / Of the beautiful Annabel Lee" • "... I lie down by the side / Of my darling, my darling, my life and my bride... / In her tomb by the side of the sea."

PREPARE TO READ

LITERARY ANALYSIS

Rhythm and Rhyme

Rhythm in a poem is its beat: the pattern of stressed and unstressed sounds. Read the following lines aloud. To hear the rhythm, stress the words or syllables in dark type.

For the **moon** never **beams** without **bring**ing me **dreams**
Of the **beau**tiful **Ann**abel **Lee**;

Rhyme is the repetition of end sounds in words. The words *me, sea,* and *Lee* rhyme. Poets often use rhyme at the end of lines. Sometimes they use rhyme within lines, as well. For example, in the line above, the words *beams* and *dreams* rhyme.

Use this chart to record the rhyming words at the end of lines in "Annabel Lee."

Stanza 1	
Stanza 2	
Stanza 3	

READING STRATEGY

Paraphrasing

Paraphrasing means restating an idea in your own words. You can do this to understand lines that may be confusing. Look at the example in the chart below. You can use this chart to paraphrase lines from the poem as you read.

Lines from poem	Paraphrase
"For the moon never beams without bringing me dreams Of the beautiful Annabel Lee"	The moon always reminds me of Annabel Lee.

Annabel Lee

Edgar Allan Poe

The narrator tells about his love for the young woman Annabel Lee. They lived by the sea when they were very young. They loved each other so much that the angels in heaven were jealous of them. But one night a cold wind chilled Annabel Lee, and she died.

◆ ◆ ◆

The angels, not half so happy in Heaven,
Went envying her and me:—
Yes! that was the reason (as all men know,
In this kingdom by the sea)
That the wind came out of a cloud, chilling
And killing my Annabel Lee.

But our love it was stronger by far than the love
Of those who were older than we—
Of many far wiser than we—
And neither the angels in Heaven above
Nor the demons down under the sea,
Can ever dissever my soul from the soul
Of the beautiful Annabel Lee:—

For the moon never beams without bringing me dreams
Of the beautiful Annabel Lee;
And the stars never rise but I see the bright eyes
Of the beautiful Annabel Lee;

Vocabulary Development

dissever (di SEV er) *v.* separate

◆ Reading Check

How did Annabel Lee die?

____

____

◆ Literary Analysis

Circle the **rhyming words** in this stanza.

____

____

____

____

◆ English Language Development

The comparative form of an adjective compares two things:

"our love was *stronger* . . . than the love of those . . ."

Most short adjectives add *–er* to make the comparative form. Circle two other comparative adjectives in the bracketed section.

◆ Literary Analysis

Read the bracketed lines aloud to hear the **rhythm**. Put emphasis on the underlined words or syllables.

◆ Reading Strategy

Paraphrase these bracketed lines.

____

____

____

____

____

◆ Stop to Reflect

Write three words to describe what the narrator's life was like after the death of Annabel Lee.

1. ______________________________
2. ______________________________
3. ______________________________

And so, all the nighttide, I lie down by the side
Of my darling, my darling, my life and my bride,
In her sepulcher there by the sea—
In her tomb by the side of the sea.

Vocabulary Development

nighttide (NĪT TĪD) *n.* nighttime
sepulcher (SEP uhl ker) *n.* vault for burial; grave; tomb

REVIEW AND ASSESS

1. Whom does the narrator blame for Annabel Lee's death?

____

Explain your answer.

____

____

____

2. Why does the narrator talk about the sea?

____

____

____

3. **Literary Analysis:** Underline the words to stress to create the rhythm in these lines:

But our love it was stronger by far than the love
Of those who were older than we—
Of many far wiser than we—

4. **Literary Analysis:** Record four sets of rhyming words in the final stanza.

Set #1	Set #2	Set #3	Set #4

5. **Reading Strategy:** Paraphrase the final stanza of the poem.

Writing

Different readers respond to a poem in different ways. Write a paragraph about your response to "Annabel Lee." To begin, fill in the following chart. In it, write two things that you noticed about rhyme, rhythm, and meaning.

Rhyme	Rhythm	Meaning
1. 2.	1. 2.	1. 2.

Draft your paragraph on the lines below. On your own paper, write your final paragraph.

PREVIEW

Maestro

Pat Mora

Summary

In "Maestro," a great musician plays the violin in concert. As he bows before an audience, he recalls the sound of his mother's voice and his father's guitar. When the audience applauds, he hears the music he and his parents played together at home.

Visual Summary

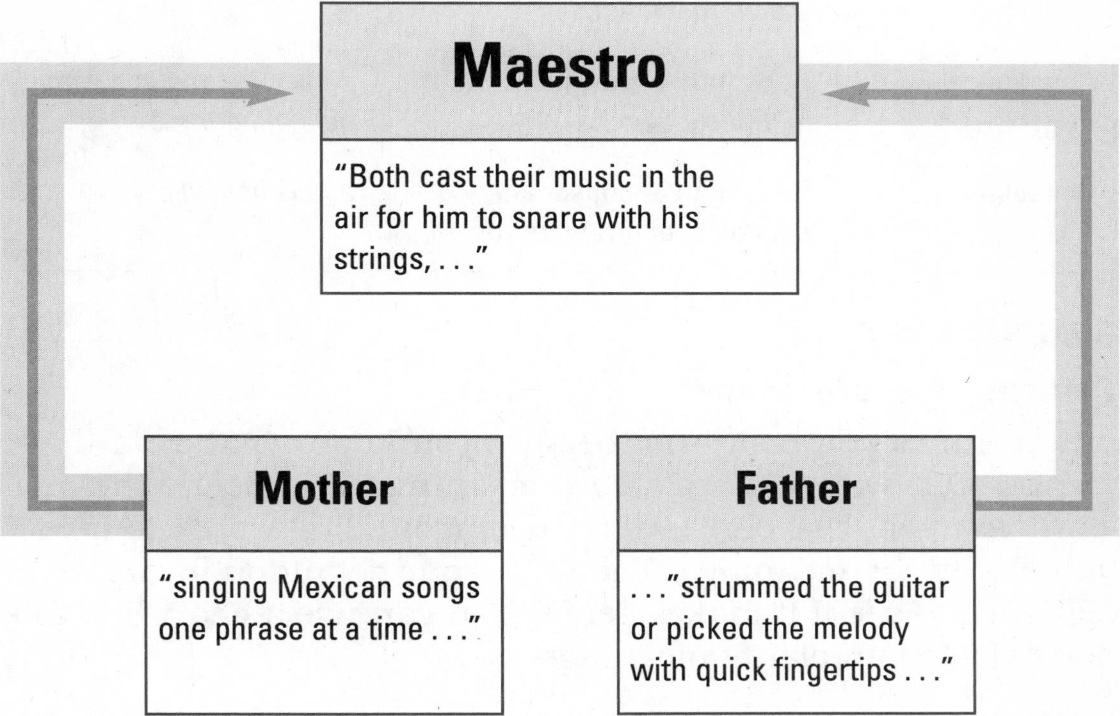

PREPARE TO READ

LITERARY ANALYSIS

Sound Devices

Poetry uses **sound devices** that make the words pleasant to hear. Rhyme is one sound device. Words that rhyme have the same ending. For example *hat* and *bat* rhyme. The following chart shows other sound devices.

Sound Device	Explanation	Example
Onomatopoeia	A word that sounds like the word it means	*strummed*
Assonance	Repetition of vowel sounds in different words	*picked the melody with quick fingertips*
Consonance	Repetition of consonant sounds in different words	*as his bow slid*

READING STRATEGY

Clarifying Word Meanings

Sometimes you might not be sure you know what a word means. One way to **clarify word meanings** is to define the word yourself. Use clues from the surrounding words to help you clarify the meanings. Then use your definition in the sentence to see if it makes sense. You can use a chart like this one to help you clarify meanings.

Unclear Word	Clues that Help Clarify	Clarified Meaning
strummed	"his father strummed the guitar" "with quick fingertips"	Strumming is a way to move your fingers over guitar strings.

Maestro

Pat Mora

In this poem a grown man remembers his childhood. An audience claps for his violin-playing. He is reminded of the Mexican music in his home when he was young. The music of his youth was his inspiration.

◆ ◆ ◆

He hears her
when he bows.
Rows of hands clap
again and again he bows
to stage lights and upturned faces
but he hears only his mother's voice

years ago in their small home
singing Mexican songs
one phrase at a time
while his father strummed the guitar
or picked the melody with quick fingertips.
Both cast their music in the air
For him to snare with his strings,
songs of *lunas*[1] and *amor*[2]
learned bit by bit.
She'd nod, smile, as his bow slid
note to note, then the trio
voz,[3] *guitarra*,[4] *violín*[5]
would blend again and again
to the last pure note
sweet on the tongue.

Vocabulary Development

maestro (MĪS troh) *n.* great musician
snare (SNAYR) *v.* catch or trap

1. **lunas** (LOO nas) *n.* Spanish for "moon."
2. **amor** (ah MOHR) *n.* Spanish for "love."
3. **voz** (VOHS) *n.* Spanish for "voice."
4. **guitarra** (gee TAHR uh) *n.* Spanish for "guitar."
5. **violín** (vee oh LEEN) *n.* Spanish for "violin."

◆ Vocabulary and Pronunciation

Bow has two meanings and pronunciations:

1. When is it pronounced "BOW," it means "to bend forward at the waist."
2. When it is pronounced "BOH," it means the tool used to play the violin.

Mark THE Text

Which meaning is used in line 2?

____

____

Find and circle the place in this poem where *bow* has the other meaning and use.

◆ Reading Strategy

Clarify the meaning of *upturned*. Draw a line between the two parts. Then switch the order of the parts, and write them here.

____

◆ Stop to Reflect

How can a musical note be sweet on the tongue? Explain.

____

____

____

____

____

REVIEW AND ASSESS

1. What is the trio that the poet describes?

____

____

2. Write three words to describe the maestro's feelings about his childhood.

   1. ____

   2. ____

   3. ____

3. **Literary Analysis:** Circle the word in this quotation that sounds like the thing it describes:

   "while his father strummed the guitar."

4. **Reading Strategy:** Clarify the meaning of *cast* as it is used in these lines in the poem:

   Both cast their music in the air

   For him to snare with his strings, . . .

Unclear Word	Clues that Help Clarify	Clarified Meaning
cast		

Writing

Write a paragraph about the Maestro's childhood. Go back to the poem and reread the lines beginning "years ago . . ."

1. In your own words, describe what happened during those years.

____

____

____

- What did he learn from his mother? You can answer using words from the poem.

____

____

- What did he learn from his father? You can answer using words from the poem.

____

____

2. How did those years influence his adult life?

____

____

____

On another piece of paper, put all your ideas together in one paragraph.

The Village Blacksmith

Henry Wadsworth Longfellow

Summary

"The Village Blacksmith," a strong, muscular man, works at his forge under a chestnut tree. He is a hard and honest worker. The children pass by on their way home from school. They like to look in at the fire. On Sundays, the blacksmith goes to church with his children. He thinks of his children's mother, who has died, and he sheds a tear. His life is a lesson to all: Life should be forged by working hard and setting good examples.

Visual Summary

The Blacksmith's Life		
He works hard at his forge every day.	Children like to look in at the fire as they pass by.	He goes to church on Sundays. He feels sad that his children's mother has died.
Lesson		
Live life well, and shape your fortune by your deeds and thoughts.		

LITERARY ANALYSIS

Figurative Language

Poets use **figurative language** to describe things in lively ways. Figurative language compares one object, person, or idea to another. Two types of figurative language are simile and metaphor.

Figure of speech	Example	Explanation
simile: a comparison using *like* or *as*	*His brawny arms/ Are strong as iron bands*	Arms are as strong as iron bands.
metaphor a comparison that does not use *like* or *as*	*At the flaming forge of life/ Our fortunes must be wrought*	Life is a burning oven Fortunes are iron that must be bent and worked.

READING STRATEGY

Using Your Senses

Poetic language often appeals to the **senses**: taste, sight, touch, smell, and sound. Words and details that appeal to the senses are called **sensory language**. You can use your senses to experience a poem more fully. As you read the poem, look for the sensory language. You can write the phrases in this chart.

Sight	• Spreading chestnut tree (broad, shady) • •
Touch	• Strong as iron hands (heavy, smooth) •
Sound	• He hears the parson pray and preach (loud, passionate) • •

The Village Blacksmith

Henry Wadsworth Longfellow

◆ Literary Analysis

Circle the **simile** in this stanza. What does this comparison tell you about the blacksmith? Write your answer on these lines.

____

____

____

____

Under a spreading chestnut tree
    The village smithy[1] stands;
The smith, a mighty man is he,
    With large and sinewy[2] hands;
And the muscles of his brawny arms
Are strong as iron bands.

◆ ◆ ◆

The blacksmith is an honest man. He earns his living working hard every day. The village children like to look into his shop and see the hammer and the fire. His work is a steady pattern in their lives.

◆ ◆ ◆

◆ Reading Strategy

Circle the words in the bracketed lines that help you to **hear** the action.

He goes on Sunday to the church,
    And sits among his boys;
He hears the parson pray and preach,
    He hears his daughter's voice,
Singing in the village choir,
    And it makes his heart rejoice.
It sounds to him like her mother's voice,
    Singing in Paradise!
He needs must think of her once more,
    How in the grave she lies;
And with his hard, rough hand he wipes
    A tear out of his eyes.

◆ ◆ ◆

◆ Reading Check

Why does the blacksmith cry?

____

____

____

____

____

The blacksmith's life is full work, joy, and sadness. But he carries on every day.

◆ ◆ ◆

◆ Background

This poem show life in a small New England village in the 1800s. The church was part of community life for many at that time.

---

1. **smithy** (SMITH ee) *n.* the workshop of a blacksmith.
2. **sinewy** (SIN yoo ee) *adj.* tough and strong.

Thanks, thanks to thee, my worthy friend,
For the lesson thou hast taught!
Thus at the flaming forge of life
Our fortunes must be wrought;
Thus on its sounding anvil shaped
Each burning deed and thought.

◆ Vocabulary and Pronunciation

The words *thee* and *thou* are no longer used in English. They are old-fashioned forms of *you*. Read these two lines, replacing *thee* and *thou* with *you*.

Vocabulary Development

forge (FOHRJ) *n.* furnace where metal is shaped
wrought (WRAHT) *v.* shaped through hammering
anvil (AN vil) *n.* a heavy block on which a blacksmith shapes metal with a hammer

REVIEW AND ASSESS

1. Was the blacksmith's life difficult or easy?

   ____

   Explain your answer.

   ____

   ____

2. Write three words to describe the blacksmith's appearance.

   1. ____
   2. ____
   3. ____

3. What sound reminds the blacksmith of his dead wife?

   ____

   ____

4. **Literary Analysis:** Complete the sentence. In the final stanza, a **metaphor** compares life to

   ____

   ____

5. **Reading Strategy:** In the following chart, list examples of sensory language from the poem. In the first column, write the sense. In the second column, write the words and phrases that appeal to that sense.

Sense	Sensory Language

Writing

In "The Village Blacksmith" the poet compares life to a blacksmith's work. Write your own metaphor comparing life to something else.

1. Make a list of possible metaphors.

Life is ______________________________

Life is ______________________________

Life is ______________________________

Life is ______________________________

Life is ______________________________

2. Circle the one you like the best.

3. Write three ways that life is like the thing you chose.

   1. ______________ ______________

   2. ______________ ______________

   3. ______________ ______________

4. Write a topic sentence that introduces your metaphor.

____

____

Write the final paragraph on your own paper.

PREVIEW

Popocatepetl and Ixtlaccihuatl

Juliet Piggott

Summary

"Popocatepetl and Ixtlaccihuatl" is a legend that explains the origin of two volcanoes near present-day Mexico City. A powerful emperor in the Aztec capital of Tenochtitlan forbids his daughter, the beautiful princess Ixtla, to marry Popo, the brave warrior she loves. Eventually, the aging emperor offers his daughter's hand to the warrior who will defeat his enemies. After a lengthy war, the emperor's men prevail. Most soldiers agree that Popo has fought hard and is responsible for the victory. But a few jealous warriors hurry back to the city and report that Popo has been killed. This news causes Ixtla to fall ill and die. Popo returns and responds by killing the guilty soldiers and refusing to become emperor. He then has two stone pyramids built outside the city. He buries Ixtla near the peak of one and then takes his place atop the taller of the two. He holds a lighted torch and watches over Ixtla's body for the rest of his days. The two volcanoes stand as reminders of the two lovers who dreamed of always being together.

Visual Summary

Elements of Legend

Larger-than-life characters	Exaggerated details
Popo, brandishing his club and shield, leads the warriors to victory.	Popo stands on top of stone pyramid for the rest of his life, holding the torch in memory of Ixtla.

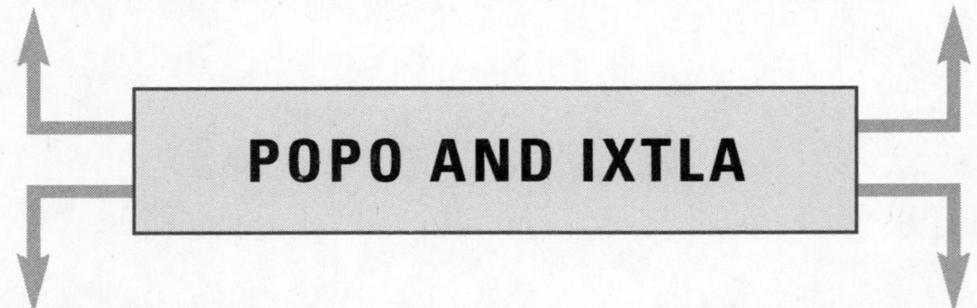

Reveals values of culture	Fantastic details
Legend reflects Aztec belief in loyalty and bravery.	Two stone pyramids built by Popo turn into two volcanoes.

PREPARE TO READ

LITERARY ANALYSIS

Legend

Legends are part of the oral tradition. They were passed down by word of mouth from generation to generation. Some people, places, or events in a legend may be based on real people, places, or events of the past.

For example, the following details from the legend of "Popocatepetl and Ixtlaccihuatl" are connected to real people, places, or events:

Detail from the Legend	Real Places or Events
• Tenochtitlan	• Once the Aztec capital, now Mexico City
• Two stone pyramids built by Popo became two snow-capped volcanoes	• Two volcanoes near Mexico city: Popocatepetl and Ixtlaccihuatl
• Popo and the other warriors fought bravely for their emperor	• Aztec warriors conquered other Mexican tribes

Details in legends become exaggerated over time. In this story, you will read about the following exaggerated details:

- smoke in the memory of the princess
- pyramids that change to volcanoes
- Popo's decision to stand on top of the pyramid forever

The qualities of the characters in legends often reveal the values and attitudes of the cultures from which they come. For example, Popo's bravery and loyalty suggest that these qualities were admired by the Aztecs.

READING STRATEGY

Rereading and Reading Ahead

Rereading and **reading ahead** can help you to understand the authors' words and ideas.

If you do not understand a certain passage, reread it. Look for connections among the words and sentences. It might also help to read ahead because a word or idea may be clarified further on.

Popocatepetl and Ixtlaccihuatl

Juliet Piggott

Have you ever looked at a mountain and wondered how it got there? People who lived long ago answered such questions by inventing legends. "Popocatepetl and Ixtlaccihuatl" is a legend that explains the origin of two volcanoes near present-day Mexico City.

The story begins with a description of Tenochtitlan and the two nearby volcanoes:

◆ ◆ ◆

Before the Spaniards came to Mexico and marched on the Aztec capital of Tenochtitlan (te NOCH tee TLAN)[1] there were two volcanoes to the southeast of that city. The Spaniards destroyed much of Tenochtitlan and built another city in its place and called it Mexico City. It is known by that name still, and the pass through which the Spaniards came to the ancient Tenochtitlan is still there, as are the volcanoes on each side of that pass. Their names have not been changed. The one to the north is Ixtlaccihuatl (EES tlah SEE WAT uhl) and the one on the south of the pass is Popocatepetl (po po kah TEE PET uhl). Both are snowcapped and beautiful, Popocatepetl being the taller of the two. That name means Smoking Mountain. In Aztec days it gushed forth smoke and, on occasion, it does so still. It erupted too in Aztec days and has done so again since the Spaniards came. Ixtlaccihuatl means The White Woman, for its peak was, and still is, white.

◆ ◆ ◆

◆ Background

The legend of "Popocatepetl and Ixtlaccihuatl" comes from the Aztec Indians of Mexico. They were great builders and engineers—their capital city of Tenochtitlan, built on a lake, had a complex system of canals for transportation and floating gardens for crops. The influence of Aztec culture continues in Mexico's art, language, and food. What legends come to us from your native land?

____

____

____

◆ English Language Development

Mark the Text

Interrupters are words or phrases that help relate ideas to one another but are not essential to the meaning of the sentence. They are set off by commas from the rest of the sentence. For example, the words "and still is" in the last sentence is an interrupter. Circle the interrupter in the underlined sentence.

1. **Tenochtitlan:** The Spanish conquered the Aztec capital in 1521.

According to an Aztec legend, there was once a very powerful Emperor in Tenochtitlan. Some thought he was wise, while others doubted his wisdom. The Emperor had a beautiful daughter. Her name was Ixtlaccihuatl, but people called her Ixtla. When the princess grew up, she became a serious young woman. She knew that the Emperor expected her to rule in his place someday.

◆ ◆ ◆

Another reason for her being so serious was that she was in love. This in itself was a joyous thing, but the Emperor forbade her to marry. He wanted her to reign and rule alone when he died, for he trusted no one, not even his wife, to rule as he did except his much loved only child, Ixtla.

◆ ◆ ◆

This is why some doubted the wisdom of the Emperor. Not allowing his daughter to marry was selfish and not truly wise. And if an emperor was not truly wise, he could not be truly great or truly powerful either.

The man with whom Ixtla was in love was a young warrior named Popocatepetl. Ixtla and his friends called him Popo. Ixtla and Popo loved each other very much, and they would have been very happy had they been allowed to marry.

In time, the Emperor became very old and ill. His enemies, the tribes that lived in the mountains, realized this. Before long, the city of Tenochtitlan was besieged. The Emperor knew that unless his enemies were driven off, Tenochtitlan would be destroyed.

Vocabulary Development

besieged (bi SEEJD) *n.* surrounded

◆ **Reading Strategy**

Read ahead to see if the Emperor makes wise decisions.

◆ **Reading Check**

Mark the Text

In the bracketed sentence, underline what the Emperor forbids Ixtla to do.

◆ **Vocabulary and Pronunciation**

Mark the Text

The word *reign* is pronounced the same as "rain." It means "to have the power of an emperor or other ruler." Circle the word in the sentence that helps you with the meaning of reign.

◆ **Reading Check**

Why doesn't the Emperor allow Ixtla and Popo to marry?

____

____

____

◆ **Reading Strategy**

Do you think the Emperor ever had wisdom? **Reread** previous passages to help answer this question. Explain your answer.

◆ **Vocabulary and Pronunciation**

In the word *succeeded,* the first *c* is pronounced like a *k,* and the second *c* is pronounced like an *s:* suk SEED ed.

Pronounce this related word: success.

In the same paragraph, circle a word in which *c* is pronounced like *k.*

◆ **Reading Check**

What reward does the Emperor promise for lifting the siege?

◆ **Literary Analysis**

What does the account of the battle suggest about the Aztecs' attitudes about war?

◆ **Reading Check**

Why do the warriors report false news?

He also knew that he was too old and too ill to lead his warriors into battle.

◆ ◆ ◆

Instead of appointing one of his warriors to lead the rest into battle on his behalf, he offered a <u>bribe</u> to all of them. Perhaps it was that his wisdom, if wisdom he had, had forsaken him, or perhaps he acted from fear. Or perhaps he simply changed his mind. But the bribe he offered to whichever warrior <u>succeeded</u> in lifting the siege of Tenochtitlan and defeating his enemies in and around the Valley of Mexico was both the hand of his daughter and the equal right to reign and rule, with her, in Tenochtitlan.

◆ ◆ ◆

And so the warriors went to war. Although each fought hard, showing great skill and courage, the war was long and fierce. Battle followed battle, and the final outcome was uncertain. As time went by, Popo emerged as the leader. <u>Brandishing</u> his club and shield, he led a great charge of warriors across the valley. The enemies fled before them for the safety of the jungles beyond the mountains. The warriors regarded Popo as the man most responsible for the victory. When they returned to Tenochtitlan, Popo would claim Ixtla as his wife at last.

But a few warriors were jealous of Popo. They slipped away from the others at night and raced back to Tenochtitlan. They reported to the Emperor that the enemies had been defeated and that Popo had been killed. The Emperor then told Ixtla the news.

Vocabulary Development

bribe (BRĪB) *n.* money or a reward offered to someone to get him to do something for the giver

brandishing (BRAN dish ing) *adj.* waving in a menacing way

He added that he did not yet know who her husband would be. Ixtla was overcome with grief. She went to her room and lay down. If Popo was dead, she did not wish to live. So she became very ill and died.

The very next day, Popo returned to Tenochtitlan. When he heard how Ixtla had died, he spoke not a word. He and the other warriors found the men who had given the false news. Popo killed each one of them in single combat. Then Popo returned to the palace. He went to Ixtla's room, lifted her body, and carried it out of the palace and out of the city. The warriors followed him.

◆ ◆ ◆

When he had walked some miles he gestured to them again and they built a huge pile of stones in the shape of a pyramid. They all worked together and they worked fast while Popo stood and watched, holding the body of the princess in his arms. By sunset the mighty edifice was finished. Popo climbed it alone, carrying Ixtla's corpse with him. There, at the very top, under a heap of stones, he buried the young woman he had loved so well and for so long, and who had died for the love of him.

That night Popo slept alone at the top of the pyramid by Ixtla's grave. In the morning he came down and spoke for the first time since the Emperor had told him the princess was dead. He told the warriors to build another pyramid, a little to the southeast of the one which held Ixtla's body and to build it higher than the other.

He told them too to tell the Emperor on his behalf that he, Popocatepetl, would never reign and rule in Tenochtitlan. He would keep watch

Vocabulary Development

edifice (ED uh fis) *n.* large structure

◆ Reading Check

Why does Ixtla die?

◆ Reading Strategy

Read ahead to find details about Popo that make him more than an ordinary man.

◆ Vocabulary and Pronunciation

Mark the Text

A pile of stones is a lot of stones all stacked together. Find and circle another phrase in this paragraph that means "a pile of stones." Then write here the word that means the same as *pile*.

◆ Literary Analysis

Do you think the warriors could have built a pyramid in one day? Explain.

◆ Literary Analysis

Put a checkmark in front of each detail that helps explain where the mountains came from.

_____ Popo had two pyramids built.

_____ Popo stood next to Ixtla's pyramid holding a torch for the rest of his days.

_____ The emperor was not very wise.

_____ Tenochtitlan was the capital.

◆ Stop to Reflect

Do you believe this explanation of the origin of the mountains?

____

Why do you think it was told?

____

____

____

over the grave of the Princess Ixtlaccihuatl for the rest of his life.

The messages to the Emperor were the last words Popo ever spoke. Well before the evening the second mighty pile of stones was built. Popo climbed it and stood at the top, taking a torch of resinous pine wood with him.

And when he reached the top he lit the torch and the warriors below saw the white smoke rise against the blue sky, and they watched as the sun began to set and the smoke turned pink and then a deep red, the color of blood.

So Popocatepetl stood there, holding the torch in memory of Ixtlaccihuatl, for the rest of his days.

The snows came and, as the years went by, the pyramids of stone became high white-capped mountains. Even now the one called Popocatepetl emits smoke in memory of the princess whose body lies in the mountain which bears her name.

Vocabulary Development

resinous (REZ in us) *adj.* full of resin, a sticky gum that oozes from pines

REVIEW AND ASSESS

1. Why are Ixtla and Popo unable to marry?

____

____

____

2. How do the Emperor's actions show his selfishness?

____

____

____

3. What effect does the Emperor's selfishness have on the safety of his kingdom? Circle the letter of the correct answer.

   (a) The kingdom ends up with no ruler.
   (b) The kingdom rests safely in Ixtla's hands.
   (c) Popo and Ixtla rule the kingdom together.
   (d) The kingdom is overthrown by enemies.

4. What leads to Ixtla's death at the end of the war?

____

____

____

5. **Reading Strategy:** Why is it sometimes a good idea to **read ahead**?

____

____

____

6. **Literary Analysis:** List three things from this story that show that it is a legend.

1. ______________________________

____

2. ______________________________

____

3. ______________________________

____

Writing

Research Summary

Read one or two articles on how volcanoes are formed. While you read, write down the main steps in the process. Then, make a list of the steps in the correct time order. Choose only the steps that cause or lead to another part of the process. For example, your list might look something like this:

- **Temperatures deep under the surface of the Earth are close to 1200 degrees C, hot enough to melt rock.**
- **As rock melts and becomes magma, it produces gas.**
- **Gas expands and needs more space, which puts pressure on the rock above it.**
- **The ground rises and expands, creating a volcano.**

Now use the steps you have listed from your research to write a summary of how a volcano is formed. How is your explanation different from the explanation in the legend of "Popocatepetl and Ixtlaccihuatl"?

____

____

____

The People Could Fly

Virginia Hamilton

Summary

In "The People Could Fly," the story is told that long ago in Africa people knew how to fly. When they were captured and sent away in slave ships, it was too crowded and the people who knew how to fly lost their wings. As the enslaved African Americans labored in the fields, they had to work very hard and were often mistreated. An old man, Toby, helps the people to fly away from their misery by whispering magic words that help them remember how to fly. He finally flies himself, leaving those who cannot fly to tell the tale to others.

Visual Summary

Details of Cultural Context

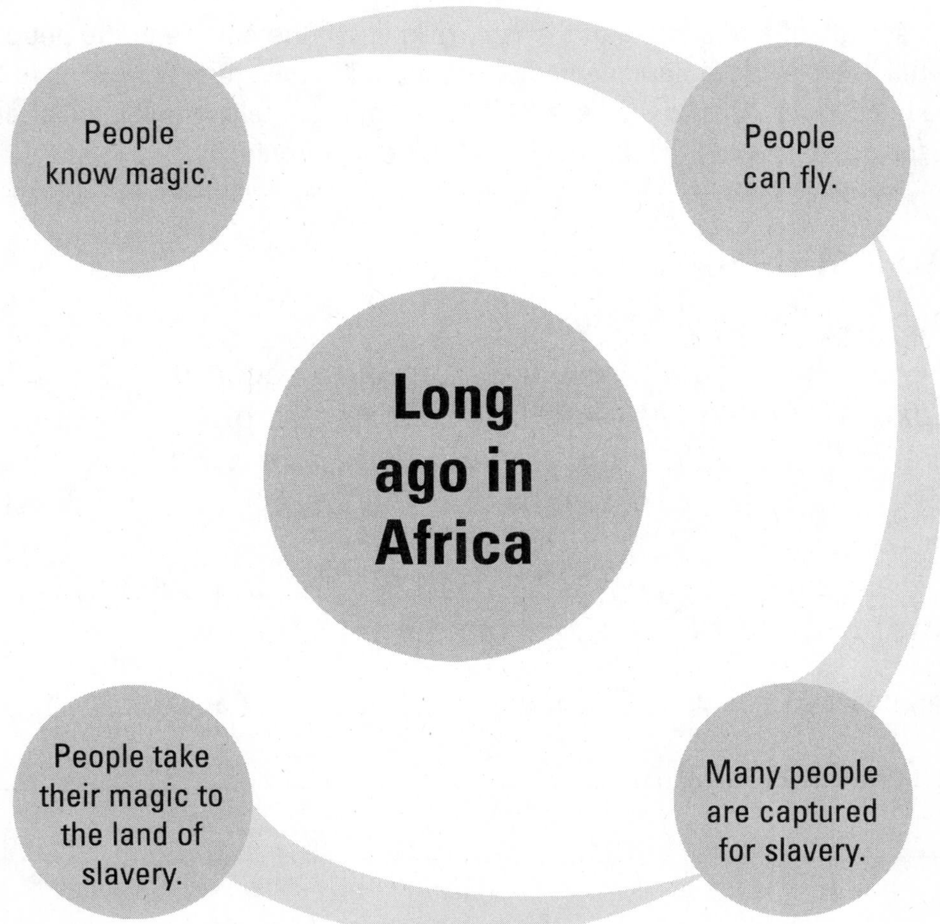

PREPARE TO READ

LITERARY ANALYSIS

Folk Tales

Many cultures have **folk tales**. Folk tales are stories that are passed from person to person by word of mouth. Folk tales communicate the ideas and values that are important to people in a culture. The following are important questions to consider:

Where do folk tales come from?
No one knows who first created folk tales. Modern writers sometimes retell folk tales. They try to capture the feeling and spirit of the stories as they have been told for hundreds of years.

What is a folk tale's message?
The message of a folk tale—or theme—tells about the culture of the people who tell it. Their beliefs and values are reflected in the story. For example, enslaved African Americans kept their hopes alive by telling folk tales about the fight for freedom and justice, such as "The People Could Fly."

READING STRATEGY

Recognizing Cultural Context

One way to appreciate a folk tale is to recognize its **cultural context**. The cultural context is the background, customs, and beliefs of the people who, first told the story. Keeping track of the cultural context of a folk tale will help you to understand what you read.

As you read "The People Could Fly," jot down details of the cultural context of the story on the lines below:

Background	Customs	Beliefs
____________	____________	____________
____________	____________	____________
____________	____________	____________

The People Could Fly

Virginia Hamilton

Have things ever seemed so bad that you wished you could just fly away and leave all your troubles behind? In the African American folk tale "The People Could Fly," an old man, Toby, helps the enslaved Africans fly away from their misery. He whispers magic words that help them remember how to fly.

As the story begins, the author tells how people in Africa a long time ago were able to fly. But they lost that ability once they were enslaved.

♦ ♦ ♦

They say the people could fly. . . .

Then, many of the people were captured for Slavery. The ones that could fly shed their wings.

♦ ♦ ♦

Many of the enslaved people got seasick on the slave ships. Missing Africa and feeling sick, the people were full of misery. They didn't think about flying then.

Even though the people who could fly didn't take their wings, they kept their power. Despite being enslaved, the magic of flying stayed with the people—but they kept it secret. Because they looked the same as the other dark-skinned people who had been coming over from Africa, it wasn't possible to know which people could fly.

♦ ♦ ♦

◆ Reading Strategy

Underline details in the bracketed passage that describe the **culture**.

◆ Reading Check

Why are the people full of misery?

____

____

____

____

____

◆ Reading Check

What special gift do some of the people have?

____

____

____

◆ **Literary Analysis**

Circle the words in this bracketed paragraph that tell you this story has been passed on orally.

One such who could was an old man, call him Toby. And standin tall, yet afraid, was a young woman who once had wings. . . . Now Sarah carried a babe. . . .

♦ ♦ ♦

The slaves work hard in the fields from sunup to sundown. The owner of the slaves is a hard, cruel man who calls himself their Master. His Overseer[1] on horseback points out slaves who are slowing down. A man called Driver[2] whips those slaves to make them work faster. The Driver's whip cuts into the slaves, hurting them badly. So they work fast to avoid the whip.

Sarah hoes and chops the row, but she carries her baby on her back. While Sarah works, the baby sleeps. When the baby grows hungry, it begins to cry. Sarah can't stop working to feed it or soothe it.

♦ ♦ ♦

"Keep that thing quiet," called the Overseer. . . . The woman scrunched low. The Driver cracked his whip across the babe anyhow. The babe hollered like any hurt child, and the woman fell to the earth.

♦ ♦ ♦

The old man, Toby, helps Sarah to her feet. She tells Toby that she must go soon. He tells her it will be soon. Sarah is so weak she can no longer stand up. She sits down in the row. The Overseer shouts at her to get up. The Driver whips her. Her dress is torn and her legs are bleeding, but she can't get up.

♦ ♦ ♦

◆ **Reading Check**

Why can't Sarah stop working to take care of her baby?

____

____

____

____

____

◆ **Reading Strategy**

List two negative things that you have learned about the culture depicted in this story.

1. __________________________

____

2. __________________________

____

____

1. **overseer** (OH ver SEE er) *n.* someone who watches over and directs the work of others.
2. **driver** *n.* someone who forced (drove) the slaves to work harder.

"Now, before it's too late," panted Sarah. "Now, Father!"

"Yes, Daughter, the time is come," Toby answered. "Go, as you know how to go!"

He raised his arms. . . . *"Kum . . . yali, kum buba tambe,"* and more magic words, said so quickly, they sounded like whispers and sighs.

♦ ♦ ♦

First, Sarah lifts one foot. Then she lifts the other. She isn't graceful. She's holding the baby. Then the magic that she knew in Africa returns. She begins to fly like a bird.

As Sarah flies away, the Overseer rides after her. Nothing can stop her. She flies until no one can see her anymore. No one talks about Sarah flying away. They aren't sure whether to believe it happened. But those who were there knew that it happened.

The next day Toby helps several more slaves fly away. The Overseer cries out to the Driver to seize the old man. The Driver gets his whip ready. The one calling himself Master comes running. He pulls out his gun, meaning to kill Toby. But Toby just laughs and sighs the ancient words to the other slaves.

♦ ♦ ♦

". . . buba yali . . . buba tambe. . . ."

There was a great outcryin. . . . Old and young who were called slaves and could fly joined hands. Say like they would ring-sing.[3] But they didn't shuffle in a circle. They didn't sing. They rose on the air.

♦ ♦ ♦

◆ Literary Analysis

In the bracketed passage, underline three details that show how the author writes in the style of a story being told.

Mark the Text

◆ Reading Check

Why do you think the Master wants to kill Toby?

____

____

____

____

____

◆ Reading Check

What are the magic words that Toby says? Write them here.

____

____

Vocabulary Development

shuffle (SHUF uhl) *v.* walk with dragging feet

3. **ring-sing:** joining hands in a circle to sing and dance.

◆ Literary Analysis

What do you think the message of this story was to enslaved African Americans?

____

____

____

◆ English Language Development

The author uses a dialect from the rural southern United States in this folk tale. She uses the dialect to make the characters seem realistic. Dialects differ in pronunciation, grammar, and word choice. For example, the author uses the word "cryin" for "crying." Circle another word in the bracketed paragraph that is written in dialect.

Mark the Text

◆ Culture Note

One way that enslaved African Americans kept their hopes alive despite the tremendous hardships they faced was to tell freedom tales—folk tales about the fight for freedom. These tales helped people to believe that some day they would find freedom from slavery and injustice. What folk tales do people tell in your native land?

____

____

____

The people flew in a flock. They left the plantation and their slavery. The flew to freedom.

Toby flies too. He takes care of the people. He isn't "cryin or laughin." He is the seer.[4] As he is flying, he sees the slaves who cannot fly. They are waiting. But Toby can't help those who can't fly. There is no time to teach them. They will have to wait for a chance to run. He calls out "goodie-bye" and flies away.

◆ ◆ ◆

So they say. The Overseer told it. The one called Master said it was a lie, a trick of the light. The Driver kept his mouth shut.

The slaves who could not fly told about the people who could fly to their children.

◆ ◆ ◆

And so the story of the people who could fly passes from generation to generation.

4. **seer** (SEE uhr) *n.* one who has supposed power to see the future; prophet.

REVIEW AND ASSESS

1. How did the people lose their wings?

2. Why does Sarah tell Toby that she must leave soon?

3. How does Toby help Sarah?

4. **Literary Analysis:** List three examples of words or phrases from the story that tell you that this story was spoken aloud.

   1. __________

   2. __________

   3. __________

(Continued)

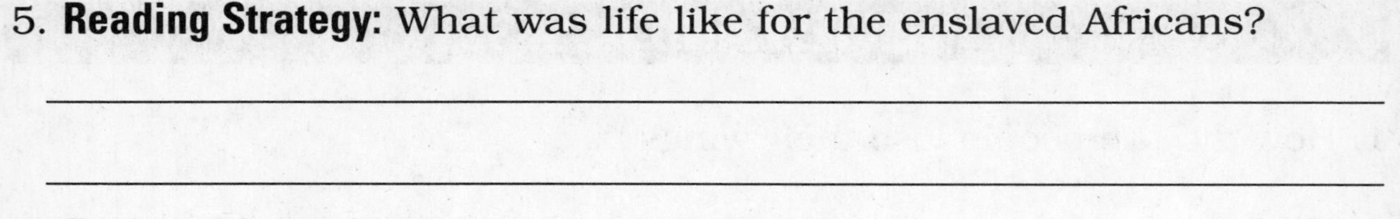

5. **Reading Strategy:** What was life like for the enslaved Africans?

Speaking and Listening

Retelling

Folk tales are stories told by ordinary people. The stories are passed along from person to person orally.

Imagine that you are going to help carry on the folk tale tradition by telling "The People Could Fly" aloud to your class. You are going to retell the story in your own words, as if you were passing it along to a younger generation Do the following:

- Review the story to remember the most important events.
- Practice reading it aloud.
- Add details of your own.
- Remember that part of the oral tradition involves adding your own personality to your retelling.
- Now practice telling the story in your own words.
- When you are ready, tell the story to the class.

Demeter and Persephone

Anne Terry White

Summary

"Demeter and Persephone" explains the Earth's seasons. When Pluto, king of the underworld, appears on Earth, Eros causes him to fall in love with Persephone. Pluto kidnaps Persephone and carries her away. When she is unable to find her daughter, Demeter, goddess of the harvest, becomes angry and makes the Earth infertile. Because humankind is threatened with starvation, Zeus asks for Persephone's release—upon the condition that she has not tasted food in the underworld. Pluto reluctantly agrees. Unfortunately, Persephone has tasted four pomegranate seeds, so she must return to Pluto for four months of every year while her mother grieves. These months are known as winter. During the months she is home, the soil is fertile and productive.

Visual Summary

Prediction Chart

CLUE		PREDICTION
• Eros shoots an arrow into Pluto's heart.	→	• Pluto will fall in love with Persephone.
• Pluto kidnaps Persephone.	→	• Demeter will be angry.
• Demeter blames the land for Persephone's disappearance.	→	• Demeter will not let anything grow on earth.
• Zeus knows where Persephone is.	→	• Zeus will send Hermes to bring Persephone back home.

LITERARY ANALYSIS

Myth

Since time began, people have tried to understand the world around them. Ancient peoples created **myths**, or stories to explain natural occurrences. For example, the ancient Greeks created myths to explain

- **the sun's daily travel across the sky.**
- **the changing seasons.**

Myths also expressed beliefs about right and wrong. Even though we can explain many things today in scientific terms, myths still make sense to us because they explain the world in human terms.

For example, Demeter [duh MEE ter] is angry because her daughter Persephone [pur SE fu nee] has been kidnapped. So she doesn't let anything grow on earth. Later, Persephone has to return to Pluto in the underword four months out of each year. Demeter causes winter during those four months. This was how the Greeks explained winter.

READING STRATEGY

Making Predictions

A **prediction** is an educated guess about what will happen. The guess is based on hints or clues in the story. In some myths, characters get into trouble because they happen to be in the wrong place at the wrong time. For example, in "Demeter and Persephone," Persephone gets kidnapped by Pluto because Eros shoots an arrow into Pluto's heart. Often, characters' troubles are the result of their own actions.

As you read, predict when a character's actions may lead to trouble. Then, read on to see if your predictions were correct.

Demeter and Persephone

Anne Terry White

Do you know what causes the changing seasons? Today, scientists explain that as the Earth revolves around the sun during the course of a year, it tilts. Part of its surface gets more sunlight, and the other part gets less. In regions getting more direct sunlight, it is summer. In areas tilting away from the sun's rays, it is winter. Thousands of years ago, the ancient Greeks explained the changing seasons with the myth of "Demeter and Persephone."

As the story begins, Pluto, the king of the underworld, becomes alarmed at the shaking of the earth.

◆ ◆ ◆

Deep under Mt. Aetna [ET nuh], the gods had buried alive a number of fearful, fire-breathing giants. The monsters heaved and struggled to get free. And so mightily did they shake the earth that Pluto, the king of the underworld, was alarmed.

"They may tear the rocks asunder and leave the realm of the dead open to the light of day," he thought. And mounting his golden chariot, he went up to see what damage had been done.

Now the goddess of love and beauty, fair Aphrodite [AF roh DĪT ee], was sitting on a mountainside playing with her son, Eros [ER os].[1] She saw Pluto as he drove around with his coal-black horses and she said:

◆ Literary Analysis

What natural event might these sentences describe?

◆ Reading Strategy

Eros, the god of love, shoots gold-tipped arrows that cause people to fall in love. **Predict** what will happen in the story.

Vocabulary Development

asunder (ah SUN der) *adv.* apart

1. **Eros:** in Greek mythology, the god of love. Identified by the Romans as Cupid.

◆ Literary Analysis

How do the Greeks explain how people fall in love?

◆ Reading Check

In the bracketed paragraph, underline the cause of Pluto's warm feelings.

◆ Reading Check

Whose daughter is Persephone?

Who kidnaps Persephone?

"My son, there is one who defies your power and mine. Quick! Take up your darts! Send an arrow into the breast of that dark <u>monarch</u>. Let him, too, feel the pangs of love. Why should he alone escape them?"

◆ ◆ ◆

Eros shoots an arrow straight into Pluto's heart. The grim Pluto has seen many fair maids. But never has his heart been touched. Now he is filled with a warm feeling. Before him is a young woman gathering flowers. She is Persephone [per SEF uh nee], daughter of Demeter [duh MEET er] goddess of the harvest. Pluto looks at Persephone and falls in love with her.

Pluto sweeps Persephone onto his chariot and speeds away. As she struggles, her girdle[2] falls to the ground, but Pluto holds her tight. Soon they reach the River Cyane.[3] Pluto strikes the bank with his trident.[4] The earth opens and darkness swallows them all—horses, chariot, Pluto, and weeping Persephone.

Demeter searches all over the earth, but no one can tell her where Persephone is. Worn out and filled with despair, Demeter returns to Sicily. There, near the River Cyane, where Pluto has gone down to the underword, a river nymph[5] brings her Persephone's girdle.

◆ ◆ ◆

The goddess knew then that her daughter was gone indeed, but she did not suspect Pluto of carrying her off. She laid the blame on the innocent land.

Vocabulary Development

monarch (MAHN ark) *n.* king or queen

2. **girdle** (GER dul) *n.* belt or sash for the waist.
3. **River Cyane** (SĪ an) a river in Sicily, an island just south of Italy.
4. **trident** (TRĪD ent) *n.* spear with three points.
5. **river nymph** (NIMF) *n.* goddess living in a river.

"Ungrateful soil!" she said. "I made you fertile. I clothed you in grass and nourishing grain, and this is how you reward me. No more shall you enjoy my favors!"

That year was the most cruel mankind had ever known. Nothing prospered, nothing grew. The cattle died, the seed would not come up, men and oxen toiled in vain. There was too much sun. There was too much rain. Thistles[6] and weeds were the only things that grew. It seemed that all mankind would die of hunger.

"This cannot go on," said mighty Zeus. "I see that I must intervene." And one by one he sent the gods and goddesses to plead with Demeter.

But she had the same answer for all: "Not till I see my daughter shall the earth bear fruit again."

◆ ◆ ◆

Zeus, of course, knows where Persephone is. He is sorry to take from his brother the one thing that brings joy to his life. But he must if mankind is to be saved. So he calls Hermes [HUR meez][7] to him and says:

◆ ◆ ◆

"Descend to the underworld, my son. Bid Pluto release his bride. Provided she has not tasted food in the realm of the dead, she may return to her mother forever."

Down sped Hermes on his winged feet, and there in the dim palace of the king, he found Persephone by Pluto's side. She was pale and joyless. Not all the glittering treasures of the underworld could bring a smile to her lips.

Vocabulary Development

intervene (IN ter VEEN) *v.* interfere

6. **thistles** (THIS uhlz) *n.* stubborn, weedy plants with sharp leaves and usually purplish flowers.

7. **Hermes:** God who served as a messenger.

◆ Literary Analysis

How did the ancient Greeks explain natural disasters?

______

______

______

◆ Reading Strategy

Since Zeus knows where Persephone is, what do you think might happen next?

______

______

______

◆ Vocabulary and Pronunciation

Some irregular verbs that have *ee* in the present form the past by changing *ee* to *e*:

Example: feed fed

What is the present form of the verb sped?

______

What is the past form of these verbs?

bleed ______

meet ______

keep ______

◆ Reading Check

Complete this sentence. Persephone may return to her mother forever, if she has not

______

______.

◆ **Reading Check**

Why isn't Persephone interested in jewels?

◆ **Reading Strategy**

Since Persephone cannot leave the underworld forever, what do you think will happen to her?

◆ **Literary Analysis**

According to the myth, why do we have winter?

"You have no flowers here," she would say to her husband when he pressed gems upon her. "Jewels have no fragrance. I do not want them."

◆ ◆ ◆

When Persephone sees Hermes and hears his message, she is filled with joy. She gets ready to leave at once. But one thing troubles her—she cannot leave the underworld forever. For she has accepted a pomegranate[8] from Pluto and has sucked the sweet pulp from four of the seeds.

Pluto helps Persephone into his chariot and Hermes takes the reins. "Dear wife," says Pluto, "think kindly of me, for I love you truly. It will be lonely here these eight months you are away. So fare you well—and get your fill of flowers!"

Hermes drives the chariot straight to the temple of Demeter. Persephone flys to her mother's arms. The sad tale of each turns into joy in the telling.

◆ ◆ ◆

So it is to this day. One third of the year Persephone spends in the gloomy abode of Pluto—one month for each seed that she tasted. Then Nature dies, the leaves fall, the earth stops bringing forth. In spring Persephone returns, and with her come the flowers, followed by summer's fruitfulness and the rich harvest of fall.

Vocabulary Development

fragrance (FRAY grentz) *n.* sweet odor; perfume

abode (uh BOHD) *n.* home

8. **pomegranate** (PAHM uh GRAN it) *n.* round fruit with a red leathery rind and many seeds.

REVIEW AND ASSESS

1. Why does Pluto take Persephone to his kingdom?

____

____

____

2. What does Demeter do when she discovers her daughter is lost? Circle the letter of the correct answer.

(a) She goes to the underworld to get her.
(b) She calls on Zeus to help her.
(c) She blames the land and punishes it.
(d) She cries a river.

3. How does Zeus solve the problem?

____

____

____

4. How do the seasons change as Persephone moves between the earth and the underworld?

____

____

____

5. **Literary Analysis:** Ancient peoples often created **myths** to explain events in nature. Complete this sentence: The myth of "Demeter and Persephone explains ______________________________

____

____.

(Continued)

6. **Reading Strategy:** Write a **prediction** you made about the following. Then tell what happened in the story.

	Prediction	**Actual Outcome**
• Persephone	______________________	______________________
	______________________	______________________
	______________________	______________________
• Demeter	______________________	______________________
	______________________	______________________
	______________________	______________________

Writing

Myth

Choose a natural event such as an earthquake or volcanic eruption. Imagine that you have never heard of any scientific explanation of the causes of the event. Write a myth that offers an explanation. Remember that you are not going to use science in your explanation. Think in terms of the gods or heroes and their actions that might have caused the event. For example, an earthquake might be caused by a god stamping his foot. Do the following:

- Begin by identifying the natural event. ______________________
- Describe people's reactions to the event. ______________________
- Think of possible ways a god might have caused the event.

____

- On a sheet of paper, prepare an outline to help you organize details and events in your myth.
- Write the myth in clear time order.

Icarus and Daedalus

Josephine Preston Peabody

Summary

In the myth of "Icarus and Daedalus," a boy's impulsive nature brings about a terrible punishment. Daedalus, once the master architect for King Minos of Crete, finds himself imprisoned on that island along with his son, Icarus. In order to escape, Daedalus puts his inventive mind to work and creates wings from feathers, thread, and wax. As he attaches the wings to Icarus' back, he warns his son not to fly too close to the sun. However, all Icarus can think about is the wonder and excitement of being able to fly. He barely hears his father's warning. Predictably, he soars too close to the sun, melts his wings, and crashes into the sea.

Visual Summary

Prediction Chart

CLUE		PREDICTION
• Daedalus is looking for a way to escape from Crete. He observes the flight of sea-gulls.	→	• Daedalus will make wings with which he and Icarus can fly to freedom.
• Daedalus warns Icarus not to fly too high or too low, but Icarus doesn't pay attention.	→	• Icarus is going to have trouble when he attempts to fly.
• Icarus flies too close to the sun.	→	• Icarus' wings will melt and he will fall into the sea and drown.

PREPARE TO READ

LITERARY ANALYSIS

Myth

People of many cultures have created **myths**, to explain natural occurrences or to express beliefs about right and wrong. The ancient Greeks believed that a person would be punished for being overly proud or arrogant. Greek mythology suggests that the gods punish humans for daring too much or for reaching too high.

For example, Daedalus may have taken too much pride in his own cleverness. He may have dared too much by thinking he could fly like a god. As a result, he is punished by the gods, who take the life of Icarus, Daedalus' young son. Icarus reaches too high when he forgets Daedalus' warning and flies toward the sun. One of the lessons in this myth is that reckless behavior can be very dangerous.

READING STRATEGY

Making Predictions

A **prediction** is an educated guess about what will happen. Use this chart to predict what will happen in the story. Then, fill in what really happens.

Prediction	What Happens

Icarus and Daedalus

Josephine Preston Peabody

Have you ever imagined what it would be like to fly through the air like a bird? Thousands of years ago, the ancient Greeks created the myth of "Icarus and Daedalus," in which a clever man figures out a way to fly by watching the sea-gulls. As the story begins, Daedalus looks for a way to escape from Crete.

◆ ◆ ◆

Among all those mortals who grew so wise that they learned the secrets of the gods, none was more cunning[1] than Daedalus. [DED uhl es]

He once built, for King Minos of Crete,[2] a wonderful Labyrinth[3] of winding ways so cunningly tangled up and twisted around that, once inside, you could never find your way out again without a magic clue. But the king's favor veered[4] with the wind, and one day he had his master architect imprisoned in a tower. Daedalus managed to escape from his cell; but it seemed impossible to leave the island, since every ship that came or went was well guarded by order of the king.

At length, watching the sea-gulls in the air—the only creatures that were sure of liberty—he thought of a plan for himself and his young son Icarus, who was captive with him.

◆ ◆ ◆

Daedalus gathers a whole bunch of feathers. He fastens them together with thread, molds them in with wax, and makes two great wings like those of a bird. He fits

◆ **Reading Check**

Mark the Text

In the bracketed sentence, circle the thing that Daedalus built for King Minos.

◆ **Reading Check**

Why did it seem impossible to leave the island?

____

____

____

____

____

◆ **Reading Strategy**

What do you **predict** Daedalus will do?

____

____

____

____

____

---

1. **cunning** (KUN ing) *adj.* skillful; clever.
2. **King Minos** (MĪ nohs) **of Crete** (KREET) King Minos was a son of the god Zeus. Crete is a Greek island in the eastern Mediterranean Sea, southeast of Greece.
3. **Labyrinth** (LAB uh RINTH) *n.* maze.
4. **veered** (VEERD) *v.* changed directions.

◆ **Vocabulary and Pronunciation**

A pair refers to two things that belong together. We usually say "a pair of _____." Write "a pair of" before each of the following words. Then say the phrase aloud.

____________________ shoes

____________________ socks

____________________ gloves

◆ **Vocabulary and Pronunciation**

To understand the expression "in at one ear and out the other," picture the action of the words. What does the expression mean?

____

____

◆ **Reading Strategy**

Predict what will happen as a result of Icarus' failure to remember his father's instructions.

____

____

◆ **Reading Strategy**

Predict what will happen if Icarus flies too high in the sky.

____

____

____

____

them to his shoulders. By waving his arms, he soon learns to fly.

◆ ◆ ◆

Without delay, he fell to work on a pair of wings for the boy Icarus [IK uh rus], and taught him carefully how to use them, bidding him beware of rash adventures among the stars. "Remember," said the father, "never to fly very low or very high, for the fogs about the earth would weigh you down, but the blaze of the sun will surely melt your feathers apart if you go too near."

For Icarus, these cautions went in at one ear and out by the other. Who could remember to be careful when he was to fly for the first time? Are birds careful? Not they! And not an idea remained in the boy's head but the one joy of escape.

◆ ◆ ◆

The day comes when the wind is right. Up they fly. They leave Crete far beneath them.

At first Daedalus and Icarus are afraid. When they look down, they feel dizzy. Icarus forgets all the instructions and soars as high as he can. His father is way below him.

◆ ◆ ◆

Vocabulary Development

rash *adj.* reckless; hasty

Alas for him! Warmer and warmer grew the air. Those arms, that had seemed to uphold him, relaxed. His wings wavered, drooped. He fluttered his young hands vainly—he was falling—and in that terror he remembered. The heat of the sun had melted the wax from his wings; the feathers were falling, one by one, like snowflakes; and there was none to help.

He fell like a leaf tossed down the wind, down, down, with one cry that overtook Daedalus far away. When he returned, and sought high and low for his poor boy, he saw nothing but the birdlike feathers afloat on the water, and he knew that Icarus was drowned.

The nearest island he named Icaria, in memory of the child; but he, in heavy grief, went to the temple of Apollo in Sicily, and there hung up his wings as an offering. Never again did he attempt to fly.

◆ Culture Note

Many cultures around the world have myths or folk tales in which people can fly. What stories about flying come to us from your native land?

____

____

____

____

◆ Reading Check

Mark the Text

In the bracketed sentence, underline what happens to Icarus' wings.

◆ Stop to Reflect

Icarus lost his life because he ignored his father's warning. In the same situation, would you have done what Icarus did? Why or why not?

____

____

____

____

____

REVIEW AND ASSESS

1. Where is Daedalus when the story begins?

____

____

2. How does Daedalus plan to escape?

____

____

3. What warning does Daedalus give to Icarus?

____

____

4. What happens to Icarus at the end of the myth?

____

____

____

5. **Literary Analysis:** What lesson does this **myth** teach?

____

____

____

6. **Reading Strategy:** What clues might lead you to **make a prediction** that Icarus will fall from the sky? List them below.

- ____

____

• ____

____

• ____

____

Writing

Myth

Greek mythology suggests that the gods punish humans for daring too much or for reaching too high. For example, Daedalus might have dared too much by thinking that people should be able to fly. The gods punish him by taking Icarus' life. Icarus reaches too high by heading toward the sun and is punished by drowning in the sea.

Write a myth about a situation today in which people might be daring too much. Use your imagination. Think about things that might seem impossible for people to do, for example:

- daring to swim across the ocean
- daring to explore the inside of a volcano
- daring to travel to Mars

Create your myth by doing the following:

- Begin by choosing a topic. ______________________________

____

- Invent a character who dares to do the impossible. Write your character's name: ______________________________
- Prepare a brief story outline to help you organize details and events in your myth.

____

____

____

____

____

- On another piece of paper, write the myth in clear time order.

Part 2

Selection Summaries in Six Languages With Alternative Reading Strategies

Part 2 contains summaries of all selections in *Prentice Hall Literature: Timeless Voices, Timeless Themes.* Summaries are in English, Spanish, Vietnamese, Cantonese, Hmong, and Cambodian. An alternative reading strategy follows each English summary.

- Use the summaries in Part 2 to preview or review the selections.
- Use the alternative reading strategies in Part 2 to guide your reading or to check your understanding of the selection.

Name ______________________________ Date ______________

"The Cat Who Thought She Was a Dog and the Dog Who Thought He Was a Cat"
by Isaac Bashevis Singer

Summary Jan Skiba, a poor peasant, lives a simple life with his wife, his daughters, a cat, and a dog in a small hut. The family does not own a mirror, and they have rarely seen their images. Because the dog and cat have never seen other dogs and cats, the dog thinks he is a cat and the cat thinks she is a dog. One day the family buys a mirror from a peddler. The mirror causes a stir. Each girl is upset about her looks and fears she'll never make a good marriage. The dog and cat, disturbed by their images, fight. Skiba decides that having a mirror is troublesome and that the family would be better off admiring the world around them than themselves. He exchanges the mirror for other goods. Life returns to normal for the family and its pets.

Use Context Clues While you are reading, you may come across a word whose meaning you don't know. The context, or the words before and after the unfamiliar word, can provide clues to help you understand the meaning of the word. Context clues may be in the same sentence in which the unfamiliar word appears or in sentences before or after the word. Notice the word *gulden* in the following sentence from the story.

They asked the peddler his price and he said a half gulden, which was a lot of money.

You probably don't know the meaning of the word *gulden,* but you do know that the peddler was giving a price. The sentence also includes the word money. From these context clues, you can figure out that a gulden is probably an amount of money.

Directions: Read the sentences below from the selection. Use context clues to determine the meaning of each underlined word. Find the meaning of the word in the following list. Write its letter in the blank.

a. one of several payments
b. very interested
c. proposal
d. faults or flaws

____ 1. After a while, Jan Skiba's wife, Marianna, made a <u>proposition</u> to the peddler. She would pay him five groshen a month for the mirror.

____ 2. Now they could see themselves clearly and they began to find <u>defects</u> in their faces, defects they had never noticed before. Marianna was pretty but she had a tooth missing in front and she felt that this made her ugly.

____ 3. That day the women became so <u>absorbed</u> in the mirror they didn't cook supper, didn't make up the bed, and neglected all the other household tasks.

____ 4. When the peddler came for his monthly <u>installment</u>, Jan Skiba gave him back the mirror and, in its stead, bought kerchiefs and slippers for the women.

"The Cat Who Thought She Was a Dog and the Dog Who Thought He Was a Cat"

by Isaac Bashevis Singer

Resumen Jan Skiba, un campesino pobre, vive una vida sencilla con su esposa, sus hijas, una gata y un perro en una pequeña choza. La familia no tiene espejo y pocas veces han visto su propia imagen. Debido a que el perro y la gata nunca han visto otros perros y gatos, el perro piensa que es un gato y la gata piensa que es una perra. Un día la familia compra un espejo a un vendedor ambulante. El espejo causa un revuelo. A ninguna de las niñas le gusta su imagen y piensan que nunca van a encontrar marido. El perro y la gata, molestos con sus imágenes, comienzan a pelear. Skiba decide que el espejo es un problema y que la familia estaría mejor si sus miembros se contentan con admirrar el mundo que los rodea, sin verse a sí mismos. Intercambia el espejo por otros productos.
La vida de la familia y sus mascotas vuelve a la normalidad.

Tóm Lược Jan Skiba, một nông dân nghèo, sống một cuộc đời giản dị với người vợ, những đứa con gái, một con mèo, và một con chó trong một túp lều nhỏ. Gia đình không có tấm gương để soi, và họ ít thấy được khuôn mặt của chính họ. Bởi vì con mèo và con chó không bao giờ thấy được những con mèo và những con chó khác, nên con chó nghĩ nó là con mèo và con mèo nghĩ nó là con chó. Một hôm gia đình mua một tấm gương soi từ người bán hàng rong. Tấm gương soi gây nên một sự xúc động. Các cô con gái đều giận dữ về dung nhan của mình và sợ rằng họ sẽ không bao giờ có được cuộc hôn nhân tốt đẹp. Con mèo và con chó phiền hà về khuôn mặt của chúng và đánh nhau. Skiba thấy rằng có tấm kính soi là có điều rắc rối và rằng gia đình nên chiêm ngưỡng thế giới xung quanh mình hơn là chiêm ngưỡng chính dung nhan của họ. Ông đem đổi tấm kính lấy một món hàng khác. Cuộc sống trở lại bình thường cho cả gia đình và các con thú.

Lus txiav kom tsawg Jan Skiba yog ib tug yawg pluag pluag ua zog khwv noj lam nyob ua neej hnub dhau hnub. Nws muaj nws tus pojniam, nws cov ntxhais, nws tus miv thiab tus aub nrog nws nyob ua ke hauv ib lub menyuam tsev me me. Nws tsev neeg mas yeej ib txwm tsis muaj tsov iav saib, mas lawv yeej ib txwm tsis pom tias lawv tus duab no zoo li cas. Tsis tag li tus aub thiab tus miv nkawd yeej tsis tau pom lwm tus aub thiab lwm tus miv los dua, ces tus aub txawm xav tias tus aub no yog tus miv, ho tus miv xav tias tus miv no yog tus aub. Muaj ib hnub ces tsev neeg no thiaj li mus yuav tau ib daim tsom iav ntawm ib tug yawg muag khoom los. Daim tsom iav ua rau lawv muaj kev ntxhov siab heev. Cov menyuam ntxhais tsis hais leejtwg, lawv kuj tsis txaus siab tias cas lawv tsis zoo nkauj txaus, mas ntshai lawv yuav nrhiav tsis tau txiv. Ob tug tsaij aub thiab miv nkawd los kuj sib caum sib tog, vim nkawd los kuj tsis txaus siab rau nkawd tias nkawd lam zoo li. Skiba pom tias vim muaj diam tsom iav es thiaj ua rau sawvdaws muaj teebmeem tag npaum li, ces cia sawvdwaws txhob muaj, es cia sawvdaws pom thiab ntshaw luag tej xwb es thiaj li zoo. Ces nws thaij li muab daim tsom iav coj mus pauv lwm yam khoom coj los siv. Ces tsev neeg ntawd thiab tej tsiaj thiaj li rov qab nyob ntsiag twb to li qub dua.

摘要　窮苦農民簡・斯基巴和太太、女兒、貓和狗生活在一間小草房裡。一家人連一面鏡子也沒有，而且他們幾乎沒看見過自己是甚麼樣子。因為狗和貓從沒見過其他狗和貓，這條狗便想他是一隻貓，貓也以為自己是一條狗。一天，這家人從一個小販那裡買來一面鏡子。這面鏡子引起不安。每個女孩都對自己的相貌感到不安，害怕自己不會有好的婚姻。狗和貓因看到鏡子中的相貌而打起來。斯基巴決定有鏡子是件麻煩事，他們羨慕周圍的世界比羨慕自己會好得多。他用鏡子換了其他東西。一家人和寵物的生活又恢復了正常。

សេចក្តីសង្ខេប ចេន ស្គីបា ជាអ្នកស្រែក័សត់ទុរគតម្នាក់រស់នៅជារបៀបសមញ្ញ ជាមួយនិងភរិយា កូនស្រី ឆ្មា និងឆ្កែ ក្នុងខ្ទមតូចមួយ ។ គ្រួសារនេះពុំមានកញ្ចក់សំរាប់ឆ្លុះមើលមុខទេ ហើយពួកគេមិនសូវដែលបានឃើញរូបរាងខ្លួននោះផង ។ ដោយហេតុថាឆ្កែនិងឆ្មាមិនដែលបានឃើញឆ្កែនិងឆ្មាផ្សេងទៀត ឆ្កែនោះយល់ថាវាជាឆ្មា ហើយឆ្មានោះយល់ថាវាជាឆ្កែ ។ ថ្ងៃមួយគ្រួសារនេះបានទិញកញ្ចក់ពីអ្នកលក់ឥវ៉ាន់កំប៉ិកកំប៉ុកម្នាក់ ។ កញ្ចក់ធ្វើឲ្យម្នាក់ៗមិនសប្បាយចិត្តសោះ ។ ក្មេងស្រីម្នាក់ៗមិនសប្បាយចិត្តនឹងរូបខ្លួនទេ ហើយបារម្ភថាទៅអនាគតនឹងមិនអាចមានគូរស្រករល្អឡើយ ។ ឆ្កែនិងឆ្មាធុញទ្រាន់នឹងរូបខ្លួនឯង ក៏ចាប់ផ្តើមខាំគ្នា ។ ស្គីបាយល់ថាការមានកញ្ចក់បណ្តាលឲ្យមានរឿងហេតុទាស់ទែងគ្នាមិនឈប់សោះ ដូច្នេះគាត់យល់ថាម្នាក់ៗគួរអួតសរសើរពីអ្នកដទៃចុះ មិនចាំបាច់អួតសរសើរពីខ្លួនឯងទេ ។ គាត់យកកញ្ចក់នេះទៅប្តូរយករបស់ផ្សេងមកវិញ ។ រឿងរ៉ាវក្នុងគ្រួសារនេះក៏បានត្រឡប់ទៅជាធម្មតាឡើងវិញ ទាំងមនុស្សទាំងសត្វ ។

Name ______________________________ Date ______________

"Two Kinds" by Amy Tan

Summary A Chinese immigrant who has started life over in the United States wants her American-born daughter to be a famous prodigy. To that end, she pushes the reluctant girl first to be an actress like Shirley Temple, then a musician like a young pianist she saw performing on TV. Despite the girl's fiasco at a talent show, her mother expects her to continue piano lessons and eventually become a famous musician. The girl balks. She asserts in a forceful and hurtful way that she's not the obedient daughter her mother wants. In conflict with her mother's expectations, the daughter says that she can only be herself. Years later, she realizes that she is two kinds of daughter—one who follows her own mind and one who is obedient.

Apply Word Identification Strategies "Two Kinds" includes a number of compound words, or words that are made up of two or more words put together. Here are two examples from the story.

hair + cut = haircut   bath + room = bathroom

A compound word may seem long and completely unfamiliar. However, if you break it into the words that make it up, you will often find that you know the meaning of one or more of the shorter words. For example, in the selection, Jing-mei finds some *handwritten* scales. Suppose you do not know the word *handwritten.* You probably recognize the word *hand,* and the word *written.* You can figure out that *handwritten* means "written by hand." Some compound words, such as *speed-reading,* have a hyphen between the words that make them up.

Directions: Examine each of the following compound words from "Two Kinds." Beside each word, write the two words that make it up. If you do not know the meaning of the compound word, try to figure it out from the two smaller words. If necessary, use a dictionary for help. Write the meaning of the compound word on the line provided

1. tiptoes ______________ ______________
   meaning: ______________________________
2. housecleaning ______________ ______________
   meaning: ______________________________
3. high-pitched ______________ ______________
   meaning: ______________________________
4. earsplitting ______________ ______________
   meaning; ______________________________
5. daydreamed ______________ ______________
   meaning: ______________________________
6. showpiece ______________ ______________
   meaning: ______________________________

"Two Kinds"

by Amy Tan

Resumen Una inmigrante china, que ha comenzado una nueva vida en los Estados Unidos, desea que su hija, nacida en ese país, se convierta en una niña prodigio famosa. Para lograrlo, obliga a su hija a convertirse en actriz, como Shirley Temple; luego en pianista para emular a un joven músico que salió en televisión. A pesar del fracaso de la niña en un concurso de talentos, su madre le exige que continúe estudiando piano para que, con el tiempo, se convierta en una pianista famosa. La niña rehúsa y reafirma, en forma enérgica e hiriente, que no es la hija obediente que su madre desea. Oponiéndose a las expectativas de su madre, declara que sólo puede ser ella misma. Años más tarde, se da cuenta de que, en el fondo, es dos clases de hija—una que hace lo desea y otra que obedece.

Tóm Lược Một người di dân Trung Hoa đang xây dựng cuộc đời mới tại Hoa Kỳ muốn đứa con gái sinh tại Mỹ trở thành một thần đồng nổi tiếng. Với cứu cánh đó, bà thúc đẩy cô cón gái tuân hành miễn cưỡng trước tiên phải là một nữ diễn viên giống như Shirley Temple, sau đó là một nhạc sĩ giống như một nhạc công đàn dương cầm mà bà thấy trình tiễn trên Truyền Hình. Bất kể đến sự thất bại của cô gái trong một buổi trình diễn của những người có năng khiếu, người mẹ vẫn hy vọng cô con gái tiếp tục học đàn dương cầm để sau cùng trở thành một nhạc công nổi tiếng. Cô gái ngần ngại trước sự việc khó khăn đó. Cô quả quyết một cách mạnh mẻ và đau đớn rằng cô không phải là một cô con gái tuân lời như mẹ cô muốn. Trái ngược với những ước vọng của mẹ, cô gái nói cô chỉ muốn trở thành một người theo ý cô. Qua nhiều năm, cô ý thức rằng cô là người con gái có hai bản tính—một bản tính chỉ theo ý muốn của riêng mình, một bản tính nghe theo lời của mẹ.

Lus txiav kom tsawg Muaj ib tug poj Suav tsiv tuaj ua lub neej tshiab nyob rau tebchaws Asmeslivkas (United States) no xav kom nws tus menyuam uas yug nyob tebchaws no tau mus ua ib tug neeg txawj txawi ntse ntse uas muaj npe heev. Vim li ntawd, nws tus ntxhais twb tsis kam kiag, los nws pheej yuam nws tus ntxhais tas zog kom mus kawm ua ib tug neeg ua yeebyam kom keej keej li Shirley Temple, thiab kom zoo li tus neeg uas ntaus piano keej keej uas nws pom tuaj ua saum samthiaj hauv TV rau luag saib. Tus menyuam twb ua yeebyam tau tsis zoo kiag, los leej niam tseem yuam tas zog kom tus menyuam mus kawm ua ib tug neeg ntaus piano kom keej thiab muaj npe nrov. Ces tus menyuam thiaj li tsum tsis kam ua. Tus menyuam thiaj hais tawv tawv thiab hais tu siab tsawv rau leej niam tias nws tsis yog ib tug ntxhais mloog niam lus li nws niam xav. Nws tsis xav ua tus neeg zoo li nws niam hais, nws tsuas ua kom tau tus neeg zoo li nws tus kheej xwb. Tau ntau xyoo, tom qab, ces nws thiaj li mam ras tias ntshai nws no yeej yog ob hom ntxhais nyob rau ib lub cev—ib hom ces yog ua li nws siab nyiam, ho ib hom ces ua ib tug ntxhais mloog niam mloog txiv lus.

摘要 一個中國移民在美國開始了新的生活，她希望在美國出生的女兒成為著名的神童。為了做到這一點，她先強迫不情願的女孩當像雪利・坦普爾那樣的演員，然後又讓她成為像她在電視上看到的年輕鋼琴家。儘管女孩對天才表演屢遭失敗，她的母親仍希望她繼續上鋼琴課，最終能成為音樂家。女孩非常執拗。她有力又令人傷心地宣佈，她不是她母親希望的那種順從女兒。在與母親期望的衝突中，女兒說她祇能做她自己。多年後，她體會到，她原來是具有雙重性格的女兒——一種是我行我素，另一種是順從。

សេចក្តីសង្ខេប អណិកជនចិនម្នាក់ដែលបានមករស់នៅសហរដ្ឋអាមេរិកចង់ឲ្យកូនស្រីរបស់គាត់ដែលកើតនៅអាមេរិកនេះក្លាយទៅជាមនុស្សល្បីល្បាញម្នាក់ ។ ដើម្បីសម្រេចបំណងនេះ ជាដំបូងគាត់បានជម្រុញឲ្យកូនស្រីគាត់ធ្វើជាតារាភាពយន្តដូចជានាង ស៊ីលី ថែមផល, បន្ទាប់មក ឲ្យធ្វើជាតន្ត្រីករដូចជាអ្នកលេងព្យាណូក្មេងម្នាក់ដែលគាត់បានឃើញក្នុងទូរទស្សន៍ ។ ទោះបីជានាងបរាជ័យក្នុងការសំដែងក៏ដោយ ម្តាយនាងនៅតែរំពឹងលើនាងលេងព្យាណូតទៅទៀត គឺលុះត្រាតែនាងបានក្លាយទៅជាតន្ត្រីករម្នាក់ដ៏ល្បីល្បាញ ។ នាងបានប្រកែកមិនធ្វើតាមចិត្តម្តាយ ។ នាងបានប្រកែកទាំងគំរលនិងមួហ្នងថា នាងមិនមែនជាកូនស្រីដ៏ល្អដែលស្តាប់បង្គាប់ដំបូន្មានឪពុកម្តាយដូចម្តាយនាងចង់បាននោះទេ ។ ដោយទំនាស់នឹងបំណងម្តាយនាង នាងក៏និយាយថា នាងនឹងអាចធ្វើអ្វីកើតលុះណាតែនាងចង់។ ច្រើនឆ្នាំក្រោយមកទើបនាងយល់ជាក់ថានាងជាកូនស្រីមានប្រភេទពីរយ៉ាង គឺទីមួយជាកូនស្រីដែលចូលចិត្តធ្វើតាមទំនើងចិត្តខ្លួនឯង និងមួយទៀត ជាកូនស្រីដែលលុះតាមឱវាទមាតាបិតា ។

Name ______________________________ Date ______________

from "Song of Myself" by Walt Whitman
"I'm Nobody" by Emily Dickinson
"Me" by Walter de la Mare

Summary These three poems discuss the idea of identity—who we are, what makes each of us different, and how we are viewed by others. The speakers in these poems accept and like themselves just as they are. In "Song of Myself," the speaker celebrates himself and all selves as equally important. In "I'm Nobody," the speaker is proud of being a "Nobody" because, she says, a "Somebody" needs the praise of other people to feel worthwhile. In "Me," the speaker compares himself to trees and flowers. Like the things in nature, he says, he will always be who he is and no other.

Read Poetry According to Punctuation Reading poetry aloud helps you hear the speaker's voice, and helps you understand the meaning of the poem.

Directions: Listen to the audiocassette recordings of the poems as you follow along in your textbook. Listen carefully for the places where the reader pauses and stops. Then, with a partner, take turns reading the poems aloud. Practice pausing briefly at commas, ellipsis points (three dots), and dashes and longer at end marks. Don't stop at the ends of lines if there is no punctuation. You may use the following chart to note the various places in the poems where you should pause.

Poems	**Pausing Points**
from "Song of Myself"	
"I'm Nobody"	
"Me"	

from "Song of Myself" by Walt Whitman
"I'm Nobody" by Emily Dickinson
"Me" by Walter de la Mare

Resumen Estos tres poemas hablan de la idea de identidad–quiénes somos, qué es lo que hace que cada uno de nosotros sea diferente, y cómo nos ven los demás. Los narradores de estos poemas se aceptan a sí mismos y están satisfechos de ser quienes son. En "Canción de mí mismo", el narrador se celebra a sí mismo y a todas las personas como igualmente importantes. En "Soy nadie", la narradora está orgullosa de ser una "nadie" debido a que, según ella, una "nadie" necesita que otros la elogien para sentirse valiosa. En "Yo", el narrador se compara a sí mismo con los árboles y las flores. Nos dice que, al igual que las cosas de la naturaleza, él siempre será quién es y no otro.

Tóm Lược Ba bài thơ này thảo luận ý kiến về sự nhận diện Ủ chúng ta là ai, việc gì làm cho mỗi chúng ta khác nhau, và người khác nhìn chúng ta như thế nào. Nhân vật trong các bài thơ này chấp nhận và ưa thích chính bản thân họ. Trong bài ồBản Nhạc của Chính Tôiố, tác giả ca tụng ông và tất cả người khác quan trọng bằng nhau. Trong bài ôTôi Không Là Aiố, tâc giả tự hào mình là ồKhông Aiố vì bà nói rằng một ồNgười Nào Đóố cần có sự khen tặng của người khác để cảm thấy mình có giá trị. Trong bài ồTôiố, tâc giả so sánh mình với cây và bông hoa. Ông nói, giống như các vật trong thiên nhiên, ông sẽ luôn luôn là chính ông và không là ai khác.

Lus txiav kom tsawg Peb zaj ntsiab lus nkauj no yog hais txog kev nrhiav tus kheej-peb yog leej twg. Yam dab tsi ua rau peb ib leeg txawv ib leeg, thiab lwm leej lwm tus pom peb zoo li cas. Cov neeg uas tau hais lus tseg rau hauv cov nkauj no txais thiab txaus siab yuav nws tus kheej. Nyob hauv "Zaj Nkauj txog Kuv Tus Kheej," tus neeg hais lus no ua kev zoo siab rau nws tus kheej thiab lwm leej lwm tus uas tseem ceeb ib yam. Nyob hauv "Kuv Tsis Yog Leej Twg," tus neeg no zoo siab ua tus neeg uas "Tsis Yog Leej Twg" vim nws hais tias tus neeg uas "Yog Leej Twg" yuav tsum qhuas lwm leej lwm tus nws thiab li zoo siab rau nws tus kheej. Nyob hauv "Kuv," tus neeg hais lus no piv nws tus kheej rau tej ntoo tej paj. Zoo li tej yam uas yog hav zoov, nws hais tias, nws yeej yuav yog nws tus kheej mus tag ib sim tsis yog ib leeg twg.

摘要　這三首詩是探討自我認同的觀念 — 我們是誰，是什麼使得我們每一個人都不同，以及我們該如何看待別人。詩裡的主人翁都接受並喜愛原來的自我。在"自我的聲音"這首詩裡主人翁歌頌他自己和所有的自我都是同樣的重要。在"我誰都不是"這首詩裡主人翁以自己"不是別人"為榮，因為她說"有的人"需要靠別人的讚美才能找到自我的價值。在"我"這首詩裡主人翁把自己比喻為樹與花。他說，就像大自然裡的事物，他永遠是他自己。

សេចក្តីសង្ខេប កំណាព្យទាំងបីនេះពិភាក្សាពីគំនិតនៃបុគ្គលិកលក្ខណៈ - តើយើងជានរណា តើអ្វីដែលធ្វើឲ្យយើងម្នាក់ៗខុសគ្នា ហើយនិងរបៀបដែលអ្នកឯទៀតមានទស្សនៈចំពោះយើង ។ អ្នកពោលនៅក្នុងកំណាព្យទាំងនេះយល់ស្របនិងចូលចិត្តខ្លួនគេដូចដែលគេបានកើតមក ។ នៅក្នុងកំណាព្យ "ចំរៀងពីខ្លួនខ្ញុំ" អ្នកពោលអបអរសាទរខ្លួនគេនិងអ្វីៗទាំងអស់ពីខ្លួនគេដែលមានសារៈសំខាន់ជាទូទៅ ។ នៅក្នុងកំណាព្យ "ខ្ញុំមិនដូចនរណាទេ" អ្នកពោលមានមោទនៈភាពដែលគាត់មិនដូចនរណា" ពីព្រោះគាត់និយាយថា "ការដែលដូចនរណាម្នាក់" ត្រូវការសរសើរពីនរណាម្នាក់ដើម្បីឲ្យមានតម្លៃ ។ នៅក្នុងកំណាព្យ "រូបខ្ញុំ" អ្នកពោលប្រៀបធៀបរូបគាត់ទៅនឹងដើមឈើនិងផ្កា ។ ដូចជារបស់នានានៅក្នុងធម្មជាតិ គាត់និយាយថា គាត់នឹងនៅតែជាខ្លួនគាត់រហូតមិនក្លាយទៅជានរណាទៀតឡើយ ។

Name ______________________________ Date ______________

"**My Furthest-Back Person**" by Alex Haley

Summary In this essay, Alex Haley describes how he traced his ancestors. Remembering family names he had heard from his grandmother, he began his search by examining old census reports. He recalled stories about the family's "furthest-back person"—an African kidnapped from his native land and sold into slavery in the United States. He thought the strange "k" sounds his grandmother had muttered over the years might be words from an African language. He discovered that one of the sounds, Kin-tay (Kinte) is the name of an old African clan. He flew to Gambia and, after traveling on foot and by boat deep into the back country, he finally found his distant relatives. An old man told him the clan's history, confirming that Haley's "furthest-back person" was a Kinte, kidnapped in Africa and sold into slavery in Annapolis, Maryland, in 1767.

Break Down Long Sentences Many of the sentences in this story are three lines long—or even longer. To help understand the long sentences, break them down into parts. Use the punctuation marks (commas, dots, dashes, colons, and semicolons) to find appropriate places to break. You may need to add a word or two to have the part make sense. Study the following example.

Sentence: I was beginning to tire, when in utter astonishment I looked upon the names of Grandma's parents: Tom Murray, Irene Murray ... older sisters of Grandma's as well—every one of them a name that I'd heard countless times on her front porch.

Sentence broken into parts: I was beginning to tire. In utter astonishment I looked upon the names of Grandma's parents. [Their names were] Tom Murray, Irene Murray. [The names included] older sisters of Grandma's as well. Every one of them [was] a name that I'd heard countless times on her front porch.

DIRECTIONS: Find at least four more sentences in the essay that are three or more lines long. Break them into parts. Compare your sentences with those of your classmates.

____

____

____

____

____

____

____

____

____

____

____

____

____

____

“My Furthest-Back Person”
by Alex Haley

Resumen En este ensayo, Alex Haley cuenta cómo logró encontrar a sus ancestros. Recordando los nombres de la familia que había oído de boca de su abuela, comenzó su búsqueda examinando viejos informes del censo. Recordó historias de la “persona más lejana” de la familia–un africano raptado de su tierra nativa y vendido como esclavo en los Estados Unidos. Pensó que los extraños sonidos “K” que hacía su abuela podrían ser palabras de un idioma africano. Descubrió que uno de los sonidos, Kin-tay (Kinte) era el nombre de un viejo clan africano. Voló a Gambia y, después de viajar a pie y en bote a un lugar recóndito del país, finalmente encontró a sus familiares lejanos. Un anciano le contó la historia del clan, confirmando que la “persona más lejana” de Haley era un Kinte, raptado en África y vendido como esclavo en Annapolis, Maryland, en 1767.

Tóm Lược Trong bài văn này, Alex Haley diễn tả cách ông tìm lại tổ tiên của ông như thế nào. Nhớ những tên gia đình do bà ông kể lại, ông bắt dầu việc tìm tiếm bằng cách xem lại các báo cáo thống kê. Ông nhớ lại những câu chuyện về ồngười trước xa xôi nhấtố của gia đình (một người Phi Châu bị bắt cóc từ nước của mình và đem bán làm nô lệ tại Hoa Kỳ. Ông nghĩ rằng cách phát âm chữ
ồKố kỳ lạ mà bà ông lẩm bẩm trong bao năm qua có thể là những chữ từ tiếng Phi châu. Ông tìm ra rằng một trong những phát âm, Kin-tay (Kinte) là tên của một bộ lạc Phi Châu cũ. Ông đi phi cơ qua Gambia và sau khi du hành bằng đường bộ và tàu sâu vào vùng hẻo lánh, cuối cùng ông tìm được họ hàng xa. Một ông già kể cho ông nghe lịch sử của bộ lạc, và xác nhận rằng ồngười trước-xa xôi nhấtố quả là một người Kinte bị bắt cóc tại Phi Châu và dem bán làm nô lệ tại Annapolis, Maryland trong năm 1767.

Lus txiav kom tsawg Nyob rau hauv daim ntawv no, Alex Haley piv txog nws kev nrov nrhiav nws poj koob yawm koob. Nco txog nws tseg neeg cov npe uas nws pog tau qhia rau nws, nws nrov mus tshawb tej qub ntauv qub ntawv. Nws nco me ntsis txog tej lus nruag uas hais txog “Tus Neeg Deb Tshaj Plaws-Tom Qab”- tus neeg dub ntawv uas tau nraug ntes mus ua qhev rau hauv tej chaws Amesliskas (United States). Nws xav txog tus niam ntawv “k” lub suab zoo li cas thaum nws pog hais nrhau tau ntau xyoo tom qab zoo li lo lus no yog los ntawm cov neeg Tawv Dub (African) cov lus. Nws nrhiav tau ib lub suab, Kin-tay (kinte) yog ib lub npe uas yog ib pab neeg Tawv Dub pawg. Nws tau caij nyuaj hoom mus rau Gambia thiab, tau mus kaw ntaw, thiab nkoj rau hauv zos. Nws mam li nrhiav tau nws cov kwv tij. Ib tug yawg laus qhia nws txog nws cov neeg lus neej tas los, qhia tau hais tias Haley “Tus Neeg Deb Tshaj Plaws-Tom Qab” yog Kinte, tau nraug ntes thiab muag los ua qhev nyob rau hauv Annapolis, Maryland rau lub xyoo 1767.

摘要　在這篇短文裡海里描述他如何尋找到他的祖先。他記得從祖母那兒聽過家族的名字，於是他開始從查閱人口普查報告著手。他回想起有關家族“最早來到的人”的故事 —— 一個從非洲自己的土地上被抓走且販賣到美國成為奴隸。他想起祖母喃喃多年奇怪的“k”音也許是來自一種非洲的語言。他發現了其中的一個音Kin-tay(Kinte)是一個非洲老部落的名字，於是他飛到了甘比亞(Gambia)。靠著一雙腳與船深入偏僻的地方終於找到了他的遠親。一位老人告訴他有關該部族的歷史，也確定了海里的“最早來到的人”是一名Kinte部落的人，他是在1767年從非洲被抓走且在馬里蘭州安那伯利斯(Annapolis)被販賣成為奴隸。

សេចក្តីសង្ខេប ក្នុងការតែងនេះ Alex Haley រៀបរាប់ពីរបៀបដែលគាត់តាមដានរកពូជពង្សរបស់គាត់ ។ ការចងចាំត្រកូលដែលគាត់បានឮពីជីដូនរបស់គាត់ គាត់ចាប់ផ្តើមការស្វែងរករបស់គាត់ដោយពិចារណាពីរបាយការណ៍នៃការស្រង់ចំនួនប្រជាជនកន្លងជាយូរមកហើយ ។ គាត់នឹកឃើញរឿងស្តីពី "ជនដែលនៅជួរដើមគេបំផុត" របស់គ្រួសារ - ជាជនជាតិអាហ្វ្រិកាំងដែលត្រូវគេចាប់ពង្រត់ពីដែនដីកំណើត ហើយលក់ធ្វើជាទាសករនៅក្នុងសហរដ្ឋអាមេរិក ។ គាត់បានគិតថាសម្លេង" ខេ "ចម្លែកដែលជីដូនរបស់គាត់បានរអ៊ូជាច្រើនឆ្នាំកន្លងមកអាចជាពាក្យចេញពីភាសាអាហ្វ្រិកាំងមួយ ។ គាត់រកឃើញថាសម្លេងមួយនៃសម្លេង ឃិនធេ (Kinte) គឺជាឈ្មោះនៃកុលសម្ព័ន្ធអាហ្វ្រិកាំងមួយ ។ គាត់ជិះយន្តហោះទៅ Gambia ហើយបន្ទាប់ពីការធ្វើដំណើរដោយជើងនិងដោយទូកចូលជ្រៅទៅភាគខាងចុងនៃប្រទេសនៅទីបំផុត គាត់បានរកឃើញសាច់ញាតិដែលជាសាច់ឆ្ងាយរបស់គាត់ ។ តាចាស់ម្នាក់បាននិយាយរឿងកុលសម្ព័ន្ធនោះប្រាប់គាត់បញ្ជាក់ថា "ជនដែលនៅជួរដើមគេបំផុត "របស់ Haley គឺជាពួក Kinte ត្រូវគេចាប់ពង្រត់ក្នុងទ្វីបអាហ្វ្រិក ហើយយកទៅលក់ឲ្យធ្វើជាទាសករ នៅ Annapolis, Maryland ក្នុងឆ្នាំ 1767 ។

Name ______________________________ Date ______________

"The Third Level" by Jack Finney

Summary Grand Central Station is supposed to have two levels. Yet Charlie finds a tunnel that takes him down to a third level, where he finds himself in the year 1894. Charlie wants to buy himself and his wife train tickets for a small town called Galesburg as it was in 1894. However, the ticket clerk will not take his modern money. Charlie later buys old-style money and tries without success to find the third level. His psychiatrist friend, Sam, says that Charlie must have imagined the third level to escape from pressures of the present. Sam later disappears. Charlie finds a letter in his grandfather's stamp collection. It is dated 1894 and addressed to Charlie. It is from Sam, who says he found the third level and has a hay and feed business in Galesburg.

Use Context to Determine Meaning When you come across a name, word, or phrase you don't know, use its context—the words, phrases, and sentences around it—to figure out its meaning. To help you identify context clues, look for words and phrases that define, compare, contrast, describe, provide examples, or offer information about the unfamiliar word or phrase.

Directions: Practice identifying context clues. On the lines provided, write the context clues for each underlined word or phrase.

1. That made my wife kind of mad, but he explained that he meant the modern world is full of <u>insecurity</u>, fear, war, worry and all the rest of it, and that I just want to escape.

   insecurity ______________________________

2. I am just an <u>ordinary</u> guy named Charley, thirty-one years old...; I passed a dozen men who looked just like me.

   ordinary ______________________________

3. Sometimes I think Grand Central is <u>growing like a tree</u>, pushing out new corridors and staircases like roots.

   growing like a tree: ______________________________

4. It's a wonderful town still, with big old frame houses, huge lawns and tremendous trees whose branches meet overhead and <u>roof the streets</u>.

   roof the streets ______________________________

"The Third Level"
by Jack Finney

Resumen Se supone que Grand Central Station tiene dos niveles. Sin embargo, Charlie encuentra un túnel que le lleva a un tercer nivel, donde se encuentra en el año 1894. Charlie desea comprar boletos de tren para ir junto con su esposa a una pequeña ciudad llamada Galesburg, tal como era en 1894. Sin embargo, el vendedor de boletos no acepta su dinero moderno. Más tarde, Charlie compra dinero antiguo e intenta, sin éxito, encontrar el tercer nivel. Sam, su amigo siquiatra, dice que Charlie seguramente imaginó el tercer nivel para escaparse de las presiones del presente. Más tarde, Sam desaparece. Charlie encuentra una carta en la colección de estampillas de su abuelo. Está fechada en 1894 y dirigida a Charlie. Es una carta de Sam, que dice que ha encontrado el tercer nivel y tiene un negocio de venta de paja y forraje en Galesburg.

Tóm Lược Trạm Grand Central đáng lẽ có hai tầng. Vậy mà Charlie tìm được một đường hầm dẫn xuống tầng thứ ba, nơi đây anh thấy mình đang ở trong năm 1894. Charlie muốn mua vé xe lửa cho anh và vợ anh đến một thị trấn nhỏ tên Galesburg như đang trong năm 1894. Tuy nhiên, người bán vé không chịu nhận tiền hiện thời của anh. Sau đó Charlie mua tiền kiểu thời xủa và cố gắng tìm tầng thứ ba nhưng không thành công. Một người bạn tâm lý học, tên Sam, cho rằng Charlie chỉ tưởng tượng đến tầng thứ ba để tránh những áp lực hiện tại. Sau đó Sam biệt tích. Charlie tìm thấy một lá thơ trong bộ sưu tầm tem của ông anh ta, thơ đề năm 1894 và gởi đến cho Charlie. Lá thơ đó của Sam nói rằng anh tìm thấy tầng thứ ba và kinh doanh bán cỏ khô và thực phẩm gia súc tại Galesburg.

Lus txiav kom tsawg Grand Central Station tig yuav tsum muaj ob xab. Tab sis Charlie nrhiav tau ib lub qhov tsua uas coj nws mus rau xab peb hauv qab, uas nws pom tau tias nws nrov qab mus rau xyoo 1894. Charlie xav yuav pib rau nws thiab nws tus poj niam nkawv mus xyuas ib lub zos me me hu ua Galesburg uas zoo li thaum uas yog xyoo 1894. Tab sis, tus neeg muag pib tsis kam txais nws cov nyiaj uas yog lus sijhawm tam sim no. Tom qab Charlie mam li yuav cov nyiaj qub qub thaum u thiab coj los nrhiav kev nrov mus rau xab peb saum ntuj tab sis nrhiav tsis tau. Nws tus phooj ywg uas kawm txog kho hlwb, Sam, hais rau nws tias nws yuav tsum xav txog xab peb xwb kom nws tsis txhob nyuaj siab txog lub sijhawm tam sim no. Tom qab tsis ntev, Sam ploj lawm. Charlie nrhiav tau ib daim ntawv nyob rau hauv nws yawg qhov chaw khaws stamp. Daim ntawv sau xyoo 1894 thiab chaw nyob xa rau Charlie. Yog los ntawm Sam, tus uas tau hais tias nws nrhia tau xab peb muaj plej pub noj kev ua luam nyob rau hauv lub zos Galesburg.

摘要 紐約大中央車站應該是兩層的建築物，但是查理卻發現有個隧道把他帶到第三層，在那兒他發覺自己竟然身在1894年。查理想為自己和妻子買前往1894年的一個叫蓋勒斯堡小鎮的火車票，但是售票員不會接受現代的貨幣，於是查理買了舊錢幣想再回去買票時卻找不到第三層了。他的精神病醫生朋友山姆說查理必須靠想像的第三層來逃避現實的壓力。不久之後山姆就消失了。查理在祖父的集郵中找到一封1894年、收信人是查理的信件。這封信寄自山姆，說他找到了第三層且在蓋勒斯堡從事家畜飼料業。

សេចក្ដីសង្ខេប ស្ថានិយកណ្ដាលចំបងត្រូវតែមានពីរជាន់ ។ ទោះយ៉ាងនេះក្ដី Charlie រកឃើញរូងដែលនាំគាត់ចុះទៅជាន់ទីបី ដែលគាត់ដឹងថាគាត់ស្ថិតនៅក្នុងឆ្នាំ 1894 ។ Charlie ចង់ទិញសំបុត្ររថភ្លើងសំរាប់ខ្លួនគាត់និងប្រពន្ធរបស់គាត់ទៅកាន់កូនក្រុងមួយហៅថា Galesburg ដូចដែលមាននៅឆ្នាំ 1894 នាកាលនោះ ។ ប៉ុន្តែអ្នកលក់សំបុត្រមិនយកលុយជំនាន់ថ្មីរបស់គាត់ទេ ។ ក្រោយមក Charlie ទិញលុយជំនាន់ចាស់ ហើយព្យាយាមដោយមិនបានជោគជ័យដើម្បីស្វែងរកជាន់ទីបី ។ មិត្តខាងចិត្តសាស្ត្ររបស់គាត់ឈ្មោះ Sam និយាយថា Charlie ត្រូវតែស្រមើស្រមៃរកជាន់ទីបីដើមភៀសខ្លួនចេញពីការកៀបសង្កត់នៃពេលបច្ចុប្បន្ន ។ ក្រោយមក Sam ក៏បាត់ខ្លួនទៅ ។ Charlie រកឃើញសំបុត្រមួយនៅក្នុងការសន្សំតែមរបស់ជីតាគាត់ ។ សំបុត្រនោះចុះថ្ងៃឆ្នាំ 1894 ហើយផ្ញើមកចំពោះ Charlie ។ សំបុត្រនោះផ្ញើមកពី Sam ដែលរៀបរាប់ ថាគាត់រកឃើញជាន់ទីបី ហើយគាត់មានជំនួញស្មៅសំរាប់ចិញ្ចឹម សត្វនៅក្នុងក្រុង Galesburg ។

Name ______________________________ Date ______________

"A Day's Wait" by Ernest Hemingway

Summary When Schatz has the flu, his father calls the doctor. The doctor says Schatz's temperature is 102 degrees. A few hours later, Schatz asks about his temperature. He is very quiet and worried, and his father cannot understand why. Finally, Schatz asks when he is going to die. His father says he is not that ill, and will not die. Schatz says boys at school in France told him a person could not live with a temperature of 44 degrees. His father then realizes Schatz has been waiting to die all day. He explains to Schatz that the French use a different kind of thermometer. On that thermometer, a normal temperature is 37 degrees. On Schatz's thermometer, normal is 98. Schatz is relieved by the explanation and becomes visibly relaxed.

Reread When you read a story, you may be puzzled at first by the way a character behaves. By the end of the story, your questions may be answered. If they are not, you can read part or all of the story again. The second time, look for specific details that will answer your questions about the character's behavior.

Directions: Use a Character Behavior Chart like the following to describe Schatz's actions. As you read the story the first time, list details that tell how Schatz behaves. If you understand why he behaves that way, check the box under "Read." If you don't understand, read the story a second time to find the answer. Then check the box under "Reread." The first action is listed for you.

BEHAVIOR	READ	REREAD
Schatz enters his father's room and closes the window.		

"A Day's Wait"
by Ernest Hemingway

Resumen Cuando Schatz se enferma de gripe, su padre llama al médico. El médico dice que Schatz tiene 102 grados de fiebre. Unas horas más tarde, Schatz pregunta cuál es su temperatura. Está muy callado y preocupado, y su padre no puede entender por qué. Finalmente, Schatz pregunta cuándo se va a morir. Su padre sabe que no está tan enfermo, y que no se va a morir. Schatz dice que los niños en la escuela en Francia le dijeron que una persona no puede vivir con una temperatura de 44 grados. Su padre se da cuenta entonces de que Schatz ha estado esperando la muerte durante todo el día. Le explica a Schatz que los franceses usan otro tipo de termómetro. En ese termómetro, la temperatura normal es de 37 grados. En el termómetro de Schatz, la temperatura normal es de noventa y ocho grados. Schatz se siente aliviado con la explicación y se tranquiliza visiblemente.

Tóm Lược Khi Schatz bị bệnh cúm, cha em gọi đến bác sĩ. Bác sĩ nói nhiệt độ trong người của Schatz là 102 độ. Vài giờ sau, Schatz hỏi về nhiệt độ của em. Em trở nên im lặng và lo âu, và cha em không hiểu tại sao. Cuối cùng, Schatz hỏi khi nào em sẽ chết. Cha em nói rằng em không bệnh nặng, và sẽ không bị chết. Schatz nói các bạn trai ở trường tại Pháp nói với em rằng người ta không thể sống được nếu nhiệt độ cao hơn 44 độ. Lúc đó cha em mới biết rằng Schatz đang chờ chết cả ngày. Ông giải thích cho Schatz rằng người Pháp dùng loại nhiệt kế khác. Trên nhiệt kế này, nhiệt độ bình thường là 37 độ. Trên nhiệt kế của Schatz, nhiệt độ bình thường là chín mươi tám. Schatz cả thấy thoải mái hơn sau khi được giải thích và tự nhiên thấy khỏe khoắn trở lại.

Lub ntsiab lus Thaum Schatz tau khaub thuas, nws txiv hu rau kws kho mob. Tus kws kho mob hais tias Schatz kub txog 102 degrees. Ob peb xuab moo tom qab Schatz nug txog seb nws kub li cas. Nws ua twjywm thiab txhawj kawg. Nws txiv tsis to taub xyov yog ua cas. Thaum kawg Schatz thiaj nug tias thaum twg nws mam tuag. Nws txiv hais tias nws tsis mob heev npaum li ntawd, thiab nws yuav tsis tuag. Schatz hais tias cov menyuam tub tom tsev kawm ntawv tim Fabkis qhia nws hias tias ib tug neeg yeej nyob tsis tau yog nws kub txog 44 degrees. Nws txiv thiaj paub tias Schatz twb tos tuag los ib hnub lawm. Nws qhia rau Schatz tias cov neeg Fabkis siv lwm yam ntsuas kub ntsuas txias (thermometer) txawv. Yam lawv siv ntawd yog nyob rau 37 degrees xwb ces zoo lawm. Hos Schatz tus ntsuas kub ntsuas txias ntawv, yog tab tom zoo no mas yuav tsum nyob rau cuaj caum yim. Schatz thiaj tso siab lug thaum hnov li ntawd.

摘要 當沙慈得了流行性感冒時，他的父親請來醫生。醫生說沙慈的體溫是102度。幾小時過後，沙慈問有關他的體溫。他異常地安靜與擔憂，他的父親不懂他為何如此。終於沙慈問到自己是否快要死去了，他父親說他並沒病得那麼重所以不會死的。沙慈於是說從前在法國時學校的男孩告訴他一個人的體溫高達44度時就不可能活了。他的父親才知道沙慈整天都在等著死亡的到臨。父親於是向沙慈解釋法國使用的是不同的溫度計。那種溫度計的人體正常溫度是37度，而沙慈用的溫度計正常溫度則是九十八度。父親的一番解說讓沙慈從擔憂中解脫並很明顯地輕鬆下來。

សេចក្តីសង្ខេប ពេលដែល Schatz កើតរោគផ្តាសាយធំ ឪពុករបស់វាហៅវេជ្ជបណ្ឌិត ។ វេជ្ជបណ្ឌិតនិយាយថាកំដៅរបស់ Schatz មាន ១០២ អង្សា ។ ពីរបីម៉ោងក្រោយមក Schatz សួរពីកំដៅរបស់វា ។ វាមិននិយាយច្រើននិងព្រួយបារម្ភណាស់ ហើយឪពុកវាមិនអាចយល់ថាមកពីហេតុអ្វីឡើយ ។ ទីបំផុត Schatz សួរថាតើវានឹងស្លាប់នៅពេលណា ។ ឪពុកវានិយាយថាវាមិនឈឺដល់ថ្នាក់នោះទេ ហើយមិនស្លាប់ទេ ។ Schatz និយាយថា ក្មេងប្រុសម្នាក់នៅសាលារៀនប្រាប់វាថាមនុស្សម្នាក់មិនអាចរស់បានទេពេលមានកំដៅដល់ ៤៤ អង្សានោះ ។ ពេលនោះទើបឪពុកវាដឹងថា Schatz បានរង់ចាំស្លាប់ពេញមួយថ្ងៃហើយ ។ គាត់ពន្យល់ប្រាប់ Schatz ថាបារាំងប្រើប្រដាប់វាស់កំដៅផ្សេង ។ នៅលើប្រដាប់វាស់កំដៅនោះ កំដៅធម្មតាគឺ ៣៧ អង្សា ។ នៅលើប្រដាប់វាស់កំដៅរបស់ Schatz កំដៅធម្មតាគឺកៅសិបប្រាំបីអង្សា ។ Schatz បានធូរស្រាលដោយសារការពន្យល់នោះ ហើយបន្ធូរអារម្មណ៍សំរាកដោយស្រួល ។

Name ____ Date ________________

"Was Tarzan a Three-Bandage Man?" by Bill Cosby
"Oranges" by Gary Soto

Summary These selections deal with childhood memories. "Was Tarzan a Three-Bandage Man?" recalls a time when the author and his friends tried to act cool by imitating their heroes. Bill's mother scolds him for walking funny to imitate a famous baseball player and putting bandages on his face like a prizefighter. In the end, Bill realizes it might have been better to admire the injurer rather than the injured. In "Oranges," a boy of twelve walks with a girl for the first time. He has two oranges and a nickel in his pocket. When he asks what she wants from a store, the girl chooses a ten-cent chocolate. He puts his nickel and an orange on the counter. Silently, the clerk accepts them.

Context Clues This article may contain some words that you don't know. You could look up each word in a dictionary. But you also may be able to figure out the meaning by using **context clues**. Look at the words and phrases that are near the word you don't know. The familiar words and phrases can help you guess the meaning of the unfamiliar word.

Directions: In each sentence below, read the word in **boldface print**. Then find another word or phrase in the sentence that can help you guess the word's meaning. Underline your clues. Write what you think the word means. You may check a dictionary if necessary. The first one has been done for you.

1. We **imitated** their walk. When they walked bowlegged, <u>we did it too</u>.
   Meaning: did the same thing as someone else
2. People with **acne** walked that way too, but it wasn't their bad skin that we admired.
   Meaning: ______________________________
3. Tough guys wore bandages over their eye, but really tough guys wore **tourniquets** around their necks.
   Meaning: ______________________________
4. Trying to be like the injured was ridiculous, since we should have been **emulating** those who caused the injuries.
   Meaning: ______________________________
5. (Supply your own sentence from the selection here.)
   ____
   ____
   Meaning: ______________________________

"Was Tarzan a Three Bandage Man?" by Bill Cosby
"Oranges" by Gary Soto

Resumen Estos títulos se ocupan de los recuerdos de la infancia. "Was Tarzan a Three-Bandage Man?" recuerda un período en el que el autor y sus amigos trataban de ser populares a base de imitar a sus héroes. La madre de Bill lo regaña por caminar de manera rara para imitar a un famoso jugador de béisbol y ponerse unas vendas en la cara como un boxeador. Al final, Bill se da cuenta de que hubiera sido mejor admirar a quien ocasionó las heridas en lugar de a quien las sufrió. En "Oranges", un niño de doce años camina con una niña por primera vez. Tiene dos naranjas y una moneda de cinco centavos en el bolsillo. Cuando le pregunta a la niña qué quiere comprar en la tienda, ella elige un chocolate que cuesta diez centavos. Pone la moneda de cinco centavos y una naranja en el mostrador. En silencio, el empleado las acepta.

Tóm lược Loạt bài này nói về những kỷ niệm của thời thơ ấu. Bài "Was Tarzan a Three-Bandage Man?" nhắc lại thời trước khi tác giả và bạn bè cố bắt chước các điệu bộ oai dũng của những người hùng lý tưởng của họ. Bà mẹ của Bill vẫn mắng Bill vì dáng đi buồn cười bắt chước một cầu thủ base-ball nổi tiếng, và dán băng đầy mặt như một người đấu thủ quyền anh. Sau cùng Bill nhận ra rằng tốt hơn hết là nên bắt chước người đả thương hơn là người bị thương. Trong bài "Oranges," một cậu bé mười hai tuổi đi dạo với một cô gái lần đầu tiên. Cậu có hai trái cam và một đồng năm xu trong túi. Cậu hỏi cô bé muốn mua gì trong tiệm thì cô đáp là muốn kẹo sô-cô-la giá là 10 xu. Cậu để đồng năm xu và một trái cam lên quầy hàng. Người bán hàng lẳng lặng nhận tiền cậu trả.

Lub ntsiab lus Cov no hais txog qhov kev xav txog thaum tseem yog me nyuam yaus. "Was Tarzan a Three Bandage Man?" nco txog lub caij thaum tus kwv sau ntawv thiab nws cov phooj yug xyaum ua ub no zoo li lwm cov tawj (hero). Bill niam cem nws qhov nws mus kev zoo li ib tug neeg txawb pob nto moo thiab muaj ntaub pav taub hau li tus sib ntaus yuav nyiaj. Thaum khawg, Bill pom hais tias tej zaum ntshai yuav zoo tshab qhov nyiam tus raug mob dua yus raug mob. Nyob hauv "Oranges," ib tus tub muaj kaum ob xyoos rhog ib tus ntxhais taug kev zaum xub thawj. Nws muaj ob lub txiv kab ntxwv thiab ib lub nickel nyob hauv nws hnab ris. Thaum nws nug tus ntxhais xav yuav ab tsi nyob hauv tsev muaj khoom no, tus ntxhais xaiv ib tus chocolate raug kaum npib liab. Nws muaj nws lub nickel thiab ib lub txiv kab ntxwv tso saum roog. Ntsiag to, tus neeg ua hauj lwm cia li txais lawm xwb.

摘要 這幾篇文章談到兒時的回憶。在 "Was Tarzan a Three-Bandage Man?" 中，作者回憶當年和朋友模仿心目中的英雄，企圖表現出很酷的樣子。比爾的母親斥責他因為模仿一位有名的棒球球員而走路很滑稽，還把繃帶貼在臉上擺出一副職業拳擊手的模樣。最後比爾發現，欽佩使人受傷的人比欽佩受傷者還好。 在 "Oranges"一文中，一個十二歲的男孩第一次和女孩走在一起。他的口袋裡有兩個柳丁和五毛錢。當他問女孩想要什麼店裡的什麼東西時，她選了一個十分錢的巧克力糖。他把五分錢和一個柳丁擺在櫃台上，收銀員默默的收下了。

សេចក្តីសង្ខេប អត្ថបទជ្រើសរើសនេះពាក់ព័ន្ធជាមួយអនុស្សាវរីយ៍ពីកុមារភាព ។ អត្ថបទ "Was Tarzan a Three-Bandage Man?" រំលឹកអំពីពេលដែលអ្នកនិពន្ធនិងមិត្តរបស់គាត់សាកល្បងដើរតួលយដោយធ្វើត្រាប់តាមតួឯកដែលពួកគេចូលចិត ។ ម្តាយរបស់ Bill ជេរគាត់ដោយសារគាត់ដើរគួរឲ្យចង់សើចធ្វើត្រាប់តាមអ្នកលេងបេសបាល់ល្បីឈ្មោះ ហើយនិងបិតបង់ស្អិតនៅលើមុខដូចជាអ្នកប្រយុទ្ធយករង្វាន់ ។ នៅទីបញ្ចប ។ ដឹងខ្លួនថាវាគួរតែសរសើរអ្នកធ្វើឲ្យគេមានរបួសប្រសើរជាងអ្នកដែលត្រូវគេធ្វើឲ្យរបួស ។ នៅក្នុងអត្ថបទ "Oranges" ក្មេងប្រុសម្នាក់ដើរជាមួយក្មេងស្រីម្នាក់ជាលើកដំបូង ។ វាមានក្រូចពីរនិងកាក់ប្រាំសេននៅក្នុងហោប៉ៅរបស់វា ។ នៅពេលដែលវាសួរនាងថាតើនាងចង់បានអ្វីពីហាងទំនិញ ក្មេងស្រីនោះរើសយកស៊ូកូឡាមួយតម្លៃដប់សេន ។ វាដាក់កាក់ប្រាំសេនរបស់វានិងក្រូចមួយនៅលើត ។ អ្នកលក់យល់ព្រមទទួលការបង់ថ្លៃទំនិញនោះដោយស្ងាត់ស្ងៀម ។

Name ______________________________ Date ______________

from *In Search of Our Mothers' Gardens* by Alice Walker

Summary In this moving and solemn tribute, the author praises her mother and other black women like her for their hard work, dedication, and inspiration. Walker views her mother as an artist whose creative spirit inspired her own life as a writer. Her mother shared herself as an artist through the stories she told and through the beautiful flower gardens she grew, despite the family's poverty. Walker admires how black women of her mother's generation managed to "hold on," despite the exhausting labors placed upon them. As a result, Walker inherited a respect for strength as well as a love of beauty in life.

Ask Questions A good way to better understand the selection is to ask yourself questions as you read. As you read, think of what you already know about the subject, and then think of what questions you would like answered.

DIRECTIONS: Think about people you know who work tirelessly. Remembering how you feel about them will help you develop a deeper understanding of the woman Alice Walker describes in *In Search of Our Mothers' Gardens*. Discuss your ideas with a small group. Then begin a KWL chart like the one shown to record interesting ideas and details you know and questions you have.

- Start the chart by filling in what you know about people who work hard.
- Add questions about what you want to know.
- As you read the excerpt from *In Search of Our Mothers' Gardens*, continue the KWL chart with what you Learn, and add new questions that come up.

What I **K**now	What I **W**ant to Know	What I've **L**earned
______________	______________	______________
______________	______________	______________
______________	______________	______________
______________	______________	______________
______________	______________	______________
______________	______________	______________
______________	______________	______________
______________	______________	______________

Resumen En este conmovedor y solemne homenaje, la autora elogia a su madre y a otras mujeres negras como ella por su trabajo esforzado, su dedicación, y su inspiración. Walker ve a su madre como una artista cuyo espíritu creativo inspiró su propia vida de escritora. Su madre se compartió a si misma como artista con los cuentos que contaba y con los hermosos jardines florales que cultivaba, a pesar de la pobreza de la familia. Walker admira cómo las mujeres negras de la generación de su madre lograron seguir adelante a pesar del trabajo extenuante que debían realizar. En consecuencia, Walker heredó el respeto por el carácter, así como el amor por la belleza en la vida.

Tóm Lược Trong bài văn cảm động và tỏ lònh tôn kính này, tác giả khen ngợi mẹ của cô và những phụ nữ da đen khác về những việc làm khó nhọc, cần mẫn, và gợi cảm của họ. Walker nhìn mẹ của mình như là một nghệ sĩ tạo nên những gợi cảm cho cuộc đời của bà là một nhà văn. Mẹ của bà được ví như một nghệ sĩ qua những câu chuyện bà kể lại và qua những vườn hoa đẹp bà trồng, bất chấp tình trạng thiếu hụt của gia đình. Walker khen ngợi những phụ nữ da đen trong thế hệ của mẹ bà làm thế nào để "bám víu", bất chấp những việc làm khó nhọc. Kết quả là, Walker có được sự chịu đựng dẻo dai cũng như tình yêu vẽ đẹp trong đời sống.

Lub ntsiab lus Nyob rau ntawm kev muab tej yam ua tsaug rau neeg uas tseem ceeb, tus sau ntawv qhuas txog nws niam thiab cov pojniam dub li nws niam uas sib zog ua haujlwm, nyiam nws txoj haujlwm, thiab muaj kev zoo siab ua nws txoj haujlwm. Walker pom nws niam zoo li ib tug neeg tis duab keej heev uas nws txawj tsim ntau yam. Tej kev no pab tau ua nws lub neej xws li tus neeg sau ntawv. Nws niam qhia nws tus kheej ib yam li ib tug neeg tis duab. Tej kev qhia no yog los ntawm cov dabneeg nws piav thiab ntawm lub vaj paj zoo nkauj uas nws cog, txawm tias lawv tsev neeg pluag npaum li cas. Nws qhuas txog cov pojniam dub uas yog nws niam ib phaum txog qhov uas muaj txojsia nyob "hold on", txawm tias ua haujlwm hnyav nkees npaum li cas. Walker nav thwm cov kev muaj zog uas nws tau txais los ntawm nws niam thiab kev hlub uas zoo nkauj rau ntawm lub neej.

摘要 在這篇動人肅穆的讚辭中，作者歌頌自己的母親以及其他像母親的黑人婦女她們的辛勤工作、奉獻與感召。Walker 視母親如一名藝術家，母親的創作精神激勵了她的寫作生涯。她的母親不管家裡有多貧困都會經由講述故事和種植美麗花朵的院子來與她家人分享她的藝術生活。Walker 非常敬佩她母親那一代的黑人婦女，不論她們承受的工作有多重都能成功地「堅持下去」。這樣的結果讓Walker承襲了一份對勞力的敬佩與懂得珍惜生命中美好的東西。

សេចក្តីសង្ខេប ក្នុងអត្ថបទរំលឹកគុណដ៏ឧឡារិកនិងមានចលនានេះ អ្នកនិពន្ធសរសើរម្តាយរបស់នាងនិងស្ត្រីស្បែកខ្មៅឯទៀតដូចជារូបនាងចំពោះការងារលំបាក ការលះបង់ ហើយនិងចិត្តចង់បានរបស់ពួកគេ ។ Walker មើលឃើញម្តាយរបស់នាងថាជាសិល្បៈករដែលបង្កើតព្រលឹងជំរុលចិត្តនាងឲ្យមានជីវិតផ្ទាល់ជាអ្នក និពន្ធ ។ ម្តាយរបស់នាងរួមចំណែកផ្ទាល់របស់នាងជាសិល្បៈករម្នាក់តាមរយៈរឿងដែលគាត់និទាន ហើយនិងតាមរយៈសួនផ្កាស្អាតៗដែលគាត់ដាំ ទោះបីជាគ្រួសារមានក្តីក្រខ្សត់ក្តី ។ Walker កោតសរសើររបៀបដែលស្ត្រីស្បែកខ្មៅនៃជួនតារបស់ម្តាយនាងប្រឹងប្រែងតស៊ូដើម្បី "រស់នៅតទៅទៀត" ទោះបីគេបានដាក់ ការងារដ៏ហត់នឿយឲ្យពួកគេក្តី ។ ជាលទ្ធផល Walker ទទួលកេរ្តិ៍ការគោរពចំពោះកម្លាំង ក៏ដូចជាសេចក្តីស្រឡាញ់នៃលំអក្នុងជីវិតដែរ ។

Name ______________________________ Date ______________

"Seventh Grade" by Gary Soto
"Melting Pot" by Anna Quindlen

Summary These two selections examine, in different ways, how people relate to each other. In "Seventh Grade," Victor goes through the first day of school trying to impress Teresa, who he hopes will be his girlfriend. Though Victor embarrasses himself in class by pretending to speak French, Teresa is fooled and impressed, much to Victor's surprise and pleasure. In "Melting Pot," the author describes how her New York neighborhood is a mixture of different ethnic groups. She sees the concept of the American melting pot existing where she lives, but only on a person-to-person basis. As groups, the neighbors may not get along, but as individuals, they often are friends.

Relate to Your Own Experience One way to get more enjoyment out of what you read is to relate the characters' experiences to your own. To help you link your experience with a character's, form a mental picture of the scenes described by the author. As you read "Seventh Grade," pause from time to time. Picture each scene in your mind. Use this page to jot down notes to describe what you imagine. Then work with a partner to draw sketches of what Gary Soto describes in each of the following scenes. If you prefer, choose some scenes from "Melting Pot" and write notes about them. Then draw sketches of the scenes you imagined.

Victor and Michael exchanging greetings on the first day of school

Victor practicing his scowling as a girl looks at him

Victor lingering in homeroom after the bell rang, hoping to bump into Teresa as she leaves

Victor sitting at a table outside, near where Teresa is sitting under a plum tree

Victor pretending to know how to speak French

Mr. Bueller shuffling papers in the classroom as Victor and Teresa talk about French

____

____

____

____

____

____

____

____

____

____

____

____

____

____

"Seventh Grade" by Gary Soto
"Melting Pot" by Anna Quindlen

Resumen Estos dos pasajes examinan, de maneras diferentes, cómo se relaciona la gente entre sí. En "Seventh Grade," Victor pasa su primer día en la escuela tratando de impresionar a Teresa, que desea sea su novia. Aunque Victor queda en ridículo en clase pretendiendo hablar en francés, Teresa le cree y queda impresionada, para sorpresa y placer de Victor. En "Melting Pot," el autor describe cómo su barrio de Nueva York es una mezcla de diferentes grupos étnicos. Ve el concepto del "crisol de razas" de los Estados Unidos en el lugar donde vive, pero sólo de persona a persona. Como grupos, los vecinos son enemigos, pero como individuos son amigos.

Tóm Lược Hai bài chọn lọc này nghiên cứu, bằng những cách khác nhau, về sự liên hệ của con người. Trong bài "Seventh Grade", Victor cố gắng lấy lòng Teresa trong trọn buổi học đầu tiên, người mà cậu hy vọng sẽ là bạn gái của cậu. Tuy Victor tự làm xấu mình trong lớp bằng cách giả vờ nói tiếng Pháp, Teresa vẫn bị lừa, và cảm phục, làm cho Victor rất đổi ngạc nhiên và hài lòng. Trong "Melting Pot", tác giả tả diễn tả vùng lân cận của cô tại Nữu Ước là một hỗn hợp giữa các giống dân khác nhau. Cô thấy quan niệm của việc hỗn hợp giống dân Mỹ tồn tại nơi cô sinh sống, nhưng chỉ trên căn bản theo từng người. Theo nhóm, những người láng giềng là kẻ thù của nhau, nhưng theo cá nhân, họ là bạn.

Lub ntsiab lus Ob zaj uas xaiv los no muab ntsuam xyuas ob peb yam seb tibneeg sib txheeb sib ze li cas. Nyob hauv qib xya "Seventh Grade" Victor mus kawm ntawv thawj hnub vim yog nws xav ua kom Teresa nyiam nws, vam tias yuav ua nws tus hluas nkauj. Txawm tias Victor yuav ua rau nws txaj muag npaum cas hauv hoob kawm ntawv vim nws pheej ua txuj uas li nws hais tau lus Fabkis los Teresa cia li ntseeg thiab nyiam nws. Qhov no ua rau Victor ceeb thiab zoo siab heev. Nyob rau "Melting Plot," tus sau qhia txog tias ntawm qhov chaw nws nyob, New York, muaj ntau yam neeg nyob ua ke. Nws pom Asmesliskas qhov kev hlawv lauj kaub tshwm sim ntawm qhov chaw nws nyob, tiamsis tsuas yog ib tug neeg nrog ib tug xwb. Yog nyob ua tej pawg, cov neeg nyob thaj tsam ntawm nws nyob ntawv yog yeeb ncuab, tiamsis ntawm tus kheej, lawv yog phooj ywg.

摘要 這兩篇選文是從不同的角度來探討人與人之間如何相處。在 "Seventh Grade" 中，維克特爾就在想法子如何讓泰瑞莎留下深刻印象中渡過了開學的第一天。他希望泰瑞莎能成為他的女朋友。雖然維克特爾很難為情地在班上假裝說法語，但是泰瑞莎卻相信了而且還很崇拜他，這令維克特爾非常驚訝且高興。在 "Melting Pot" 中，作者則描述她紐約的鄰居是由各種不同的族裔混合而成。她看到一種美國民族大熔爐的觀念存在她居住的地方，但僅於個人對個人而已。以種族團體來看，鄰居都是敵人；但以個人來看，他們又都是好朋友。

សេចក្តីសង្ខេប អត្ថបទជ្រើសរើសទាំងពីរនេះពិនិត្យមើលតាមរបៀបខុសគ្នានូវរបៀបដែលមនុស្សទាក់ទងគ្នាទៅវិញទៅមក ។ នៅក្នុង "Seventh Grade" Victor ឆ្លងកាត់ថ្ងៃទីមួយនៅសាលារៀនដោយព្យាយាមធ្វើឲ្យ Teresa ចាប់អារម្មណ៍ ដែលវាសង្ឃឹមថានឹងបាននាងធ្វើជាសង្សាររបស់វា ។ ថ្វីបើវាបានធ្វើឲ្យខ្លួនវាខ្មាស់គេនៅក្នុងថ្នាក់ដោយធ្វើឫកជានិយាយភាសាបារាំង Teresa បានវង្វេងនិងចាប់អារម្មណ៍ ធ្វើឲ្យ Victor ភ្ញាក់ផ្អើលនិងសប្បាយចិត្តជាខ្លាំង ។ នៅក្នុង "Melting Pot" អ្នកនិពន្ធរៀបរាប់ពីរបៀបដែលសង្កាត់នៅក្រុងញូយករបស់នាងលាយច្របល់ដោយក្រុមសាសន៍ផ្សេងៗ ។ នាងឃើញគោលគំនិតនៃការលាយចូលគ្នារបស់អាមេរិកាំងកើតឡើងនៅកន្លែងដែលនាងរស់នៅតែលើគោលការនៃជនម្នាក់ទៅជនម្នាក់ទៀតប៉ុណ្ណោះ ។ ក្នុងក្រុមរបស់សង្កាត់ជាសត្រូវនិងគ្នា ប៉ុន្តែនៅជាបុគ្គល ពួកគេជាមិត្តនិងគ្នា ។

Name ______________________________ Date ______________

"Fable" by Ralph Waldo Emerson
"If—" by Rudyard Kipling
"Thumbprint" by Eve Merriam

Summary These three poems focus on the ideas of individuality and wholeness. In "Fable," a squirrel resents that a mountain has called it a "little prig." The squirrel responds by saying that although a mountain is big, it is not as lively as a squirrel and it cannot crack a nut. In other words, individuals possess their own special talents that make them no better or worse than other individuals. In "If—," the speaker details the positive qualities that a person must possess to be considered a successful and complete individual. In "Thumbprint," the speaker celebrates her singularity through the special design of curved lines that make up her unique thumbprint.

Paraphrase Sometimes the language of poetry is different from familiar, everyday language. The words themselves might be unfamiliar, or the order of the words might be unusual. As you read these poems, identify and list examples of poetic language. Then write more familiar words or word order for the phrases you list. Create a chart like the one below. A few phrases from Rudyard Kipling's poem have been modeled for you. Choose more from his poem, and choose some from Ralph Waldo Emerson's and Eve Merriam's poems as well.

Poetic Language	More Familiar Language
If you can keep your head when all about you / Are losing theirs and blaming it on you	If you can stay calm when others cannot
If you can force your heart and nerve and sinew / To serve your turn long after they are gone	If you can keep on going when your body feels worn out

"Fable" by Ralph Waldo Emerson
"If—" by Rudyard Kipling
"Thumbprint" by Eve Merriam

Resumen Estos tres poemas se centran en las ideas de individualidad y de totalidad. En "Fable," una ardilla se ofende porque una montaña le ha llamado "pequeña malcriada." La ardilla responde diciendo que, aunque una montaña es grande, no tiene la vivacidad de una ardilla y no puede cascar una nuez. Es decir, los individuos poseen sus propios talentos especiales que ni les hacen mejores ni peores que otros individuos. En "If—," el narrador detalla las cualidades positivas que una persona debe poseer para ser considerada como un individuo triunfador y completo. En "Thumbprint," el narrador celebra su singularidad por medio del diseño especial de líneas curvas que constituyen su huella digital pulgar exclusiva.

Tóm Lược Ba bài thơ này chú trọng về cá nhân và tập thể. Trong bài "Fable", một con sóc không thích vì bị một hòn núi gọi mình là "thằng tự phụ tí hon". Con sóc trả lời lại rằng mặc dù hòn núi lớn, nhưng không sống động như con sóc và không thể làm bể được hột đậu. Nói một cách khác, mỗi cá nhân đều có tài nghệ đặc biệt riêng làm cho họ không hơn hay kém người khác. Trong "If—", tác giả nói lên chi tiết những phẩm chất mà con người có để troỏ thành một cá nhân thành công và hoàn toàn. Trong bài "Thumbprint", tác giả ca ngợi tính kỳ lạ của mình qua những đường cong đặc biệt đã tạo ra dấu tay duy nhất của bà.

Lub ntsiab lus Peb zaj paj huam saum no tsom lub tswv yim uas hais txog yus tus kheej tag nrho tibsi. Nyob rau "Fable," ib tug luav tsis nyiam tias lub roob hu nws ua ib tug "little prig." Tus luav teb tias txawm lub roob loj los nws twb tsis ciaj li tus luav thiab nws twb tsoo tsis tau ib lub noob kom tawg pleb. Yog yuav hais ces, ib tug neeg twg nws yeej txawj nws tes taw uas ua rau nws yeej tsis zoo lossis phem tshaj lwm tus. Nyob rau "If—," tus neeg hais lus qhia txog tej kev lossis tej uas ib tug neeg yuav tsum muaj nws thiaj yuav yog ib tug tsheej neeg thiab thiaj vam meej. Nyob rau "Thumbprint," tus neeg hais lus muaj kev zoo siab uas nws tseem tsis tau yuav txiv los ntawm cov kab nkaus uas muaj ntawm nws tus ntiv tes xoo.

摘要 這三首詩著重在個體和全體的概念上。在"Fable" 中，有隻松鼠很氣憤一座山說牠是「自命不凡的小傢伙」。松鼠回答說雖然山是巨大的但卻不像松鼠那般充滿活力而且也沒法打開堅果。換言之，每一個個體都擁有他們自己特殊的才能使得他們不比其他的個體較差或較好。在 "If–" 中，主人翁則詳述一個人必須擁有被視為是成功及完整個體的正面特質。在 "Thumbprint" 中，主人翁讚美她那經過特殊設計的曲線所構成獨一無二的大姆指指紋。

សេចក្តីសង្ខេប កំណាព្យទាំងបីនេះផ្តោតអារម្មណ៍លើគំនិតនៃមនុស្សម្នាក់ៗនិងភាពទាំងមូល ។ នៅក្នុង "Fable" សត្វកង្ហែនមួយតូចចិត្តនិងភ្នំមួយហៅវាថា "កូនចោរល្អិត" ។ សត្វកង្ហែនឆ្លើយតបដោយនិយាយថាថ្វីបើភ្នំធំមែន តែឯងមិនរស់រវើកដូចជាសត្វកង្ហែនមួយ ហើយឯងមិនអាចបំបែកគ្រាប់ឈើបានទេ ។ ន័យម្យ៉ាងទៀតគឺជនម្នាក់ៗមានការប៉ិនប្រសប់ពិសេសរៀងខ្លួនដែលធ្វើឲ្យពួកគេមិនឲ្យល្អជាងឬអាក្រក់ជាងជនឯទៀតឡើយ ។ នៅក្នុង "If—" អ្នកពោលរៀបរាប់ក្បោះក្បាយនូវគុណភាពល្អដែលជនម្នាក់ត្រូវមានដើម្បីឲ្យគេគិតថាជាជនមានជោគជ័យនិងគ្រប់លក្ខណៈម្នាក់ ។ នៅក្នុង "Thumbprint" អ្នកពោលបង្ហាញពីភាពតែមួយរបស់គាត់តាមរយៈការរចនាពិសេសនៃបន្ទាត់កោងដែលបង្កើតជាស្នាមមេដៃតែមួយដូចគ្នារបស់នាង ។

Name ______________________________ Date ______________

"Mother to Son" by Langston Hughes
"The Courage That My Mother Had" by Edna St. Vincent Millay
"The Hummingbird That Lived Through Winter" by William Saroyan

Summary These three selections focus on the themes of courage and persistence. In "Mother to Son," the speaker talks of the hardships she has endured. She uses her own experiences to warn her son not to give up when he faces similar obstacles. In "The Courage That My Mother Had," the poet praises the courage her deceased mother showed when she was living. Though her mother left her a golden brooch, the poet would prefer the treasure of her mother's courage for herself because she needs it now. "The Hummingbird That Lived Through Winter" tells about an elderly, sight-impaired man lovingly nursing an ailing hummingbird back to life, exhibiting a love for all living creatures.

Question: After reading a selection, you need to determine what you understand and don't understand about it. You can write down questions that you may have, and then seek help from your teacher or a classmate.

Directions: Use the chart below to record what you do and do not understand about each selection. Then discuss your questions with another person.

Selection	What I Understand	What I Do Not Understand

"Mother to Son" by Langston Hughes
"The Courage That My Mother Had" by Edna St. Vincent Millay
"The Hummingbird That Lived Through Winter" by William Saroyan

Resumen Estas tres historias se concentran en el tema del coraje y la persistencia. En "Mother to Son", el personaje habla de las dificultades que ha tenido que superar. Usa sus propias experiencias para advertir a su hijo que no desista cuando se enfrenta a obstáculos similares. En "The Courage That My Mother Had", iel poeta alaba el coraje que demostró tener su madre durante su vida. A pesar de que la madre le dejó un prendedor de oro, la poetisa preferiría el coraje de su madre porque en este momento lo necesita. "The Hummingbird That Lived Through Winter" cuenta la historia de un anciano con problemas en la vista, que se ocupa de cuidar a un picaflor enfermo, demostrando un profundo cariño por todos los seres vivientes.

Tóm lược. Loạt bài này chú trọng vào đề tài tính kiên trì và lòng dũng cảm. Trong "Mother to Son," người kể chuyện nói về những khổ cực bà đã phải cam chịu. Bà dùng kinh nghiệm của bà để dạy con trai là không nên bỏ cuộc khi gặp những khó khăn tương tự. Trong bài "The Courage That My Mother Had," thi sĩ ca tụng sự can đảm của bà mẹ quá cố lúc bà còn sống. Mặc dù bà mẹ để lại cho thi sĩ một cái ghim trâm quý bằng vàng, nhưng thi sĩ cho rằng mình muốn có lòng can đảm của mẹ hơn vì thi sĩ đang cần đức tính đó. Bài "The Hummingbird That Lived Through Winter" kể chuyện một ông già mắt kém ân cần săn sóc một con chim bị đau trở lại bình thường, chứng tỏ lòng thương yêu mọi sinh vật của cụ.

Lub ntsiab lus Cov xaiv ntawm peb qhov no yog hais txog zaj lus siab taw thiab rau siab. Nyob hauv "Mother to Son," tus sau piav qhia txog kev txom nyem nws tau raug los. Nws siv nws qhov kev kawn los qhia kom nws tus tub tsis thob tsuv thaum ntsib tej yam teeb meem zoo li nws. Nyob hauv "The Courage That My Mother Had," tus kwv paj huam qhia ntxiv txog nws niam lub siab taw thaum ua neej nyob. Tseem hais tias nws niam tseg nws niam tus koob khawm kub rau nws los tus kwv sau paj huam tseem xav tau nws niam qhov siab taw duav rau qhov nws muaj svs tam sis no. "The Hummingbird That Lived Through Winter" piav txog ib tug neeg laus tsis pom kev tau pab hlub tu ib tug noog hummingbird ciaj rov los, qhia txoj kev hlub rau tas nrho cov tsiaj muaj sia.

摘要　這三篇文章都是談論勇氣和毅力。在 "Mother to Son" 中，敘述者談到她以前經歷的苦難。她以自己的經驗警告兒子，在遇到類似的障礙時不要輕言放棄。在 "The Courage That My Mother Had" 中，詩人讚美她過世的母親在生前所表現的勇氣。雖然詩人的母親留給她一個金色胸針，她卻寧願擁有母親的勇氣寶藏，因為她現在正需要這份勇氣。"The Hummingbird That Lived Through Winter" 描述一位視力受損的老人慈愛地照顧一隻生病的蜂鳥，使它起死回生，展現出他對所有生物的關愛。

សេចក្ដីសង្ខេប អត្ថបទជ្រើសរើសទាំងបីនេះផ្ដោតអារម្មណ៍លើប្រធាននៃរឿងក្លាហាននិងការតស៊ូព្យាយាម ។ នៅក្នុងអត្ថបទ "Mother to Son" អ្នកនិពន្ធនិយាយអំពីការលំបាកវេទនាដែលនាងបានហែលឆ្លង ។ នាងប្រើការពិសោធន៍ផ្ទាល់របស់នាងដើម្បីព្រមានកូនប្រុសរបស់គាត់កុំឲ្យលះបង់ចោលនៅពេលណាដែលប្រឈមមុខជាមួយឧបសគ្គស្រដៀងគ្នានេះ ។ នៅក្នុងអត្ថបទ "The Courage That My Mother Had" កវីនិពន្ធអួតសរសើរសេចក្ដីក្លាហានរបស់ខ្មោចម្ដាយរបស់គាត់ដែលបានបង្ហាញឲ្យឃើញកាលពីពេលដែលម្ដាយគាត់នៅរស់ ។ ថ្វីបើម្ដាយរបស់គាត់ទុកបន្សល់កន្ទាស់សក់មាសឲ្យគាត់ក្ដីកវីនិពន្ធប្រាថ្នាកំណប់នៃសេចក្ដីក្លាហានរបស់ម្ដាយគាត់សំរាប់ខ្លួនគាត់ពីព្រោះគាត់ត្រូវការវានៅពេលឥឡូវនេះ ។ អត្ថបទ "The Hummingbird That Lived Through Winter" និទានអំពីបុរសជរាដែលមានភ្នែកអន់ខ្សោយម្នាក់ចិញ្ចឹមដោយថ្នាក់ថ្នមនូវកូនសត្វចាបមានសម្លេងពិរោះដែលឈឺមួយឲ្យជារស់រានមានជីវិតឡើងវិញសំដែងបង្ហាញអំពីសេចក្ដីស្រឡាញ់ចំពោះសត្វលោកទាំងអស់ ។

Name ______________________________ Date ______________

"The Third Wish" by Joan Aiken

Summary Mr. Peters discovers a swan tangled in thorns. He frees the swan, which turns into a little man—the King of the Forest. Mr. Peters requests three wishes as a reward. The King obliges, giving him three leaves to wish upon, but warns that wishes often leave people worse off than before. Mr. Peters wishes for a beautiful wife and receives Leita, a former swan. Over time, Leita grows unhappy because she misses her sister, who is still a swan. Mr. Peters uses his second wish to turn Leita back into a swan. He and the two swans remain close. One morning, old Mr. Peters is found dead in bed, smiling, with a leaf and feather in his hands.

Clarify Sometimes when you read, the meaning of a passage may not be clear. To help you understand it better, you can write down questions that you have about the passage. Then try reading the section again. As you read, look for details that will answer your questions. Also, use a dictionary to look up words you do not understand.

Use a chart like the one below to help clarify the meaning of passages in "The Third Wish." First record your questions about each passage. Then reread the passage and tell what you now understand that you did not understand before.

Questions (What I Don't Understand)	**Answers** (What I Now Understand)

"The Third Wish"
by Joan Aiken

Resumen El Sr. Peters descubre a un cisne enredado entre espinas. Libera al cisne, que se transforma en un pequeño hombrecito–el Rey del Bosque. El Sr. Peters pide tres deseos como recompensa. El Rey se los concede, dándole tres hojas para pedir sus deseos, pero le advierte a menudo que los deseos dejan a la gente peor que antes. El Sr. Peters desea una esposa hermosa y recibe a Leita, una mujer que había sido cisne. Con el correr del tiempo, Leita se empieza a sentir infeliz ya que extraña a su hermana, que todavía es un cisne. El Sr. Peters hace uso de su segundo deseo para volver a transformar a su esposa en un cisne. Él y los dos cisnes siguen siendo amigos. Una mañana, encuentran al Sr. Peters muerto en su cama, con una sonrisa en los labios y una hoja y una pluma en sus manos.

Tóm Lược Ông Peters tìm được một con thiên nga bị vướng trong bái gai. Ông thả tự do cho con thiên nga, rồi nó biến thành một người đàn ông nhỏ nhắn—là Vua của Rừng. Ông Peters yêu cầu được thưởng bằng ba điều ước. Không thể từ khước, nhà vua cho ông ta ba cái lá để ước, nhưng cảnh cáo rằng những lời ước thường làm cho con người trở nên tệ hại hơn trước. Ông Peters ước có một người vợ đẹp và được Leita, trước đây là thiên nga. Thời gian trôi qua, Leita trở nên buồn bã vì cô nhớ đến người em, vẫn còn là thiên nga. Ông Peters dùng điều ước thứ nhì biến Leita trở lại thành thiên nga. Ông ta và hai con thiên nga sống gần gũi nhau. Một sáng nọ, người ta tìm thấy Peters nằm chết trên giường, miệng mỉm cười, với một cái lá và một lông chim trong tay.

Lub ntsiab lus Mr. Peters nrhiav pom ib tus noog swan (noog uas muaj caj dab ntev) daig ib cov xov pos ya tsis tau. Nws tso tus noog tawm, tus noog txawm phis ua ib tug txiv neej me me. Nws yog tus huab tais uas kav lub hav zoov ntawv. Mr. Peters thov peb yam ua khoom plig. Tus huab tais ntawv kam thiab muab peb daim nplooj ntoos rau nws thov, tabsis ceeb toom rau nws tias cov kev thov feem ntau ua rau neeg haj yam tsis muaj lossis phem tshaj qhov qub. Mr. Peters thov kom nws tau ib tug pojniam zoo nkauj ces nws txawm tau Leita, uas yog ib tug qub noog. Ntev mus Leita siab nyob tsis tus vim nws nco nws tus niam hluas uas tseem yog ib tug noog. Mr. Peters siv nws qhov kev thov thib ob kom Leita rov qab ua noog. Nws thiab ob tug noog ntawv txawm nyob ze ua ke. Muaj ib tag kis sawv ntxov, tus yawg laus Mr. Peters tau tuag saum nws lub txaj, ntsej muag luag ntxi thiab ntawm nws txais tes nws tuav ib daim nplooj ntoos thiab ib tug plaub noog.

摘要 彼得先生發現一隻被荊棘纏住的天鵝。他釋放了天鵝，天鵝變成一個小人一森林之王。彼得先生要求國王以三個願望作為回報。國王應他的請求給了他三片許願用的葉子，並且警告說許願通常留給人們的是比從前更壞的情況。彼得先生許願有個美麗的妻子，他於是得到以前是隻天鵝的萊塔。時間漸漸過去，萊塔因想念她的姊妹而鬱鬱寡歡。而且她的姊妹還仍是一隻天鵝。彼得先生使用他第二個願望讓萊塔變回原來的天鵝。之後他與兩隻天鵝依然保持親近。有一天早上，彼得老先生被發現手中握著一片葉子和羽毛微笑地死在床上。

សេចក្តីសង្ខេប លោក Peters រកឃើញក្ងានមួយជាប់នៅក្នុងដុបបន្លា ។ គាត់ជួយយកក្ងាននោះចេញ រួចក្ងាននោះប្រែក្លាយទៅជាបុរសតូចម្នាក់ ដែលជាស្តេចព្រៃ ។ លោក Peters សុំសេចក្តីប្រាថ្នាបីយ៉ាងជារង្វាន់ ។ ស្តេចព្រៃត្រូវតែឲ្យតាមសំណូមពរដោយឲ្យគាត់នូវស្លឹកឈើបីសន្លឹកសំរាប់ការប្រាថ្នានោះ ប៉ុន្តែហាមថាជាញឹកញាប់សេចក្តីប្រាថ្នាធ្វើឲ្យមនុស្សអាក្រក់ជាងពីដើម ។ លោក Peters ប្រាថ្នាឲ្យមានប្រពន្ធស្អាតម្នាក់ ហើយបានទទួលនាង Leita ដែលជាអតីតក្ងាន ។ ជាបន្តមកទៀត នាង Leita កាន់តែកើតការមិនសប្បាយចិត្តដោយសារនាងនឹកប្អូនស្រីរបស់នាងដែលនៅតែជាសត្វក្ងាននៅឡើយ ។ លោក Peters ប្រើសេចក្តីប្រាថ្នាទីពីររបស់គាត់ធ្វើឲ្យនាងប្រែទៅជាក្ងានវិញ ។ គាត់នឹងក្ងានទាំងពីរនៅជាប់ជាមួយគ្នា ។ នៅព្រឹកមួយ គេឃើញតាចាស់ Peters ស្លាប់នៅលើគ្រែដោយញញឹម ដោយមានកាន់ស្លឹកឈើនិងស្លាបសត្វមួយក្នុងដៃ ។

Name ______________________________ Date ______________

"A Boy and a Man" by James Ramsey Ullman
from *Into Thin Air* by Jon Krakauer

Summary Both selections deal with the drama of mountain climbing. In "A Boy and a Man," Rudi Matt risks his life to save a man who has fallen in an icy crevasse, or deep crack, in the Alps. The man, renowned mountaineer Captain John Winter, is surprised to discover that Rudi is only sixteen. He seeks Rudi's advice on climbing the Citadel, a peak upon which Rudi's father died while climbing. Rudi makes Winter promise not to tell his mother that he was mountain climbing. In the second selection, Jon Krakauer describes his dangerous trek up the Icefall on Mt. Everest, detailing how the ice made the climb an uncertainty. Krakauer's experience leaves him awestruck at the task of reaching Everest's peak.

Predict As you read a story, you can be an active reader by trying to **predict**, or guess, what will happen next. Your predictions should not be wild guesses, however. Good story predictions are always based on details and hints that the author gives you along the way.

Use the chart below to predict events from "A Boy and a Man" and from *Into Thin Air.* After each prediction, record the details and hints that led you to make that prediction.

My Prediction	Details and Hints
"A Boy and a Man"	
from *Into Thin Air*	

"A Boy and a Man" by James Ramsey Ullman
from *Into Thin Air* by Jon Krakauer

Resumen Ambos textos hablan del drama del alpinismo. En "A Boy and a Man," Rudi Matt arriesga su vida para salvar a un hombre que ha caído en una grieta profunda en los Alpes. El hombre, el renombrado montañista Capitán John Winter, se sorprende al descubrir que Rudi tiene tan sólo dieciséis años. Le pide consejo a Rudi para subir al Citadel, un pico en el cual murió el padre de Rudi mientras lo escalaba. Rudi hace que Winter le prometa no decirle a su madre que ha estado escalando montañas. En el segundo texto, Jon Krakauer describe su peligrosa subida al Icefall del Monte Everest, relatando cómo el hielo hizo incierta la subida. La experiencia de Krakauer le dejó embelesado con la idea de llegar a la cumbre del Everest.

Tóm Lược Cả hai bài chọn lọc này nói về thảm kịch của việc leo núi. Trong bài "A Boy and a Man", Rudi Matt đã liều thân để cứu một người đàn ông bị té vào một vực thẳm nước đá, hay chỗ nứt sâu, trong dãy núi Alps. Người đàn ông, là Đại Úy John Winter leo núi nổi tiếng, rất kinh ngạc khi khám phá ra rằng Rudi chỉ mới mười sáu tuổi. Ông nhờ Rudi làm cố vấn trong việc leo núi Citadel, một đỉnh núi mà trước đây cha của Rudi đã bỏ mình khi leo. Rudi buộc Winter phải hứa không được nói với mẹ cậu rằng cậu là một người leo núi. Trong bài thứ nhì, Jon Krakauer diễn tả cuộc hành trình nguy hiểm lên đỉnh Icefall trên ngọn Everest, trình bày chi tiết nước đá làm cho việc leo núi khó khăn như thế nào. Kinh nghiệm của Krakauer đã để lại cho ông một mối kinh hoàng leo lên đỉnh Everest.

Lub ntsiab lus Ob zaj uas tau xaiv los saum no hais txog neeg kev nce roob. Nyob rau "A Boy and a Man," Rudi Matt muab nws txoj sia pheej hmoov mus pab ib tus txiv neej uas poob rau ib lub qhov dej tob tob uas khov tag lawm nyob rau hauv Alps. Tus txiv neej nce roob uas muaj meej mom zoo hu ua Captain John Winter ntawv tau ib plaws thaum nws paub tias Rudi muaj kaum rau xyoo xwb. Nws mug Rudi txog kev yuav ua cas nce lub ntsis roob Citadel uas Rudi txiv tau tuag thaum nws nce. Rudi kom Winter cog lus tsis pub qhia nws niam tias nws nce roob. Nyob rau zaj dab neeg thib ob uas tau xaiv los no, Jon Krakauer qhia txog kev txaus ntshai thaum nws nce lub roob siab siab Mt. Everest uas khov dej tag lawm, thiab nws qhia ntxiv tias roob khov tag ua rau kev nce tsis paub xyov yuav ua li cas li. Krakauer cov kev txawj ua rau nws kov yeej kom nws nce mus txog saum ntsis roob Everest.

摘要 這兩篇選文都是有關爬山的戲劇性文章。在"A Boy and a Man"中，魯迪・麥特冒著生命的危險在阿爾卑斯山脈拯救一位掉落到冰隙（或深裂縫）中的人。這個人就是有名的登山家 Captain John Winter，他非常驚訝地發現魯迪才十六歲。他請教魯迪攀登 Citadel 峰的事，Citadel 峰就是魯迪父親攀登出意外身亡之峰。魯迪要 Winter 允諾不會告訴他的母親他曾爬過山。在第二篇選文中，Jon Krakauer 描述他的艱險攀登埃佛勒斯峰（聖母峰）的冰瀑布之旅，細述冰如何使得攀登變得不確定。Krakauer 的經驗讓他自己對登上埃佛勒斯峰這項艱巨的任務感到不可思議。

សេចក្តីសង្ខេប អត្ថបទជ្រើសរើសទាំងពីរនេះដោះស្រាយជាមួយវិនាដកម្មនៃការឡើងភ្នំ ។ នៅក្នុងរឿង "A Boy and a Man" លោក Rudi Matt ប្រថុយជីវិតគាត់ដើម្បីសង្គ្រោះបុរសម្នាក់ដែលបានធ្លាក់ក្នុងស្នាមប្រេះជ្រៅរបស់ទឹកកកនៅភ្នំ Alps ។ បុរសនោះគឺអនុសេនីយឯក John Winter ដែលល្បីឈ្មោះលើផ្លូវភ្នំ គាត់មានការភ្ញាក់ផ្អើលដែលដឹងថា Rudi មានអាយុតែដប់ប្រាំមួយឆ្នាំប៉ុណ្ណោះ។ គាត់សួរដំបូន្មានពី Rudi ស្តីពីការឡើងភ្នំ Citadel ជាកំពូលភ្នំដែលឪពុករបស់ Rudi ស្លាប់នៅពេលឡើងលើនោះ ។ Rudi បង្ខំលោក Winter ឲ្យសន្យាថាមិនប្រាប់ម្តាយរបស់វាថាវាជាអ្នកឡើងភ្នំឡើយ ។ ក្នុងអត្ថបទជ្រើសរើសទីពីរ លោក Jon Krakauer រៀបរាប់ពីដំណើរប្រកបដោយគ្រោះថ្នាក់របស់គាត់ឡើងលើកំពូល Icefall លើភ្នំ Everest ដោយរៀបរាប់ល្អិតល្អន់ពីរបៀបដែលទឹកកកធ្វើឲ្យការឡើងនោះមិនជាក់ច្បាស់ ។ ការពិសោធន៍របស់លោក Krakauer បន្សល់ឲ្យគាត់នូវការស្ញប់ស្ញែងពីកិច្ចការទៅដល់កំពូលភ្នំ Everest ។

Name ______________________________ Date ______________

"The Charge of the Light Brigade" by Alfred, Lord Tennyson
from *Henry V*, "St. Crispian's Day Speech" by William Shakespeare
"The Enemy" by Alice Walker

Summary All of these poems deal with war. In "The Charge of the Light Brigade," a brigade of six hundred cavalry soldiers charges into an enemy position heavily fortified with cannon. Many of the soldiers are killed, but their bravery will be honored always. In the excerpt from *Henry V*, King Henry speaks of the glory that will come to soldiers who fight in a battle to be fought on St. Crispian's Day. Those who survive the battle and live to old age will proudly tell battle stories to their sons. In "The Enemy," the tiny fist of a dead child holds the "crumpled heads / of pink and yellow flowers." This is a harsh reminder that when a country goes to war, the children suffer.

Reading Poetic Contractions A contraction is a shortened form of a word or words. For example, the contraction *aren't* is short for the words *are not*. Notice that an apostrophe (') takes the place of the missing *o* in the contraction. Often in poetry, you find special contractions, called **poetic contractions,** that you do not find in ordinary writing. For example, in "The Charge of the Light Brigade," the author uses the contraction *sab'ring*, a shortened form of the word *sabering*. When you come across such a contraction, look at it closely to figure out what letter or letters are missing. Then read the word as if all the letters were there.

Use the chart below to record the word or words that are shortened in each poetic contraction. The first one is done for you.

Contraction	Missing Letter or Letters	Full Word or Words
sab'ring	e	sabering
call'd		
rememb'red		
ne'er		
accurs'd		

"The Charge of the Light Brigade" by Alfred, Lord Tennyson
from *Henry V*, "St. Crispian's Day Speech" by William Shakespeare
"The Enemy" by Alice Walker

Resumen Todos estos poemas tratan del tema de la guerra. En "The Charge of the Light Brigade", una brigada de seiscientos soldados de caballería carga contra una posición enemiga que se encuentra fuertemente defendida con cañones. Muchos de los soldados mueren, pero su valentía será honrada siempre. En el fragmento de *Henry V*, el rey Henry habla de la gloria que cubrirá a los soldados que peleen en la batalla que tendrá lugar el Día de St. Crispian. Quienes sobrevivan a la batalla y lleguen a viejos les contarán con orgullo las historias de la batalla a sus hijos. En "The Enemy", el diminuto puño de un niño muerto sostiene las "cabezuelas estrujadas de flores rosadas y amarillas". Esto nos recuerda amargamente que cuando un país está en guerra, sus niños sufren.

Tóm Lược Tất cả các bài thơ này đề cập đến chiến tranh. Trong bài "The Charge of the Light Brigade" một lữ đoàn gồm sáu trăm lính kỵ binh tấn công vào vị trí quân thù được phòng thủ bởi súng đại bác nặng. Nhiều người lính bị giết, nhưng sự dũng cảm của họ sẽ được tôn vinh đời đời. Trong đoạn trích từ bài *Henry V*, Vua Henry nói về sự vinh quang sẽ đến với những người lính chiến đấu trong trận đánh St. Crispian's Day. Những người đó vẫn còn sống sau trận đánh và sống đến già sẽ kể lại một cách tự hào những câu chuyện chiến đấu cho các con trai của họ. Trong bài "The Enemy," bàn tay nhỏ của một đứa bé đã chết còn nắm giữ "những nụ hoa bị nhàu nát màu hồng và vàng." Điều này nhắc chúng ta nhớ rằng khi một đất nước có chiến tranh, trẻ em thường là những người bị đau khổ.

Lub ntsiab lus Tag nrho cov paj huam no hais txog kev ua tsov ua rog. Nyob rau "The Charge of the Light Brigade," ib pawm tub rog uas muaj rau pua leej caij nees mus tom lawv tus yeeb ncuab qhov chaw uas muaj phom loj tiv thaiv ntau heev. Cov tub rog raug tua ntau leej heev tiamsis lawv kev tawv qhawv yuav nco mus tas ib txhis. Nyob rau ib co lus ntawm phau ntawv *Henry V*, huab tais Henry has txog yuav muaj kev qhuas rau cov neeg uas sib tua nyob rau lub rog thaum St. Crispian hnub. Cov uas sib tua rog es tsis tuag yuav nyob mus txog hnub laus thiab yuav zoo siab qhia txog tej kev ua rog no rau lawv tej tub. Nyob rau "The Enemy," tus menyuam mos liab uas tuag lawm tuav hauv nws xib teg "crumpled heads / of pink and yellow flowers." Qhov no yog ib qho hnyav phem heev kom peb nco qab tias thaum twg ib lub tebchaws mus ua rog, cov menyuam yog cov uas txom nyem.

摘要 這些詩都與戰爭有關。在 "The Charge of the Light Brigade" 中，六百名騎兵戰士勇猛衝向敵人設有重重加農砲的防禦陣營。許多士兵都戰死了，但他們的英勇事蹟將永遠被敬重。節錄自 *Henry V* 的演說中，亨利國王說榮耀將屬於那些在 St. Crispian 日作戰的士兵們。而那些從戰場上存活下來且活到老年時將會很光榮地告訴他們的兒子有關這次戰役的故事。在 "The Enemy" 中，一個死去孩子的小拳頭中握著「弄縐的粉紅色和黃色花頭」。這一怵目驚心的景象提醒我們當一個國家陷入戰爭中，孩子總是最受傷害的。

សេចក្ដីសង្ខេប កំណាព្យទាំងអស់នេះជាប់ទាក់ទងជាមួយសង្គ្រាម ។ នៅក្នុង "The Charge of the Light Brigade" កងពលមួយដែលមានទាហានសេះប្រាំមួយរយនាក់វាយលុកចូលទីតាំងសត្រូវដែលគាំទ្រយ៉ាងមាំដោយកាំភ្លើងធ្លាប់ជាច្រើន ។ ទាហានក្នុងចំណោមនោះជាច្រើនត្រូវស្លាប់ ប៉ុន្តែសេចក្ដីក្លាហានរបស់ពួកគេនឹងត្រូវគេគោរពជានិច្ច ។ នៅក្នុងសេចក្ដីដកស្រង់ពីរឿង *Henry V* លោក King Henry និយាយពីកិត្តិយសដែលនឹងមានចំពោះទាហានដែលប្រយុទ្ធក្នុងសមរភូមិនៅថ្ងៃ St. Crispian ។ អ្នកដែលនៅរស់រានមានជីវិតពីសមរភូមិនោះ ហើយរស់នៅរហូតដល់ចាស់នឹងនិទានរឿងក្នុងសមរភូមិដោយមោទនៈភាពប្រាប់ចៅរបស់ពួកគេ ។ នៅក្នុង "The Enemy" កូនកណ្ដាប់ដៃរបស់ក្មេងតូចដែលស្លាប់ទៅក្ដោប "ត្រួយផ្កាញីញក់ពណ៌ផ្កាឈូកនិងពណ៌លឿង" ។ នេះជាការរំលឹកដ៏អាណោចអាធម្មមួយថាពេលណាប្រទេសមានសង្គ្រាម កូនក្មេងមានការឈឺចាប់ ។

Name ______________________________ Date ______________

"The Californian's Tale" by Mark Twain
"Valediction" by Seamus Heaney

Summary Both selections deal with the effect a woman's absence has on a home. In "The Californian's Tale," a California gold prospector comes to the well-kept home of Henry, who invites the traveler in. Henry credits the niceness of his home to his young wife, who is away until Saturday night. He urges his guest to stay until she returns. Henry's friends come over on Saturday and give Henry a drink with a drug that puts him to sleep. They explain that Henry's wife has been dead for nineteen years. They go through the annual act of pretending she's returning, so that Henry won't go wild. In "Valediction," the speaker mourns the absence of the lady who once brightened his home but for whom he now grieves.

Summarize When you read a story, you can check your understanding along the way by summarizing different sections as you complete them. To summarize, first jot down all the important events and details that appear in a section of the story you are reading. Then, write a brief summary based on your notes.

Use the chart below to summarize sections of "The Californian's Tale." Record the main events and details in each section. Then use them to summarize the section. The beginning of the story has been done for you.

Main Events and Details	Summary
Thirty-five years ago Twain prospected on the Stanislaus. Once heavily populated, the area was now empty.	Mark Twain prospected on the Stanislaus, an area once heavily populated. Now the region has few people.

"The Californian's Tale" by Mark Twain
"Valediction" by Seamus Heaney

Resumen Ambos textos hablan del efecto de la ausencia de una mujer en un hogar. En "The Californian's Tale," un buscador de oro en California llega a la bien cuidada casa de Henry, quien invita al viajero a entrar. Henry atribuye el atractivo de su hogar a su joven esposa, que está de viaje hasta la noche del sábado. Le pide a su huésped que se quede hasta que ella vuelva. El sábado vuelven a la casa los amigos de Henry y le dan a Henry una bebida con una droga que lo hace dormir. Explican que la esposa de Henry murió hace diecinueve años. Para que Henry no se enloquezca, todos los años hacen el ritual de fingir que ella va a volver. En "Valediction," el narrador lamenta la ausencia de la mujer que solía dar vida a su hogar, de cuya pérdida se siente acongojado.

Tóm Lược Cả hai bài chọn lọc này nói về ảnh hưởng của sự vắng mặt của người đàn bà trong gia đình. Trong "The Californian's Tale", một người tìm vàng California đi đến ngôi nhà được giữ gìn ngăn nắp của Henry, là người đã mời ông đến. Henry khen ngợi những việc gọn đẹp trong nhà ông đều do một tay người vợ trẻ làm ra, bà đã đi vắng và sẽ trở về tối thứ Bảy. Ông yêu cầu khách ở nán lại chờ đến khi vợ về. Các bạn của Henry đến thăm trong ngày thứ Bảy và cho Henry uống thuốc ngủ. Họ giải thích rằng người vợ của Henry đã mất mười chín năm rồi. Theo lệ mỗi năm họ giả vờ rằng bà sẽ trở về để Henry không làm việc xằng bậy. Trong bài "Valediction", tác giả để tang sự vắng mặt của người đàn bà đã có lần làm khang trang căn nhà của ông nhưng giờ đây làm cho ông nhung nhớ.

Lub ntsiab lus Ob zaj xaiv los no hais txog thaum tug pojniam tsis nyob hauv tsev lawm yuav ua rau lub tsev zoo li cas. "The Californian's Tale," ib tug neeg khaws kub hauv California tuaj rau ntawm Henry lub tsev uas tu tau zoo nkauj heev. Nws txawm cawm tus neeg ntawv los hauv tsev. Henry muab tej kev qhuas tu lub tsev zoo ntawv tag nrho rau nws tus pojniam hluas hluas uas tsis nyob hauv tsev lawm uas yuav yog vas xaum mam rov los. Nws hais kom nws tus qhua nyob es nws pojniam los tso. Henry tus phooj ywg rov tuaj hnub vas xaum thiab muab tshuaj rau hauv dej lom Henry tsaug zog lawm. Lawv qhia tias Henry tus pojniam twb tuag tau kaum cuaj xyoos lawm. Lawv ua txuj tias nws yuav rov qablos kom Henry nyob tsis tsheej. Nyob rau "Valediction," tus hais lus quaj rau tus pojniam uas nws tau muaj ib zaug uas tau ua rau nws lub tsev tshav ntuj nrig tabsis tam sim no yog tus uas nws nyiav.

摘要 這兩篇選文都是關於家中少了女人的影響。在 "The Californian's Tale" 中，一位加州黃金探勘者來到亨利保持得非常整齊的家，亨利邀請這名旅人入內。亨利將整齊的家歸功於年輕的妻子，他的妻子離家要到禮拜六晚上才會回來。亨利於是渴望他的客人留下來等到她回來。亨利的朋友禮拜六過來並給亨利喝下摻有安眠藥的飲料。他們解釋亨利的妻子已經死了十九年了。他們每年都得來這麼一次假扮她的歸來，因為只有如此亨利才不會崩潰。在 "Valediction" 中，主人翁哀悼一位辭世的女士，這位女士曾為他的家帶來歡樂但現在他感到悲傷。

សេចក្តីសង្ខេប អត្ថបទជ្រើសរើសទាំងពីរដោះស្រាយជាមួយឥទ្ធិពលរបស់ការមិនបង្ហាញខ្លួនរបស់ស្រីម្នាក់នៅក្នុងផ្ទះ ។ នៅក្នុងរឿង "The Californian's Tale" អ្នករុករកមាសរដ្ឋ California មកផ្ទះដែលថែរក្សាយ៉ាងល្អរបស់លោក Henry ដែលជាអ្នកអញ្ជើញអ្នកដំណើរចូលផ្ទះ ។ លោក Henry ឲ្យគុណសម្បត្តិនៃភាពស្អាតល្អរបស់ផ្ទះទៅប្រពន្ធក្មេងរបស់គាត់ ដែលទៅឆ្ងាយរហូតដល់យប់ថ្ងៃសៅរ៍ទើបមកវិញ ។ គាត់អង្វរឲ្យភ្ញៀវរបស់គាត់ស្នាក់នៅរហូតដល់នាងមកវិញ ។ មិត្តរបស់លោក Henry មកលេងនៅថ្ងៃសៅរ៍ហើយឲ្យស្រាមានលាយថ្នាំដល់លោក Henry ផឹកធ្វើឲ្យគាត់ដេកលក់ ។ ពួកគេពន្យល់ថាប្រពន្ធរបស់លោក Henry បានស្លាប់អស់ពេលដប់ប្រាំបួនឆ្នាំហើយ ។ ពួកគេធ្វើតាមរបៀបនេះរៀងរាល់ឆ្នាំដោយធ្វើហាក់ដូចជានាងត្រឡប់មកវិញដើម្បីកុំឲ្យលោក Henry ច្រួលច្រាល ។ ក្នុងរឿង "Valediction" អ្នកពោលរួមទុក្ខចំពោះការបាត់ខ្លួននៃលោកស្រីម្នាក់ដែលពីដើមបានធ្វើឲ្យផ្ទះគាត់រុងរឿង ប៉ុន្តែឥឡូវនេះគឺជាអ្នកដែលគាត់កើតទុក្ខដោយទឹករលឹក ។

Name ______________________________ Date ______________

"Stopping by Woods on a Snowy Evening" by Robert Frost
"Four Skinny Trees" by Sandra Cisneros
"Miracles" by Walt Whitman

Summary These three selections celebrate the wonders of nature, each in a different way. In "Stopping by Woods on a Snowy Evening," a traveler pauses to watch snow fall in woods that belong to someone else. The traveler cannot stay, however, because of promises to keep and miles yet to be traveled. In "Four Skinny Trees," the narrator admires the determination of four scrawny trees outside her window that possess the secret strength to keep growing and going on. The trees inspire the narrator to continue going on, too. In "Miracles," the speaker celebrates all aspects of nature—both indoors and outdoors—which some people might consider ordinary, but which he sees as miracles.

Respond to Levels of Meaning Often when you read a piece of literature, you can find several meanings in it. You may find one meaning that other readers find as well. But you may also find a personal meaning that other readers don't necessarily experience.

Work with a partner. First, read the three selections together. Then, discuss what each selection means to each of you personally. How do you both feel about the work? Use the chart to record your individual feelings, and then see how similar or different they are.

Selection	What It Means to Me	What It Means to My Partner
"Stopping by Woods ..."		
"Four Skinny Trees"		
"Miracles"		

"Stopping by Woods on a Snowy Evening" by Robert Frost
"Four Skinny Trees" by Sandra Cisneros
"Miracles" by Walt Whitman

Resumen Cada uno de estos tres textos celebra las maravillas de la naturaleza de una manera diferente. En "Stopping by Woods on a Snowy Evening," un viajero se detiene a mirar caer la nieve en un bosque que pertenece a otra persona. El viajero no puede quedarse, ya que tiene promesas que cumplir y muchas millas por caminar. En "Four Skinny Trees," el narrador admira la determinación de cuatro árboles raquíticos frente a su ventana que poseen la fuerza secreta para seguir creciendo y continuar adelante. Los árboles inspiran al viajero a también continuar adelante. En "Miracles," el narrador celebra todos los aspectos de la naturaleza–tanto dentro de la casa como afuera–cosas que algunas personas quizás consideren normales, pero que él ve como milagros.

Tóm Lược Ba bài văn chọn lọc này khen ngợi những sự kỳ diệu của thiên nhiên, mỗi bài một vẽ khác nhau. Trong "Stopping by Woods on a Snowy Evening", một người du hành đứng nhìn tuyết rơi trong rừng cây của người khác. Mặc dầu vậy, người du hành không thể ở nán lại, vì những lời hứa phải giữ và nhiều dặm đường xa phải đi. Trong "Four Skinny Trees", người viết chuyện khen ngợi sự quyết tâm của bốn cây gầy còm bên ngoài cửa sổ của bà đã phô trương sức mạnh tìm ẩn làm cho cây tiếp tục mọc và lớn lên. Các cây này cũng tạo hứng khởi cho bà để tiến tục tiến lên. Trong bài "Miracles", tác giả ngợi khen tất cả các cảnh trí của thiên nhiên--cả trong nhà lẫn ngoài trời--những loại mà một số người cho là bình thường, nhưng theo ông chúng kỳ diệu.

Lub ntsiab lus Peb zaj xaiv los no muaj kev zoo siab rau tej yam ntuj tsim teb raug uas ib txwm muaj, ib zaj hais lawm ib yam. Nyob hauv "Stopping by Woods on a Snowy Evening," ib tug tibneeg ncig saib tebchaw nres saib te (snow) poob ntawm ib lub hav zoov uas muaj tswv kav. Tus tibneeg ncig tebchaws ntawv nyob tsis tau, txawm li cas los xij peem, vim yuav tau ua raws li cov lus cog tseg thiab tseem tshuav kev deb heev mus. Nyob rau "Four Skinny Trees," tus neeg uas sau nyiam plaub tsob ntoo me me ua zoo li twb yuav tuag nraum zoov nws lub qhov rais uas cawm tau kom muaj zog loj hlob zuj zus mus. Cov ntoo ntawv txawm ua rau tus neeg ntawv pheej lam nyob zuj zus mus thiab."Miracles," tus hais lus muaj kev zoo siab rau txhua yam uas muaj sia—tsis hais hauv tsev lossis nraum zoov uas neeg yuav pom tias nws zoo li txhua yam xwb, tiamsis rau nws mas yog ib qhov txawv heev.

摘要 這三篇選文各以不同的方式來歌頌大自然的神奇。在 "Stopping by Woods on a Snowy Evening" 中，一位旅人暫停佇足欣賞白雪降在私人林地中的景色。旅人不能停留因為必須遵守他的諾言何況還有好幾哩路要趕呢。在 "Four Skinny Trees" 中，解說者佩服她窗外那四棵瘦巴巴的樹的決心，它們擁有神秘的力量支撐它們不斷地成長。這些樹也激勵解說者繼續不斷努力求進。在 "Miracles" 中，主人翁讚美大自然的各個種類一室外與室內一這些也許有人覺得普通無奇，但在他看來卻是神奇。

សេចក្តីសង្ខេប អត្ថបទជ្រើសរើសទាំងបីនេះបង្ហាញពីភាពអស្ចារ្យរបស់ធម្មជាតិតាមរបៀបខុសគ្នាក្នុងអត្ថបទនិមួយៗ ។ ក្នុងរឿង "Stopping by Woods on a Snowy Evening" អ្នកដំណើរឈប់បង្អង់ដើម្បីមើលទឹកកកធ្លាក់នៅក្នុងព្រៃដែលជារបស់នរណាម្នាក់ទៀត ។ ទោះយ៉ាងនោះក្តី អ្នកដំណើរមិនអាចនៅទីនោះបានទេ ដោយមានកិច្ចសន្យាត្រូវធ្វើនិងមានដំណើរវែងឆ្ងាយទៅទៀត ។ នៅក្នុង "Four Skinny Trees" អ្នកពោលសរសើរសេចក្តីប្តេជ្ញារបស់ដើមឈើសង្គមបួនដើមនៅក្រៅបង្អួចរបស់នាងដែលមានកម្លាំងសម្ងាត់ដើម្បីធំលូតលាស់បន្តទៅទៀត ។ ដើមឈើនោះជំរុលចិត្តអ្នកពោលឲ្យបន្តការធំលូតលាស់ទៅទៀតដែរ ។ ក្នុងរឿង "Miracles" អ្នកពោលបង្ហាញពីលក្ខណៈទាំងអស់របស់ធម្មជាតិ គឺទាំងនៅក្នុងផ្ទះនិងនៅក្រៅផ្ទះ ដែលមនុស្សខ្លះអាចចាត់ទុកថាធម្មតា ប៉ុន្តែគាត់មើលឃើញថាជាភាពអព្ភូតហេតុ ។

Name ______________________________ Date ______________

"The Night the Bed Fell" by James Thurber

Summary In this hilarious story, James Thurber recalls the chain of events that led to chaos one night when he was a youth. His father had gone to the attic to sleep, despite his mother's protests that the wobbly bed might collapse. During the night, young James accidentally tipped over his own cot. The noise caused his mother to scream, which woke up a visiting cousin, Briggs, who immediately poured camphor—a strong-smelling medicine—on himself, thinking he had stopped breathing. The camphor made the room smell so foul that Briggs broke a window to get air. James's mother, still thinking her husband had fallen, went to the attic. The father was puzzled by all the commotion. Eventually the confusion was sorted out.

Identify Causes and Effects In many stories, there is a pattern of causes and effects. A **cause** is the reason something happens. An **effect** is what happens as a result of the cause. For example, in Thurber's story, Father wants to be away where he can think. Therefore, he goes to the attic to sleep. His desire to be alone is the cause; sleeping in the attic is the effect.

Think about the things that happen in "The Night the Bed Fell." Record each important cause and the effect that it leads to.

Cause		Effect
______________	>	______________
______________	>	______________
______________	>	______________
______________	>	______________
______________	>	______________
______________	>	______________
______________	>	______________
______________	>	______________
______________	>	______________
______________	>	______________
______________	>	______________
______________	>	______________
______________	>	______________
______________	>	______________
______________	>	______________
______________	>	______________

"The Night the Bed Fell"
by James Thurber

Resumen En esta divertida historia, James Thurber recuerda los sucesos que llevaron al caos una noche cuando era joven. Su padre había ido a dormir al desván a pesar de las protestas de su madre de que la maltrecha cama podría desplomarse. Durante la noche, el joven James volcó accidentalmente su propia cama. El ruido hizo gritar a su madre, despertando a Briggs, un primo que estaba de visita, quien inmediatamente derramó sobre sí mismo alcanfor — una medicina con un olor muy fuerte —, pensando que había dejado de respirar. Debido al alcanfor, la habitación olía tan mal que Briggs rompió una ventana para que entrara aire. La madre de James, que seguía pensando de que su marido se había caído, subió al desván. El padre estaba perplejo ante toda la conmoción. Finalmente, se logró aclarar la confusión.

Tóm Lược Trong câu chuyện buồn cười này, James Thurber nhớ lại một chuổi việc xảy ra tạo nên cuộc hỗn loạn trong một đêm khi ông còn trẻ. Cha ông đi lên gác ngủ, bất chấp việc kháng cự của mẹ ông là cái giường ọp ẹp có thể bị sập. Trong đêm, James lăn nên bị té khỏi ghế bố. Tiếng động làm cho mẹ ông la lên, làm cho người bà con đến thăm tên Briggs thức dậy, anh lập tức tự đổ dầu nóng Camphor—một loại dầu có mùi rất nồng—lên mình, vì nghĩ rằng anh đã ngưng thở. Mùi dầu camphor làm cho cả căn phòng bị ngạc nên Briggs tông một cửa sổ ra để thở. Mẹ của James, vẫn nghĩ rằng chồng bà bị té, vội chạy lên gác. Người cha đang lo nghĩ vì các hỗn loạn. Việc rắc rối này sau đó đã được giải quyết.

Lub ntsiab lus Nyob rau zaj dab neeg ua txaus luag no, James Thurber nco txog tej yam uas ua rau sawvdaws paub tsis meej ib hmo thaum nws tseem yau. Nws txiv nce mus pw saum nthab (attic) txawm tias nws niam qhia tias lub txaj tsis khov, pheej co uas tej zaum yuav vau. Thaum tsaus ntuj menyuam tub James dawm nws lub txaj uas tsis yog lam txhob txwm ua. Lub suab ua rau nws niam qw, qhovntawd ua rau Briggs, tus kwvtij uas tuaj xyuas nws tsim dheev tam sim ntawv. Nws cia li ua ib qhov tshuaj uas tsw muaj ceem heev ncuav rau nws tag, xav tias nws tsis ua pa lawm. Cov tshuaj camphor ntawv ua rau lub hoov ntawv tsw phem heev uas Briggs thiaj tau tsoo ib lub qhov rais kom tau cua. James niam txawm xav tias nws tus txiv poob qab txag thiab nce mus saum nthab. Leej txiv xav tsis thoob txog tej kev uas ua rau nws sawv no. Thaum kawg cov kev tsis sib to tau ntawv mam li rov to taub.

摘要 在這則愉快熱鬧的故事中，James Thurber 回憶起當他還年少時，一次一連串的事件導致了一個混亂的夜晚。儘管他的母親認為那張搖搖晃晃的床有倒塌之虞，他的父親卻已經上去閣樓睡覺了。半夜小 James 意外地弄翻他的小床。床倒聲導致母親尖叫而尖叫聲吵醒了來訪的表哥布利格斯，他立即將樟腦——一種味道強烈的藥品一倒在自己身上，因為他以為自己已經停止呼吸了。樟腦使得房間難聞死了，布利格斯於是打破窗戶透氣。James 的母親仍以為是她的丈夫摔下床。當她上到閣樓時，父親被所有的騷動搞得一團霧水。最後這些疑惑總算解決了。

សេចក្ដីសង្ខេប ក្នុងរឿងគួរឲ្យចង់សើចនេះ James Thurber រំលឹកពីហេតុការណ៍បន្តគ្នាដែលនាំឲ្យមានការច្របូកច្របល់នៅយប់មួយកាលគាត់នៅក្មេង ។ ឪពុកគាត់បានឡើងទៅលើឡៅដើម្បីដេក ទុកជាមានការជំទាស់ពីម្ដាយរបស់គាត់ថាគ្រែរញ្ជួយនោះអាចបាក់ក្ដី ។ នៅពេលយប់នោះយុវជន James ទាក់ជើងដោយចៃដន្យជាមួយពៅអីរបស់វា ។ សម្លេងនោះនាំឲ្យម្ដាយរបស់គាត់ស្រែកឡើងធ្វើឲ្យភ្ញាក់ជីដូនមួយគាត់ឈ្មោះ Briggs ដែលមកលេង ជីដូនមួយនោះក៏ចាក់ថ្នាំទេពិរូដែលជាថ្នាំមានក្លិនខ្លាំងទៅលើខ្លួនព្រោះគិតថាគាត់បានឈប់ដកដង្ហើម ។ ថ្នាំទេពិរូធ្វើឲ្យបន្ទប់ធំក្លិនឈ្ងក់ទើប Briggs វាយបង្អួចបើកដើម្បីឲ្យខ្យល់ចូល ។ ម្ដាយរបស់ James ទៅកាន់លើឡៅ ព្រោះនៅតែគិតថាប្ដីរបស់គាត់បានធ្លាក់ ។ ឪពុកគាត់មានការងឿងឆ្ងល់ចំពោះការជ្រួលច្របល់ទាំងអស់នេះ ។ ដាយថាហេតុ ការយល់ច្រឡំនេះត្រូវបានដោះស្រាយ ។

Name ______________________________ Date ______________

"All Summer in a Day" by Ray Bradbury

Summary A class of nine-year-old children, living on the planet Venus, looks forward to seeing the sun for the very first time. A seemingly endless seven-year rainfall is predicted to stop for a short time. The children taunt a frail classmate, Margot, who came from Earth and had seen the sun from there. They don't believe her reports about what the sun is like. As a cruel joke, the children lock Margot in a closet before going out to play in the sun for the only hour of sunshine after seven years. When the rain resumes, and the children sadly return indoors, they realize that Margot has missed the sunshine. Knowing how cruel they have been, they slowly go to the closet to let Margot out.

Envision Setting and Actions When you **picture a setting and actions,** you picture what is happening and where it is happening. As you read, pay close attention to story details that describe the setting. If you were standing in that setting, what would you see? Hear? Touch? Smell? Taste? Also pay attention to details that describe the action. Picture everything that is happening around you.

Record details about "All Summer in a Day" in the chart below.

"All Summer in a Day"

What I see ______________________________

____

What I hear ______________________________

____

What I feel ______________________________

____

What I smell ______________________________

____

Resumen Una clase de niños de nueve años que viven en el planeta Venus tienen la esperanza de ver el sol por primera vez. Se predice que una lluvia interminable de casi siete años va a parar por un corto tiempo. Los niños se burlan de una compañera de clase enferma, Margot, que llegó desde la Tierra y había visto al sol desde allí. Ellos no le creen lo que dice sobre el sol. Como una broma cruel, los niños encierran a Margot en un armario antes de salir a jugar al sol durante la única hora de sol en siete años. Cuando comienza de nuevo a llover, y los niños vuelven de nuevo adentro, se dan cuenta que Margot se ha perdido ver los rayos de sol. Sabiendo lo cruel que han sido, lentamente van al armario y dejan salir a Margot.

Tóm lược Một lớp học gồm có các em chín tuổi sống trên hành tinh Venus đang chờ được thấy mặt trời lần đầu tiên. Một trận mưa dai dẳng kéo dài cả 7 năm trời mà lúc đó hình như sắp tạnh. Các em trêu trọc một học trò mảnh khảnh cùng lớp từ trái đất tới, tên là Margot, cô đã từng nhìn thấy mặt trời từ nơi cô tới. Bọn trẻ không tin chuyện cô kể về mặt trời. Đùa cợt quá độ, bọn trẻ nhốt cô bé vào tủ trước khi cả bọn kéo nhau ra chơi dưới ánh nắng mặt trời, một cơ hội chỉ lâu độ một tiếng đồng hồ trong bẩy năm trời. Khi trời lại bắt đầu mưa, lũ trẻ chợt nhận ra là Margot đã bị mất cơ hội chơi đùa dưới ánh mặt trời. Biết là mình đã đùa quá ác, lũ trẻ mở tủ thả Margot ra.

Lub ntsiab lus Ib pab me nyuam yaus kawn ntawv muaj cuaj xyoo nyob lub ntiaj tev Venus tos xyuas lub hnub thawj zau. Lawv qhia hais tias kob nag los tsis txawj tu tau xya xyoo yov tu tsis ntev no. Cov me nyuam yaus pheej ua phem rau lwm ib tus phooj ywg kawn ntawv uas nws tsis tsuav muaj zog, Margot, nws tuaj hauv ntiaj teb tuaj thiab nws tau pom lub hnub lawn thaum nyob nrav. Lawm tsis ntseeg nws piav txog lub nhub zoo li cas li. Hais txog qhov phem, cov me nyuam yaus muaj Margot kaw rau ib qhov chaw ua ntej lawm yuav mus ua si thaum tib teev ua lub hnub thiaj tawm tuaj tib zaug hauv xya xyoo. Thaum nag rov qab los, cov me nyuam yaus tu siab rov qab nkaj los hauv tsev, lawm mam nco hais tias Margot tsis tau pom lub hnub ci. Paub hais tias lawm ua phem, lawm thiab maj mam mus qhib tso Margot tawm los.

摘要 金星上有一班九歲的孩子非常盼望看到生平第一次的太陽。根據氣象預報，一場下了七年的雨即將暫停一會兒。這群孩子逗弄一位身體虛弱的同學瑪歌，她來自地球，曾經看過太陽。他們不相信她對太陽所做的報告，而對瑪歌開了一個殘酷的玩笑。在他們跑到七年才會出現一小時的陽光下玩耍之前，先把她鎖在衣櫃裡。等到天又下起雨來，孩子們難過的回到室內，發現瑪歌已經錯過了陽光。他們發覺自己非常殘酷，慢慢走到衣櫃前把瑪歌放出來。

សេចក្តីសង្ខេប ថ្នាក់នៃក្មេងអាយុប្រាំបួនឆ្នាំដែលរស់នៅលើពិភព Venus ទន្ទឹងរង់ចាំមើលព្រះអាទិត្យជាលើកដំបូងបំផុត ។ ការធ្លាក់ភ្លៀងប្រាំពីរឆ្នាំដែលហាក់ដូចជាគ្មានទីបញ្ចប់ត្រូវបានគេទាយទុកថានិងឈប់មួយក្នុងពេលដ៏ខ្លី ។ ក្មេងៗនិយាយឡកឡឺយឲ្យ Margot ជាមិត្តរួមថ្នាក់ទន់ខ្សោយម្នាក់ដែលមកពីផែនដីហើយដែលធ្លាប់ឃើញព្រះអាទិត្យនៅទីនោះ ។ ពួកគេមិនជឿរបាយការណ៍របស់នាងអំពីរូបរាងរបស់ព្រះអាទិត្យទេ ។ ជាការលេងសើចយ៉ាងអាក្រក់អាក្រីក្មេងៗចាក់សោរMargot ទុកនៅក្នុងទូមុនពេលចេញទៅលេងនៅក្រោមពន្លឺព្រះអាទិត្យដែលមានរយៈពេលតែមួយម៉ោងប៉ុណ្ណោះក្នុងរយៈពេលប្រាំពីរឆ្នាំ ។ នៅពេលដែលភ្លៀងរាំង ហើយក្មេងៗត្រឡប់ចូលក្នុងបន្ទប់វិញដោយទុក្ខទោម្នេញពួកគេដឹងថា Margot មិនបានឃើញរស្មីព្រះអាទិត្យទេ ។ ដោយដឹងថាជាភាពអាក្រក់អាក្រីដែលពួកគេបានធ្វើ ពួកគេទៅកាន់ទូដោយយឺតៗដើម្បីដោះលែងឲ្យ Margot ចេញ ។

Name ______________________________ Date ______________

"The Highwayman" by Alfred Noyes

"The Real Story of a Cowboy's Life" by Geoffrey C. Ward

Summary In "The Highwayman," a dashing highwayman tells Bess, his beloved, that he'll return to her after a short while. Tim, the horse keeper, overhears the conversation and informs authorities who then tie Bess with a musket aimed at her heart. When the highwayman returns, Bess pulls the trigger, to warn him of danger, and is killed. The highwayman comes back to avenge her death, but is shot and killed. "The Real Story of a Cowboy's Life" describes the dirty and dangerous work of a cattle drive. Among numerous difficulties are settlers angered over cattle crossing their land and nighttime stampedes that sometimes cause cowboys' deaths. However, a cowboy's life is also full of small pleasures like the beauty of the animals crossing the plains and the songs of the other cowboys.

Identify Causes and Effects In many stories, there is a pattern of causes and effects. A **cause** is the reason something happens. An **effect** is what happens as a result of the cause. Think about the things that happen in each of the three selections. Record each important cause and the effect that follows.

"The Highwayman"

Cause		Effect
______________________________	>	______________________________
______________________________	>	______________________________
______________________________	>	______________________________

"The Real Story of a Cowboy's Life"

Cause		Effect
______________________________	>	______________________________
______________________________	>	______________________________
______________________________	>	______________________________

"The Highwayman" by Alfred Noyes
"The Real Story of a Cowboy's Life" by Geoffrey C. Ward

Resumen En "The Highwayman", un atrevido salteador de caminos le dice a Bess, su amada, que volverá a ella en poco tiempo. Tim, el caballerizo, oye la conversación e informa a las autoridades, quienes atan a Bess y ponen un mosquete apuntándole al pecho. Cuando el bandolero vuelve, Bess aprieta el gatillo para advertirle del peligro, cayendo muerta. El salteador regresa para vengar su muerte, pero resulta muerto de un tiro. "The Real Story of a Cowboy's Life" describe el trabajo sucio y peligroso de un vaquero. Entre las numerosas dificultades están los pobladores molestos por el cruce de ganado por sus tierras y las estampidas nocturnas que a veces causan la muerte de vaqueros. Sin embargo, la vida del vaquero está también llena de pequeños placeres como la belleza de los animales que cruzan la llanura y las canciones de los otros vaqueros.

Tóm lược Trong "The Highwayman," một gã cướp đường rành nghề nói với Bess, là người yêu của anh ta, rằng anh ta sẽ trở về gặp cô sau một thời gian ngắn. Tim, kẻ giữ ngựa, nghe trộm cuộc đối thoại và báo tin nhà cầm quyền đến trói Bess cùng khẩu súng trường nhắm vào tim cô. Khi gã cướp đường trở lại, Bess kéo cò súng, báo động sự nguy hiểm,và cô bị giết. Gã cướp đường quay lại trả thù cho cái chết của cô ấy, anh bị trúng đạn và bị giết. "The Real Story of a Cowboy's Life" mô tả mộ công việc bẩn thỉu vàn nguy hiểm của nghề chặ xúc vật. Một trong những khó khăn là khi những người lập nhgiệp tức giận đàn xúc vật vượt qua đất dai của họ và ban đêm chúng chay tán loạn đôi khi làm chêt của những người chăn bò. Tuy vậy, đời một người chăn bò (cowboy) lại có nhiều thú vui nho nhỏ như được ngắm vẻ đẹp của thú vật đang đi qua đồng cỏ và nghe những bài át của các bạn chăn bò khác.

Lub ntsiab lus Nyob rau "The Highwayman," ib tug neeg tub sab uas tsis ntshai li hais rau Bess, uas yog nws tus hlub tias, nws mam rov qab los ib pliag. Tim, yog tus uas saib cov nees, hnov nkawv sib tham thiab nws mus qhia tub ceev xwm, tuaj muab Bess khi thiab muab ib rab phom taw rau ntawm nws hauv siab. Thaum tus tub sab rov qab los, Bess nyem rab phom kom nws paub hais tias muaj kev tsis zoo lawm, qhov no ua rau nws tau tuag. Tus tub sab rov qab tuaj pauj qhov ua rau Bess tuag ntawv tiamsis ho ua rau nws tau tuag. "The Real Story of a Cowboy's Life" qhia txog kev lo av thiab kev tsis zoo ntawm kev un ib tug neeg lawv nyuj. Muaj ntau yam kev nyuaj xws li, cov neeg chim heev thaum cov nyuj hlav lawv cov av thiab thaum hmo ntuj uas nyuj taum plov rau ub rau no ua rau tus neeg caij nees (cowboy) ntawv tuag. Tab sis, ib tug tub yug nyuj lub neej los muaj ntau qhov kev zoo siab ib yam li pom qhov zoo kauj ntawm cov tsiaj hla tiaj zaub thiab cov zaj nkauj ntawm lwm tus tub yug nyuj.

摘要 在 "The Highwayman" 中，一名不怕死的攔路強盜告訴愛人貝絲他不久將回到她身邊。照顧馬匹的湯姆無意間聽到這段對話並告知有關當局，於是當局派人把貝絲與瞄準她胸口的滑膛槍綁在一起。當攔路強盜回來時，貝絲以拉板機來警告他有危險，但自己卻死了。攔路強盜想回來為她的死報仇卻也被射殺了然而，一位牛仔的生活也充滿了小小的歡樂，例如動物横越平原的美麗景象以及其他牛仔的歌聲。"The Real Story of a Cowboy's Life"描述追趕牛群是一種既骯髒又危險的工作。而在這數不清的困難中最具代表性的是移民者痛恨牛群横越他們的土地以及晚間牛群驚慌奔竄，有時會造成牛仔的死亡。然而，一位牛仔的生活也充滿了小小的歡 樂，例如動物横越平原的美麗景象以及其他牛仔的歌聲。

សេចក្តីសង្ខេប នៅក្នុង "The Highwayman" បុរសពនេចរដែលប្រញាប់ប្រញាល់ម្នាក់និយាយប្រាប់នាង Bess ដែលជាសង្សាររបស់គាត់ថាគាត់នឹងត្រឡប់មកវិញនៅពេលមួយសន្ទុះទៀត ។ Tim ដែលជាអ្នកថែសេះ លួចស្តាប់ការសន្ទនានោះ ហើយផ្តល់ដំណឹងដល់អាជ្ញាធរដែលបន្ទាប់មកទៀតចង Bess ដោយភ្ជង់ដាវសាបចំបេះដូងនាង ។ នៅពេលបុរសពនេចរត្រឡប់មកវិញ Bess ទាញកៃកាំភ្លើងដើម្បីឲ្យសញ្ញាគាត់ពីគ្រោះថ្នាក់ ហើយត្រូវគេសម្លាប់ទៅ ។ បុរសពនេចរត្រឡប់មកវិញដើម្បីសងសឹកឲ្យនាង ប៉ុន្តែត្រូវគេបាញ់សម្លាប់ទៅ ។ នៅក្នុង "The Dying Cowboy" យុវជនឃ្វាលគោម្នាក់ដែលជិតស្លាប់សុំឲ្យគេកប់គាត់នៅស្រុកកំណើត នៅក្បែរផ្នូរខ្មោចឪពុកគាត់ ដោយមិនឲ្យកប់នៅក្នុងវាលស្មៅដាច់ស្រយាលទេ ។ ទោះយ៉ាងនេះក្តី អ្នកឃ្វាលគោដែលស្តាប់បណ្តាំរបស់គាត់មើលឃើញថាវាលស្មៅជាកន្លែងស្អាតល្អ ហើយគេក៏កប់គាត់នៅទីនោះទៅ ។ "The Real Story of a Cowboy's Life" រៀបរាប់ពីការងារស្មោកគ្រោកនិងមានគ្រោះថ្នាក់នៃការកៀងហ្វូងគោ ។ នៅក្នុងចំណោមការពិបាកជាច្រើននោះគឺមានកំហឹងរបស់អ្នកតាំងទីរស់នៅពីរឿងហ្វូងគោដើរកាត់ដីរបស់ពួកគេ និងការផ្អើលរត់របស់ហ្វូងគោនៅពេលយប់ ដែលជួនកាលអាចបណ្តាលឲ្យអ្នកឃ្វាលគោស្លាប់បាន ។ ទោះជាយ៉ាងនេះក្តី ជីវិតរបស់បុរសឃ្វាលគោពោរពេញទៅដោយសេចក្តីរីករាយដូចជាសំរស់របស់សត្វពាហនៈឆ្លងកាត់ខ្ពង់រាប ហើយនិងចម្រៀងរបស់បុរសឃ្វាលគោឯទៀត ។

Name ______________________________ Date ______________

"Amigo Brothers" by Piri Thomas
"The Walk" by Thomas Hardy
"Justin Lebo" by Phillip Hoose
"The Rider" by Naomi Shihab Nye

Summary Finding a way around a problem is a central theme of these selections. The "Amigo Brothers" are best friends who must fight against each other for a championship. They train separately and they worry about hurting each other. In the ring, they throw their toughest punches, learning that their friendship will endure no matter who wins. The speaker in "The Walk" finds a way to appreciate a walk to a hilltop even without the company of a special companion. Justin Lebo overcomes difficulties while making bikes to give to less fortunate boys. He learns to collaborate with his parents and others who can help him with money, know-how, and bike parts. He tolerates publicity because it helps him meet his goal, giving joy to others. The speaker in "The Rider" learns to leave loneliness behind while riding around the neighborhood on a bicycle.

Make Inferences When you **make an inference,** you take a guess about something not stated directly in the story. For example, in "The Rider," the speaker never says that she feels lonely. However, you could make that inference for two reasons: She wonders if riding a bicycle can rid a person of loneliness, and she is riding a bicycle. From those two clues you infer that she may feel loneliness herself.

Make an inference about a character or event in each selection. Give the reasons that lead you to make each inference.

"Amigo Brothers"

Inference	Reasons
______________________	______________________
______________________	______________________

"The Walk"

Inference	Reasons
______________________	______________________
______________________	______________________

"Justin Lebo"

Inference	Reasons
______________________	______________________
______________________	______________________

"The Rider"

Inference	Reasons
______________________	______________________
______________________	______________________

"Amigo Brothers" by Piri Thomas
"The Walk" by Thomas Hardy
"Justin Lebo" by Phillip Hoose
"The Rider" by Naomi Shihab Nye

Resumen El tema central de estos textos es buscar la manera de resolver un problema. "The Amigo Brothers" son amigos íntimos que deben enfrentarse por un campeonato de boxeo. Se entrenan por separado y están preocupados de lastimarse el uno al otro. En el cuadrilátero lanzan sus golpes más fuertes, aprendiendo que su amistad durará gane quien gane. El narrador de "The Walk" encuentra la manera de apreciar un paseo a la cima de una colina, a pesar de no tener un acompañante especial. Justin Lebo supera dificultades al construir bicicletas para regalarles a los muchachos menos afortunados. Aprende a colaborar con sus padres y con otros que puedan aportarle dinero, conocimientos, y piezas de bicicleta. Tolera la publicidad, ya le ayuda a conseguir su objetivo, alegrando el corazón de otros. El narrador de "The Rider" aprende a dejar atrás la soledad mientras recorre su barrio en bicicleta.

Tóm lược Tìm cách giải quyết cho một vấn đề là chủ đề chính của những lựa chọn này. "Amigo Brothers" là những người bạn thân nhất họ phải đánh lộn với nhau để dành chức vô địch. Họ tập luyện riêng rẽ và lo ngại rằng họ sẽ làm cho những người bạn khác buồn. Trên vũ đài, họ đấm những cú đấm mạnh nhất, họ hiểu rằng tình hữu nghị của họ vẫn tồn tại bất kể ai chiến thắng. Diễn giả trong "The Walk" tìm ra một cách để cảm kích khi đi bộ lên đỉnh đồi mà không có ai theo mình. Justin Lebo vượt qua những khó khăn trong khi chế tạo ra xe đạp cho những đứa con trai kém may mắn. Ông học cùng làm việc với cha mẹ ông và những người khác có thể giúp ông bằng tiền, bí quyết để làm, và các bộ phận của xe đạp. Ông chịu đựng sự công khai vì điều đó giúp ông đạt được mục đích, mang niềm vui đến mọi người. Diễn giả "The Rider" cố gắng quên sự cô đơn khi chạy xe đạp trong khu láng giềng.

Lub ntsiab lus Kev nrhiav ib txoj kev los daws teebmeem yog lub hauv plawv txha kaj qaum ntawm cov dab neeg uas xaiv los no. "The Amigo Brothers," yog ob tug phooj ywg uas zoo tshaj plaws uas yuav tsum tau sib ntaus seb leejtwg tau thib ib. Nkawv nyias xyaum nyias thiab ntshai tsam nkawv ho ua rau ib tug raug mob. Thaum nkag nkag rau hauv lub kauj sib ntaus, nkawv ntaus lub nrig uas hnav tshaj plaws, thiab kawm tau hais tias, kev phooj ywg yuav thev tau txawm tias leejtwg yog tus yeej. Tus hais lus nyob rau "The Walk" nrhiav tau kev los ua tsaug rau qhov uas nws taug kev mus txog saum roob txawm tias tsis muaj leejtwg tseem ceeb nrog nws mus. Justin Lebo kov yeej ntau yam kev nyuaj siab thaum nws tsim cov luv tees mus pub rau cov menyuam tub uas tsis muaj. Nws kawm koom tes nrog nws niam thiab txiv thiab lwm tus uas yuav muaj nyiaj pab nws, cov uas paub kho luv tees, thiab cov khoom uas yuav kho luv tees. Nws ua siab loj rau tej kev luam ntawv tawm rau neeg paub vim qhov no pab nws mus txog nws txoj hau kev, uas yog pub kev zoo siab rau lwm tus. Tus hais lus nyob rau zaj "The Rider" kawm txoj kev uas nyob nws tib leeg xwb, los mus caij luv tees ncig thaj tsam uas nws nyob ntawv.

摘要 這些選文的主旨在於如何從問題中找出一條解決之道。"Amigo Brothers" 是兩個最要好的朋友必須為一場冠軍賽互相爭奪。他們分開受訓而且擔心會傷到彼此。當比賽的鈴聲響起，他們各使出最重的拳擊，因為他們知道無論誰贏都不會影響他們的友誼。在 "The Walk" 中，主人翁找到一條能用心體驗欣賞一路走到山頂的路，甚至不需要一位特別的同伴隨行。當 Justin Lebo 想要為不幸的男孩們製造腳踏車時，他克服了困難。他學會如何與他的父母及那些能提供錢、懂得如何製造腳踏車和提供腳踏車零件的人合作。他忍耐做宣傳工作只因為如此能幫助他達成目標，將歡樂帶給其他的人。在 "The Rider" 中，主人翁則是學著在家附近騎腳踏車而將孤寂拋在腦後。

សេចក្តីសង្ខេប ការរកឃើញផ្លូវចេញពីបញ្ហាជាសាច់រឿងគោលរបស់អត្ថបទជ្រើសរើសនេះ ។ "Amigo Brothers" គឺជាមិត្តល្អដែលត្រូវប្រយុទ្ធគ្នាដើម្បីភាពជាជើងឯក ។ ពួកគេហាត់ហ្វឹកហ្វឺនដាច់ផ្សេងពីគ្នា ហើយពួកគេបារម្ភខ្លាចធ្វើឲ្យឈឺដល់គ្នាទៅវិញទៅមក ។ នៅក្នុងសង្វៀន ពួកគេដាល់គ្នាយ៉ាងខ្លាំងក្លាបំផុតដោយដឹងថាមិត្តភាពរបស់ពួកគេនឹងស្ថិតស្ថេរទោះជានរណាឈ្នះក្តី ។ អ្នកពោលនៅក្នុង "The Walk" រកឃើញមធ្យោបាយដើម្បីអរគុណការដើរឡើងកំពូលទួលទោះបីដោយគ្មានគូគ្នាដែលរួមជាមួយជាពិសេសក្តី ។ Justin Lebo យកឈ្នះលើការលំបាកនៅពេលធ្វើកង់ដើម្បីឲ្យដល់ក្មេងកំសត់ទុរគត ។ គាត់រៀនធ្វើការសំរបសំរួលជាមួយឪពុកម្តាយគាត់និងអ្នកឯទៀតដែលអាចជួយលុយ ដែលដឹងពីរបៀបធ្វើ ហើយនិងគ្រឿងកង់ ។ គាត់ទទួលស្គាល់ការផ្សាយសាធារណៈពីព្រោះវាជួយគាត់ឲ្យសំរេចតាមគោលដៅ ដោយផ្តល់សេចក្តីរីករាយដល់អ្នកឯទៀត ។ អ្នកពោលនៅក្នុង "The Rider" រៀនបំភ្លេចចោលភាពត្រម៉ង់ត្រម៉ោចនៅពេលជិះកង់ជុំវិញសង្កាត់ ។

Name ______________________________ Date ______________

"Our Finest Hour" by Charles Osgood

Summary In this humorous essay, journalist Charles Osgood describes the series of mistakes that occurred the night he was a substitute anchor on the *CBS Evening News* telecast. First, the lead story that Osgood introduced did not appear on the monitor; a different story ran instead. The next report didn't appear on the monitor, either. Then, a cue for a commercial brought no commercial. Later, a news story that no one had pre-screened was abruptly cut during its broadcast. After another mishap, a worker's outrage was picked up by a microphone. To top off Osgood's embarrassment, that night journalists from China visited the studio to observe the broadcast.

Distinguish Fact From Opinion As you read, it is important to recognize when writers are stating facts and when they are stating opinions. A **fact** is a statement that can be proven true. An **opinion** is a statement that expresses someone's personal feelings or taste, and cannot be proven true or false.

Read each statement from "Our Finest Hour." Tell whether it is a fact or an opinion. If it is a fact, tell how you could prove it. If it is an opinion, tell what word or words in the statement express a personal feeling.

1. Anchoring is easy enough, most of the time.
   Fact or opinion? Why?

   ____

   ____

2. A reporter was beginning a story.
   Fact or opinion? Why?

   ____

   ____

3. When the commercial was over, I introduced a piece from Washington.
   Fact or opinion? Why?

   ____

   ____

4. All in all, it was not the finest broadcast CBS News had ever done.
   Fact or opinion? Why?

   ____

   ____

5. They must have had a really great impression of American electronic journalism.
   Fact or opinion? Why?

   ____

   ____

"Our Finest Hour"
by Charles Osgood

Resumen En este ensayo humorístico, el periodista Charles Osgood describe la cadena de errores que ocurrió la noche en que fue locutor suplente de la transmisión del noticiero de CBS. Para empezar, la primera noticia que Osgood introdujo no apareció en el monitor; en su lugar, apareció una noticia diferente. El siguiente informe tampoco apareció en el monitor. Después, tras la señal de un aviso comercial, el aviso no apareció. Más tarde, una noticia que nadie había revisada de antemano fue cortada abruptamente durante la emisión. Después de otro desastre, el micrófono captó la voz de un empleado maldiciendo. Para terminar de avergonzar a Osgood, esa noche la transmisión estaba siendo observada por un grupo de periodistas venidos de China.

Tóm Lược Trong bài văn trào phúng này, ký giả Charles Osgood diễn tả một chuỗi lầm lỗi xảy ra trong ngày ông làm xướng ngôn viên phụ cho đài truyền hình trong chương trình CBS Evening News. Trước hết, dẫn đầu câu chuyện là việc giới thiệu chương trình của Osgoods đã không được trình chiếu trên màn ảnh, thay vào đó lại là một câu chuyện khác. Việc báo cáo tiếp theo cũng không có trên màn ảnh. Kế đến, phần cuối dành cho quảng cáo lại không có quảng cáo. Sau đó, một câu chuyện mới chưa được thông qua trước bị cắt đứt thình lình trong khi đang trình chiếu. Sau khi có một chuyện không hay nữa xảy ra, tiếng chưởi thề của một nhân viên bị phát ra trên máy phóng thanh. Việc xấu hổ nhất của Osgood là tối hôm ấy có các nhà báo Trung Hoa viếng thăm phòng làm việc để quan sát việc trình chiếu trên đài truyền hình.

Lub ntsiab lus Nyob rau daim ntawv txaus luag no, ib tug neeg sau ntawv hu ua Charles Osgood qhia txog cov uas lawv ua yuam kev hmo uas nws mus hloov tus neeg tshaj tawm xov xwm nyob rau CBS thaum tsaus ntuj. Qhov thib ib, zaj uas nws piav tsis pom tshwm rau lub monitor (lub zoo li lub T.V); tabsis muaj lwm zaj ho tshwm. Zaj thib ob uas nws tham los kuj tsis tshwm rau ntawm lub monitor li thiab. Ces cov kev tshaj tawm uas yuav tsum los txuas tsis los txuas li thiab. Tom qab ib zaj lus tshaj tawm uas tsis tau muaj neeg tso ciali ho tawm tuaj lub sijhawm ntawv. Tom qab uas yuam kev ib qho ntxiv, ib tug neeg uas ua haujlwm npau taws hais lus phem los lub paj taub tseem rub tau tawm rau neeg mloog thiab. Tseem ua kom Osgood txaj muag tshaj thiab mas yog ib tug neeg sau ntawv uas tuaj suav teb tuaj tseem tuaj xyuas lawv lub chaw tso tawm xov xwm hmo ntawv thiab.

摘要 在這則幽默的短文中，新聞記者 Charles Osgood 描述在 CBS 晚間新聞電視廣播當代理主播的那晚所發生的一連串失誤。首先 Charles Osgood 介紹頭條新聞故事，螢光幕上出現的卻是不同的新聞故事。下一個播報的新聞也沒在螢光幕上出現。然後提示是廣告時間了卻沒有廣告。之後沒經審查過的一段新聞故事在播報中又突然被切斷。又接著另一個小小錯誤之後，一個工作人員的咒罵聲經由麥克風傳了出來。而最令 Osgood 發窘的是剛好那一晚來自中國的記者們來到了演播室參觀新聞廣播工作。

សេចក្ដីសង្ខេប ក្នុងអត្ថបទកំប្លែងនេះ អ្នកកាសែត Charles Osgood រៀបរាប់ពីកំហុសជាបន្តបន្ទាប់ដែលកើតឡើងនៅយប់ដែលគាត់ធ្វើជាអ្នកគាំទ្រជំនួសនៅក្នុងការផ្សាយទូរទស្សន៍របស់ *CBS Evening News* ។ មុនដំបូង រឿងនាំមុខដែលលោក Osgood បង្ហាញនោះមិនលេចចេញនៅលើកញ្ចក់មើលទេ គឺបង្ហាញពីរឿងផ្សេងទៀត ។ របាយការណ៍បន្ទាប់មកទៀតក៏មិនចេញនៅលើកញ្ចក់មើលដែរ ។ បន្ទាប់មកសញ្ញាសំរាប់ផ្សាយពាណិជ្ជកម្មមិនបង្ហាញការផ្សាយពាណិជ្ជកម្មដែរ ។ ក្រោយមករឿងថ្មីមួយដែលគ្មាននរណាបានរៀបចំជាមុនត្រូវកាត់ចេញមួយរំពេចនៅក្នុងពេលផ្សាយ ។ បន្ទាប់ពីរឿងអកុសលមួយទៀត គេចាប់បានការស្តីបន្ទោសរបស់អ្នកធ្វើការតាមប្រដាប់និយាយ ។ ដើម្បីបំពេញការអៀនខ្មាស់របស់លោក Osgood ឲ្យដល់បន្ទុក នៅយប់នោះមានអ្នកកាសែតមកពីប្រទេសចិនបានទៅទស្សនាបន្ទប់ផ្សាយដើម្បីសង្កេតមើលការផ្សាយ ។

Name ______________________________ Date ______________

"Cat on the Go" by James Herriot

Summary Veterinarian James Herriot relates his experiences with an unusual cat. Herriot and his assistant perform surgery to save the stray cat after it is brought near death to his office. Herriot and his wife Helen then nurture the cat in their home. One evening the cat disappears, and is found later at a church meeting. Another night, the cat is found at a darts championship. After a third incident, the Herriots realize that the cat enjoys visiting places at night before returning home. They are devastated, however, when the cat's real owners unexpectedly show up one day to reclaim it. After giving up the pet, the Herriots visit it about a month later, and are thrilled that it recognizes them.

Understand Bias In their writings, writers show bias—the knowledge and interest that they have in their subject. You can see bias in the details they use, such as descriptions of characters and their actions. For example, when James Herriot says of the cat Oscar, "He was a warm and cherished part of our home life," you can tell the writer really loves and enjoys animals.

Explain what you can tell about writer James Herriot from each of his statements below from "Cat on the Go."

1. I had no more desire to pour ether onto that comradely purring than he had.
   What it tells about Herriot:
   ____
   ____

2. I am fond of cats but we already had a dog in our cramped quarters and I could see difficulties.
   What it tells about Herriot:
   ____
   ____

3. This time Helen and I scoured the marketplace and side alleys in vain and when we returned at half past nine we were both despondent.
   What it tells about Herriot:
   ____
   ____

4. Ever since our cat had started his excursions there had been the gnawing fear that we would lose him, and now we felt secure.
   What it tells about Herriot:
   ____
   ____

5. Feeling helpless and inadequate, I could only sit close to her and stroke the back of her head.
   What it tells about Herriot:
   ____
   ____

"Cat on the Go"
by James Herriot

Resumen El veterinario James Herriot relata sus experiencias con un gato insólito. Herriot y su asistente operan al gato callejero, que fue traído casi muerto a su consultorio, para salvarle la vida. Herriot y su esposa Helen cuidan al gato en su casa. Una noche el gato desaparece, y más tarde es encontrado en una reunión en la iglesia. Otra noche, el gato aparece en un campeonato de dardos. Tras un tercer incidente, los esposos Herriot se dan cuenta de que al gato le gusta visitar lugares por la noche antes de volver a casa. Se sienten desconsolados cuando los verdaderos dueños del gato aparecen un día para reclamarlo. Un mes después de entregar el gato, los Herriot lo visitan y quedan encantados cuando el gato los reconoce.

Tóm Lược Bác sĩ thú y James Herriot có kinh nghiệm quan hệ đến một con mèo không tầm thường. Herriot và phụ tá của ông đã giải phẩu cứu một con mèo hoang khi nó gần chết và được mang đến phòng mạch. Herriot và vợ của ông nuôi dưỡng con mèo trong nhà của họ. Có một buổi chiều con mèo mất tích, và được tìm thấy sau đó tại phòng họp trong nhà thờ. Một đêm khác, thì lại tìm thấy nó nơi thi đua phóng tên. Sau lần thứ ba, ông bà Herriot biết được rằng con mèo thích đi thăm viếng nhiều nơi trước khi về nhà. Mặc dầu vậy, họ bị thất vọng, khi có một ngày nọ chủ thật của con mèo xuất hiện thình lình và nhận lại nó. Sau khi giao trả con vật, khoảng một tháng sau, gia đình Herriot đến thăm và rất vui mừng vì nó nhận ra họ.

Lub ntsiab lus Ib tug neeg kho tsiaj hu ua James Herriot piav txog nws qhov kev uas tau ua dhau los lawm hais txog ib tug miv uas txawv heev. Herriot thiab tus uas pab nws nkawv tau phais thiab cawm tau ib tug miv tsis muaj tswv uas twb yuav tuag thaum lawv coj tuaj rau hauv nws qhov chaw ua haujlwm. Herriot thiab nws tus pojniam thiaj tu tus miv hauv nkawv tsev. Muaj ib hmos tus miv ploj lawm thiab muaj neeg pom nws tom ib lub rooj sab laj hauv tsev thov ntuj. Muaj ib hmos ho pom tus miv tom chaw sib tw cuam hmuv. Tom qab uas ua ob peb zaug li, Herriots mam paub tias tus miv nyiam mus ncig xyuas chaw hmo ntuj ua ntej nws yuav los tsev. Nkawv xav tias lawv txhob txwm ua rau nkawv xwb thaum tus miv nws tus tswv muaj ib hnub cia li tuaj coj tus miv rov qab lawm. Tom qab ib hlis uas nkawv muab tus miv rov qab rau nws tus tswv lawm, Herriot nkawv mus xyuas tus miv thiab zoo siab heev thaum uas nws tseem cim tau nkawv.

摘要 這篇是關於獸醫 James Herriot 與一隻特別的貓的經驗。Herriot 和他的助手在為一隻帶到醫院時已頻臨死亡的貓動過手術後拯救了這隻迷失的貓。之後 Herriot 和他的妻子海倫就在他們的家飼養這隻貓。一天晚上貓咪不見了，後來在教堂的聚會上被發現。另外一晚則是在擲飛鏢冠軍賽中被尋獲。在第三次意外發生後，Herriot 終於知道這隻貓喜歡在夜晚回家前到一些地方逛逛。但有一天當這隻貓的真正主人意外地出現聲稱擁有該貓時，他們很難過。在送走貓咪大約一個月後，Herriot 一家人去看牠且非常震驚貓咪還認得他們。

សេចក្តីសង្ខេប អតីតយុទ្ធជន James Herriot តភ្ជាប់ការពិសោធន៍របស់គាត់ទៅនិងឆ្មាចម្លែកមួយ ។ លោក Herriot និងអ្នកជំនួយរបស់គាត់ធ្វើការវះកាត់ដើម្បីជួយឆ្មាវង្វេងផ្ទះបន្ទាប់ពីវាជិតស្លាប់ហើយត្រូវគេនាំមកការិយាល័យគាត់ ។ បន្ទាប់មកលោក Herriot និងប្រពន្ធគាត់ឈ្មោះ Helen ចិញ្ចឹមបីបាច់ឆ្មានោះនៅផ្ទះពួកគាត់ ។ នៅល្ងាចមួយ ឆ្មានេះបាត់ខ្លួន ហើយក្រោយមកត្រូវគេរកឃើញនៅក្នុងការជួបជុំឯវិហារ ។ យប់មួយទៀត គេឃើញឆ្មានោះនៅឯកន្លែងប្រកួតជើងឯកខាងចោលកូនព្រួញដែក ។ នៅក្រោយហេតុការណ៍ទីបី គ្រួសារលោក Herriot ដឹងថាឆ្មានោះចូលចិត្តដើរលេងតាមកន្លែងនានានៅពេលយប់មុនពេលវាត្រឡប់មកផ្ទះវិញ ។ យ៉ាងណាក៏ដោយ ពួកគេខូចចិត្តពេលម្ចាស់ពិតប្រាកដរបស់ឆ្មាបង្ហាញខ្លួនដោយមិនដឹងជាមុននៅថ្ងៃមួយដើម្បីទាមទារឆ្មាវិញ ។ បន្ទាប់ពីឲ្យសត្វសម្លាញ់ទៅគេវិញ គ្រួសារ Herriot ទៅលេងឆ្មានេះនៅពេលមួយខែក្រោយមក ហើយមានការរំភើបដែលវានៅចាំពួកគេ ។

Name ______________________________ Date ______________

"The Luckiest Time of All" by Lucille Clifton
"in Just-" by E. E. Cummings
"The Microscope" by Maxine Kumin
"Sarah Cynthia Sylvia Stout Would Not Take the Garbage Out" by Shel Silverstein
"Father William" by Lewis Carroll

Summary These selections celebrate unusual personalities. In "The Luckiest Time of All," a woman tells how she met her husband by running off to see the circus when she was young. She was chased by a dog and rescued by her future husband. "in Just-" describes different individuals who are out enjoying a spring day. "The Microscope" describes how Anton Leeuwenhoek invented the microscope, despite people's sneers at him and his odd pursuit. In "Sarah Cynthia...," the title character refuses to take out the garbage and, as a result, winds up with a pile of garbage from coast to coast. In "Father William," an elderly yet lively father offers humorous answers to his son's questions about how he has managed to stay fit all these years.

Recognize Author's Purpose Authors usually write with a specific purpose in mind. Sometimes they want to *amuse* or *entertain* you. Sometimes they wish to *inform* or *educate* you about a topic. Sometimes they want to *reflect* or *reminisce* about an experience. Sometimes they wish to *persuade* you to accept their opinion or to *take action* on an issue.

The author's purpose in all of the selections in this grouping is to amuse and entertain readers.

Below each selection title, write a passage that demonstrates the purpose of amusing and entertaining readers. The first one has been done for you.

1. "The Luckiest Time of All"
   But the stone was gone from my hand and Lord, it hit that dancin dog right on his nose!

2. "in Just-"
   ____
   ____
   ____

3. "The Microscope"
   ____
   ____
   ____

4. "Sarah Cynthia Sylvia Stout Would Not Take the Garbage Out"
   ____
   ____

5. "Father William"
   ____
   ____
   ____

"The Luckiest Time of All" by Lucille Clifton
"in Just-" by E. E. Cummings
"The Microscope" by Maxine Kumin
"Sarah Cynthia Sylvia Stout Would Not Take the Garbage Out" by Shel Silverstein
"Father William" by Lewis Carroll

Resumen Estas selecciones celebran personalidades inusuales. En "The Luckiest Time of All," una mujer cuenta cómo conoció a su marido durante una escapada para ver el circo cuando era joven. Un perro la persiguió y su futuro marido la rescató. "In Just-" describe a diferentes personas que han salido a disfrutar de un día primaveral. "The Microscope" describe como Anton Leeuwenhoek inventó el microscopio, a pesar de las burlas de la gente y de su extraña búsqueda. En "Sarah Cynthia...," el personaje del título se niega a sacar la basura y termina con una pila de basura de costa a costa. En "Father William," un viejo pero vivaz padre responde en forma humorística cuando su hijo le pregunta cómo se las ha arreglado para mantenerse en buen estado físico durante tantos años.

Tóm Lược Những bài chọn lọc này ca tụng những cá tánh không bình thường. Trong bài "The Luckiest Time of All", một người đàn bà kể lại việc đã gặp chồng bà như thế nào khi lén xem hát xiệc lúc bà còn trẻ. Bà bị chó rượt và được người chồng tương lai cứu thoát. Bài "In Just-" diễn tả những cá nhân khác nhau cùng ra ngoài trời thưởng thức một ngày xuân. "The Microscope" diễn tả Anton Leeuwenhoek làm thế nào để sáng chế ra kính hiển vi, bất chấp người ta chê cười về ông và việc đeo đuổi kỳ lạ của ông. Trong "Sarah Cynthia...", nhân vật trong tựa bài từ chối đem rác ra ngoài, kết quả là, trong nhà có một đống rác lớn từ đầu đến cuối nhà. Trong "Father William", một cá già dùng những câu buồn cười để trả lời những câu hỏi của con về làm thế nào ông giữ được khỏe mạnh trong những năm nay.

Lub ntsiab lus Cov tau xaiv los no hais txog kev zoo siab txog tej kev yus coj uas txawv heev uas tsis tau pom dua li. Nyob rau "The Luckiest Time of All," ib tug pojniam qhia txog tias nws ntsib nws tus txiv li cas thaum nws khiav mus saib circus (cov neeg uas tuaj ua kev lom zem rau neeg saib) thaum nws tseem yau. Muaj ib tug aub caum nws tiamsis tus txiv neej uas yuav yog nws tus txiv los cawm tau nws. "In Just-," qhia txog ntau yam tib neeg txawv uas nyiam tawm rooj mus ua si thaum caij nplooj hlav. "The Microscope," qhia txog tias Anton Leeuwenhoek tsim lub teeb uas tsom tej yam khoom me me (microscope) li cas txawm tias neeg saib tsis taus nws tias, ua cas es yuav mus ua tej yam txawv ua luaj. Nyob rau "Sarah Cynthia...," tus neeg hais tas los lub npe tsis kam coj khib nyiab mus pov tseg thiab yog vim li ntawv, thiaj li muaj tej pawg khib nyiab nyob ib sab ntug dej hiav txwv rau ib sab ntug dej hiav txwv. Nyob rau "Father William," ib tug txiv uas laus heev lawm tiamsis tseem khov heev teb nws tus tub tej lus nug tias nws ua li cas es thiaj li noj qab nyob zoo tseem khov kho ntau xyoo tag npaum no.

摘要 這些選文是頌揚人的特性。在 "The Luckiest Time of All" 中，一位女士告訴我們她年輕時跑去看馬戲團表演如何遇到她的丈夫。當時她被一隻狗追著跑，最後是她未來的丈夫救了她。"in Just-" 則描述不同 的個人外出享受一個春日。"The Microscope" 描述安東・柳威弗克是如何不管人們對他及他怪異研究的譏笑下發明顯微鏡的。在 "Sarah Cynthia…," 中，題目上的人物拒絕丟掉垃圾，結果最後是遍及全國各地的一堆垃圾。在 "Father William" 中，當兒子問到父親有關他這些年來是如何成功地保持健康的身體時， 年老但仍充滿活力的父親給了兒子一個幽默的回答。

សេចក្តីសង្ខេប អត្ថបទជ្រើសរើសទាំងនេះបង្ហាញពីចរិកលក្ខណៈខុសធម្មតា ។ ក្នុងរឿង "The Luckiest Time of All" នារីម្នាក់និទានពីរបៀបដែលគាត់ជួបនឹងប្តីរបស់គាត់ ពេលរត់ទៅមើលក្រុមសៀកកាលគាត់នៅក្មេង ។ ឆ្កែមួយដេញខាំគាត់ហើយអានាគតប្តីរបស់គាត់បានជួយគាត់ ។ រឿង "In Just-" រៀបរាប់ពីបុគ្គលខុសគ្នាដែលចេញ ទៅលេងសប្បាយជាមួយថ្ងៃនៃរដូវរំហើយ ។ រឿង "The Microscope" រៀបរាប់ពីរបៀបលោក Anton Leeuwenhoek បង្កើតប្រដាប់អតិសុខុមទស្សន៍ ទុកជាប្រជាជននិយាយមើលងាយគាត់និងការតាមរុករកចម្លែករបស់គាត់ក្តី ។ ក្នុងរឿង "Sarah Cynthia..." តួឯកប្រកែកមិនយកសំរាមទៅចោល ហើយជាលទ្ធផលត្រូវបានទទួលគំនរសំរាមពីច្រាំងមួយទៅច្រាំងមួយទៀត ។ ក្នុងរឿង "Father William" ឪពុកដែលនៅសកម្មមានអាយុច្រើនម្នាក់ផ្តល់ចម្លើយកំប្លែងទៅកូនប្រុសរបស់គាត់អំពីរបៀបដែលគាត់នៅតែមាំមួយគ្រប់ឆ្នាំទាំងអស់នេះ ។

Name ______________________________ Date ______________

"Zoo" by Edward Hoch
"The Hippopotamus" by Ogden Nash
"How the Snake Got Poison" by Zora Neale Hurston

Summary These three selections look humorously at the world through the eyes of animals. In "Zoo," a professor comes to Earth bringing a spaceship full of animals from other planets. Humans pay to see the creatures. Ironically, the animals believe that they are visiting a zoo of odd creatures on Earth, and pay the professor as well! In "The Hippopotamus," the speaker suggests that though a hippo looks strange to us, we probably look equally strange to the hippo. "How the Snake Got Poison" explains how snakes were given poison as a means of protection against other creatures. But the snake starts using the poison too often, so he is given a rattle to warn creatures that the snake is there.

Evaluate an Author's Message Most authors have a message that they convey in their writing. As a responsible reader, you must decide what that message is. What is the author trying to teach you about people, or about life in general, through the characters and events in the writing?

Read each passage below. Identify the author's message. The first one has been done for you.

"Zoo"

1. "There are bars to protect us from them .... Next time you must come with us. It is well worth the nineteen commocs it costs .... It was the very best Zoo ever ...."

   Author's message: Feelings of superiority are often the result of an individual's perspective, or how one views others.

"Zoo"

2. "And the crowd slowly filed by, at once horrified and fascinated by these strange creatures that looked like horses but ran up the walls of their cages like spiders. 'This is certainly worth a dollar,' one man remarked, hurrying away."

"The Hippopotamus"

3. We laugh at how he looks to us / And yet in moments dank and grim / I wonder how we look to him.

   Author's message: ______________________________

   ____

"How the Snake Got Poison"

4. "When you hear feets comin' you ring yo' bell and if it's yo' friend, he'll be keerful. If it's yo' enemy, it's you and him."

   Author's message: ______________________________

   ____

"Zoo" by Edward Hoch
"The Hippopotamus" by Ogden Nash
"How the Snake Got Poison" by Zora Neale Hurston

Resumen Estas tres selecciones ven con humor al mundo a través de los ojos de los animales. En "Zoo", un profesor viene a la Tierra y trae una nave espacial llena de animales de otros planetas. Los humanos pagan para ver a los animales. Irónicamente, los animales creen que están visitando un zoológico de criaturas raras en la Tierra, y también le pagan al profesor. En "The Hippopotamus", el autor sugiere que a pesar de que el hipopótamo parece ser algo extraño para nosotros, probablemente también nosotros parecemos ser algo extraño al hipopótamo. "How the Snake Got Poison" explica cómo las serpientes recibieron el veneno para protegerse contra otras criaturas. Pero, la serpiente comienza a usar el veneno demasiado a menudo, por lo tanto, recibe un cascabel para alertar a las otras criaturas que está allí.

Tóm lược. Ba bài được chọn trong loạt bài này tả cái nhìn thế giới một cách hài hước qua cặp mắt của các thú vật. Trong "Zoo," một giáo sư đại học xuống Trái Đất và đem theo một phi thuyền đầy những thú vật từ các hành tinh khác đến. Loài người trả tiền để được đi coi các sinh vật ấy. Mỉa mai thay, các thú vật lại tin rằng chúng đang thăm viếng một sở thú có những sinh vật cổ xưa trên Trái Đất, và chúng cũng trả tiền cho ông giáo sư để được đi coi những sinh vật ấy! Trong bài "The Hippopotamus," người kể chuyện đề nghị là mặc dầu con hippo trông lạ hoắc, có lẽ chúng ta cũng trông lạ hoắc đối với con hippo. Bài "How the Snake Got Poison" cắt nghĩa tại sao loài rắn lại được có nọc độc để tự vệ chống lại những sinh vật khác. Nhưng con rắn lại dùng nọc qúa thường xuyên, nên trời lại cho nó phát lên tiếng lách cách để báo cho các sinh vật khác là có nó ở gần đó.

Lub ntsiab lus Peb qhov no yog cov tsiaj pom peb lub ntiaj tev txaus luag. Nyob hauv "Zoo," ib tus kws qhia ntawv los hauv ntiaj teb coj ib lub dab hlau muaj tsiaj puv nkaus los lwm lub ntiaj teb los. Neeg them nyiaj tuaj xyuas cov tsiaj. Qhov txaus luag, cov tsiaj xav hais tias lawn tua xyuas chaw yug tsiaj uas muaj cov tsiaj txawv nyob ntiaj teb, thiab them nyiaj qhov tus kws qhia ntawv tib si! Nyog "The Hippopotabus," tus piav hais tias txawm tus ntxnw dej ntsia txawv rau peb, peb los yeej ntsia txawv rau tus ntxnw dej thiab. "How the Snake Got Poison" piav tias nab muaj taug kom pab thaiv lawv rau lwm tus tsiaj. Tab sis nab siv nws cov taug ntaun dhau, ces thiab muaj tus tw tswb kom qhia lwm tus tsiaj paub hais tias nab nyob ntawv.

摘要　這三篇文章幽默地透過動物的眼光來看世界。在"Zoo" 一文中，一位教授把其他星球的動物從太空船帶到地球。人類付錢來看這些動物。諷刺的是，這些動物以為牠們正在參觀一個地球上奇怪生物的動物園，也付錢給這位教授！在 "The Hippopotamus"一文中，敘述者指出雖然河馬在我們看起來很奇怪，可是我們在河馬眼中可能也一樣奇怪。"How the Snake Got Poison" 解釋蛇獲得毒藥，以便保護自己不受其他動物侵害。可是蛇使用毒藥的次數太多，結果獲得一個響環，使其他生物警覺蛇就在附近。

សេចក្ដីសង្ខេប អត្ថបទជ្រើសរើសទាំងបីនេះឃើញហាក់ដូចជារីករាយនៅនាពិភពលោកតាមរយៈភ្នែករបស់សត្វពាហនៈ ។ នៅក្នុងអត្ថបទ "Zoo" សាស្ត្រាចារ្យម្នាក់មកកាន់ភពផែនដី ដោយនាំនូវយានអវកាសដែលពេញទៅដោយសត្វមកអំពីពិភពឯទៀត ។ មនុស្សម្នាបង់ប្រាក់ដើម្បីមើលសត្វទាំងនោះ ។ គួរឲ្យសង្វេគ ពពួកសត្វទាំងនេះជឿថាពួកវានឹងទៅលេងសួនសត្វនៃសត្វចម្លែកនៅលើភពផែនដី ហើយបង់ប្រាក់ឲ្យសាស្ត្រាចារ្យនេះផងដែរ! នៅក្នុងអត្ថបទ "The Hippopotamus" អ្នកពោលស្នើយោបល់ថាថ្វីបើសត្វដំរីទឹកឃើញរាងចម្លែកចំពោះយើងៗ ក៏មុខជាឃើញរាងចម្លែកដូចគ្នាចំពោះដំរីទឹកដែរ ។ អត្ថបទ "How the Snake Got Poison" ពន្យល់ប្រាប់អំពីរបៀបដែលគេឲ្យពិសទៅពស់ដើម្បីធ្វើជាគ្រឿងការពារទល់និងសត្វឯទៀត ។ ប៉ុន្តែពស់ចាប់ផ្ដើមប្រើពិសញឹកញាប់ណាស់ពេកដូច្នេះទើបគេឲ្យចង្រ្កង់វាដើម្បីព្រមានសត្វនានាថាពស់នៅទីនោះ ។

Name ______________________________ Date ______________

"After Twenty Years" by O. Henry

Summary A New York police officer walking his beat one night comes upon a man, Bob, who says he's waiting to meet a friend, Jimmy Wells, whom he hasn't seen in twenty years. Bob, who left New York twenty years ago to make a fortune out West, is confident that loyal, honest Jimmy will honor their appointment. Once the officer leaves, another man arrives and greets Bob. After talking briefly, Bob realizes that the other man is not Jimmy. He is a plainclothes officer, who arrests Bob for suspicion of a crime commited in Chicago. He hands Bob a letter from Jimmy, the first officer, who explains that he didn't have the heart to arrest Bob himself.

What Happens Next? We all like to predict what will happen next, whether it is in a movie, in real life, or in stories that we read.

Directions: As you read "After Twenty Years," pause from time to time to ask yourself what will happen next. Keep track of your predictions in this chart. When you find out what actually does happen, record that information on the chart, too. A sample entry has been given.

Event	My Prediction	What Actually Happens
The policeman walks his beat.	He will see someone.	He sees a man in a darkened doorway.

"After Twenty Years"
by O. Henry

Resumen Una noche, un policía de Nueva York que hace su recorrida habitual se encuentra con un hombre llamado Bob, que dice que está esperando a un amigo, Jimmy Wells, a quien no ve desde hace veinte años. Bob, que se fue de Nueva York hace veinte años para hacer fortuna en el Oeste, confía en que el leal y honesto Jimmy acudirá a la cita. Cuando el policía se ha ido, llega otro hombre y saluda a Bob. Después de conversar, Bob se da cuenta de que el otro hombre no es Jimmy. Es un policía de paisano que arresta a Bob como sospechoso de un crimen cometido en Chicago. Le entrega a Bob una carta de Jimmy, quien le explica que no tuvo valor para arrestar él mismo a Bob.

Tóm Lược Trong một đêm nọ có một viên cảnh sát Nữu Ước cầm dùi đang đi bộ đến một người đàn ông, Bob, đang chờ gặp một người bạn tên Jimmy Wells, là người mà ông đã không gặp mặt trong suốt hai mươi năm. Bob, đã rời Nữu Ước hai mươi năm trước để làm giàu tại miền Tây xa xôi, ông tin tưởng rằng người bạn trung thành và thành thật Jimmy sẽ đến đúng hẹn. Khi viên cảnh sát đi xa, có một người đàn ông khác đến và chào Bob. Sau khi nói chuyện qua loa, Bob biết rằng người đàn ông đó không phải là Jimmy. Ông ta là một cảnh sát chìm, đến để bắt Bob về việc tình nghi phạm tội tại Chicago. Ông ta trao cho Bob một lá thơ của Jimmy, là viên cảnh sát đầu tiên, ông giải thích rằng không có can đảm tự đến bắt Bob.

Lub ntsiab lus Ib tug tub ceev xwm hauv New York taug kev li txhua hmo mus ntsib ib tug txiv neej hu ua Bob, nws hais tias nws tuaj tos ntsib nws ib tug phooj ywg hu ua Jimmy. Nws tsis taupom Jimmy tau nees nkaum xyoo lawm. Bob, tsiv hauv New York tau nees nkaum xyoo rau sab hnub poob seb hmoov puas zoo muaj nyiaj thiab cia siab tias Jimmy tus uas nws ntseeg thiab tus uas ua ncaj ncees yuav tuaj ntsib nws raws li nkawv tau sib teem tseg. Thaum tus tub ceev xwm mus lawm muaj ibtug txiv neej los ntsib Bob. Tom qab ua nkawv tham ib pliag, nws mam paub tias tus txiv neej no tsis yog Jimmy. Nws tsuas yog tsis hnav kaub ncaws tub ceev xwm xwb, nws ntes Bob vim nws ntseeg tias Bob yog tus uas ua tub sab tua neeg nyob rau hauv Chicago. Nws muab ib daimntawv uas sau los ntawm Jimmy, uas yog thawj tug tub ceev xwm yog tus sau, qhia tias nws tsis muaj nplooj siab yuav ntes Bob nws tus kheej.

摘要 有一天晚上一名紐約警員走在執勤的巡邏路線上碰到一個名叫鮑勃的人，他說自己正等著與二十年沒見名叫吉米・威爾斯的朋友會面。二十年前離開紐約到西部去闖天下的鮑勃有信心高尚誠實的吉米會前來赴約。那名警員才離開，另一個人就到達並與鮑勃打招呼。經過簡短的談話之後，鮑勃認出這個人並不是吉米而是一名便衣警察，他是來逮捕因在芝加哥涉嫌犯罪的鮑勃。他交給鮑勃一封吉米的信，吉米就是第一次出現的警員；吉米在信中向他說明自己不忍心親自逮捕他。

សេចក្ដីសង្ខេប នាយប៉ូលិសក្រុងនូយ៉កម្នាក់ដើរដោយរំភើបនាយប់មួយទៅកាន់បុរសម្នាក់ឈ្មោះ Bob ដែលនិយាយថាគាត់កំពុងរង់ចាំជួបមិត្តគាត់ម្នាក់ឈ្មោះ Jimmy Wells ដែលគាត់មិនដែលបានជួបអស់ពេលម្ភៃឆ្នាំហើយ ។ Bob ដែលចាកចេញពីក្រុងនូយ៉កកាលពីម្ភៃឆ្នាំមុនដើម្បីទៅរកលាបនៅទិសខាងលិចជឿទុកចិត្តលើ Jimmy ដែលស្មោះត្រង់និងភក្ដីនឹងគោរពការណាត់ជួបរបស់ពួកគេ ។ បន្ទាប់ពីនាយប៉ូលិសចេញទៅ បុរសម្នាក់មកដល់ហើយរាក់ទាក់ជាមួយ Bob ។ បន្ទាប់ពីការនិយាយគ្នាត្រួសៗ Bob ដឹងថាបុរសនោះមិនមែនជា Jimmy ទេ។ គាត់ជានាយប៉ូលិសដែលមានឯកសណ្ឋានប៉ូលិស ហើយចាប់ Bob ពីបទសង្ស័យថាបានប្រព្រឹត្តបទឧក្រិដ្ឋមួយនៅក្រុងស៊ីកាគោ ។ គាត់ហុចសំបុត្រមួយពី Jimmy ដែលជានាយប៉ូលិសលើកដំបូងទៅឲ្យ Bob សំបុត្រនោះពន្យល់ថាគាត់មិនដាច់ចិត្តចាប់ Bob ដោយខ្លួនគាត់ទេ ។

Name ______________________________ Date ______________

"Rikki-tikki-tavi" by Rudyard Kipling

Summary In India, a mongoose named Rikki-tikki-tavi is washed from his burrow by a flood. He is adopted by the family of a young boy named Teddy. Exploring the garden of his new home, Rikki meets Nag and Nagaina, two deadly cobras. Rikki instinctively recognizes the snakes as enemies who are meant to be killed. Later that day, Rikki rescues Teddy by killing a small poisonous snake. That night, Rikki overhears the cobras' plot to enter the house and kill Teddy's family. Rikki attacks Nag in the bathroom, fighting until Teddy's father shoots the cobra dead. The next day, Rikki finds Nagaina's eggs and begins crushing them. When the cobra threatens to kill Teddy, Rikki chases her into the rat hole in which she lives and kills her. Teddy's family and the garden animals hail Rikki as a hero.

Predict Trying to figure out what will happen next is one way to stay interested in a story. You can use prior knowledge, or what you already know before you start reading, to help yourself make predictions. For example, if you find out that a cobra is one of the characters in a story, you can use what you already know about cobras to predict what will happen. You can also use clues from the story to help predict the outcome.

Directions: As you read "Rikki-tikki-tavi," stop occasionally and think about what might happen next. Record your predictions and your reasons for making them in this chart. In the last column, keep track of whether you were right. A sample entry has been made.

What I Predict	Why I Predict It	Was I Right?
The mongoose will survive the flood that washed him from his burrow.	The opening paragraph says that "Rikki-tikki did the real fighting," so he must have survived.	Yes.

"Rikki-tikki-tavi"
by Rudyard Kipling

Resumen En la India, una mangosta llamada Rikki-tikki-tavi es expulsada de su guarida por una inundación. Es adoptada por la familia de un niño llamado Teddy. Mientras explora el jardín de su nueva casa, Rikki se encuentra con Nag y Nagaina, dos cobras mortíferas. Rikki instintivamente reconoce que las cobras son enemigos que deben morir. Más tarde ese mismo día, Rikki rescata a Teddy matando una pequeña víbora venenosa. Esa noche, Rikki oye a las cobras hablando de entrar a la casa y matar a la familia de Teddy. Rikki ataca a Nag en el baño, luchando con ella hasta que el padre de Teddy mata a la cobra de un tiro. Al día siguiente, Rikki encuentra los huevos de Nagaina y comienza a romperlos. Cuando la cobra amenaza con matar a Teddy, Rikki la persigue hasta el agujero en el que vive y la mata. La familia de Teddy y los animales del jardín saludan a Rikki como un héroe.

Tóm Lược Tại Ấn Độ, có một con chồn ăn thịt rắn tên Rikki-tikki-tavi bị nước lụt cuốn trôi ra khỏi hang. Nó được gia đình một cậu bé tên Teddy đem về nuôi. Trong lúc đi vòng quanh ngôi vườn trong nhà mới, Rikki gặp được Nag và Nagaina, là hai con rắn hổ rất độc. Rikki cảm nhận ra ngay các con rắn này là kẻ thù, có nghĩa là phải giết chết. Sau đó trong ngày, Rikki giết một con rắn độc nhỏ để cứu Teddy. Tối hôm đó, Rikki nghe lóm được hai con hổ mang đang bàn kế vào nhà để giết gia đình Teddy. Rikki tấn công Nag trong nhà tắm, đánh nhau đến khi cha của Teddy bắn con hổ mang chết. Ngày hôm sau, Rikki tìm được trứng của Nagaina và đè bẹp chúng. Khi con hổ mang dọa giết Teddy, Rikki rượt nó chạy vào ổ chuột nơi con rắn sống và giết chết nó. Gia đình Teddy và các thú trong vườn chào đón Rikki như một người anh hùng.

Lub ntsiab lus Nyob rau teb chaws India, ib tug luj (mongoose) hu ua Rikki-tikki-tavi raug dej tshoob tawm ntawm nws lub qhov los thaum dej nyab. Ib tug menyuam tub hu ua Teddy thiab nws tsev neeg tau yuav nws coj los tu. Saib ncig lub vaj paj ntawm nws lub chaw tshiab Rikki ntsib Nag thiab Nagaina, ob tug nab raj kubsai uas muaj taug txaus ntshai heev. Rikki cia li paub tam sim tias ob tug nab raj kub sai no yog yeeb ncuab thiab yuav tsum muab tua povtseg. Hnub ntawv thaum lig zog Rikki pab cawm tau Teddy uas nws muab tus nab me zog muaj taug ntawv tua. Hmo ntawv Rikki hnov ob tug nab raj kub sai nkawv tham txog yuav nkag mus hauv lub tsev thiab mus tua Teddy tsev neeg. Rikki nrog Nag sib tog hauv chaw da dej, sib tog sib tog txog thaum Teddy txiv los tua tus nab ntawv tuag. Hnub tom qab Rikki nrhiav pom Nagaina cov qe thiab pib muab lawv nyem kom tawg. Thaum tus nab hem tias nws yuav tua Teddy, Rikki caum nws mus rau hauv lub qhov nas tsuag uas yog tus nab qhov chaw nyob lawm thiab muab nws tua tuag. Teddy tsev neeg thiab cov tsiaj hauv vaj paj qw nrov hais tias nws yog ib tug keej heev (phab ej).

摘要 在印度有一隻被洪水從地洞裡沖出來的蒙鼠叫 Rikki-tikki-tavi。牠被一個少男名叫泰迪的家庭收養。Rikki 在牠新家的院子一番探險之後遇到了 Nag 和 Nagaina 兩條致命的眼鏡蛇。Rikki 直覺地認出這些蛇就是該被殺掉的敵人。那天稍晚，Rikki 殺死一條有毒的小蛇而拯救了泰迪。那晚 Rikki 無意中聽到眼鏡蛇要進入屋內殺死泰迪一家人的陰謀。Rikki 在浴室攻擊 Nag，纏鬥直到泰迪的父親射殺了這條眼鏡蛇為止。第二天 Rikki 發現了 Nagaina 下的蛋並踩碎牠們。當 Nagaina 揚言要殺掉泰迪時，Rikki 追趕 Nagaina 進入她住的鼠洞並殺了她。泰迪一家人及院子裡的動物都把 Rikki 視為英雄。

សេចក្តីសង្ខេប ក្នុងប្រទេសឥណ្ឌា សត្វស្រកាឈ្មោះ Rikki-tikki-tavi ត្រូវទឹកជំនន់បោកគួចចេញពីរន្ធវា ។ វាបានគេយកមកចិញ្ចឹមដោយគ្រួសារក្មេងប្រុសម្នាក់ឈ្មោះ Teddy ។ ដើររុករកក្នុងសួនច្បារនៃផ្ទះថ្មីរបស់វា Rikki ជួប Nag និង Nagaina ជាពស់ពញ្ញក់សាហាវពីរក្បាល ។ Rikki ស្គាល់ពីកំណើតថាពស់ជាសត្រូវដែលគេត្រូវសម្លាប់ចោល ។ នៅល្ងាចថ្ងៃនោះ Rikki ជួយសង្គ្រោះ Teddy ដោយសម្លាប់កូនពស់មានពិសមួយ ។ នៅយប់នោះ Rikki លបស្តាប់ពួពស់ពញ្ញាក់ដាក់ផែនការណ៏ចូលក្នុងផ្ទះសម្លាប់គ្រួសារ Teddy ។ Rikki វាយប្រហារ Nag ក្នុងបន្ទប់ទឹក ប្រយុទ្ធរហូតដល់ឪពុករបស់ Teddy បាញ់ពស់ពញ្ញក់ស្លាប់ទៅ ។ នៅថ្ងៃបន្ទាប់ Rikki រកឃើញពងរបស់ Nagaina ហើយចាប់ផ្តើមកំទេចពងទាំងនោះចោល ។ ពេលដែលពស់ពញ្ញក់គំរាមចង់សម្លាប់ Teddy Rikki ដេញពស់នោះចូលក្នុងរន្ធកណ្តុរដែលជាកន្លែងពស់រស់នៅហើយសម្លាប់ពស់នោះទៅ ។ គ្រួសារ Teddy និងសត្វនៅក្នុងសួនសាទរគោរព Rikki ថាជាវីរបុរស ។

Name ____ Date ___________________

"Papa's Parrot" by Cynthia Rylant

Summary This touching story examines the relationship between a father and his son. A boy named Harry once enjoyed visiting and helping at his father's candy store, but as he grows older, he goes there less often. In Harry's absence, the father keeps a parrot in the shop, talking to the parrot instead of his son. Harry is embarrassed by his father's behavior, and continues to stay away from the shop. When his father falls ill, Harry goes to the store to help out. To his astonishment, he hears the parrot repeatedly say, "Where's Harry? Miss him." Harry realizes the bird is echoing his father's words. Understanding that his father misses their time together in the shop, Harry goes to visit him in the hospital.

Identify with a Character The characters you read about in stories are not much different from characters you meet in real life. In fact, as you read a story, you might even recognize some attitudes, feelings, or qualities of your own in the characters of the story.

Directions: Choose one of the characters in "Papa's Parrot." Then choose one of the story events. Put yourself in that character's place as the event took place. Think about how you would have felt if you had been there. Write a diary entry based on the event, from the point of view of the character. Use the lines provided to make notes and to write your diary entry.

Character: ____

Story Event: ____

How You Feel: ____

____

____

____

Dear Diary,

____

____

____

____

____

____

____

____

____

____

____

"Papa's Parrot"

by Cynthia Rylant

Resumen Esta emocionante historia cuenta la relación entre un padre y su hijo. Un niño llamado Harry solía disfrutar sus visitas para ayudar en la tienda de caramelos de su padre, pero a medida que crece, deja de ir tan a menudo. Ante la ausencia de Harry, el padre mantiene a un loro en la tienda, hablándole al loro en lugar de a su hijo. A Harry le da vergüenza el comportamiento de su padre y continúa alejado de la tienda. Cuando su padre se enferma, Harry va a la tienda a ayudar. Se sorprende al escuchar al loro decir repetidamente, "¿Dónde está Harry? Lo extraño." Harry se da cuenta que el loro repite las palabras de su padre. Al darse cuenta que su padre extraña las horas que compartían en la tienda, Harry visita a su padre en el hospital.

摘要　這個感人的故事探討一對父子的關係。一個名叫亨利的男孩以前很喜歡去父親開的糖果店幫忙，可是等他逐漸長大後就越來越少去。亨利不在的時候，他父親在店裡養了一隻鸚鵡，與其和自己的兒子說話，他開始和鸚鵡說話。亨利對父親的行為感到很難為情，繼續躲著糖果店不去。他的父親生病以後，亨利去店裡幫忙，結果很驚訝的聽到那隻鸚鵡不斷說，「亨利在哪裡？很想念他。」亨利發覺那隻鸚鵡是在重複他父親的話。等到他明白父親很懷念他們一起在店裡的時光，亨利就去醫院探望父親。

សេចក្ដីសង្ខេប រឿងរំភើបចិត្តនេះពិចារណាអំពីទំនាក់ទំនងរវាងឪពុកនិងកូនប្រុសរបស់គាត់ ។ កុមារា Harry ដែលកាលមួយនោះចូលចិត្តទៅលេងនិងជួយធ្វើការនៅហាងចាបហួយរបស់ឪពុកវា ប៉ុន្តែនៅពេលដែលវាធំឡើង វាមិនសូវទៅទីនោះញឹកញាប់ទេ ។ ការមិនបង្ហាញខ្លួនរបស់ Harry ទើបឪពុកនោះចិញ្ចឹមសេកមួយនៅក្នុងហាង ហើយនិយាយទៅកាន់សេកនេះជំនួសកូនប្រុសរបស់គាត់ ។ Harry មានការអៀនខ្មាស់ចំពោះអាកប្បកិរិយារបស់ឪពុកវានេះ ហើយវាមិនមកជិតហាងនោះជាបន្តទៅទៀត ។ នៅពេលដែលឪពុកវាធ្លាក់ខ្លួនឈឺ Harry ទៅកាន់ហាងដើម្បីជួយធ្វើកិច្ចការ ។ វាមានការភ្ញាក់ផ្អើល ដោយឮសេកនិយាយដដែលៗថា "តើ Harry នៅឯណា? នឹកវា" ។ Harry ដឹងថាសត្វស្លាបនោះត្រាប់តាមពាក្យរបស់ឪពុកវា ។ ដោយយល់ថាឪពុករបស់វានឹកពេលដែលពួកគេនៅជាមួយគ្នា Harry ក៏ទៅលេងនិងគាត់នៅឯមន្ទីរពេទ្យ ។

Tóm lược Câu chuyện rất cảm động này kể lại mối liên hệ giữa một người cha và đứa con trai của ông. Một cậu bé tên là Harry trước thường thích đi thăm và giúp đỡ bố cậu ở tiệm bán kẹo. Nhưng càng lớn lên, cậu càng đi lại thăm viếng ít hơn. Khi vắng Harry, người cha nuôi một con vẹt trong cửa hàng, và ông thường chuyện trò với con vẹt. Thấy bố có hành động như thế, Harry rất xấu hổ, và càng lánh xa cửa tiệm. Khi người bố bị đau, Harry đến tiệm để giúp đỡ bố. Anh rất ngạc nhiên khi nghe con vẹt cứ nhắc đi nhắc lại, "Where's Harry? Miss him." Harry mới nhận ra rằng con vẹt chỉ nhắc lại những lời bố mình thốt ra mà thôi. Anh chợt hiểu là bố đã tiếc nhớ những ngày có con trai giúp đỡ trong tiệm, và anh đến nhà thương để thăm bố.

Lub ntsiab lus Zaj dab neeg txaus tu siab no hais txog kev sib raug zoo ntawm ib tug txiv thiab ib tug tub. Muaj ib tug tub lub npe hu ua Harry, thaum ub nws nyiam mus xyuas thiab pab nws txiv ntawm nws txiv qhov chawj muag npawm npoos qab zis, tab sis thaum nws loj tuaj ces nws tsis tshua mus ntxiv lawn. Lub caij Harry tsis tuaj, nws txiv yug ib tug noog iam (parrot) tham nrog nws ua lis nws tus tub. Harry pom li ntawv, nws txaj muaj, ces nws cia li tsis tuaj ntxiv lawm. Thaum nws txiv mob, Harry thiav tau mus pab tog tsev muaj khoom. Nws ceeb ntawm hnov tus iam pheej hais tias, "Where's Harry? Miss him." Harry mam paub hais tias tus noog muaj nws txiv cov lus lom hais xwb. Pom hais tias nws txiv nco nws txog thaum lub caij nkawv nyob ua ke hauv tsevj muaj khoom, Harry tiaj mus xyuas nws txiv tau tsev kho mob.

Name ____ Date ________________

"Suzy and Leah" by Jane Yolen

Summary This story is told through a series of diary entries written by two girls during World War II. Leah, a German-Jewish refugee of World War II, has been sent to America with her brother. The rest of her family has been killed in Germany. Suzy, an American girl, visits the refugee shelter and brings treats and clothing to the refugees. But she does not try to understand what the refugees have suffered. She is puzzled and offended by Leah's shyness and distrust of others. When Leah goes to the hospital with appendicitis, Suzy visits her. After secretly reading Leah's diary, Suzy understands her better, and offers her own diary for her new friend to read.

Make Inferences It wouldn't be much fun to read a story in which the author told you everything straight out. It's more fun to put the clues together and figure out what the author is telling you about the characters or the setting. For example, if an author says, "Bob was very poor," that doesn't give you much to figure out. However, the author might say, "Bob's shoes were so full of holes that Bob had to stuff newspaper inside them so his feet wouldn't touch the ground." This gives you the chance to infer that Bob was poor.

Directions: Choose two paragraphs from "Suzy and Leah." List three details from each paragraph. For each detail, tell what it suggests about the character or the setting.

Paragraph 1

Paragraph beginning with the words ______________________________

Detail #1: ______________________________

What it suggests: ______________________________

Detail #2: ______________________________

What it suggests: ______________________________

Detail #3: ______________________________

What it suggests: ______________________________

Paragraph 2

Paragraph beginning with the words ______________________________

Detail #1: ______________________________

What it suggests: ______________________________

Detail #2: ______________________________

What it suggests: ______________________________

Detail #3: ______________________________

What it suggests: ______________________________

"Suzy and Leah"
by Jane Yolen

Resumen Esta historia se cuenta a través de una serie de escrituras en el diario de dos niñas durante la segunda guerra mundial. Leah, una refugiada judía alemana ha sido enviada a Estados Unidos con su hermano. El resto de la familia fue asesinada en Alemania. Suzy, una niña norteamericana, visita la casa de refugiados y le lleva regalos y ropa a los refugiados. Pero, no trata de entender lo que los refugiados han sufrido. Se siente sorprendida y ofendida por la timidez de Leah y la manera en que desconfía de otras personas. Cuando Leah va al hospital con apendicitis, Suzy la visita. Después de leer en secreto el diario de Leah, Suzy la comprende mejor y le ofrece a su nueva amiga su propio diario para que lo lea.

Tóm lược Câu chuyện này được kể lại qua một loạt những trang nhật ký của hai cô thiếu nữ trong thời Đại Thế Chiến Kỳ II. Leah, người Đức gốc Do Thái khi tỵ nạn Thế Chiến thứ II được gia đình gửi sang Hoa Kỳ để sống với người anh của cô. Những người còn lại trong gia đình cô thì đều bị giết tại Đức. Suzy, một cô gái Hoa kỳ đi thăm trại tỵ nạn, cô đem quà và quần áo đến cho người tỵ nạn. Nhưng cô không hiểu họ đã chịu đựng những khổ nhục gì. Cô rất thắc mắc và không được hài lòng khi thấy Leah nhút nhát và không tin tưởng vào ai cả. Khi Leah phải vào nhà thương để mổ ruột dư, Suzy vào thăm. Cô lén đọc được nhật ký của Leah, lúc bấy giờ mới hiểu bạn hơn, và tình nguyện đưa nhật ký của mình cho Leah đọc.

Lub ntsiab lus Zaj lus no hais raws nyias tus kheej cov ntawv sau ntawm ob tug ntxhais thaum tsov rog ntiaj teb zaum ob. Leah, ib tug neeg thoj nam German-Jewish ntawm tsov rog ntiaj teb zaum ob, raug xav mus Amerika nrog nws tus nus. Dua li lwm tus ntawm nws tsev neeg raug tua nyob Germany tas. Susy, ib tug ntxhsais Amerika, nws tuaj xyuas neeg thoj nam qhov chaw thiab nqa ub no thiab ris tsho tuaj rau cov neeg thoj nam. Tab sis nws tsis xav kawm paub hais tias ua cas cov neeg thoj nam txom nyem npaum li cas. Nws xav tsis tawm thiab chim ntawm qhov Leah txaj muag thiab tsis ntseeg lum tus neeg rhauv. Thaum Leah mob plab nyhuv tws, nws mus tom tsev kho mob, Suzy los tuaj xyuas nws thiab. Thaum nws nyiag twm Leah phau ntawv sau txog nws tus kheej tas, Susy thiab paub nws zoo tshaj, thiab muaj nws phau los rau nws tus phoog ywg tshiab twm.

摘要 這個故事是透過二次世界大戰期間兩個女孩之間的日記來敘述的。莉亞是二次世界大戰期間一位德國猶太裔的難民，和兄弟一起被送到美國，他們的家人都在德國被殺了。蘇西是一個美國女孩，帶著好吃的東西和衣服去訪問難民營。可是她不想嘗試了解難民所受的苦難，而對於莉亞的害羞和其他人的不信任感到困惑而不舒服。莉亞因為盲腸炎住院以後，蘇西去醫院看她。等到蘇西偷偷看了莉亞的日記後，才更了解莉亞，也把自己的日記拿給這位新朋友看。

សេចក្តីសង្ខេប រឿងនេះត្រូវបាននិទានតាមរយៈកំណត់ហេតុប្រចាំថ្ងៃមួយខ្សែដែលសរសេរដោយកុមារីពីរនាក់នៅក្នុងកម្លុងសង្គ្រាមលោកលើកទីពីរ ។ Leah ដែលជាជនភៀសខ្លួនជាតិជ្វីហ្វ-អាល្លឺម៉ង់នៃសង្គ្រាមលោកលើកទីពីរ ត្រូវបានគេបញ្ជូនទៅអាមេរិកជាមួយបងប្រុសរបស់នាង ។ គ្រួសារឯទៀតរបស់នាងត្រូវគេសម្លាប់នៅក្នុងប្រទេសអាល្លឺម៉ង់ ។ Suzy ដែលជាកុមារីជាតិអាមេរិកាំងនាងទៅលេងជំរកជនភៀសខ្លួនហើយនិងនាំយកចំណីអាហារនិងសំលៀកបំពាក់ទៅឲ្យជនភៀសខ្លួន ។ ប៉ុន្តែនាងមិនព្យាយាមយល់អំពីអ្វីដែលជនភៀសខ្លួនបានឈឺចាប់ទេ ។ នាងមានការងឿងឆ្ងល់និងអាក់អន់ចិត្តដោយសារ ការអៀនខ្មាស់និងការមិនជឿទុកចិត្តអ្នកឯទៀតរបស់ Leah ។ នៅពេលដែល Leah ទៅដេកពេទ្យដោយមានរោគពោះវៀនជុះខ្នែង Suzy ទៅមើលនាង ។ បន្ទាប់ពីបានអានកំណត់ហេតុប្រចាំថ្ងៃរបស់ Leah Suzy យល់អំពីនាងគ្រាន់បើជាមុន ហើយឲ្យកំណត់ហេតុប្រចាំថ្ងៃផ្ទាល់របស់នាងទៅមិត្តថ្មីដើម្បីអាន ។

Name ______________________ Date ______________

"Ribbons" by Laurence Yep
"The Treasure of Lemon Brown" by Walter Dean Myers

Summary In "Ribbons," Stacy, a Chinese-American girl, is offended when her grandmother, a recent immigrant from Hong Kong, disapproves of her ribboned ballet shoes. Later Stacy learns that, as a child, her grandmother had been forced to bind her feet with ribbons, a Chinese tradition believed to enhance a woman's beauty. Stacy explains to her grandmother the purpose of ballet shoes, dances for her, and bonds with her. In "The Treasure of Lemon Brown," Greg, a teenager, leaves home one night to avoid his father's lecture on the importance of school. In an abandoned building, Greg meets Lemon Brown, a homeless man who was once a noted musician. Brown proudly shows Greg old newspaper reviews of his performances, which his son had been carrying when he died in the war. Greg returns home with a new respect for his father.

Ask Questions Sometimes it is difficult to understand what you are reading. One way to make it easier is to ask yourself questions as you read. When you come across a difficult passage, ask yourself why the author is including it. Does it tell you more about the setting, the characters, or the theme? Does it give a hint about what might happen next? How does this part relate to what has happened before?

Directions: As you read "Ribbons" and "The Treasure of Lemon Brown," practice this reading strategy by writing questions and answers in the ovals below. One sample has been given.

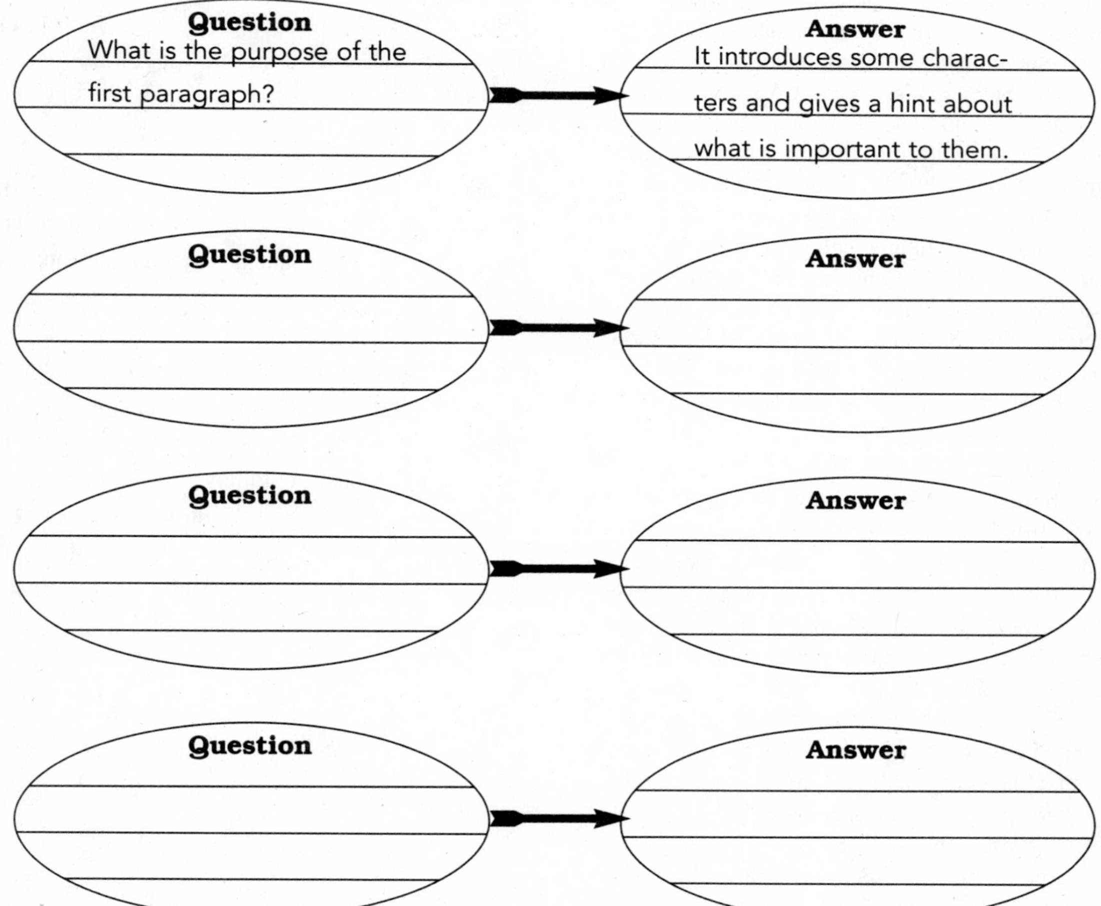

"Ribbons" by Laurence Yep
"The Treasure of Lemon Brown" by Walter Dean Myers

Resumen En "Ribbons," Stacy, una niña estadounidense de ascendencia china, se ofende cuando su abuela, que ha inmigrado recientemente de Hong Kong, desaprueba sus zapatillas de ballet con cintas. Más tarde Stacy se entera de que, cuando su abuela era niña, la forzaban a atarse los pies con cintas, una tradición china que se creía realzaba la belleza femenina. Stacy le explica a su abuela el propósito de las zapatillas de ballet, baila ante ella, y establece un vínculo con ella. En "The Treasure of Lemon Brown," el adolescente Greg se va de casa una noche para no tener que oír la lección de su padre sobre la importancia de la escuela. En un edificio abandonado, Greg se encuentra con Lemon Brown, un hombre sin hogar que fue antes un músico afamado. Brown le muestra con orgullo a Greg reseñas de periódicos de sus actuaciones, que su hijo llevaba consigo cuando murió en la guerra. Greg vuelve a casa con un nuevo respeto por su padre.

Tóm Lược Trong bài "Ribbons", Stacy, một cô gái người Mỹ gốc Hoa, bị phiền lòng khi bà của cô, mới di cư đến từ Hông Kông, không chấp thuận đôi giày ba lê có gắn nơ của cô. Sau đó, Stacy biết rằng, khi còn nhỏ, bà của cô đã bị bắt buộc bó chân bằng dây nơ, một phong tục của người Tàu để làm tăng thêm vẽ đẹp cho người phụ nữ. Stacy giải thích cho bà nghe về mục đích của đôi giày ba lê, dùng để nhảy múa đối với cô, và gắn bó với cô. Trong "The Treasure of Lemon Brown", Greg, một thiếu niên, bỏ nhà một đêm để tránh không nghe cha cậu giảng về sự quan trọng của trường học. Trong một tòa nhà bỏ hoang, cậu gặp Lemon Brown, một người đàn ông không nhà đã có lần là một nhạc sĩ viết nhạc. Brown khoe Greg những báo cũ nói về những cuộc trình diễn của ông, mà con của ông luôn mang theo trong mình khi tử trận. Greg trở về nhà với một lòng kính phục mới đối với cha cậu.

Lub ntsiab lus Nyob hauv "Ribbons," Stacy yog ib tug menyuam ntxhais uas yog neeg Suav nyob rau teb chaws Amesliskas. Nws xav txawv heev taws thaum nws niam tais uas nyuam qhuav tuaj Hong Kong tuaj tsis nyiam nws phab khau las voos uas muaj hlua ntaub khi. Tom qab Stacy mam li paub tias thaum nws niam tais me, lawv muab hlua ntaub yuam khi rau nws phab kaw taw, qhov no yog ib qhov uas neeg suav ntseeg tias yuav ua rau ib tug neeg zoo nkauj. Stacy ua zoo qhia rau nws niam tais tias, phab khau muaj hlua ntaub khi ntawv yog los pab tuav nws phab kaw taw thaum nws ua las voos. Nyob rau "The Treasure of Lemon Brown," Greg, ib tug menyuam tub khiav tawm hauv nws lub tsev thaum hmo ntuj mus kom nws tsis txhob tau mloog nws txiv qhia tias kev kawm ntawv tseem ceeb npaum li cas. Hauv ib lub tsev uas neeg muab tso pov tseg lawm, Greg mus ntsib Lemon Brown uas yog ib tug neeg tsis muaj vaj muaj tsev uas thaum ub yog ib tug kws txawj paj nruag. Brown zoo siab muab tej ntawv xov xwm qub thaum ub txog nws tej kev ua paj nruag rau neeg saib los qhia rau Greg, uas nws tus tub tseem nqa rawv thaum nws tus tub mus tuag tom tshav rog. Greg rov qab los tsev thiab saib nws txiv muaj nqe zog tuaj.

摘要 在"Ribbons"中，一名華裔美國女孩史泰絲，當她最近才從香港移民來美的祖母反對她的繫絲帶巴蕾舞鞋時，她的心靈受到了傷害。史泰絲之後才知道當她祖母還是個小女孩時就被迫用布帶纏腳，這是中國的傳統認為能增加女人的美。史泰絲跟祖母解釋巴蕾舞鞋的用途是讓她能跳舞，並在這之後她與祖母之間的感情更加連繫在一起。在"The Treasure of Lemon Brown"中，蓋瑞格是一名十來歲的孩子，有一晚為了避開父親訓誡有關學校的重要性而逃家。在一處廢棄的建築物內蓋瑞格遇見了一名流浪漢 Lemon Brown，他曾是個有名的音樂家。Brown 很驕傲地給蓋瑞格看他從前演奏時被刊登的舊報紙，當他的兒子戰死沙場時也曾帶著這張舊報紙。蓋瑞格帶著重新對父親的尊敬回到了家。

សេចក្តីសង្ខេប ក្នុងរឿង "Ribbons" នាង Stacy ដែលជានារីជាតិអាមេរិកាំងកំណើតចិន ត្រូវគេធ្វើឲ្យអាក់អន់ចិត្ត ពេលដែលជីដូននាងដែលជាជនអន្តោប្រវេសន៍ថ្មីៗពីក្រុងហុងកុង មិនយល់ព្រមនិងស្បែកជើងរបាំបាលេមានចងបូររបស់នាង ។ ក្រោយមក Stacy ដឹងថាកាលនៅពីក្មេង ជីដូននាងធ្លាប់បានគេបង្ខំឲ្យរុំជើងគាត់ជាមួយបូរ ដែលជាទំនៀមទម្លាប់ចិនព្រោះគេជឿថាដើម្បីបង្កើនសំរស់របស់នារី ។ Stacy ពន្យល់ប្រាប់ជីដូននាងអំពីគោលបំណងនៃស្បែកជើងបាលេ នាងរាំឲ្យគាត់មើល ហើយនិងធ្វើឲ្យចុះសំរុងគ្នាជាមួយគាត់ ។ ក្នុងរឿង "The Treasure of Lemon Brown" Greg ដែលជាក្មេងជំទង់ម្នាក់ ចាកចេញពីផ្ទះនាយប់មួយដើម្បីគេចពីការឲ្យមេរៀនរបស់ឪពុកវាស្តីពីសេចក្តីសំខាន់របស់សាលារៀន ។ ក្នុងអាគារដែលគេបោះបង់ចោលមួយ Greg ជួប Lemon Brown ដែលជាបុរសគ្មានទីលំនៅម្នាក់ដែលពីដើមជាអ្នកសរសេរអក្សរភ្លេង ។ Brown បង្ហាញ Greg ដោយអំនួតនូវកាសែតចាស់បង្ហាញឡើងវិញនូវការសំដែងរបស់គាត់ដែលកូនរបស់គាត់ធ្លាប់បានបន្តក្បែ

Name ______________________________ Date ______________

"Stolen Day" by Sherwood Anderson

Summary This story looks at the relationship of a parent and child, particularly a son's need to feel his mother's love. The boy is fascinated and frightened by a neighbor's disease of inflammatory rheumatism. Imagining he also has it, the boy is scared and leaves school to go home. Once home, however, his mother does not treat him as if he has a serious disease. The boy is sure that he will die and is bothered by his mother's busyness and seeming lack of pity. He recalls how she had once show great compassion for a drowned child, and aches for the same show of compassion for himself.

Identify with the Characters: Identifying with characters can help you appreciate their stories and the themes or ideas the story conveys. When you identify with a character, you put yourself in the character's place, and think about how you would act.

Think about the boy from the story "Stolen Day." Try to identify with him by answering these questions on the lines provided.

1. How is the boy's situation in life similar to your own?

____

____

2. In what ways, if any, are his problems similar to any that you have faced in your life?

____

____

3. When have you felt joy, sorrow, and other emotions similar to those that the character experiences?

____

____

4. Which, if any, of the boy's values and interests do you share?

____

____

5. Do you identify with any of the other characters in the story (Walter, the mother, the siblings)?

____

____

"Stolen Day"
by Sherwood Anderson

Resumen Esta historia examina la relación de un padre y su niño, particularmente la necesidad de un hijo de sentir el amor de su madre. El niño se siente fascinado y asustado por la enfermedad de reumatismo inflamatorio de un vecino. Imaginándose que él también sufre de la enfermedad, el niño se asusta y se va de la escuela hacia su casa. Sin embargo, una vez que llega a casa, la madre no lo trata como si tuviera una enfermedad seria. El niño está seguro que morirá y le molesta la falta de pena de su madre y la manera en que se mantiene ocupada. Recuerda cómo una vez ella había sentido mucha compasión por un niño que se había ahogado y ansía la misma compasión hacia él.

Tóm lược Chuyện này quan sat mối liên hệ giữa bố mẹ và con cái, đặc biệt là nói về chuyện một đứa con trai phải cần có tình thương của người mẹ như thế nào. Cậu bé vừa bị mê hoặc vừa cảm thấy sợ hãi khi thấy người hàng xóm bị mắc bệnh viêm thấp. Cậu tưởng tượng là mình cũng bị mắc bệnh đó, nên sợ hãi bỏ trường về nhà. Khi cậu về đến nhà thì mẹ cậu không xử sự như cậu có bệnh nặng. Cậu bé tin chắc là mình sắp chết và đau khổ vì mẹ bận rộn dường như không chú trọng đến mình. Cậu nhớ lại có lần mẹ cậu đã tỏ ra thương cảm một cậu bé chết đuối, và cậu mong mẹ cũng nhiều thương cảm như vậy với chính cậu.

Lub ntsiab lus Zaj lus no qhia txog qhov sib ntseeg ntawm niam txiv thiab me nyuam, qhov tseem ceeb tus tub xav tau nws niam qhov hlub. Tus tub xav txog thiab ntshai txog ib tug neeg nyob ntawm nws ib sab tsev qhov mob txog npaws pob txha (inflammatory rheumatism). Xav hais tias yog nws muaj qhov mob ntawv thiab ne, tus tub tau ntshai thiab nws tawm ntawv los mus tsev. Tab sis thaum nws los tsev nws niam tsis xyuas nws zoo li tias nws yog ib tus muaj mob loj li. Tus tub tseeg tias nws yov tuag thiab txhawj txog nws niam qhov tsis knom li thiab zoo li nws niam tsis muaj qhov lub neeg. Nws xav txog thaum nws niam tseem muaj siab lub ntawm ib tus me nyuab pom dej tuag, thiab mob siab txog thaum nws niam tseem lub nws thiab.

摘要　這個故事探討父母和孩子之間的關係，特別是兒子需要感受到母親的關愛。這個男孩對於鄰居的風濕炎一方面感到著迷，一方面也很害怕。他想像自己也得了這種病，心裡非常害怕，就離開學校跑回家去。可是等他回家以後，他媽媽對待他並不像他得了絕症一樣。這個男孩確定他很快就會死掉，因此對於媽媽的忙碌和缺乏憐憫感到很苦惱。他回想她曾經對一個淹死的小孩表現很大的同情心，而他現在也渴望獲得一樣的同情心。

សេចក្តីសង្ខេប រឿងនេះពិនិត្យមើលអំពីទំនាក់ទំនងរបស់មាតា/បិតានិងកូនជាពិសេសគឺសេចក្តីត្រូវការរបស់កូនប្រុសដើម្បីឲ្យមានអារម្មណ៍អំពីសេចក្តីស្នេហារបស់ម្តាយវា ។ កុមារានោះមានការចាប់ចិត្តជាខ្លាំងនិងភ័យខ្លាចចំពោះជម្ងឺរលាកសន្លាក់ឆ្អឹងរបស់អ្នកជិតខាង ។ ដោយស្រមៃថាវាមានរោគនោះដែរ កុមារានោះមានការភ័យខ្លាចហើយចាកចេញពីសាលាទៅផ្ទះវិញ ។ ទោះយ៉ាងនេះក្តី នៅពេលវាទៅដល់ផ្ទះ ម្តាយរបស់វាមិនថែរក្សាវាដូចជាវាមានជម្ងឺធ្ងន់ធ្ងរឡើយ ។ កុមារានោះជឿប្រាកដថាវានឹងស្លាប់ហើយមានក្តីរំខានចិត្តចំពោះភាពរវល់និងភាពខ្វះការអាណិតអាសូររបស់ម្តាយរបស់វា ។ វារំលឹកអំពីកាលមួយនោះដែលគាត់បានបង្ហាញការអាណិតអាសូរដ៏អស្ចារ្យចំពោះក្មេងលង់ទឹកម្នាក់ ហើយនិងទៅជាឈឺបង្ហាញថាមានការអាណិតអាសូរដូចគ្នាសំរាប់ខ្លួនវា ។

Name ______________________________ Date ______________

"How to Enjoy Poetry" by James Dickey

Summary In this expository essay, the writer explores what poetry is, what it can do, and his own feelings about poetry. James Dickey loves poetry. He wants to help others enjoy it, too. To start enjoying poetry, Dickey suggests to readers that they skip their experiences with poetry in classrooms, textbooks, tests, and libraries; instead, he thinks the way to start is by going straight to personal experiences. He talks about the connections that words have with our hearts. He explains how rhyme and rhythm leave lasting impressions on people. He suggests ways that readers can think about poetry. He even encourages writing poetry. Reading poetry, he says, can change your life—the deeper a person's encounters with poetry, the deeper their experiences with life.

Recognize the Organization One way to read and understand nonfiction more effectively is by noting how the information is organized. In "How to Enjoy Poetry," author James Dickey chooses to list his advice for reading poetry in chronological order. That is, he tells you what you should do first, next, and so on. Notice how, early in his essay, he writes, "The first thing to understand about poetry is ...." That phrase is a clue that Dickey is presenting his suggestions in chronological order.

Copy the chart below. As you read Dickey's essay, jot down in chronological order his tips for enjoying poetry. Start with the advice that he offers first.

"How to Enjoy Poetry"
Tip #1:
Tip #2:
Tip #3:
Tip #4:
Tip #5:
Tip #6:
Tip #7:
Tip #8:
Tip #9:
Tip #10:

"How to Enjoy Poetry"
by James Dickey

Resumen En este ensayo, el poeta James Dickey expresa sus ideas sobre la poesía y cómo pueden apreciarla mejor los lectores. Para que la poesía tenga vida, dice Dickey, es necesario que el lector responda emocionalmente. Sugiere que los lectores se abran todo lo posible a su propia existencia, y también a contemplar algo que "no es usted," como un cubo de hielo. Dickey elogia el poderoso ritmo del lenguaje de un poema, diciendo que el desafío de escribir rimas es "como una competencia con uno mismo." Dickey concluye que, a medida que los encuentros de los lectores con la poesía se hacen más profundos, las experiencias de sus propias vidas se harán también más profundas. "Usted entenderá entonces el mundo en su interacción con las palabras, el mundo recreado por las palabras y por las imágenes," dice Dickey.

Tóm Lược Trong bài luận này, nhà thơ James Dickey bày tỏ những ý kiến của ông về thơ văn và làm thế nào để được đọc giả khen ngợi nhiều hơn. Dickey nói, để cho bài thơ sống động, đọc giả cũng phải biểu lộ cảm xúc. Ông đề nghị các đọc giả nên cởi mở càng nhiều càng tốt cho sự hiện hữu của họ, và cũng nên suy tưởng đến vài điều "không phải là quý vị", là cục nước đá chẳng hạn. Dickey khen ngợi sức mạnh của những nhịp vần trong bài thơ, ông nói rằng sự thử thách khi viết văn vần"giống như một bài thi cho chính quý vị". Dickey kết luận rằng khi sự gặp gỡ của đọc giả đối với thơ văn sâu hơn, những kinh nghiệm cuộc đời của chính họ cũng sâu thêm. Dickey nói "Quý vị sẽ bắt đầu thấu hiểu được thế giới khi dùng chữ, nó có thể được tạo lại bằng từ ngữ, bằng vần điệu, và hình ảnh".

Lub ntsiab lus Nyob rau daim ntawv no, tus neeg sau ntawv hu ua James Dickey qhia txog nws qhov kev xav li cas rau kev sau paj huam thiab yuav ua li cas cov neeg nyeem thiaj li muaj siab xav saib paj huam muaj nuj qes lossis nyiam heev. Dickey hais tias, yuav ua kom paj huam nyob muaj mus mas, tus neeg nyeem yuav tsum muaj kev raug siab. Nws pab tawm tswv yim tias, kom tus neeg nyeem yuav tsum qhib lawv tus kheej kom loj li loj tau, thiab saib tej yam uas "tsis yog koj," xws li lub nab kuab dej khov. Dickey qhuas txog paj huam ua cov suab ntawm cov lus muaj zog heev, thiab hais tias qhov kev sib tw ntawm kev sau phaj huam kom sib dhos muaj txwm mas "zoo li kev sib tw ntawm yus tus kheej." Dickey hais thaum kawg tias thaum tus neeg nyeem ntawv los ntsib paj huam uas muaj kev tob, cov uas lawv yuav ua ntawm lawv lub neej los tob ib yam nkaus. "Koj mam li to taub lub ntiajteb no thaum nws los mus do nrog lo lus, xws li nws rov mus tsim los ntawm lus, lub suab, thiab tus duab," Dickey hais li ntawv.

摘要 在這篇短文裡，詩人 James Dickey 表現他對詩的看法以及詩如何能讓讀者開拓更大的鑑賞力。為了讓詩有活力，Dickey 說讀者感情上的回響是必要的。他建議讀者儘可能地敞開自己達到他們自己的存在並且能專注「你以外的」某些事物，例如一個冰塊。Dickey 讚美詩在語言押韻方面散發出的力量，並說作詩的挑戰是「像把自己也包在裡面的容器」。Dickey 總結說一旦讀者與詩的邂逅愈深則讀者對他們自己的生活體驗也會愈深。「由詩與文字的互動以及詩由文字、韻律和意象的再創作中你會慢慢地了解到詩的世界。」Dickey 說。

សេចក្តីសង្ខេប ក្នុងតែងសេចក្តីនេះ កវី James Dickey សង្កត់បញ្ជាក់ពីទស្សនៈរបស់គាត់លើកំណាព្យកាព្យឃ្លោង និងពីរបៀបដែលអ្នកអានអាចចូលចិត្តអស្ចារ្យថែមទៀតបាន ។ លោក Dickey និយាយថា ដើម្បីឲ្យកំណាព្យរស់រវើក គេតំរូវឲ្យមានការឆ្លើយតបដោយទឹកចិត្តរបស់អ្នកអាន ។ គាត់ឲ្យយោបល់ថាអ្នកអានត្រូវបើកចំហរខ្លួនគេឲ្យច្រើនដែលអាចធ្វើបានចំពោះការបើកចំហរដែលមានរបស់គេផ្ទាល់ ហើយថែមទាំងសម្លឹងមើលអ្វីដែល"មិនមែនជាអ្នក" ដូចជាដុំទឹកកក ។ លោក Dickey សរសើរចុងជួនដែលមានថាមពលនៃភាសារបស់កំណាព្យដោយនិយាយថាការប្រកួតប្រជែងនៃការសរសេរពាក្យជួនគឺ"ដូចជាការប្រឡងជាមួយខ្លួនឯង" ។ លោក Dickey សារុបសេចក្តីថានៅពេលដែលការជួបជាមួយកំណាព្យរបស់អ្នកអានកាន់តែជ្រៅ ការពិសោធន៍នៃជីវិតផ្ទាល់របស់ពួកគេនឹងធ្វើឲ្យជ្រៅដែរ ។ លោក Dickey និយាយថា"អ្នកនឹងទៅជាយល់ពីពិភពលោកនៅពេលដែលវាឆ្លងឆ្លើយជាមួយពាក្យ ដោយហេតុថាវាអាចត្រូវគេបង្កើតឡើងវិញដោយពាក្យ ដោយចុងជួន និងដោយរូបភាព" ។

Name ______________________________ Date ______________

"No Gumption" by Russell Baker
from *An American Childhood* by Anne Dillard

Summary In these autobiographical pieces, the authors recall memorable childhood experiences. In "No Gumption," Baker describes how, in 1932 during the Depression, his mother was concerned with his laziness. She encouraged him, at age eight, to sell magazines in town, first on the streets, and then door to door. Unable to sell any, Russell was then shown up by his younger sister, whose determination enabled her to sell all Russell's magazines. Later, an A grade on a school composition inspired Russell to choose a writing career, which he saw as requiring no gumption. In *An American Childhood*, the author describes how she and friends, as children, threw a snowball at a passing car. The driver chased the children on foot for ten blocks until finally catching up with them. While Dillard was unimpressed by the driver's scolding words, she was astonished that he had chased them over such a long distance.

Understand the Author's Purpose Authors write for different purposes, or reasons. Some wish to *inform*, some wish to *entertain*, and others wish to *persuade*. Sometimes a writer has more than one purpose in mind when writing. Russell Baker and Anne Dillard each manage to inform, entertain, and persuade at various points in their essays.

Answer these questions about the two essays.

1. Where does Baker *entertain* you with a humorous description of himself?

____

____

2. Where does he *inform* you about the kind of town he lived in as a boy?

____

____

3. Where does he try to *persuade* you that he had no gumption?

____

____

4. Where does Dillard *entertain* you with a humorous description of the chase?

____

____

5. Where does she *inform* you about the children in her neighborhood?

____

____

6. Where does she try to *persuade* you that she is as tough as the boys?

____

____

"No Gumption" by Russell Baker
from *An American Childhood* by Anne Dillard

Resumen En estos escritos autobiográficos, los autores recuerdan experiencias memorables de su niñez. En "No Gumption," Baker cuenta cómo en 1932, durante la Depresión, su madre se preocupaba por su pereza. Ella le sugirió que , a la edad de ocho años, vendiese revistas en el pueblo, primero en las calles y después puerta a puerta. Tras no ser capaz de vender ninguna, Russell fue puesto en evidencia por su hermana menor, cuya determinación le permitió vender todas las revistas de Russell. Más tarde, una nota de A en una composición escolar inspiró a Russell a elegir el oficio de escritor, que según él no requería coraje. En *An American Childhood*, la autora describe cómo ella y sus amigos, cuando niños, arrojaron una bola de nieve a un coche que pasaba. El conductor persiguió a los niños a pie durante diez cuadras hasta alcanzarlos. Aunque a Dillard le importaron poco las palabras de regaño del conductor, quedó asombrada de que les persiguiera a una distancia tan larga.

Tóm Lược Trong những bài nói về tiểu sử này, các tác giả nhớ lại những kinh nghiệm không quên thời ấu thơ. Trong "No Gumption", năm 1932 trong thời kỳ Suy Thoái Trầm Trọng, Baker diễn tả mẹ ông lo lắng như thế nào vì sự lười biếng của ông. Bà khuyến khích ông, lúc đó được tám tuổi, đi bán tạp chí trong thành phố, đầu tiên là trên đường phố, và sau đó đi bán từng nhà. Không thể bán được tờ nào, sau đó Russell lại bị em gái qua mặt, em ông nhất quyết có thể bán được tất cả tạp chí của Russell. Sau này, việc luôn được điểm A tại trường về môn luận văn gợi cho Russell chọn nghề viết văn, mà theo ông không cần đòi hỏi về tánh bặt thiệp. Trong bài *An American Childhood*, tác giả diễn tả làm thế nào bà và các bạn, lúc còn nhỏ, đã thảy banh tuyết vào xe chạy qua. Người tài xế ngừng xe lại chạy xuống rượt đám trẻ khoảng mười đoạn đường cho đến khi bắt được chúng. Dillard không màng về những lời chửi rủa của người tài xế trong lúc đó, bà chỉ quá kinh ngạc vì ông ta đã rượt đuổi một đoạn đường quá xa.

Lub ntsiab lus Ob zaj ntawv uas sau txog ob tug tibneeg lub neeg no, tus neeg sau ntawv nco txog tej yam uas nws tau ua thaum nws tseem me. Nyob rau "No Gumption," Baker piav qhia tias, thaum 1932 lub sijhawm uas nyiaj tsis muaj nqe (Depression), nws niam nyuaj siab txog nws txoj kev tub nkeeg. Nws niam pab txhawb nws kom nws mus muag ntawv magazine thaum nws muaj yim xyoo. Nws mus muag hauv zos, thaum nws nyuam qhuav pib nws mus muag tom kev, tom qab ntawv nws mam muag qhov rooj rau qhov rooj. Russell muag tsis tau li. Nws tus muam thiaj yuav qhia rau Russell tias nws ua tau. Vim nws ntseeg tias nws yuav tsum ua tau xwb nws thiaj li muag tag nrho Russell cov ntawv magazines. Tom qab thaum Russell tau tus A ntawm daim ntawv uas nws sau tom tsev kawm ntawv. Qhov ntawv thiaj ua rau nws txiav txim siab ua ib tug neeg sau ntawv, vim nws pom tias qhov no tsis muaj kev thawb kom yus yuav tsum ua. Nyob rau *An American Childhood*, tus sau ntawv qhia txog nws thiab nws cov phooj ywg. Thaum lawv tseem yau lawv txawb ib lub snowball rau ib lub tsheb uas tsav los dhau. The tsav tsheb caum lawv tau kaum block, thaum kawg nws caum tau lawv. Txawm tias Dillard tsis mloog tus tsav tsheb tej lus cem los nws ceeb tias tus yawg ntawv tseem caum lawv los deb kawg.

摘要 這是兩篇自傳體文章，作者回憶童年時期的經歷。在 "No Gumption" 中，Baker 描述在 1932 年經濟大蕭條的期間他的母親如何對他的怠惰擔心。他八歲時母親鼓勵他到鎮上去賣雜誌，剛開始是在街上兜售接著便挨家挨戶推銷。Russell 並沒賣出任何一本，他妹妹於是決定讓哥哥看看她有辦法賣掉他的所有雜誌的能力。之後 Russell 學校的作文得了個 A 等因之激發他選擇一個寫作生涯。因為他覺得寫作並不需要精明幹練。在 *An American Childhood* 中，作者則描寫童年時期她與其他的朋友向路過的車輛投擲雪球，一名駕駛如何跑了十條街追趕他們直到最後追上他們。Dillard 雖然不覺得那名駕駛罵的話有多了不起，但還是非常驚訝他追他們那麼長的距離。

សេចក្ដីសង្ខេប ក្នុងអត្ថបទពីប្រវត្តិរបស់អ្នកនិពន្ធទាំងនេះ អ្នកនិពន្ធរំលឹកការពិសោធន៍ពីវ័យក្មេងដែលអាចចងចាំបាន ។ ក្នុងរឿង "No Gumption" លោក Baker រៀបរាប់ពីរបៀបដែលម្ដាយគាត់មានការបារម្ភពីភាពខ្ជិលច្រអូសរបស់គាត់ ក្នុងឆ្នាំ ១៩៣២ ក្នុងកម្លុងពេលសេដ្ឋកិច្ចចុះដុនដាប ។ ម្ដាយគាត់លើកទឹកចិត្តគាត់ដែលកាលនោះមានអាយុប្រាំបីឆ្នាំ ឲ្យលក់ទស្សនាវដ្ដីនៅក្នុងក្រុង មុនដំបូងនៅតាមផ្លូវ បន្ទាប់មកទៅតាមផ្ទះ ។ ដោយមិនអាចលក់ដាច់សោះ ប្អូនស្រីរបស់ Russell បានបង្ហាញការប្ដេជ្ញាចិត្តដែលអាចឲ្យនាងលក់ទស្សនាវដ្ដីទាំងអស់របស់គាត់បាន ។ ក្រោយមក ការទទួលពិន្ទុ A នៅក្នុងការប្រឡងនៅសាលារៀនជំរុលចិត្ត Russell ឲ្យរើសយកអាជីវកម្មជាអ្នកនិពន្ធ ដែលគាត់ឃើញថាជាការតំរូវដែលគ្មានការបង្ខំ ។ ក្នុងរឿង *An American Childhood* អ្នកនិពន្ធរៀបរាប់ពីរបៀប ដែលគាត់និងមិត្តរបស់គាត់កាលនៅក្មេងបានចោលពំនូតទឹកកកទៅលើឡាន ដែលបើកកាត់ ។ អ្នកបើកឡាននោះរត់ដេញតាមក្មេងៗចំនួនដប់កំណាត់ផ្លូវរហូតតាមទាន់ពួកកូនក្មេងនៅទីបំផុត ។ ខណៈដែល Dillard មិនចាប់អារម្មណ៍និងពាក្យស្ដីបន្ទោសរបស់អ្នកបើកឡាន នាងភ្ញាក់ផ្អើលដែលអ្នកបើកឡានបានដេញតាមពួកគេយ៉ាងឆ្ងាយបែបនេះ ។

Name ______________________________ Date ______________

"Nolan Ryan" by William W. Lace

Summary This selection looks at the habits and balanced lifestyle of major-league baseball pitcher Nolan Ryan. Ryan continues the good habits he learned in early life: eating only wholesome, low-fat foods and working out daily even in the off-season. Ryan takes care of his mental health, as well, by keeping up his interests in other things. His family and his commitment to the community are a big part of his life. He raises cattle on several different ranches and participates in charity work whenever he can. He has a generosity of spirit until he's on the mound and his drive to win takes over, making him a fierce competitor. Ryan's character makes him an exciting person to watch, on or off the baseball field.

Set a Purpose for Reading Before you read a selection, it is helpful to know why you are reading it. You can decide that for yourself by setting a purpose for reading. First, learn the topic of the selection. Next, think of specific questions you would like answered by reading the selection. Then, as you read, look for details that will help you answer your questions.

For the selection, list four questions you have about the topic. Then, as you read the selection, see if you can answer each question.

Question 1: ______________________________

Question 2: ______________________________

Question 3: ______________________________

Question 4: ______________________________

Answer 1: ______________________________

Answer 2: ______________________________

Answer 3: ______________________________

Answer 4: ______________________________

"Nolan Ryan"
by William W. Lace

Resumen Esta selección se ocupa de los hábitos y el estilo de vida equilibrado del conocido lanzador de béisbol Nolan Ryan. Ryan continúa los buenos hábitos que aprendió al principio de su vida: comer solamente comidas nutritivas, con poca grasa y hacer ejercicios todos los días, inclusive fuera de la temporada. Ryan cuida su salud mental también, manteniéndose interesado en otras cosas. Su familia y su compromiso con la comunidad son una gran parte de su vida. Se dedica a criar ganado en varios ranchos y participa en actividades caritativas cuando puede. Tiene generosidad de espíritu hasta que llega a la loma del lanzador y lo posesiona el deseo de ganar, convirtiéndolo en un formidable competidor. El carácter de Ryan lo convierte en una persona interesante para observar, en el campo de béisbol o fuera de él.

Tóm lược Chuyện này chú trọng tới những thói quen và đời sống quân bình của một cầu thủ ném bóng tên là Nolan Ryan trong một đội banh baseball thượng hạng. Ryan luôn luôn giữ những thói quen tốt đã học được từ khi còn nhỏ tuổi: ăn những thức ăn lành, ít ăn đồ mỡ màng, và tập thể thao hàng ngày ngay cả những khi không phải là mùa chơi banh. Ryan cũng giữ gìn sức khỏe tâm thần của mình nữa, bằng cách tiếp tục chú tâm đến những việc khác ngoài công việc chính của mình. Gia đình ông và những chú tâm đến cộng đồng của ông chiếm một phần quan trọng trong đời sống của ông. Ông nuôi trâu bò trong vài trang trại và dự vào những việc làm từ thiện bất cứ lúc nào ông làm được. Ông có một tấm lòng rộng rãi phóng khoáng, trừ khi đã ngồi trên lưng con trâu đua là ông chỉ còn chú trọng đến thắng trận đua, thành ra ông là người thi tài rất đáng nể. Tính tình của ông Ryan làm cho ông trở thành một đấu thủ rất hào hứng trên sân banh trong các cuộc tranh tài baseball.

Lub ntsiab lus Qhov no ntsia txog tus thawj cuam pob Nolan Ryan cov haum lwn nws niaj hnub ua thiab tuav nws lub neeg kom tus. Ryan nws tseem rau siab ua qhov zoo uas nws kawm thaum ub los: noj los noj qov huv zoo, noj yam tsis muaj rog thiab nes hnub ua kom fws tawj tseem hais tias thaum caij so los li. Ryan tseem saib xyuas kom nws siab ntsws tus, uas muab nws cov kev xav mus xav rau lwm yam thiab. Nws tsev neeg thiab nws qhov pab zej zog yog ib qhov loj nyob hauv nws lus neej. Nws yug tsiaj rau ntau thaj teb thiab nws ho mus koom ua hauj lwm pab dawb thaum nws khoom. Nws muaj lub siab dawb txog ntua thaum nws yov pob cuam es nws qhov xav yeej mam los txeeg, ua kom nws yog ib tug sib twv txaus ntshai. Ryan tus yeeb yam ua kom nws yog ib tug neeg cus plaws zoom ntsia thaum nyob thiab twm ntawm chaw ntau pob.

摘要　這篇文章描述職棒投手諾倫萊恩的習慣和均衡的生活方式。萊恩一直保持從小學到的好習慣：只吃有益健康的低脂食物，即使在非球賽的季節仍然每天鍛鍊身體。萊恩也會對其他事物保持興趣，照顧自己的精神健康。他的家人以及他對社區的投入都是他生活中很重要的一部份。他在幾個牧場養了牛群，並且盡可能參與慈善工作。他平常為人慷慨，可是等他一站上投手板，一股想要獲勝的衝勁就會使他變成一個凌厲的競爭者。萊恩的性格使別人很喜歡看他，不管是在棒球場上還是棒球場外。

សេចក្ដីសង្ខេប អត្ថបទជ្រើសរើសនេះពិចារណាមើលអំពីទម្លាប់និងជីវភាពរស់នៅដែលមានលំនឹងរបស់អ្នកចោលបាល់នៃកីឡាបេសបាល់ចំបងឈ្មោះ Nolan Ryan ។ Ryan បន្តទម្លាប់ល្អដែលគាត់បានចាប់ផ្ដើមនៅក្នុងជីវិតរបស់គាត់៖ បរិភោគចំណីអាហារដែលមានសុខភាពនិងមានជាតិខ្លាញ់តិច ហើយហាត់ប្រាណប្រចាំថ្ងៃ ទោះបីជានៅក្រៅរដូវលេងបាល់ក្ដី ។ Ryan រក្សាសតិអារម្មណ៍របស់គាត់ផងដែរដោយរក្សាចំណាប់ចំណូលចិត្តរបស់គាត់ជាមួយរឿងឯទៀតៗ ។ គ្រួសារនិងការរួមចំណែករបស់គាត់ចំពោះសហគមន៍គឺជាភាគធំមួយនៃជីវិតរបស់គាត់ ។ គាត់ចិញ្ចឹមសត្វនៅក្នុងកសិដ្ឋានផ្សេងៗគ្នាជាច្រើន ហើយនិងចូលរួមក្នុងការងារជាអំណោយ នៅពេលណាដែលគាត់អាចធ្វើបាន ។ គាត់មានទឹកចិត្តអាណិតមេត្តារហូតទាល់តែដល់ពេលគាត់នៅក្នុងរង្វង់ចោលបាល់ ហើយគាត់ប្ដេជ្ញាយកជ័យជំនះមកជំនួសវិញ ទើបធ្វើឲ្យគាត់ក្លាយទៅជាគូប្រកួតយ៉ាងសាហាវម្នាក់ ។ លក្ខណៈរបស់ Ryan ធ្វើឲ្យគាត់ទៅជាជនដែលគួរឲ្យចង់មើល ទោះនៅក្នុងឬនៅក្រៅធ្លាកីឡាក៏ដោយ ។

Name ____ Date ____________________

from *Barrio Boy* by Ernesto Galarza
"I Am a Native of North America" by Chief Dan George
"Rattlesnake Hunt" by Marjorie Kinnan Rawlings
"All Together Now" by Barbara Jordan

Summary In the excerpt from *Barrio Boy*, the author tells of his entrance into first grade as a fearful Mexican boy trying to learn English. Thanks to a dedicated teacher, he ultimately triumphs. In "I Am a Native of North America," the author recalls his father's great love of the earth and its precious gifts, contrasting his culture with that of white society, which he sees as lacking love. In "Rattlesnake Hunt," the author describes how she overcame her fear of snakes by joining a snake expert on a rattlesnake hunt. In "All Together Now," Barbara Jordan appeals to American parents to teach their children to tolerate racial and ethnic differences in order to cultivate a love for all humanity.

Identify the Author's Main Points In an essay, an author usually makes several main points. A main point is a general and important idea. It is supported by specific details such as facts, statistics, stories, and examples.

For each selection below, list one main point that the author makes. Then cite at least two details that help support the main point.

from *Barrio Boy*

(a) Main Point ____

(b) Supporting Details ____

"I Am a Native of North America"

(a) Main Point ____

(b) Supporting Details ____

"Rattlesnake Hunt"

(a) Main Point ____

(b) Supporting Details ____

"All Together Now"

(a) Main Point ____

(b) Supporting Details ____

from *Barrio Boy* by Ernesto Galarza
"I Am a Native of North America" by Chief Dan George
"Rattlesnake Hunt" by Marjorie Kinnan Rawlings
"All Together Now" by Barbara Jordan

Resumen En el pasaje de *Barrio Boy,* el autor cuenta que cuando ingresó al primer año era un temeroso muchacho mexicano que quería aprender inglés. Gracias a un maestro dedicado, finalmente logra triunfar. En "I Am a Native of North America," el autor rememora el gran amor de su padre por la tierra y sus invalorables regalos, contraponiendo su cultura a la de la sociedad de raza blanca, que él considera falta de amor. En "Rattlesnake Hunt," la autora describe cómo logró sobreponerse al miedo a las víboras yendo a cazar víboras de cascabel con un experto. En "All Together Now," Barbara Jordan exhorta a los padres a que les enseñen a sus hijos a tolerar las diferencias raciales y étnicas para cultivar el amor por toda la humanidad.

Tóm Lược Trong đoạn văn trích từ *Barrio Boy,* tác giả kể lại lúc bắt đầu vào học lớp một khi ông là một em bé Mễ Tây Cơ sợ hãi cố gắng học Anh văn. Cám ơn người giáo viên tận tâm, cuối cùng ông đã thắng. Trong "I Am a Native of North America", tác giả nhớ lại tình yêu vũ trụ bao la của cha ông và những món quà quí giá của nó, ngược lại với phong tục tập quán của ông là xã hội của người da trắng, nơi mà ông thấy thiếu đi tình yêu thương. Trong bài "Rattlesnake Hunt", tác giả diễn tả để không còn sợ rắn nữa bà đã làm bằng cách gia nhập với những người chuyên môn trong một cuộc đi săn rắn lục lạc. Trong "All Together Now", Barbara Jordan cầu khẩn các cha mẹ người Mỹ nên dạy cho con họ sự thông cảm về màu da và sự khác nhau giữa các chủng tộc để từ đó trao đổi tình thương cho tất cả mọi người.

Lub ntsiab lus Nyob rau *Barrio Boy,* tus sau qhia txog thaum nws nkag mus kawm ntawv hoov ib uas nws ntshai heev uas yog hoob xyaum kawm ntawv Askiv. Ua tsaug rau ib tug kws qhia ntawv ua muaj siab heev, nws tau kov yeej lawm. Nyob rau "I Am a Native of North America," tus sau nco txog nws txiv txoj kev hlub rau lub ntiajteb no thiab cov khoom plig zoo heev. Muaj nws tej kab lig kev cai uas tsis zoo li cov neeg tawv dawb uas nws pom tias tsis muaj kev hlub. Nyob rau "Rattlesnake Hunt," tus sau qhia txog qhov uas ua rau nws tsis ntshai nab los ntawm kev koom nrog ib tug neeg paub txog nab zoo heev must nrhiav nab tua. Nyob rau "All Together Now," Barbara Jordan hu nug cov niam txiv Asmesliskas kom lawv qhia lawv cov menyuam kom yuav tsum ua zoo rau txhua tus neeg uas nqaij tawv txawv, thiaj li yuav cog tau kev hlub tau rau noob neeg.

摘要 這是一篇節錄自 *Barrio Boy* 的文章，作者敘述有關他以一名墨西哥男孩而要進入小學一年級學習英文的恐懼經驗。因為一位熱心的老師，他最終是成功了。在"I Am a Native of North America"中，作者追憶他的父親那世上最偉大的愛而且這愛是最珍貴的禮物，相反的他認為不同於他的文化的白種社會則似乎缺少愛。在 "Rattlesnake Hunt" 中，作者描述她自己如何從參與一位獵響尾蛇專家的活動中克服對蛇的恐懼。在 "All Together Now" 中，Barbara Jordan 喚起美國的父母教育孩子對不同的人種和民族要有寬容的心才能培養一種對全人類的愛。

សេចក្តីសង្ខេប ក្នុង សេចក្តីដកស្រង់ពី *Barrio Boy* អ្នកនិពន្ធនិទានពីការចូលរៀនថ្នាក់ទីមួយរបស់គាត់ថាជាក្មេងប្រុសមិចសិកកាំងដែលខ្លាចម្នាក់សាកល្បងរៀនអង់គ្លេស ។ ដោយអរគុណចំពោះគ្រូដែលចេះលះបង់ម្នាក់ វាមានជោគជ័យដ៏អស្ចារ្យ ។ ក្នុង "I Am a Native of North America" អ្នកនិពន្ធរំលឹកពីស្នេហាដ៏អស្ចារ្យ របស់ឪពុកគាត់ចំពោះផែនដីនិងអំណោយមានតម្លៃរបស់ផែនដីធ្វើឲ្យផ្ទុយគ្នារវាង វប្បធម៌របស់គាត់ជាមួយសង្គមស្បែកស ដែលគាត់មើលឃើញថាខ្វះសេចក្តីស្នេហា ។ ក្នុង"Rattlesnake Hunt" អ្នកនិពន្ធរៀបរាប់ពីរបៀបដែលនាងយកឈ្នះលើការខ្លាចពស់របស់នាងដោយចូលរួមជាមួយអ្នកជំនាញការខាងពស់ក្នុងការរកចាប់ពស់កណ្តឹង ។ ក្នុង "All Together Now" អំពាវនាវដល់មាតាបិតាអាមេរិកាំង ឲ្យបង្រៀនកូនចៅរបស់គេឲ្យអត់អោនដល់សាសន៍និងជាតិពន្ធខុសគ្នាដើម្បីបណ្តុះ ស្នេហាសំរាប់មនុស្សលោក ។

Name ______________________________ Date ______________

"A Christmas Carol: Scrooge and Marley" Act I by Charles Dickens
dramatized by Israel Horovitz

Summary On Christmas Eve, stingy Ebenezer Scrooge rejects all holiday celebration. He refuses to visit his nephew's family or to give to charity. He even chases away a caroler, and only reluctantly agrees to give his clerk, Bob Cratchit, the next day off. That night at home, Scrooge is visited by the ghost of his dead business partner, Jacob Marley. The ghost warns Scrooge to open his heart to humanity or suffer serious consequences. After telling Scrooge that three spirits will visit him on successive nights, Marley disappears. Later, the first spirit, the Ghost of Christmas Past, comes and takes Scrooge back in time. Scrooge is upset to see himself first as a lonely schoolboy, and then as a young man whose fiancee leaves him because of his obsession with money. The ghost then disappears, and Scrooge goes to sleep.

Picture As you read a play, it helps if you picture the production in your mind. You can do that with the help of stage directions, which appear in italic type enclosed in brackets. Always read stage directions carefully. Use details about the setting to imagine what the stage looks like in each scene. Use details about the characters to imagine how the actors move and speak on stage.

Use the chart below to record important stage directions in Act I. Tell how each direction helps you envision the play. The first one has been done for you.

Stage Direction	How It Helps Me Picture the Play
Ghostly music in the auditorium. A single spotlight on JACOB MARLEY, D.C. He is ancient; awful, dead-eyed	The scene is eerie, and Jacob Marley is frightening.

"A Christmas Carol: Scrooge and Marley" Act I by Charles Dickens dramatized by Israel Horovitz

Resumen En Nochebuena, el avaro Ebenezer Scrooge se rehúsa a celebrar las fiestas. Se niega a visitar a la familia de su sobrino y a dar a la caridad. Incluso rechaza a un cantor de villancicos y apenas acepta a regañadientes darle el día siguiente libre a Bob Cratchit, su asistente. Esa noche, Scrooge es visitado en su casa por el fantasma de su socio muerto, Jacob Marley. El fantasma le advierte a Scrooge que abra su corazón a la humanidad, o sino sufrirá graves consecuencias. Después de decirle a Scrooge que tres espíritus le visitarán en noches sucesivas, Marley desaparece. Más tarde, el primer espíritu, el Fantasma de las Navidades Pasadas, viene y lleva a Scrooge hacia atrás en el tiempo. Scrooge se siente transtornado al verse primero como un escolar solitario, y después como un joven cuya novia lo deja a causa de su obsesión por el dinero. El fantasma desaparece y Scrooge se duerme.

Tóm Lược Trước lễ Giáng Sinh, một người keo kiệt tên Ebenezer Scrooge bỏ hết tất cả việc ăn mừng các ngày lễ. Ông từ chối đến thăm gia đình người cháu hoặc giúp đỡ hội từ thiện. Ông còn rượt luôn cả người hát nhạc thánh ca, và chỉ đồng ý một cách miễn cưỡng cho ông Bob Cratchit, là thư ký của ông được nghỉ ngày hôm sau. Tối hôm đó tại nhà, Scrooge được một hồn ma tên Jacob Marley trước đây là người cộng sự đến thăm. Hồn ma khuyên Scrooge nên cởi mở tấm lòng với nhân loại hay sẽ bị hoạn nạn về sau. Sau khi nói với Scrooge sẽ có ba hồn ma khác đến thăm trong những đêm kế tiếp, Marley biến mất. Sau đó, hồn ma thứ nhất, là hồn của lễ Giáng Sinh kiếp trước, đến và đem Scrooge về thời đó. Scrooge buồn chán vì thấy chính mình trước đó là một cậu học sinh cô đơn, và tiếp đến là một người đàn ông bị vị hôn thê bỏ vì ham tiền. Sau đó hồn ma biến mất, và Scrooge đi ngủ.

Lub ntsiab lus Thaum hmo Christmas Eve ntawv, ib tug neeg qia dub hu ua Ebenezer Scrooge tsis kam txais kev zoo siab ntawm tej hnub cai no. Nws tsis kam mus saib nws tus xeeb ntxwv tsev neeg lossis muab khoom plig pub neeg. Nws caum cov neeg uas tuaj hu nkauj kom lawv khiav, thiab twb yuav luag tsis kam nws tus neeg uas pab nws ua haujlwm hu ua Bob Cratchit no so es tsis txhob tuaj ua haujlwm. Hmo ntawv thaum tsaus ntuj, Scrooge tau ntsib nws tus qub phooj ywg uas thaum ub ua haujlwm ua kev hu ua Jacob Marley, uastau tuag ua dab lawm. Tus dab ceeb toom rau nws tias, qhib koj lub siab rau tibneeg lossis yuav raug kev tsis zoo. Tom qab uas nws qhia hais tias tseem muaj peb tug ntsuj plig yuav los xyuas nws hmo tom qab, ces Marley cia li pawv lawm. Tom qab tus ntsuj plig thib ib uas yog ntsuj plig Christmas yav tas, los thiab coj Scrooge mus rau cov sijhawm tom qab. Scrooge tsis xav siab thaum nws yog ib tug tub kawm ntawv uas tsis muaj phooj ywg, thiab thaum nws twb tiav hlua uas nws tus hluas nkauj tseem khiav tso nws cia vim nws vwm rau nyiaj txiag. Tus ntsuj plig txawm ploj, ces Scrooge mus pw lawm.

摘要 在聖誕節前夕，吝嗇的 Ebenezer Scrooge 拒絕所有節日慶祝。他拒絕探訪他外甥一家人或施捨窮人。他甚至趕走報佳音的人，僅勉強地同意給他的職員鮑勃・克拉挈特第二天的休假。那晚在 Scrooge 家，他死去的生意伙伴 Jacob Marley 的鬼魂來拜訪他。鬼魂提醒 Scrooge 要對別人敞開心房否則將遭受嚴重的後果。在告訴 Scrooge 連續幾晚將有三個靈魂來訪之後 Marley 就消失不見了。然後第一個靈魂，過去的聖誕鬼魂來帶 Scrooge 回到從前，Scrooge 很難過地看到自己一開始是個孤獨的學校男孩，之後他成長為青年，但他的未婚妻因他腦中只有錢而離開他。那鬼魂之後消失了而 Scrooge 也上床去睡覺。

សេចក្តីសង្ខេប នៅយប់មុនបុណ្យគ្រិស្តម៉ាស់ Ebenezer Scrooge បដិសេធការធ្វើបុណ្យឈប់សំរាកទាំងអស់ ។ គាត់បដិសេធមិនទៅលេងគ្រួសារក្មួយរបស់គាត់ ឬឲ្យទានឡើយ ។ គាត់ថែមទាំងដេញពួកអ្នកច្រៀងចំរៀងសរសើរទៀតផង ហើយយល់ព្រមឲ្យស្មៀនគាត់ឈ្មោះ Bob Cratchit ឈប់សំរាប់នៅថ្ងៃបន្ទាប់ដោយស្ទាក់ស្ទើរប៉ុណ្ណោះ ។ នៅផ្ទះនាពេលយប់នោះ ខ្មោចដៃគូរកស៊ីរបស់គាត់ឈ្មោះ Jacob Marley បានមកលេងលោក Scrooge ។ ខ្មោចនោះព្រមានលោក Scrooge ឲ្យមានចិត្តល្អដល់មនុស្សលោក បើពុំដូច្នោះទេនឹងទទួលលទ្ធផលធ្ងន់ធ្ងរជាមិនខាន ។ បន្ទាប់ពីប្រាប់លោក Scrooge ថាមានព្រលឹងបីនាក់នឹងមកលេងនិងគាត់នៅយប់ជោគជ័យនេះ រួចហើយព្រលឹងលោក Marley ក៏រលាយបាត់ទៅ ។ ក្រោយមក ខ្មោចអតីតគ្រិស្តម៉ាស់ដែលជាព្រលឹងទីមួយ មកនាំលោក Scrooge ត្រឡប់ទៅពេលអតីតកាលវិញ ។ លោក Scrooge មិនសប្បាយចិត្តដោយឃើញខ្លួនឯងពីមុនជាសិស្សសាលាកំសត់ឯកោម្នាក់ បន្ទាប់មកជាយុវបុរសម្នាក់ដែលគូដណ្តឹងរត់ចោលពីព្រោះតែការងុបនិងលុយរបស់គាត់ ។ បន្ទាប់មកខ្មោចនោះក៏រលាយបាត់ទៅ ហើយលោក Scrooge ត្រឡប់ទៅដេកវិញ ។

Name ______________________________ Date ______________

"A Christmas Carol: Scrooge and Marley" Act II by Charles Dickens
dramatized by Israel Horovitz

Summary In Act I, Ebenezer Scrooge revisited the Christmases of his past, where he recalled a lonely childhood and a young adulthood in which he benefited from the kindness of a generous supervisor. In Act II, he visits first his Christmas Present—and sees how poorly he is regarded by his nephew and his wife and by the family of his clerk, Bob Cratchit. He moves on to the Christmas of his future. There, he looks in on three vagrants who have made off with the trappings of his deathbed, including even the shirt on his back. Determined to change both present and future, Scrooge awakens on Christmas day and sets off to provide richly for family, friends, and strangers alike.

Question As you read a play, you may have questions about the characters or their actions. You might wonder what a character meant by a particular comment. You might not understand why a character behaved as he or she did. When you have questions, it is best to write them down. Then, as you read on, see if you can find the answers.

Use the left column of the chart below to record questions about things you don't understand as you read Act II. Then, as you find answers, record them in the right column.

What I Don't Understand	What I Now Understand

"A Christmas Carol: Scrooge and Marley" Act II by Charles Dickens
dramatized by Israel Horovitz

Resumen En el Primer Acto, Ebenezer Scrooge volvió a visitar las navidaded de su pasado, donde recordó su niñex solitaria y su juventud, durante la cual se benefició de la bondad de un generoso Supervisor. En el Segundo Acto, visita primero sus Navidades Presentes—y descubre el mal concepto que tienen de él su sobrino y su esposa y la familia de su empleado, Bob Cratchit. Pasa entonces a las Navidaded Futuras. Allí observa a tres vagabundos que se han robado lo que encontraron junto a su lecho de muerte, hasta la camisa que llevaba puesta. Resuelto a cambiar su presente y su futuro, Scrooge se despierta el día de Navidad y comienza a dar valiosos obsequios a familiares, amigos y extraños por igual.

Tóm Lược Trong màn I, Ebenezer Scrooge thăm viếng lại những mùa giáng sinh của quá khứ, nơi đó ông nhớ lại thời ấu cô đơn và thời niên thiếu nhờ tấm lòng tốt của một bậc Bề Trên rông lượng. Trong màn II, trước tiên ông thăm viếng Giáng Sinh Hiện Tại—và thấy mình bị vợ chồng đứa cháu trai và gia đình của người thư ký Bob Cratchit xét đoán tồi tệ làm sao. Ông di chuyển qua Giáng Sinh Tương Lai. Tại đó ông nhìn thây ba người lang thang đang ăn cấp bộ đồ tang trên giường cxhết của ông, kể cả cái áo ông đang mặc nữa. Quyết định thay đổi cả hiện tại và tương lai, Scrooge tỉnh dậy vào ngày Giáng Sinh và cung cấp tiền bạc cùng thực phẩm dồi dào đồng dều cho gia đình, bạn bè, và cả những người xa lạ nữa.

Lus txiav kom tsawg Nyob rau Zaj I, Ebenezer Scrooge nrog tus plig Christmas yav tag los rov qab mus rau lub neej yav tag los, uas nws porn thaum nws yog ib tug menyuam yaus nyob ntsuag ntsuag no. Nyob Zaj II ces nws nrog tus plig Christmas tamsis no mus porn thaum nws yog menyuam hluas es muaj ib tug yawg saib xyuas nws ua haujlwm ua siab zoo zoo thiab pab pab nws kawg, nws kuj mus pom pob khoomplig uas luag yuav rau nws zaum xub xub thawj — thiab nws mus pom tias nws tus tub xeebntxwv thiab tus tub xeebntxwv tus pojniam, thiab tus neeg ua haujlwm pab nws hu ua Bob Cratchit tsev neeg mas lawv saib nws tsis muaj nqis Ii. Tag ces nws thiaj nrog tus plig Christmas yav tom ntej mus. Ces nws mus pom thaum nws tuag es muaj peb tug neeg pluag pluag thov khawv tseem tuaj nyiag tej ub tej no ntawm lub txaj nws pw tuag, muaj ib tug tseem tuaj chua nyiag kiag lub tsho ntawm nws hnav thaum nws tuag mus lawm. Tag kis ntawd thaum nws sawv los uas yog hnub Christmas kiag, ces nws thiaj Ii txiav txim tias nws mas yuav tsum hloov nws lub neej tamsis no thiab hloov nws lub neej yav torn ntej. Ces nws thiaj Ii tawm tsev nqa ub nqa no mus pab tej phooj tej ywg, mus pab tej rnuaj tej pluag, tus nws paub thiab tsis paub los nws pab tag tib si.

摘要 在第一幕中，艾伯奈澤・斯克盧奇重訪了過去的聖誕節，使他記憶起孤獨的童年和年輕時的自己。那時他受到慷慨上司的恩惠。在第二幕中，他首先看到了他現在的聖誕節一還看到在他的外甥和太太、以及職員鮑勃・克拉切特一家人的眼中一他多麼可憐。他又來到他未來的聖誕節。在那裡，他看到三個流浪漢拿著他停屍床上的裝飾物逃之夭夭，甚至包括他身上穿著的襯衫。決心改變現狀和將來，斯克盧奇在聖誕節這天醒來，開始把大量的錢財分給家人、朋友和陌生人。

សេចក្តីសង្ខេប ក្នុងឈុតទី ១ លោក Ebenezer Scrooge បានមើលទិដ្ឋភាពនៃបុណ្យគ្រិស្តម៉ាស់ពីអតីតកាលរបស់គាត់ឡើងវិញ ដោយលោកបានទឹកឃើញនូវកុមារភាពនិងយុវភាពកំសត់ឯកោរបស់គាត់ ហើយគាត់ត្រូវបានទំនុកបំរុងដោយនាយចៅហ្វាយចិត្តសប្បុរសម្នាក់ ។ នៅក្នុងឈុតទី ២ មុនដំបូងលោកមើលបុណ្យគ្រិស្តម៉ាស់នាពេលបច្ចុប្បន្ន-- ហើយឃើញថាលោកជាមនុស្សកំសត់ណាស់បើប្រៀបទៅនឹងក្មួយគាត់និងប្រពន្ធរបស់គេ ព្រមទាំងគ្រួសារស្មៀនរបស់គាត់ឈ្មោះ Bob Cratchit ។ បន្ទាប់មកទៀត លោកក្រឡេកមើលទៅបុណ្យគ្រិស្តម៉ាស់នាពេលអនាគតរបស់គាត់ ។ ពេលនោះលោកឃើញមនុស្សខ្ជាត់ព្រាត់បីនាក់ចាកចេញពីផ្ទះលោកដោយបានលួចយករបស់របរនៅលើគ្រែ ដែលលោកកំពុងតែដេកស្លាប់នោះ សូម្បីតែអាវយឺតដែលជាប់និងខ្លួនលោកក៏ចោរទាំងនោះលួចយកដែរ ។ ដោយតាំងចិត្តកែប្រែទាំងបច្ចុប្បន្នកាលនិងអានាគតកាលរបស់គាត់ៗភ្ញាក់ដឹងខ្លួននៅថ្ងៃបុណ្យគ្រិស្តម៉ាស់ ហើយចេញដំណើរទៅធ្វើអំណោយដល់បងប្អូនញាតិមិត្ត និងអ្នកក្រៅផងដែរ ។

Name ______________________________ Date ______________

"The Monsters Are Due on Maple Street" by Rod Serling

Summary It is an ordinary day in an ordinary town. Suddenly, a flash of light appears overhead and all electrical devices in town stop working or go on and off haphazardly. The townspeople, in their panic, look for someone to blame. They accuse one another of being the alien behind the strange happenings. One particularly disturbed man even shoots another. The blaming and confusion continue and increase. No one is safe from the mob that is seeking answers. While all this happens on Maple Street, two aliens watch from their spacecraft, which is sitting atop a nearby hill. They discuss how the most dangerous enemy humans confront is themselves.

Predict As you read a play, it can be fun to predict, or guess, what will happen next. The most reliable predictions are those based on story details you've already read. Before you make a prediction, ask yourself: What has each character done so far? What type of person is each character? If I were a character in the story, what might I do next?

Use the chart below to record your predictions in the story. For each prediction, explain why you think it will happen.

What I Predict Will Happen	Why I Think It Will Happen

"The Monsters Are Due on Maple Street"

by Rod Serling

Resumen Es un día cualquiera una ciudad como todas. De pronto, un rayo de luz aparece en lo alto, y todos los dispositivos electrico dejan de funcionar o se encienden y se apagan al azar. Los habitantes de la ciudad, en medio de su paánico, tratan de culpar a alguien. Se acusan mutuamente de ser el extraterrestre que ocasiona los extraños sucesos. Un hombre especialmente alterado, dispara contra otro. La confusión las acusaciones contiúan y aumentan. Nadie está a salvo de la turba que exige una respuesta. Mientras todo esto sucede en la calle Maple, dos extraterrestres observan desde su nave espacial, en una colina cercana. Comentan que el enemigo más peligroso de los seres humanos son ellos mismos.

Tóm Lược Đó là một ngày bình thường trong một thành phố bình thường. Đột nhiên, một tia chớp xuất hiện trên đầu mọi người và tất cả những máy móc sử dụng điện trong thành phố đều ngừng hoạt động hoặc tắt mở một cách bất chợt. Cư dân trong thành phố, trong nỗi kinh hoàng, cố tìm ra người để quy trách. Họ lên án lẫn nhau là người của hành tinh khác sau những biến cố kỳ lạ. Đặc biệt có một người gây phiền toái cho người khác thậm chí còn bắn chết một người nữa. Những sự lên án lẫn nhau và những sự lộn xộn vẫn tiếp tục và gia tăng. Không có ai còn an toàn giữa đám đông người hỗn loạn đang đi tìm câu trả lời. Trong khi tất cả những điều này xảy ra trên đường Maple, thì hai người từ hành tinh khác đang quan sát từ phi thuyền của họ, đang đậu trên đỉnh đồi gần đó. Họ thảo luận rằng kẻ thù nguy hiểm nhất mà loài người đối phó chính là con người.

Lus txiav kom tsawg Hnub ntawd nyob rau lub zos ntawd los kuj zoo ib yam nkaus li txhia hnub, sawvdaws nyob mus mus los los li qub. Tiamsis tos nco na ha, dab tsi cia li tib laim dhau plaws lawv taub hau, ces tej khoom siv faisfab cia li tuag tag, qee cov khoom ces cia li cig tuag cig tuag. Cov neeg hauv zos kuj ceeb thiab ntshai heev, ib tug liam ib tug tias tus ntawd yog tus ua. Lawv sib liam tias yeej yog muaj neeg txawv ntiajteb los ua rau kom qee tus yeej yog muaj neeg txawv ntiajteb los ua rau kom qee tus neeg hauv lawv vim li ntawd, thiaj li tau tua ib tug neeg hauv lawv zos ua kom zos ua kom muaj tej yam txawv txawv li ntawd rau lawv. Vim li ntawd, thiaj muaj ib tug yawg uas pheej tsis meej pem pes tsawg thiaj li tau tua inb tug neeg hauv lawv zos pov tseg. Ces hajyam ua rau lawv sib liam mus mus los los vwm tag. Tsis hais leej twg los puav leej txhawj thiab ntshai heev vim tsam cov neeg xav paub tias yog leejtwg tiag. Thaum cov neeg tabtom sib ceg liam ntxhov nyho li no ntawm txoj kev Maple Street, ciav pom muaj ob tug neeg txawv ntiajteb nyob ntawm ib lub nkoj dav-hlua loj tsaws saum lub roob tsis deb ntawm lawv pes tsawg ntawd ntsia ntsia lawv. Ces ob tug neeg txawv ntiajteb ntawd thiaj sib tham tias neeg tus yeebncuab phem tshaj plaws rau neeg ces rov qab yog neeg tus kheej xwb.

摘要 這是一個普通的城鎮中普通的一天。突然，一道亮光劃破夜空，鎮上所有的電器都停止了工作或偶然地開啟和關閉。恐慌中，鎮上的人們尋找著該責怪誰。他們互相譴責對方是這些怪事背後的外星人。特別不安的一個人甚至還開槍打死了另一個人。人們的責怪和混亂在持續和發展。在尋求答案的暴眾中沒有一個人是安全的。這一切發生在楓樹街的同時，兩個外星人坐在停泊在附近山頂的航天器裡，靜靜地觀察著。他們在討論最危險的敵人一人類怎樣面對自己。

សេចក្តីសង្ខេប រឿងនេះកើតឡើងនៅថ្ងៃធម្មតាមួយ ក្នុងទីក្រុង ។ រំពេចនោះពន្លឺផ្លេកបន្ទោរបានបាញ់ផ្ទះភ្លែតទៅលើមេឃ ធ្វើឲ្យឧបករណ៍ភ្លើងទាំងអស់ក្នុងក្រុងឈប់ដើរ ឬឆេះរលត់ភ្លឹបភ្លែតៗ ។ អ្នកភូមិភ័យពេកក៏ស្តីបន្ទោសដាក់គ្នាទៅវិញទៅមក ។ ពួកគេបានចោទគ្នាថា មានគ្រួសារខ្លះជាជនដែលមកពីភពដទៃហើយកំពុងបង្ករឿងនេះ ។ បុរសម្នាក់ភ័យខ្លាំងពេកក៏បាញ់បុរសម្នាក់ទៀត ។ ការបន្ទោសគ្នានិងភាពច្របូកច្របល់រីកវរបន្តទៅទៀតនិងកាន់តែកើនឡើង ។ គ្មាននរណារួចខ្លួនពីការស្វែងរកចម្លើយរបស់មនុស្សចលាចលនោះឡើយ ។ ខណៈដែលរឿងនេះកំពុងកើតឡើងលើវិថី ជនមកពីភពក្រៅពីរនាក់សម្លឹងមើលចេញពីយានអវកាសរបស់គេដែលចតនៅលើកំពូលភ្នំនៅក្បែរនោះ ។ ពួកគេពិគ្រោះគ្នាថាសត្រូវដែលមានគ្រោះថ្នាក់ដែលមនុស្សប្រឈមមុខជាមួយគឺពួកមនុស្សខ្លួនគេនោះឯង ។

Name ______________________________ Date ______________

"The Cremation of Sam McGee" by Robert Service
"Washed in Silver" by James Stephens
"Winter" by Nikki Giovanni

Summary These three poems demonstrate the impact that nature has on our lives. "The Cremation of Sam McGee," is the story of the Tennessee miner who died of the cold during the Gold Rush in the Yukon. The narrator tells the tale of the final trip across the frozen landscape with Sam's corpse. But when the corpse is warmed by the fire, Sam comes back to life! In "Washed in Silver," poet James Stephens describes the transforming power of the moonlight that shines on the landscape, and how he himself blends into the silvery light. The poem "Winter" describes how creatures large and small, including humans, have the natural instinct to prepare for the cold months.

Identify the Speaker The **speaker** in a narrative poem is the person telling the story. Sometimes the speaker is a character who takes part in the story's action. At other times he or she may be an observer who merely reports the action. Either way, you can learn about the speaker from the way he or she tells the story. The things the speaker says, and the way the speaker says them, are important clues to the speaker's personality and to the meaning of the poem.

Read each statement below made by the speaker in "The Cremation of Sam McGee." Then explain what the comment seems to indicate about the speaker's personality. The first one has been done for you.

1. Why he left his home in the South to roam 'round the Pole, God only knows.

   What it indicates about the speaker: He doesn't think that traveling to the Pole is an activity meant for everyone.

2. Well, he seemed so low that I couldn't say no.

   What it indicates about the speaker: ______________________________

3. A pal's last need is a thing to heed, so I swore I would not fail.

   What it indicates about the speaker: ______________________________

4. In the days to come, though my lips were dumb, in my heart how I cursed that load.

   What it indicates about the speaker: ______________________________

5. The trail was bad, and I felt half mad, but I swore I would not give in.

   What it indicates about the speaker: ______________________________

6. Then I made a hike, for I didn't like to hear him sizzle so.

   What it indicates about the speaker: ______________________________

"The Cremation of Sam McGee" by Robert Service
"Washed in Silver" by James Stephens
"Winter" by Nikki Giovanni

Resumen Estos tres poemas demuestran el impacto que la naturaleza tiene en nuestras vidas. "The Cremation of Sam McGee", es la historia de un minero de Tennessee quien murió de un resfriado durante la fiebre del oro en el Yukón. El autor cuenta la historia del viaje final a lo largo de la planicie helada con el cuerpo de Sam. Pero cuando el fuego calienta el cuerpo, Sam revive. En "Washed in Silver", el poeta James Stephens describe el poder de transformación de la luz de la luna que brilla sobre la planicie y cómo él mismo se mezcla en la luz plateada. El poema "Winter" describe cómo las criaturas grandes y pequeñas, incluyendo a los humanos, tienen el instinto natural de prepararse para los meses fríos.

Tóm lược Những bài thơ này cho ta nhìn thấy ảnh hưởng của thiên nhiên trong đời sống của chúng ta. Bài "The Cremation of Sam McGee," kể chuyện về một người thợ mỏ ở Tennessee đã thiệt mạng vì trời lạnh buốt trong thời gian Chạy Tìm Vàng trong miền Yukon (Gold Rush in the Yukon). Người thuật chuyện kể lại chuyến đi sau cùng qua miền đá đông lạnh với xác của ông Sam đã diễn ra như thế nào. Nhưng khi xác chết được lửa nóng làm ấm lên thì Sam sống lại! Trong bài "Washed in Silver," thi sĩ James Stephens tả quyền lực biến đổi của ánh trăng khi soi sáng lên phong cảnh tạo vật, và ông tả cảnh ông hoà mình vào ánh trăng bạc ra sao. Bài thơ "Winter" nói về mọi sinh vật, kể cả loài người, đã biết dùng bản năng tự nhiên của mình để sửa soạn cho những tháng rét mướt mùa đông.

Lub ntsiab lus Peb qhov paj huam no qhia ntawm lub ntiaj teb ua lis cas rau peb lub neej. " The Cremation of Sam McGee," yog ib zaj dab neeg txog Tennessee tus neeg khawb qhov hlau uas tuag vim qhov no thaum lub caij Gold Rush nyob Yukon. Tus kws sau tham txog qhov hlas zaum kawg nrog tus tuag Sam lub cev raws cov roob hav uas khov daus tas. Tab sis thaum lub cev los ziab hluav taws sov tuaj, Sam cia li ciaj rov los! Nyob hauv "Washed in Silver," kws paj huam James Stephens piav txog cov duab hli ci iab rau roob hav, thiab ua kom nws tus kheeg ploj raws zoo lis kab teeb nyiaj. Qhov paj huam "Winter" qhia hais tias cov tsiaj loj thiab me, neeg tib si, yeej muaj qhov paub npaj txog rau thaum hlis no.

摘要 這三首詩顯示大自然對我們生活的影響力。"The Cremation of Sam McGee" 描述一位田納西的礦工在淘金熱的時候凍死在育康一地。敘述者描述他帶著山姆的屍體最後一次穿越冰凍的大地。可是當屍體感受到火的溫暖，山姆竟然活了過來！"Washed in Silver"一詩中，詩人詹姆士史蒂芬描述照在大地的月光具有轉化的力量，而他如何融進這一片銀色的月光。"Winter"一詩描述大大小小的生物，包括人類在內，都有自然的本能會為寒冬天作準備。

សេចក្តីសង្ខេប កំណាព្យ ទាំងបីនេះបង្ហាញចំណុចប៉ះពាល់ដែលធម្មជាតិមានមកលើជីវិតរបស់យើង ។ កំណាព្យ "The Cremation of Sam McGee," ជារឿងរបស់អ្នកជីករ៉ែនៃរដ្ឋ Tennessee ដែលស្លាប់ដោយសារភាពត្រជាក់នៅក្នុងកម្លុងការប្រជែងដណ្តើមមាស (Gold Rush) នៅក្នុង Yukon ។ អ្នកពោលនិទានរឿងនៃដំណើរចុងក្រោយឆ្លងកាត់ដែនដីត្រជាក់កកជាមួយសាកសពរបស់ Sam ។ ប៉ុន្តែនៅពេលដែលសាកសពនោះត្រូវកំដៅដោយភ្លើង Sam រស់ឡើងវិញ! ។ ក្នុងកំណាព្យ "Washed in Silver" កវីនិពន្ធ James Stephens រៀបរាប់អំពីឋាមពលប្រែរូបរបស់លោកខែដែលចែងចាំងទៅលើទេសភាព ហើយនិងរបៀបដែលខ្លួនគាត់រលាយចូលទៅក្នុងពន្លឺពណ៌ប្រាក់ ។ កំណាព្យ "Winter" រៀបរាប់ពីរបៀបដែលសត្វលោកទាំងធំទាំងតូចដោយរួមទាំងមនុស្សផងមានសភាវគតិធម្មជាតិដើម្បីប្រុងប្រៀបសំរាប់ខែត្រជាក់ ។

Name ______________________________ Date ______________

"Seal" by William Jay Smith
"The Pasture" by Robert Frost
"Three Haiku" by Matsuo Bashō, translated by Daniel C. Buchanan

Summary These descriptive poems paint pictures with words. "Seal"—a poem whose words are arranged in the shape of a seal—describes the actions of a seal. The animal dives with a zoom and swims "Quicksilver-quick," past sting ray and shark. Soon, the seal resurfaces and "...plops at your side / With a mouthful of fish!" In "The Pasture," the poet states in a conversational tone that he is going to the pasture. He's going "to rake the leaves away" or to fetch a calf that's young and still totters on its legs when the mother licks it. He invites the reader also to come to the pasture. The poems that make up the selection "Three Haiku" describe the beauty of nature. One of the poems describes sunrise. Another depicts spring, and the third one reflects upon an evening graced by the fragrance of blossoms.

Read According to Punctuation Punctuation marks are like traffic lights. They tell you when to stop and go. In poetry, it is not always obvious from the structure of the lines where you should pause and stop as you read. You should not necessarily stop at the end of a line. To help you read, pay close attention to the **punctuation**. Stop at a period, even if it's in the middle of a line. Pause at a comma or a dash. Read with emphasis at an exclamation point.

Read each of the three poems. Find places where punctuation helps you understand how to read the passage. Record each example in its proper place in the chart. One example has been done for you.

Punctuation Signals and Passages
Stop at a Period
____
____
____
____
Pause at a Comma or Hyphen
____
____
____
____
Read with Emphasis at an Exclamation Point
See how he dives from the rocks with a zoom!
____
____
____

"Seal" by William Jay Smith
"The Pasture" by Robert Frost
"Three Haiku" by Matsuo Bashō, translated by Daniel C. Buchanan

Resumen Estos poemas descriptivos pintan imágenes con las palabras. "Seal"– un poema cuyas palabras están dispuestas en forma de foca – describe los actos de una foca. El animal se zambulle súbitamente y nada rápidamente, sobrepasando a la raya y al tiburón. Muy pronto la foca reaparece y se tumba a su lado con la boca llena de peces. En "The Pasture," el poeta expresa en un tono informal que va a ir al prado. Va a rastrillar las hojas o a recoger a una ternera muy joven que todavía trastabilla cuando su madre la lame. Invita al lector a acercarse también al prado. Los poemas que componen "Three Haiku" describen la belleza de la naturaleza. Uno de los poemas hace la descripcibn del amanecer. Otro representa la primavera, y el tercero es una reflexión sobre el atardecer perfumado por la fragancia de los capullos.

Tóm Lược Những bài thơ tả cảnh này tô điểm các hình ảnh bằng ngôn ngữ. "Seal"-- một bài thơ mà các chữ được sắp xếp theo hình dáng của một con hải cẩu -- diễn tả những hành động của con vật này. Hải cẩu lặn rất nhanh và bơi "nhanh như xẹt", qua mặt cá đuối và cá mập. Chẳng bao lâu, con hải cẩu trồi lên mặt nước và "...ốp xuất hiện ngay cạnh bạn, với miệng đầy cá!" Trong bài "The Pasture", nhà văn bày tỏ theo cách đối thoại là ông sẽ đi đến mục trường. Ông sẽ "cào lá đi" hay đuổi một con bò con còn chưa đứng vững đi nơi khác trong khi mẹ nó đang liếm nó. Ông cũng mời đọc giả đến mục trường. Bài thơ tạo ra sự lựa chọn "Three Haiku" diễn tả vẽ đẹp của thiên nhiên. Một trong các bài thơ diễn tả cảnh mặt trời mọc. Bài khác diễn tả mùa xuân và bài thứ ba phản ảnh một cảnh chiều tà bằng những mùi hương hoa.

Lub Ntsiab Lus Cov paj huam uas sau tau zoo no muab lus los kos ua duab. "Seal" – ib zag paj huam uas cov lus muab tso zoo li tus tsiaj seal (cov tsiaj noj ntses uas nyiam nyob saum nqhuab thiab hauv hav dej) – thiab qhia txog tias tus tsiaj seal coj li cas. Tus tsiaj dhia rau hauv dej thiab ua luam dej "Ceev li ceev," ("Quicksilverquick") hla dhau tus ntses sting ray (ntses loj dav tw ntev nyob hiav txwv) thiab tus ntses shark (ntses noj neeg). Tsis ntev xwb, tus seal rov tshwm saum nplaim dej thiab "…nrov npluv tshwm nyob ntawm koj ib sab lawm/Thiab tau tib qhov ncauj ntses!" Nyob rau "The Pasture," tus neeg sau paj huam hais lo lus zoo li sib tham tias nws yuav mus rau tom lub tiaj zaub yug tsiaj. Nws yuav muab "sua cov nplooj pov tseg" los sis mus coj tus me nyuam nyuj uas tseem mos uas nws cov tes taw tseem tshee tshee thaum leej niam yaim nws. Nws tseem caw tus neeg nyeem kom nrog nws mus tom thaj tiaj zaub thiab. Cov paj huam uas raug xaiv nrog yog "Three Haiku" qhia txog kev zoo nkauj ntawm ntuj ib txwm tsim muaj. Ib txog paj huam hais txog hnub tawm. Hos ib txog hais txog lub caij nplooj pib hlav, thiab txoj thib peb piav txog ib hnub uas hnub qaij muaj paj tawg tsw qab zoo nkauj nrog.

摘要　這些敘述詩是用文字來構思圖景。"Seal" 一詩則用文字排列成海豹的樣子。內容是描述海豹的活動情形。海豹急速跳入水中並「如水銀般地快速游過黃貂魚和鯊魚身旁。過一會兒，海豹浮上水面而且「…撲通一聲墜落在你身邊，嘴裡還塞滿了魚」。在 "The Pasture" 中，詩人以會話的語調來敘述他將要去牧場。他將要「掃除落葉」或帶回一隻當母牛舐牠時還仍搖搖擺擺的稚嫩小牛。他邀請讀者也來同遊牧場。從俳句中選出的 "Three Haiku" 這三首俳句描述的是大自然的美麗。其中一首描寫日出。另一首描寫春天，第三首則表現出一個花香增色的夜晚。

សេចក្តីសង្ខេប កំណាព្យរៀបរាប់ទាំងនេះលំអរូបភាពជាមួយពាក្យ ។ កំណាព្យ "Seal" ជាកំណាព្យមួយដែលពាក្យត្រូវគេរៀបជារាងដូចសត្វស្មៀល ដែលរៀបរាប់ពីសកម្មភាពសត្វស្មៀលមួយ ។ សត្វនោះលោតជាំផ្លូងចូលទឹកយ៉ាងលឿនហើយហែល"យ៉ាងលឿនដូចរលកប្រាក់" ហួសត្រីកាំប្រម៉ានិងឆ្លាម ។ មិនយូរប៉ុន្មានសត្វស្មៀលផុសឡើងលើទឹកវិញ ហើយ"ផ្ងប់នៅក្បែរអ្នក ដោយមាត់ពេញទៅដោយត្រី!" ។ ក្នុងកំណាព្យ "The Pasture" កវីថ្លែងក្នុងទំនុកចរចារថាគាត់នឹងទៅកាន់វាលស្មៅ ។ គាត់នឹង"កោយស្លឹកឈើចោល" ឬទៅយកកូនគោដែលនៅក្មេង ហើយ នៅតែត្រេតទ្រេតឈរមិនជាប់នៅពេលដែលមេវាលិតវា ។ គាត់អញ្ជើញអ្នកអានទៅកាន់វាលស្មៅផងដែរ ។ កំណាព្យដែលប្រឌិតការជ្រើសរើស "Three Haiku" រៀបរាប់ពីសោភ័ណភាពរបស់ធម្មជាតិ ។ កំណាព្យមួយនៃកំណាព្យទាំងអស់រៀបរាប់ពីថ្ងៃរះ ។ កំណាព្យមួយទៀតពណ៌នាពីរដូវលំហើយ និងកំណាព្យទីបីឆ្លុះបញ្ចាំងពីពេលល្ងាចដែលលំអដោយក្លិនក្រអូបនៃផ្ការីក ។

Name ______________________________ Date ______________

"Martin Luther King" by Raymond Richard Patterson
"Annabel Lee" by Edgar Allan Poe

Summary These poems use words designed to call up intense, often vivid feelings, about someone who has died. In his poem about the late civil rights leader Martin Luther King, Jr., Patterson's choice of words shows how the passion of King's beliefs made him admirable and keeps him memorable, even after his death. "He showed what Man can be/Before death sets him free." The poem "Annabel Lee" tells of the deep love between the young woman Annabel Lee, who lived by the sea, and a young man. When Annabel Lee dies from a chill, her lover grieves her death. But he believes that their love is so profound that their souls are never truly separated.

Paraphrase When you **paraphrase** the lines of a poem, you restate the ideas in your own words. Paraphrasing can help you discover how well you understand the passage. When you paraphrase, you change the poetic language into language you might use in prose writing or conversation. A paraphrase does not have to rhyme, even if the original lines of the poem do. Above all, remember not to change the meaning of the lines when you paraphrase them.

Read each passage below from the three poems. Restate the same idea in your own words. The first one has been done for you.

Original Passage	Paraphrase
1. His love so deep, so wide, He could not turn aside.	He had too much love in him to ignore the problems of others.
2. His passion, so profound, He would not turn around.	
3. He taught this suffering Earth, The measure of Man's worth.	
4. So that her highborn kinsmen came / And bore her away from me.	
5. With a love that the winged seraphs of Heaven / Coveted her and me.	
6. ... The stars never rise but I see the bright eyes / Of the beautiful Annabel Lee.	

"Martin Luther King" by Raymond Richard Patterson
"Annabel Lee" by Edgar Allan Poe

Resumen Estos poemas usan palabras para crear sentimientos intensos, a menudo vívidos, sobre alguien que ha fallecido. En el poema sobre el asesinado líder de los derechos civiles Martin Luther King, Jr., la selección de palabras de Patterson muestra cómo la pasión de las creencias de King hicieron que fuera admirable y memorable, inclusive después de su muerte. "Demostró lo que puede un hombre ser/Antes de que la muerte lo libere." El poema "Annabel Lee" habla del profundo amor entre una mujer joven llamada Annabel Lee, quien vivía a orillas del mar y un hombre joven. Cuando Annabel Lee muere de un resfriado, su amante llora su muerte. Pero, cree que el amor entre ellos es tan profundo que sus almas nunca estarán verdaderamente separadas.

Tóm lược Những bài thơ này dùng những chữ súc tích để gợi lên những cảm xúc căng thẳng, mạnh mẽ mà người ta thường cảm thấy khi thấy một người qua đời. Trong bài thơ nói về vị lãnh tụ về nhân quyền đã quá cố Martin Luther King, Jr., Patterson đã chọn những từ ngữ tả lên được lòng tin mãnh liệt của ông King làm cho ông đáng kính phục và mọi người phải nhớ đến ông mãi, ngay cả sau khi ông đã qua đời. "He showed what Man can be/Before death sets him free." Bài thơ "Annabel Lee" kể lại câu chuyện một người đàn bà trẻ sống ở ven biển tên là Annabel Lê đã có lòng thương yêu sâu đậm một chàng trai trẻ như thế nào. Khi Annabel Lee chết vì bị cảm lạnh, người yêu của cô than tiếc vô cùng. Nhưng anh vẫn tin rằng vì tình yêu của họ sâu đậm như vậy chắc chắn linh hồn họ chẳng bao giờ thật sự xa cách nhau.

Lub ntsiab lus Cov paj huam no siv ib cov lus uas kom kub siab, mob siab txog tej tus neeg uas nws tau tuag lawn. Nyob hauv nws zaj paj huam hais txog tus thawj coj neeg cov cai Martin Luther King, Jr. uas tuag lawn, Patterson xaiv ib cov lus uas qhia kom pom hais thiab txawm nws twb tuag lawn los, King qhov muaj lub siab ntsheej nws, ua kom nws raug nyiam thiab nco mus ntev. "He showed what Man can be/Before death sets him free". Qov paj huam "Annabel Lee" hais txog kev sib hlub tob ntawm tus poj niam hluas Annabel Lee, uas nws tsev nyob ze ntawm dej hiav txwv, thiab ib tug tub hluas. Thaum Annabel Lee mob daus no tuag, nws tus neeg hlub quaj tus siab heev. Tab sis nws ntsheeg hais tias nkawv txoj kev sib hlub tob heev, nkawv ob tus plig yov tsis sib ncaim li.

摘要　這幾首詩使用一些特定的字眼喚起一股對過世的人強烈而鮮明的情感。在描述已故的民權領袖馬丁路德金恩的詩中，佩特森所選擇的字顯示金恩信仰的熱情使他受人景仰，甚至在去世後仍然受到緬懷。〈他顯示人可以有何作為/在死亡使他自由之前。〉"Annabel Lee"一詩則是描述一位住在海邊的年輕女子和一個年輕男子之間的深刻愛情。安妮柏李因為風寒去世後，她的情人非常哀傷。可是他相信他們的愛情非常深刻，因此彼此的靈魂其實不會分開。

សេចក្តីសង្ខេប កំណាព្យទាំងនេះប្រើពាក្យដែលគេរចនាឡើងដើម្បីរំលឹកអំពីចេតនារម្មណ៍ដែលរស់រវើកជាញឹកញាប់អំពីនរណាម្នាក់ដែលបានស្លាប់ទៅ ។ នៅក្នុងកំណាព្យរបស់គាត់អំពីមេដឹកនាំសិទ្ធិប្រជាពលរដ្ឋចុងក្រោយគឺលោក Martin Luther King, Jr. ពាក្យជំរើសរបស់លោក Patterson បង្ហាញពីរបៀបនៃចំណង់នៃជំនឿរបស់លោក King ធ្វើឲ្យគាត់ទៅជាគួរឲ្យសរសើរហើយនិងរក្សាការចងចាំចំពោះគាត់ ទោះបីជានៅក្រោយពេលគាត់ស្លាប់ទៅហើយក្តី ។ "គាត់បង្ហាញពីអ្វីដែលបុរសអាចធ្វើបាន/នៅមុនពេលមរណៈភាពដោះលែងគាត់ឲ្យមានសេរីភាព" ។ កំណាព្យ "Annabel Lee" និទានអំពីស្នេហាដ៏ជ្រៅរវាងយុវនារី Annabel Lee ដែលរស់នៅក្បែរសមុទ្រ ហើយនិងយុវបុរសម្នាក់ ។ នៅពេលដែល Annabel Lee ស្លាប់ដោយសារភាពត្រជាក់កក គូស្នេហារបស់នាងកើតទុក្ខរីងរៃចំពោះមរណៈភាពរបស់នាង ។ ប៉ុន្តែនាយជឿជាក់ថាសេចក្តីស្នេហារបស់ពួកគេជ្រៅក្រៃលែងដែលព្រលឹងរបស់ពួកគេមិនបែកគ្នាជាពិតប្រាកដ ។

Name ______________________________ Date ______________

"Full Fathom Five" by William Shakespeare
"Onomatopoeia" by Eve Merriam
"Maestro" by Pat Mora

Summary The focus in these poems is on different types of music, real or imagined. In "Full Fathom Five," a son is told that his father lies dead beneath the sea. However, the father is transformed into the beautiful pearls and coral of the depths; and sea nymphs, or goddesses, ring bells in his honor. "Onomatopoeia" is about the sounds water makes when it flows from a rusty spigot. There is a stream of noise that becomes its own symphony. In the poem by Pat Mora, the maestro plays the violin in concert. As he bows before an audience he recalls the lyrical sound of his mother's voice. Each time the audience applauds, instead of hearing the clapping he hears in his mind the music that he and his parents played together at home.

Listen as You Read Poetry Poems are meant to be read, but even more so, they are meant to be heard. When you read a poem, read it out loud in order to **listen** to the musical language. Listen for rhyme, rhythm, and repetition of sounds and words. Don't just silently read a passage such as, "Full fathom five thy father lies." Say the line aloud, and hear the effective repetition of the *f* sound four times.

Read each passage below aloud. Describe the special or unusual sounds you hear. The first one has been done for you.

Passage	What I Hear
1. Full fathom five thy father lies.	the repetition of the *f* sound four times
2. "Hark! Now I hear them—ding-dong, bell."	
3. slash, / splatters, / scatters, / spurts, / finally stops sputtering / and plash!	
4. gushes rushes splashes / clear water dashes.	
5. while his father strummed the guitar / or picked the melody with quick fingertips.	
6. *voz, guitarra, violin* / would blend again and again	

"Full Fathom Five" by William Shakespeare
"Onomatopoeia" by Eve Merriam
"Maestro" by Pat Mora

Resumen Estos poemas hablan de diferentes músicas, reales o imaginarias. En "Full Fathom Five," se le dice al hijo que su padre yace muerto en el fondo del mar. Sin embargo, el padre se transforma en las hermosas perlas y corales de las profundidades; y las ninfas del mar, o diosas, tañen campanas en su honor. "Onomatopoeia" se refiere a los sonidos del agua que fluye de un grifo herrumbrado. Hay una corriente de sonido que se transforma en sinfonía. En el poema de Pat Mora, el maestro toca el violín en un concierto. Al inclinarse ante la audiencia, recuerda el sonido lírico de la voz de su madre. Cada vez que la audiencia aplaude, en lugar de oir las palmas oye en su mente la música que él y sus padres solían tocar en casa.

Tóm Lược Những bài thơ này chú trọng đến những loại nhạc khác nhau, thật sự hay tưởng tượng. Trong bài "Full Fathom Five", một người con được cho biết rằng cha của anh nằm chết dưới đáy biển. Tuy nhiên, người cha đã hóa thành những viên ngọc trân châu và san hô dưới lòng biển; và những vị hải tinh, hay các vị thần linh, rung những tiếng chuông mừng sự có mặt của ông. "Onomatopoeia" nói về những âm thanh do nước làm ra khi chảy ra từ một vòi nước rỉ sét. Một loạt âm thanh trở thành một bản nhạc hòa tấu. Trong bài thơ bởi Pat Mora, người nhạc trưởng chơi đàn vĩ cầm trong cuộc hòa nhạc. Khi cuối đầu chào khán giả, ông nhớ lại giọng ca của mẹ mình. Mỗi khi khán giả vỗ tay khen ngợi, thay vì nghe tiếng vỗ tay ông nghe trong tiềm thức tiếng hòa nhạc của ông cùng cha mẹ tại nhà.

Lub Ntsiab Lus Qhov uas cov paj huam no hais txog yog tej yam yas suab txawv, tseeb los yog xav xwb. Nyob rau "Full Fathom Five," muaj neeg qhia rau ib tug tub tias nws paub tias nws txiv tuag pw ncee lees hauv qab pas dej hiav txwv. Txawm li cas los xij peem, nws txiv txia mus ua tej lub qe qaum pob zeb ci zoo nkauj thiab tej ntxhuab zoo nkauj tuaj hauv qab pas dej tob; thiab ntxhais nkauj zag, lossis poj saub, xav tias yuav tau raws li nws qhov kev xav tau muaj meej mom. "Onomatopoeia" yog hais txog cov suab dej ntws/nrog los ntawm tus kais dej uas xeb lawm. Muaj tej tug dej uas muaj suab nws cia li ua nws qhov suab nrov. Nyob rau txoj paj huam uas Pat Mora sau, tus xib fwb qhia suab qoj lub Violin (lub xem xaus cov neeg tawv dawb siv) nyob rau saum lub sam thiaj nquam paj nruag. Thaum nws nyo hau rau cov neeg tuaj saib, nws nco dheev txog nws niam lub suab hu nkauj zoo. Ib zaug twg cov neeg npuaj tes, nws tsis hnov cov suab npuaj tes tabsis nws hnov nyob rau hauv nws lub siab cov yas suab uas nws thiab nws niam nws txiv lawv tshuab/qoj ua ke nyob tom tsev.

摘要　這些詩的焦點是放在不同種類的音樂，有現實或虛幻的。在 "Full Fathom Five" 中，兒子被告知父親葬身海底。然而父親已化身為深海美麗的珍珠與珊瑚；海中年輕的大自然女神為他的榮耀鳴鐘。"Onomatopoeia" 是關於水從生的水龍頭出來所造出的聲音。滔滔不絕的聲音自成一首交響樂曲。而在 Pat Mora 的詩中，音樂大師在音樂會中演奏小提琴。當他向聽眾鞠恭致意時，他憶起母親悅耳的聲音。每回聽眾鼓掌時，他聽到的不是掌聲而是在他內心深處與父母在家演奏時的樂聲。

សេចក្ដីសង្ខេប ចំណុចដែលគេយកចិត្តទុកដាក់ខ្លាំងនៅក្នុងកំណាព្យទាំងនេះគឺនៅលើប្រភេទខុសគ្នានៃភ្លេង ពិតឬស្រមើស្រមៃ ។ ក្នុងកំណាព្យ "Full Fathom Five" គេប្រាប់កូនប្រុសម្នាក់ថាឪពុករបស់វាដេកស្លាប់នៅក្រោមសមុទ្រ ។ តែឪពុកវាបានប្រែក្លាយទៅជាគុជនិងផ្កាថ្មដ៏ល្អនៅបាតសមុទ្រ និងអារក្ខទេវីសមុទ្រ ឬទេពធីតា រោទិ៍ជួងដើម្បីជាកិត្តិយសរបស់គាត់ ។ កំណាព្យ "Onomatopoeia" គឺអំពីសម្លេងដែលទឹកបង្កើតឡើងនៅពេលដែលវាហូរពីចំពួយច្រេះចាប់មួយ ។ មានខ្សែទឹកនៃសម្លេងដែលក្លាយទៅជាភ្លេងមហោរីដោយខ្លួនវា ។ នៅក្នុងកំណាព្យដោយ Pat Mora អ្នកដឹកនាំតន្ត្រីលេងវីយូឡុងនៅក្នុងការប្រគុំភ្លេង ។ នៅពេលដែលគាត់ឱនគោរពនៅមុខអ្នកស្តាប់ គាត់នឹកឃើញសម្លេងដែលធ្វើឲ្យអណ្តែអណ្តូងរបស់ម្តាយគាត់ ។ ពេលអ្នកស្តាប់ទះដៃសរសើរម្តងៗ នៅក្នុងចិត្តគាត់ៗទៅជាឮសម្លេងភ្លេងដែលគាត់និងឪពុកម្តាយគាត់លេងភ្លេងជាមួយគ្នានៅផ្ទះទៅវិញ ។

Name ______________________________ Date ______________

"Fog" by Carl Sandburg
"Life" by Naomi Long Madgett
"Loo-Wit" by Wendy Rose
"The Village Blacksmith" by Henry Wadsworth Longfellow

Summary Each of these poems makes a comparison. In "Fog," Carl Sandburg compares fog to a cat, giving fog the cat's quiet, stealth-like qualities. In "Life," Naomi Madgett shows how a watch is like a life. She demonstrates the passage of time by characterizing the watch as a lively toy used to amuse an infant. As time goes by and the end of life draws near, the watch runs down, unwinding. In "Loo-Wit," a volcano takes on the characteristics of an old woman. The land surrounding the volcano's crater, or the woman's throat, is described as patches of her skin. "The Village Blacksmith" compares life to the blacksmith's forge, where everything we do works to shape us into who we are.

Respond to Poetry When poets speak to you in their work, they do not want you merely to read or listen. They also want you to **respond**. When you respond to a poem, you consider how its ideas relate to your own life and experiences. You think about whether or not you agree with the poet's ideas. You allow the poem to inspire you to ask questions, and then you try to answer those questions.

Complete the outline below with your responses to each poem.

I. "Fog"

How I feel about the poet's ideas:

____

II. "Life"

How I feel about the poet's ideas:

____

III. "Loo-Wit"

How I feel about the poet's ideas:

____

IV. "The Village Blacksmith"

How I feel about the poet's ideas:

____

"The Village Blacksmith" by Henry Wadsworth Longfellow
"Fog" by Carl Sandburg
"Loo-Wit" by Wendy Rose
"Life" by Naomi Long Madgett

Resumen Cada uno de estos poemas ofrece una comparación. En "Fog", Carl Sandburg compara la niebla a un gato, brindando a la niebla las cualidades tranquilas y sigilosas del gato. En "Life", Naomi Madgett muestra cómo un reloj es como una vida. Demuestra el paso del tiempo caracterizando al reloj como un divertido juguete que se usa para entretener a un bebé. A medida que pasa el tiempo y se acerca el final de la vida, el reloj se para, dejando de girar. En "Loo-Wit", un volcán adquiere las características de una anciana. La tierra que rodea al cráter del volcán, o la garganta de la mujer, se describe como trozos de su piel. "The Village Blacksmith", compara la vida a la fragua del herrero, donde todo lo que hacemos nos transforma en quienes somos.

Tóm lược Mỗi bài thơ trong loạt này đều làm một sự so sánh. Bài "The Village Blacksmith" so sánh đời sống cũng tựa như cái lò của người thợ rèn, trong đó chúng ta rèn luyện để trở thành con người hiện hữu của chúng ta. Trong bài "Fog," Carl Sandburg so sánh sương mù với con mèo, gán cho sương mù đặc tính trầm lặng, len lén của mèo. Trong bài "Loo-Wit," ngọn núi lửa cũng có đặc tính như một bà già. Mảnh đất chung quanh chỗ chũng của núi, hoặc cổ họng của bà già, trông cũng như những mảnh da của bà. Trong bài "Life," Naomi Madgett cho ta thấy chiếc đồng hồ cũng giống như đời sống. Thi sĩ chứng minh sự trôi chẩy của thời gian bằng cách tả chiếc đồng hồ như một thứ đồ chơi sống động dùng để giúp vui cho con nít. Thời gian trôi qua và khi gần đến giai đoạn cuối cùng của cuộc đời, đồng hồ quay chậm lại, lò xo rãn ra.

Lub ntsiab lus Ib zaj ntawm cov paj huam no yuav los ua ib zaj pivtxwv. "The Village Blacksmith" piv neeg lub neej rau tus ntaus hlau lub qhov cub, uas puas tsav yam peb ua kom tau raws peb hais tias peb yog leeg twg. Nyob hauv "Fog," Carl Sandburg piv tus qav rau tus miv, muaj miv qhov ntsiag to rau tus qav, suab ntsiag to yog qhov tseem ceeb. Nyob hauv "Loo-Wit," lub roob hluav taws piv ib yam li tus pom laus. Cov as nyob ncig ntawm lub roob hluav taws, los yog tus poj niam lub caj pas, zoo li ab tsi npog nws daim tawv. Nyob hauv "Life," Naomi Madgett qhia hais tias lub moos zoo lis neeg lub neej. Nws hais txog lub caij nyoog, piv lub moos zoo li ib yam khoom ua si uas muaj sia rau ib tug me nyuam tau dag luag. Ib sij hawm dhau mus ces lub neej kawg los ze zus, lub moos yov nres, tsis tig lawm.

摘要 這幾首詩都做了一個比喻。"The Village Blacksmith" 把生命比喻成鐵匠的熔鐵爐，而我們的所做所為都塑造了我們的樣子。 在 "Fog"一詩中，卡爾森柏把霧比喻成貓，賦予它一股安靜而隱密的特質。在 "Loo-Wit" 中，一座火 山被比擬成一位老婦人。火山口附近的土地，或是 老婦人的喉嚨，被形容成 她小塊的皮膚。在 "Life"一詩中，奈歐米梅吉把手錶比 喻成生命。她把手錶形容成一個逗弄嬰兒的玩具，顯示了時光的流逝。等到時光飛逝而生命走到盡頭時，手錶的發條也鬆了。

សេចក្តីសង្ខេប កំណាព្យនិមួយៗនៃកំណាព្យទាំងនេះធ្វើការប្រៀបធៀប ។ កំណាព្យ "The Village Blacksmith" ប្រៀបធៀបជីវិតទៅនិងចង្ក្រានរបស់ជាងដែកជាកន្លែងដែលយើងធ្វើកិច្ចការអ្វីទាំងអស់ដើម្បីកែទ្រង់ទ្រាយរបស់យើងឲ្យទៅជារូបយើងសព្វថ្ងៃនេះ ។ ក្នុងកំណាព្យ "Fog" លោក Carl Sandburg ប្រៀបធៀបអ័ព្ទទៅនិងឆ្មាមួយដោយឲ្យអ័ព្ទមានគុណភាពស្ងាត់ស្ងៀមលាក់លៀមរបស់ឆ្មា ។ នៅក្នុងកំណាព្យ "Loo-Wit" ភ្នំភ្លើងមួយដើរតួជាស្ត្រីចាស់ម្នាក់ ។ ដីនៅជុំវិញមាត់ភ្នំភ្លើងឬបំពង់ករបស់ស្រីចាស់នោះ ត្រូវបានគេរៀបរាប់ថាជាសំណុំស្បែករបស់គាត់ ។ ក្នុងកំណាព្យ "Life" Naomi Madgett បង្ហាញពីរបៀបដែលនាឡិកាដៃដូចជីវិតរស់នៅ ។ នាងបង្ហាញពីរយៈនៃពេលវេលាដោយធ្វើលក្ខណៈរបស់នាឡិកាដៃដូចជាល្បែងលេងដែលមានជីវិតដែលគេប្រើដើម្បីលួងក្មេងតូចៗ ។ ពេលវេលាចេះតែកន្លងទៅហើយនិងចុងបញ្ចប់នៃជីវិតកាន់តែខិតចូលមកជិត នាឡិកាដើរយឺតឡើងដោយអស់ឡាន ។

Name ______________________________ Date ______________

"Popocatepetl and Ixtlaccihuatl" by Juliet Piggott

Summary This Mexican legend explains the origin of the volcanoes Popocatepetl and Ixtlaccihuatl. An aging Aztec emperor plans for his daughter, Ixtla, to succeed him as ruler. She loves the warrior Popo, but her father forbids her to marry anyone. However, when his empire is threatened by enemy tribes, he changes his mind. He decrees that Ixtla will marry the warrior who can defeat his enemies. All the warriors wish to marry the princess, but Popo is the one who defeats the enemy. After the battle, some jealous warriors run ahead to tell the emperor that Popo is dead. Hearing the news, Ixtla dies. A mournful Popo has a giant pyramid of stones built and buries Ixtla at the top. Then, from atop a second pyramid, he watches over her grave for the rest of his life.

Predict As you read a legend, you may be able to guess, or **predict**, things that will happen in the story. To make a good prediction, pay close attention to story details. Think about everything that has happened so far in the legend. Think what you have learned about the characters so far. By doing so, you will be better able to predict what characters may do next or what may happen to them.

As you read "Popocatepetl and Ixtlaccihuatl," make predictions about future events. Tell why you think each event will occur. Then, once you finish the story, record what actually happens.

My Prediction:

____

Why It May Happen:

____

What Actually Happens:

____

My Prediction:

____

Why It May Happen:

____

What Actually Happens:

____

My Prediction:

____

Why It May Happen:

____

What Actually Happens:

____

"Popocatepetl and Ixtlaccihuatl"
by Juliet Piggott

Resumen Esta leyenda mexicana explica el origen de los volcanes Popocatepetl e Ixtlaccihuatl. Un anciano emperador azteca tiene planeado que su hija, Ixtla, le suceda en el poder. Ella ama al guerrero Popo pero su padre le prohíbe casarse con nadie. Sin embargo, cuando su imperio se ve amenazado por tribus enemigas, cambia de parecer. Decreta que Ixtla ha de casarse con el guerrero que logre derrotar a sus enemigos. Todos los guerreros desean casarse con la princesa, pero es Popo quien derrota al ejército. Después de la batalla, algunos guerreros celosos se adelantan para decirle al emperador que Popo ha muerto. Al oír la noticia, Ixtla se muere. El apesadumbrado Popo hace construir con piedras una pirámide gigantesca y entierra a Ixtla en la cumbre. Desde la cima de una segunda pirámide, dedica el resto de su vida a vigilar su tumba.

Tóm Lược Câu chuyện thần thoại Mễ Tây Cơ giải thích nguồn gốc của hai ngọn núi lửa Popocatepetl và Ixtlaccihuatl. Một ông hoàng Aztec đã già muốn nhường ngôi lại cho con gái, Ixtla. Nàng yêu chiến sĩ Popo, nhưng cha nàng cấm không cho lấy ai. Tuy nhiên, khi vương quốc của ông bị các bộ lạc khác đe dọa, ông thay đổi ý kiến. Ông phán rằng Ixtla sẽ được gã cho chiến sĩ nào đánh bại quân giặc. Tất cả các chiến sĩ đều muốn cưới công chúa, nhưng Popo là người đánh bại được quân giặc. Sau trận chiến, vài chiến sĩ ganh tỵ chạy về trước báo cho ông hoàng hay rằng Popo đã chết. Nghe được tin này, công chúa Ixtla cũng chết theo. Chàng Popo đau khổ xây một kim tự tháp khổng lồ bằng đá để chôn Ixtla trên đỉnh. Sau đó từ đỉnh kim tự tháp thứ nhì, chàng nhìn qua mộ nàng cho đến hết cuộc đời chàng.

Lub ntsiab lus Zaj Mexican lus ntsuag thaum ub no qhia txog ntawm lub roob hluav taws (volcanoes) Popocatepetl thiab Ixtlaccihuatl. Ib tug huab tais laus hu uas Aztec npaj tseg kom nws tus ntxhais Ixtla, los tuav nws qhov chaw ua huab tais. Tus ntxhais hlub tus tub rog Popo tab sis nws txiv tsis pub nws yuav leejtwg li. Tabsis thaum nws lub tebchaws raug yeeb ncuab tuaj thab plaub, nws pauv nws lub siab. Nws tshaj tawm tias Ixtl yuav tau yuav tus tub tua rog uas tawm tsa yeej nws tus yeeb ncuab. Tag nrho cov tub rog xav yuav tus ntxhais huab tais, tabsis Popo yog tus uas tua yeej cov yeej ncuab. Tom qab ntawm chav tua rog, ib tug txiv neeg uas khib heev mus ua ntej mus qhia tus huab tais tias Popo tuag lawm. Thaum hnov li no, Ixtla thiaj li tuag. Popo quaj thiab ua ib lub tsev loj loj siab siab uas xuas pob zeb ua thiab muab Ixtla pw rau saud. Ces ntsia saum ib theem tsev ntxiv, nws ntsia ntsoov lub ntxa mus tas nws tiam neej.

摘要 這篇墨西哥傳說故事是在說明 Popocatepetl 和 Ixtlaccihuatl 火山的起源。一個年老的皇帝 Aztec 已為女兒 Ixtla 規劃好將來要繼承他的皇位。她愛上一名戰士 Popo，但她父親禁止她嫁任何人。當他的帝國遭到敵對部族的威脅時，他改變了心意並宣佈哪個戰士能擊敗敵人就把女兒 Ixtla 嫁給他。所有的戰士都希望能迎娶公主，但只有 Popo 是唯一擊敗敵人的。戰役之後，一些忌妒的戰士們跑在前頭告訴皇帝 Popo 已經死了。聽到這消息Ixtla也傷心致死。哀傷的 Popo 蓋了一座巨大的石造金字塔並將Ixtla埋在最上層。之後 Popo 從第二座金字塔上面看守她的墳墓以了結餘生。

សេចក្តីសង្ខេប រឿងព្រេងមិចសិកកាំងនេះពន្យល់ពីដើមកំណើតរបស់ភ្នំភ្លើង Popocatepetl និង Ixtlaccihuatl ។ ស្តេចចក្រពត្រ្តចាស់ម្នាក់ឈ្មោះ Aztec គ្រោងការណ៍សំរាប់បុត្រីរបស់ព្រះអង្គឈ្មោះ Ixtla ដើម្បីជួយព្រះអង្គឲ្យធ្វើជាអ្នកកាន់អំណាច ។ នាងស្នេហាអ្នកចម្បាំងឈ្មោះ Popo ប៉ុន្តែបិតានាងហាមនាងមិនឲ្យរៀបការជាមួយនរណាឡើយ ។ ទោះយ៉ាងនេះក្តី នៅពេលដែលចក្រភពរបស់ទ្រង់ទទួលការគំរាមកំហែងពីសត្រូវជាពួកកុលសម្ព័ន្ធ ទ្រង់ក៏ដូរព្រះទ័យ ។ ទ្រង់ចេញក្រិត្យថា រាជធីតា Ixtla នឹងរៀបការជាមួយអ្នកចម្បាំងណាដែលអាចយកឈ្នះលើសត្រូវបាន ។ អ្នកចម្បាំងទាំងអស់ប្រាថ្នាចង់រៀបការជាមួយរាជធីតា ប៉ុន្តែ Popo គឺជាអ្នកចម្បាំងដែលយកឈ្នះលើសត្រូវបាន ។ នៅក្រោយសង្គ្រាម អ្នកចម្បាំងដែលច្រណែនខ្លះបានរត់ទៅមុនដើម្បីទូលស្តេចចក្រពត្រថា Popo ស្លាប់ហើយ ។ គ្រាន់តែឮដំណឹងនេះភ្លាម រាជធីតា Ixtla ក៏ស្លាប់ទៅ ។ Popo ដែលកើតទុក្ខសោកសង្រេងបានឲ្យគេសង់ពៀរ៉ាមីដពីថ្មធំសម្បើមមួយដើម្បីបញ្ចុះសពនាង Ixtla នៅលើកំពូល ។ បន្ទាប់មកគាត់នៅលើកំពូលពៀរ៉ាមីដទីពីរដើម្បីសម្លឹងមើលផ្នូររបស់រាជធីតារហូតដល់គាត់អស់ជីវិត ។

Name ______________________________ Date ______________

"The People Could Fly" by Virginia Hamilton
"All Stories Are Anansi's" by Harold Courlander
"The Lion and the Statue" by Aesop
"The Fox and the Crow" by Aesop

Summary Folk tales and fables demonstrate how stories are used to explain ideas and teach lessons. In "The People Could Fly," African slaves escape plantations by floating into air and flying to freedom. "All Stories are Anansi's" tells how a clever spider gained ownership of all stories by capturing the hornets, the great python, and the leopard for the Sky God. "The Lion and the Statue" shows a lion and man arguing their strength. Readers learn that people often see things only as they want them to be. In "The Fox and the Crow," a hungry fox plays upon a crow's vanity by flattering the crow into singing. The crow opens its mouth to sing, and drops a piece of cheese right to the fox!

Recognize Storyteller's Purpose When you **recognize a storyteller's purpose,** you understand why the story was written. Some tales are told in order to entertain or amuse the audience. Others are told to inform or educate listeners. Still others are told to persuade the audience to accept an opinion, or to teach listeners a lesson about life.

For each of the selections below, identify the storyteller's purpose and tell what you learned from the story.

1. **"The People Could Fly"**
   Storyteller's purpose:
   ____
   What I learned:
   ____
2. **"All Stories are Anansi's"**
   Storyteller's purpose:
   ____
   What I learned:
   ____
3. **"The Lion and the Statue"**
   Storyteller's purpose:
   ____
   What I learned:
   ____
4. **"The Fox and the Crow"**
   Storyteller's purpose:
   ____
   What I learned:
   ____

"The People Could Fly" by Virginia Hamilton
"All Stories Are Anansi's" by Harold Courlander
"The Lion and the Statue" by Aesop
"The Fox and the Crow" by Aesop

Resumen Las fábulas y los cuentos demuestran cómo las historias se usan para explicar ideas y enseñar lecciones. En "The People Could Fly", esclavos africanos se escapan de las plantaciones flotando por el aire y volando hacia la libertad. "All Stories are Anansi's" nos dice cómo una araña muy inteligente se convirtió en dueña de todas las historias al capturar al avispón, al gran pitón y al leopardo para el Dios del Cielo. "The Lion and the Statue" muestra a un león y a un hombre comparando su fuerza. Los lectores aprenden que a menudo uno ve las cosas solamente como las quiere ver. En "The Fox and the Crow", un zorro hambriento se aprovecha de la vanidad de un cuervo al convencer al cuervo que cante. El cuervo abre la boca para cantar y deja caer un pedazo de queso en el lugar donde está el zorro.

Tóm lược Những mẩu chuyện bình dân và những chuyện ngụ ngôn cho thấy là người ta thường dùng câu chuyện để cắt nghĩa những tư tưởng của chúng ta và cũng dùng để giảng dậy. Trong "The People Could Fly," những người nô lệ Phi châu trốn khỏi các trang trại bằng cách nổi bổng lên không trung và bay tìm tự do. Bài "All Stories Are Anansi's" kể chuyện môt con nhện tinh lanh đã chiếm làm sở hữu tất cả chuyện tích bằng cách đi chiếm đoạt những con ong, một con trăn khổng lồ, và con báo đem lên cho Thượng Hoàng. Bài "The Lion and the Statue" tả sư tử và người cãi cọ xem ai khoẻ hơn. Người đọc sẽ nhận ra rằng người ta ai cũng chỉ nhìn sự vật theo ý mình muốn mà thôi. Trong bài "The Fox and the Crow," một con cáo đói lợi dụng tính khoe khoang của con quạ mà khen nó để lừa cho nó hát lên. Con quạ mở miệng để hát thì đánh rơi miếng phó mát vào ngay miệng cáo!.

Lub ntsiab lus Sawv daws cov dab neeg thiab zaj lus qhia paub hais tias dab neeg siv los qhia txuj ci thiab qhia lus cob qhia. Nyob hauv "The Peaple Could Fly," cov qhev African nyiag khiav tawm ntawm hav teb ya mus saum ntuj thiab ya mus qhov chawj thaj yeeb (freedom). "All Stories Are Anansi's" hais txog cov zaj dab neeg ntawm ib tug kab laum sab ntse uas nws txhom tau cov daiv, tus nab daj, thiab tus tsov txaij rau tus huab tais qaum ntuj. "The Lion and the Statue" hais txog ib tug tsov thiab ib tug neeg sib cav txog nkawv qhov zog loj. Cov twm ntawv kawm tau hais tias neeg tsuas xav ntsia pom yam lawv xav pom xwb. Nyob hauv "The Fox and the Crow," ib tug hma tshaib plab nws muaj tus noog dub qhov kab theeb ntxhias kom tus noog hais kwv txhiaj. Tus noog qhib qhov ncauj hais, ces nws ua ib qho cheese (cheese) poob ncaj nraim rau tus hma!

摘要 民間故事和寓言顯示人們如何拿故事來解釋觀念及傳達教訓。在"The People Could Fly"一文中，非洲奴隸在空中漂浮而逃離大農場，飛向自由。"All Stories Are Anansi's" 告訴我們一隻聰明的蜘蛛為天空之神捕捉大黃蜂、大蟒蛇和美洲豹，因此能擁有一切的故事。"The Lion and the Statue" 敘述一隻獅子和一個人爭論誰的力量比較大。讀者會發現人們對事情通常都有一廂情願的看法。在 "The Fox and the Crow" 一文中，一隻飢餓的狐狸利用烏鴉的驕傲，奉承烏鴉開口高歌。這隻烏鴉一張開嘴巴，就把嘴中的乳酪掉進狐狸的嘴裡！

សេចក្តីសង្ខេប រឿងនិទានតៗគ្នានិងរឿងល្បើកបង្ហាញពីរបៀបដែលគេប្រើរឿងដើម្បីពន្យល់អំពីគំនិតនិងបង្រៀនមេរៀន ។ នៅក្នុង "The People Could Fly" ទាសករអាហ្វ្រិកាំងភៀសខ្លួនពីចំការដំណាំធំៗដោយបណ្តែតតាមអាកាសហើយហោះទៅកាន់សេរីភាព ។ "All Stories Are Anansi's" និទានពីរបៀបពីងពាងឆ្លាតវៃមួយដែលបានទទួលសិទ្ធិជាម្ចាស់នៅគ្រប់រឿងទាំងអស់ដោយចាប់បានឃ្មុំ ពស់ថ្លាន់ធំសម្បើម ហើយនឹងខ្លាររខិនឲ្យព្រះមេឃ (Sky God) ។ "The Lion and the Statue" បង្ហាញអំពីតោនិងបុរសជជែកគ្នាអំពីកម្លាំងរបស់ពួកគេ ។ អ្នកអានដឹងថាមនុស្សតែងតែឃើញបញ្ហានានាតាមដែលពួកគេចង់បានតែប៉ុណ្ណោះ ។ នៅក្នុង "The Fox and the Crow" កញ្ជ្រោងដើរល្បិចតាមជំនោររបស់ក្អែកដោយបញ្ជោរក្អែកឲ្យច្រៀង ។ ក្អែកនោះបើកមាត់ច្រៀងហើយធ្លាក់ដុំឈីសទៅឲ្យកញ្ជ្រោង!

Name ______________________________ Date ______________

"Phaëthon, Son of Apollo" by Olivia Coolidge
"Demeter and Persephone" by Anne Terry White
"Icarus and Daedalus" by Josephine Preston Peabody

Summary These three selections relate Greek myths. In "Phaëthon, Son of Apollo," the sun god Apollo grants Phaëthon's request to drive his chariot across the sky so that the boy can prove he is Apollo's son. Phaëthon loses control, and is killed after Zeus destroys the carriage to save the earth. In "Demeter and Persephone," Persephone, daughter of the harvest goddess Demeter, is rescued from the underworld. Because she has eaten food there, Persephone can stay on earth for only eight months a year. The myth explains why nothing grows there just before spring. In "Icarus and Daedalus," Daedalus builds wings for himself and his son to escape the king. When Icarus flies too close to the sun, he dies.

Predict As you read a myth, you may be able to guess, or **predict**, things that will happen in the story. To make a good prediction, pay close attention to story details. Think about everything that has happened so far in the myth. By doing so, you will be better able to predict what will happen next.

As you read the three myths, make predictions about future events. Tell why you think each event will occur.

1. "Phaëthon, Son of Apollo"

My Prediction: ______________________________

Why It May Happen: ______________________________

____

2. "Demeter and Persephone"

My Prediction: ______________________________

Why It May Happen: ______________________________

____

3. "Icarus and Daedalus"

My Prediction: ______________________________

Why It May Happen: ______________________________

____

"Phaëthon, Son of Apollo" by Olivia Coolidge
"Demeter and Persephone" by Anne Terry White
"Icarus and Daedalus" by Josephine Preston Peabody

Resumen Estos tres textos relatan mitos griegos. En "Phaëthon, Son of Apollo," el dios sol Apollo accede al pedido de Phaëthon de conducir su carro por el cielo para que el muchacho pueda probar que es el hijo de Apollo. Phaëthon pierde el control y muere cuando Zeus destruye el carruaje para salvar a la tierra. En "Demeter and Persephone," Persephone, la hija de Demeter, la diosa de las cosechas, es rescatada del infierno. Por haber comido allí, Persephone sólo puede permanecer en la Tierra ocho meses al año. El mito explica por qué nada crece allí hasta los albores de la primavera. En "Icarus and Daedalus," Daedalus hace alas para sí y para su hijo para escaparse del rey. Icaro vuela demasiado cerca del sol y muere.

Tóm Lược Ba bài chọn lọc này liên hệ đến những chuyện truyền kỳ Ai Cập. Trong "Phaëthon, Son of Apollo", vua mặt trời Apollo chấp thuận sự yêu cầu của Phaëthon cho phép đánh xe ngựa của ông đi qua bầu trời để chàng trai chứng minh rằng chàng là con của Apollo. Phaëthon bị mất thăng bằng, và chết sau khi Zeus phá hủy chiếc xe để cứu quả đất. Trong "Demeter and Persephone", Persephone con gái của nữ thần gặt hái Demeter, được cứu từ dưới lòng đất. Vì đã dùng thực phẩm tại đó, nên Persephone chỉ có thể ở trên địa cầu tám tháng trong một năm. Truyền thuyết giải thích lý do vì sao không vật gì mọc được trước mùa xuân. Trong bài "Narcissus", nàng Echo bị chết sau khi thất bại trong việc chiếm được tình yêu của chàng đẹp trai Narcissus, là người cũng chết sau khi yêu cái bóng phản chiếu của chính mình. Trong "Icarus and Daedalus", Daedalus làm cánh cho mình và con trai trốn khỏi nhà vua. Khi Icarus bay quá gần mặt trời, cậu bị chết.

Lub ntsiab lus Peb zaj uas xaiv los saum no hais txog cov neeg Greek tej zaj uas cov laus tau hais tseg. Nyob rau "Phaëthon, Son of Apollo," tus Vajtswv uas kav lub hnub hu ua Apollo no kam ua raws li Phaëthon tej lus thov kom tso nws tsav nws lub laub cab neeg (Chariot) ncig saum ntuj es tus tub ntawv thiaj qhia tau tseg tias nws yog Appollo tus tub. Lub laub cab neeg plam ntawm Phaëthon mus thiab nws raug tua tom qab uas Zeus muab lub laub cab neeg ntawv ua puas ntsoog es nws thiaj li cawm tau lub ntiajteb. Nyob rau "Demeter and Persephone," Persephone, yog ib tug ntxhais vaj uas kav qoob loo hu ua Demeter no tus ntxhais, tau muaj neeg cawm nws hauv qab teb los. Vim tias nws tau noj mov hauv qab teb, Persephone tsuas nyob tau yim lub hli tauj ib xyoo xwb. Cov zaj dab neeg uas cov laus tau hais tseg qhia txog tias vim li cas thiaj tsis muaj dabtsis tuaj ua ntej lub caij uas nplooj ntoos hlav. Nyob rau "Icarus and Daedalus," Daedalus ua tis rau nws thiab nws tus tub kom nkawv khiav dim ntawm tus huab tais. Thaum Icarus ya ze lub hnub dhau lawm, he thiaj tau tuag.

摘要 這三篇選文都與希臘神話故事有關。在 "Phaëthon, Son of Apollo" 中，太陽神 Apollo 答應 Phaëthon 的請求讓他駕著他的馬車橫越天空以證明自己是 Apollo 的兒子。Phaëthon 失去控制，Zeus 為了拯救地球因而摧毀了馬車也殺死了 Phaëthon。在 "Demeter and Persephone" 中，收穫女神 Demeter 的女兒 Persephone 是從地獄被拯救出來的。因為她已經吃了那裡的食物，Persephone 一年只能在地上停留八個月。神話故事解釋了為什麼春天之前地上什麼也不長。在 "Icarus and Daedalus" 中，Daedalus 為他自己和兒子製造了飛行翼以便逃 離國王。當 Icarus 飛得太靠近太陽時，他死了。

សេចក្តីសង្ខេប អត្ថបទជ្រើសរើសទាំងបីនេះទាក់ទងនិងប្រពៃណីរបស់ជាតិ Greek ។ ក្នុងរឿង "Phaëthon, Son of Apollo" ព្រះអាទិត្យឈ្មោះ Apollo ប្រទានតាមសំណូមពររបស់ Phaëthon ដើម្បីបររថរបស់ទ្រង់កាត់មេឃដើម្បីឲ្យក្មេងប្រុសនោះអាចបញ្ជាក់ថាខ្លួនគេជាបុត្ររបស់ព្រះអាទិត្យ ។ Phaëthon មិនអាចបញ្ជារថបាន ហើយត្រូវស្លាប់ទៅបន្ទាប់ពី Zeus បំផ្លាញរថនោះដើម្បីសង្គ្រោះផែនដី ។ ក្នុងរឿង "Demeter and Persephone" នាង Persephone ដែលជាបុត្រីរបស់ទេពធីតាប្រមូលផលឈ្មោះ Demeter ត្រូវគេសង្គ្រោះរួចពីឋានក្រោម ។ ពីព្រោះនាងបានញាំុចំណីនៅទីនោះ Persephone អាចនៅលើផែនដីតែប្រាំបីខែក្នុងមួយឆ្នាំប៉ុណ្ណោះ ។ ប្រពៃណីចែងថាហេតុនេះហើយទើបគ្មានអ្វីដុះនៅទីនោះមុនរដូវផ្ការីកបន្តិច ។ ក្នុងរឿង "Icarus and Daedalus" នាយ Daedalus កសាងស្លាបសំរាប់ខ្លួនគាត់និងកូនប្រុសរបស់គាត់ដើម្បីភៀសខ្លួនពីស្តេច ។ ពេល Icarus ហើរទៅជិតព្រះអាទិត្យហួស គាត់ក៏ស្លាប់ទៅ ។

Answers to Part 1
Unit 1

The Cat Who Thought She Was a Dog and the Dog Who Thought He Was a Cat

p. 6 Reading Strategy Students should circle *poor farmer.*

p. 6 Vocabulary and Pronunciation Responses will vary, depending on the students' native tongues.

p. 6 Reading Strategy Students should circle *traveled from door to door, buying and selling things.*

peddler: someone who travels door to door, buying and selling things

p. 7 Vocabulary and Pronunciation Students should listen to the pronunciations of native English speakers in your area and should circle "1 syllable" or "2 syllables," whichever applies.

p. 7 Vocabulary and Pronunciation *displeased:* not pleased

disbelief: the opposite of belief

disappear: the opposite of appear

p. 7 Culture Note Responses will vary, based on student knowledge. Ask students to share their ideas.

p. 8 Vocabulary and Pronunciation Any words students circle will depend on their native languages. For example, native Spanish speakers may circle *family*, which is similar to the Spanish *familia*, and *envied*, which is similar to the Spanish *envidiado.* Students whose native languages do not use the Roman alphabet should still consider sound-alike words with similar meanings.

p. 8 Literary Analysis Possible response: The beauties of nature are more important than your own appearance; the world is more important than you.

p. 8 Literary Analysis Possible response: A person's actions toward others are more important than his or her appearance; being kind and generous is more important than how you look.

Review and Assess

1. Possible response: poor, happy, loving
2. Marianna Skiba—missing tooth; first daughter—nose too snub and broad; second daughter—chin too narrow and long; third daughter—freckles; Kot—realizes she is not a dog.
3. Jan gives back the mirror because it has disrupted the house, and he realizes it is not good to spend so much time looking at one's self.
4. The following words help readers understand the meaning of the word *trinket:* jewelry and kerchiefs
5. *glimpse:* a quick look
6. Students should check the first, fourth, and fifth sentences.

Two Kinds

p. 13 Culture Note Responses will vary, depending on the students' experiences.

p. 13 Reading Strategy Students should circle *super, talent,* and *ed.*•

Possible completed sentence: A *supertalented* child is a child with more than normal talent.

p. 13 Vocabulary and Pronunciation Responses will vary, depending on the students' native tongues.

p. 14 Vocabulary and Pronunciation Students should circle *when* and *why.*

p. 14 English Language Development Students should correct the first sentence to "I only ask you to be your best" or "I only ask that you be your best." They should correct the other to "Do you think (that) I want you to be a genius?"

p. 14 Vocabulary and Pronunciation Students should say the word and then write the meaning.

Possible meaning: bass: the lower sounds of music or singing

p. 15 Reading Strategy Students should circle *un* and *able*.

un-: not ; *-able:* able

p. 15 Vocabulary and Pronunciation Students should circle *scale, cat,* and *cans*.

p. 15 Vocabulary and Pronunciation Students should circle the *ph*.

p. 15 English Language Development Students should circle *worser* and cross out the *r* to make it *worse*.

p. 16 Culture Note Responses will vary, depending on the customs of students' native lands.

p. 16 Culture Note Responses will vary, depending on the students' native tongues.

p. 16 Vocabulary and Pronunciation Students should circle *stomach*.

p. 17 English Language Development Students should circle *stronger*.

p. 17 English Language Development Students should circle both sets of quotation marks in the mother's remarks and both sets in Jing-mei's remarks, for a total of eight sets of quotation marks.

The author shows a change of speaker by indenting and sometimes also by using explanations (dialogue tags) such as "she shouted in Chinese" and "I shouted."

p. 17 Literary Analysis Students should circle *I wanted to see it spill over.* They should also circle *anger.*

p. 18 Reading Check Students should number four things that Jing-mei does that disappoint her mother: (1) She does not get straight A's or (2) become class president. (3) She does not get accepted to Stanford University. (4) She even drops out of college.

p. 18 Reading Strategy Students should put a line between *forgive* and *ness*.

Possible meaning: the act or state of forgiving

p. 18 Vocabulary and Pronunciation The correct answer is *C*. Students should circle *notes* and *played*.

Review and Assess

1. Students should circle *famous* and *herself*.
2. Kind 1: those who are obedient

   Kind 2: those who follow their own mind
3. She is both an obedient daughter who wants love and approval and an independent daughter who has gone her own way.
4. *unlike:* not similar to

   childish: like a young person

   childhood: state or condition of acting like a young person
5. Possible motives for pushing Jing-mei to be famous: hope, pride, love

   Possible motives for arranging the talent show: pride, competitive spirit

   Possible motives for offering the piano: love, forgiveness

   Possible motives for agreeing to take piano lessons: desire for attention, respect for mother, need to please mother, need to gain approval

   Possible motives for refusing to take more lessons: shame, fear, need for independence

   Possible motives for saying hurtful words: anger, shame, desire to win the battle and end the piano lessons

My Furthest-Back Person (The Inspiration for *Roots*)

p. 23 English Language Development A *sixteen-year-old* African; a *British-held* fort.

p. 23 Culture Note The census just after the Civil War was taken in 1870.

p. 23 Reading Strategy Students might put a line after the first comma, the second comma, *astonishment*, the colon, the second *Murray, well,* and *heard*. Accept reasonable variations: for example, some students may not put a line after *heard*. Students should circle C, Haley's great-grandparents.

p. 24 English Language Development Students should circle *didn't* and *hadn't* and change them to *did not* and *had not*.

p. 24 English Language Development Students should add a *d* in each *an'* to make *and*, a *g* in *choppin'* to make *chopping*, and an *h* in *'im* to make *him*.

p. 25 Vocabulary and Pronunciation Students should say *Kamby* with the same /*a*/ sound that they use for the first /*a*/ in *Gambia*. Most students will circle *yes*.

p. 25 Stop to Reflect The correct answer is *D*; he said he has to get to the Gambia River, and the paragraph before said the Gambia River flows near the old kingdom of Mali in Africa.

p. 25 Reading Strategy Students might put a line after *something, fantasized* (or after the dash), *country*, the first comma, and the second comma. Accept reasonable variations.

Students should circle *very old men* and *who could tell centuries of the histories of certain very old family clans.* Accept reasonable variations.

A *griot* is a very old African man who can tell centuries of the histories of certain very old African family clans.

p. 26 Vocabulary and Pronunciation In this context, a *bank* is the side of a river.

Students should circle two of the following words: *upriver, left, ashore.*

p. 26 Culture Note Kunta Kinte was about 16 years old.

p. 26 Literary Analysis In the text, students might circle *sob, bawling*, and *weeping.*

In the margin, students should circle *joy.* Haley is proud to have made this journey and made a critical connection to his own history.

p. 27 English Language Development Students should circle *teeth*, and write its singular form: tooth.

p. 28 English Language Development Students' answers will vary based on their native language.

p. 28 Literary Analysis Students should circle *cargo, choice*, and *healthy*. Also accept *Gambia, Africa*, and/or *slaves* if students can explain these answers adequately.

Review and Assess

1. Kunta Kinte was an African who was the first person in Alex Haley's family to come to America.
2. He was kidnapped near the Gambia River, shipped to Annapolis, Maryland, and sold into slavery.
3. Students should include at least five details of information.

   details of grandmother's story (African said his name was *Kin-tay*, banjo was *ko*, river was *Kamby Bolong*; *Kin-tay* chopping wood for a drum when kidnapped)—Cousin Georgia—Kansas City, Kansas

   language sounds like Mandinka; *ko* is *kora*, an old African stringed instrument; *Kamby Bolong* is likely Gambia River—Dr. Jan Vansina—Wisconsin

   Kin-tay is pronunciation of *Kinte*, clan name going back to old kingdom of Mali—Dr. Philip Curtin—Wisconsin (on phone to Dr. Vansina)

   Griots in back country tell Kinte family history; family villages of Kintes include Kinte-Kundah and Kinte-Kundah Janneh-Ya—Gambians in capital—Gambia (Africa)

   Kinte clan began in Old Mali; one member, Kairaba Kunta Kinte, settled in Juffure in Gambia; his youngest son, Omoro, wed Binta Kebba; they had 4 sons; eldest, Kunta Kinte, disappeared soon after the king's soldiers came, when he was 16 and had gone to chop wood for a drum—Kebba Kanga Fofana (griot)—Juffure, Gambia

   Col. O'Hare's Forces (British "king's soldiers") sent to James Fort in Gambia mid-1967—government records—Britain

   Lord Ligonier under Capt. Thomas Davies sailed on the Sabbath, July 5, 1767, from Gambia River to Annapolis; cargo included 3265 elephants' teeth, 800 pounds of cotton, 32 oz. Gambian gold, 140 slaves—British shipping records—Britain

   Lord Ligonier arrived in Annapolis Sept. 29, 1767; only 98 slaves survived—Annapolis Historical Society—Annapolis, Maryland

   sale of slaves from Gambia River, Africa, announced—microfilm copy of *Maryland Gazette*, Oct. 1, 1767, p. 2—Annapolis, Maryland
4. Students might draw a line after *upriver*, the first comma, *ashore*, and the second comma. Accept reasonable alternatives; for example, students might include a comma after the first *village*.

   The travelers left their boat in Albreda.

   Juffure was the village where the *griot* lived.
5. Possible responses: They are about his own family. They prove his grandmother's stories, which fascinated him as a boy. They are a source of pride to him as an

African American. They reflect the origins of so many African American families. They show the pain and suffering of slavery.

A Day's Wait

p. 33 Vocabulary and Pronunciation Students should circle *headache.*

p. 33 Vocabulary and Pronunciation Students should circle *downstairs* and put a line between *down* and *stairs.* *Downstairs:* down the stairs; on a lower floor of the house

p. 33 Vocabulary and Pronunciation *Advertisement:* ad; *bicycle:* bike

p. 34 English Language Development Students should circle "past tense of *lie,* meaning 'to be resting.'"

p. 34 Culture Note Responses will vary, depending on the students' native tongues.

p. 34 Vocabulary and Pronunciation Responses will vary, depending on the students' native tongues. For example, Spanish speakers may list *medicina* and médico for *-med-; escribir* and *inscribir* for *-scrib-/-scrip-;* and *visibilidad* and vision for *-vid-/-vis-.*

p. 35 Literary Analysis Students should circle *he asks whether taking the medicine will do any good* and *isn't taking it easy.* Accept all reasonable internal conflicts. Possible response: Schatz's inner struggle seems to be between his desire to face his illness bravely and his fear and worry about what will happen to him.

p. 35 Vocabulary and Pronunciation The correct answer is relax. Students should use the context of the conversation: *temperature is all right* and *nothing to worry about.*

p. 36 Culture Note Answers will vary. Students should support their opinion.

Review and Assess

1. The correct answer is *C.*
2. Students' wordings will vary. On the thermometers used in France, no one can live with a temperature of 44 degrees. So when Schatz heard the doctor say that his temperature is 102 degrees, he thinks he is sure to die.
3. Possible response: loving, patient, sympathetic, rugged
4. Schatz is (A) scared and (B) worried, BUT he tries to be (C) brave and (D) unselfish. Students may flip the order of *A* and *B* and/or the order of *C* and *D.*

   Possible examples of (A) and (B): Schatz is white faced; there are dark circles under his eyes; he is very stiff and tense; he seems detached and has trouble paying attention to his father's reading; he is evidently holding tightly onto his emotions; the next day he cries.

   Possible examples of (C) and (D): Schatz does not express his fears and holds tightly onto his emotions; he says he'd rather stay awake (i.e., to face death); even though it would be a comfort to have someone with him at this scary time, he tells father to leave because he knows it might bother the father to see his son die and orders people out of the room so that they don't catch the illness.
5. *evidently:* easily seen; clearly
   prescribed: ordered in writing; written in advance
   detached: unconnected

Was Tarzan a Three Bandage Man?

p. 41 Reading Strategy The correct answer is *A.*

Students might circle some or all of the following: *pigeon-toed walker, walked pigeon-toed,* and *a painful form of . . .*

p. 41 English Language Development Students should circle *fastest* and *faster.* They should label *fastest* superlative and *faster* comparative.

The comparative form compares how Robinson runs now with how he would run if he didn't walk like that.

p. 42 Culture Note Responses will vary, depending on the popular sports in students' native lands.

p. 42 Reading Strategy *emulate:* to admire and imitate

Students might circle [Bill and his friends] *wear a Band-Aid* and/or *the Band-Aid is just for show. . . .*

p. 42 Vocabulary and Pronunciation Students should correct *nuthin'* to *nothing*, *kinda* to *kind of*, *coverin'* to *covering*, and *somethin'* to *something*. Some students may omit correction of kinda and coverin', the two terms already explained in the note.

p. 43 Reading Check The correct answer is *A*.

p. 43 Reading Check The correct answer is *B*. She will have the father make him need not a mere bandage but far more serious stitches for his wounds.

p. 43 English Language Development Students should circle *wouldn't* (or just the *n't* part) and *no*. They might correct the sentence to "I wouldn't want to mess with a (*or* any) two-bandage man."

p. 43 Literary Analysis Students should circle *Our hero worshipping was backwards*.

Review and Assess

1. Possible response: Bill and his friends admire the sports stars and want to be like them. Imitating the sports stars is a fad of sorts and is considered "tough" and "cool" among the boys' peers.
2. T: The mother thinks Bill's behavior is silly.

   F: The mother is a friend of Jackie Robinson's mother.

   F: The mother thinks Bill's feet will fall off.

   T: The mother has a good sense of humor.

   F: The mother knows the names of all the popular sports heroes.
3. Suggested responses: Wearing the bandages does not really make anyone good at fighting. He is confusing the boys imitating the boxers with the actual boxers. He is confusing looking tough with being tough.
4. Suggested responses: Was the movie hero Tarzan tough and cool? Is the movie hero Tarzan worthy of imitation too?
5. Students should circle *a skin condition*.
6. *Purpose: to tell a funny, interesting story;* Possible examples: the boys imitating Jackie Robinson's pigeon-toed walk; the mother's remark, "He'd be faster if he didn't walk like that"; Bill imitating Buddy Helm's bowlegged walk; the boys wearing bandages to look like boxers; and so on.

   Purpose: to describe something important to him; Possible examples: Cosby indicating these athletes were "shining heroes" to him as a boy; showcasing his mother's wit or sense of humor; talking about what he did with his close friends of childhood (Fat Albert and the others).

   Purpose: to make a point about life or people's behavior; Possible examples: "Then, athletes were sports stars even before they started to incorporate themselves"; "Our hero worshipping was backwards."

Unit 2

In Search of Our Mother's Gardens

p. 48 Vocabulary and Pronunciation Students should circle *sunup* and draw a line between *sun* and *up*. *Sunup* means "the time that the sun rises; sunrise; or dawn."

p. 48 Reading Strategy Students should circle A.

p. 48 Reading Check C.

p. 49 Culture Note Answers will vary according to each student's country of origin. If students do not know the capital city of their native country, encourage them to use an encyclopedia or other reference source to find out.

p. 49 English Language Development Students should circle *plainly*. *Plainly* means "clearly."

p. 50 Vocabulary and Pronunciation Students may circle *bulbs* or *prune*. *Bulbs* commonly refers to objects used to generate electric light. (Light bulbs and planting bulbs share a similar shape.) *Prune* commonly refers to a fruit.

p. 50 Reading Strategy Answers will vary according to each student's country of origin.

p. 51 Reading Strategy B. *Intruded* means "interrupted." Students may say that the meaning of the root *-trud-* suggests that being intruded upon is like being pushed.

p. 51 Vocabulary and Pronunciation Students should circle all the *ls* in *literally*.

Review and Assess

1. She thinks they owe their creative spirit to the women who have lived before them.
2. Students should check *She and her husband worked hard . . .* and *No matter how plain their house. . . .*
3. The correct answer is *B*.
4. The correct answer is *D*.
5. Students may list: her mother's perseverance in planting a garden wherever she lived; her strength in caring for it; her ability to make it beautiful; and her ability to work hard for her family.
6. *-liter-: literate*/able to read; *literacy*/ability to read.

   -nym-: synonyms/ words that mean the same thing; *antonyms*/words that have opposite meanings.

   -magni-; magnify/to enlarge; *magnificent*/large in beauty, wonder or power.

Seventh Grade

p. 56 Culture Note Most students will say it is easier to study their native language because they begin with a stronger foundation. However, some students may note that the grammar and vocabulary of even a native language may be complex to learn.

p. 56 English Language Development They are going to study French. He is going to visit France one day.

p. 57 English Language Development Students should mark the dialogue as follows:

Michael: What classes . . ;
Victor: French . . . ; Michael: Spanish . . ;
Victor: I'm not . . . .

p. 57 Vocabulary and Pronunciation Students should circle the *l* in *calmly* and pronounce the word as *KAHM lee.*

p. 57 Reading Strategy Students may say *on the sly* means "sneakily." Students should circle catch her eye, on page 57. *Catch her eye* means "to get her attention by getting her to look at him."

p. 58 Literary Analysis Possible response: Students may like Victor because he is trying his best, but is not able to be as smooth as he wants.

p. 58 Vocabulary and Pronunciation *Crush* can mean to break or to reduce in size.

p. 59 Culture Note Students should circle *wewe*. Students answers will vary based on their native language.

p. 59 English Language Development Accept any answers that would help a students remember the spelling of the word. Some students may decide that the silent *g* in sign is like a silent stop sign.

p. 60 Stop to Reflect Teresa might be able to help Victor in Math. Possible response: They may become friends.

p. 60 Culture Note Students' answers will vary based on their native language.

p. 60 Vocabulary and Pronunciation Students should circle the letter *t*.

Review and Assess

1. Victor signs up for French because Teresa was taking French, too.

   Victor is slow to leave homeroom because Teresa was still there, talking to the teacher.

   Victor goes outside during lunch because he thinks Teresa is eating outside.

   Victor pretends to know French to impress Teresa.

   Victor gets French books at the library because he wants to learn French so Teresa won't discover he does not speak the language.
2. Possible responses: Victor is embarrassed when he tries scowling. Victor is embarrassed when he says "Teresa" is a noun. Victor is embarrassed when he pretends to speak French.
3. Possible responses: Seventh grade is a time of fun, anxiety, uncertainty, or of a blooming interest in girls/boys, or of feeling self-conscious.
4. Possible responses: Amused: the incident of scowling; the boy's language when he tries to speak French. Understanding; the French teacher is kind to Victor; some of

Victor's embarrassed, self-conscious feelings.

5. *Making a face* means moving the features on your face to show an expression.

   Catch her eye means "to get her attention by getting her to look."

Melting Pot

p. 65 Literary Analysis For personal experiences, students may circle *my children* or *her mother was raised as an American.* For personal feelings, students may circle *isn't surprised.* For informal language students may circle *the parents don't speak perfect English.*

p. 65 Culture Note Possible responses: Good point: Children will be better prepared to interact with members of the community. Bad point: Children will not have the opportunity or skills to speak with the relatives in their native country. Children will lose the chance to be bilingual.

p. 66 English Language Development *Moneyed* probably means "wealthy."

p. 66 Vocabulary and Pronunciation Students should circle *though* and *neighborhood.*

p. 67 Vocabulary and Pronunciation *Panes* means sheets of glass. *Pains* means aches. Students should circle *one* and *great.*

p. 67 Stop to Reflect Because she is "one of them."

p. 68 Reading Check Students should mark *calamari* with *A.* Students should mark *sushi* with *B.* Students should mark *bait* with *C.*

p. 68 Reading Strategy 1. described in a very general way; 2. a very tense place; 3. two things that don't mix easily.

p. 68 Literary Analysis Yes, she is happy. Students should write the sentence *I am one of them, and one of us.*

Review and Assess

1. People who call America a melting pot mean that the country's values and traditions are generated by the mixing of many different groups. No one culture retains its values—instead a new set of values and traditions comes from the mixing of cultures.
2. Students should check *It is most like a melting pot when people deal with each other person-to-person.*
3. Students should identify these conflicts: old-timers vs. young professionals; old immigrants vs. new immigrants.
4. Anna Quindlen is a young professional because she has a career and small children. She is an old-timer because she has lived in the community for a long time. She is an old immigrant because her grandparents immigrated to America.
5. *Taking over* means "taking control."
6. Possible response: Personal experience: Quindlen describes what it was like when she moved on to the block eight years earlier.

   Personal feelings: Quindlen defends her neighborhood.

   Informal language: half a dozen elderly men; I like you.

   Humor: The antiques store used to be a butcher shop.

The Hummingbird that Lived Through Winter

p. 73 Culture Note Possible responses: Good point: They will feel comfortable among people who share customs and language. Bad point: They may not learn the new language or customs.

p. 73 Vocabulary and Pronunciation Students should circle *eighty.*

p. 73 Vocabulary and Pronunciation The correct answer is *B. The dead of winter* is the time when nothing grows because it is so cold.

p. 74 Reading Check Many students may say this is a good enough description. Others may say that the description does not include the color of the bird.

p. 74 English Language Development The present participle of the verb *lie* is *lying.*

p. 74 Literary Analysis Students should circle *wonderful, suspended,* and *most alive.* Student should draw boxes around *helpless* and *pathetic.* The correct answer is *D.*

p. 75 Literary Analysis Students may circle *signs of fresh life;* the *warmth of the room; the vapor . . . ;* or *the change.*

p. 75 Reading Strategy Students should draw a line between *rest* and *less. Restless* means without resting, or without being able to rest.

p. 76 Think Ahead Students may predict that he will live because he is shown such care.

p. 76 English Language Development Students may circle *swiftly* or *gently.* The adjective *swift* is changed to *swiftly* with the addition of *-ly.* The adjective *gentle* is changed to *gently* by dropping the *e* and adding *-ly. Swiftly* means "quickly." *Gently* means "with care."

Review and Assess

1. Possible responses: 1. Dikran blows warm air on the bird. 2. He feeds it honey. 3. They let the bird go.
2. Possible response: Students may say that Dikran knows it is better for a bird to be free than for it to be house bound.
3. Students should place a check before the following statements: *He can barely see; He loves and respects nature; He respects the freedom of living things.*
4. Students should place a check before the following statements. Each statement is followed by an appropriate explanation. *Hope or renewal/* He lives through winter. *The fragile or delicate nature of life:* The tiny bird could have died. The beauty and wonder of nature: *His recovery is amazing; the birds in spring are beautiful.*
5. Hummingbird: a bird that hums. Helpless: Without being able to help. Heartbreaking: Something that breaks a heart; something that is painfully sad.

Unit 3

The Third Wish

p. 81 Reading Strategy (a) untangle. Students should circle *trying* and *entangled.*

p. 81 Culture Note Answers may vary, but students should describe the creatures and their powers.

p. 81 Literary Analysis Possible response: Mr. Peters expects three wishes because he knows the pattern of older fairy tales. Characters usually do not know what to expect.

p. 82 English Language Development Students should write *elves* and *halves.*

p. 82 Reading Check Students should circle the words *a little lonely* and *had no companion.*

p. 82 Vocabulary and Pronunciation Students should circle the *gh* combination in *thought* and label it as *silent.* Students should also circle the *gh* combination in *laughing* and label it as *f.*

p. 82 Literary Analysis He gets his wish. He gets a wife almost instantly.

p. 83 Stop to Reflect Possible response: She may really be a swan.

p. 83 Literary Analysis (d) He knows what happens in fairy tales.

p. 83 Vocabulary and Pronunciation Students should circle *rhymes with fears.*

p. 84 Vocabulary and Pronunciation It means clothing.

p. 84 Read Fluently Possible response: Rhea is her swan-sister.

p. 84 English Language Development Students should circle the question marks after the words *do you,* after *the last,* after *a swan,* and after *a girl.*

p. 85 Vocabulary and Pronunciation Students should circle the *w* in *two.*

p. 85 Literary Analysis Students should circle *no.* Students should circle the last sentence that describes Mr. Peters holding the withered leaf.

Review and Assess

1. He rescues a swan tangled in the weeds.
2. (b) He seems fed up with granting wishes and makes fun of human beings.
3. Possible response: His third wish was to be together in spirit with his wife. He knew she was still his companion.

4. Students should check *We are never comfortable . . . , Love sometimes means letting go . . . , What we wish for . . .* and *There are many different . . .*
5. In the first column students should list *three wishes; animals transforming;* and *unexpected outcomes.* In the second column students should list a *car; radio;* and *the offer of a trip around the world.*
6. (c) dark; (d) the side of a road or waterway.

The Charge of the Light Brigade

p. 90 Literary Analysis (a) the sound of horses' hooves.

p. 90 English Language Development Students should circle *Forward, the Light Brigade! Charge for the guns!* Quotation marks show these words are being spoken. Students should circle *A.*

p. 90 Stop to Reflect (d) Good soldiers do not question orders.

p. 91 Reading Check Students should answer *yes.* Students should circle *All that was left of them, Left of six hundred.*

p. 91 Vocabulary and Pronunciation In line 30 students should label *charge* with an *n* for noun. In the title, students should also label *charge* with an *n* for noun. In line 6 students should label *charge* with a *v* for verb. In line 32 students should label *charge* with an *n* for noun.

Review and Assess

1. Students should check *They are riding . . . They are lightly armed . . . They are attacking.*
2. (a) They go forward bravely without question.
3. Many of the soldiers are killed.
4. (b) He is proud of their bravery.
5. On the first line students should write *cannon; them.* On the second line students should write *trapped.* On the third line students should write *battle.*
6. Fired on as frequently as rain drops in a storm.

The Californian's Tale

p. 96 Vocabulary and Pronunciation Students should circle *horn* and *strike.* Students should define *horn* as *a device used to make a loud noise,* and *strike* as *to hit.*

p. 97 Literary Analysis People were invited in and made welcome. Students should circle the last sentence of the paragraph.

p. 97 Vocabulary and Pronunciation A stand for washing. It holds a tub or sink or container for water.

p. 98 English Language Development Students should circle *seemed* and label it *reg.* In the next sentence students should circle *drank* and *was* and label them *irreg.*

p. 98 English Language Development Students should circle *She'll.* Students should write the words *She will* on the line.

p. 98 Read Fluently Possible response: He may be lonely.

p. 99 Stop to Reflect Student should write *No.* Possible Response: He may be embarrassed.

p. 99 Vocabulary and Pronunciation Students might circle *gaity, Henry,* and *she.*

p. 100 Literary Analysis very; extremely.

p. 100 Vocabulary and Pronunciation Students should circle *fiddle, banjo,* and *clarinet.*

p. 101 Literary Analysis Students should circle *clarinet, rattling dance-music,* and *big boots.*

p. 101 English Language Development Students should circle *gentlemen,* and write the singular form *gentleman.*

p. 101 Reading Strategy (a) Henry lost his mind when he lost his wife, and he gets worse on the anniversary of that loss. His friends play along to try to help him get through it.

p. 102 Stop to Reflect (d) all of the above

Review and Assess

1. (d) It is pretty and shows a woman's touch.
2. Students should write a *T* in front of *Henry talks about . . . , Henry lost his wife . . . , Henry's wife was well liked . . . , and Henry's wife was an educated woman . . .* Students should write an *F* in front of *Henry's wife was an orphan* and *Henry's wife knew little about . . .*
3. The miners pretend she is coming home to help Henry through this rough time of the year.
4. (a) It could be lonely but those who were there were often kind and friendly.
5. On the first line students should write *friendly; folksy.* On the second line the student should write *colorful; descriptive.* On the third line the student should write *rural; homey.* On the forth line the student should write *gathering together; playing musical instruments.*
6. Thirty-five years ago I panned for gold but I never found any.

Four Skinny Trees

p. 107 Reading Check (a) thin and scrawny. Students should circle *skinny* and *pointy.*

p. 107 Vocabulary and Pronunciation (a) stay; endure; refuse to give up

p. 108 Reading Strategy (c) alone in a difficult world

Review and Assess

1. Both the speaker and the trees are skinny.
2. The speaker and the trees grow up in a poor city neighborhood.
3. Students should put a check in front of *strength, hope,* and *pride.*
4. For the first sentence students might write *Children do not belong in ghettos but often are raised there.* For the second sentence students might write *Individual strengths are often hidden.* For the third sentence students might write *Inner strength helps us reach high goals.*
5. Students should circle *(a) roots* and *(b) the trees' branches*

Unit 4

The Night the Bed Fell

p. 133 Vocabulary and Pronunciation unhappy; unfriendly; unknown.

p. 133 Vocabulary and Pronunciation out of your mind: not in a good state of mind; out of practice: not used to something

p. 113 Literary Analysis Students should circle *He thinks he needs to wake up every hour. Otherwise, he might suffocate to death.*

p. 114 Reading Strategy Students should explain why they do or do not think it is significant.

p. 114 Vocabulary and Pronunciation Students should circle *tiptoe.*

p. 114 Reading Check Top Floor Attic: Mr. Thurber; Next Room: James and Briggs; In Hall: Rex, the dog; Across the Hall: Roy; Floor Below Attic: Mrs. Thurber and Herman

p. 115 Reading Strategy Students should explain what they think might happen. Yes. It is a significant event. It starts the whole chain of events.

p. 115 English Language Development Students should circle *sniffing* and *himself.*

p. 115 Literary Analysis Students should circle *Gugh.*

p. 116 Vocabulary and Pronunciation Possible answers: write, wrong.

p. 116 Literary Analysis Students should circle the following: *He thinks the house is on fire; mother thinks he is trapped under his bed; "He's dying!" . . . I'm all right!, Briggs yelled.*

p. 116 English Language Development Students should circle *father.*

p. 116 Stop to Reflect Students should explain why they do or do not think it is funny.

Review and Assess

1. The correct answer is (a).
2. He does these things because he is afraid he will stop breathing at night.
3. Mother: She thinks her husband is trapped under the bed. Cousin Briggs: He

thinks he is suffocating and everyone is trying to save him. Rex the Dog: He jumps on Briggs, thinking he is the culprit.

4. He probably exaggerated Briggs' fear of suffocation. The story of his Aunt Sarah leaving money for burglars outside her house might be an exaggeration. The story about his Aunt Gracie is probably an exaggeration when he says she piled shoes "about her house." The story of the dog jumping on Briggs might also be an exaggeration.
5. Students should check the following: The father goes up to the attic to sleep; Young James Thurber's cot collapses; The mother fears the attic bed fell and hurt or killed the father; Brother Herman yells to try to calm mother; Cousin Briggs pours camphor all over himself; Rex attacks Briggs; The father thinks the house is on fire and comes downstairs. Students should circle *Young James Thurber's cot collapses* as the event that causes all of the confusion.

All Summer in A Day

p. 121 English Language Development Students should circle the question marks and put a box around the exclamation mark.

p. 121 Literary Analysis Students should circle the following: *Venus has known nothing but rain.*

p. 121 Reading Check They're the children of the men and women who came to Venus from Earth to set up a space colony.

p. 122 Vocabulary and Pronunciation Possible answers: our, sour, tower, power

p. 122 Reading Strategy Margot: quiet and shy; William: bold and mean

p. 122 English Language Development Students should circle *drenched* and draw an arrow to *windows* from *drenched.*

p. 123 Reading Strategy Students should circle the following contrasts: *[Margot has] lived on Venus for only five years. Before that, she lived on Earth./The rest of the children have lived all of their lives on Venus. She remembers the sun./Because they were only two when they saw the sun, they don't remember it.* Possible answer: Margot's past experience might be considered a "crime" to the others because she is able to remember something they wish they could remember. They are probably jealous.

p. 123 English Language Development die and dying.

p. 123 Reading Strategy Students should circle the following: *Margot's parents are thinking of moving back to earth.* This probably makes the children hate her because they are jealous.

p. 123 Reading Check Margot came to Venus five years ago, when she was four. She came from Earth.

p. 124 Reading Strategy Students should circle the following words: *protesting, pleading,* and *crying.* The other children are mean.

p. 124 English Language Development Not able to be believed.

p. 124 Culture Note Students should name a similar game.

p. 125 Vocabulary and Pronunciation calm: the *l* is silent; climb: the *m* is silent; island: the *s* is silent; overwhelm: the *h* is silent.

p. 125 Vocabulary and Pronunciation The first *g* is soft and the second *g* is hard.

p. 126 Stop to Reflect Students will probably say that she will feel very angry and sad.

Review and Assess

1. For seven years, it has rained constantly.
2. She is from Earth and remembers the sun; are mean to her; regret.
3. The correct answer is (b).
4. Students should check the following: Children can be mean to one another; Outsiders are often treated badly; If you are mean, you may regret it later.
5. 1. "Sometimes there were light showers; sometimes there were heavy storms; but always there was rain." 2. "She doesn't play games with the other children in the echoing tunnels of their underground city." 3. "It was the color of flaming bronze and it was very large. And the sky around it was a blazing blue tile color."

6. *Similarities:* Margot and her classmates 1. live on Venus 2. are nine years old 3. are eager to see the sun
Differences: 1. Margot remembers the sun. Her classmates do not remember the sun. 2. She has been living on Venus for only five years. Her classmates have been living on Venus their entire lives. 3. Margot did not get to see the sun because she was locked away in a closet. Her classmates went out and played in the sun.

The Highwayman

p. 131 Vocabulary and Pronunciation It is the light that shines from the moon.

p. 131 Stop to Reflect Students should circle (a). The details that point to the answer are *a French cocked-hat, a bunch of lace at his chin, a coat of claret velvet, breeches of brown doeskin,* and *a jeweled twinkle.*

p. 132 English Language Development claret-velvet coat; blood-red lips.

p. 132 Literary Analysis He's probably jealous and dislikes the highwayman. He might try to get the highwayman in trouble.

p. 132 Reading Strategy The highwayman has probably robbed someone.

p. 133 Culture Note Responses will vary, depending on students' native tongues.

p. 133 Literary Analysis Students should circle the following: *they gag Bess and tie her to her bed by the window. They tie a gun called a musket to her, with the barrel below her heart.*

p, 133 Vocabulary and Pronunciation knight: night; know: no; knew: new.

p. 133 Read Fluently The correct answer is (c).

p. 134 Literary Analysis The following words add to the suspense: *Nearer he came and nearer!; Her eyes grew wide for a moment; she drew one last deep breath.* Students might wonder if Bess will be able to let the highwayman know that the soldiers are after him.

p. 134 Literary Analysis He wants to go back to fight the soldiers because of what they did to Bess. Students should circle the following: *he spurred like a madman; with white road smoking behind him and his rapier brandished high.*

p. 134 Reading Check Bess shot herself while trying to sound off a gun shot to warn the highwayman that the soldiers were after him.

p. 135 Reading Check The correct answer is (c).

Review and Assess

1. He doesn't want anyone to see him because he is wanted by the law.
2. Highwayman: dashing, romantic, loyal; Bess: beautiful, romantic, brave, loyal; Tim: jealous.
3. The correct answer is (d).
4. The following details help build suspense: 1. Tied up and gagged, Bess desperately wants to warn her love of the danger that awaits him. 2. "The highwayman came riding/The redcoats looked to their priming." 3. "Nearer he came and nearer! Her face was like a light."
5. Tim probably told the authorities that the highwayman was at the inn because he is jealous of their love.
6. Cause: Bess pulls the trigger because she is trying to sound off a gun shot to warn the highwayman that the soldiers are waiting to get him. Effects: Bess kills herself. The highwayman hears the warning shot and rides away.

Amigo Brothers

p. 140 Vocabulary and Pronunciation Jim.

p. 140 Reading Check What: division finals; When: seventh of August, two weeks away.

p. 140 Reading Strategy The wall is probably created by the tension they feel because they have to compete against each other.

p. 141 Vocabulary and Pronunciation sis

p. 141 Literary Analysis Students should circle *Antonio nodded* and underline *Antonio.*

p. 141 Reading Check No. Students should circle *only one of us can win.*

p. 141 Vocabulary and Pronunciation gotta: got to; don'tcha: don't you

p. 142 Literary Analysis Felix: he had figured out how to psyche himself for tomorrow's fight; Antonio: Antonio was also thinking of the fight/Antonio went to sleep hearing the opening bell for the first round. The narrator is omniscient or "all knowing."

p. 142 Vocabulary and Pronunciation affect; effect

p. 142 Vocabulary and Pronunciation The correct answer is (b). The words *dressing gowns to match their trunks* helps explain the meaning.

p. 143 Culture Note about 61 kilos.

p. 143 Vocabulary and Pronunciation Students should circle *right.*

p. 143 Reading Strategy The correct answer is (c). The words *He [Felix] missed a right cross as Antonio slipped the punch and countered with one-two-three lefts that snapped Felix's head back* help you make the inference.

p. 144 English Language Development Students should circle *came* and *taught.*

p. 144 Vocabulary and Pronunciation Students should circle the *ou* in *sound* and *round.*

p. 145 Reading Check Neither boy is winning.

p. 145 Culture Note Answers will vary.

p. 145 Reading Strategy The correct answer is (d). Students should circle *No matter what the decision, they knew they would always be champions to each other.*

p. 145 Reading Check The announcer points to no one as the winner because the boys have already left the ring, arm in arm.

Review and Assess

1. The correct answer is (b).
2. How it brings them together: they worked out together and went running together. How it drives them apart: They have to compete against each other, and only one person can win.
3. Tall-A; short—F; dark—F; fair—A; boxes better when he comes in close—F; boxes more gracefully—A; has better moves as a boxer—F; keeps boring down on his opponent—F
4. Friendship is more important than winning.
5. Felix: 1. Felix knew they could not "pull their punches," or hold back when they fought 2. he had figured out how to psyche himself

   Referee: The referee was stunned by their savagery.

   Crowd: The fear soon gave way . . .
6. Antonio and Felix work very hard to fulfill their dreams about boxing; The Golden Gloves is an important tournament in the world of boxing.

Unit 5

Our Finest Hour

p. 151 Reading Check Students should circle the following words: *means sitting there in the studio and telling some stories into the camera and introducing the reports and pieces that other reporters do.* Students should circle (a) the main announcer.

p. 152 Vocabulary and Pronunciation Students should circle *second time.*

p. 152 Literary Analysis They thought they had fixed the problem, but they had not. A political story from Washington, D. C. was supposed to be introduced, but pictures of people in France pretending to be dead to show the dangers of smoking came up on the monitor.

p. 152 English Language Development 1. had seen 2. decided 3. come

p. 153 Literary Analysis Students should circle the following: *French people pretending to be dead* and *myself, bewilderment and all.* The fact that he sees himself is funny because he's feeling bewildered by what is happening, he doesn't realize they are coming back to him, and then he sees himself with a look of bewilderment on his face.

p. 153 Vocabulary and Pronunciation Students should circle (b).

p. 153 Vocabulary and Pronunciation The practice of reporting.

Review and Assess

1. Students should circle answer (d).
2. Students should circle *calm* and *professional.*
3. No. His words are a follow-up to the fill-in producer yelling "What is going on?" so he was probably having fun with what had happened.
4. **Supposed to Happen:** He introduced his first report. **Actually Happened:** He saw himself on the monitor and then a different story was introduced. **Supposed to Happen:** He introduced a political story from Washington, D. C. **Actually Happened:** Pictures of people in France pretending to be dead to show the dangers of smoking came up on the monitor. **Supposed to Happen:** Osgood introduced a story about rafting. **Actually Happened:** Nothing happened on the monitor.
5. Any of the following details show that the author's purpose is mainly to entertain:
   - Osgood starts by explaining that he introduced his first report and then builds to make his point that a story came on that was not the story he introduced.
   - Then, Osgood explains that a political story from Washington, D. C. was supposed to be introduced, but pictures of people in France pretending to be dead to show the dangers of smoking came up on the monitor.
   - He explains how the monitor shows him with a bewildered look on his face.
   - He tells us how the fill-in producer screamed so loud "half of America" could hear him.
   - He ends his story by telling us the humorous way that the head of CBS responded to the incident.

Cat on the Go

p. 158 Culture Note sittin' = sitting; 'e = he; 'im = him

p. 158 Literary Analysis Students should circle the following: *I went home for a blanket and brought 'im round to you.*

p. 158 Vocabulary and Pronunciation "WOONd" and "injury" are used here.

p. 158 Reading Strategy Students should circle answer (b).The words *terrible wound* show us that the cat is very badly hurt. The words *There's nothing anybody can do about . . . about that* also show us that it seems like a hopeless situation for the cat.

p. 159 Think Ahead Some students may think he will survive because his purrs are a positive sign.

p. 159 Reading Strategy Students should circle (a) try.

p. 159 Stop to Reflect He needs to sit still so that he can rest and heal.

p. 159 Reading Check The correct answer is (b).

p. 160 Literary Analysis He is playful and friendly.

p. 160 English Language Development Students should circle *Mothers'* and label it *pl* for *plural.*

p. 160 Literary Analysis Students should circle *seemed to enjoy himself, enjoyed the slides,* and *was very interested in the cakes.*

p. 161 English Language Development Students should circle *getting* in the sentence *He likes getting around. . . .*

p. 161 Vocabulary and Pronunciation Students should circle *ue.* The following words rhyme with tongue: hung, lung, rung, and sung.

p. 161 Literary Analysis Possible answer: considerate and generous.

p. 162 Vocabulary and Pronunciaton Students should circle *ah* and *'im.* ah = I; 'im = him.

p. 162 Vocabulary and Pronunciaton Students should circle these words and label as follows: walked-R, opened-R, strode-I, took-I, leaped-R; put-I, stroked-R

Review and Assess

1. The correct answer is (c).
2. He purrs after being seriously injured. He likes to be a cat-about-town.

3. The Herriots are very sad about returning Oscar, but they also realize that he should be with his original owners because they had him first and they love him very much.
4. The correct answer is (b).
5. Oscar the Cat: friendly and affectionate; James Herriot: skilled as a doctor and a good storyteller; Helen Herriot: caring
6. Oscar was always visiting people and places. Let's try this. The two boys screamed with excitement.

The Luckiest Time of All

p. 167 Vocabulary and Pronunciation It used to be a show that traveled throughout the south.

p. 167 Reading Strategy Students should circle the following text: *somethin like the circus.*

p. 167 Culture Note She probably calls her "Sweet Tee" as a loving term to show that she is precious and dear to her.

p. 168 English Language Development Ovella and I walked through every place we had walked through before.

p. 168 Vocabulary and Development Elzie did not want to lose her lucky stone. When the dog was loose, it chased Elzie.

p. 169 Read Fluently Elzie says she is luckier than anybody for meeting her husband, but then in the last sentences she says that *most* of the time she thinks she's lucky. There are probably times when she's frustrated with her husband, so she's being funny when she says "Least mostly I think it."

Review and Assess

1. Students should circle two of the following words: adventurous, fun-loving, and shy. Adventurous: they want to join Silas Greene to see the world. Fun-loving: They want to join in on the excitement when they see the dancing dog and people throwing money for the dog. Shy: Elzie says she felt shy when she walked toward Amos.
2. Students should circle the following words: heroic, thoughtful, protective, nice.
3. It was unlucky because it hit the dog's nose and the dog chased her. It's lucky because the dog-chase led to her meeting her husband.
4. One example is when she calls the dog the "cutest one thing in the world next to you." Another example is when she refers to Amos as the "finest fast runnin hero in . . . Virginia." Another example is when she says the dog "lit out after me and I flew."
5. After all those years, she can look back and see how important that funny experience was in her life. She can realize how different life probably would have been for her if she had not had that experience. Certain moments probably stand out in her mind more than other moments, so her use of hyperbole helps stress those particular moments and add more excitement to her story.
6. (c) spotted; (b) holding gently

How the Snake Got Poison

p. 174 English Language Development Students should circle *suit (verb): to go well with.*

p. 174 Read Fluently Students should circle *Ah* for *I* and *de* for *the.*

p. 174 Culture Note The following are the dialect words and their meanings: Ah=I, nothin'=nothing, stompin'=stomping, lak=like, dat=that, dis=this, yo'=your, mouf=mouth, tromps= tramp, yo'self=yourself.

p. 175 Literary Analysis The snake feels he needs protection so he won't be stomped on and so that his generation won't be killed off, but the small animals feel they need protection from the snake so he won't kill them and their generations.

p. 175 Vocabulary and Pronunciation The correct answer is (b) We're scared.

p. 175 Reading Strategy Students should circle (b). Students should explain why they agree or disagree.

Review and Assess

1. God gives the snake poison so that he'll be protected and so that his generation won't be killed off.
2. The correct answer is (c) by warning friends.

3. The story couldn't end that way because in reality snakes are poisonous and have rattles.
4. The small animals complain that the snake's poison is killing their generations. The snake explains that he has to protect himself because all he sees is feet coming to step on him and he can't tell who is his enemy and who is his friend.
5. Students should check the following: *A snake's rattles protect small animals from the snake; All types of animals created by God deserve to remain on earth; Animals have special traits or abilities to help them survive.*

Unit 6

Rikki-tikki-tavi

p. 180 Reading Check Students should circle *a small furry animal that kills snakes*. The word *bungalow* is also explained in this paragraph. Students should put a box around the word *bungalow* and circle the words *one-story house*.

p. 180 English Language Development Students should circle *he revived* to indicate that the mongoose was in the process of waking up.

p. 180 Vocabulary and Pronunciation Students should write *generosity; liberality in giving*

p. 181 English Language Development Students should circle adjective: not friendly, unkind.

p. 181 Literary Analysis (b) rising action

p. 182 Reading Strategy Rikki thinks he will fight Nag later.

p. 182 Reading Check Students should circle *It must be the head.* Possible response: Yes, because Rikki is a born snake killer.

p. 183 Vocabulary and Pronunciation Students should circle *up and down; round in great circles; shaken to pieces; behind him*

p. 183 Vocabulary and Pronunciation Students should circle *bang-stick*. The term is appropriate because it accurately describes what a shotgun looks like and sounds like.

p. 183 Reading Strategy (a) try to kill Nagaina. Even with Nag dead, Nagaina is still a danger.

p. 184 Vocabulary and Pronunciation (b) able to reach out and bite easily

p. 184 English Language Development Students should circle *Look at your friends; Look at your eggs; Go and look; Give it to me*. Students should write *you* before each command.

p 185 Literary Analysis Nagaina is killed by Rikki. Killing the last villain helps fix the problem.

p. 185 English Language Development Students should write *knives; leaves; wolves; beliefs.*

Review and Assess

1. Students should circle *brave, nosey.*
2. Mongooses are born to kill snakes; Rikki wants to protect Teddy from the cobra.
3. (d) He wants to clear the garden of deadly cobras.
4. 1. Nag eats a baby bird. 2. Nagaina sneaking up behind Rikki to do him harm. 3. Karait striking at Rikki.
5. The climax is when Nag is killed.
6. Students should write *We learn that Rikki is a natural predator of snakes; Rikki hears Nagaina mention the eggs are soon to hatch; Nagaina snuck up behind Rikki.*

After Twenty Years

p. 190 Vocabulary and Pronunciation (c) a regular path or round that a person makes

p. 190 Reading Strategy Students should circle *the man* and *spoke*. Students should then use lines to separate the beginning and end of the sentence.

p. 190 English Language Development Students should circle the double quotation marks before *Until* and *It*, and after *ago* and *then*. Students should circle the single quotation marks before *Big* and after *Joe*.

p. 191 Vocabulary and Pronunciation Students should write *18; 20; 20; 20.*

p. 191 Vocabulary and Pronunciation (a) absolutely; yes indeed

p. 191 Reading Check Students should circle *I've had to compete with some of the sharpest wits going to get my pile . . .*

p. 192 Literary Analysis Students should circle *with collar turned up to his ears.* This may mean the man is not Jimmy Wells.

p. 192 Stop to Reflect (c) Both a and b seem likely.

p. 193 Literary Analysis Most students will be surprised by this ending. The ending makes sense because it allows Jimmy to do his duty by having Bob arrested, while not making himself arrest his old friend.

Review and Assess

1. Bob and Jimmy agreed to meet at a specific time and place.
2. (b) They were close in childhood but have taken different paths in life.
3. Students should check *He wants to keep a promise . . . , He wants to show off . . . , He is curious . . .*
4. Jimmy is unable to arrest Bob himself because of the friendship and bond they once had.
5. Jimmy recognizes Bob as a criminal, the reader learns that Jimmy is the police officer, and Jimmy has another officer pose as himself to arrest Bob.
6. The police officer knows about the restaurant and when it was torn down; The police officer is probing Bob for details of his success out west.
7. Students should circle *a man leaned.* Students should draw lines between *store* and *a*, and between *leaned* and *with*. The man leaned in the doorway of a darkened hardware store. An unlit cigar was in his mouth.

Papa's Parrot

p. 198 Stop to Reflect Students should circle *Though* and *merely*. (b) Harry's

p. 198 Vocabulary and Pronunciation (a) visitors; companionship

p. 199 Literary Analysis Students should circle *embarrassed* and label it *D*. Students should circle *he keeps* and label it *I*.

p. 199 Vocabulary and Pronunciation Students will have varying answers.

p. 199 Reading Check Students should circle all words in quotation marks. Students should label *H* any phrase followed by *Harry said* or *Harry mumbled.* Students should label the other circled words *R*.

p. 200 Reading Fluently (a) annoyed

p. 200 Stop to Reflect His father

Review and Assess

1. Students should check *He has outgrown the store . . . , He and his friends now . . . , He is embarrassed . . .*
2. (d)
3. Harry learns that his father is lonely and misses him.
4. Students should write *Harry Tillian liked his papa.* Students should write *Mr. Tillian looked forward to seeing his son.*
5. Students should write *he keeps walking.* Students should write *Harry had always stopped in to see his father at work.*
6. Students should write *yes* or *no* and explain their responses.

Ribbons

p. 205 English Language Development Students should circle the exclamation marks.

p. 205 Reading Check Students should circle *Chinese for grandmother.* Students should write *mother*

p. 205 Reading Strategy Students should circle *What's wrong with her feet?* Students might ask *Why is she sensitive?*

p. 206 Vocabulary and Pronunciation Students should circle one *l* and *t*.

p. 206 Reading Check Ballet Lessons; her room

p. 206 English Language Development Students should circle *had brought; have bought; will have caught.*

p. 207 Literary Analysis Students should circle *Grandmother is a hero.*

p. 207 Reading Check Students should circle *grandmother; mom; daughter.*

p. 207 Vocabulary and Pronunciation Students should read the words aloud.

p. 207 English Language Development Students should circle *dropped.*

p. 208 Think Ahead That something is wrong with Grandmother's feet.

p. 208 Reading Strategy Students should circle *What happened to your feet?* Students might ask *Was that very painful?*

p. 208 Literary Analysis (a) People try to spare their loved ones from pain.

p. 209 Literary Analysis Students should check *People will undergo . . . , People will do painful things . . .*

p. 209 Vocabulary and Pronunciation Students should circle *children.*

p. 209 Stop to Reflect The invisible ribbon is a bond between the women.

Review and Assess

1. Students should check *Grandmother is a brave woman . . . , Grandmother values freedom . . .*
2. (d) She can talk more with Ian, who has learned more Chinese.
3. Grandmother thinks the ribbons are for binding Stacy's feet.
4. (d) the loving family ties between Stacy, her mother, and Grandmother.
5. Students should check *Love and understanding . . . , We don't want those we love . . . , The best way to know a person . . .*
6. Students may ask questions such as *Why is grandmother so secretive? Because she is trying to shield her granddaughter. Why does grandmother treat Stacy differently than Ian? Because that is Chinese culture. What did grandmother's feet look like? Deformed.*

The Treasure of Lemon Brown

p. 214 Vocabulary and Pronunciation 1. team 2. teem 3. principal 4. principle

p. 214 Reading Check Students should circle *dark* or *angry.*

p. 214 Vocabulary and Pronunciation (b) to read steadily and often

p. 215 Stop to Reflect Students may say that Greg's father was trying to encourage Greg to work hard.

p. 215 Vocabulary and Pronunciation Students should circle *For a moment; listened carefully but it was gone; as soon as the rain let up; about to look*

p. 215 Reading Strategy Students will have varying questions.

p. 216 English Language Development Students should write *Do you not have a home? Are you after my treasure? As I said, I have a razor. What do you mean, if I have one? Every man has a treasure. If you don't know that you are foolish.*

p. 216 Reading Strategy Students will have varying questions.

p. 216 Vocabulary and Pronunciation Students should circle *flashlight* and *wallpaper.* Students should write *A flashlight is a small portable light that illuminates in a flash. Wallpaper is decorated paper that covers a wall.*

p. 217 Vocabulary and Pronunciation Students should circle the *e* in *He,* the *ee* and *ie* in *eerie,* the *e* in *Maybe,* the first *e* in *scene,* the *e* in *be,* the first *e* in *even,* and the *ee* and *i* in *eerier.*

p. 217 Read Fluently (c) proud

p. 217 Literary Analysis Students should circle *Brown felt like his son would be able to do something if he knew his father had.* (c) Greg's father telling how he studied hard to pass the postal test.

p. 218 English Language Development Students should insert the word *Of* before the word 'Course.

p. 218 Stop to Reflect Lemon's experiences may allow Greg to realize the accomplishments of his father and will bring Greg and his dad closer together.

p. 218 English Language Development Students should change *foolishest* to *most foolish.*

p. 219 Stop to Reflect Possible response: Greg smiles because he can now appreciate his father's lecture. He is looking forward to listening to his father.

Review and Assess

1. (d) He is blocks from home, and the rain is very heavy.
2. (c) They have heard that Brown has a treasure and want to steal it.

3. poor: homeless/lives in empty old building; dresses in rags

   talented: got good reviews for playing harmonica and singing blues

   loved family: traveled all over, working hard, to support his wife and son

   proud: gave clippings of reviews of his performances to his son

   sad: grieves for loss of wife and son
4. his old harmonica and clippings of old reviews of his performances
5. Students should put a check in front of *A person's achievements are a treasure that can be passed down* and *Just about everyone has a treasure of some kind.*
6. Possible question: What is Lemon Brown's treasure? Answer: an old harmonica he used to play when he performed, and clippings of old reviews of his performances

   Possible question: Why does the treasure have special meaning to him? Answer: He gave it to his son, who treasured it and had it with him when he was killed in the war.

   Possible question: What does Greg learn from Lemon Brown? Answer: to value his father's proud achievements and concern for Greg

Unit 7

I Am a Native of North America

p. 224 Culture Note White Society differs from Native Americans in that it values material possessions. The societies are similar in that they both enjoy social gatherings.

p. 224 Reading Check People learned to live with one another; learned to serve one another; learned to respect the rights of one another.

p. 224 Reading Strategy Students should circle *nature was considered a gift and treat nature well.*

p. 225 Reading Strategy Students should circle *They stripped the land and poisoned the water and air.*

p. 225 English Language Development Students should circle *lowest* and *greatest.*

p. 225 Literary Analysis Without love we become weak.

p. 226 Vocabulary and Pronunciation (c) physical

p. 226 Reading Strategy Students should write *Many young people have forgotten the old ways. They have been made to feel ashamed of their Indian ways.*

p. 226 Reading Check Native Americans must forgive the terrible sufferings the white society brought.

Review and Assess

1. Native American and White Society
2. Native Americans view nature as a gift that should be respected.
3. The author's idea of brotherhood is love and forgiveness.
4. Under *Native American Culture* students should write *People learn to respect the rights of their neighbors through communal living; People love and respect nature.* Under *White Society* students should write *People live near one another but do not know or care about their neighbors; People abuse nature.*
5. The author provided support for his main idea by explaining how well the Native American culture lived. He compares how the Native Americans used their natural resources to how the white society abused them.

All Together Now

p. 231 Vocabulary and Pronunciation (c) The major groups into which human beings are divided based on physical features.

p. 231 Reading Check No. People bring peace between races, not laws.

p. 231 Literary Analysis Students should underline *Each of us can decide to have one friend of a different race or background.*

p. 232 English Language Development Students should underline *One thing is clear . . . their inner reality.*

p. 232 Reading Strategy Students should underline *Babies come into the world as blank as slates* and *Children learn ideas and attitudes from the adults*

p. 232 Literary Analysis Students should circle *Parents can actively encourage their children to be in the company of people who are of other racial and ethnic backgrounds.*

Review and Assess

1. people
2. Civil Rights Act of 1964; Voting Rights Act of 1965. Laws cannot create tolerance; people's attitudes have to change.
3. The author means babies are innocent and can be taught anything by their parents and teachers.
4. The author is dedicated to bringing people together. She wants people to work towards racial peace.
5. Possible response: Do the supporting details make sense? Do they persuade me to accept the author's point of view? Students' responses to the second question may vary, but they should explain their answers.

How to Enjoy Poetry

p. 237 Literary Analysis Students should underline *When you really feel it, a new part of you happens, or an old part is renewed, with surprise and delight at being what it is.*

p. 237 English Language Development Students should underline *go together* and *some go.*

p. 237 Vocabulary and Pronunciation *Deep* means to explore something in a serious way, focusing on things that are not easily noticed.

p. 238 Reading Strategy Students should underline *Poetry can describe the sun and stars in different ways and from different perspectives.*

p. 238 Literary Analysis Dickey explains how to begin writing poetry.

p. 238 Reading Check The writer says you need to begin with yourself to start enjoying poetry.

p. 239 English Language Development Students should circle *more memorable*

p. 239 Stop to Reflect Yes. Both reading and writing poetry help you to look at your own life differently. Reading and writing poetry help you make connections between things that you have never connected before.

Review and Assess

1. (c) poetry comes to you from outside you and something from within you must meet it
2. Giving to poetry means allowing yourself to get into the words and feel their meanings.
3. Rhythm and rhyme are important to poetry because they make the words more memorable and more pleasant to read.
4. Dickey explains that poetry can uncover a new part of you, and he explains how poetry comes to you from the outside.
5. 1. When you really feel poetry, a new part of you happens. 2. To understand poetry is to know it comes to you from outside. 3. You must make a gut connection with the poetry.

from An American Childhood

p. 244 English Language Development Students should circle *thought.*

p. 244 Culture Note Students' responses will vary.

p. 244 Vocabulary and Pronunciation Students should circle *waited for cars* and *with snowballs.* Students should write *the meaning of pelted is to be hit with something thrown.*

p. 245 Reading Strategy Students should circle *He was in city clothes: a suit and tie, street shoes.* The purpose for including this information is to describe the challenge this driver took on when he decided to chase the kids in the snow.

p. 245 English Language Development Students should circle *across, over, up, through, between*

p. 245 Stop to Reflect Students answers will vary.

p. 246 Literary Analysis Dillard's description of the events tells us she enjoys challenges and seeks excitement.

p. 246 Reading Strategy Dillard wants to show the level of difficulty and the toll the chase has taken on the pursuer.

p. 246 English Language Development (b) calmed down and came back to reality. Dillard means the man began to start thinking clearly.

p. 247 Reading Check Dillard feels the most satisfying thing about her experience is that she went all out and did her very best in a challenging situation.

Review and Assess

1. Dillard enjoys the competition and mental and physical aspects of football.
2. Dillard is outgoing. Dillard is competitive.
3. Dillard feels the man was a worthy opponent. She tells us this by describing how difficult the chase was for everyone involved.
4. A passage that entertains: *He ran after us, and we ran away . . . we were running for our lives.* A passage that teaches a lesson: *Then she realized that the man knew the same thing she did: You have to throw yourself into an activity with all your energy if you want to win.* A passage that explains something about the author: *Your fate. . . . Nothing girls did could compare to it.*

Unit 8

A Christmas Carol: Scrooge and Marley, Act 1, Scenes 1 & 2

p. 252 Reading Strategy Students should respond with their own ideas of what a ghost looks like.

p. 252 Vocabulary and Pronunciation (b) joke

p. 253 Vocabulary and Pronunciation A poulterer sells poultry.

p. 253 Reading Check The story takes place on Christmas Eve, 1843.

p. 253 Vocabulary and Pronunciation (b) spending money only when necessary

p. 254 Reading Strategy Students should circle *ancient, awful, dead-eyed*

p. 254 English Language Development Students should underline *asking*

p. 254 Reading Check He doesn't think his nephew should be merry because he is poor.

p. 254 Vocabulary and Pronunciation Students should circle *dismal.*

p. 255 Literary Analysis Bah! Humbug!

p. 255 English Language Development Students should circle all the exclamation marks in the passage and then read the passage with emotion and excitement.

p. 255 Vocabulary and Pronunciation Students should circle *family, refuses, after*

p. 256 English Language Development It is six o'clock, so the clock rings six times.

p. 256 Literary Analysis Students should circle *Cratchit smiles faintly.*

p. 256 Reading Check Cratchit gets one day off a year.

p. 256 Reading Check Cratchit wants to say Merry Christmas. Scrooge hates Christmas.

p. 257 Reading Strategy The scenery changes from an office to a street scene. Music is heard. People walk by.

p. 257 Literary Analysis Scrooge is grumpy and snaps at passing boys. The other characters are happy and cheerful.

Review and Assess

1. Jacob Marley is Scrooge's former business partner. He is a ghost in this play.
2. Scenes 1 and 2 take place in Scrooge's place of business, a countinghouse.
3. Scrooge is stingy and he doesn't want to pay Cratchit for a day when he doesn't work.
4. *Things Scrooge Says:*

   Bah! Humbug!

   Every idiot who goes about with "Merry Christmas" on his lips, should be boiled with his own pudding, and buried with a stake of holly through his heart.

   Things Scrooge Does:

   He refuses to go to his nephew's for Christmas dinner.

   He refuses to give the kind men a donation for the poor.
5. Reading Strategy:
   - How he moves: Possible response: He walks slowly, with a cane. He is bent over.

- His facial expressions: Possible response: He frowns. He says mean things under his breath. He tries to hit people with his cane.

A Christmas Carol: Scrooge and Marley, Act 1, Scenes 3–5

p. 262 Vocabulary and Pronunciation When something disappears, it goes out of view or existence.

p. 262 Reading Check He sees Jacob Marley's face on the door knocker.

p. 262 Reading Strategy Students should circle *horrible to look at, pigtail, vest, suit as usual, drags an enormous chain, is transparent*

p. 263 Literary Analysis Students should draw a sketch of the scene as it is described.

p. 263 Culture Note Students should tell what the names of the coins and bills are in their country.

p. 263 Reading Check He screams a ghostly scream and takes off his head.

p. 263 Stop to Reflect He did not care for other people during his life. All he cared about was money.

p. 263 Reading Strategy Students should use their imaginations to picture this figure. Possible response: A child with the head of an old man.

p. 264 Vocabulary and Pronunciation Students should circle *do, through*

p. 264 Literary Analysis Students should circle *panicked*

p. 264 English Language Development Students should circle *open, soft, downy, country. Open* follows a linking verb.

p. 265 English Language Development Students should circle *crying, singing, weeping, dancing, playing*

p. 265 Reading Check Students should underline *he thinks of the young caroler whom he shooed away from his office earlier that night. He says he wishes he had given him something.*

p. 265 Reading Check He thinks about Cratchit. He wishes that he had been kinder to him.

p. 265 Reading Strategy They describe how the boy Ebenezer is replaced by a man Ebenezer. The co-workers disappear and a young woman in mourning clothes appears.

p. 266 Reading Check money.

p. 266 Reading Check The world is hard on people who are poor and it punishes people who try to be rich.

p. 266 English Language Development Students should circle *nobler, wiser*

p. 267 Reading Check She is releasing him from marrying her.

p. 267 Vocabulary and Pronunciation Students should circle *ch* and *tu*

p. 267 Reading Check The ghost of Christmas Past appears, Scrooge sees himself as a lonely boy in the schoolhouse. Scrooge sees his former boss and coworkers. Scrooge sees himself and a woman.

Review and Assess

1. Marley's ghost has to carry the chain because he didn't care for other people in life.
2. The Ghost of Christmas Past visits Scrooge after Marley leaves.
3. Scrooge as a young boy: Scrooge cries.

   Scrooge as a twelve-year-old boy: He says he loved his sister.

   Scrooge with his coworkers: He wishes he had been kinder to Cratchit.

   Scrooge with his fiancée: He yells "No!"
4. Scrooge was a lonely boy. Scrooge had a sister whom he loved. Scrooge was engaged at one time.
5. He panics.

Unit 9

The Cremation of Sam McGee

p. 272 Reading Strategy Students should underline *it stabbed like a driven nail.* The cold air is being compared to a driven nail as it stabs through the parka into the body.

p. 272 Reading Check Sam McGee was miserable because he was from the south and wasn't used to cold weather.

p. 272 Reading Strategy Students should circle *chilled clean through to the bone.*

p. 272 Reading Check Last remains refers to a dead body.

p. 273 Literary Analysis Sam dies from the cold.

p. Stop to Reflect Possible response: The fire may warm Sam back to life.

p. 274 Literary Analysis Students should check *Character, Setting,* and *Plot.* Sam the *character* is speaking, the cold *setting* is described, and the plot is covered by Sam speaking and the narration.

Review and Assess

1. unbearably cold
2. He is trying to earn money.
3. He promises to cremate Sam's body.
4. Sam felt so bad, the narrator felt obligated to keep his promise.
5. Sam McGee sitting up getting warm.
6. 1. setting: The cold Arctic. 2. characters: Sam McGee. 3. rhythm: Well he seemed so low that I couldn't say no.
7. Students should complete the *What it means* part with *it was unbearably cold; a very bright smile;* and *I tried not to be afraid.*

Annabel Lee

p. 279 Reading Check She died from the cold.

p. 279 Literary Analysis Students should circle *me, sea, chilling, killing,* and *Lee.*

p. 279 English Language Development Students should circle *older than* and *wiser than.*

p. 279 Literary Analysis Students should read the bracketed lines aloud putting emphasis on the underlined words.

p. 280 Reading Strategy Every night I lay down by my wife's grave.

p. 280 Stop to Reflect 1. Lonely. 2. Angry. 3. Bitter

Review and Assess

1. The narrator blames the angels and the cold for Annabel Lee's death. The narrator believes the angels were jealous of the love between him and Annabel.
2. The narrator talks about the sea because the young lovers lived near the sea.
3. Students should underline *love, stronger far, love those, older, we, many, wiser,* and *we*
4. Students should list *beams/dreams,* and *rise/eyes, sea/Lee* and *nighttide/bride/side* as the sets of rhyming words in the final stanza.
5. The moon and stars remind me of Annabel Lee.

Maestro

p. 285 Vocabulary and Pronunciation *Bow* means to bend forward at the waist. Students should circle the word *bow* in line 16.

p. 285 Reading Strategy *Upturned* means to be facing upwards. Students should write the words *turned up.*

p. 285 Stop to Reflect A song can be sung so beautifully that one might describe it as tasting great rather than sounding great. *Sweet on the tongue* is an example of this.

Review and Assess

1. The voice, the guitar, and the violin.
2. Sentimental, happy, proud.
3. Students should circle the word *strummed.*
4. Under *Clues that help Clarify,* students should write *in the air; to snare.* Beneath *Clarified Meaning,* students should write *to be tossed up in the air.*

The Village Blacksmith

p. 290 Literary Analysis Students should circle *his brawny arms are strong as iron bands.* This comparison tells us that the blacksmith has great strength.

p. 290 Reading Strategy Students should circle the words *he hears the parson pray and preach, he hears his daughter's voice.*

p. 290 Reading Check The blacksmith cries because he is remembering his wife who has passed away.

p. 291 Vocabulary and Pronunciation Students should replace *thee* and *thou* with *you.*

Review and Assess

1. The blacksmith's life is difficult. His daily work involves dealing with extreme heat and lifting heavy materials.
2. Rough; large; strong.
3. His daughter singing reminds the blacksmith of his dead wife.
4. The correct answer is a furnace.
5. In the spaces under *Sense*, students should write *Sight; Touch; Sound.* In the spaces under *Sensory Language*, students should write *Spreading chestnut tree; Strong as iron hands; He hears the parson pray and preach.*

Unit 10

Popocatepetl and Ixtlaccihuatl

p. 296 Background Answers will vary.

p. 296 English Language Development Students should circle *on occasion.*

p. 297 Reading Strategy Students should read ahead to see if the Emperor makes wise decisions.

p. 297 Reading Check Students should underline *forbade her to marry.*

p. 297 Vocabulary and Pronunciation Students should circle *rule.*

p. 297 Reading Check The Emperor trusted no one.

p. 298 Reading Strategy Answers will vary. The Emperor must have had wisdom to rule for so long. The Emperor never had wisdom if he forbade his daughter to marry.

p. 298 Vocabulary and Pronunciation Students should say the word *success.* Students should circle *Mexico.*

p. 298 Reading Check As a reward, the emperor offers the hand of his daughter and the equal right to reign and rule Tenochtitlan.

p. 298 Literary Analysis Aztecs regarded warriors as heroes and war as a battle for honor.

p. 298 Reading Check The warriors report false news because they were jealous of Popo's success.

p. 299 Reading Check Ixtla dies because she believes her love has been killed in battle.

p. 299 Reading Strategy Student should read ahead to find details about Popo that make him more than an ordinary man.

p. 299 Literary Analysis The warriors could not have built the pyramid in one day. This is part of the folk tale that makes it sound miraculous.

p. 299 Reading Check Popo buries Ixtla's body at the top of the pyramid.

p. 300 Literary Analysis Students should check *Popo had two pyramids . . . , Popo stood next to Ixtla's . . .*

p. 300 Stop to Reflect No. This is an Aztec folk tale that was written as a fictional account of the mountains' origins.

Review and Assess

1. The emperor forbids them to marry.
2. By offering his daughter as a reward, he does not recognize her wishes.
3. Students should circle (a) The kingdom ends up with no ruler.
4. Ixtla dies because she believes the man she loves has been killed in battle.
5. Reading ahead sometimes helps you better understand what is happening earlier.
6. Possible responses: smoke in the memory of the princess; pyramids that change to volcanoes; Popo's decision to stand on top of the pyramid forever.

The People Could Fly

p. 305 Reading Strategy Students should underline *people who could fly; slavery; slave ships, magic of flying,* and *dark-skinned.*

p. 305 Reading Check The people are full of misery because they can't fly any more. They are miserable because they have been enslaved.

p. 305 Reading Check Some people have the special gift of being able to fly.

p. 306 Literary Analysis Students should circle the words *call him Toby; standin',* and *Now.*

p. 306 Reading Check Sarah can't feed her baby because the overseer is watching.

p. 306 Reading Strategy Possible responses: violence; abuse; treating people and babies badly.

p. 307 Literary Analysis Students should underline *said so quickly* and *sounded like whispers and sighs.*

p. 307 Reading Check Possible response: The master wants to kill Toby because Toby is helping slaves escape.

p. 307 Reading Check The magic words are *buba yali* and *buba tambe.*

p. 308 Literary Analysis The message is that people should have hope and they will be saved.

p. 308 English Language Development Students should circle *goodie-bye.*

p. 308 Culture Note Students' answers will vary based on their native culture. Encourage students to share the stories with the class.

Review and Assess

1. The people lose their wings when they become slaves.
2. Sarah tells Toby she must leave soon because she thought she would die.
3. Toby helps Sarah by chanting a spell and helping her fly.
4. Possible responses include: *say; hollerin',* and *Couldn't believe it, call him Toby; standin', Call her Sarah,* and *Now.*
5. Life was painful and hard. They wanted to be free and they wanted to be safe.

Demeter and Persephone

p. 313 Literary Analysis The events might describe volcanic eruptions.

p. 313 Reading Strategy Eros will shoot an arrow and someone will fall in love. Some students may predict that this love will stop the monsters from shaking the earth.

p. 314 Literary Analysis The Greeks say that people are hit by Eros' arrow and fall in love.

p. 314 Reading Check Students should underline *Eros shoots an arrow straight into Pluto's heart* and *a young woman gathering flowers.*

p. 314 Reading Check Persephone is the daughter of Demeter, the goddess of the harvest. Pluto kidnaps Persephone.

p. 315 Literary Analysis The ancient Greeks believed that natural disasters were caused by the gods.

p. 315 Reading Strategy Students may predict that Zeus will save Persephone.

p. 315 Vocabulary and Pronunciation The present form of the verb *sped* is *speed.* The past form of the given words are as follows: *bleed*/bled; *meet*/met; *keep*/kept.

p. 315 Reading Check tasted food in the realm of the dead.

p. 316 Reading Check She likes things with fragrance. Jewels have no fragrance.

p. 316 Reading Strategy Students may predict that Persephone will be very unhappy or that she will die.

p. 316 Literary Analysis We have winter because Demeter doesn't allow things to grow while her daughter, Persephone, is with Pluto.

Review and Assess

1. Pluto takes Persephone to his kingdom because he is in love with her.
2. The correct answer is *C.*
3. Zeus solves the problem by asking Hermes to bring Persephone back.
4. When Persephone is on earth, there is spring and summer. When she is in the underworld the earth has fall and winter.

5. The myth of Demeter and Persephone explains the cycle of the seasons.
6. Possible responses: **Persephone:** *Prediction:* Students may have predicted she would die. *Outcome:* She did not die; but she was not completely happy either. **Demeter:** *Prediction:* Students may have predicted that Demeter would get Persephone back. *Outcome:* Demeter was able to get Persephone back for part of the year.

Icarus and Daedalus

p. 321 Reading Check Students should circle *a wonderful Labyrinth.*

p. 321 Reading Check It seemed impossible to leave because every ship was guarded.

p. 321 Reading Strategy Students should say what they think Daedalus will do.

p. 322 Vocabulary and Pronunciation a pair of shoes; a pair of socks; a pair of gloves.

p. 322 Vocabulary and Pronunciation It means he was not paying attention to what he heard.

p. 322 Reading Strategy If he doesn't remember his father's instructions he might be badly hurt or even die.

p. 322 Reading Strategy The heat of the sun could melt his feathers apart.

p. 323 Culture Note Ask students to try to name at least one story.

p. 323 Reading Check Students should underline the following: *The heat of the sun had melted the wax from his wings; the feathers were falling.*

p. 323 Stop to Reflect Students should say what they would do in the same situation.

Review and Assess

1. He is in Crete.
2. He plans to create wings so he can fly away.
3. He warns him not to fly too low or too high.
4. Icarus drowns at the end of the myth.
5. The myth teaches us the importance of being careful and cautious, and it teaches us to pay attention to others when they are teaching us how to do something that can be dangerous.
6. The following are some clues from the story: His father's instructions "went in at one ear and out by the other." / Icarus forgets all the instructions and soars as high as he can. / His father is way below him.

Answers to Part 2

"The Cat Who Thought She Was a Dog and the Dog Who Thought He Was a Cat" by Isaac Bashevis Singer

Use Context Clues (page 329)

1. c
2. d
3. b
4. a

"Two Kinds" by Amy Tan

Apply Word Identification Strategies (page 331)

Sample Responses:

1. tip and toes; meaning: walks on the tips of the toes
2. house and cleaning; meaning: cleaning the house
3. high and pitched; meaning: a pitch (or sound) that is high
4. ear and splitting; meaning: hurts (or splits) the ear
5. day and dreamed; meaning: dream during the daytime
6. show and piece; meaning: a piece that is shown off

from "Song of Myself" by Walt Whitman
"I'm Nobody" by Emily Dickinson
"Me" by Walter de la Mare

Read Poetry According to Punctuation (page 333)

Students might make notes that they do not pause at the end of a line with no punctuation, pause briefly at commas, pause briefly at ellipses and dashes, and pause longer at end punctuation.

"My Furthest-Back Person" by Alex Haley

Break Down Long Sentences (page 335)

Sample Responses:

1. Sentence: And when a main reading room desk attendant asked if he could help me, I wouldn't have dreamed of admitting to him some curiosity hanging on from boyhood about my slave forbears.

   Sentence broken into parts: A main reading room desk attendant asked if he could help me. I wouldn't have dreamed of admitting to him some curiosity. [The curiosity was] hanging on from boyhood about my slave forbears.
2. Sentence: Then, intensely, he queried me about the story's relay across the generations, about the gibberish of "*k*" sounds Grandma had fiercely muttered to herself while doing her housework, with my brothers and me giggling beyond her hearing at what we had dubbed "Grandma's noises."

   Sentence broken into parts: He queried me about the story's relay across the generations. [He queried me] about the gibberish of "*k*" sounds Grandma had fiercely muttered to herself while doing her housework. My brothers and I giggled beyond her hearing at what we had dubbed "Grandma's noises."
3. Sentence: The first native Gambian I could locate in the U.S. was named Ebou Manga, then a junior attending Hamilton College in upstate Clinton, N.Y.

   Sentence broken into parts: The first native Gambian I could locate in the U.S. was named Ebou Manga. [He was] then a junior attending Hamilton College in upstate Clinton, N.Y.
4. Sentence: I suppose I physically wavered, and they thought it was the hate; rustling whispers went through the crowd, and a man brought me a low stool.

   Sentence broken into parts: I suppose I physically wavered. They thought it was the hate. Rustling whispers went through the crowd. A man brought me a low stool.

"The Third Level" by Jack Finney

Use Context to Determine Meaning (page 337)

Sample Responses:

1. fear, war, worry and all the rest of it
2. a dozen men who looked just like me
3. pushing out new corridors and staircases like roots
4. tremendous trees whose branches meet overhead

"A Day's Wait" by Ernest Hemingway

Reread (page 339)

Some of the behaviors that students may have questions about are:

1. When his father comes downstairs, Schatz is dressed, even though his father told him to go back to bed. On rereading the story, students might recognize that the boy was afraid of being sick.
2. Schatz does not follow what his father is reading to him. After rereading, students might realize that the boy is not listening because he is thinking about his illness.
3. The father goes outside for awhile. When rereading the story, students might recognize that the father was not very worried about his son's illness.
4. The boy refuses to let anyone come into the room to visit him. After reading the story again, students will probably recognize that the boy wanted to be alone to die.

"Was Tarzan a Three-Bandage Man?" by Bill Cosby "Oranges" by Gary Soto

Context Clues (page 341)

Sample Responses:

2. meaning: bad skin
3. meaning: bandages around the neck
4. meaning: trying to be like the injured
5. One possible sentence: Although baseball and football stars inspired us, our real heroes were the famous prize fighters, and the way to emulate a fighter was to walk around with a Band-Aid over one eye. Meaning: were our heroes

Unit 2

from *In Search of Our Mothers' Gardens* by Alice Walker

Ask Questions (page 343)

What I Know: Some students will focus on specific people they have known that work hard. Others might write about the motivations or lifestyles of hard workers.

What I Want to Know: Many students will wonder about the reason that some people work hard. Others might want to know how they can become hard workers themselves. Or, students may want to find out ways that they can avoid the kind of work they see some people do.

What I've Learned: Students may notice that many hard workers are so because they have no other choice in life, but that they also try to make things as beautiful as possible. Others will learn that work is not something to avoid—that there are certain pleasures that come from a hard-working life.

"Seventh Grade" by Gary Soto
"Melting Pot" by Anna Quindlen

Relate to Your Own Experience (page 345)

Students should record their ideas about what is happening in each scene. Student responses will vary based on their own experiences. Encourage students to relate their own experiences as much as possible.

"Fable" by Ralph Waldo Emerson
"Thumbprint" by Eve Merriam
"If—" by Rudyard Kipling

Paraphrase (page 347)

Sample Responses:

1. From Kipling—Poetic language: If you can dream—and not make dreams your master;/if you can think—and not make thoughts your aim. Paraphrase: If you can dream and think without making your own thoughts your main goal.
2. From Merriam—Poetic language: On the pad of my thumb/are whorls, whirls, wheels/in a unique design:/mine alone. Paraphrase: My thumbprint has its very own design.
3. From Emerson—Poetic language: If I cannot carry forests on my back,/Neither can you crack a nut. Paraphrase: I am not a mountain, but you are not a squirrel.

"Mother to Son" by Langston Hughes
"The Courage That My Mother Had" by Edna St. Vincent Millay
"The Hummingbird That Lived Through Winter" by William Saroyan

Question (page 349)

Sample Responses:

Hughes: Students might understand worn stairs or wandering in the dark. They might not understand what a crystal stair is, and they might not understand the mother's tone.

Millay: Students will probably understand that the poet is praising her mother's courage and wishing that she had it. They might be confused by this image of the mother: "Rock from New England quarried;/Now granite in a granite hill."

Saroyan: Students will probably understand the old man's nature, and his love for living things. They may not understand why the man let the hummingbird go, or what the man means when he says that each bird is "our bird."

Unit 3

"The Third Wish" by Joan Aiken

Clarify (page 351)

Students may have a variety of questions about this selection. Some of the questions and answers might include:

1. What is causing the crying, struggling, and thrashing? After rereading, the students learn it is the swan.
2. Why does the swan look at the man with hate in his eyes? After rereading, students may be able to see that the bird was frightened.
3. Where did the little green man with a golden crown come from? After rereading, students should be able to recognize that the swan and the little green man are the same creature.
4. Why is Mr. Peters content in his old age? After finishing the story, students may see that his contentment came because he understood the swans and had loved Leita.

"A Boy and a Man" by James Ramsey Ullman
from *Into Thin Air* by Jon Krakauer

Predict (page 353)

Sample Responses:

"A Boy and a Man"

1. Rudi will be unable to save the man because the time it takes to get help will leave the man frozen.
2. Rudi will be able to save the man because he is so determined and willing to sacrifice his own comfort.
3. Rudi and Captain John Winter will climb the Citadel together as a way of honoring Rudi's father.

from *Into Thin Air*

1. The writer will be injured because of all the danger mentioned in the story.
2. The writer will be able to speed across the tower because he is so eager to do it, and because he loves the challenge.
3. Krakauer safely returns from Mount Everest because he survived to write his account.

"The Charge of the Light Brigade" by Alfred, Lord Tennyson
from *Henry V*, "St. Crispian's Day Speech" by William Shakespeare
"The Enemy" by Alice Walker

Reading Poetic Contractions (page 355)

1. Missing Letter or Letters: e; Full Word or Words: called
2. Missing Letter or Letters: e; Full Word or Words: remembered
3. Missing Letter or Letters: v; Full Word or Words: never
4. Missing Letter or Letters: e; Full Word or Words: accursed

"The Californian's Tale" by Mark Twain
"Valediction" by Seamus Heaney

Summarize (page 357)

Sample Responses:

1. Main events and details: Twain describes the lonely land around him. Summary: The land was so lonesome that the only sounds were those of insects.
2. Main events and details: Twain visits the cottage and finds it very pleasing compared to the experiences he's been through. Summary: Twain found a pleasing cottage and was happy to be away from the drudgery of the past weeks. The cabin was refreshing and homey.
3. Main events and details: Twain surveys the bedroom and notices many nice details. Summary: The bedroom was nicer than anything he had seen for a long time, with fine features.
4. Main events and details: Twain washes his face. Summary: As he washed his face and looked around the room, he found a picture.
5. Main events and details: The cottage owner tells Twain about his wife's return, and praises her beauty. Summary: The cottage owner praises his wife and can't wait for Twain to meet her, but he won't meet her because he is leaving.

"Stopping by Woods on a Snowy Evening" by Robert Frost
"Four Skinny Trees" by Sandra Cisneros
"Miracles" by Walt Whitman

Respond to Levels of Meaning (page 359)

The purpose of this exercise is to show how two different people can have different responses to a selection. Encourage students not to be shy in sharing their responses. Remind them that sharing responses can help both people to understand a selection better.

Unit 4

"The Night the Bed Fell" by James Thurber

Identify Causes and Effects (page 361)

Sample Responses:

1. Cause: Briggs fears that he will stop breathing in the night.
   Effect: He puts a glass of camphor by his bed.
2. Cause: Aunt Sarah Shoaf fears a burglar bringing chloroform.
   Effect: She piles her money, silverware, and other valuables outside her bed with a note.
3. Cause: Aunt Gracie Shoaf fears burglars.
   Effect: She throws shoes down the hall.
4. Cause: Narrator sleeps in a bad army cot.
   Effect: Cot crashes.
5. Cause: Cot crashes.
   Effect: Mother wakes and screams.
6. Cause: Mother screams.
   Effect: Herman wakes and shouts with mother.
7. Cause: Herman shouts.
   Effect: Briggs wakes up, thinking that he is suffocating.
8. Cause: Briggs wakes up, thinking that he is suffocating.
   Effect: Briggs pours camphor on himself, making the room smell terribly.
9. Cause: The room smells terribly.
   Effect: Briggs breaks open the window with his hand.
10. Cause: Briggs breaks open the window with his hand.
    Effect: Narrator wakes up, fearing he is in a bad situation.
11. Cause: Mother tries to get the door to the attic open.
    Effect: Father wakes up, fears the house is on fire, and yells, "I'm coming!"
12. Cause: Father yells, "I'm coming!"
    Effect: Mother thinks he's talking to God and is dying.
13. Cause: Dog doesn't like Briggs.
    Effect: Roy has to hold the dog down.
14. Cause: Father comes downstairs.
    Effect: Mother weeps.
15. Cause: Father wanders around in the night.
    Effect: Father catches a cold.

"All Summer in A Day" by Ray Bradbury

Picture Setting and Actions (page 363)

Sample Responses:

See: Rain, "the drum and gush of water, with the sweet crystal fall of showers and the concussion of storms so heavy they were tidal waves come over the islands."

Hear: Rain, "they always awoke to the tatting drum . . . "; No rain, " the silence was so immense and unbelievable that you felt your ears had been stuffed or you had lost your hearing altogether."

Feel: Warmth of the sun, "But they were running and turning their faces up to the sky and feeling the sun on their cheeks like a warm iron; they were taking off their jackets and letting the sun burn their arms. "

Smell: "The door slid back and the smell of the silent, waiting world came in to them."

"The Highwayman" by Alfred Noyes
"The Real Story of a Cowboy's Life" by Geoffrey C. Ward

Identify Causes and Effects (page 365)

Sample Responses for "The Highwayman":

1. Cause: The Highwayman comes to see Bess.
   Effect: The Highwayman promises to return to get her.
2. Cause: The horsekeeper overhears.
   Effect: He warns the authorities.
3. Cause: King George's men come to the inn.
   Effect: Bess is captured.
4. Cause: Bess gets her hand on the gun so she can warn the Highwayman.
   Effect: She kills herself to save him.
5. Cause: The Highwayman returns to avenge Bess's death.
   Effect: He is killed by King George's men.

Sample Responses for "The Real Story of a Cowboy's Life":

1. Cause: The cowboys traveled through dusty ground.
   Effect: They would rinse their mouths to clean out the dirt.
2. Cause: One jittery cow would act up.
   Effect: An entire herd would stampede.
3. Cause: The herds ruined settlers crops and brought disease.
   Effect: The cowboys and settlers weren't friendly.
4. Cause: Herds came to their destination.
   Effect: Cowboys would relax in town.

"Justin Lebo" by Phillip Hoose
"The Rider" by Naomi Shihab Nye
"Amigo Brothers" by Piri Thomas
"The Walk" by Thomas Hardy

Make Inferences (page 367)

Sample Responses:

1. In "Amigo Brothers," students might infer that the boys are great friends because they do not want to hurt each other in the fight.
2. Readers of "The Walk" might infer that the speaker was able to enjoy himself because he does not think of his old companion as being left behind.
3. In "Justin Lebo," students may infer that Justin is goodhearted because he wants everyone at the boys' home to have a bike and because he works hard to make it happen.
4. Students may infer from "The Rider" that the speaker is lonely because she wonders if biking can eliminate loneliness and she is riding a bike herself.

Unit 5

"Our Finest Hour" by Charles Osgood

Distinguish Fact From Opinion (page 369)

Sample Responses:

1. Opinion. The words "easy enough" and "most of the time" show that this is a personal opinion.
2. Fact. You could prove this by finding the reporter and the story.
3. Fact. You could prove this by looking at the piece after the commercial.
4. Opinion. The terms "all in all" and "not the finest" express personal feelings and cannot be proven.
5. Opinion. The term "really great impression" cannot be defined or proven—it expresses personal opinion.

"Cat on the Go" by James Herriot

Understand Bias (page 371)

Sample Responses:

1. He found the cat a pleasant creature.
2. He was a generous pet owner and had probably already taken in strays.
3. He was hoping to find the cat.
4. He wanted to know that the cat would be okay.
5. Herriot is kind and gentle.

"The Luckiest Time of All" by Lucille Clifton

"Father William" by Lewis Carroll

"The Microscope" by Maxine Kumin

"in Just—" by E. E. Cummings

"Sarah Cynthia Sylvia Stout Would Not Take the Garbage Out" by Shel Silverstein

Recognize Author's Purpose (page 373)

Sample Responses:

2. "and eddieandbill come/running from marbles and piracies and it's/spring"
3. "We ought to ship him off to Spain/He says he's seen a housefly's brain."
4. "At last the garbage reached so high/That finally it touched the sky."
5. "But, now that I'm perfectly sure I have none [brain],/Why, I do it again and again."

"Zoo" by Edward Hoch

"The Hippopotamus" by Odgen Nash

"How the Snake Got Poison" by Zora Neale Hurston

Evaluate an Author's Message (page 375)

Sample Responses:

2. We often treat things that are different from us as a commodity.
3. We view things from our own perspective, but often fail to think of things from other perspectives.
4. People treat you differently depending on whether you are a friend or an enemy.

Unit 6

"After Twenty Years" by O. Henry

What Happens Next? (page 377)

Students may write predictions after the following events:

1. The man walks up to the policeman.
2. The man tells the policeman that he is supposed to meet his old friend Jimmy here.
3. The man pulls out a diamond-studded watch.
4. The policeman leaves.
5. "Jimmy" shows up.

Encourage students to compare their predictions with what actually happens.

"Rikki-tikki-tavi" by Rudyard Kipling

Predict (page 379)

Students may write the following predictions:

1. The mongoose will become a friend to the family because they choose to take care of him when he is nearly dead.
2. Rikki-tikki-tavi will save the family from a snake because the father mentions how safe the mongoose is, and how the mongoose could defend Teddy from a snake.
3. Nag will cause further trouble for the family and the mongoose because he has eaten the baby bird.
4. The mongoose will defeat Nag because Nag is afraid of him.
5. Nagaina will kill Teddy or the mongoose as revenge for the death of Nag.

Encourage students to compare their predictions with what actually happens.

"Papa's Parrot" by Cynthia Rylant

Identify with a Character (page 381)

Encourage students to explore their own feelings by writing a detailed diary entry.

"Suzy and Leah" by Jane Yolen

Make Inferences (page 383)

Sample Responses:

Paragraph beginning with the words "Today I walked"

Detail #1: "A line of rickety wooden buildings"

Suggests: The refugee camp has poor accommodations.

Detail #2: "Just like in the army"

Suggests: The refugees are treated as if they are part of the war.

Detail #3: "A fence lots higher than my head. With barbed wire on top."

Suggests: The refugees are kept like prisoners because people fear they may escape.

Paragraph beginning with the words "I put on the blue dress"

Detail #1: "I put on the blue dress."

Suggests: Leah has nothing else to wear.

Detail #2: "The color reminded me of your eyes and the blue skies over our farm before the smoke from the burning darkened it."

Suggests: Leah is homesick, remembering her life before the war.

Detail #3: "I had no mirror until we got to the school"

Suggests: The conditions in the refugee camp aren't very good.

"Ribbons" by Laurence Yep
"The Treasure of Lemon Brown" by Walter Dean Myers

Ask Questions (page 385)

Sample Responses:

1. "Ribbons." Question: Why is there a break after Dad stops the ballet lessons?
   Answer: The break shows a passage of time and the narrator's perspective.
2. "The Treasure of Lemon Brown." Question: What is the purpose of the third paragraph (beginning "Greg had sat in the small, pale green kitchen")?
   Answer: It gives the reader some history and context without telling all the background.
3. "The Treasure of Lemon Brown." Question: What is the purpose of the final paragraph?
   Answer: It concludes the story by giving a hint about Greg's feelings at the end.

"Stolen Day" by Sherwood Anderson

Identify with the Characters (page 387)

Sample Responses:

1. Some students might talk about the boy's age and his relationship with his family. Others might talk about his school situation.
2. Many students will be able to identify with a fear of being sick, especially fear that comes from seeing other sick people.
3. Students will probably identify with the boy's longing for his mother's affection or his jealousy over her care for the drowned child.
4. Some students will understand the boy's love of fishing, but others may not be able to identify with it. A lot of students will share his concerns about health and family.
5. Some students will identify more with the boy's family—the teasing siblings and the busy mother, for example. Others may suffer from a permanent health condition and might identify most with Walter.

Unit 7

"How to Enjoy Poetry" by James Dickey

Recognize the Organization (page 389)

Sample Responses:

1. Understand that poetry comes from outside you, but requires something inside you to live.
2. Don't let the poet write down to you; read up to him.
3. Remember that poetry is new to each reader.
4. Start simply.
5. Open yourself as wide as you can.
6. Read the list of images and think about your own life.
7. Think about the rhythm.
8. Try writing poetry yourself.
9. Try to understand how the world interacts with words
10. Recognize connections between things.

"No Gumption" by Russell Baker
from *An American Childhood* by Anne Dillard

Understand the Author's Purpose
(page 391)

Sample Responses:

1. "I loved to pick through trash piles and collect empty bottles, tin cans with pretty labels, and discarded magazines. The most desirable job on earth sprang to mind. 'I want to be a garbage man.'"
2. "There were two filling stations at the intersection with Union Avenue, as well as an A&P, a fruit stand, a bakery, a barber shop, Zuccarelli's drugstore, and a diner shaped like a railroad car."
3. "My idea of a perfect afternoon was lying in front of the radio rereading my favorite Big Little Book *Dick Tracy Meets Stooge Viller*."
4. "We smashed through a gap in another hedge, entered a scruffy backyard and ran around its back porch and tight between houses to Edgerton Avenue."
5. "The oldest two Fahey boys were there—Mikey and Peter—polite blond boys who lived near me on Lloyd Street . . . Chickie McBride was there, a tough kid, and Billy Paul and Mackie Kean too, from across Reynolds, where the boys grew up dark and furious, grew up skinny, knowing, and skilled."
6. "Some boys taught me to play football . . . Best, you got to throw yourself mightily at someone's running legs. Either you brought him down or you hit the ground flat out on your chin, with your arms empty before you. It was all or nothing."

"Nolan Ryan" by William W. Lace

Set a Purpose for Reading (page 393)

Sample Responses:

Question 1: Who is Nolan Ryan?

Question 2: Why is he called a Texas treasure?

Question 3: What is Ryan like?

Question 4: Does Ryan have any records?

Answer 1: Nolan Ryan is a great major-league baseball pitcher.

Answer 2: He is a successful player with an admirable lifestyle. He is modest and uncomplicated.

Answer 3: He is a balanced person with interests and commitments beyond baseball. He takes care of his health and his family.

Answer 4: Ryan holds almost 50 major league records, including strikeouts and no-hitters.

"Rattlesnake Hunt" by Marjorie Kinnan Rawlings
from *Barrio Boy* by Ernesto Galarza
"I Am a Native of North America" by Chief Dan George
"All Together Now" by Barbara Jordan

Identify the Author's Main Points
(page 395)

Sample Responses:

from *Barrio Boy*

Main point: Entering a new situation can be frightening.

Supporting Details: 1) The day the speaker enrolls, he and his mother have to go into the building without knowing exactly what to expect. 2) Ernesto has to sit in the front row.

"I Am a Native of North America"

Main point: Real love is the only thing that can heal cultural divides.

Supporting Details: 1) The speaker's father grew up in a house of love and learned to love people. 2) Our spirits feed on love.

"Rattlesnake Hunt"

Main point: Facing your fears is the best way to conquer them.

Supporting Details: 1) The author goes on a rattlesnake hunt even though she is afraid. 2) The author learns about how rattlers work.

"All Together Now"

Main point: We need to build a more tolerant society.

Supporting Details: 1) History shows that racism continues. 2) Children can be taught to be tolerant and to enjoy people who are different from themselves.

"A Christmas Carol: Scrooge and Marley" Act I by Charles Dickens dramatized by Israel Horovitz

Picture (page 397)

Sample Responses:

1. Stage Direction: A ghostly bell rings in the distance. MARLEY moves away from SCROOGE, now, heading D. again. As he does, he "takes" the light: SCROOGE has disappeared into the black void beyond.

   How it Helps Me Picture the Play: Scrooge is a dark character and his mystery continues.
2. Stage Direction: We see SCROOGE'S clerk, BOB CRATCHIT, who sits in a dismal tank of a cubicle, copying letters.

   How it Helps Me Picture the Play: Bob Cratchit's work situation is dreary and unending.
3. Stage Direction: SCROOGE will walk alone to his rooms . . . There will be occasional pleasant greetings tossed at him. SCROOGE, in contrast to all, will grump and mumble.

   How it Helps Me Picture the Play: Scrooge's movement and his grumpiness contrast with the cheerful, spirited people around him.
4. Stage Direction: SCROOGE fastens the door and walks across the hall to the stairs . . . he checks each room; sitting room, bedrooms, slumber-room. He looks under the sofa, under the table: nobody there.

   How it Helps Me Picture the Play: Scrooge lives in a large house, but there is nobody there with him.
5. Stage Direction: Outside the window, specters fly by, carrying money-boxes and chains. They make a confused sound of lamentation.

   How it Helps Me Picture the Play: The scene is spooky, and Scrooge is haunted by it.

"A Christmas Carol: Scrooge and Marley" Act II by Charles Dickens dramatized by Israel Horovitz

Question (page 399)

Sample Responses:

1. Students might not understand why Scrooge is so hateful. As they read the play, they will understand his past, and the reasons for his misery.
2. Students might not understand why the ghosts keep appearing to Scrooge. As they read, they will understand that the ghosts are used to help Scrooge understand the spirit of Christmas.
3. Students might not understand why the ghost of Christmas Present takes Scrooge to the Cratchit's home. As they read, they will see that Tiny Tim's condition will change Scrooge's heart.
4. Students might not understand how Bob Cratchit can drink a toast to the cruel Scrooge. As readers keep reading, they see that Bob Cratchit has a heart that is kind enough to include Scrooge.
5. Students might not understand how Scrooge can save the situation for Tiny Tim. As they read, they will understand that the ghosts still give Scrooge the chance to change his ways and Tiny Tim's outcome.

The Monsters Are Due on Maple Street by Rod Serling

Predict (page 401)

Sample Responses:

1. Students might predict that the play will deal with strange events based on the fifth dimension because of the narrator's comments at the beginning of the play.
2. Students might predict that the monsters will destroy the humans based on the lack of electricity and phone service after the meteor.

3. Students might predict that Tommy will communicate with the monsters since he is the one that believes that they are real from the beginning.
4. Students might predict that Goodman is one of the aliens because he didn't pay attention to the meteor, and his car is the only one in the neighborhood that starts.
5. Students might predict that the people themselves are the real monsters since they are so quick to judge Goodman.
6. Students might predict that the dark approaching figure is going to be a friend rather than a monster based on the paranoia that everyone is feeling.

Unit 9

"The Cremation of Sam McGee" by Robert Service "Washed in Silver" by James Stephens "Winter" by Nikki Giovanni

Identify the Speaker (page 403)

Sample Responses:

2. He can't deny a request from a friend.
3. He is loyal to his dying friend.
4. Though he never spoke it, he was unhappy about carrying McGee's body.
5. He is worn out, but he perseveres.
6. He is sensitive to hearing his friend's body burn.

"Seal" by William Jay Smith "The Pasture" by Robert Frost "Three Haiku" by Matsuo Bashō, translated by Daniel C. Buchanan

Read According to Punctuation (page 405)

Sample Responses for Stop at a Period:

I'm going out to fetch the little calf that's standing by the mother. ("The Pasture")

On sweet plum blossoms the sun rises suddenly. (Haiku 1)

On that nameless mountain lie thin layers of mist (Haiku 2)

Temple bells die out. (Haiku 3)

Sample Responses for Pause at a Comma or Hyphen:

Back up he swims past Sting Ray and Shark, out with a zoom, a whoop, a bark; ("Seal")

Quick-silver quick, softer than spray, down he plunges and sweeps away ("Seal"

I shan't be gone long.—You come too. ("The Pasture")

Sample Responses for Read with Emphasis at an Exclamation Point:

He plops at your side with a mouthful of fish! ("Seal")

Look, a mountain path! (Haiku 1)

A perfect evening! (Haiku 3)

"Martin Luther King" by Raymond Richard Patterson "Annabel Lee" by Edgar Allen Poe

Paraphrase (page 407)

Sample Responses:

2. His passion was so great that he had to follow it.
3. He showed the suffering world how great a man can be.
4. She died. OR Her dead ancestors took her to be with themselves.
5. The angels were jealous of our love and that's why they took her.
6. The bright stars remind me of the eyes of Annabel Lee.

"Full Fathom Five" by William Shakespeare "Onomatopoeia" by Eve Merriam "Maestro" by Pat Mora

Listen as You Read Poetry (page 409)

Sample Responses:

2. the sounds of the bell ringing ding-dong
3. the repetition of the *s* sound 6 times
4. the repetition of the *sh* sound 4 times
5. the repetition of the short *i* sound 6 times
6. the repetition of the *g* sound 3 times

"Fog" by Carl Sandburg
"Life" by Naomi Long Madgett
"Loo-Wit" by Wendy Rose
"The Village Blacksmith"
by Henry Wadsworth Longfellow

Respond to Poetry (page 411)

Students may agree or disagree with the poets' ideas, but encourage them to give reasons for their response. Responses should include personal experiences that relate to each poem.

Unit 10

"Popocatepetl and Ixtlaccihuatl"
by Juliet Piggott

Predict (page 413)

Sample Responses:

Prediction 1: The Princess Ixtla will marry Popo.

Why It May Happen: They love each other.

What Actually Happens: She dies because she thinks he has been killed in a battle.

Prediction 2: Popo will defeat the enemy tribes.

Why It May Happen: He is a fine warrior.

What Actually Happens: He defeats the enemy tribes.

Prediction 3: The Princess Ixtla will die.

Why It May Happen: She is very sick because she believes Popo is dead.

What Actually Happens: The Princess dies and her mournful lover buries her at the top of a mound of stones.

"The People Could Fly"
by Virginia Hamilton
"All Stories are Anansi's"
by Harold Courlander
"The Lion and the Statue" by Aesop
"The Fox and the Crow" by Aesop

Recognize Storyteller's Purpose (page 415)

Sample Responses:

1. The storyteller's purpose is to show the suffering of the slaves, and the way they dealt with it. Students might learn more about conditions on a plantation.
2. The storyteller's purpose is to show how the spider became the owner of all stories. Students might learn about the kinds of animals in Western Africa.
3. The purpose of the storyteller is to teach the lesson that sometimes people represent reality the way they want it to be. Students might recognize that they do this themselves sometimes.
4. The storyteller's purpose is to teach the lesson that flatterers aren't always trustworthy. Students might realize that they sometimes use flattery for the wrong reason.

"Phaëthon, Son of Apollo"
by Olivia Coolidge
"Demeter and Persephone"
by Anne Terry White
"Icarus and Daedalus"
by Josephine Preston Peabody

Predict (page 417)

Sample Responses:

1. Students might predict that something bad will happen to Phaëthon because he is prideful and insists on being the best at everything. Others might insist that his strength will keep him from harm.
2. Students might predict that Persephone will return to her mother forever. Others might predict that she will have eaten with Pluto and will be unable to escape him.
3. Students might predict that tragedy will come to Icarus because of carelessness that his father warns him against.